Praise for *America's Unwritten Constitution*

"Filled with thought-provoking material and fun vignettes, suitable for a wide audience. . . . Amar's approach is refreshing. . . . Amar makes a creative case that America's written Constitution and its unwritten Constitution, since the beginning of the nation, have fit snugly together to form a single, more perfect union."
—*Washington Post*

"In his ambitious new book, *America's Unwritten Constitution*, he examines the paradox of needing to go beyond the text in order to faithfully follow the text. . . . His is a 'holistic' interpretation, one that rejects reading passages or clauses of the text in isolation from the document as a whole. He is masterfully creative in finding overarching themes that tie the disparate clauses together in novel and sometimes counterintuitive ways. . . . A highly engaging and thought-provoking book." —*Wall Street Journal*

"In *America's Unwritten Constitution*, [Amar] contends that the written Constitution points to an unwritten one, and he argues that we can interpret with both intellectual honesty and analytical rigor." —*New York Times Book Review*

"The Constitution has been described as both binding law and aspirational treatise. . . . Akhil Amar, a Yale law professor and one of contemporary America's most brilliant constitutional scholars, [suggests] in his latest, and best, book, *America's Unwritten Constitution*, that the issue is not an 'either-or' question." —*Boston Globe*

"*America's Unwritten Constitution* is full of fascinating history, as well as novel and often persuasive analysis. . . . An ambitious book, and an impressive one. It tackles many of the most important and controversial issues in constitutional law. Amar's arguments are uniformly informative and ingenious. . . . This book demonstrates with force and clarity that the relation between authoritative written texts of the past and conceptions and practices that have developed over time is a central concern not only of religious doctrine but also of secular law." —*Commonweal*

"[An] ambitious work. . . . Amar's great contribution is to relate some of the great thematic developments of constitutional history to the words of the Constitution itself. . . . *America's Unwritten Constitution* is not a treatise intended to guide legal practitioners or political scientists. Its aim is the more majestic one of articulating some of the grand underlying themes of American constitutional law and grounding them in the constitutional text. It aspires to be what Thucydides called 'a possession for all time,' and it succeeds. Readers today, as well as those of future generations, will read it to their profit." —*The Federal Lawyer*

"[Amar lays] out his argument in case-by-case details that are scholarly and legalistic but always readable. . . . [An] ingenious mixture of history, legal anecdotes and hypothetical cases." —*Kirkus*

"Yale law professor Amar follows his highly regarded historical-textual analysis of *America's Constitution* with a companion volume on the history, culture, and legal tenets of the 'unwritten constitution,' the traditions and precedents that inform constitutional interpretation. . . . Sophisticated readers will be rewarded for traveling with Amar as he covers a great deal of ground." —*Publishers Weekly*

"Deeply researched and carefully argued, this book is nothing less than a sophisticated and comprehensive theory of constitutional jurisprudence that resists being construed along narrow political lines. Indispensable for law students and scholars, this will also be enjoyed by general readers who are passionate about constitutional law." —*Booklist*

"Akhil Amar's splendid new book, *America's Unwritten Constitution*, combines an unmatched eye for detail with a unique capacity for overarching perspective and masterfully elegant synthesis. It is a wonderfully readable companion to Amar's unparalleled earlier volume, *America's Constitution: A Biography*. Together, these two works convey as little else can the majesty and sweep of America's constitutional project."
　—**Laurence H. Tribe, Carl M. Loeb University Professor and Professor of Constitutional Law, Harvard Law School**

"In *America's Unwritten Constitution*, Professor Amar adds to his already masterful bibliography what will instantly become a classic examination of constitutional law. As the Constitution itself stood in need of a seminal biography, so too the vast and varied domain of our Nation's constitutional law cried out for a guidebook. Professor Amar has now brilliantly provided both."
　—**Ken Starr, President of Baylor University; Solicitor General of the United States, 1989–1993; Independent Counsel, 1994–1999**

"Akhil Amar brings the patience of a historian, the ardor of a lover, and (yes, sometimes) the panache of a conjurer to America's unwritten Constitution. If you want to argue with him, you will have to summon all these qualities yourself. This is a serious and provocative book." —**Richard Brookhiser, author of *James Madison***

"This book is brilliant, creative, ambitious, comprehensive, imaginative, and thought-provoking. It is a must-read for anyone interested in Constitutional Law."
　—**Steven G. Calabresi, Class of 1940 Research Professor, Northwestern University School of Law; Co-Founder of the Federalist Society**

"This is an engrossing, epic work of enduring importance—not only a treasure trove for scholars of American law, history, and politics, but also an inspiring, empowering guidebook for activists. It compellingly demonstrates how to harness the Constitution's full meaning in order to promote its thrilling vision of liberty and justice for all. No matter what your prior knowledge of this field, and no matter what your ideological perspective, this magnificent book will enhance your understanding and appreciation of our cherished Constitution. If I had to choose a single work to recommend to either my constitutional law students or my civil libertarian colleagues, this would be it."
　—**Nadine Strossen, Former President, American Civil Liberties Union; Professor, New York Law School**

AMERICA'S
UNWRITTEN
CONSTITUTION

ALSO BY AKHIL REED AMAR

America's Constitution

The Bill of Rights

The Constitution and Criminal Procedure

AMERICA'S UNWRITTEN CONSTITUTION

The Precedents and Principles We Live By

AKHIL REED AMAR

BASIC BOOKS

A MEMBER OF THE PERSEUS BOOKS GROUP

New York

Copyright © 2012 by Akhil Reed Amar
Hardcover first published in 2012 by Basic Books,
A Member of the Perseus Books Group
Paperback first published in 2015 by Basic Books

Books published by Basic Books are available at special discounts for
bulk purchases in the United States by corporations, institutions, and
other organizations. For more information, please contact the Special Markets Department at the Perseus Books Group, 2300 Chest-
nut Street, Suite 200, Philadelphia, PA 19103, or call (800) 810-4145,
ext. 5000, or e-mail special.markets@perseusbooks.com.

Designed by Janet Tingey

The Library of Congress has cataloged the hardcover as follows:
Amar, Akhil Reed.
America's unwritten constitution : the precedents and principles we
live by / Akhil Reed Amar.
p. cm.
Includes bibliographical references and index.
ISBN 978-0-465-02957-0
1. Constitutional history—United States. 2. Constitutional law—
Social aspects—United States. I. Title.
KF4541.A875 2012
342.7302'9—dc23
2012012363

ISBN 978-0-465-06490-8 (paperback)
ISBN 978-0-465-03309-6 (e-book)

10 9 8 7 6 5 4 3 2

"For God, for country, and for Yale"
and also—always—for family

CONTENTS

INTRODUCTION

THE EIGHT THOUSAND WORDS OF America's written Constitution only begin to map out the basic ground rules that actually govern our land. For example, the idea that racial segregation is inherently unequal does not explicitly appear in the terse text. The First Amendment prevents "Congress" from abridging various freedoms, but the Amendment does not expressly protect these freedoms from abridgment by the president or state governments. None of the Constitution's early amendments explicitly limits state governments. Although everyone today refers to these early amendments as "the Bill of Rights," this phrase, too, is unwritten. The phrases "separation of powers," "checks and balances," and "the rule of law" are also absent from the written Constitution, but all these things are part of America's working constitutional system—part of America's *unwritten* Constitution.

Consider also the axiom that all voters must count equally—one person, one vote—in state elections and in elections to the U.S. House of Representatives. No clause of the written Constitution expressly proclaims this axiom. At the Founding, this axiom was not widely honored in practice; nor did it sweep the land at any time over the next 175 years. And yet today, this unwritten rule—a rule supported by every Supreme Court justice, by both major parties, by opinion leaders of all stripes, and by an overwhelming majority of ordinary citizens—forms the bedrock of the American system of government.

Of course, much (though not all) of America's "unwritten Constitution" does involve written materials, such as venerable Supreme Court opinions, landmark congressional statutes, and iconic presidential proclamations. These materials, while surely written texts, are nonetheless distinct from the written Constitution and are thus properly described by lawyers and judges as parts of America's unwritten Constitution.

America's unwritten Constitution encompasses not only rules specifying the substantive content of the nation's supreme law but also rules clarifying the methods for determining the meaning of this supreme law. Since the written Constitution does not come with a complete set of instructions about how it should be construed, we must go beyond the text to make sense of the text.

Without an unwritten Constitution of some sort, we would not even be able to properly identify the official written Constitution. In the late 1780s, several different versions of the text circulated among the citizenry, each calling itself the "Constitution." Each featured slightly different punctuation, capitalization, and wording. Which specific written version was and is the legal Constitution? To find the answer, we must necessarily go beyond these dueling texts themselves and consider things outside the texts. (When we do, we shall discover that the hand-signed parchment now on display in the National Archives is not and never was the official legal version of the Constitution, though this celebrated parchment does, happily, closely approximate the official text.) With a proper analytic framework in place, we shall also be poised to resolve a debate that has recently erupted about whether the Constitution contains a consciously Christian reference to Jesus in the phrase "the Year of our Lord"—a phrase that appeared in many but not all of the self-described written Constitutions making the rounds in the 1780s.

WHAT, EXACTLY, IS THE UNWRITTEN Constitution and how can we find it? How can Americans be faithful to a written Constitution even as we venture beyond it? What is the proper relationship between the document and the doctrine—that is, between the written Constitution and the vast set of judicial rulings purporting to apply the Constitution? In particular, how should we think about various landmark cases—from *Brown v. Board of Education* and *Gideon v. Wainwright* to *Reynolds v. Sims* and *Roe v. Wade*—that critics over the years have assailed as lacking proper foundations in the written Constitution?

This book tackles these and related questions. In brief, I argue that the written Constitution itself invites recourse to certain things outside the text—things that form America's unwritten Constitution. When viewed properly, America's unwritten Constitution supports and supplements the written Constitution without supplanting it.

Consider the Constitution's Ninth Amendment, which affirms the reality of various rights that are not textually "enumerat[ed]"—rights that are concededly not listed in the document itself. To take this amendment seriously, Americans must go beneath and beyond the Constitution's textually enumerated rights. For instance, even though the text fails to specify a criminal defendant's entitlement to introduce reliable physical evidence of his innocence, surely this textual omission should not doom a defendant's claim of right.

The Ninth Amendment is not the only textual portal welcoming us to journey beyond the Constitution's text, and the trail of unenumerated rights is only one of several routes worth traveling in search of America's unwritten Constitution. In the pages that follow, we shall revisit many of our Constitution's most important topics, from federalism, congressional practice, executive power, and judicial review to race relations, women's rights, popular constitutionalism, criminal procedure, voting rights, and the amendment process.

With case studies drawn from these and other areas, we shall see how America's two Constitutions, written and unwritten, cohere to form a single constitutional system. The written Constitution cannot work as intended without something outside of it—America's unwritten Constitution—to fill in its gaps and to stabilize it. In turn, America's unwritten Constitution could never properly ignore the written Constitution, which is itself an integral part of the American experience. Over the centuries, various extratextual practices and precedents that have done justice to the text have flourished while other extratextual practices and precedents that have done violence to the text have faded away.

No Supreme Court opinion has ever openly proclaimed that its members may properly disregard or overturn the written Constitution. According to the Court, judicial precedents may in appropriate situations be judicially overruled; various statutes may be invalidated by courts or repealed by Congress; unwritten customs may ebb away; unenumerated rights may occasionally be pruned back. But the written Constitution itself operates on a higher legal plane, and a clear constitutional command may not as a rule be trumped by a mere case, statute, or custom.

Other elements of our unwritten Constitution—well-established legislative and executive practices and deeply embedded American political norms—similarly evince fidelity to the written Constitution. Congress members, presidents, cabinet officers, state legislators, and governors all pledge allegiance to the terse text. Ordinary citizens celebrate this document—at times to the point of idolatry, revering it without reading it.

Indeed, the very concept of a written Constitution forms part of our national language and lies at the heart of our national birth-story. At the precise historical moment that British colonists in the New World declared their independence from the British crown, they also freed themselves from traditional British ideas of constitutionalism. Between 1776 and 1789, Americans adopted a series of written "constitutions," first at the state level and then continentally. Each of these documents audaciously sought to compress basic legal ground rules into a single text that would outrank the vast mass of ordinary law. Most of these constitutions also aimed to speak in a special way to and for ordinary citizens. In 1787–1788, the process of ordaining the last and most momentous of these written instruments, a continent-wide "Constitution for the United States of America," directly involved far more voters than had any previous constitutional event in world history.

The standard British understanding of a "constitution" was quite different at that time, and remains so today. The "British Constitution" has never consisted of a single foundational document. Nor has it ever been reducible to a clearly defined set of specially enacted legal texts. Rather, for centuries the term "British Constitution" has referred to the traditions, practices, understandings, principles, and institutions that collectively structure the basic British system of government and way of life. In short, Britain has long lived under an entirely "unwritten Constitution." Ever since 1776, America has rejected this British model.

But America's revolutionary break with the British model was only partial, not total. In several ways, the terse text has always pointed beyond itself, inviting readers to fill in its gaps by consulting extratextual sources such as judicial opinions, executive practices, legislative enactments, and American traditions. America's written Constitution thus bids us to heed her unwritten Constitution, which in turn refers us back, in various ways, to its written counterpart. Like the Chinese symbols yin and yang, America's written Constitution and America's unwritten Constitution form two halves of one whole, with each half gesturing toward the other.

Equipped with this comprehensive understanding of the American constitutional system, we can begin to bridge the deep divide in our current constitutional culture. Today, some judges, politicians, pundits, and scholars plant their flag on the high ground of constitutional text and original intent, while others proudly unfurl the banner of a "Living Constitution." Too often, each side shouts past the other, and both sides overlook various ways in which the text itself, when properly approached, invites recourse to certain nontextual—unwritten—principles and practices. We are all textualists; we are all living constitutionalists.

TWO POINTS ABOUT THIS BOOK's scope and structure deserve emphasis at the outset.

First, although this book uses legal materials and legal reasoning to show the reader why various constitutional interpretations are legally correct or incorrect, nonlawyers should not be daunted. Nothing here requires any special legal training or background. This is a book for general-interest readers who care about the Constitution, whether they be schoolteachers, college students, journalists, political activists, or merely civic-minded citizens. Whenever actual judicial cases, congressional statutes, presidential proclamations, state laws, House and Senate rules, and the like are discussed, I provide enough background to enable the reader to grasp the relevant issues.

At various points, I posit hypothetical fact patterns to help the reader see the proper shape of a given unwritten constitutional rule. Hypotheticals are the grist of legal reasoning and form an implicit or explicit part of virtually every legal case ever decided and every legal issue ever analyzed outside a courtroom. Even if a judge is sure that the plaintiff in the case at hand—call it case A—deserves to win, the judge must decide how broadly or narrowly to rule. If she adopts a broad rule, plaintiffs in later cases B and C will also deserve to win under the sweeping logic she announces. By contrast, a narrow rule in case A might mean that plaintiffs in later cases B and C will likely or surely lose. When case A is decided, the distinct fact patterns of cases B and C may not yet have arisen. Perhaps these fact patterns will never arise. But precisely because cases B and C could in principle later materialize, a good judge will think carefully about these now-hypothetical cases in crafting the proper rule for the case at hand—case A.

For similar reasons, I shall routinely illustrate the proper scope of an unwritten constitutional principle by asking the reader to ponder a fact pattern that has yet to arise and that perhaps may never arise. Often these hypotheticals are closely related to fact patterns that have already occurred and cases that have already been decided. The hypothetical merely presents the relevant issue in a cleaner way that clarifies analysis. The hypotheticals showcased in this book are thus not the stuff of science fiction. They do not involve Martian invasions or antigravity pills. They aim not to bend the reader's mind, but to sharpen it. Specifically, several of these hypotheticals are designed to show the reader that we today can sometimes be quite sure that a future case must and will be decided a particular way, even though the text of the Constitution does not provide an explicit answer, and even though no identical court case has yet been decided. Nevertheless, we can be confident of the right answer to this not-yet-decided case because there truly is an unwritten Constitution alongside the written Constitution—and because there is a great deal more to this unwritten Constitution than merely the sum total of all previously decided judicial cases.

Second, this book is about method as well as substance. Before we can confidently say *what* government officialdom may and may not properly do under various unwritten constitutional rules, we must figure out *how* to find these unwritten rules. Fortunately, there are a handful of interpretative tools—constitutional compasses and lenses—that can be used to locate and bring into sharp focus the unwritten substantive do's and don'ts. The written Constitution does not enumerate these methodological tools. Thus, these interpretive instruments are themselves components of America's unwritten Constitution.

Indeed, these lenses and compasses are perhaps the most important components of America's unwritten Constitution, and they form the organizational spine of this book. Fair warning: This book is not arranged by substantive subject matter. I do not, for example, devote one chapter to religious freedom, another to separation of powers, and yet another to voting rights. Rather, each chapter opens with a brief explanation of a particular way of approaching America's unwritten Constitution—using a distinct *methodological* tool—and then proceeds to offer a few illustrative (but not exhaustive) examples of the specific unwritten substantive rules that this particular methodological tool helps us find and define.

In actual constitutional practice, faithful interpreters make use of multiple tools to think about any given constitutional issue. The distinct methodological instruments thus work together, in much the same way that distinct chapters work together to form a book and distinct vertebrae work together to form a spine.

Consider, for example, America's preeminent right, the freedom of speech. Textually, this freedom appears in the First Amendment, but if everything depended solely on this explicit patch of constitutional text, which became part of the Constitution in 1791, then the First Congress in 1789 and 1790 would have been free to pass censorship laws had it so chosen. But surely the First Congress had no such power. And surely states have never had proper authority to shut down political discourse, even though the First Amendment does not expressly limit states. The robust, wide-open, and uninhibited freedom of American citizens to express their political opinions is a basic feature of America's unwritten Constitution that predates and outshines the First Amendment. Or so I claim.

I do not prove this specific claim in a single chapter devoted solely to free speech. Rather, free speech pops up at several points in the book, each time in connection with a different method for finding America's unwritten Constitution. In Chapter 1, I invite readers to read between the lines of the Constitution—to see what principles are implicit in the document, read as a whole, even if these principles are nowhere explicitly stated in any specific clause. In the middle of this chapter I show that free speech is one implicit principle among many. In Chapter 2, I invite readers to pursue a wholly different methodological line of inquiry—to look away from the text altogether, if only momentarily, and instead ponder the specific historical procedures and protocols by which the Constitution was in fact enacted. It turns out that this method gives us a second and distinct reason for believing that an unwritten constitutional right of free speech preceded and surpassed the First Amendment. Chapter 3 offers a third way of thinking about unwritten constitutionalism, focusing on the actual rights that ordinary twenty-first-century Americans embody and embrace in their daily lives. One of those rights is the freedom of speech. Further support for a robust right of free speech appears when we take yet another methodological tack by reading the Constitution through the lens of modern case law—the approach showcased in Chapter 4. Later chapters illustrate still more ways to find the unwritten Constitution, and in these chapters free speech occasionally pops up yet again.

ULTIMATELY, THIS BOOK EXPLAINS NOT merely what America's Constitution, written and unwritten, says on a wide variety of topics, but, even more critically, how to make proper constitutional arguments—how to think constitutional law and how to do constitutional law. Some of these ways of thinking and doing are well understood today; others are not. Thus this book offers a new vision of the nature of constitutional interpretation—a new vision, that is, of the tools and techniques for going beyond the written Constitution while remaining faithful to it.

Although this book makes no claim to encompass every aspect of America's unwritten Constitution, the chapters that follow seek to illuminate many of the best avenues for understanding this expansive and sometimes elusive entity. Alongside my book *America's Constitution: A Biography,* which mapped the written Constitution in considerable detail, the current volume aims to offer readers a vivid and panoramic account of the American constitutional experience.

AMERICA'S
UNWRITTEN
CONSTITUTION

CHAPTER 1

READING
BETWEEN THE LINES

America's Implicit Constitution

THE IMPEACHMENT TRIAL OF ANDREW JOHNSON (1868).

The United States Senate deciding the fate of President Andrew
Johnson, in a trial presided over by Chief Justice Salmon P. Chase.

O N THE AFTERNOON OF MARCH 5, 1868, as the nation's capital saw its first fair day in nearly a month, the Senate galleries filled to capacity. According to one press account, the ladies in the audience sparkled "with all the bright colors of brilliant toilettes." Sitting in the presiding officer's chair, Chief Justice Salmon P. Chase solemnly summoned each senator to step forward and take an oath to do "impartial justice."[1]

Usually, the chief justice does not chair Senate proceedings. Typically, senators take no special judicial oath. On many a day, elegant spectators do not throng the Capitol galleries. But this was no ordinary day. For the first time in history, the Senate was convening as a court of presidential impeachment. Andrew Johnson, the seventeenth president of the United States, stood formally accused of high crimes and misdemeanors warranting his ouster from office.[2]

No one knew who would prevail in the days ahead. An overwhelming majority of the House of Representatives had put forth eleven articles of impeachment, indicting Johnson for his wild anticongressional rhetoric and fierce defiance of congressional legislation—but conviction would require a two-thirds vote in the Senate. Johnson had many allies in the upper chamber. But did he have enough?

One by one, senators approached the chair and were sworn in. Rhode Island's Henry B. Anthony went first, followed by Delaware's James A. Bayard Jr. In 1801, Congressman James A. Bayard Sr. had brokered a deal making Thomas Jefferson president. Back then, Bayard Jr. had been an infant. Now he would have his own chance to shape a president's fate.

As Bayard Jr. took his oath, some in the chamber likely thought back to the legendary Bayard-Jefferson affair. They may have also recalled that Jefferson, as the vice president of the United States from 1797 to 1801, had himself presided over the Senate, thus occupying the very chair now filled by Chase. Johnson, too, had once sat in this seat, as Abraham Lincoln's vice president in early 1865. Did any of these stray thoughts cross Chase's mind as he sat in the Jefferson/Johnson chair? Did it further cross Chase's mind that, if he played his part well in the impeachment trial, he might himself win the presidency in November, and thereafter fill an even more powerful chair once occupied by Jefferson and Johnson?

Chase continued to go down the alphabet. Several dozen senators—including Thomas Hendricks, Reverdy Johnson (no relation to Andrew), John Sherman, William Sprague (Chase's own son-in-law), Charles Sumner, and Peter Van Winkle—stepped forward and took their judicial oaths. Then came the moment many had been waiting for: The secretary called the name of Ohio's senior senator, Benjamin Franklin Wade, the official Senate president pro tempore. As Wade approached the chair, Hendricks—the senior senator from Indiana and a supporter of President Johnson—rose to his feet to object. The crowd hushed.

It took Hendricks less than two minutes to explain why Wade could not properly take the requisite oath. Under the presidential-succession statute then on the books, the Senate president pro tempore stood next in line after Johnson. (No vice president existed in 1868. When Lincoln was killed at war's end, Vice President Johnson had become President Johnson, and his old seat had thereafter remained empty.) Thus, were the Senate to convict Johnson, Wade would move into the White House. With so much to gain from a guilty verdict, Wade should not sit in judgment over Johnson. "I submit," intoned Hendricks, that "he [Wade] is not competent to sit as a member of the court."

Sherman immediately leaped to Wade's defense. As unflinching in debate as his famous older brother, General William Tecumseh Sherman, was in warfare, Ohio's junior senator gave no quarter: "This question... is answered by the Constitution of the United States, which declares that each State shall be entitled to two senators on this floor, and that the court or tribunal for the trial of all impeachments shall be the Senate of the United States. My colleague [Wade] is one of the senators from the State of Ohio; he is a member of this Senate, and is therefore made one of the tribunal to try all cases of impeachment." Sherman bluntly added that no one had objected moments earlier to the swearing-in of President Johnson's son-in-law, Tennessee Senator David Patterson.[3]

The constitutional game was now afoot. For the rest of that day and well into the next, senators did what they did best—speechify—on the nice constitutional questions before them: Should Wade sit in judgment when he obviously had an enormous personal stake in the outcome? But wouldn't his recusal effectively deprive Ohio of its equal share in the Senate on the most momentous issue then facing America?

HOW SHOULD THE SENATE HAVE decided the deep questions raised on March 5, 1868? It is tempting to say that senators should simply have followed the plain meaning of the written Constitution. But constitutional quicksand awaits all who insist on reading every clause of the document literally. Seemingly firm textual ground at times simply dissolves underfoot. For example, Article I, section 3, declares that "the Vice President of the United States shall be the President of the Senate" and that the Senate enjoys the "sole Power to try all Impeachments." There are only two textual exceptions. First, "when the President of the United States is tried, the Chief Justice shall preside" over the Senate impeachment trial. Second, when the vice president is "Absen[t]" from the Senate or acting as America's chief executive (because, say, of a temporary presidential disability), a Senate-chosen officer—a "Senate...President pro tempore"—may substitute. Read literally, all this seems to say that whenever the *vice president* is impeached, he *himself* may chair this Senate trial. But can it really be true that a man may sit in judgment of his own case?[4]

Clause-bound literalism cannot provide the infallible constitutional compass we crave. Yet surely faithful interpreters should not simply toss the written Constitution aside or treat it as an infinitely malleable plaything. How, then, should we proceed?

For starters, we must learn to read between the lines—to discern America's implicit Constitution nestled behind the explicit clauses. In short, we must come to understand the difference between reading the Constitution *literally* and reading the document *faithfully*.

The best way for us to get a feel for this difference is through a series of detailed historical case studies and hypotheticals. Later in this chapter, we shall return to the events of March 5, 1868, but before we do, let's tweak the actual facts of this episode so that we may better understand the underlying constitutional issues.

"President of the Senate"

SUPPOSE THAT ANDREW JOHNSON had been impeached exactly three years earlier. On March 5, 1865, Johnson was the newly installed vice president and thus the Senate's ordinary presiding officer. Abraham Lincoln still lived. Could Vice President Johnson have properly insisted in 1865, as Senator Wade would insist in 1868, that the Constitution explicitly authorized him to wield power in impeachment proceedings? How should the Senate have responded if Johnson, stubbornly standing on the literal language of the Constitution, had proclaimed that as the nation's vice president (and thus the "President of the Senate" according to Article I, section 3), he was entitled to chair his own impeachment trial?

The key that unlocks the door is the simple idea that no clause of the Constitution exists in textual isolation. We must read the document as a whole. Doing so will enable us to detect larger structures of meaning—rules and principles residing between the lines. Often, these implicit rules and principles supplement the meaning of individual clauses. For example, although no single clause explicitly affirms a "separation of powers," or a system of "checks and balances," or "federalism," the document writ large does reflect these constitutional concepts. This much is old hat. But as we shall now see, there are times when the document, read holistically and with attention to what it implies alongside what it expresses, means almost the *opposite* of what a specific clause, read in autistic isolation, at first seems to say.

IN CLOSE PROXIMITY TO THE declaration in Article I, section 3, that "the Vice President of the United States shall be President of the Senate," we find the following language in Article I, section 5: "Each House may determine the Rules of its Proceedings." These two clauses should be harmonized in a way that does justice to the central purpose of each. For instance, were the Senate to pass a rule that "no vice president may ever preside over the Senate," then the Senate-proceedings clause would simply swallow up the Senate-president clause. We should not allow this to happen. But neither should we allow the reverse: We should not permit the Senate-president clause to swallow up the Senate-proceedings clause.

Here, then, is a sensible synthesis: The Senate should adopt a rule prohibiting the vice president from chairing *any vice-presidential impeachment proceeding*. This rule would not categorically bar all vice presidents from ever presiding over the Senate. This rule would not even bar vice presidents from ordinarily presiding over the Senate. The rule would merely say that in certain unusual situations, the chamber's usual presiding officer must absent himself from the chair as a matter of ethics and first principles.[5]

The long-standing practice of federal courts—which, like the practices of other branches can inform our understanding of first principles—confirms the soundness of this proposed reconciliation of the two clauses. The Constitution explicitly envisions a chief justice and implicitly authorizes this figure to preside over the Supreme Court, as a rule. However, in a case directly involving his own financial interests, the chief justice should step aside. In the landmark 1816 case of *Martin v. Hunter's Lessee*, involving competing claimants to a tract of valuable Virginia real estate, Chief Justice John Marshall properly absented himself from the bench because he had a stake in some of the land at issue. Had Marshall not stepped aside, his colleagues would have been justified in demanding his recusal—not across the board, but in the case at hand. Centuries before *Martin*, the celebrated English chief justice Sir Edward Coke had famously ruled, in a lawsuit known as *Bonham's Case*, that adjudicators must be free from financial self-interest. According to Coke, no man should be a judge in his own case.[6]

Exactly where, a skeptic might ask, does America's Constitution say that? Even if senators (or justices) are constitutionally permitted to follow the venerable legal maxim *nemo judex in causa sua*, are they constitutionally obliged to do so? If so, what is the source of this constitutional obligation?

To answer these questions, we will need to weave together several threads of law, history, and logic.

ONE THREAD MAY BE FOUND in Sir William Blackstone's *Commentaries on the Laws of England*, a canonical four-volume treatise first published in the late 1760s. Both before and after Independence, American lawyers and activists of all stripes relied heavily and preeminently on the *Commentaries* for instruction on basic English legal principles, many of which applied with full force in America. Sifting through nearly a thousand American political tracts printed between 1760 and 1805, one scholar has found that no European authorities were cited more frequently than Montesquieu and Blackstone, each of whom was invoked almost three times as often as the next man on the list, John Locke.[7]

Near the outset of the *Commentaries*, Blackstone explained that even seemingly absolute legislative language sometimes contained implicit exceptions. Certain things simply went without saying. To be sure, Blackstone made clear that judges must never ignore the "main object" of a law, however misguided that object might appear to them. "[I]f the parliament will positively enact a thing to be done which is unreasonable, I know of no power that can control it....[W]here the main object of a statute is unreasonable the judges are [not] at liberty to reject it; for that were to set the judicial power above that of the legislature, which would be subversive of all government." Blackstone then introduced a key qualification: Judges (and other interpreters) should construe laws so as to avoid absurdity or unreasonableness when dealing with exceptional situations that the legislature did not envision when it crafted general language. "Where some collateral matter arises out of the general words, and happens to be unreasonable, there the judges are in decency to conclude that this consequence was not foreseen by the parliament, and therefore they are at liberty to expound the statute by equity, and only *quoad hoc* [as to this collateral matter] disregard it."

Elsewhere in the opening section of the *Commentaries*, Blackstone elaborated this venerable canon of legal interpretation. "[T]he rule is, where words bear...a very absurd signification, if literally understood, we must a little deviate from the received sense of them....[S]ince in laws all cases cannot be foreseen or expressed, it is necessary, that when the general decrees of the law come to be applied to particular cases, there should be somewhere a power vested of excepting those circumstances, which (had they been foreseen) the legislator himself would have excepted."

To illustrate these basic ground rules of legislation and interpretation, Blackstone offered an elegant—and for our purposes, stunningly apt—example. "Thus if an act of parliament gives a man power to try all causes [cases], that arise within his manor of Dale; *yet, if a cause should arise in which he himself is party, the act is construed not to extend to that; because it is unreasonable that any man should determine his own quarrel.*"[8]

A SECOND THREAD RELEVANT TO the proper rules of constitutional interpretation may be found in a fascinating verbal exchange that occurred in mid-August 1787 at the Philadelphia Convention that framed the U.S. Constitution. Delegates Elbridge Gerry and James McHenry proposed the insertion of an explicit clause forbidding Congress to enact ex-post-facto laws—laws, that is, seeking to retroactively criminalize actions that were wholly innocent when done. Two of the Convention's best lawyers, both of whom would eventually be named to the Supreme Court by George Washington, bristled at the proposal. An explicit constitutional prohibition, they argued, was unnecessary and would reflect poorly on the legal sophistication of the draftsmen. The impermissibility of punishing conduct that was innocent when done was a first principle of justice and the rule of law. As such, it went without saying, they claimed.

Oliver Ellsworth, who would later serve as America's third chief justice, "contended that there was no lawyer...who would not say that ex-post-facto laws were void of themselves. It cannot be necessary to prohibit them." Future associate justice James Wilson agreed. The insertion of such an artless reminder would invite negative "reflexions on the Constitution—and proclaim that we are ignorant of the first principles of Legislation, or are constituting a Government which will be so." Fellow lawyers Gouverneur Morris and William Samuel Johnson concurred that the insertion of an ex-post-facto clause would be an "unnecessary" precaution.

On the other side of the issue stood, among others, delegates Daniel Carroll, Hugh Williamson, and John Rutledge. (Rutledge was yet another lawyer and future Supreme Court justice.) Various state constitutions had included express prohibitions of ex-post-facto laws, and Williamson declared that an explicit clause in the federal document "may do good here, because the Judges can take hold of it." Ultimately the Philadelphia delegates voted with these men to include an express prohibition on ex-post-facto laws. If some future Congress ever tried to violate first principles, this explicit clause would give judges something hard and concrete—something textual and specific—to "take hold of."[9]

Yet no one at Philadelphia was recorded as challenging Ellsworth's and Wilson's emphatic legal claim, in the Blackstonian tradition, that even without the clause, the best reading of the Constitution would construe the document as *implicitly* prohibiting all congressional statutes seeking to impose retroactive criminal punishment. As Blackstone had explained to his legions of readers on both sides of the Atlantic, unless the supreme legislature made crystal clear its specific intent to command an absurd or unjust result, the supreme law was to be interpreted so as to avoid patent absurdity or gross injustice.

Ellsworth and Wilson understood that this well-settled English rule of legal interpretation properly applied to America as well, but with a twist. In England, the supreme legislature was Parliament, and the supreme law was the corpus of parliamentary statutes. In America, the supreme law-maker would be the American people themselves, who were being asked by the Philadelphia framers to ordain and enact the supreme law of the Constitution. Unless that supreme law—the Constitution—specifically and pointedly authorized Congress to pass ex-post-facto criminal laws, the proper presumption would be that the document withheld this author-ity from Congress. Such unjust congressional enactments would simply fall outside the ambit of proper "legislative Power" vested in Congress by the Constitution. Blackstone's own language on ex-post-facto laws harmo-nized perfectly with Ellsworth's and Wilson's remarks. In a chapter on "the Nature of Laws in General," Blackstone had suggested that ex-post-facto statutes were not even laws, "properly" speaking.[10]

As finally proposed by the Philadelphia framers and eventually enacted by the American people, the Constitution's opening sentence proclaimed that one of the document's paramount objects was "to establish Justice." Here was additional textual support in the written Constitution itself for the Ellsworth-Wilson position, following Blackstone, that all the docu-ment's clauses had to be construed against the backdrop of the first prin-ciples of justice. Such principles could be contravened only by pointed tex-tual language or undeniably clear enacting intent.

LET'S NOW WEAVE TOGETHER THE threads on the table. Given the constitutional clauses and bits of historical evidence that we have consid-ered thus far, the Constitution as a whole should not be construed to allow a vice president to preside over his own impeachment trial. The image shocks our widely shared sense of fairness and justice. No one should be a judge in his own case. The result seems absurd. The point is elementary and elemental. It goes without saying.

Had the Constitution specifically commanded such a result in pointed language—say, in a clause proclaiming that "the vice president shall preside over the Senate *even in cases of his own impeachment*"—then there would be conclusive textual evidence that America's sovereign, the people, had specifically focused on the matter and had decided that the result was neither unjust nor absurd. But Article I, section 3, does not speak with this kind of unmistakable specificity.

If it could be shown that the Constitution's framers and ratifiers generally understood its bland rule about the Senate's regular presiding officer to apply even when that regular presiding officer was himself being impeached, then deference to this widespread understanding might be warranted. However, there is no evidence that Americans envisioned and embraced this result while drafting and ratifying this clause. On the contrary, there is strong reason to presume that they thought that Blackstone's approach—summarizing and illustrating the background interpretive canons of Anglo-American law—would obviously apply here. There is no relevant difference between Blackstone's lord of the manor Dale and America's vice president. In neither case should nonspecific language be construed to authorize a grotesque perversion of fair procedure.

ONE MORE THREAD ADDS FURTHER strength and texture to our emerging argument against vice-presidential self-dealing. It turns out that Article I, section 3, contains yet another relevant passage: "When the President of the United States is tried [in the Senate, sitting as an impeachment court], the Chief Justice shall preside."

True, these words say nothing explicit about the vice president. But if we give the matter even the slightest thought, it quickly dawns on us that the central purpose of this passage was to oust the vice president from the chair. In presidential impeachment trials, the chief justice should preside *precisely because the vice president should not.* This central purpose lay visible on the surface of the earliest version of this clause at Philadelphia, before the clause was rewritten for stylistic and organizational reasons: "The Vice President shall be ex officio President of the Senate, except when they sit to try the impeachment of the President, in which case the Chief Justice shall preside."[11]

The reason that the vice president should never preside in a presidential impeachment also springs to mind upon a moment's reflection: The vice president would have an intolerable conflict of interest. The problem would not be, as some modern observers might initially assume, that the vice president would be unduly inclined to favor his running mate, the president. Rather, the problem at the Founding was the exact opposite: The vice president was apt to be the leading *rival* of the president. Under the framers' version of the electoral college, presidential and vice-presidential candidates did not formally run as a partisan ticket. (That system emerged only after the ratification of the Twelfth Amendment in 1804.) Whoever came in second in the presidential election automatically became vice president—and would in turn automatically move into the top spot upon an impeachment court's conviction of the president. No man with so much to gain by a guilty verdict should preside over the trial.[12]

If the vice president may not sit in the chair when the president is on trial, surely it follows even more strongly—*a fortiori*, as lawyers would say—that the vice president may not properly preside over his own trial.[13]

Granted, a brazen legalistic counterargument might be made on behalf of this gross impropriety, as follows: The Constitution could have explicitly provided that the vice president would be ineligible to preside whenever *either* the president *or the vice president himself* was on trial, but the document did not so provide. The framers apparently did focus on the conflict-of-interest problem, and they decided that the problem existed only in cases of *presidential* impeachment.

Arguments like this give legal reasoning a bad name. There is simply no evidence that the framers or ratifiers clearly envisioned and specifically endorsed the ridiculous image of a vice president presiding over his own trial.

At Philadelphia, the impeachment debate centered almost entirely on issues of *presidential* impeachment. The very idea of creating the position of vice president did not emerge until the last days of the Convention, and what little attention this office did receive was often subsidiary to other issues of more pressing concern to the delegates. Even without access to then-secret Philadelphia records, a careful eighteenth-century reader could deduce from the final text itself that the vice presidency had received incomplete attention in the drafting process. While expressly authorizing compensation for House and Senate members in Article I, for presidents in Article II, and for Supreme Court (and other federal) judges in Article III, the document failed to even mention compensation for the vice president. Surely we should place no weight on this thoughtless omission; it would be silly to deny compensation to vice presidents on the theory that the document demands this odd result by negative implication. So, too, we should place no weight on the omission of an explicit recusal clause for vice presidential impeachments; it would be silly to read the chief-justice clause as authorizing, by mere negative implication, a vice president to sit in judgment of himself.[14]

In the year-long ratification process, there is no record of anyone saying that the vice president would be obliged to vacate the Senate chair *only* in cases of presidential impeachment. At no point did the Constitution's friends champion the odd idea that although a vice president should obviously not preside when he stood to gain an office, he nevertheless should preside when he stood to lose one.

Instead, leading Federalists explicitly invoked the *nemo judex in causa sua* principle in a variety of contexts and with a forcefulness that confirmed that this principle was a premise of the entire constitutional project. In *The Federalist* No. 10, James Madison, writing under the pen name "Publius," declared that "[n]o man is allowed to be a judge in his own cause; because his interest would certainly bias his judgment, and, not improbably, corrupt his integrity." In *The Federalist* No. 80, Alexander Hamilton (also writing as "Publius") reiterated and broadened the claim: "No man ought certainly to be a judge in his own cause, or in any cause in respect to which he has the least interest or bias."[15]

Had the specific issue of vice-presidential impeachment procedure ever come into sharp focus in the ratification debates, an able lawyer such as Wilson or Ellsworth would have had at his disposal a decisive Blackstonian defense of the constitutional text as actually drafted—a defense running something like this: In the case of a man literally presiding over his own case, it obviously went without saying that such a thing was impermissible. *Nemo judex in causa sua* was a foundational feature of civilized legal systems—not merely in late eighteenth-century America and England, but across the planet and over the centuries. The very image of a man presiding at his own trial bordered on the ludicrous: No one could be in two places at once—both in the chair and in the dock. Even if such eccentric geometry were physically possible, it would be legally absurd. To have explicitly prohibited such a thing would have been worse than a waste of ink. Had the draftsmen at Philadelphia dignified this scenario with an explicit textual prohibition, they would have invited public ridicule and needlessly cluttered the document. In the case of a *presidential* impeachment, however, the matter was not so self-evident. Strictly speaking, a vice president in the Senate chair would not be judging his own case, but someone else's. Here, the impropriety might be somewhat more debatable, and the application of the *nemo judex in causa sua* principle perhaps more contestable. So it made good sense for the Constitution to specifically resolve that issue in an explicit clause ousting the vice president from the chair and filling it instead with a more impartial officer, the chief justice.[16]

ON MARCH 5, 1868, WHEN AMERICANS FIRST WITNESSED Chief Justice Salmon P. Chase presiding over the Senate in a presidential impeachment trial, some may have wondered whether the framers had specified the best officer for such an occasion. As many of the politicians and spectators who packed the Senate chamber understood, Chase himself yearned to be president and had long bent his enormous energies toward that end. At the 1860 Republican Convention in Chicago, Chase had finished third in the presidential balloting. Early in 1861, Lincoln had tapped Chase to be his treasury secretary. But even while serving under Lincoln, Chase had dreamed of displacing him. The ubiquitous one-dollar greenbacks issued by the wartime Treasury Department had featured Chase's visage, not Lincoln's. In the opening months of 1864, Chase had angled, unsuccessfully, to position himself atop the November ticket.

Before naming Chase to the Court in late 1864, Lincoln had expressed "only one doubt" about Chase's fitness for the job. "He is a man of unbounded ambition, and has been working all his life to become President. That he can never be; and I fear that if I make him chief-justice he will simply become more restless and uneasy and neglect the place in his strife and intrigue to make himself President. If I were sure that he would go on the bench and give up his aspirations and do nothing but make himself a great judge, I would not hesitate a moment."[17]

Lincoln knew his man. Chase continued to hunger for the top executive post after he had secured the highest judicial job. Even as Johnson's trial was unfolding, its presiding officer was making plans to seek the upcoming Democratic nomination for the presidency—the very spot that the defendant was hoping to secure for himself.[18]

Was Chase, therefore, under an unwritten constitutional obligation to recuse himself at Johnson's impeachment trial? Should the Senate have tried to muscle him out when he did not stand down? Had we only an unwritten maxim, *nemo judex in causa sua*, to guide us, the answer might seem uncertain.

But the letter and spirit of the written Constitution made plain that Chase did not need to step aside. Merely harboring presidential ambitions—even intense and plausible presidential ambitions—was not a constitutionally disqualifying conflict of interest. Rather, this abstract sort of conflict of interest was obviously built into the very structure of the impeachment machinery designed by the framers. *This* kind of conflict of interest *was* something that America's supreme legislature, the people, *had* doubtless envisioned and embraced as a *necessary* part of the *main object* of Article I's impeachment clauses.

While the Constitution structured presidential impeachment as a judicialized proceeding—rife with the language of "Trial," "Case," "Judgment," and "convict[ion]," and to be presided over by the nation's highest judicial officer—the document also placed power to administer this judicialized system in the hands of regular politicians in the House and Senate. In the impeachment process, the president's trial bench and jury would consist not of professional judges or common citizens, but of uncommon political leaders, many of whom would likely harbor strong political ambitions—including, in some cases, presidential aspirations. From the outset, the Senate was expected to function as a nursery for future presidents and presidential aspirants. As the Founders' system predictably played out, most of the early presidents (including Johnson himself) had previously served as senators.[19]

Nor were chief justices expected to be men wholly uncontaminated by presidential hopes and dreams. At the Founding, presidents were widely seen as executive magistrates akin to judicial magistrates. Before the Philadelphia framers finally hit upon the idea of creating a standing office of vice president, delegate Gouverneur Morris had proposed that in case of presidential death or disability, presidential powers should devolve upon the chief justice. The men who eventually became America's first two chief justices, John Jay and John Rutledge, had both received substantial support in the presidential election of 1789, finishing third and fourth, respectively—directly behind George Washington and John Adams. America's fourth chief justice, John Marshall, was probably the Federalists' most eligible presidential prospect at the time of his nomination and confirmation. Recent scholarship suggests that, only days before his nomination to the Court in early 1801, Marshall, who was then secretary of state, had schemed to secure the presidency for himself in the constitutional confusion created by the tangled Adams-Jefferson-Burr election of 1800. If we consider more recent history, it is worth remembering that Chief Justice William Howard Taft was an ex-president, that Chief Justice Charles Evans Hughes had been the Republican Party nominee for the presidency, and that Chief Justice Earl Warren had been the Republican Party nominee for the vice presidency.[20]

Thus, in constituting senators and the chief justice as the president's impeachment court, the Founders surely envisioned presidential aspirants as proper judges of sitting presidents. The decisive difference between such figures and the vice president was that a senator or a chief justice would become chief executive only through a standard presidential election, whereas the vice president would *automatically* ascend upon the president's conviction—he would gain power *solely* because of the judicial verdict of the impeachment court. Giving the gavel to the vice president would therefore create an intolerable conflict of interest; giving the gavel to the chief justice would not.

GAVELS ASIDE, WHAT ABOUT THE role that Ohio Senator Benjamin Wade, the Senate president pro tempore, sought play as an impeachment judge and juror at Johnson's trial? In the event of Johnson's conviction, who would automatically ascend to the powers of the presidency solely because of that verdict? Benjamin Wade.

Recall that, from the moment President Lincoln died and Vice President Johnson moved up to replace him, the vice presidency stood vacant, and could not be refilled until the next presidential election. (This would change only with the Twenty-fifth Amendment, adopted after President John F. Kennedy's assassination a century later.) Thus, were the Senate to oust Johnson, someone other than the vice president would need to take over as chief executive. Anticipating scenarios of this sort, the Philadelphia framers had drafted a specific succession clause authorizing Congress to create a statutory line of succession. In 1792, Congress enacted a law placing the Senate president pro tempore first in the statutory line of succession and the House speaker second.[21]

Initially, we might wonder how America's written Constitution, which so carefully provided that the vice president should never preside over a president's impeachment trial, could have allowed almost the same thing—arguably, something even worse—by giving the Senate president pro tempore an actual vote in a presidential impeachment trial, when he, too, could hardly be an impartial judge. In fact, the written Constitution did no such thing. The Constitution's succession clause required Congress to designate an "officer"—presumably an executive-branch *cabinet* officer—to fill whatever succession gap might open up. The Congress in 1792 simply misunderstood the Constitution's command and instead specified legislative figures—who were not, properly speaking, "officers" within the meaning of the succession clause.* Stressing the letter and spirit of the key word, "officer," Congressman James Madison and others opposed the 1792 act on constitutional grounds, but neither Madison nor anyone else at the time explained in detail how the act, in addition to all its other flaws, would pervert the Constitution's carefully designed impeachment structure. In 1792 lawmakers were not focusing intently on the unusual situation of a double vacancy created by the impeachment and conviction of a vice-president-turned-president, as distinct from many of the other possible scenarios—of death, mental disability, physical disability, kidnapping, resignation, and so on—that might leave the nation simultaneously bereft of both president and vice president.[22]

---

* The political backstory here is that Treasury Secretary Alexander Hamilton's congressional allies in 1792 did not wish to boost Hamilton's cabinet rival, Secretary of State Thomas Jefferson. So Congress did what came naturally—excluding both cabinet officers from the line of succession and instead privileging its own chieftains.

With this old law on the books, however, Senator Wade found himself in an awkward position at the outset of Johnson's trial. Senators sympathetic to Johnson demanded that Wade recuse himself in obedience to the venerable *nemo judex* principle. As they saw it, Wade's status as Johnson's legal successor made it impossible for Wade to take the requisite impeachment oath to do "impartial justice" and thereafter to sit as a proper judge and juror in what the Constitution itself labeled a "Trial."[23]

Wade's defenders countered that his recusal would deprive the state of Ohio of its constitutional entitlement to two votes in the Senate chamber at a particularly important moment. Counterbalancing the venerable principle of *nemo judex in causa sua* was a common-law doctrine called "the rule of necessity." This rule allowed a judge with an otherwise disqualifying self-interest to hear a case if his participation were truly necessary or if all other judges would likely have a comparable conflict of interest. For example, the Constitution says that federal judicial salaries may not be decreased. Were Congress nevertheless to try to cut these salaries, would every federal judge be barred from hearing a judicial challenge to the cut? Judges over the centuries have answered this question differently; but the modern Supreme Court has proclaimed itself competent to hear such cases under the necessity exception to the *nemo judex in causa sua* principle. Similarly, Wade's senatorial allies explicitly argued that necessity required his participation, lest his state lose its constitutionally guaranteed equality in the Senate.[24]

In theory, Wade could have kept his Senate seat and his full constitutional voting privileges, and also avoided a personal conflict of interest, simply by renouncing his statutory right to succeed Johnson. Yet renunciation would not really have cured the self-interest problem; rather, it would have made House Speaker Schuyler Colfax the constitutional heir apparent, even though Colfax himself had played a prominent role earlier in the impeachment process, when the House in effect had acted as a grand jury, indicting Johnson for alleged high crimes and misdemeanors. A self-interested grand-jury foreman hardly seems much better than a self-interested trial judge or juror. Had *both* Wade and Colfax renounced their succession claims, there would have been no one left to replace Johnson, creating a vacuum that would have only widened the constitutional crisis.

Although Congress was formally free to repeal and replace the 1792 act in 1868, any replacement law would have come about with Johnson's impending removal in mind. Thus the new law would have lacked the virtues of a succession statute enacted impersonally and impartially, behind a suitably thick veil of ignorance obliging lawmakers to focus on long-term succession principles rather than short-term politics.

In short, no constitutionally perfect option existed in early March 1868. Both Wade's supporters and his critics made good points, and the real problem was that an old law made no sense, but could not be fixed in time for the trial.

After hours of public debate, the Senate eventually decided to seat Wade on March 6. Wade thereafter sat in judgment over Johnson and at the trial's end voted in a self-serving way—to convict. Rumor had it that by then Wade had already selected his would-be cabinet. But his self-interested vote did not tip the balance. Johnson ultimately had enough votes to remain in power. The final vote to convict was 35 to 19—just shy of the two-thirds needed to oust Johnson and crown Wade.

Looking back on the Wade affair, late nineteenth-century Americans found little to commend in the flawed 1792 statute that had created the conflict of interest. In 1886, Congress repealed the 1792 act, replacing it with a proper system of cabinet succession that excluded House and Senate members from the line of presidential succession and thereby freed the impeachment process from the specter of self-interested adjudication.

This might seem a happy ending to our saga, but history does not always yield happy endings. In 1947 Congress changed the succession rules yet again, inserting the House speaker and Senate president pro tempore (in that order) ahead of various cabinet officers in the line of succession.[25]

THE TAKE-HOME LESSON OF OUR story thus far is that sound constitutional interpretation involves a dialogue between America's written Constitution and America's unwritten Constitution. The latter, at a minimum, encompasses various principles implicit in the written document as a whole and/or present in the historical background, forming part of the context against which we must construe the entire text. The constitutional analysis in the preceding pages has not flowed from a literalistic and clause-bound reading of the written Constitution, which of course contains no clause that explicitly prohibits the vice president from presiding over his own impeachment trial. But neither has our argument strayed far from the written Constitution. Rather, we have been exploring a variety of unwritten sources that intertwine with the written text—sources such as Blackstone's canonical *Commentaries* summarizing late eighteenth-century rules of interpretation; Founding-era speeches and essays; preconstitutional and postconstitutional practices and precedents; principles and purposes implicit in various patches of constitutional text; and, above all, structural deductions from the constitutional system viewed holistically.

Standing alone, the written Constitution would appear to be inadequate. Were it read in a literal and flatfooted way, some of its clauses would seem indeterminate or even perverse when measured against the larger purposes of the document itself.

Standing alone, an unwritten Constitution would appear to be illegitimate. Were it to degenerate into an assortment of "constitutional rules" conjured up out of thin air, it would do violence to the fundamental choice of the American people over the centuries to ordain and amend a single written text that sets forth the nation's supreme law.

Neither America's written Constitution nor America's unwritten Constitution stands alone. Rather, the two stand together and support each other. The unwritten Constitution, properly understood, helps make sense of the written text. In turn, the written text presupposes and invites certain forms of interpretation that go beyond clause-bound literalism.[26]

If anyone thinks that all the interpretive puzzles we have been pondering would have happily disappeared had the framers simply been more textually explicit by inserting into the written Constitution a clause declaring that "no man may be a judge in his own case," think again. A clause along these lines would hardly have been self-defining. Would such a clause have (implicitly) recognized a countervailing principle of necessity? When would such a counterprinciple, whether implicit or explicit, come into play? (Recall that some judges have hesitated to sit in cases involving issues of judicial compensation, while other judges have sat without compunction; and that senators in 1868 sharply disagreed about whether Wade's participation in the Johnson impeachment could be justified by "necessity.") How broadly or narrowly should we define the judge's "own case"? For instance, what about a lawsuit where a judge's brother was the lawyer for one of the parties? (In *Dred Scott v. Sanford*, Justice Benjamin Curtis sat in judgment and famously dissented, voting to support the legal claims of plaintiff Dred Scott, whose lawyer was the justice's brother, George Ticknor Curtis. Today, this decision to sit would probably set off an avalanche of criticism by legal ethicists.) How broadly should we define being a "judge"? (While Chief Justice Marshall did not sit in judgment in the 1816 Virginia land case of *Martin v. Hunter's Lessee*, he did draft the legal petition to his colleagues in his own quite recognizable handwriting, and he may have discussed the relevant legal issues with his brethren in their common boardinghouse. Here, too, modern legal ethicists would probably insist on stricter standards.) Thus, even an explicit textual affirmation of the *nemo judex in causa sua* principle in the Constitution itself would have left open a range of questions whose answers could not simply be deduced from the words themselves.[27]

To see the limits of clause-bound textualism from another angle, recall that the Constitution does contain an explicit ex-post-facto clause. Even so, the clause has given rise to many questions on which the text is hardly decisive. What if a law does not change the substantive rules of criminal conduct but does retroactively modify evidentiary rules of proving criminality—say, by allowing certain kinds of evidence that were inadmissible at the time the crime was committed? What if a law retroactively authorizes a harsher punishment for conduct that was universally understood to be a heinous crime at the moment of its commission? What if a law merely creates a new set of courts that did not exist at the time of the crime? At the Philadelphia Convention, James Wilson overstated his case when he proclaimed that an explicit ex-post-facto clause would be "useless." If nothing else, the clause has usefully eliminated whatever small uncertainty might have existed about certain core cases involving retroactive criminalization of actions that were wholly innocent when done. But Wilson was right to say that, even with the inclusion of an explicit clause, the written text would not suffice to answer all hard constitutional questions: "Both sides will agree to the principle & will differ as to its application."[28]

At these junctures, where isolated clauses shade off into indeterminacy or perversity, we must raise our sights and see the big picture: the Constitution as a whole.

"Congress shall have Power"

TO BETTER UNDERSTAND THE KIND of interpretive approach needed when we seek to find the implicit Constitution hiding behind the document's explicit words, let's now undertake a completely different case study. Having just worked through various unusual constitutional issues that arose at a unique hour of American history—the opening moments of the first-ever presidential impeachment trial—some readers might wonder whether the tool of holistic reading is of help in handling the more mundane matters that routinely arise in ordinary courtrooms. In fact, this tool did much of the work in perhaps the most canonical Supreme Court case ever decided. Precisely because this great case had nothing to do with presidential impeachment, and involved a wholly different set of issues— issues concerning the breadth of congressional lawmaking power and the reserved powers of states, issues that continue to arise in routine litigation in twenty-first-century courts—a close look at the Court's landmark decision will make clear that the technique of reading between the lines has widespread application.

WERE SOME FUTURE GENERATION EVER to erect a monument to America's greatest judicial decisions—a case-law version of Mount Rushmore—*McCulloch v. Maryland* would surely make the final cut. So would *Marbury v. Madison* and *Brown v. Board of Education*, but unlike most other landmark cases, *McCulloch* deserves its place in the pantheon for its style as well as its substance. To read *McCulloch* is to behold the art of constitutional interpretation at its acme.

The *McCulloch* case arose when Maryland tried to impose a targeted tax on the Bank of the United States—a bank that Congress had initially set up in 1791 and had revived in the wake of the War of 1812. In an opinion by Chief Justice Marshall writing for a unanimous bench in 1819, the *McCull-*

och Court decided two important issues. First, the Court held that Congress had acted within its constitutional powers in creating and renewing the national bank. Second, the justices ruled that no state could, in the absence of congressional consent, impose a tax on that bank.

This much is well understood by both modern civics textbooks and modern Court opinions. But the actual chain of constitutional argumentation that Marshall forged to reach these results has become twisted in the modern retelling. Prominent modern citations to *McCulloch* are miscitations, treating the opinion as if it rested on certain explicit constitutional clauses. In fact, Marshall repeatedly relied not on explicit clauses but on the implicit meaning of the Constitution as a whole.

Begin with the first issue decided by *McCulloch*—the question of congressional power to create a national bank. Ask a lawyer or a knowledgeable layperson to name the basis for Marshall's decision, and he will probably point you unhesitatingly to the necessary-and-proper clause. This clause—the concluding language of Article I, section 8, of the Constitution—declares that "Congress shall have Power ...To make all Laws which shall be necessary and proper for carrying into Execution the foregoing Powers."

According to conventional wisdom, *McCulloch* read this specific clause as giving the federal government important additional powers—powers above and beyond those conferred on the central government by the preceding ("foregoing") clauses of Article I, section 8, such as the powers to regulate interstate commerce and to raise armies. In a notable 2005 case, *Gonazales v. Raich*, Justice Antonin Scalia cited *McCulloch* for exactly this point. (The issue in *Raich* was whether Congress had power to criminalize medicinal marijuana use in a situation where a state had legalized medicinal use. By a vote of six to three, the Court sided with Congress.) All told, the various justices who wrote opinions in *Raich* cited *McCulloch* ten times, and while they disagreed about many things, no one took issue with Justice Scalia's claims that *McCulloch* had relied on the necessary-and-proper clause and had read that clause as adding to the other powers enjoyed by the central government.[29]

In fact, *McCulloch* did no such thing. *McCulloch* said something closer to the opposite—that perhaps the necessary-and-proper clause conferred no additional power on the federal government.[30]

Before Marshall in *McCulloch* said a single word about this clause, he declared that the Constitution as a whole seemed to empower Congress to create a national bank and that anyone who thought otherwise must shoulder the burden of proof. According to Marshall, even "in the absence" of a necessary-and-proper clause, congressional power should be read in a generous and commonsensical way so as to achieve the basic purposes for which the American people had established the Constitution. Marshall believed that, had the Constitution not contained a necessary-and-proper clause, Congress would nonetheless enjoy considerable flexibility in exercising its "great powers," including the powers to regulate interstate commerce and to raise armies. Such flexibility, wrote Marshall, surely encompassed the power to create a national bank.

True, Marshall did devote several pages to the necessary-and-proper clause. Marshall claimed that Maryland (which was attacking the bank) had invoked the clause to *limit* what would otherwise be the broad natural sweep of the earlier enumerated powers of Congress. It was enough for Marshall to show—and it was all he purported to show—that the necessary-and-proper clause did not subtract anything from the earlier enumerations of federal power. Whether the clause added power, Marshall pointedly declined to say. Perhaps, he suggested, the clause did expand power. "Its terms purport to enlarge, not to diminish." Or perhaps, he mused, the clause simply was meant to "remove all doubts" that all the other congressional powers should be read with suitable breadth. Either way—whether the clause was a plus or merely a zero so far as federal power was concerned—it was not a minus, said Marshall. The clause "cannot be construed to restrain" the earlier enumerated powers.

There is a reason why *McCulloch* has been so widely misread. The necessary-and-proper clause is a concrete and seemingly specific text. Like the ex-post-facto clause, it is something, we instinctively feel, that judges and other faithful interpreters may properly "take hold of." By contrast, we may worry that once a judge goes beyond a specific clause, he might simply make things up, faithless to his constitutional oath. The thought that Marshall may have been faithless in perhaps the most canonical Court decision of all time unnerves us. So Marshall is depicted as a narrow textualist, building his constitutional church on the solid rock of an explicit clause.[31]

Marshall in *McCulloch* was indeed a faithful interpreter, but he was not a clause-bound textualist. Rather, he elegantly blended a close reading of the written Constitution with a sensitive understanding of America's unwritten Constitution.

He began by stressing that not everything in the Constitution was, or could sensibly be, explicit. Some things were merely implied. "Among the enumerated powers, we do not find that of establishing a bank....*But there is no phrase in the instrument which...excludes incidental or implied powers; and which requires that every thing granted shall be expressly and minutely expressed*" (emphasis added). Later in this section, he reiterated that he read the Constitution as generally giving Congress an "*implied*" authority "of selecting means for executing the enumerated powers" (emphasis added).

The need for such implications was not due to poor draftsmanship at Philadelphia. Rather, Marshall insisted, this need derived from the very essence of the Constitution as an embodiment of American popular sovereignty. If every aspect of constitutional law—every constitutional power, every constitutional limit on power, every minor constitutional exception and niggling qualification to a general constitutional rule, every constitutional principle entitled to weight in constitutional interpretation—had to be expressly and minutely included in the text of the Constitution itself, the document would, said Marshall, "partake of the prolixity of a legal code." (He had in mind here something like today's tax code.) Such a detailed and labyrinthine text "would probably never be understood by the public." At that point, the essence of America's Constitution as the people's law— as a terse, accessible text that had been understood, debated, and ratified by the people, and that could thereafter be understood, interpreted, and, if necessary, amended by the people—would have been fatally compromised.

If not the necessary-and-proper clause, then which enumerated powers authorized Congress to create a national bank? The chief justice did almost all the heavy lifting in a single paragraph that did little more than gesture toward a cluster of clauses. None of these clauses did Marshall closely parse. Several he only paraphrased:

Although, among the enumerated powers of government, we do not find the word "bank" or "incorporation," we find the great powers to lay and collect taxes; to borrow money; to regulate commerce; to declare and conduct a war; to raise and support armies and navies. The sword and the purse, all the external relations, and no inconsiderable portion of the industry of the nation, are entrusted to its government....A government, entrusted with such ample powers, on the due execution of which the happiness and prosperity of the nation so vitally depends, must also be entrusted with ample means for their execution.

Viewed one by one, virtually every clause that Marshall invoked can be dismissed if read in a narrow, literalistic, autistic way—the way Congressman James Madison read them in 1791, when he (unsuccessfully) argued in the House of Representatives against the constitutionality of the first national bank. Strictly speaking, the law creating the bank did not *itself* lay taxes or borrow money. As a matter of strict logic, one can imagine an army without a bank, and a bank without an army. And so on.[32]

Marshall's constitutional genius was to grasp that Americans had not ratified the Constitution clause by clause, enumerated power by enumerated power. The people had ratified the Constitution as a whole, and thus the federal government's powers needed to be read as a whole rather than as a jumble of discrete clauses. In Marshall's words, the question of federal power should "depend on a fair construction of the *whole instrument*" (emphasis added), read through the prism of the general purposes that the American people had in mind when they framed and ratified the document.

In one of *McCulloch*'s most quotable—if least understood—lines, Marshall stressed (with italics) that "we must never forget, that it is *a constitution* we are expounding." Three intertwined ideas lay close to the surface of this reminder. First, the Constitution could not remain true to its nature as a document from and for the people were it to become overly long and intricate. Here, the distinction was between "a constitution" and a code. Second, the Constitution warranted rules of interpretation that were different from those of the earlier Articles of Confederation, which, Marshall reminded his readers, had openly purported to "exclude[] incidental or implied powers." Here, the distinction was between "a constitution" and a pure confederation based entirely on state sovereignty. Third, the Constitution was a "whole instrument." Here, the distinction was between "a constitution" and an assortment of clauses read in disjointed fashion.

McCulloch's pivotal paragraph exemplified Marshall's trademark brand of holistic analysis. The great chief proceeded in three steps. Step One: The central purpose of the Constitution was to safeguard national security across a vast continent. This was apparent when one pulled back from specific clauses and saw the big picture—in Marshall's words, "[t]he sword and the purse." (Though Marshall did not mention it, this purpose was also evident in the words "common defence" and "general Welfare," which appeared both in the Constitution's Preamble and at the outset of Congress's enumerated powers.) Step Two: Creating a national bank fit sensibly within that central purpose, given all the ways that a continental bank might facilitate continental defense. In particular, Marshall underscored that a national bank with branches across the land could ensure that American soldiers—who might need to march from "the St. Croix to the Gulph of Mexico, from the Atlantic to the Pacific"—would be paid on site and on time. (As a veteran of Valley Forge, Marshall knew deep in his bones how all could be lost if men at a decisive time and place deserted or deteriorated for want of funds or supplies.) Step Three: This kind of sensible fit with the Constitution's broad purposes, as opposed to a mathematically perfect nexus between a statute and a specific empowering clause, was all that was required. Had the Constitution's words "imperiously require[d]" a tighter fit, judges would "have only to obey." Absent an explicit constitutional command to this effect, the commonsensical connection between a national bank and national defense (not to mention national fiscal operations more generally) would easily suffice.

WITH THIS ANALYSIS OF ENUMERATED powers in mind, let's now return to Marshall's discussion of the necessary-and-proper clause. Why, we might wonder, didn't Marshall try to expand federal authority still further by arguing that the necessary-and-proper clause added something extra to the previous enumerations? Given that the clause, as Marshall read it, did not subtract from the earlier enumerations, what was its purpose if it did not add some extra power?

Marshall suggested that perhaps the clause was merely *declaratory* of what would have been the best reading of the Constitution even had this clause not existed. Viewed this way, the clause aimed neither to increase nor decrease federal power but rather to add clarity and remove doubt. With this clause in place, it would be plain to all that, in sharp contrast to the old Confederation's Congress, the new Constitution's Congress would have some latitude in implementing its enumerated powers.

This was how the clause had been presented to the American people by leading Federalists during the ratification period. In the first major battleground state to hold a ratifying convention, Pennsylvania, James Wilson explained that the clause "say[s] no more than that the powers we have already particularly given, shall be effectually carried into execution." Writing as "Publius," Alexander Hamilton in *The Federalist* No. 33 admitted that the clause "might be chargeable with tautology or redundancy" because it was added merely for clarity and "greater caution" to guard against a stingy reading of the other enumerated powers. Madison/Publius echoed the point in *The Federalist* No. 44. Even without this explicit clause, "there can be no doubt that all the particular powers requisite as means of executing the general powers would have resulted to the government *by unavoidable implication*" (emphasis added).[33]

Seen this way, the clause calls to mind the ex-post-facto clause, which was also understood by leading Federalists as simply making explicit what would otherwise have been merely (but clearly) implicit. Indeed, the link between the two clauses was even tighter, for the necessary-and-proper clause included an important textual reminder that congressional laws should be "proper." Marshall understood *propriety* in this context to mean that congressional laws had to fit with the "spirit of the constitution" and not merely its "letter." A law that was merely a "pretext" should not be upheld under the necessary-and-proper clause, Marshall insisted.

Note what this means. As Marshall took pains to prove, the necessary-and-proper clause subtracted nothing from federal power. The clause "cannot be construed to restrain" the earlier enumerated powers of Congress. Therefore, Marshall believed that the earlier enumerations themselves included a propriety requirement—albeit an implicit one. Just as Blackstone, in a passage paraphrased at Philadelphia by Ellsworth and Wilson, had insisted that ex-post-facto laws were not "*properly*" viewed as true laws, so Marshall insisted that all federal laws were governed by a propriety requirement, and would have been so governed even if the necessary-and-proper clause had never existed.

An illustrative hypothetical to highlight the difference between "proper" and "improper" congressional action: Suppose that in June 1789, the First Congress had enacted a law restricting the transportation across state lines of certain "noxious" items. Ordinarily, such a law would fall squarely within the letter and spirit of Congress's enumerated power to "regulate Commerce...among the several States." Suppose, however, that this law had defined "noxious" items to consist solely of "newspapers and pamphlets recommending that the people elect a different set of Representatives to Congress in 1790." Would such a law truly fit the spirit of the Constitution? Would this law be constitutionally "proper," or instead be an impermissible "pretext"?

In confronting this hypothetical, most modern Americans would instinctively reach for the First Amendment. But in June 1789, the First Amendment had yet to be proposed by Congress or ratified by the states.

No matter. The free-expression core of that amendment was itself merely declaratory—making textually plain what was otherwise strongly implicit. When we read the Constitution as a "whole instrument," we readily see that it was designed to establish a regime of fair elections and thus robust political expression. In such a republic, the people would freely choose their congressmen, and Congress would have no proper power to squelch or skew electoral discourse, especially discourse about whether incumbent congressmen should be reelected. In light of the entire Constitution's basic structure, our hypothetical law should be seen as an improper, and therefore unconstitutional, use of an express enumerated power—even in the absence of the First Amendment, and, indeed, even had the Constitution omitted the purely declaratory word "proper." From day one, the Constitution prohibited certain kinds of federal censorship even though the underlying prohibition could be said to be purely implicit.[34]

LET US NOW TURN to the second question decided by *McCulloch*, and Marshall's argument that no state could unilaterally tax the federal bank (or any other proper federal instrumentality). Today, many treat this part of *McCulloch* as relying solely on the text of the Constitution's supremacy clause, which declares that "the Laws of the United States which shall be made in Pursuance" of the Constitution prevail over "Contrary" state laws. In 1983, Justice Harry Blackmun, joined by three colleagues, wrote that "the Supremacy Clause, of course, is the foundation of *McCulloch v. Maryland*, where the Court laid down the principle that the property, functions, and instrumentalities of the Federal Government are immune from taxation by its constituent parts."[35]

In fact, *McCulloch* invoked the supremacy clause in a more subtle way. Marshall treated the issue of state taxation of a federal agency as governed not so much by the decisive words of a single clause as by the deeper principles animating the document as a whole. Marshall insisted on reading between the lines to vindicate the document's spirit, rather than focusing solely on its letter:

> *There is no express provision for the case*, but the [bank's] claim has been sustained on a principle which so entirely pervades the constitution, is so intermixed with the materials which compose it, so interwoven with its web, so blended with its texture, as to be incapable of being separated from it, without rending it into shreds. This great principle is, that the constitution and the laws made in pursuance thereof are supreme; that they control the constitution and laws of the respective States, and cannot be controlled by them. (Emphasis added.)

Marshall had at least three reasons for conceding that no "express provision" applied. First, nothing in the congressional statute creating the bank explicitly immunized it from state taxation, though such immunity was surely implicit. (It went without saying.) Second, the 1781 Articles of Confederation—the compact among the thirteen states that the Constitution had displaced—had included language in Article IV, paragraph 1, that spoke directly and specifically to the issue of state taxation of federal property: "[N]o imposition, duties or restriction shall be laid by any state, on the property of the united states." No clause in the Constitution itself was comparably explicit. Third, the Constitution, in Article I, section 10, declared that "[n]o State shall, without the Consent of Congress," impose certain taxes on tonnage, imports, and exports. Maryland argued that these clauses should be read to set forth the *only* kinds of state taxes that were unconstitutional, and that otherwise states should be free to tax as they pleased.

Marshall sidestepped these mild clausal embarrassments by reminding readers of the principles that pervaded the Constitution as a whole, as distinct from those that had animated the Articles of Confederation. The Confederation had been proudly premised on state sovereignty: Its Articles had opened by proclaiming that "[e]ach state retains its sovereignty, freedom, and independence, and every Power, Jurisdiction, and right, which is not by this confederation *expressly* delegated to the United States" (emphasis added). In a document that prioritized states' rights so emphatically and sweepingly, the immunity of federal agencies and federal property from state taxation was something that needed to be, and therefore was, stated expressly. As Marshall made clear at the outset of his *McCulloch* opinion, the Constitution stood on wholly different ground. It was not premised on state sovereignty. It pointedly omitted any language requiring that all limits on state power be "expressly" stated. In *this* document, no counterpart language to the old Article IV, paragraph 1, was needed. The impropriety of state taxes on proper federal agencies went without saying.[36]

Marshall proceeded to elaborate how state taxation of federal instrumentalities inverted first principles of logic and legitimacy. Logically, the whole was greater than the part; thus, no mere part of the union could undo what the union as a whole had done. States were represented in the Congress that had created the bank, but the union was not symmetrically represented in the Maryland legislature. In burdening the bank, Maryland was in effect taxing unrepresented out-of-staters who had financed the federal institution—New Yorkers, Pennsylvanians, and so on, who had no vote in Maryland. If the Revolution and the Declaration of Independence meant anything, surely they stood for the proposition that in America, there should be no taxation without representation.[37]

Here, as elsewhere, Marshall exemplified not clause-bound literalism, but holistic constitutional interpretation. From start to finish in *McCulloch*, he showed us by example how to read between the lines.

"Speech"

IF STATES MAY NOT OBSTRUCT a duly authorized federal bank, what about state obstructions of other legitimate federal functions? In particular, what about state obstructions of national political discourse? To answer these questions, we will need to move past *McCulloch*'s specific facts and venture into another legal quadrant altogether. Here, too, we shall see that faithful constitutional interpreters must transcend clause-bound literalism by fixing their eyes on the document as a whole.

A not-entirely-hypothetical hypothetical: Suppose that in 1858, an antislavery congressman from Illinois returned to his district to address his constituents. In vivid but wholly nonviolent, nondefamatory language, our hypothetical congressman proclaimed slavery "a vast moral evil and a monstrous injustice—a hateful and ungodly institution that corrupts the white man, tyrannizes the black man, and mocks the divine order in which all men are created equal." Our imaginary congressman—let's call him Lincoln Abraham—went on to opine that voters in every slave state should press their state lawmakers to "act now to put slavery on a path of extinction," and that Congress should enact federal legislation subsidizing these state reforms. Suppose further that Abraham printed his passionate speech as a campaign pamphlet and personally sent copies of this pamphlet, through private channels, to political allies outside Illinois, including friends and relatives in North Carolina. Finally, let's suppose that North Carolina then indicted Abraham for the crime of encouraging slave discontent.

History buffs will recognize this fictional case as only a slight twist on what actually happened in the late 1850s. Many slave states criminalized peaceful antislavery or egalitarian expression and tried to shut down core political speech by antislavery leaders, including northern congressmen.[38]*

---

* For example, a North Carolina statute, enacted in 1830 and revised in 1854, made it a crime to circulate "any written or printed pamphlet or paper...the evident tendency whereof is to cause slaves to become discontented with the bondage in which they are held...and free negroes to be dissatisfied with their social condition." First-time offenders could be whipped, pilloried, and imprisoned for at least a year. Repeat offenders could be put to death. In 1860, North Carolina's legislature decided that this law was too soft on crime, and instead authorized capital punishment of first offenders. In 1859, a North Carolina grand jury did in fact indict, and demand the extradition of, various northern political leaders who had lent

But surely the Constitution circa 1858, properly construed, did not allow states to criminalize political discourse between public servants and the voters they served. Our imaginary Representative Abraham's remarks exemplify a species of speech at the very heart of the American system of government—political opinions communicated by a congressman to his constituents and fellow citizens on the most pressing political issue of the era. No state could bar this sort of speech, or prevent voters from other districts from listening in if they so desired. If a state may not shut down a national bank, neither may a state shut down a national debate about national policy. True, the Constitution as of 1858 did not in any single clause explicitly say that North Carolina could not suppress a political address by an Illinois congressman. But read as a whole and in context, the document certainly implied at least that much.[39]

For a strict textualist, the First Amendment (which had of course become part of the federal Constitution long before the 1850s) is entirely beside the point. The first word of the First Amendment is "Congress." *Congress* may make no law abridging freedom of speech or of the press. No words of the First Amendment place any explicit restriction on *states*.

But this hardly means that state legislatures in antebellum America were by negative implication free to run roughshod. As we have seen, arguments from negative implication can sometimes seriously mislead us and point us toward constitutionally outlandish results. It is absurd to think (by negative implication) that the only time that the vice president must recuse himself is when the president is being impeached. It is erroneous to think (by negative implication) that the only proper limits on Congress's enumerated powers are those expressly and minutely set forth in the terse text. It is unreasonable to think (by negative implication) that the only taxes that states are prohibited from imposing are the ones explicitly banned by the Constitution. Likewise, it is wrong to think that Congress is the only government entity that must respect freedom of speech or of the press.[40]

Today, almost no well-trained lawyer reads the First Amendment in so

---

their names in support of Hinton Helper's provocative (and presciently titled) antislavery pamphlet *The Impending Crisis*. More than sixty Republican congressmen had endorsed the pamphlet and had proposed to distribute an abridged version as a campaign tract.

narrow and literalistic a fashion. If a federal judge attempts to impose a gag order on reporters in the courtroom, or if the president tries to muzzle the press in order to prevent embarrassing leaks, lawyers immediately grab hold of the First Amendment, even if Congress is not directly involved and the other branches of the federal government purport to be acting under their own inherent powers. The famous 1971 Pentagon Papers case, *New York Times Co. v. United States*, was decided under the First Amendment, even though the case pivoted not on a statute enacted by Congress but on the unilateral actions of the president—Richard Nixon, who was trying to censor *The New York Times*. Modern lawyers instinctively heed the admonition of the Ninth Amendment, whose language cautions against drawing hasty negative inferences when reading the Bill of Rights.

The First Amendment's first word, "Congress," is now read as a synecdoche: The right of free expression applies against all branches of the federal government and rightly so. If the president and federal courts cannot censor citizens even with the backing of a congressional law, it would be odd to think that they can do so without such a law. Limits on the less electorally accountable branches of the federal government follow *a fortiori* from those imposed on Congress.

While it makes good sense to read the First Amendment as guarding against all *federal* abridgments of free speech, it would be far more troubling to construe the amendment as creating rights against states. That amendment was originally designed by Federalists in the First Congress to placate Anti-Federalists anxious about the wide scope of federal powers and eager to protect legitimate states' rights. Reading the Bill of Rights as giving the federal government (especially federal courts) broad extra powers to limit state governments does somersaults with that original understanding. Madison himself, the main sponsor of the First Amendment, drafted a separate amendment that would have safeguarded the rights of speech and press (and certain other rights) against states; but that proposed amendment failed to clear the Senate, where states'-rights sentiment ran strong.[41]

Thus, the First Amendment is not the ultimate source of the Constitution's limits on state censorship. But surely nothing in that amendment insulates state speech regulation from federal oversight if such oversight is authorized by other clauses or by the Constitution as a whole. Members of Congress—and by extension, other agents of the federal government—are prohibited from *abridging* free expression, but not from *protecting* it.[42]

THERE IS ANOTHER FREE-SPEECH CLAUSE in the Constitution that deserves our attention as we ponder the fate of our imaginary Representative Abraham. Though the original Constitution contained no clause explicitly affirming the rights of ordinary citizens to speak and publish freely, it did guarantee, in Article I, section 6, that "Senators and Representatives... shall not be questioned" outside Congress for "any Speech or Debate in either House." Thanks to this clause, no government entity (except the House of Representatives itself, pursuant to its own internal disciplinary rules) could ever punish, tax, hold liable, or otherwise obstruct a House member for a House speech. In performing its vital function as America's preeminent debating society and policy-making forum, Congress could never be muzzled by the federal courts, by the president and his minions, *or by state legislatures, state executives, or state courts.*

In safeguarding congressional speech from state censorship, this clause built squarely on foundations laid by the Articles of Confederation, which had similarly provided that "[f]reedom of speech and debate in congress shall not be impeached or questioned in any Court, or place out of Congress." The main objective of this precursor clause was to protect congressional speech from state-law interference—an objective that lived on in the later language of the Constitution. If anything, the need to protect congressional speech from state assaults was even greater in a document designed to make the new Congress far more independent of states than the old Congress had been.

The stunningly broad immunity that this clause gave to congressional speech surpassed the protection that the First Amendment afforded to ordinary citizen speech. Even if a representative on the House floor intentionally spewed malicious falsehoods about some hapless citizen, the speaker was nonetheless shielded from the ordinary defamation laws applicable to ordinary speakers. No criminal prosecution, state or federal, could ever be brought against a representative even when a floor speech had been designed to incite and had in fact incited immediate lawless violence, or had spilled military secrets in wartime.

Counterbalancing this extraordinary breadth and absolutism of protection were several notable limits in Article I, section 6. First, only sitting congressmen—political leaders who had won widespread respect and cleared high electoral hurdles—could claim this privilege. Second, Congress itself had broad authority to prevent improper speech from taking place on the floor. Parliamentary rules of order and decorum could be invoked to cut off an abusive or irresponsible speaker—in midsentence, if necessary. Third, Congress could punish miscreant members after the fact, with sanctions ranging up to temporary imprisonment in the Capitol and expulsion from Congress.

Although the letter of the Article I speech clause confined itself to congressional utterances within the Capitol, the spirit of the clause radiated more broadly. Given that the fictional Lincoln Abraham would have been untouchable by North Carolina had he simply addressed his colleagues, his constituents, and his fellow Americans from the House floor, it would be odd to think that he should lose protection merely because he made it easier for his far-flung audience to hear his ideas. Surely the right to hear what was actually said on the floor of the people's House should not be limited to those Americans who happened to live in or close to the District of Columbia. Had Abraham first delivered his speech in the House and then merely repeated it verbatim in his district and in his pamphlet, a strong case could be made for absolute protection of his mere repetition and republication.[43]

But let's suppose that our imaginary Abraham was not merely repeating in his district and in his pamphlet words that he had first uttered in the House. Although Abraham would then fall outside the particularly absolute version of freedom of speech built into the congressional free-speech clause, he could still lay claim to the basic free-speech right of all Americans: the right to voice his nonviolent, nondefamatory political opinions to any citizen willing to listen, a right implicit in the very structure of the Constitution.

HERE, AT LAST, we reach the heart of the matter. The entire Constitution was based on the notion that the American people stood supreme over government officials, who were mere servants of the public, not masters over them. Under first principles of popular-sovereignty theory and principal-agent law (which governs, for example, employer-employee relations), it was improper—not to mention impudent—for mere public servants in either the federal or the state governments to prohibit their legal masters, the sovereign citizenry, from floating political opinions and weighing political proposals among themselves. The voters had an inalienable right to voice and hear nonviolent, nondefamatory criticisms of (and apologies for) incumbent legislators, state and federal, and also had a foundational right to voice and hear vigorous arguments about legal institutions such as slavery and legal reforms such as abolition. The entire structure of the American system presupposed these rights.[44]

The federal system also presupposed that Illinois speakers had a right to communicate with willing listeners in North Carolina, who in turn had a right to import this speech from out of state, just as they had a right to other forms of interstate commerce. No state official could unilaterally bar this commerce in ideas and opinions. Nor could Congress have "properly" prohibited this species of interstate commerce, even prior to the adoption of the First Amendment, whose free-expression language was largely declaratory, adding textual emphasis to a principle already evident in the Constitution's basic structure.

Indeed, in deciding whether to ratify the Constitution in the late 1780s, the American people held a year-long continental conversation among themselves that featured remarkably robust and uninhibited interstate political speech and publication free from any notable government censorship, even though much of the expression was sharply critical of existing governmental authorities and legal institutions (including slavery). Even before the First Amendment, the very act of constitutional ordainment itself gave legal validity to a robust right of political expression. Without such a right, the Constitution might never have come into existence, and the people's vaunted right to alter or abolish government might have become a grim joke rather than a proud reality.

We shall return to this issue in the next chapter, where we shall more systematically analyze various unwritten elements that were part of the very process by which the people ordained, and, later, amended, the written Constitution. For now, it is worth emphasizing that nothing in the strong antislavery words uttered by our hypothetical Lincoln Abraham differed in any relevant way from passionate utterances that occurred abundantly and without legal repression during the great constitutional conversation of 1787–1788.

"executive Power"

WE HAVE PLAYED LONG ENOUGH with the imaginary Lincoln Abraham. Let us now confront the flesh-and-blood Abraham Lincoln. To what extent could a Lincoln-hating slave state—say, North Carolina—have lawfully obstructed the president in the early days of his administration by trumping up criminal charges against him and demanding that he immediately come south to face trial? With this hypothetical—our last one in this chapter—we shall see once again the need to read each constitutional clause in the context of the document as a whole.

HAD NORTH CAROLINA simply indicted Abraham Lincoln for the political opinions put forth in his speeches and publications, the president could of course have claimed the same inalienable rights of expression enjoyed by our hypothetical Lincoln Abraham or any other citizen. But let's suppose that North Carolina instead cooked up charges that did not on their face arraign the president merely for his political opinions. Imagine, for instance, a grand jury indictment charging that Lincoln had secretly conspired to incite bloody slave uprisings and the mass murder of innocents by sending arms, ammunition, and funds to John Brown and his fanatic partners in crime.[45]

No provision of the Constitution explicitly shields a sitting president from state criminal prosecution—or from state imprisonment upon conviction, for that matter. Also counseling against presidential immunity is our old friend, the argument from negative implication. As we have already seen, Article I, section 6, does explicitly shield senators and representatives from state (or federal) lawsuits based on their floor speeches. That section also shields congressmen from certain civil-litigation tactics involving physical arrests—arrests that might improperly prevent the targeted lawmakers from attending Congress. No comparably worded clause of the Constitution expressly protects the president from state (or federal) litigation that might intrude upon the proper performance of his duties. According to the negative-implication argument, when the Founders meant to create special shields for federal functionaries, they did so explicitly. On this logic, a sitting president must face a jury of his peers just like the rest of us.

Perhaps—but only if this result makes sense of the document as a whole and its deep structures and principles. After all, the argument from negative implication is itself only an implication. No explicit constitutional clause says that Article I, section 6, enumerates the only constitutional immunities deserving of recognition. No explicit constitutional clause says that "the president shall enjoy no privileges or immunities save those expressly enumerated." On the contrary, Article II begins, sweepingly, by vesting the president with "[t]he executive Power" of the United States. As a textual matter, the question is whether immunity from a state criminal proceeding (and from potential state imprisonment) should be understood as an implied component of federal "executive Power." The argument for reading immunity into this Article II phrase is hardly a wild textual stretch: It may be rather difficult (to put it mildly) for a president to fulfill the many and varied duties of his office from a state criminal courtroom or a state prison cell.

True, the president's immunity was not textually specified to the same degree as was Congress's. The framers may well have felt a special need to mark the contours of congressional immunities in black and white because as a practical matter the protection of these immunities would be committed to the other two branches in ordinary law enforcement and adjudication. Whatever implicit immunities were appropriate for those other branches, the framers might have assumed, would be effectively self-enforcing and hence needed little textual reinforcement. Presidents armed with the federal executive power could simply use their executive muscles to resist improper state arrest warrants and the like issued against them;

and federal judges could similarly protect themselves from pesky litigation by simply refusing to entertain certain improper federal-court suits and by reversing meddlesome state-court judgments.[46]

Federal courts over the centuries have done just that, holding repeatedly that no federal judge may be sued under state defamation law for any utterance in a judicial opinion—in effect recognizing a judicial freedom of speech in a federal court remarkably similar to the congressional freedom of speech in the Capitol.

Remarkably similar except, of course, for the fact that the judicial immunity is entirely an implication from the Constitution's general structure, whereas the congressional immunity is explicit in the Constitution's text. Much as Ellsworth, Wilson, and Blackstone argued that certain well-settled background principles of the rule of law went without saying, so, too, the Supreme Court has insisted that judicial free speech is an implicit element of the basic Anglo-American system of law. As the Court explained at the turn of the twentieth century,

> a series of decisions, uniformly to the same effect, extending from the time of Lord Coke to the present time, established the general proposition that no action will lie against a judge for any acts done or words spoken in his judicial capacity in a court of justice.... "This provision of the law is not for the protection or benefit of a malicious or corrupt judge, but for the benefit of the public, whose interest it is that the judges should be at liberty to exercise their functions with independence and without fear of consequences."[47]

Granted, no federal judge or congressman enjoys blanket immunity from state criminal prosecution. Neither does any cabinet officer; nor does the vice president.* If any of these federal figures becomes the victim of a state criminal-law vendetta, he must ultimately rely on federal courts

---

* At the time that he served as the Senate's presiding officer during the 1805 impeachment trial of Supreme Court Justice Samuel Chase (no relation to Salmon), Vice President Aaron Burr stood indicted by both New York and New Jersey for having killed Alexander Hamilton in an 1804 duel at Weehawken. During the Chase impeachment, newspapers quipped that ordinarily "it was the practice in Courts of Justice to arraign the *murderer* before the *Judge*, but *now* we behold the *Judge* arraigned before the *murderer*."

to protect him. In some situations, the trial itself, though based on state criminal law, may properly be removed from a state to a federal courthouse because a federal officer stands accused. In other situations, the Supreme Court may simply review and reverse any state-court conviction obviously based on state discrimination against federal officials.[48]

The presidency, however, is constitutionally unique. Here, the power of an entire branch of the federal government centers in one man. (This is the plain meaning of the above-noted opening clause of Article II.) Congress can operate at full speed even if an indicted or imprisoned member is absent. So can the federal judiciary. Cabinet secretaries exist mainly to help the president himself and can be temporarily replaced by undersecretaries. Effective substitutes for the vice president are also easy to find; the VP's main constitutional duty is to preside over the Senate, and in his absence this chair can be filled by a senator. Article II, by dramatic contrast, revolves around one man who is expected at all times to be at the ready to do whatever may be needed at a critical moment to keep the nation afloat and on course. When the president is told that he must—upon pain of imprisonment—appear at a particular state criminal hearing at a particular place and time, the executive branch itself is being held hostage, perhaps at an hour of national danger when even a small distraction may spell national disaster. Not only is the president unable to devote his entire attention to the business of the American people, but someone other than the president—some local judge or local prosecutor or local jury, perhaps with pretextual or partisan motives—is usurping the authority to define the national executive agenda.[49]

Of course, in such situations the vice president may take over. But if so, the votes of millions across the continent are being set aside by a local body of grand jurors and petit jurors from one city or county.* In these scenarios, the part is undoing the decision of the whole, turning the constitutional

---

* Pop quiz: Name Lincoln's vice president in his first term. Hint: The answer is not Andrew Johnson, but someone whom few Americans today can easily recall—a fact that should remind us that vice presidents are not always perfect substitutes for presidents. This was especially true prior to a pair of mid-twentieth-century amendments—the Twenty-second and Twenty-fifth Amendments, to be precise—that have elevated the constitutional and electoral status of vice presidents.

order topsy-turvy. A courageous president faithfully discharging his constitutional duty may at times need to take actions that render him hugely unpopular in one city, county, state, or even region. No single locality should be allowed to prevent or punish this faithful discharge of national duty. Abraham Lincoln became president by dint of a national vote of confidence, and only a comparable national process could properly dislodge him from the presidency.

The Constitution provided for just such a process to dislodge a miscreant president: impeachment. In this process, nationally accountable bodies would make the pivotal decisions to intrude upon, and, if necessary, oust, a nationally elected executive. The House, acting as a special grand jury, would represent not one city or county but all America, as would the Senate in its capacity as impeachment judge and jury. In addition, the American people themselves would have regular opportunities to judge the president at election time and to send him packing if they found him wanting. Once out of office, an ex-president could stand trial for his alleged crimes without undue prejudice to the national business.[50]

Even if the underlying criminal conduct alleged by a state against the president did not rise to the level of an offense that warranted impeachment and removal, House and Senate members might in certain situations properly view the president's decision to invoke immunity as itself grossly corrupt and hence impeachable. Imagine a scenario of national peace and prosperity where the president did have spare time, and where the state criminal charges proffered against him seemed on their face to be entirely nonpretextual, based on strong evidence, and susceptible of quick adjudication in an ordinary criminal trial. In such a case, congressmen might believe that an honorable president would waive immunity and clear his name. If the president refused to take this path, that refusal itself might cast doubt on his probity and fitness to hold high office.[51]

This interpretation of constitutional structure finds considerable support in constitutional history. In two separate *Federalist* essays, Hamilton/ Publius suggested that any proper criminal trial of the president should take place only after his impeachment and removal by Congress. The president "would be liable to be impeached, tried, and upon conviction [in an impeachment court] removed from office; and would *afterwards* be liable to prosecution and punishment in the ordinary course of law" (emphasis added). He would "at all times" be "liable to impeachment, trial, dismissal from office, incapacity to serve in any other, and to the forfeiture of life and estate by *subsequent* prosecution in the common course of law" (emphasis added).[52]

Other leading Federalists expressed similar views. At the Philadelphia Convention, Gouverneur Morris declared that "a conclusive reason for making the Senate instead of the Supreme Court the Judge of impeachments, was that the latter was to try the President *after* the trial of the impeachment" (emphasis added). During the North Carolina ratifying convention of 1788, Governor Samuel Johnston spoke even more sweepingly: "[M]en who were in very high offices could not be come at by the ordinary course of justice; but when called before this high tribunal [of impeachment] and convicted, they would be stripped of their dignity, and reduced to the rank of their fellow-citizens, and then the courts of common law might proceed against them."[53]

Several other Founding statesmen and statements muddied the waters. At one point in the Pennsylvania ratifying convention, James Wilson declared that "far from being above the laws, he [the president] is amenable to them in his private character as a citizen, and in his public character by impeachment." The structural argument for presidential immunity does not flatly contradict Wilson's generalization, but it does qualify and clarify Wilson's rhetoric by highlighting that impeachment should ordinarily occur first (unless a president opts to waive his immunity, which he might do precisely in order to avoid an impeachment). The subtle issues of timing and the exact relationship between impeachment and the regular criminal-law process were topics that Wilson (unlike Hamilton, Morris, and Johnston) did not come close to addressing.[54]

Wilson also boasted that the Constitution did not give the president even "a single privilege," but this rhetorical exaggeration in the heat of debate has not stood the test of time. Beginning with George Washington, presidents have repeatedly and with the approval of other branches asserted various privileges—including, for instance, privileges to withhold information related to national security, secret international diplomacy, and internal executive-branch deliberations. The last of these privileges was explicitly endorsed by a unanimous Supreme Court in the 1803 case of *Marbury v. Madison* (in a passage that has escaped the notice of most modern law professors).[55]

Shortly after the Constitution was ratified, a brief discussion took place in the Senate about whether a sitting president could be criminally prosecuted. Vice President John Adams and Senator Oliver Ellsworth agreed that "you could only impeach him [the president] and no other process whatever lay against him." Otherwise, "you put it in the power of a common justice to exercise [coercive] authority over him and stop the whole machine of Government." If, for example, the president were to commit murder in the streets, he would be promptly impeached and removed, and "when he is no longer President you can indict him." Writing several years later, Thomas Jefferson—not usually an ally of Adams and Ellsworth—offered a similar analysis: "[W]ould the executive be independent of the judiciary, if he were subject to the commands of the latter, & to imprisonment for disobedience; if the several courts could bandy him from pillar to post, keep him constantly trudging from north to south & east to west, and withdraw him entirely from his constitutional duties?"[56]

In 1833, Justice Joseph Story published a landmark treatise on American constitutional law, and he, too, offered a structural defense of presidential immunity: "There are...incidental powers, belonging to the executive department, *which are necessarily implied* from the nature of the functions, which are confided to it. Among these, must necessarily be the power to perform them, without any obstruction or impediment whatsoever. The president cannot, therefore, be liable to arrest, imprisonment, or detention, while he is in the discharge of his office." Though Story went on to hedge his bets on the issue of presidential immunity, it would be hard to find a clearer defense of honoring not only what the Constitution says explicitly, but also what it says implicitly.[57]

IF A SITTING PRESIDENT may simply brush aside a state prosecutor, may a sitting governor do so as well? After all, many state constitutions purport to vest their governors with "executive power." Despite this surface similarity, the structural case for gubernatorial immunity is quite weak and in general has not carried the day as a matter of state constitutional law.

Governors differ from presidents along several dimensions. First, most state constitutions over the years have created prosecutorial structures strongly independent of, and designed to counterbalance the power of, state governors. Today, the great majority of states elect their attorneys general and governors independently, whereas at the federal level the attorney general answers directly to the president and has done so without interruption since the days of George Washington. Structurally, state executive and prosecution powers do not truly revolve around a single, unitary executive as they do under the federal Constitution. Second, presidents are entrusted with vast powers of diplomacy and national security on which the very existence of the nation may depend. Governors have no comparable authority. In this respect, the executive power of a state is inherently different from the executive power of the United States. Intruding upon a sitting governor is not the same as distracting or disabling a president during a potential international crisis. Third, when a state prosecutor brings suit under state law in state court against a sitting state governor, the specter of the part undermining the whole does not arise as it does when a single state tries to undo the effects of a national presidential election.[58]

The fact that presidents may properly enjoy certain implicit privileges that governors do not (and vice versa) reminds us that even though advocates for certain implicit presidential privileges may stress the words "executive Power"—and indeed I invoked these very words a few pages back—this phrase is not always the weight-bearing workhorse it might seem. Like other textual arguments, the appeal to the Article II clause vesting the president with "executive Power" is at times merely a handy textual label affixed to an argument whose main force derives from constitutional structure and spirit—that is, from America's implicit Constitution.[59]

BUT WHAT ABOUT THE RULE OF LAW? Does presidential immunity from state prosecution and imprisonment improperly place the president above the law? In a word, no. For this immunity is itself implicit in America's highest law, the Constitution.

Consider, one last time, the Article I, section 6, clause guaranteeing congressional freedom of speech and debate. No one today sensibly says that this particularly absolute form of congressional free speech places congressmen above the law. The law itself provides for this privilege and does so for sound reasons of public policy. So, too, with federal judicial immunities from state libel law, immunities that are implicit in the Constitution's structure and history rather than explicit in the Constitution's text. The same thing is true of any presidential immunity derived from the Constitution itself—an immunity that of course applies equally to all presidents, liberal and conservative alike. This immunity does not arise from some sort of aristocratic birth privilege. Rather, it exists for those who have been democratically selected to serve as the nation's first officer. Here, what might at first seem like a mere private privilege really serves a larger public purpose, safeguarding the rights of the American people to choose their president, unfettered by any clever state effort to nullify that national choice.

It is worth reiterating that none of the immunities that we have considered allows unchecked lawlessness. These immunities simply create alternative legal structures of decision and judgment. Congress itself may punish congressional speakers who abuse the Article I speech privilege. Appellate tribunals may review, reverse, and chastise judges who wantonly defame others, and abusive judges may also be removed from office by an impeachment court. Likewise, presidents may be judged by America's high court of impeachment; and once out of office they may be tried on bona fide state charges, just like the rest of us (with all the standard rights of other citizens and of other federal officers to protect them from state vendettas).[60]

The real question is not "Are presidents above the law?" but rather "What is the law for presidents?" Rightly understood, the law itself says that sitting national executives should be judged nationally and impartially. Though the Constitution does not say this in so many words, no single state criminal judge or jury may properly preside over an unconsenting incumbent president, just as no vice president may properly preside over his own impeachment. No party may properly judge his own case, and no part may properly judge the whole. Principles such as these make sense of the entire document.

THIS CHAPTER HAS HOPPED WITH abandon from one specific constitutional topic to another to another. Substantively, the topics—the proper composition of impeachment courts, the scope of congressional lawmaking power and the limits on state authority to tax federal entities, the sweep of free-speech rights, and the immunity of sitting presidents from criminal prosecution—share little in common and are rarely discussed together. Some topics (such as the limited authority of states to tax federal entities) are pure issues of governmental structure; others (such as the freedom of speech) raise classic questions of individual right. Some matters (for example, impeachment) would almost never come before regular courts, while others (for instance, the scope of congressional lawmaking power) are the stuff of daily adjudication.

There is a method—*le mot juste*—in this madness. A single methodological idea unifies all the foregoing case studies and hypotheticals. On each topic, clause-bound literalism fails. Sometimes the key clause in isolation is simply indeterminate. (The phrase "executive Power" can be read narrowly or broadly on the issue of presidential immunity from prosecution.) Other times, the most salient clause, in isolation, sends a rather misleading message. (The First Amendment speaks only of "Congress," but surely presidents, federal courts, and states must also honor citizens' rights to express political opinions.) On occasion the Constitution's true meaning is very nearly the opposite of what the applicable clause seems to say quite expressly. (The vice president does not properly preside over his own impeachment.) This chapter's unifying idea is that we must read the Constitution as a whole—between the lines, so to speak.

The Constitution does not expressly command us to do this. The rule of holistic construction is itself unwritten. But it is a rule deeply faithful to the written Constitution, even as it tells readers to transcend narrow literalism.

This technique is not the only proper way to find America's unwritten Constitution. In the next chapter, we shall deploy a quite different technique for staying true to the written Constitution while going beyond it—a technique that views "the Constitution" not as a document, but as a deed.

CHAPTER 2

HEEDING THE DEED

America's Enacted Constitution

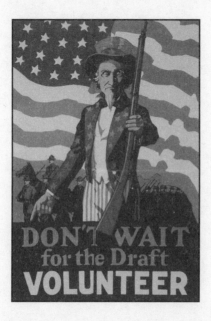

DON'T WAIT FOR THE DRAFT (1917).

By the time of World War I, the constitutional propriety of a national draft seemed well settled, even though most Americans in the late 1780s and early 1790s had envisioned a federal army composed of volunteers, not citizen conscripts. While nothing in the text of any subsequent amendment explicitly or implicitly addressed the issue of conscription, the very process by which the Fourteenth Amendment was enacted in the wake of the Civil War provided strong—albeit unwritten—support for a national draft.

I N THE FATEFUL YEAR FOLLOWING the unveiling of the Philadelphia delegates' proposed Constitution in September 1787, specially elected ratifying conventions across the continent enacted the proposal into law, much as the houses of an ordinary legislature might enact a statute. The specific enacting procedures and protocols that brought forth the Constitution are rich with meaning. They invite interpretation.

The sort of interpretation I have in mind here is not interpretation of *what* the Constitution says as a text, explicitly or implicitly. Rather, it is interpretation of *how* the Constitution became law. To do this sort of interpretation, we must first inform ourselves about the procedures through which Americans in 1787–1788 enacted the Constitution, and must then explore the implications and entailments—the deep meaning—of these enactment procedures. Similarly, we must probe and ponder the later procedures and protocols that generated various constitutional amendments. After all, amendments, too, are interpretable instances of constitutional enactment. On a surprisingly wide range of issues—the freedom of speech, the status of majority rule, the role of religion, the scope of suffrage rights, and the legality of conscription—we shall see that how the Constitution was originally enacted and later amended is every bit as meaningful as what the text as a whole expresses and implies.

"the freedom of speech"

THE LAW OF OUR LAND came to life on a continent awash with speech and through a process that teemed with talk of the freest sort. In an extraordinary efflorescence of accusations, addresses, allegories, analyses, appeals, arguments, assemblies, boasts, books, canards, cartoons, complaints, conversations, costumes, debates, deliberations, denials, diatribes, effigies, encomiums, essays, exaggerations, exegeses, exhortations, flags, harangues, insults, lamentations, letters, misstatements, opinions, paintings, pamphlets, parades, petitions, plays, pleas, poems, prayers, prophesies, quips, sermons, songs, speeches, squibs, symbols, toasts, and writings of every sort, Americans practiced an amazingly vigorous freedom of expression in the course of enacting the Constitution. Sharp-elbowed political maneuvering there was aplenty; widespread punishment of exuberant expression there was not.[1]

Although much of the action took place informally and "out of doors"—in taverns, town squares, newspapers, and neighborhoods—the state ratification conventions were parley places par excellence. Assembling outside the confines of everyday government, these specially elected, single-purpose conventions were viewed as personifying the American people themselves. Conventions thus enjoyed a democratic mandate to say yea or nay to the Constitution superior to any authority that could be claimed by mere state legislatures filled with ordinary lawmakers elected in the ordinary way. Even in conventions where one side—Federalist or Anti-Federalist—entered with an apparently decisive majority, delegates on the other side, as a rule, freely spoke their piece. Often a speech or argument on a particular issue prompted an apt counterargument. At times, delegates even pronounced themselves persuaded by something said by men on the other side.[2]*

Americans understood what they were doing as they were doing it, exulting in the luxuriant freedom of expression being acted out before their eyes and ears by their hands and mouths. Future justice James Wilson, America's preeminent theorist of popular sovereignty, put it best at the outset of the Pennsylvania ratifying convention, before any state had agreed to the Philadelphia plan: "[I]n our governments, the supreme, absolute, and uncontrollable power remains in the people, [who] possess over our constitutions control in *act* as well as right.... *These important truths, sir, are far from being merely speculative. We, at this moment, speak and deliberate under their immediate and benign influence.*" Wilson returned to this enactment theme several days later. In America, he explained, sovereignty "continues,

---

* One key episode of persuasion occurred early in the pivotal Massachusetts ratifying convention. Samuel Adams, who had entered the convention as a skeptic, asked why the framers' plan departed from the general American tradition of annual legislative elections. When Fisher Ames offered up an explanation, Adams pronounced himself satisfied on the point. Ultimately, Adams voted yes and his swing may have been decisive for several other delegates who followed his lead in this critical convention. The final vote was nail-bitingly close, with 187 yeas prevailing over 168 nays.

resides, and remains, with the body of the people. *Under the practical influence of this great truth, we are now sitting and deliberating*, and under its operation, we can sit as calmly and deliberate as coolly, in order to change a constitution, as a legislature can sit and deliberate under the power of a constitution, in order to alter or amend a law."[3]

On this issue, American constitutional theory and practice broke sharply with long-standing English law. In England, Parliament, not the citizenry, was sovereign, and ordinary Englishmen did not in law or in fact enjoy a broad freedom to criticize incumbent officials or the government as a whole. English freedom of the press meant only that printers were free from government licensing schemes and other sorts of prepublication censorship. If English printers in the late 1780s upbraided powerful men or institutions, these printers were vulnerable, both in theory and in practice, to postpublication punishment or liability. Across the Atlantic, by contrast, citizens criticized officials, officialdom, and social institutions (including slavery) with abandon—sometimes under pen names, sometimes more openly. In the years between the winning of American independence and the Constitution's ratification, few legal sanctions actually operated to limit boisterous political expression.[4]

In a famous Virginia tract penned during the Adams administration, James Madison reminded his audience of this history as he denounced the repressive Alien and Sedition Acts of 1798: "[T]he practice in America must be entitled to…respect. In every state, probably, in the Union, the press has exerted a freedom in canvassing the merits and measures of public men, of every description, which has not been confined to the strict limits of [English] common law. On this footing the freedom of the press has stood; on this foundation it yet stands." As an exclamation point, Madison reminded his audience that *without this robust freedom of expression, perhaps the Constitution itself would not have come into being.* Had sedition laws "forbidding every publication that might bring the constituted [government] agents into contempt or disrepute, or that might excite the hatred of the people against the authors of unjust or pernicious measures, been uniformly enforced against the press, might not the United States have been languishing, at this day, under the infirmities of a sickly Confederation?"[5]

Though the Philadelphia drafters had incautiously failed to include an explicit clause affirming a sweeping right of free speech for ordinary citizens, such a right was nonetheless an intrinsic and indispensable, albeit unwritten, element of the Constitution as actually enacted. This right therefore existed as a core component of America's Constitution even before the adoption of the Bill of Rights, which textually codified Americans' right to express themselves via speech, press, petition, and assembly.[6]

Most Americans today associate the right of free expression with the First Amendment. It is helpful to remember how that amendment came to be. The original Philadelphia plan contained no explicit guarantee of citizen free speech and no standard Bill of Rights resembling various state constitutional bills of rights already on the books. In the great ordainment debate of 1787–1788, Anti-Federalists highlighted this defect. Federalists listened, and some were persuaded. A consensus began to emerge that a Bill of Rights should indeed be added once the Constitution came into effect.

The text that we call the Bill of Rights and the subset of that text that we call the First Amendment thus came about as a direct result of this epic national conversation. Aptly, the textual guarantee of freedom of speech arose thanks to the actual practice—the popular incarnation and acting out (or, if you will, the enactment)—of freedom of speech in the Constitution-making process. The text itself harks back to this earlier experience by referring to "*the*" freedom of speech and of the press as a preexisting right that is merely affirmed and declared—not created—by the First Amendment.

EXACTLY WHAT SORT OF CONSTITUTIONAL ARGUMENT is this argument from enactment? At root, enactment arguments form a subspecies of historical argument, but a particularly interesting subspecies, partaking of some of the strengths more typically associated with arguments based on the Constitution's specific text and overall structure.

Many standard historical arguments are only loosely connected to the actual constitutional text. For example, suppose a constitutional historian were to argue for a broad constitutional right of citizens to be free from federal censorship by noting that a handful of leading Federalists in 1787–1788 asserted that the Philadelphia plan withheld from Congress any general enumerated power over freedom of the press. Skeptics might point out that there were other men at the time who said something different; or might ask how many people in the ratification process actually heard this handful of Federalist apologists; or might wonder how many people were in fact persuaded by this Federalist argument; or might worry about where the Constitution's text specifically prevents Congress from using those powers that are enumerated—such as the powers to govern the territories and the national seat, to regulate interstate commerce, and to adopt tax laws—in ways that threaten the press.

By contrast, the argument from enactment offers a tighter, more intrinsic connection to the Constitution. The claim is not that free speech generally prevailed on the ground in postcolonial America. (In fact, loyalist speech was suppressed during the Revolution.) Rather, the special twist is that the very act of constitutional ordainment itself occurred in and through a regime of boisterous, virtually uncensored free speech. In this respect, the argument from enactment history functions like a standard textual argument, which also focuses tightly on the Constitution itself. But the enactment approach understands the Preamble's self-reference to "this Constitution" as a deed as well as a text—a doing, an ordainment, a constituting, a performative utterance. In short, an *enactment*, reflected in the text itself: "We the People...do ordain and establish this Constitution." Exactly who did this and how? These are the questions highlighted by the enactment approach.

To put the point a slightly different way, an enactment argument can perhaps be seen as a textual argument of sorts—an interpretation of the tiny but powerful workhorse word "do" in the Preamble. The argument from enactment prompts us to understand what was in fact *done* by the people in the very process of ordaining and establishing the Constitution. And what was done—as Wilson and Madison highlighted during and shortly after the event—was a remarkable embodiment of free speech, speech that was inextricably intertwined with the very deed of ordainment itself.

Enactment arguments also share one of the great strengths of various classical arguments derived from the Constitution's general structure: a focus on the Constitution as a whole rather than on some small clause or part. Whereas many standard textual arguments are small-bore and clause-bound, enactment arguments are panoramic, drawing our attention to how the entire Constitution came into being. In this sense, an enactment argument is the ultimate structural argument, with a historical twist.

Howsoever we classify enactment arguments—whether we view them as historical, or textual, or structural—we need to see that the written Constitution and the unwritten Constitution cohere to form a single system. While the Preamble's text does not quite say, in so many words, that "the process by which this document is being enacted is itself part of the Constitution, and thus a source of constitutional law and constitutional principle," the Preamble text surely gestures toward this idea, directing our gaze to the specific set of events by which the Constitution's text itself came to life. In turn, these events point back to the legal text that was born in this process. Here, too, we see how neither America's written Constitution nor America's unwritten Constitution stands alone. Rather, the two stand together and buttress one another.

"sufficient for the Establishment of this Constitution"

THE REMARKABLE FREEDOM OF SPEECH that flourished in 1787–1788 culminated in a series of votes to enact into law the plan proposed by the Philadelphia delegates. But what master voting rule determined the legal winner in this process? In other words, exactly how many yes votes were legally necessary to enact the Constitution? How many no votes would have legally reversed the outcome? To answer these questions and understand the profound implications of the answers, we must once again read the Constitution not merely as a text, but also as a deed.

A quick glance at the terse text would seem to suggest that a supermajority principle was at work in 1787–1788, with the ratification bar set higher than a simple majority but lower than unanimity. According to the words of Article VII, "the Ratification of the Conventions of nine [out of thirteen] States, shall be sufficient for the Establishment of this Constitution." But a closer examination, attentive to how Americans in fact enacted the Constitution within each state, underscores the remarkable centrality and salience of simple majority rule. This centrality is all the more remarkable precisely because the word "majority" is unwritten; it appears nowhere in the text of Article VII. But, as we shall now see, simple majority rule clearly does appear in the deed—the doing, the enactment—of Article VII.

THE NINE-THIRTEENTHS RULE OF ARTICLE VII differed from a standard voting rule in one critical respect: The (nine or more) states voting yes would not bind the (four or fewer) states voting no. Article VII made clear that in the event of nine or more yeses, the proposed Constitution would take effect only "between the States so ratifying." (As the enactment process in fact occurred in 1787–1788, two states—Rhode Island and North Carolina—declined to ratify and thus stood outside the new Union when the Constitution went into effect.) Typical voting rules, by contrast, specify conditions under which the yes voters bind the no voters. For instance, if a majority of each house of Congress votes for a proposed law and the president signs it, that law ordinarily binds even the congressmen who voted against it (as well as their constituents, of course).

Viewed from this angle, Article VII can be reconceptualized as an interstate unanimity rule of sorts: The new document would bind only those states that would agree to be bound. The logic here was straightforward. Prior to the Constitution's ratification, the Articles of Confederation, which all thirteen states had ratified during the Revolution, provided the framework for interstate relations. Those Articles declared that each of the thirteen states was a legally sovereign entity. The Confederation itself was merely a "league of friendship," a multilateral treaty among the thirteen sovereigns. The Philadelphia framers were proposing to dissolve this treaty via a process in which nine or more states would quit the old Confederation and recombine into a new indivisible union. Obviously, each sovereign state in this process had to be free to decide for itself. No consenting sovereign, or combination of consenting sovereigns, could properly bind any nonconsenting sovereign to the new legal order.

Within each state, however, the yes voters in the ratifying convention did claim the right to bind the no voters. But subject to what voting rule? How high was the bar set *inside* each state ratifying convention? This was the critical question hiding beneath the surface of Article VII, which spoke directly to the interstate voting rule but said nothing about the intrastate voting rule.

Once we shift our gaze from Article VII's text to the actual state enactment practice set in motion by that article, four key facts come into
view. First, every state convention operated under simple majority rule.
(In three of America's largest states, the yes voters in convention mustered
only the slimmest of majorities—187 to 168 in Massachusetts, 89 to 79 in
Virginia, and 30 to 27 in New York, the cliffhanger to end all cliffhangers.)
Second, each state convention followed majority rule even though the federal Constitution's text contained not a single word specifying this as the
proper metric. (Evidently, it went without saying.) Third, this rule operated even in states whose constitutions arguably required something more.
Fourth, when each convention vote actually took place, Anti-Federalists
generally accepted the legitimacy of simple majority rule. When outvoted,
the naysayers—many of whom passionately opposed the Constitution—
acquiesced, often without a peep.

MASSACHUSETTS MERITS SPECIAL ATTENTION. Here, as in every other state, a vote to ratify the federal Constitution was a vote to modify the
existing state constitution in certain respects. The Bay State constitution
had come into operation in 1780 only after having cleared an extraordinari-
ly high bar—a two-thirds vote of the state electorate. A plausible structural
argument from symmetry would have insisted that any modification of
the 1780 rules must likewise clear a two-thirds bar. The amendment clause
of the 1780 document could also be read to privilege the two-thirds principle. It provided that a new constitutional convention would meet in 1795
if "two-thirds of the qualified voters...who shall assemble and vote" so
desired.[7]

Note the amendment clause's key date: 1795. The Bay State's eventual
ratification of the federal Constitution *in 1788* necessarily occurred outside
the confines of this clause, which was thus treated as a nonexclusive provision setting forth merely one way, rather than the only way, by which state
constitutional reform could properly occur. (Here, too, Americans at the
Founding rejected the argument from negative implication.) But even if
the Massachusetts amendment clause in its entirety did not apply—even if
1788 could properly substitute for 1795, and even if the legislature could call
the convention without waiting for any request from the "qualified vot-

ers" assembled in their respective townships—it was yet another leap for Federalists to substitute simple majority rule for the two-thirds principle.

One notable Anti-Federalist essayist, "A Republican Federalist," argued that although the amendment clause need not be viewed as exclusive, it certainly had to be read as exemplary. Why should the voting rules for 1788 differ wildly from those laid out for 1795? If simple majority rule in a state convention meeting pursuant to a standard state statute could suffice in 1788, then presumably the same thing would be true in 1795. But that result, emphasized the essayist, would render the amendment clause "a nullity."[8]

This was hardly an incontrovertible interpretation. The state amendment clause could also be viewed merely as specifying certain procedures applicable when the legislature resisted constitutional reform and refused to call a constitutional convention on its own motion. Since, in 1787–1788, the legislature was willing to act on its own authority, the amendment clause was arguably irrelevant.

But only arguably, for the "Republican Federalist" essayist had a colorable claim on the other side. The likely author of this essay was James Warren—speaker of the Massachusetts House of Representatives, husband of the formidable writer Mercy Otis Warren, and brother-in-law of the late James Otis, an early hero in the patriot cause of the 1760s. Here, then, was a large figure making a large legal assertion. Yet when the hour of decision arrived in the Massachusetts convention itself, no diehard Anti-Federalist delegate tried to make a last stand on this legal ground. On the contrary, as soon as the final vote was announced, several of the convention's leading Anti-Federalist spokesmen stood up and graciously conceded defeat, explicitly and repeatedly emphasizing in their brief remarks that the convention "majority" had lawfully decided the matter. When word of the ratification reached young John Quincy Adams, who had previously inclined against the proposed Constitution, the future president wrote in his diary that "I think it is my duty to submit.…In our Government, opposition to the acts of a majority of the people is rebellion to all intents and purposes."[9]

Neighboring New Hampshire closely tracked the Massachusetts model. Here, too, a state constitutional amendment clause could be read to require a two-thirds vote of the state electorate. Here, too, the Federalists treated the clause as irrelevant. Here, too, the state legislature acted on its own authority to summon a ratifying convention. Here, too, the convention ultimately gave the Federalists victory only by a slim majority (via a vote of 57 to 47, to be precise). Yet here, too—and this is the most remarkable fact, given the intense passions kindled by the Philadelphia plan—Anti-Federalist delegates gamely acquiesced when narrowly outvoted.

WHEREAS NEW HAMPSHIRE WAS ONE of the last states to say yes, Pennsylvania had been one of the first—and Keystone State Anti-Federalists had barked much louder. But in the end they did not bite.

When outvoted in a state convention held late in 1787, disaffected Anti-Federalist delegates in Pennsylvania published a slashing protest that included ominous language asserting that the entire convention proceedings had been illegal under the state constitution of 1776. Foreshadowing the later experiences in Massachusetts and New Hampshire, Pennsylvania Federalists had simply sidestepped an explicit state constitutional amendment clause that pivoted on a two-thirds rule of sorts. According to that clause, in 1783 and "in every seventh year thereafter," a convention was to meet if two-thirds of a special group—the "council of censors"—so decreed. Operating outside the clause in the autumn of 1787, an impatient state legislative majority had used aggressive parliamentary tactics to ram through a bill authorizing a specially elected state ratifying convention, which then used simple majority rule in the ultimate ratification vote. In response to the Federalists' political hardball and haste, the outvoted Anti-Federalist delegates contended that the convention had no "authority to do any act or thing, that can alter or annihilate the constitution of Pennsylvania (both of which will be done by the new constitution) *nor are their proceedings in our opinion, at all binding on the people.*"[10]

But like the Massachusetts and New Hampshire amendment clauses, Pennsylvania's clause could plausibly be construed merely as laying down rules to be followed if the legislature resisted constitutional change, while leaving the legislature free at all times to call a convention on its own motion. Thus, even the disaffected Pennsylvania dissenters seemed disinclined to double down on their claim that the state amendment clause was exclusive, or to lay great stress on its two-thirds pivot. Indeed, in one passage the dissenters appeared to concede that the state constitution could legitimately be modified if "a majority of the people should evidence a wish for such a change."[11]

This critical concession positioned the dissenters in the mainstream of American constitutional thought in the late 1780s. Across the continent, patriots from all points on the political spectrum had come to believe that, regardless of the specific wording of various state constitutional clauses, the people had an inalienable legal right to alter or abolish inadequate governmental systems, and that such a legal right could be exercised by a simple majority of the people in any given state.

Nice questions of institutional detail arose within the broad outlines of the majority-rule principle. For instance, must a majority of the voters weigh in directly, or could a convention majority suffice? (This was an especially fair question in Massachusetts and New Hampshire, where the general electorate had directly authorized state constitutions in the early 1780s.) What if the convention delegates themselves were selected in an election with low turnout? (This was a key complaint of the disgruntled Pennsylvanians.) But these nice questions should not obscure the widespread agreement circa 1787 on the special status of majority rule in making and amending state constitutions.

The special link between American-style popular sovereignty and majority rule had appeared in a canonical legal text even before the Declaration of Independence. Virginia's famous Declaration of Rights, adopted in June 1776, had asserted "as the basis and foundation of government" the principles that "all power is vested in, and consequently derived from, the people," and that whenever "any government shall be found inadequate…, *a majority of the community hath an indubitable, inalienable, and indefeasible right to reform, alter, or abolish it,* in such manner as shall be judged most conducive to the public weal." Virtually every other state followed Virginia's lead with one or more legal odes to popular sovereignty; but none specified the majority-rule-in-amendment principle with comparable clarity.[12]

Over the next decade, several states seemed to deviate from simple majority rule in their practices of constitutional formation and/or their provisions for constitutional amendment. But by 1787, the intellectual and political momentum had shifted decisively toward the advocates of majority rule. On the Federalist side, leaders such as Wilson, Madison/Publius,

Hamilton/Publius, and Gouverneur Morris all insisted that the right of the people to alter or reform their government at all times resided in a simple majority. Leading Anti-Federalists, such as George Mason (the author of the 1776 Virginia Declaration), Patrick Henry, and "the Federal Farmer," emphatically agreed.[13]

Though some Americans doubtless remained outside this crystallizing consensus, the enactment practice set into motion by Article VII bespoke a remarkable convergence: Ultimately, both Federalists and Anti-Federalists in each of the thirteen states deemed it sufficient that the state legislature had summoned a specially elected convention which had then voted yes by majority rule. As Wilson remarked in the Pennsylvania ratifying convention, "Who are the majority in this assembly?—Are they not the people?"[14]

WHEN THE PHILADELPHIA FRAMERS unveiled their proposed Constitution in September 1787, the nonexclusivity of state constitutional amendment clauses and the sufficiency of majority rule in the process of state constitutional change were powerful political and legal theories, but not much more. A year later, these theories were established political and legal facts. Over the ensuing years, state after state has emulated the remarkable examples set in 1787–1788. Thus, Pennsylvania and Delaware legislators summoned new state conventions in 1790 and 1791, respectively, to reform state constitutions via simple-majority votes, even though these two states' 1776 constitutions had specified different and arguably exclusive supermajoritarian amendment procedures. Since then, states from every region have followed suit, amending their constitutions via an assortment of popular-sovereignty and majority-rule procedures nowhere specified in, and at times arguably contrary to, old constitutional texts. Fully two centuries of state constitutional reform have thus tracked specific enactment practices set in motion by Article VII—practices nowhere specified in the federal Constitution's text, yet clearly part of the very process by which that text sprang to life.[15]

Let us also note one additional set of questions raised by the centrality of majority rule in the Founding enactment process: If majority rule was indeed—or, if you like, in deed—the unwritten voting principle for every state ratifying convention, wasn't majority rule also, and for similar reasons, the unwritten voting rule for the House and the Senate? And if so, does this mean that today's Senate has the right to change its current filibuster rules by a simple majority vote—even though the written Constitution does not say all this in so many words? As we shall see in Chapter 9, the particular manner in which the Constitution was enacted in each state ratifying convention in 1787–1788 does in fact have precisely this enormous implication.

"our Lord"

A HARDCORE TEXTUALIST might at first dismiss the very idea of an unwritten Constitution as hopelessly confused and undisciplined, if not downright illegitimate. On this view, America's written Constitution is a crisply defined text with a neatly bounded and universally identifiable set of words. Everyone knows, or can easily learn, what is within its four corners and what is not. Moreover, the document refers time and again to itself—to "this Constitution"—as a written text. A companion resolution drafted by the Philadelphia Convention in mid-September 1787 likewise used the phrase "the preceding Constitution" to refer to a particular piece of prose to be laid before the American people via specially elected ratifying conventions. Both in those conventions themselves and in the larger continental conversation out of doors in 1787–1788, Americans everywhere promiscuously and unselfconsciously used the word "Constitution" to refer to that particular piece of prose. Americans in every subsequent generation have followed suit. By contrast, an "unwritten Constitution" seems maddeningly vaporous, lacking the sharpness of an easily recognizable set of words. What warrant is there for venturing even an inch beyond the four corners of the document itself, or for describing anything outside the text as part of our actual "Constitution"?[16]

The enactment argument turns the tables on this hardcore textualist. The Preamble's language prominently directs readers to the ratification process as the very foundation of the entire document's legal authority. Similar language appears in the Constitution's eye-catching final provision, Article VII: "The Ratification of the Conventions of nine States, shall be sufficient for the Establishment of this Constitution." Any self-proclaimed textualist who fails to focus on the ratification process has ignored proverbial neon signs found in the opening and closing sentences of the text itself.

Indeed, what happened during the enactment process established the official content and contours of the document. Several slightly differently worded, differently capitalized, and differently punctuated texts—each calling itself "this Constitution"—were floating around after mid-September 1787. Which of these was the *real* written Constitution? Exactly where did the real document's *official legal text* begin and end? As it happens, the document's boundaries are not self-evident on the face of the text itself. Unless we look beyond the text, we cannot even determine which ink marks are, in fact, the official written Constitution. In a startling twist, it turns out that the corners and crispness of the written Constitution exist thanks to events outside the text—events that form part of the seemingly squishy "unwritten Constitution."[17]

Even more startling, events outside the iconic parchment under glass at the National Archives definitively establish that *this* particular piece of prose was not the official copy of the Founders' written Constitution. The American people never formally ratified the handwritten, hand-signed parchment that almost everyone today uses as the authoritative version of the Founders' Constitution. Even the Senate is on record that this revered parchment is of no legal significance.

Fortunately, the document that *was* officially ratified by Americans in the late 1780s—a text printed in New York several days after the close of the Philadelphia Convention—bears a close resemblance to the familiar National Archives parchment. Although the ratified version features different punctuation and capitalization, its words are almost (but not absolutely) identical to those penned onto the iconic parchment. For most purposes, the National Archives version suffices. But on one particularly hot issue in contemporary culture wars—involving the parchment's reference to Jesus as "our Lord"—the Constitution's official text diverges, thereby casting light on first principles of church and state.

ON SEPTEMBER 15, 1787, the delegates to the Philadelphia Convention finally reached agreement on a complete text. After months of deliberations carefully veiled from outside scrutiny, the Convention was ready to go public with its proposed Constitution. But how? In a world without fax machines, photocopiers, or even mimeographs, eighteenth-century Americans generally relied on two technologies to generate hard copies of legal texts: engrossing (handwriting) and letterpress printing. The men at Philadelphia availed themselves of both technologies on September 15.

Maryland delegate James McHenry recorded the following entry in his daily journal: "Ordered [Constitution] to be engrossed and 500 copies struck [printed]—Adjourned till monday the 17th." Convention President George Washington's September 15 diary entry confirms McHenry's: "[A]djourned 'till Monday that the Constitution which it was proposed to offer to the People might be engrossed—and a number of printed copies struck off."[18]

Both engrossing and printing were carried out under the direction of the Convention's Committee of Style, which on September 17 presented the assembly with a single four-page engrossed parchment for endorsement. After the text was read aloud and a last-minute alteration was agreed to and penned in, thirty-nine of the forty-two delegates present added their signatures to the parchment. The Convention then charged Secretary William Jackson to deliver the proposed Constitution to the Congress that was organized under the existing Articles of Confederation and sitting in New York City.[19]

Although it is possible that each Philadelphia signer carefully examined the parchment before endorsing it, such a tedious practice would have painfully slowed the signing ceremony. No more than a few delegates could have examined the engrossed copy simultaneously. More likely, each delegate simply referred to his own printed copy of the draft Constitution that the Committee of Style had distributed on September 12, a document that had served thereafter as the Convention's working paper. Perhaps some delegates assumed that the parchment was identical to the September 12 draft, as revised between the 12th and the 15th—an assumption apparently confirmed by the oral reading of the engrossed document. In fact, this assumption was false: The two versions differed in small ways—such as punctuation and capitalization—that were unlikely to be detected by any delegate listening to the reading of the engrossed copy while carefully following along by consulting his own copy of the September 12 print.

On September 18, the five hundred printed copies that had been authorized three days earlier were struck by the Philadelphia print shop of John Dunlap and David C. Claypoole and distributed to the remaining delegates. Like the September 12 draft print, however, the September 18 print punctuated and capitalized the constitutional text rather differently from the engrossed parchment signed on September 17.

On September 20, William Jackson reached New York and laid before Congress the Philadelphia delegates' proposed Constitution. Whether or not the parchment was read aloud—the records on this point are murky—here, too, delegates probably relied on their own printed copies. On September 28, Congress unanimously voted to forward the proposed Constitution to the states for ratification. Accordingly, Secretary of Congress Charles Thompson, evidently using the September 18 print as his guiding template, arranged for one hundred copies to be printed for transmission to the states. For this project, Thompson used the print shop of John McLean, a New York publisher with ties to the Philadelphia printer John Dunlap.[20]

Virtually no one in the several states had access to the signed parchment that remained in the files of Congress in New York. Rather, the September 28 print was carefully reprinted in lots of up to ten thousand for mass distribution to the citizenry. This was the version submitted to the people of the United States as they chose their delegates to various ratifying conventions. This was the version that those ratifying conventions in turn used. And this was the version, with minor stylistic variations, that nine out of thirteen ratifying conventions expressly included in their formal instruments of ratification submitted to Secretary Thompson.[21]

By 1789, eleven state conventions had ratified the new Constitution— enough for it to go into effect under Article VII. One of the first acts of the new Congress was to authorize the printing of "a *correct* copy of the Constitution of the United States." Published in 1789 by Francis Childs and John Swaine, "printers to the United States," this copy followed (with minor deviations) the printed archetype of September 28, 1787, and not the engrossed parchment.[22]

Unfortunately, in the confused administrative transition from government under the Articles to government under the Constitution, no single copy of the September 28 print was preserved as a definitive master copy.

Nevertheless, according to a 1961 Senate document that investigated the matter in great detail, this lapse "created no question for many years." The text "printed in the session laws of 1789, which was undoubtedly reproduced from a copy of the print of September 28, 1787, was accepted as the real thing." For decades, "this printed archetype was the model followed in official editions of the laws and other governmental issues." Although editing discrepancies crept into some official editions, "the frequent prints for the use of the Houses of Congress in what became the Senate and House Manuals reproduced the printed archetype with great fidelity."[23]

Meanwhile, what had become of the Philadelphia parchment that now graces the National Archives? For many years, the parchment was all but forgotten, buried in the disorganized files of the old Confederation. In 1818, Congress provided for the publication of the theretofore-secret official journal of the Philadelphia Convention. Secretary of State John Quincy Adams oversaw the compilation of the primary documents, and the product of his labors was published in 1819. Though this publication failed to include the text of the engrossed parchment, the work of organizing loose files had apparently uncovered its original four pages. The following year, the State Department published an edition of the engrossed text as an item of historical interest.[24]

Two factors explain the parchment's later ascendancy. First, repeated reprinting of the September 28 print resulted in increasing numbers of discrepancies due to compounded printers' errors; yet no single copy of the print had been preserved as an official touchstone. As a result, the parchment increasingly came to serve as the definitive standard. Second, in the late 1870s the State Department brought the hand-signed engrossed parchment of the Declaration of Independence, fresh from its famous public display in Philadelphia as part of America's first World's Fair in 1876, into the same depository as the hand-signed engrossed parchment of the Constitution. The centennial magic of the Declaration apparently rubbed off on its constitutional counterpart.[25]

In effect, the parchment Constitution was gilt by association. In popular folklore it became *the* Constitution, the icon of a nation desperately in need of unifying symbols in the wake of the Civil War. This time, it was the September 28 print that was forgotten in the excitement. In 1878, the parchment was reproduced under the direction of Congress as the apparent official text of the Constitution. Since then, this copy has become the dominant one, reprinted routinely in congressional manuals and in the United States Code. The engrossed parchment has been on grand display alongside the engrossed Declaration for most of the past century, and the printed archetype has faded into the mists of history.[26]

WILL THE REAL WRITTEN CONSTITUTION please stand up? Which precise piece of prose should count as the official text of the Founders' supreme law?

If we narrowly read the hand-signed parchment and the September 28 print as two self-contained texts, the parchment fares rather well: Although each document repeatedly refers to *itself* as "this Constitution," only the parchment can boast the actual attesting signatures of George Washington, Benjamin Franklin, and dozens of other notable framers.

But if we read these texts more broadly and understand the importance of the enactment process outside the text, the parchment must yield pride of place to the print. Clearly, "this Constitution" was designed to be "ordained and established" not by Washington and his fellow notables, but by "the People" at large, who would legally enact the text via "Ratification of the Conventions of nine States." The iconic parchment never came before the people. Only the September 28 print did, and this was the particular piece of prose that was in fact ratified by all the state conventions—eleven in the initial enactment process of 1787–1788, and two more thereafter.[27]

For almost all legal purposes, the variance of punctuation and capitalization between print and parchment should make no difference whatsoever.* As John Marshall recognized in *McCulloch*, Americans enacted the Constitution as a whole, and faithful interpreters should thus aim to make sense of the entire document. Sensible readers should hesitate to place great weight on syntactical specks and grammatical nits if such minutiae run counter to the Constitution's general spirit and structure. In short, we must never forget that it is "a Constitution"—and not a clause or a comma or a capital letter in isolation—we are expounding.

---

* Bowing to general practice, this book and its predecessor volume, *America's Constitution: A Biography*, generally quote the parchment version.

This reminder has special bite because in at least one spot a printer's error slipped into the official September 28 print. Article I, section 8, empowered Congress to constitute as many "tribunals inferior to the supreme court" as Congress saw fit, and Article III's opening sentence likewise referred to the possibility of several "inferior courts." In the very next sentence, however, the plural "s" got dropped by the printer, with the official September 28 print referring to "the judges, both of the supreme and inferior court"—an obvious goof. A few state ratifying conventions caught the typo and corrected the blunder in their official instruments of ratification.[28] (For what it's worth, the iconic parchment consistently used the plural "courts.")

For some, the glitch in the formal text might be cause for great concern. The official clause says "court" and not "courts"—and for an ultra-strict and clause-bound textualist, that's that, and we are stuck with the singular noun whether it makes sense or not. But once we reject this extreme approach and embrace a more holistic and commonsensical view of the entire document—as a text that was meant to be read and enacted by ordinary citizens, not supersleuths with magnifying glasses and microscopes—we are free to admit that this one clause contains a simple printer's error, and move on. Typos happen, and faithful readers who seek to honor and preserve the text as a workable whole should place no weight on what is obviously an isolated and meaningless misprint.

This point can also be cast into the framework of the preceding chapter, which focused in part on background rules of legal construction against which the Constitution's explicit text should be read. Much as laws should be construed so as to avoid absurd results not foreseen or intended by the legislature, so, too, obvious scriveners' errors in official legal texts—errors that escaped the eyes and would frustrate the basic purposes of the enacting lawmaking body—should be disregarded.

IT IS POETIC that the Constitution's official text consists of a typeset print rather than a handwritten, hand-signed parchment. The parchment is unique—truly one of a kind. The print is democratic, precisely because each copy was not one of a kind, but one of an infinitely replicable set. All prints were created equal, with no one person's typeset copy different from, or superior to, anyone else's. With a printed version, a vast multitude of ordinary Americans across the land could literally read from the same page. The parchment was a ceremonial artifact made for show—to be preserved for the ages in pristine form. (Today it is kept safe in a magnificent museum in argon gas under bulletproof glass, untouchable by ordinary human hands.) The print was a legal workhorse made for use—to be read and reread by ordinary Americans at their convenience. Inexpensive and abundant in 1787, printed copies could be annotated, underlined, rolled up, folded, and passed from hand to hand. Whenever a given copy became too worn or scribbled over, another identical copy would presumably lie within easy reach.

In our starstruck world, the signatures at the bottom of the parchment make the engrossed original a national treasure: What other artifact—besides, perhaps, the parchment Declaration of Independence—contains the autographs of so many famous people in so tight a cluster commemorating so momentous an occasion? (Tellingly, during World War II both parchment documents were brought for safekeeping to Fort Knox, the legendarily secure storehouse of other national treasure.)

But precisely because the Philadelphia framers' autographs were so personal, some obvious questions arise concerning the legal significance of the signature section. Indeed, the opening words of the signature section have sparked a sharp debate among modern authors and activists. Some argue that these opening words are imbued with deep legal meaning. Others seek to dismiss the parchment's finishing flourish as irrelevant—a modest literary touch at most, or merely an eighteenth-century commonplace of no deep significance.

Here is what all the shouting is about. Immediately below the single sentence of Article VII and above the thirty-nine attesting autographs, the parchment contains the following words: "done in Convention by the Unanimous Consent of the States present the Seventeenth Day of September in the Year of our Lord one thousand seven hundred and Eighty seven and of the Independence of the United States of America the Twelfth In witness whereof We have hereunto subscribed our Names."

On one side of the debate stand those who claim that these words prove that, legally speaking, America is a religious nation and indeed a Christian country. On this view, the written Constitution acknowledges the Lordship of Jesus Christ in the phrase, "in the Year of our Lord." If this rather sectarian exemplar of government-sponsored ceremonial religion is permissible—indeed, part of the Constitution itself!—then surely other, more ecumenical references to God by government are also appropriate.

This argument took center stage shortly after a federal appellate court opinion in 2002 deployed the First Amendment's establishment clause in a particularly aggressive fashion to limit governmental endorsement of religion. Congress responded with a statute whose preface blasted the appellate decision by name and pointed directly to "the Constitution's use of the express religious reference 'Year of our Lord' in Article VII." According to the statute's preface, a strict insistence that government should not invoke God would render the Constitution itself unconstitutional—an "absurd result," huffed an outraged Congress.[29]

On the other side of the debate stand those who seek to minimize, or dismiss entirely, the parchment's reference to God. First, they note, contra Congress, that the "Year of our Lord" phraseology is not part of Article VII itself, but is rather the opening provision of a distinctly separate attestation section. This section, they claim, contains no operative legal rules akin to those found in virtually every other part of the Constitution. Second, these debaters suggest that the word "Lord" should not be read as a strong constitutional endorsement of religion in general or Christianity in particular. Had the parchment simply used the date, "1787," virtually no one would think twice or suggest that the mere use of this common-era dating system itself made any strong theological statement. The same would hold true had the parchment said "A.D. 1787" or even "1787, *Anno Domini.*" Surely, the argument runs, the mere translation of *Anno Domini* into English should not be seen as a grand religious gesture. In both England and America, before and after the Revolution, it was common practice to use the words "in the Year of our Lord" in official legal documents.[30]

Each side in this debate makes some valid points. But both sides miss the biggest points: The words "in the Year of our Lord" do not merely lie outside of Article VII. They lie outside of the official written Constitution—that is, the legal one—altogether. Nevertheless, these words are an important part of America's unwritten Constitution and as such need not be read in a manner that drains them of all religious significance.

Let us put aside, for a moment, the iconic parchment, which is only a ceremonial document, and focus instead on the official printed Constitution—the democratic one, the legal one, the one actually ratified by the people. The September 28 print sent out to the state ratifying conventions did contain a typeset list of the Philadelphia signatures, preceded by the very same dating words that have caused all the shouting.[31]

But are these words part of the legal Constitution itself, or are they actually something else, akin to other documents that accompanied the written Constitution yet were not part of it? Here we reach the crux of the matter.

Had we only the self-contained constitutional text to guide us, the answer might seem uncertain. Although the written Constitution clearly does refer to itself as a bounded text, it does not clearly define its own textual boundaries. The Preamble is certainly part of the written Constitution, for it says so in its very textual self-reference to "this Constitution." Ditto for Article VII, whose single closing sentence contains the same self-reference. Obviously, everything between the Preamble and Article VII likewise counts as part of the written Constitution—and the words "this Constitution" recur repeatedly in this middle material.[32]

By contrast, a letter to the Confederation Congress signed by George Washington on behalf of the Philadelphia Convention, and dated September 17, 1787, is obviously not part of the written Constitution, but was merely designed to accompany the Constitution as added explanation and commentary. Tellingly, this letter does not use the self-referential phrase "this Constitution" but instead speaks of "the Constitution, which we now present" and "that Constitution which has appeared to us the most adviseable." Yet another companion document dated September 17, 1787—the resolution of the Philadelphia Convention submitting the Constitution to Congress—likewise referred to "the preceding Constitution."[33]

Is, then, the language after the single sentence of Article VII—the language containing the phrase "the Year of our Lord" and all the signatures—properly part of "this Constitution," or instead merely companion language of personal attestation accompanying "the preceding Constitution"? The text of this section itself contains no references to the "Constitution" either as part of the same ("this") document or as an entirely different ("that") document.

Still, the text of this section does contain some tip-offs. It says that "We" the undersigned have "hereunto subscribed our Names" as "witness[es]" to an act "DONE in Convention." This is not at all the language of the Constitution itself. The Constitution speaks of "We the people" acting publicly—not "We," a handful of delegates meeting behind closed doors. The Preamble looks forward to a formal legal deed of ordainment and establishment that the citizenry will "do," not backward to an informal deed of draftsmanship already "DONE" by some notables who summered in Philadelphia. All these textual tip-offs suggest that the attestation-and-signature language below Article VII is not part of the official Constitution itself. Rather, this language is exactly like the accompanying Convention resolution and Washington letter—companion words of explanation framing the legal canvass but forming no part of it, strictly speaking.

Yet, unlike both the Convention resolution and the Washington letter, which were written on entirely separate sheets of paper in Philadelphia, the attestations and signatures appear on the ceremonial parchment itself. In the September 28 print, the attestation-and-signature language was not crisply demarcated as a distinct accompanying document. It was not printed on a wholly separate piece of paper, but rather appeared near the top of the final sheet of a four-page set. The sheet began with the final paragraph of Article VI and the entirety of Article VII, which was closely followed by the attestation-and-signature language, which was in turn closely followed by the Philadelphia Convention resolution, the Washington letter, and the forwarding resolution of the Confederation Congress. On this sheet, the attestation-and-signature section was thus tightly wedged between words that clearly were part of the Constitution and words that clearly were not—blurring the precise point where the written Constitution officially ended. It is therefore somewhat difficult to definitively determine the boundaries of the written Constitution based solely on textual analysis and visual inspection of the September 28 print.

But once we recall the importance of enactment, we can slice the Gordian knot with one clean stroke: Of the nine states that printed the texts of the Constitution that they were ratifying, a majority—five—ended the text with the single sentence of Article VII and thus severed off the witness and signature flourish. Evidently, all five states understood that the witness and signature language was not part of the official written Constitution itself. No matter how we count, this closing flourish was never ratified by the nine-state minimum required by Article VII.[34]

TO INSIST THAT THE PARCHMENT'S final flourish is no part of our official *written* Constitution is only to begin proper analysis, once we acknowledge the existence of an *unwritten* Constitution worthy of respect. What should we make of the fact that thirty-nine framers subscribed to language with explicit Christian overtones? And how should we understand the additional fact that a majority of the ratifying conventions—seven, to be precise—used the "Year of our Lord" phraseology in dating their own acts of assent in 1787, 1788, and 1790? Don't these facts give rise to an enactment argument in support of the "Christian nation" interpretation of America's Constitution?[35]

Those who venture beyond the written Constitution must understand not only where to start, but also when to stop, and why. True, the unwritten Constitution may properly supplement the written word. Not every textual gap in the written Constitution should be read as a purposeful, pregnant omission. The unwritten Constitution can also discourage flatfooted over-readings of textual provisions that were meant to be followed faithfully, not literally. But the unwritten Constitution should never contradict the plain meaning and central purpose—what Blackstone called the "main object"—of an express and basic element of the written Constitution. Supplementing the text is one thing; supplanting it, something altogether different. Proper enactment arguments intertwine with, but never strangle, the Constitution's text.[36]

Yet strangulation of the text would indeed ensue if we insisted that America's unwritten Constitution proclaims that Christ is King. Were the Lordship of Jesus Christ truly a full-fledged (albeit unwritten) constitutional principle comparable to the constitutional principle *nemo judex in causa sua*, then the carefully chosen language of Article VI would be reduced to gibberish: "The Senators and Representatives…and all executive and judicial Officers…of the United States [and various state officials] shall be bound by Oath or Affirmation, to support this Constitution; but no religious Test shall ever be required as a Qualification to any Office or public Trust under the United States."

The central meaning of this clause—not some uncommon, counterintuitive, quirky, peripheral application, but its basic thrust, its main object—is that no federal public servant may ever be forced to pass a religious test.

For example, no one may be forced as a condition of federal service to affirm that Jesus Christ is Lord. But if the Lordship of Christ were indeed a basic constitutional principle, Article VI would require every covered federal public servant to pledge to support a Christian Constitution while simultaneously proclaiming that no religious test whatsoever should ever be imposed on these very same federal public servants! Congress in 2002 thus got the matter exactly backward: They were the ones whose reading of the "Year of our Lord" language would make the Constitution itself unconstitutional—a truly "absurd result."

Even if the Article VI clause banning federal religious tests did not exist, religious neutrality would still be a clear, central, and striking element of the written Constitution as a whole—especially once we attend to what the Constitution did *not* say. Though not all textual omissions were purposeful, some surely were. For instance, the document nowhere described the system of government it created as a *confederation* or a *league*. Nowhere did it use the word *sovereignty* to describe the legal status of states. Nor did it require that all federal power be *expressly* enumerated. All of these italicized words had been high-profile and weighty textual features of the Articles of Confederation. Thus, the pointed absence of these words from the written Constitution was no mere oversight or irrelevance. These were pregnant and purposeful omissions, as Federalists freely admitted—indeed, proudly stressed—during the ratification process.*

Similarly, although the Declaration of Independence, the Articles of Confederation, and several state constitutions had explicitly and prominently invoked God in their opening and/or closing passages, the federal Constitution conspicuously did not. Thus, neither the Preamble nor any other constitutional clause explicitly mentioned the "Creator" or "Nature's God" or "the Supreme Judge of the World," as had the Declaration of Independence and the New York Constitution of 1777 (which incorporated the Declaration); or "the Great Governor of the World," as had the

---

* We cannot always determine which textual omissions were pointed and purposeful, and which other omissions were not, solely by examining the text itself. Background history and context will often be decisive in helping us to decide how much (if any) weight to give to the fact that a certain word, phrase, rule, or principle is not explicit in the text. Once again, we see how an unwritten Constitution (here, based on history and context) is necessary to make full sense of the written Constitution.

Articles of Confederation; or the "Great Governor of the Universe," as had the Pennsylvania Constitution of 1776; or "the Great Legislator of the Universe,...the Supreme Being, the great Creator and Preserver of the universe," as had the Massachusetts Constitution of 1780. The South Carolina Constitution of 1778 used the word "God" nine times—a word that explicitly appeared in every revolution-era state constitution save Virginia's. But this word appeared nowhere in the federal Constitution—a pointed omission if ever there was one.

That said, a religiously neutral Constitution should not be confused with an antireligious or anti-Christian Constitution. Just as no unbeliever could be barred from federal service for his atheism, no true believer could be excluded for his abiding faith.

For example, while most Founding-era state constitutions expressly included the phrase "so help me God" or some analogous reference to "God" in their obligatory oaths, the Article II presidential oath omitted all mention of God. This omission was surely pointed and purposeful, with the result that no duly selected president could be obliged to utter the word "God" or profess his belief in any supreme being. But neither did Article II bar the use of the word "God" or the phrase "so help me God" or "in Jesus' name" at a presidential oath ceremony if the oath-taker opted to add an allusion to the Almighty. Over the years, many (but not all) presidents have chosen to utter the words "so help me God" alongside the oath as prescribed verbatim by Article II. Similarly, presidents have often taken their oaths with a hand upon the Christian Bible, even though Article II makes no mention of a Bible (in sharp contrast to eighteenth-century English-law requirements for the monarch's oath ceremony). The invocations of God and the introductions of Bibles at presidential inaugurations are properly recognized as personal religious choices. Thus, these grand ceremonies have dramatized that the Constitution's essence is religiously neutral but not antireligious. This spirit of neutrality welcomes all types—believers, doubters, and deniers alike—into federal service and does not seek to prohibit personal and voluntary professions and exemplifications of religious belief, even in prominent public settings.[37]

This is exactly how we should understand the parchment's "Year of our Lord" language—which perhaps was, at least for some signers, a personal and voluntary profession of belief in the most prominent public setting imaginable. Each of the thirty-nine signers was signing for himself, and in that signing moment was properly allowed to profess his faith, if he so chose. Many signers with quill in hand likely gave no thought to the "Year of our Lord" language and its theological overtones. But other signers may well have mused on things eternal, and on their personal relationships to God, at the precise instant when they added their names to a plan that they hoped would sharply bend the arc of human history toward justice. Modern commentators who try to minimize the "Year of our Lord" language by denying even the possibility of its religious significance may well misread at least some of the signers.[38]

Precisely because the signatures were so personal, the words of Lordship did not need to mean the same thing for all signers. Each man was signing as a human being, as a "witness." Were these words of Lordship true law, they might well need to have an unvarying, impersonal, objective, official meaning. But these words were not words of law. Each signer at Philadelphia could decide for himself on the meaning, or lack thereof, of these words, much as the words "so help me God" have probably meant different things to the different human beings who have uttered these words in their presidential oath ceremonies.[39]

The best interpretation of the signatures thus clarifies one major feature of the written Constitution: America's supreme law was (and remains) not aggressively antireligious but merely religiously neutral.

But what are we to make of the fact that seven states included the phrase "Year of our Lord" in dating their own respective decisions to ratify the document? In these seven instances, the phrase was not unofficial and personal, as with the signatures of the Philadelphia delegates. Rather, the phrase was part of an official legal action—indeed, an action that was at the heart of the enactment process by which the Constitution acquired its legal authority. How does this enactment fact about the unwritten Constitution square with the meaning of the written Constitution?

Actually, it squares quite nicely. The written Constitution's principle of religious neutrality applied to the federal document itself and to federal public service, but states were far freer to favor religion in general or even one sect in particular. Thus, the oath provision of Article VI began by obliging both *state and federal* public servants to pledge allegiance to the United States Constitution, but then proceeded to bar religious tests only for *federal* public servants. Here was another pointed and purposeful omission, allowing states to continue to use religious tests for state officials. As of 1787, almost every state did in fact use religious tests. Nine states incorporated these tests into the very texts of their written constitutions.[40]

The Founders' framework for both free-expression law and church-state law, a framework most people today associate with the written text of the First Amendment, was thus largely settled, thanks to America's unwritten Constitution, well before the First Amendment was even drafted. In various ways, the First Amendment merely codified extant, albeit unwritten, constitutional principles implicit in the original text and/or incarnated in the enactment process.

If anything, the text of the First Amendment underprotected the deep principles of free speech and free press by expressly safeguarding free expression against Congress without explicitly mentioning Americans' broad free-expression rights against states. (Recall the discussion of this precise point in Chapter 1, in our Lincoln Abraham hypothetical.) In partial mitigation, nothing in the First Amendment limited the power and duty of Congress to protect citizens from any state effort to stifle the free political expression that was essential to republican government.

By contrast, the text of the First Amendment did tell Congress to lay off the states in matters of religion. The amendment prohibited Congress merely from "*abridging*" free expression (thus allowing Congress to *promote* free expression, where necessary and proper), but limited Congress more symmetrically on the topic of religion. Congress could not pass any law "*respecting*" religious establishments—that is, any law either establishing a national church or disestablishing state churches. Generally speaking, religion simply lay beyond the scope of enumerated federal power, leaving the states free to do as they pleased, even to prefer religion in general or one denomination in particular.

Thanks to the intertwining of America's written and unwritten Constitution, this system—a religiously neutral federal regime alongside state freedom to aid preferred sects—was already largely in place before the First Amendment was even drafted. The emphatic words of Article VI banning federal religious tests prefigured the First Amendment, as did various elements of an *unwritten* Constitution: the pointed *absence* of "God" in the Preamble; the notable *lack* of any enumerated federal power over religion in Article I; the striking *nonappearance* of religious elements in the Article II presidential oath; and the *omission* of the words "our Lord" in the official written Constitution, in stark contrast to the presence of those two words in various official state ratification instruments that lay *outside* the Constitution's formal text.

IF THE FIRST AMENDMENT was not the first word on the constitutional law of church and state, neither was it the last. The Fourteenth Amendment, adopted in the wake of the Civil War, added additional words that barred states from preferring whites over blacks or Gentiles over Jews. Thanks to this amendment, citizens of all races and all creeds now stand equal before the states, and no state may abridge any citizen's fundamental rights, freedoms, privileges, and immunities—including the privilege to choose her religion (or atheism) freely without state compulsion or favoritism. States today are no longer allowed to proclaim the Lordship of Christ or the preferred status of an official Protestant church, just as they are no longer permitted to proclaim an official policy of white supremacy—interrelated principles to which we shall return in later chapters.

"The United States shall guarantee to every State...a Republic[]"

AND SPEAKING OF THE FOURTEENTH AMENDMENT...we must recognize that this momentous part of America's Constitution supplemented and superseded the Founders' constitutional compromises not only through its text, but also via its deed—via the very process by which it became an amendment. Though hardly unique in this respect, the Fourteenth Amendment provides an especially vivid illustration of the fact that the Constitution's amendments have at times embodied transformative deeds. These deeds—these post-Founding enactments—are as much a part of America's unwritten Constitution as are the enactments of the Founders themselves.

But before we can honor the unwritten principles constitutionalized by these amendatory enactments, we must first identify those principles—and to do that we must once again dive into some fascinating facts beyond but adjacent to the official text.

WHEN THE STATE GOVERNMENTS that had forcibly attempted to secede in 1860–1861 professed a willingness to return to the fold at war's end in 1865, a justifiably wary Congress declined to seat the ex-Confederate states' federal representatives and senators until Congress could assure itself that the new South was now playing and would continue to play by the Constitution's rules. The old South had not played by the rules—hence "the recent unpleasantness" that had left more than a half million dead. In the First Reconstruction Act, Congress outlined what the ex-Confederate states should do to regain admission to Congress. The act became law on March 2, 1867, and applied to the entire South except Tennessee. (The Volunteer State had been welcomed back to Congress in July 1866, immediately after having voted to ratify the proposed Fourteenth Amendment; no other former rebel state had followed Tennessee's example.)[41]

Three interrelated instructions formed the foundation of the First Reconstruction Act. First, each ex-Confederate state should adopt a new state constitution via an electoral process enfranchising virtually all adult male residents, regardless of race. Second, each new state constitution should guarantee a right to vote in ordinary elections to this same broad swath of adult male residents. Third—and most important for our purposes—the new governments elected under the new state constitutions should ratify the Fourteenth Amendment, which Congress had proposed in June 1866, and which had already been ratified by three-fourths of the loyal states plus Tennessee.[42]

How should we understand the legal status of this landmark statute? To the strict textualist, the First Reconstruction Act lies entirely outside the written Constitution. Yet surely the act was a critical part of the process by which the Fourteenth Amendment was actually adopted. Without this landmark statute, it is doubtful that ex-Confederate states would have promised and practiced universal male suffrage; and without this broad suffrage base, it is doubtful that these states would have ever agreed to ratify the Fourteenth Amendment (or, for that matter, the later Fifteenth Amendment guaranteeing race-blind suffrage in every state).

More to the point, the First Reconstruction Act bluntly directed ex-Confederate states to ratify the Fourteenth Amendment with all deliberate speed. In much the same way that free speech and majority rule were the basic protocols and processes that brought forth the original Constitution in the 1780s, so the Reconstruction Act's directive to the former Confederacy was the basic legal matrix that brought forth the Fourteenth Amendment. The act was the amendment's legal birth canal, so to speak. Properly understood, the statute was thus part of the public meaning of that amendment as an embodied enactment—an 1860s re-do of the 1780s "We...do."

From this enactment perspective, Americans in the 1860s should be understood as having given birth to a new constitutional principle, albeit one that did not explicitly appear in the Fourteenth Amendment's text. Under this new unwritten principle, the federal government would properly enjoy sweeping authority to hold state governments to the highest contemporary standards of democratic inclusiveness.

ALTHOUGH THIS IS NOT THE ONLY possible interpretation of the Fourteenth Amendment enactment process, it is more explanatory than alternative accounts, which are on one side too complacent and on the other too eccentric.

In a too-complacent view, the Fourteenth Amendment's enactment created no new constitutional norm, because the Founders themselves had already provided the federal government with authority to hold states to proper democratic standards. The Constitution's Article I, section 5, allowed each house of Congress to judge the elections of its members, and Article IV instructed the federal government to "guarantee to every State in this Union a Republican Form of Government." Together, these clauses empowered each house to refuse to seat a self-proclaimed representative or senator if the relevant house deemed the underlying election constitutionally inadequate under correct principles of republican government.

True enough, but many framers would have been startled to learn that Congress could use these clauses to require states to enfranchise blacks—indeed, illiterate, unpropertied ex-slaves, at that! State franchise law, as defined by state constitutions and traditional state practice, underpinned the federal system as originally designed. Antebellum Congresses did not rest on a nationally defined suffrage base but simply piggybacked on state suffrage law. The federal House of Representatives was chosen by those persons in each state who were eligible under state law to vote for state assemblies. Likewise, the United States Senate was chosen by state legislatures that ultimately derived their powers from voting rules established by state law.

At the Founding, the Article IV republican-government clause could plausibly be read as reinforcing this state-law bedrock, not undermining it: The federal government would simply guarantee existing state constitutional practices against the possibility of unrepublican amendment or violent overthrow—as might happen, for example, if a governor's minions revised the state constitution to create a hereditary dictatorship, or if a state military cabal wrested control from duly elected civilian authorities. On this narrow view of Article IV, the federal government could prevent a state from backsliding whenever agitators tried to transform an existing republican regime into an unrepublican one, but federal authorities could not oblige a state to make any great democratic leaps forward. So long as states faithfully followed the basic structural practices in place in 1787, federal officials would not interfere.

In the 1780s and in every decade thereafter, a significant number of states had denied free blacks the vote. Many Founding-era states also had property requirements for voting. Before the Civil War, some states began to experiment with franchise-restricting literacy tests. By what right, asked President Andrew Johnson and his conservative allies in the mid-1860s, did the Reconstruction Congress claim authority to impose on the ex-Confederate states an utterly novel federal requirement of race-blind universal male suffrage? Would the state ratifying conventions in 1787–1788—especially in the South—have agreed to the federal Constitution if ratifiers had clearly understood that Congress could radically redefine the most basic and jealously protected political structures of state constitutions?

In truth, the enactment of the Fourteenth Amendment pivoted on a fresh interpretation of the republican-government clause, an interpretation that had not been firmly established by the Founding Fathers. The too-complacent view misses the key fact that a new principle of broad national control over undemocratic state franchise law was born as part of the Fourteenth Amendment's enactment process.

Enter the eccentrics, who claim that because the Fourteenth Amendment was ratified by dint of a congressional statute that went beyond the Constitution as understood by the framers, the amendment was never properly adopted. The supposed Fourteenth Amendment is therefore a nullity![43]

To be clear: No justice on the current Court takes this position. Nor has any justice in history ever publicly written anything of the sort in *United States Reports*, the official compilation of Supreme Court opinions. Nor has any president proclaimed this view, if we put aside the curious case of Andrew Johnson, who said all manner of things while the amendment was pending, but ultimately allowed his own secretary of state to proclaim the amendment validly enacted. Nor does any mainstream constitutional scholar today deny the Fourteenth Amendment's legal validity.[44]

This universal consensus reigns for a reason. Without this consensus, the project of American constitutionalism as we know it might well implode. That project revolves around a canonical text—the written Constitution— that all (noneccentric) citizens and public servants acknowledge as the official supreme law of the land. Though interpreters may sharply disagree about the document's meaning, all point to the same basic text, which provides firm common ground for constitutional conversation and contestation. This text—with countless millions of copies in circulation, all of which include the words of the Fourteenth Amendment—is the national focal point, the common denominator for all constitutionalists, whether Democrat or Republican, liberal or conservative, private citizen or public servant.

Granted, some small imprecision at the outer edges of the text would not doom the project of written constitutionalism. Disagreement about whether the words "our Lord" are part of the canonical legal text or merely part of its ceremonial parchment counterpart does not threaten to unravel the entire constitutional fabric. The words at issue are peripheral in every respect: The attestation clause as written does not claim to have any enforceable legal bite, the Supreme Court has never quoted this clause for any purpose whatsoever, and many constitutional experts have literally never given the clause a moment's thought.

By contrast, the Fourteenth Amendment stands at the very center of the Constitution, both textually and functionally. In 1955, Justice Felix

Frankfurter remarked that "claims under the Fourteenth Amendment" were "probably the largest source of the Court's business."[45] Since then, the practical significance of the amendment has only grown—indeed, skyrocketed. The amendment was the vehicle by which the post-1955 Supreme Court eventually (and correctly) came to apply virtually all the provisions of the original Bill of Rights against state and local governments. Today the lion's share of "Bill of Rights" cases litigated in courts are actually Fourteenth Amendment cases. The Fourteenth Amendment was also the truest source of congressional power to adopt sweeping civil rights laws in the late twentieth century—laws that changed the course of world history.

Long before the Warren Court revolution and the Second Reconstruction of the 1960s, the validity of the Fourteenth Amendment was definitively established. All three branches of the federal government pledged allegiance to the Fourteenth Amendment in the late 1860s and early 1870s, as did the citizenry and state governments at the time. Ever since, the amendment's legality has been a basic premise of the American constitutional system. For example, the federal Income Tax Amendment was explicitly proposed by Congress in 1909 and ratified by state legislatures by 1913 as "Article XVI" of the Constitution, plainly indicating that "Article XIV" and "Article XV"—that is, the Fourteenth and Fifteenth Amendments—were already valid parts of the Constitution.

To understand the stakes here, recall that the Civil Rights Act and the Voting Rights Act of the 1960s were notable efforts to enforce the Fourteenth and Fifteenth Amendments. Without the epic changes wrought by these laws, Americans in 2008 would never have elected Barack Obama president. If these amendments are truly invalid, then presumably the Second Reconstruction of the late twentieth century was likewise invalid and the results of that Reconstruction are also illegitimate. On this view, the very status of Barack Obama as president would be constitutionally dubious.

Only cranks think this way.

The eccentrics fail to understand that the Reconstruction generation faithfully interpreted the Founders' project, even as Reconstructors went beyond various specific expectations that were widespread in the late 1780s. True, the First Reconstruction Act did supplement the Founders' rules.

But it did not supplant them. Rather, it interpreted and extended them in the unique context of a Civil War that, constitutionally, should never have happened. (The original Constitution emphatically denied state authority to unilaterally secede.) To the extent that Reconstructors stretched the text of various Founding-era clauses, these men did so in order to make the best sense of—and ultimately to preserve—the document as a whole.

Whatever various framers may have expected or predicted, the *text* of the republican-government clause did not unambiguously limit the federal role to merely policing against state retrogression. The leading modern book on the clause reports that some Founders "expected the concept of republican government to change over time, hopefully perfecting the experiment begun by the Revolution."[46]

In any event, the southern states *had* clearly regressed between 1789 and 1866. In 1789, antislavery speech was broadly allowed, whereas in the late antebellum period it was officially outlawed and/or suppressed by massive extralegal violence in much of the South, where the Republican Party had in effect been criminalized in the 1850s. In 1860, Lincoln received not a single popular vote—not one!—south of Virginia. One does not find such perfectly one-sided election returns or such savagely skewed pubic debates in true republics. Prior to the Founding, no large set of colonial or state officials had ever taken up arms to assail a freely elected government. In the years just before Reconstruction, a vast conspiracy of southern officials calling itself "the Confederacy" had done just that in arrogant defiance of the free-election essence of republican government. In 1789, southern states did not lag miles behind most northern states in the percentage of free males eligible to vote. By 1866, a yawning chasm had abruptly opened up between the ex-gray states and most true-blue states. In many a northern state, the law circa 1866 barred only a tiny proportion of free adult males, often less than 3 percent, from voting. In the ex-confederacy before the First Reconstruction Act, comparable disenfranchisement rates ranged from about 25 percent to over 50 percent—roughly ten to twenty times the typical northern rate.[47]

Thus, even though the ex-Confederate states claimed that they were simply perpetuating long-standing suffrage rules—in many places, free blacks had never been allowed to vote—the perpetuation of these old voting rules in the late 1860s threatened to create a wholly new and qualitatively different sort of disfranchisement. Free blacks accounted for a minuscule proportion of the total free population of most southern states prior to 1860. But once slaves won their freedom, thanks to Lincoln's Emancipation Proclamation and the subsequent Thirteenth Amendment, free blacks mushroomed almost overnight to become a vastly larger segment, a significantly greater proportion of free folk than had ever been excluded from the franchise in the antebellum era.[48]

Though it cannot be said that the Founders' republican-government clause clearly required that these new freemen be enfranchised, neither can it be said that the clause clearly blessed the *unprecedented* disfranchisement of a *vast* number of *free* men. The written text did not clearly specify what should happen in this unanticipated scenario, and the unwritten antibacksliding principle could also be interpreted either way. Contrary to the complacent view, the First Reconstruction Act represented a new principle that was not clearly established in 1789; but contrary to the eccentric view, the act reflected a plausible application of Founding texts and principles to a situation that the Founders had simply failed to address with specificity.

IN ASSESSING THE CONSTITUTIONAL PROPRIETY of the Reconstruction Act, we must keep three additional things in mind. First, the nation needed strong medicine to ensure that recently rebellious states would never again commit the ultimate act of unrepublicanism by waging war on a freely elected regime. Even if the act's requirement of universal male suffrage in the old South was not an *intrinsic element* of republican government, it was an *appropriate instrument* of republican government, and thus good enough under *McCulloch*. Just as a continental bank, though not logically necessary for a continental army, was nevertheless quite useful to support such an army, so black suffrage in the South was quite useful to buttress the wholly proper republican-government project of ensuring due southern respect for the results of free elections. With blacks voting in the South, a second unilateral secession movement would be highly unlikely to prevail.

Second, the Reconstruction Act's additional directive that ex-Confederate states ratify the Fourteenth Amendment was also an appropriate instrument to further the republican-government ideal. The amendment required every state to honor concrete elements of a proper republican government, such as equal citizenship, free speech, free assembly, free religious exercise, and fair trials. Although in 1789 these concrete elements were perhaps not universally understood as necessary components of republican government, neither were they universally understood as wholly beyond the proper meaning of republicanism. Here, too, Reconstructors did not violate Founding principles even as they went beyond them, clarifying what the original text and late eighteenth-century history had left unclear. The Founders' question mark properly gave way to the Reconstructors' exclamation point.[49]

Third, Congress adopted the Reconstruction Act only after three-quarters of the true-blue states had already ratified the amendment—enough to make the amendment fully valid had Congress chosen simply to exclude ex-Confederate states from the Article V amendment tally (just as Congress in early 1865 had excluded all ex-Confederate states from the electoral-college tally in tabulating the presidential election results of 1864). Although the Reconstruction Congress ultimately opted to include ex-Confederate states in the amendment process, Congress need not have done so. Read holistically, the Constitution envisioned a federal union of republican states, and states without proper republican governments could not justly complain if they were simply excluded from the Article V state-count and treated as de facto federal territories pending reestablishment of proper republican governments.[50]

In the end, Congress did not go this far. Instead, Congress improvised a two-stage strategy that relied heavily on the verdict of true-blue states in the first stage of enactment, but then gave ex-gray states an important role during the final stage of enactment. The pivot in this two-stage enactment process was the First Reconstruction Act, an act adopted only after a deep and wide democratic consensus had been reached in the only states where true republicanism—with free speech, broad electorates, and fair elections—had generally prevailed in the preceding decade. Via the First Reconstruction Act, Congress ingeniously used the constitutional amendment process itself both as a good test of the South's genuine commitment to republican government and as a good vehicle for restoring truly republican southern states to their proper status as constitutional entities in good standing.

JUST AS THE WRITTEN FOUNDING text of the republican-government clause was legitimately open to either a narrow or a broad reading during Reconstruction, so, too, the unwritten Reconstruction enactment principle glossing that Founding text could plausibly be read narrowly or broadly by still later faithful constitutional interpreters. Read narrowly, the enactment principle inherent in the First Reconstruction Act gave Congress broad power to hold states to a high standard of democracy only when state failures to meet these standards imperiled the entire constitutional project. Read more broadly, the enactment principle gave Congress wide discretion to determine when to intervene in states that fell short of the highest standards of contemporary democracy. Read even more broadly, the enactment principle visible in the Reconstruction amendment process empowered other branches of the federal government in addition to Congress. On this broadest reading, the 1860s enactment experience glossed the words of a 1780s clause about state republican government—and nothing in those words said that only the federal Congress, as opposed to federal courts, could give teeth to the demanding principle of state republicanism. Likewise, nothing in these words limited the federal role to moments of extreme national urgency.

As we shall see in Chapter 4, it is a broad view of this Reconstruction gloss that best explains one of the most dramatic subsequent episodes in the history of American constitutionalism—the insistence of the Warren Court that every state abide by the apportionment rule of "one person, one vote."

"Armies…being necessary to the security of a free State"[31]

ONE FINAL AND EYE-OPENING FEATURE of the Reconstruction enactment process merits attention: The First Reconstruction Act explicitly authorized the Union Army (?!) to oversee the process of bringing the South into proper constitutional alignment. This military deployment might well have startled many a Founder who romanticized state militias while viewing a continental army with deep suspicion; the deployment nevertheless represented a plausible effort to faithfully execute the Founders' project in the unprecedented crisis kindled by the Confederates' unconstitutional efforts to secede.

Here, too, we can read the unwritten principle springing to life in the 1860s narrowly or broadly. Read narrowly, the Fourteenth Amendment's enactment process might seem to have nothing to say about the scope of the federal government's power to directly conscript citizens into the army. After all, the army that oversaw the Fourteenth Amendment ratification process in the old South was a virtually all-volunteer army. But seen though a wider-angled lens, the enactment experience of the late 1860s does indeed help us understand why a national military draft is nowadays deemed permissible.

The Founding-era texts and original understandings provide only modest support for a federal draft. Although Article I empowers Congress to "raise and support Armies," this clause was generally understood in the 1780s to authorize the raising of *volunteer* armies. Direct national conscription to populate the federal army was no more envisioned than, say, direct national conscription to populate the federal judiciary. Rather, the prevailing notion was that whatever military conscription might occur would take place through a militia system elsewhere outlined in Article I. (Similarly, Article III envisioned that judicial conscription might occur via a jury-duty regime that bore certain resemblances to the militia-duty system.)

In this militia system, states could train and organize militia conscripts according to rules laid down by Congress, and the federal government could summon these militiamen into national service whenever manpower was needed to execute the laws, suppress insurrections, or repel invasions. One notable libertarian safeguard for conscripted militiamen was a guarantee in Article I that state governments would choose militia officers, who would presumably be tied by various preexisting and postcombat social and political networks to the militiamen whom they commanded. Any direct federal draft would outflank this localist-libertarian safeguard, blurring the very distinction between an "army" soldier and a "militia" member as these constitutional words and concepts were widely understood by Americans in 1789.[52]

Consider also the preambulatory language of the Second Amendment. By declaring that "a well regulated Militia" was "necessary to the security of a free State," the amendment appeared to proclaim that the militia, and not the army, was the nation's constitutionally preferred defense structure. Any efforts to maneuver around the militia and its built-in localist-libertarian safeguards could plausibly be viewed as offending the animating spirit of this amendment's preamble. Although the philosophy of *McCulloch v. Maryland* smiled upon congressional laws genuinely aimed at securing national defense, the case had also frowned on federal policies that dishonored the "spirit" of the Constitution or that were improper "pretexts."

In the 1810s, direct national conscription was condemned as unconstitutional by no less a figure than Daniel Webster, but in the 1860s the party of Lincoln migrated to a different vision. Over the course of the nineteenth century, the word "army" in ordinary language had begun to shed its eighteenth-century connotations of a strictly volunteer force. In 1793, the world witnessed the first modern national draft—Revolutionary France's *levée en masse*. But even in 1860, it was doubtful that military developments abroad—developments that the American people had never legally endorsed or voted to incorporate into America's constitutional system—effectively authorized Congress to deviate from the basic meaning of key constitutional words such as "army" and "militia," as these words had been understood by those who had ratified the original Constitution and Bill of Rights in the pre-Napoleonic era.[53]

Then came secession, which shattered the Founding vision. With so many state militias arrayed under Confederate banners, it seemed to many Americans that the Founding-era text's smug confidence in state militias had been misplaced. Many faithful constitutionalists came to believe that, if the nation was to survive its darkest hour and win the war in the most direct way, a national draft might indeed be constitutionally "necessary" and not a mere "pretext," as *McCulloch* had expounded these words. In 1863, Congress passed and President Lincoln signed into law a national draft of sorts.[54]

Nevertheless, Chief Justice Roger Taney readied himself to hold this law unconstitutional in the event that a proper judicial case raising the issue came before him. (It didn't, and Taney's draft draft remained in his desk.)

Because the 1863 law allowed individual draftees to buy their way out—by providing a substitute or paying a fee—many supporters claimed the law was technically a tax and not a system of direct conscription. Even after Antietam and the Emancipation Proclamation, the constitutionality of a pure system of national conscription remained doubtful.[55]

The constitutional doubts that lingered in 1863 should today be dispelled, thanks to the enactments of the Fourteenth and Fifteenth Amendments. These enactments simply could not have occurred without the vigorous and visible work of the Union Army under the First Reconstruction Act—also commonly referred to as the Military Reconstruction Act. Here was direct proof, via military measures inextricably intertwined with the very act of constitutional amendment and publicly endorsed by the American people themselves through the amendment process, that it was indeed "necessary and proper" for Congress to enjoy broad discretion in the raising and deployment of federal troops.[56]

True, by 1867, most draftees had been released from service. Thus, the army that oversaw Reconstruction was not a conscripted army. But neither was it the Founders' vaunted militia. The high-profile deployment of the Union Army to guarantee a regime of true republican governments undercut the central ideological premise of the Second Amendment's preamble: No longer could it be insisted that the localist militia was always America's constitutionally preferred force structure to vindicate the Constitution's deepest values and secure its most sacred principles. And without a heavy thumb on the militia pan of the balance scale, there would be no decisive reason to read Article I in a stingy way that would deny Congress broad discretion over the army's basic organizational structure.

Nothing in the 1860s vision repudiated the Founders' explicit written commands, even as this unwritten vision superseded earlier unwritten understandings. Nowhere did the Founders' text *explicitly* provide that the army clauses should be construed narrowly lest they undercut America's militia system. Nowhere did the Founders' text *explicitly* bar a national army draft if such a draft were deemed necessary to execute the laws, suppress insurrections, or repel invasions. Nowhere did the Founders' text *explicitly* say that every conscript must be officered locally. Rather, these things were arguably implicit in Article I as glossed by Amendment II.

These unwritten understandings should ultimately give way to a later principle of the unwritten Constitution celebrating the army as a proper engine of national defense and republican government.

This Reconstruction-era view does not render the Founders' militia clauses wholly redundant. These clauses continue to operate to raise the effective political cost if Congress ever seeks to conscript Americans directly into the army. Thus, Congress may indeed outflank the militia clauses of Article I, but in order to execute this detour, supporters of an army draft will need to overcome political critics singing the praises of the good old militia system—a ready-made alternative rendered especially salient by the militia clauses of Article I.

Although libertarians, localists, and traditionalists might object whenever a draftee is forced to serve directly under a nationally chosen officer rather than a state-chosen military commander, egalitarians might well have a different view of the matter. Under the reconstructed Constitution, the federal government might deem it proper for white draftees to serve under black officers—an arrangement that would have shocked many a Founder (especially a southern Founder) but that would poetically personify the theme of racial equality at the heart of the Fourteenth and Fifteenth Amendments.

It is these acts of amendment during Reconstruction, rather than the formal texts of the Founding, as understood by the Founders, that best justify the current legal gloss on the army clause of Article I. Under this gloss, the army clause is now read as giving Congress general power to conscript soldiers. Thus, Congress today need not rely on the state governments if Congress believes that a military draft is warranted—whether in wartime or peacetime, and whether or not the nation's very survival is at stake.[57]

The definitive judicial pronouncement on this issue occurred in the *Selective Draft Law Cases* of 1918, in which the Supreme Court unanimously affirmed the lawfulness of army conscription. The Court placed primary emphasis on the Founding text, claiming that the Article I clause empowering Congress "to raise and support armies" meant that federal lawmakers could fill the army as they saw fit. But this argument slighted various Founding-era understandings that sharply differentiated between an "army" that was expected to be filled with volunteers and a general "militia" structure that would instead require all able-bodied men of military age to serve.

Near the end of its opinion, the Court also mentioned both the Civil War draft experience and the Fourteenth Amendment. The Court's main gesture toward the Fourteenth Amendment consisted of a textual argument. The amendment's opening words defining national citizenship, said the Court, affirmed national primacy and thus confirmed the propriety of the national government's direct authority over its citizens.[58]

But long before the Fourteenth Amendment, the Founders' Constitution had explicitly referred to national citizenship. Although the original document did not clearly define the term, Articles I and II, for example, required that every federal representative, senator, or president must be "a Citizen of the United States." How did the more detailed definition of national citizenship in the Fourteenth Amendment decisively change the Founding-era basics of a citizen's military responsibility? After all, the Fourteenth Amendment affirmed the citizenship of women as well as men. Did the amendment thereby make women—who could not even vote in the 1860s—draftable? Wasn't the amendment's opening section organized around the concept of civil rights, as crisply contradistinguished from political rights such as voting and military service? Textually, the amendment said nothing whatsoever about the "army" or the "militia." Without more, it seems a stretch to read the brisk words of the citizenship clause as purposefully inverting the elaborate rules about armies and militias laid down in Article I.

The Court's instinct was sound, but its execution was faulty: It tried to squeeze its Reconstruction argument into a textual frame, with emphasis on the written Constitution. Alongside the written document there lies an unwritten Constitution—and as we have seen, one obvious element of that unwritten system resides in the very process by which the written Constitution was ordained and later amended. Though the Fourteenth Amendment's text said nothing explicit about armies or militias, the amendment's enactment process did indeed—that is, in deed—embody a new role for the army.

Today it is altogether fitting and proper to read the Founders' text through the prism of the Reconstructors' deeds. Faithful constitutionalists are free to reject early interpretations of the Article I military clauses that were based primarily on the Founders' nostalgic preference for militias over armies—a preference repudiated by the Reconstruction enactment process itself, which gave the Union Army prominent pride of place over the militia. Hence the lawfulness today of a national draft, regardless of what the framers may have expected or intended.

IN THIS CHAPTER, we have accepted the Preamble's invitation to note what "We the People" were actually "do[ing]," and to heed how we did it, when "We" ordained and later amended the Constitution at epic moments in our national history. "We" Americans also routinely "do" a variety of things as normal persons in our daily lives. It turns out that these deeds and actions—not ordainment deeds, but ordinary deeds; not momentous public enactments, but mundane private activities—also invite interpretation, and add another layer to America's unwritten Constitution. Therein lies our next tale.

CHAPTER 3

HEARING THE PEOPLE

America's Lived Constitution

HOME SWEET HOME (1877).

Be it ever so humble, the home looms large in American culture
and also in America's Constitution, both written and unwritten.

NOTHING IN THE WRITTEN CONSTITUTION explicitly guarantees the right to have a pet dog, to play the fiddle, to relax at home, to enjoy family life with your loved ones, to raise your children, or to wear a hat. Yet these and countless other liberties are generally upheld by American governments, absent compelling reasons for abridgment. Many of Americans' most basic rights are simply facts of life: "This is how we, the people, do things in America and we therefore have the right to keep doing these things."

This chapter explores the constitutional status of textually unnamed or underspecified rights—first, by applying the methods of the preceding two chapters, and then by bringing a third method into the picture. In addition to reading between the lines of the text and pondering the specific procedures by which the text was enacted and amended, we must take account of—and take a count of—how ordinary Americans have lived their lives in ordinary ways and thereby embodied fundamental rights.

With case studies drawn from a wide cross-section of constitutional law—from criminal procedure to privacy law, property law, and punishment law—we shall see that judges should pay and do pay close attention to how various rights are embodied in citizens' daily rhythms and embedded in powerful customs. Examples of such lived rights include the rights of a criminal defendant to testify and present evidence in his own defense, a right to enjoy consensual conjugal happiness in one's home, and a right not to be punished in a cruel manner that violates modern national norms.

Though the written Constitution is quite supple when properly supplemented by a sensitive account of lived rights, the document is not infinitely malleable. Some claims of right are simply implausible, such as the claim that the Constitution calls for the exclusion of reliable physical evidence if such evidence is found by the government in a search or seizure that violates the Fourth Amendment. Any honest account of America's Constitution must illustrate not only which unwritten constitutional rules and principles can properly be found, but also which ones cannot, and why.

"the accused shall enjoy the right..."

WHEN IT COMES TO RIGHTS, the written Constitution gestures beyond itself, pointing to the existence of entitlements that are not "enumerate[ed]"—not expressly listed—in the written Constitution itself. Thus, the Ninth Amendment proclaims that "[t]he enumeration in the Constitution, of certain rights, shall not be construed to deny or disparage others retained by the people." But this amendment does not give us much detail about where and how these unenumerated rights are to be found. Similarly, the opening section of the Fourteenth Amendment declares that "[n]o State shall make or enforce any law which shall abridge the privileges or immunities of citizens of the United States," but does not itemize these unabridgeable rights or specify where they are to be discovered.

We have already begun to develop tools to find the source and define the scope of unenumerated rights. First, let's recall that we must peer behind the written Constitution to locate rights that may be *implicit* in its words. Though unenumerated—that is, not expressly declared in a specific constitutional clause—implicit rights are nonetheless full-fledged constitutional entitlements on any sensible reading of the document.

To see the importance of implicit rights and the ease with which they may be properly derived, consider the following Hollywood-style hypothetical: A defendant on trial for murder in the District of Columbia claims that he is innocent and that someone else—a man with close ties to the prosecutor's office—is the real culprit. Miraculously, the defendant has acquired decisive forensic evidence that he seeks to lay before the jury: a knife matching the victim's fatal stab wound, with her dried blood on the blade and the real culprit's fingerprints and DNA on the handle. The defendant is also poised to testify about the culprit's motive. However, the prosecutor moves to exclude the knife from the trial and thereby prevent the jury from even learning of the weapon's existence because the defense team obtained the knife via daring acts of deception and trespass committed by a private investigator. The prosecutor points to a statute generally prohibiting the introduction of illegally acquired evidence. When the defendant counters by asserting that he has a basic constitutional right to establish his innocence, the prosecutor responds that there is no such right specifically enumerated in the Constitution, and that the statute thus governs the case. How should the judge rule?

For the defendant, of course. No matter what the prosecutor might say, the Ninth Amendment gives defense counsel a knock-down rejoinder.

For example, the prosecutor might try to rest his case on the explicit words of the Sixth Amendment: "In all criminal prosecutions, the accused shall enjoy the right to a speedy and public trial, by an impartial jury...and to be informed of the nature and cause of the accusation; to be confronted with the witnesses against him; to have compulsory process for obtaining witnesses in his favor, and to have the assistance of counsel for his defence." These words explicitly guarantee the rights to confront the government's *witnesses* and to subpoena *witnesses* for the defense, but there is no comparably specific language in the Sixth Amendment (or any other clause of the Constitution) guaranteeing the defendant a right to introduce *physical evidence*, such as a knife. Thus, the prosecutor's argument would run, the words of the Sixth Amendment negate the very existence of the supposed constitutional right claimed by the defendant.

We have seen this sort of move—a sweeping argument from negative implication—before. Although such moves might make sense in some constitutional situations, this is not one of them.[1]

The Ninth Amendment, after all, instructs us precisely *not* to read the Sixth Amendment (or any other constitutional listing of rights, for that matter) in a stingy, negative-implication, rights-denying fashion: "The enumeration in the Constitution, of certain rights"—such as the rights to confront and to compel witnesses—"shall not be construed to deny or disparage others retained by the people," such as the right to establish one's own innocence, even in contexts not directly involving witnesses.

But where, our hypothetical prosecutor might ask, does this putative right to verify one's innocence come from? Even if the Sixth Amendment does not negate the existence of such a right, our prosecutor would insist that surely the amendment does not affirm this right, which is nowhere specifically mentioned in the amendment's text.

Here, too, our prosecutor errs. When properly construed alongside the Ninth Amendment, the Sixth Amendment does indeed affirm and presuppose a defendant's basic right to defend himself with truthful evidence.

The Ninth Amendment tells us to look beyond "enumeration" when interpreting—"constru[ing]"—the Constitution. It reminds us that not everything in the Constitution is textually itemized and specified. Some of what is in the Constitution is implied rather than expressed. Part of the meaning that can be extracted from the document lies between the lines and beneath the words. Thus, even as the Ninth Amendment emphatically warns against certain *anti*-rights readings of the written Constitution based on mere negative implication, the amendment warmly invites certain *pro*-rights readings based on positive implications.

Earlier, we saw how an implicit principle may properly follow *a fortiori* from an explicit provision—in particular, how the ineligibility of the vice president to preside over his own impeachment trial follows a fortiori from a clause that explicitly prevents a vice president from presiding over a president's impeachment trial. The a fortiori idea is not limited to issues of government structure, such as impeachment, but also applies in the domain of constitutional rights.

For example: Since the First Amendment prevents the president from censoring publishers even when Congress has purported to authorize him to do so, surely it follows a fortiori that the Constitution prevents him from censoring publishers on his own say-so. Since the Fifth Amendment bars the government from placing a defendant twice in jeopardy for the same offense, surely it follows a fortiori that the Constitution bars the government from placing him thrice in jeopardy. Moving closer to our Hollywood hypothetical, since the Sixth Amendment guarantees a defendant the right to use legal force to compel an uncooperative witness to testify, surely it follows a fortiori that the Constitution entitles a defendant to put a cooperative witness on the stand. And—returning to the precise facts of our hypothetical—since the Sixth Amendment entitles a defendant to use legal force against others to establish his own innocence, via subpoenas compelling testimony from uncooperative witnesses, surely it follows a fortiori that the defendant has a right to introduce reliable physical evidence already in his possession that also establishes his innocence.

When we read between the lines and dig beneath the words, we see that the deep purpose of the Sixth Amendment is to ensure a fair trial for the defendant, a trial enabling him to show that he did not do what the government has accused him of having done—in short, a trial allowing him to make "his defence," in the concluding words of the amendment. The enumerations of specific rights, such as the rights to confront and compel witnesses and to be informed of the specific criminal charges leveled by the government, imply and presuppose this fundamental unifying structure—the spirit of the Sixth Amendment—which simply went without saying in much the same way that it went without saying that no man could be a judge in his own case.[2]

Indeed, these two implicit precepts—the right to demonstrate one's innocence and the rule that no man may judge his own case—derive from the same taproot of simple justice. In one of the Supreme Court's earliest discussions of enumerated and unenumerated rights, Justice Samuel Chase in 1798 suggestively linked the two ideas, condemning both "a law that punished a citizen for an innocent action" and "a law that makes a man a Judge in his own cause" as laws "against all reason and justice." It "cannot be presumed," Chase declared, that the American people had ever authorized their governments to make such laws.[3]

A defendant's right to truthfully defend himself with reliable evidence and testimony would exist even if the Sixth Amendment had never been adopted. This root right would sensibly be understood as implicit in the very structure of the original Constitution's Judicial Article, which speaks of "Trial[s]," "Courts," "Law," "Equity," "Judges" and "judicial Power," among other things. All these words in turn must be read against the Preamble's promise that the Constitution would "establish Justice," not subvert it. What is the purpose of a criminal "Trial," in a "Court" worthy of the name, if not to allow a defendant a fair opportunity to show that he is innocent of the charges leveled against him? The very structure of the trial attests to this purpose: Strictly speaking, a trial is triggered when a defendant pleads "not guilty" and ends when the trier (typically a jury) renders a verdict of "guilty" or "not guilty."[4]

But if all this is so, then it follows that much of the Sixth Amendment was itself arguably superfluous. Its textually specified rules of confrontation, compulsory process, and so on could have been properly inferred from the Philadelphia Constitution's Judicial Article alone, even if the Bill of Rights had never been adopted. In this respect, the Sixth Amendment was hardly unique. As we have seen, the Article I, section 8, necessary-and-proper clause was widely viewed (by Publius and the *McCulloch* Court, among others) as merely declaratory of the true scope and limits of federal power deducible from the rest of the Constitution, properly construed. So, too, the core of the First Amendment's free-speech clause merely codified a principle of free political expression that was both implicit in the Philadelphia Constitution as a whole (recall our fictional Lincoln Abraham) and evident in the very enactment of the document (as we saw at the outset of the previous chapter).[5]

Nor is this brief list exhaustive. Still other explicit rules and principles of the Bill of Rights were also implicit in the Constitution as a whole. Indeed, the First Congress, which drafted the Bill of Rights, highlighted this fact by explicitly prefacing the document with official language proclaiming that some of its provisions were "declaratory" of existing law. And let's also remember that at the Philadelphia Convention, future justices James Wilson and Oliver Ellsworth had similarly insisted, à la Blackstone, that the Article I, section 9, clause prohibiting Congress from passing ex-post-facto laws was logically unnecessary and merely declaratory.[6]

Thus far, we have focused on how the original Constitution as modified and glossed by the initial amendments, especially the Ninth Amendment, operates to limit federal power and to protect rights against *federal* officials. With regard to unenumerated rights against states, the key clause comes from the Fourteenth Amendment, which was adopted after the Civil War to ensure that states would never again abuse their citizens in ways that the old South had done, with disastrous consequences. It's worth repeating this clause, this time with emphasis: "*No State* shall make or enforce *any* law which shall abridge the privileges or immunities of citizens of the United States." With these words, Reconstruction Republicans ringingly proclaimed that all the fundamental rights, freedoms, privileges, and immunities applicable against federal officials would also apply against states. Thanks to this amendment, the basic (albeit unenumerated) right of a man to prove his innocence obtains not just in federal courts but in state courts, too—as do all other basic rights, both explicit and implicit, affirmed in the original Constitution and its first nine amendments.[7]

ALTHOUGH THE NINTH AMENDMENT offers little detailed guidance about how to find unenumerated rights, it does give us one powerful textual clue: Proudly echoing the Preamble, the amendment speaks of un-enumerated rights of "*the people.*" Proper unenumerated rights should be *popular* rights—rights that the American people (and not merely a few judges, following their own subjective sensibilities) have in some way or another endorsed, embraced, enacted, or embodied.

The implicit constitutional rights that we have just surveyed easily pass this popularity test. After all, the people themselves ratified the original Constitution and all its textual amendments. If these texts (implicitly) affirm various rights, then these rights are rights that the people themselves have (implicitly) endorsed. The robust free-speech right elaborated in Chapter 2 can also be seen as an obvious right of "the people," for this robust right pervaded the very process by which the "We the People" enacted the Constitution.

But *implying* rights in an incomplete textual listing and *enacting* rights in the process of adopting the Constitution are not the only ways that the American people themselves can demonstrate that they claim and hold dear a particular unenumerated right. We must also consider *lived* rights.

Simply put, many of the Ninth Amendment rights of the people and the Fourteenth Amendment privileges and immunities of citizens may be found in everyday American life—in the practices of ordinary Americans as they go about their affairs and in the patterns of laws and customs across the land. The rights of *the people* include various rights that the people themselves live out; the fundamental privileges and immunities *of citizens* encompass those things that the citizens themselves treat as fundamental in their rhythms and routines.

Thus, the hero of our Hollywood-style hypothetical need not rely solely on the implicit logic of the written Constitution. The Ninth and Fourteenth Amendments also invite him to root his claim of right directly in principles of truth, justice, and the American way as understood and practiced by the American people.[8]

OUR HYPOTHETICAL IS JUST THAT—an imaginary scenario—precisely because American governments have not routinely attempted to prevent defendants from introducing trustworthy exculpatory evidence. A close look at the rules that have actually operated to govern criminal defendants in American courtrooms across the centuries will deepen our understanding of why our hypothetical hero deserves to prevail.

At the Founding, criminal defendants were never allowed to take the stand to testify on their own behalf. This categorical disqualification rule, which operated in both the new federal courts and every state court, derived from then-dominant understandings of truth and justice. It was widely thought that the testimonial performances of accused men would often be false—perjured fables cooked up by guilty defendants.[9]

Criminal defendants were not the only ones at that time who were disqualified from testifying. In general, no "interested party" could take the stand in American courts. In civil lawsuits, this included both the plaintiff and the defendant as well as anyone else who stood to gain or lose something as a result of the verdict. The underlying Founding-era vision was that witnesses should be governed by evidentiary rules akin to the recusal rules that applied to judges and juries. Just as no man should be a judge in his own case, neither should he be a witness in his own case. Only in the nineteenth century did this vision yield to a more modern conception allowing those with obvious biases to testify, thus leaving it up to the impartial trier of fact—the judge or the jury, as the case might be—to sift and sort the conflicting accounts.

In the early republic, almost all states followed common-law or state constitutional rules similar to the federal Fifth Amendment's self-incrimination clause, rules that prevented the government from obliging a criminal defendant to testify against himself. These bans on compelled self-incrimination intermeshed with Founding-era testimonial disqualification rules. If *allowed* to testify, criminal defendants might feel *obliged* to testify. Unless crafted with care, a formal right to testify might morph into a practical duty to testify, a duty in tension with the right against compelled self-incrimination. The pressure to testify would be particularly acute if jurors were permitted to assume the worst about a defendant who chose to remain silent when given the option to take the stand: "If he really is innocent, why won't he testify and tell us his story under oath?" By preventing all defendants from taking the stand, the old rule precluded this sort of jury speculation.

If he were allowed to testify, a guilty defendant might of course perjure himself in an effort to avoid conviction. At the Founding, many believed that lying under oath was an especially grievous offense against both man and God—a willful and wicked act that might cause the perjurer to lose his immortal soul or suffer some other horrible punishment in the afterlife. But fallen and frail human beings, especially criminals, could not always be counted on to take the long view. If defendants were permitted to testify under oath, a person who up to that point was merely guilty of, say, an unplanned assault might go on to commit what many eighteenth-century Americans viewed as the even greater offense of premeditated perjury. Alas, a liar might lose his soul even if he saved his skin. And this sad outcome would have been induced by the legal system itself, which in effect would have led men into temptation by creating a perjury trap for petty criminals—a trap potentially triggering cosmic punishment vastly disproportionate to their underlying pretestimonial offenses. As a matter of tenderness and justice to defendants, it was thought better to spare them any temptation to perjure themselves than to allow them to testify.[10]

In an age when no other interested witness was allowed to take the stand, it was doubtful that juries would properly credit a criminal defendant's sworn testimony even if he was telling the truth. At the Founding, any proposed right of a criminal defendant to testify under oath at his own trial would have posed unique risks while offering uncertain benefits to its supposed beneficiaries.

Over the ensuing decades, background legal norms and cultural understandings evolved. Perjury came to be seen as more continuous with other human failings. On the civil side of the courthouse, new rules began to allow persons to take the stand even if they had something to gain or lose by their testimony. In 1864, Maine became the first state to allow all criminal defendants to testify under oath at trial. The federal government followed suit in 1878, and by the turn of the twentieth century only Georgia persisted in barring criminal defendants from the stand. Many jurisdictions also aimed to ease the burden on nontestifying defendants by instructing jurors not to draw adverse inferences against mute defendants. (An innocent defendant, after all, might wish to remain silent for any number of reasons—for example, because he was apt to stutter, sweat, or become confused upon close interrogation, and thus look guilty even though he was in fact truthfully attesting to his innocence.)[11]

And here is the punch line: In a trio of modern cases—*Ferguson v.*

Georgia in 1961, *Griffin v. California* four years later, and *Rock v. Arkansas* in 1987—the Supreme Court constitutionalized this new American consensus by proclaiming a right of every criminal defendant, state or federal, to take the stand if he wants to do so, and if not, a right to a jury instruction that no inference of guilt should be drawn from his silence.

AT THIS POINT IN OUR STORY, we should pause to savor the significance of the reversal in the relevant rules over time: At the Founding, no criminal defendant could testify at his own trial, but today, every defendant has a clear constitutional right to do so. No constitutional clause has expressly dictated this about-face. Yet the reversal is plainly justified and notably uncontroversial. In the 1987 *Rock* case, justices spanning the ideological and methodological spectrum unanimously agreed that a defendant ordinarily had a constitutional right to take the stand, even as the Court splintered over the precise contours of this right. (The Court majority held that a defendant had a right to testify even though he had previously undergone hypnosis to recover repressed memories. The dissenters thought that hypnotically refreshed testimony could be barred under a general evidentiary rule, applicable to other witnesses, that this sort of hypnosis rendered a witness's testimony uniquely unreliable and uniquely impervious to cure via vigorous cross-examination.) No major political party or mainstream national politician has taken aim at the defendant's constitutional right to testify or attacked "activist" judges for recognizing such a right—even though the right is not enumerated in the written Constitution, and even though Founding-era practice was precisely to the contrary.[12]

Three factors explain and justify the modern constitutional consensus. First, nothing in the written Constitution prohibits the recognition of an unenumerated right to testify in one's own criminal case. The new right supplements the text but does not supplant it—and of course both the Ninth and Fourteenth Amendments invite supplementation of enumerated rights with unenumerated rights. The Fifth Amendment also comes into play here, with its sweeping, albeit nonspecific, promise of fair federal courtroom procedures—"due process of law," a phrase repeated in the Fourteenth Amendment and thereby made applicable to state and local governments as well.

It is possible to imagine putative unenumerated rights that would contradict the text and thereby justifiably provoke strong resistance if they were to win official recognition. Consider, for instance, a criminal defendant who concedes that a fair federal trial can be held in the state where the crime occurred, but nevertheless claims an unenumerated right to relocate the trial across state lines—a right, in effect, to one peremptory challenge of the prosecutor's initial choice of venue. Were judges to recognize this particular claim of right, the new right would negate the core meaning and clear command of the Judicial Article, which mandates that "the Trial of all Crimes...shall be held in the State where the said Crimes shall have been committed."[13]

By contrast, no textual violation occurred when courts recognized a criminal defendant's right to testify. Of course, to say that an unwritten right to testify is logically compatible and textually consistent with a written right to stay mute is to say very little. An infinite number of putative constitutional rights, many quite outlandish, could pass a simple noncontradiction test. For instance: "Criminal defendants have an unenumerated constitutional right to government-provided soft drinks every Thursday." Surely this alleged right and countless others do not deserve recognition as proper Ninth or Fourteenth Amendment entitlements or as entailments of due process of law.[14]

A second key factor thus differentiates the criminal defendant's right to testify from other claims that have, justifiably, not prevailed: Before this entitlement won official recognition as an unenumerated constitutional right, it had established itself in everyday American practice and in the lives of the American people. Only in the late twentieth century did the Court proclaim this right, decades after Americans began exercising it on a daily basis in virtually every courthouse in the country.

Indeed, the entitlement to testify has roots as old as the written Constitution itself, even though the specific right announced by the modern Court ran counter to Founding-era practice (as the justices in *Ferguson* candidly acknowledged). The sea-change that occurred in the late nineteenth century, when the old rules barring defendant testimony gave way to new rules welcoming defendants to tell their stories under oath, did not mark a revolution in first principles of law and justice. Rather, the new rules merely involved the application of old principles to a new context. True, the new rules directly reversed the old rules in specific application. But the alternative—hidebound continuation of the old rules—would have raised serious problems of its own for interpreters seeking general legal coherence and fidelity to Founding principles. The Founders, after all, had disallowed criminal defendant testimony largely because this testimony was at the time deemed distinctly unreliable, as indeed was all testimony from interested parties at that time. But in a changed mid-nineteenth-century world in which other biased persons—civil plaintiffs and civil defendants, for example—were for the first time being allowed to testify, the premises of the old criminal-procedure rule no longer made sense. If a jury could be trusted to discount for the bias of interested witnesses in civil cases, the same held true in criminal cases. Given that the Fifth and Sixth Amendments had been drafted to give criminal defendants greater and more explicit rights than civil defendants, it was perverse to allow civil defendants to take the stand while denying this privilege to criminal defendants. Once civil defendants could testify to escape civil liability, the right of criminal defendants to testify to escape criminal conviction followed a fortiori.

Even if it were conceded that a criminal defendant's right to testify was a wholly new invention of the late nineteenth century, with absolutely no connection to Founding-era principles or practices, this concession would hardly doom the right as a proper candidate for protection under the Ninth and Fourteenth Amendments. One of the core unenumerated rights of the people under the Ninth Amendment is the people's right to discover and embrace new rights and to have these new rights respected by government, so long as the people themselves do indeed claim and celebrate these new rights in their words and/or actions.

This reading of the Ninth Amendment is consistent with but not compelled by the amendment's text and original public meaning. In the Founding era, there were at least two plausible ways of construing the amendment's clipped reference to unlisted rights "retained by the people." On one reading, the word "retained" suggested a historical test: The people were entitled to various preexisting and customary rights already in place at the Founding, rights that they would continue to possess—that is, "retain." On another reading, the word "retain" sounded more in logic and political theory than in history. Rights were logically superior to and/or philosophically prior to government, and thus were conceptually withheld from government—"retained"—when government was established. Even if a given right only became analytically clear or won recognition in practice after the adoption of the Ninth Amendment, this right would still supersede governmental power and was thus fully covered by the amendment's letter and spirit.[15]

In choosing between these two plausible readings of the Ninth Amendment, faithful interpreters should embrace the second, which helps the written Constitution cohere with settled contemporary practice—with the actual world of American constitutional law that recognizes and reverences many utterly uncontroversial rights (such as the right of a criminal defendant to testify at his own trial), even though these rights are unenumerated and emerged long after the Founding. Those who respect the terse text and want it to succeed in its general project should hesitate to reject a perfectly plausible reading that ultimately strengthens the text by connecting it with the basic rights claimed and practiced by each generation of Americans.

But even if this reading of the Ninth were rejected, no matter. Here we come to the third and final factor that explains and justifies the modern recognition of unenumerated rights whose emergence postdates the Founding. Although the original public meaning of the Ninth Amendment is somewhat murky, the key clause of the Fourteenth Amendment is quite clear. The core "privileges" and "immunities" of "citizens" safeguarded by the amendment encompass not merely pre-1868 rights recognized in canonical sources such as the federal Bill of Rights and the Declaration of Independence, but also post-1868 rights that Congress may identify in civil rights laws enacted under section 5 of the amendment, which reads as follows: "The Congress shall have power to enforce, by appropriate legislation, the provisions of this [amendment]."

This amendment was drafted by Congress for Congress. Its rights provisions were phrased in broad, open-ended language precisely to enable future Congresses to protect basic civil rights, both old and new. And Congress was not the only branch with authority to recognize new rights. Judges, too, were expected to play their part in the process to pay heed to emerging privileges and immunities embodied, among other places, in evolving American laws and practices.[16]

The Fourteenth Amendment promised that basic rights, freedoms, privileges, and immunities would constrain not just states but also the federal government. Although the amendment's key clause, which appears in the second sentence of section 1, explicitly applied to states—"No State shall…"—readers must take special care to avoid the negative-implication trap lurking in this passage. By dint of section 1's opening sentence, the amendment also obliged federal officialdom to respect fundamental civil rights. That opening sentence made clear that all American-born persons were "citizens of the United States." For the Reconstruction Republicans who drafted and ratified this amendment, what it meant to be a citizen was, *ipso facto*, to have certain basic rights, freedoms, privileges, and immunities. While specific language—"No state shall…"—was needed to make clear that *state* abuses would thenceforth be prevented by the *federal* Constitution, basic rights vis-à-vis the federal government went without saying. Long before the Civil War, *McCulloch* had made clear that Congress had no power to do improper things. An amendment that explicitly says that states may not abuse citizens should thus never be twisted to imply that Congress may.[17]

A more faithful negative implication flows from the amendment's above-quoted section 5: Congress enjoys broad power to "enforce" rights, old and new, but no power to abridge these rights. In general, the amendment was thus designed to favor whichever federal enforcement branch, Court or Congress, had the broader view of a given civil right, whether old or new.[18]

LET US NOW RETURN to our Hollywood-style hypothetical, for the hypothetical contains a few additional elements that will help us further appreciate how America's lived Constitution of actual practice has dramatically shaped the evolving law of constitutional criminal procedure.

The best tack for our hypothetical prosecutor to take would be to concede that unenumerated rights exist and to further concede that a criminal defendant ordinarily does have an unenumerated right to testify and to present reliable exculpatory evidence. But our prosecutor could argue that the specific facts of our hypothetical case justify a limited exception to these general rights, an exception that itself has roots in basic American ideals of fair play—that is, in America's unwritten Constitution. With this tack, our prosecutor would at least be playing the right game. But he would still deserve to lose.

Suppose the prosecutor pointed to simple symmetry as the relevant, albeit unwritten, constitutional principle. Ordinarily, a defendant should be allowed to present his own witnesses and evidence, because the prosecution is allowed to present its own witnesses and evidence; but, our prosecutor could argue, since the exclusionary rule generally prevents the government from introducing evidence that the police acquired illegally, a symmetric extension of the exclusionary rule should bar the defendant from introducing evidence that his team acquired illegally.

Symmetry can indeed be seen as an implicit element of the Constitution's criminal-procedure provisions. For example, the defendant's Sixth Amendment right of compulsory process generally entitles him to the same subpoena power enjoyed by the prosecutor—a pure symmetry rule. The prosecutor may typically confront defense witnesses, and the defendant is symmetrically entitled under the Sixth Amendment to confront prosecution witnesses. When the jury convicts the defendant, the prosecutor gets to keep the win and need not retry the case; symmetrically, the Fifth Amendment double-jeopardy clause entitles the defendant to keep the win if the jury acquits.[19]

Symmetry can also help explain and justify the Court's celebrated twentieth-century recognition that an indigent felony defendant is entitled to an attorney at government expense. Since the government pays for its own counsel (i.e., the prosecutor), it must symmetrically finance counsel for the defendant if he so requests. However, Founding-era practice fell short of this standard. The First Congress—the same Congress that drafted the Bill of Rights—provided appointed counsel to all capital defendants, but relegated other defendants to a different version of the symmetry principle: The judge—a government-paid official—was supposed to provide legal advice to any unrepresented defendant who requested assistance.[20]

As the years passed and the American adversarial system took firm hold, it became increasingly clear that this quaint judge-as-counsel model was unworkable. A judge could not both properly umpire the game and effectively coach the defense team. In a 1938 case captioned *Johnson v. Zerbst*, the Court read the Sixth Amendment clause entitling federal criminal defendants to "the Assistance of Counsel" to include, by implication, a right to a government-provided lawyer. A quarter-century later, the Warren Court, in the landmark case of *Gideon v. Wainwright*, held that the Fourteenth Amendment guaranteed state criminal defendants the same basic rights as federal criminal defendants, including the right to government-paid counsel.

By the time *Gideon* famously declared the right to appointed counsel for all felony defendants, this right was already settled practice in every federal court as well as in forty-five of the states encompassing roughly 90 percent of the national population. (Even in the five outlying states, appointed counsel was made available to all capital defendants and to various defendants in noncapital cases of special complexity, and in some states to all defendants in certain cities and counties.) In short, a basic right to appointed counsel was already part of the fabric of America's lived Constitution. Of the twenty-five states that filed or signed onto legal briefs in the *Gideon* case, twenty-two sided with the indigent defendant, as the *Gideon* Court proudly noted.[21]

The shift from Founding-era-style symmetry to *Gideon*-style symmetry suggests that the symmetry idea, without more, is not an entirely self-defining concept—and that the specific shape that the symmetry principle has taken in Supreme Court case law over the years has reflected evolving lived customs and popular understandings. Even today, *Gideon* and its progeny do not oblige government to finance both prosecutors and public defenders equally; nor does this line of cases entitle defendants to government subsidies for defense-team private investigators remotely comparable to governmental expenditures for the prosecutor's investigatory team—a.k.a. the police.

As important as the symmetry principle is in various contexts, it does not exhaust all the rights, enumerated and unenumerated, that a criminal defendant may properly claim. Both at the Founding and today, the prosecutor may not oblige the defendant to take the stand. Under one reading of symmetry, there would be nothing wrong with a rule likewise disabling the defendant from putting himself on the stand. This was indeed Founding-era practice. But as we have seen, current law gives the defendant more than mere symmetry. Only the defense can call the defendant to the stand.

Even more flamboyantly asymmetric, and more illustrative of first principles, is the rule—applicable in every criminal court in America, state and federal—that the prosecution must bear the burden of proof and indeed must prove the case against the defendant beyond reasonable doubt. If it is equally likely that the defendant is innocent or guilty, the trier of fact must acquit. Imagine a case where it is absolutely certain that one of two identical twins did the deed, but it is utterly uncertain which one. Neither may be convicted, because America's Constitution is premised on the asymmetric idea that it is better to let a guilty man walk free than to convict an innocent man.

Perhaps Blackstone overstated when he exuberantly proclaimed in his *Commentaries* that it was "better that *ten* guilty persons escape, than that *one* innocent suffer." But today almost no one believes that the Court overstated or overreached when it made clear in a celebrated 1970 case, *In re Winship*, that the Constitution recognized the right of every criminal defendant, state or federal, to be acquitted in the absence of "proof beyond a reasonable doubt" of his guilt. The *Winship* Court cited opinions stretching back into the nineteenth century clearly foreshadowing its holding, and also stressed that its ruling codified the lived Constitution of American practice. In the Court's words, the reasonable-doubt standard has played "a vital role in the American scheme of criminal procedure," commanding "virtually unanimous adherence" in both state and federal courts, and forming part of the "historically grounded rights of our system." Yet the *Winship* Court also candidly acknowledged that the crystallization of the specific verbal formula "beyond a reasonable doubt" did not occur in America until 1798—that is, a decade *after* the ratification of the original Constitution and seven years *after* the adoption of the Ninth Amendment. *Winship* thus provides yet another example of an uncontroversial, unenumerated, post-Founding fundamental right.[22]

Winship also provides a decisive rebuttal to our hypothetical prosecutor's claim that a defendant can be barred from introducing evidence establishing his innocence simply because the prosecution is sometimes barred from introducing decisive evidence proving his guilt. The fact that the guilty sometimes go unpunished is hardly an acceptable reason for punishing the innocent instead. As *Winship* makes clear, the first principles of the entire criminal-justice system aim to make it highly unlikely that an innocent man will suffer erroneous conviction.

Not only does our hypothetical prosecutor dishonor these first principles, but he also errs in trying to extend a dubious doctrine, the so-called "exclusionary rule." Under this doctrine, the modern Supreme Court has routinely prevented prosecutors from introducing reliable evidence of guilt if such evidence was obtained in an unconstitutional search or seizure. Although the Court has promulgated this rule in the name of the Constitution, nothing in the document's letter or spirit says or implies anything like the exclusionary rule; no Founder ever embraced anything of the sort; and for the first century after the Declaration of Independence, no court in America, state or federal, ever practiced or preached any type of exclusionary rule. Reliable physical evidence invariably came into court, with no questions asked about whether the police had behaved properly in acquiring this evidence. As one mid-nineteenth-century English court bluntly said, summarizing the traditional Anglo-American rule, "it matters not how you get it; if you steal it even, it would be admissible in evidence."[23]

Unlike the Court's rulings in *Winship*, *Gideon*, and several other twentieth-century criminal-procedure cases that we have just surveyed, the modern exclusionary rule draws no strength from the deeply rooted American ideal of protecting innocent defendants from erroneous convictions. Instead, the rule perversely benefits the guilty as such. The guiltier a person turns out to be—the bigger the pile of reliable evidence the police find in the search—the bigger the windfall to the defendant when the evidence is tossed out.[24]

If a search target is innocent, the police find no incriminating evidence and so there is nothing to exclude—which means that the rule does nothing to deter the police from harassing a person whom they know to be innocent. Were the exclusionary rule the only legal remedy, it would be open season on the innocent. Fortunately, the rule is not the only available remedy; other remedies exist to protect the innocent from abusive searches and seizures, and many of these remedies have strong roots in Founding practices and principles. But once these remedies are properly in place, there is little need for an exclusionary rule whose incremental effect is to benefit *only* guilty persons.

Suppression of reliable evidence was a rare practice in America before 1914, when the Supreme Court, in *Weeks v. United States*, read the exclusionary rule into the Constitution as a limit on the federal government (but not states). Prior to *Weeks*, only one state (Iowa) was on record supporting the basic doctrine of exclusion. After *Weeks*, some states—via legislation, or, more typically, state court reinterpretation of state bills of rights—began to embrace the exclusionary rule to rein in errant state officials. Other states, however, continued to strongly resist the idea that probative evidence should be suppressed—an idea that seemed particularly troubling in cases involving violent crimes such as murder, rape, and robbery. (*Weeks*, by contrast, had involved a rather less scary criminal, whose offense had been sending illegal lottery tickets through the U.S. mail.)[25]

The decisive moment in the history of the exclusionary rule occurred in 1961, when a bare majority of the Court in *Mapp v. Ohio* decided to impose the exclusionary rule on all fifty states. On the eve of *Mapp*—a case in which police officers had entered a house looking for a bombing fugitive but ended up finding only pornography—twenty-four states rejected the entire concept of exclusion and four others practiced only limited exclusion. Altogether, these twenty-eight states accounted for roughly 55 percent of the nation's population. Unlike *Gideon*, *Winship*, and the right-to-testify cases, *Mapp* did not merely codify a preexisting national consensus. In other words, *Mapp* had no deep roots in America's lived Constitution—or in America's explicit or implicit Constitution, for that matter.[26]

Even today, nearly a century after *Weeks* and more than a half-century after *Mapp*, the exclusionary rule remains controversial in many circles, with critics on the bench, in Congress, in the Justice Department, in state houses and governors' offices, in the legal academy, on the airwaves, and throughout American culture more generally. Thus the real question is not whether the exclusionary rule should be expanded to punish innocent persons such as our hypothetical defendant, but whether the rule should be drastically narrowed, having never won the broad and deep support of the American people—having never, in short, achieved true *popularity*.

Later, we shall probe the exclusionary rule in more detail. For now, it suffices to say that even with the exclusionary rule in full effect, our hypothetical prosecutor's proposal to extend the rule against defendants cannot stand. Recall that at the Founding, reliable physical evidence was universally admissible; criminal defendants had an absolute right (and prosecutors likewise had unfettered power) to introduce reliable physical evidence, even if the evidence had been acquired improperly. Although the modern exclusionary rule has stripped prosecutors of their power to introduce improperly acquired evidence, defendants have not thereby forfeited their ancient rights. A defendant's entitlement to show that he is innocent of all the charges the government has trumped up against him is surely one of the basic, albeit unenumerated, rights that has always been retained by the people under the Ninth Amendment and is likewise protected as a core privilege or immunity under the Fourteenth Amendment. Various new unenumerated rights are one thing—a perfectly proper thing, thanks in part to these two amendments. But new limits on ancient rights are something very different, something that the Ninth and Fourteenth Amendments, rightly read, do not support.

THE BIG LESSON IN our wide-ranging story thus far is that unenumerated rights have bloomed profusely and may properly continue to bloom even in a domain—constitutional criminal procedure—where the written Constitution lays down what might seem to the untrained eye to be an exclusive grid of specific rules. In this domain, explicit texts and implicit rights have blended together with lived rights, creating results sure to surprise the blinkered literalist. In sum, a document whose text says merely that a criminal defendant cannot be compelled to testify now also entitles him to take the stand if he wishes; the government must provide defense lawyers to all indigent felony defendants even though the Founders neither clearly enumerated nor fully established this right; prosecutors must prove guilt "beyond reasonable doubt," a phrase that postdates the Bill of Rights; defendants must be allowed to present physical evidence, notwithstanding the fact that the text says nothing about this; and, above all, government must honor the values of truth and innocence, words that nowhere appear in America's written Constitution.[27]

"due process"

LIVED RIGHTS ALSO BLOSSOM IN domains where the document speaks with much less specificity. Such rights have been particularly important in a quadrant of case law that lawyers and judges refer to under the curious label "substantive due process."

Perhaps the most illustrious instance of judicial protection of a lived right occurred in the 1965 case of *Griswold v. Connecticut*. Connecticut had purported to criminalize the use of contraception, even by married couples in the privacy of their own bedrooms, prompting the Supreme Court to strike down the state law as unconstitutional. Seven of the nine justices voted to recognize a right of sexual privacy within marriage. Today the decision's bottom-line result is accepted—indeed, celebrated—by judges, politicians, academics, journalists, and ordinary citizens from virtually every point on the political compass. Yet disagreement persists about exactly why the result in *Griswold* was so obviously right.

Writing for the *Griswold* majority, Justice William O. Douglas famously proclaimed that a general "right of privacy" could be found nestled between the lines of the Bill of Rights. This approach, deducing implicit constitutional rights by probing explicit constitutional clauses to identify their unifying spirit and purpose, is of course a splendid way to identify unenumerated rights. But Douglas, a justice notorious for his nonchalance, did a sloppy job proving his specific case, breezing through clauses that did in fact foreshadow modern privacy ideology (in particular, the Third and Fourth Amendments) while stretching other clauses past the point of plausibility.

Douglas began his breezy tour of the Bill of Rights by emphasizing the First Amendment rights of "association" and "assembly." (The first word was itself merely implicit in the amendment, while the second appeared explicitly via its cognate in the First Amendment's affirmation of "the right of the people peaceably to assemble.") Unfortunately for Douglas's general argument, the original meaning of the amendment's assembly and association principles had little to do with the private domain of human sexuality. The core Founding-era right of "the people" to "assemble" centered on citizens' entitlement to gather in public conventions and other political meeting grounds. This original vision was miles removed from the erotic urges of a man and a woman seeking to "assemble" on a bed. Douglas also relied on the self-incrimination clause of the Fifth Amendment, which provides that no person "shall be compelled in any criminal case to be a witness against himself." Douglas claimed this clause affirmed "a zone of privacy," but this, too, was a stretch. With a grant of immunity from prosecution, the government may, consistent with the self-incrimination clause, compel a person to divulge the most intimate sexual details. (Just ask Monica Lewinsky.)[28]

Writing separately in *Griswold*, Justice John Marshall Harlan II found a sturdier basis for invalidating the Connecticut law, which ran afoul of the actual lived experiences of ordinary Americans: "Conclusive, in my view, is the utter novelty of [Connecticut's] enactment. Although the Federal Government and many States have at one time or another had on their books statutes forbidding the distribution of contraceptives, *none, so far as I can find, has made the use of contraceptives a crime*" (emphasis added). For Harlan, a right of married spouses to use contraceptive devices in the privacy of their bedroom was a basic element of America's lived Constitution.[29]

Alas, Harlan overlooked the words of the Fourteenth Amendment that best made his case and best fit the facts before him: "No State shall make or enforce any law which shall abridge the privileges or immunities of citizens of the United States." Instead, Harlan leaned on the amendment's adjoining passage: "[N]or shall any State deprive a person of life, liberty, or property, without due process of law." Harlan's reliance on the due-process clause is understandable but unfortunate—understandable, because many pre-*Griswold* cases had used this clause, whereas very few had rested on the privileges-or-immunities clause; unfortunate, because the Court's ultimate responsibility is not to thoughtlessly exalt the case law but to thoughtfully expound the Constitution.

When we carefully examine the Constitution, we see that the clause relied on by Harlan seems quite unpromising. This clause suggests that government may indeed deprive persons of life, liberty, or property, so long as proper legal procedures are followed. However, Harlan and his colleagues failed to identify any procedural problem with the Connecticut law, which had been duly enacted by the state legislature in conformance with standard legislative protocols (such as bicameralism) and was being duly enforced in keeping with ordinary legal procedures (impartial judges, properly selected juries, fair rules of evidence, and so on).* The Court's real objection to the law was not procedural but substantive. No law, regardless of the niceness of its procedures, could properly intrude into the private space of consensual conjugal relations in the marital bedroom. The outlandish Connecticut law flunked a privacy test, not a process test.

Although the constitutional language that Harlan invoked seems precisely off-point, the clause that he overlooked was spot-on. That clause bars all state abridgments of basic "privileges" and "immunities," regardless of procedural pedigree. The entire turn of this clause naturally invites readers to ponder the need to insulate private domains from governmental intrusion. Conceptually and etymologically, "privacy" and "privilege" are linked, and the clause further suggests that certain areas should simply be "immun[e]" from governmental intrusion or regulation.

Harlan built his edifice on a phrase—"substantive due process"—that borders on oxymoron. Substance and process are typically understood as opposites. The phrase comes from judges, and the underlying concept has been deployed by judges in some of the most notorious Court opinions in American history, including the proslavery 1857 ruling in *Dred Scott v. Sanford* and the pro-sweatshop 1905 decision in *Lochner v. New York*. Because of the tainted lineage of the substantive-due-process doctrine, Douglas and most of the other justices in the *Griswold* majority loudly denied that they were relying on this doctrine or doing anything like what the Court had done in the so-called "*Lochner* era," in which the justices had invalidated a wide range of laws aiming to protect workers from employer exploitation.[30]

By contrast, the privileges-or-immunities clause comes directly from the Constitution itself—and therefore from the citizenry that ratified this language. The clause naturally directs interpreters to muse upon the wisdom

---

* In Chapter 7, we shall ponder one possible failure of the political process associated with the Connecticut contraception law—a process failure arising from the fact that no woman ever voted for this law, even though the law imposed special and potentially self-entrenching burdens of unwanted pregnancy upon women. No member of the *Griswold* Court, however, highlighted the gender issue.

of ordinary citizens rather than the case law of judges. Many of the privileges and immunities *of* citizens may be found by paying heed *to* citizens—what they do, what they say, what they believe. This is in fact what Harlan did in his pivotal sentence when he directed attention to the "conclusive" fact that citizens in virtually every state and every era had in fact practiced consensual marital sex wholly free from governmental intrusion.

Some have argued that the due-process clause holds special promise as a sturdy guarantor of rights because it appears twice in the written Constitution—first in the Fifth Amendment announcing a right against the federal government, and later in the Fourteenth Amendment proclaiming a right against states. But as we saw earlier, the Fourteenth Amendment's privileges-or-immunities clause, in tandem with companion language safeguarding citizenship rights in the amendment's opening sentence, also vests citizens with fundamental entitlements against both federal and state officials. Just as the amendment incorporated the federal Constitution's basic set of rights against states, so it also incorporated the Reconstruction-era vision of rights back against the federal government. The amendment's big idea was that the basic rights of American citizenship, rights both substantive and procedural, should apply fully and equally against all American governments—federal, state, and local.[31]

Skeptics have wondered why, if the Fourteenth Amendment's privileges-or-immunities clause truly was designed to incorporate basic constitutional rights against states, including the Fifth Amendment right to due process, the Fourteenth Amendment immediately went on to explicitly restrict state abridgments of "due process." The simple answer is that the Fourteenth Amendment's opening sentence, and its companion language guaranteeing privileges and immunities, protected only citizens. The amendment's due-process clause aimed to make clear that even noncitizens—all "persons," including aliens—were entitled to fair procedures.[32]

Some devotees of substantive due process have argued that their preferred clause directs the reader's gaze to the crucial and attractive concept of "liberty." Justice John Paul Stevens, who eventually took Justice Douglas's seat on the Court, was particularly fond of referring to "the Liberty Clause" of the Constitution.[33] Nice try, but not quite. The clause speaks of "life, liberty, [and] property" as a trio. The clause is thus no more a liberty clause than a property clause. If governments under this clause may restrict property so long as they follow proper procedures, then the same grammatically holds true for liberty. If, conversely, fair procedures do not suffice when liberty is restricted—the approach favored by Harlan and Stevens—then the same would logically hold true for property. This could take us back to the bad old days of *Dred Scott* and *Lochner*, when the Court in fact did use the clause, outrageously, to insulate various property holders, including slaveholders and sweatshop owners, from perfectly reasonable governmental regulations endorsed by a broad swath of ordinary citizens.

Thus, the best textual foundation for a lived-Constitution approach of the sort that Harlan championed in *Griswold* was not the overworked due-process clause but the overlooked privileges-or-immunities clause. Though Harlan reached the right result and for many of the right reasons, he missed a golden opportunity to illustrate how tightly America's written and unwritten Constitutions intermeshed on the facts of the case.

THE EXTREME OUTLANDISHNESS of the Connecticut contraception law, when measured against the actual experience of Americans at all times and in all places, made *Griswold* an especially easy unenumerated-rights case under a lived-Constitution analysis—too easy, in fact. Most officious laws will not be quite so eccentric and intrusive, yet many may still merit condemnation as contrary to basic rights as ordinary Americans have come to understand and practice these rights.

Consider, for instance, laws prohibiting the *distribution* of contraceptive devices to *unmarried* adults. There was a time in America when such laws were routine, but the sexual revolution of the mid-twentieth century rendered the statutes of this sort still on the books after 1970 at odds with actual social practices and norms of ordinary law-abiding Americans. Unsurprisingly, it was precisely in the early 1970s—in the 1972 case of *Eisenstadt v Baird*, to be specific—that the Supreme Court struck down these outlier statutes. Unfortunately, in so doing the Court once again overlooked the privileges-or-immunities clause, thus making it harder for ordinary Americans to see the obvious connection between the Court's commonsensical holding and the Constitution's plain meaning.[34]

Many loving couples in modern America have at times engaged in oral sex and anal sex as forms of contraception, channeling their romantic urges into nonprocreative expressions of physical intimacy. In 2003, the Court struck down a Texas statute and a handful of other state laws that purported to criminalize some of these intimate acts. Justice Anthony Kennedy's landmark opinion in the case, *Lawrence v. Texas*, is widely celebrated today for its soaring philosophical ode to liberty and equality.[35]

Lofty language aside, Kennedy also wove into his opinion strong threads that recalled Justice Harlan's more modest empirical approach: "Laws prohibiting sodomy do not seem to have been enforced against consenting adults acting in private [for much of American history]. It was not until the 1970s that any State singled out same-sex relations for criminal prosecution, and only nine States have done so....Over the course of the last decades, States with same-sex prohibitions have moved toward abolishing them." Noting that as of 2003, only thirteen states had laws on the books prohibiting consensual adult sodomy, four of which enforced their laws only against homosexual conduct, Kennedy stressed that "in those States where sodomy is still proscribed, whether for same-sex or heterosexual conduct, there is a pattern of nonenforcement with respect to adults acting in private." In short, enforcement of sodomy laws against private adult consensual conduct ran hard against the actual lived practices of twenty-first-century Americans.

On the other side of the empirical spectrum, the Court's 1973 ruling in *Roe v. Wade* cannot be justified by recourse to the actual practices of Americans at that time. According to Harvard University law professor Laurence Tribe, every state except perhaps New York had laws on the books at odds with *Roe*'s sweeping vision of abortion rights.[36]

This fact alone does not doom *Roe*. A right may properly exist and deserve judicial enforcement on grounds that do not depend on America's lived Constitution. For example, if a right is expressly enumerated in the terse text or reflects a principle plainly implicit in the written Constitution (whether in a specific clause or in the instrument as a whole), or forms an integral part of the process by which the document was enacted or amended, then such a right is a full-fledged constitutional entitlement worthy of protection even if it runs counter to actual practice.

But if a right is not an express, implied, or enacted entitlement, or part of America's lived Constitution, then in what way, precisely, is it a genuinely *constitutional* right? Justice Harry Blackmun's opinion for the Court in *Roe* failed to squarely address this question. Remarkably, his opinion seemed almost uninterested in explaining what clause or clauses of the Constitution supported the specific right announced by the Court in the name of the document. He did not even quote the constitutional patch of text on which he claimed to be relying—the Fourteenth Amendment's due-process clause. Had he bothered to examine this clause, he would have found the word "process" to be a large stumbling block to his openly substantive approach to abortion rights. Notably, nearly four decades after it was handed down, *Roe* still roils and polarizes, unlike many of the other unenumerated-rights cases that we have encountered. (In Chapter 7, we shall probe an entirely different and far more plausible line of defense of abortion rights, focusing not on privacy and substantive due process à la *Roe*, but instead on principles of gender equality and women's rights, principles that *Roe* itself overlooked.)

In other areas where litigants have made unenumerated-rights claims far in advance of actual American practice, the Court has generally declined to rush in. For example, a strong philosophical claim might be made on behalf of a right of any competent adult to end his own life at the time and in the manner of his own choosing and to enlist professional medical assistance in implementing his free choice. Nothing could be more private—none of the government's business!—than the question of how and when one chooses to leave this world, advocates of this right have argued. Yet in 1997, the Court in *Washington v. Glucksburg* unanimously reversed an exuberant circuit court opinion that had declared a broad constitutional right to die. After setting forth the facts of the case, the *Glucksburg* Court launched its analysis as follows:

We begin, as we do in all due-process cases, by examining our Nation's history, legal traditions, and practices. In almost every State—indeed, in almost every western democracy—it is a crime to assist a suicide. The States' assisted-suicide bans are not innovations. Rather, they are longstanding expressions of the States' commitment to the protection and preservation of all human life. Indeed, opposition to and condemnation of suicide—and, therefore, of assisting suicide—are consistent and enduring themes of our philosophical, legal, and cultural heritages.[37]

The justices have likewise declined to recognize a constitutional right of a patient to use an otherwise illegal drug such as marijuana when a licensed physician has prescribed the drug in order to alleviate intense pain. Although such a right has considerable moral appeal to many thoughtful analysts and may one day come to persuade a majority of Americans and their elected lawmakers, that day has not yet arrived. On this issue, as on many other issues involving unenumerated rights, the Court has shown little interest in leaping far ahead of America's lived experience.[38]

"houses"

ANY SERIOUS ACCOUNT OF AMERICANS' lived experience must attend to the private places in which most Americans actually live—their homes—and to the sorts of private lives that are lived in these places. The idea of "home life" has long been integral to American culture, and thus to America's unwritten Constitution. The opening picture of this chapter presents an idealized mid-nineteenth-century depiction of home life; many of the themes and elements of this specific depiction of "home sweet home" have deep roots in the Founding era and continue to have strong resonance in our time. True, the word "privacy" looms larger in modern constitutional discourse than it did in the Founders' era; but prototypes of modern privacy theory can be found in several of the sources that ultimately led to the framing and ratification of the Ninth Amendment and its broad affirmation of unenumerated rights.

ON NEW YEAR'S EVE, 1787, Federalist Noah Webster (of later dictionary fame) spoofed Anti-Federalists, many of whom smelled tyranny around every corner—they had already begun to compose long lists of proposed amendments to the Constitution explicitly guaranteeing specific rights they deemed at risk. These Anti-Federalists had not gone nearly far enough, wrote Webster as he offered up his own Swiftian amendment proposal: "That Congress shall never restrain any inhabitant of America from eating and drinking, at seasonable times, or prevent his lying on his left side, in a long winter's night, or even on his back, when he is fatigued by lying on his right."[39]

Webster was not alone in resisting the Anti-Federalist push for a detailed Bill of Rights. In most states, leading Federalists argued that no enumeration could possibly list all rights and that any omitted right might be at greater risk if stingy interpreters ever construed the list in negative-implication fashion. In the First Congress, Federalist Theodore Sedgwick declared that if the aim were truly to itemize all the people's rights, Congress would need to specify "that a man should have a right to wear his hat if he pleased, that he might get up when he pleased, and go to bed when he thought proper."[40]

In the end, the Founding generation rejected the broad Federalist argument that a Bill of Rights was unnecessary and dangerous. (It surely didn't help that the Federalists had also argued, quite inconsistently, that the Philadelphia Constitution already contained a de facto Bill of Rights, in Article I, section 9.) But in the drafting of the Bill, the Webster-Sedgwick concern did persuade the First Congress to stress, via the Ninth Amendment, that the new Bill of Rights did not aim to enumerate exhaustively all the rights that were retained by the people.

Some of the very intrusions that Webster and Sedgwick smugly assumed that governments would never attempt—or at least close cousins of these intrusions—have in fact come to pass, often at the hands of state or local officials rather than the dreaded federal government. The framers of the Ninth Amendment and its Fourteenth Amendment counterpart, the privileges-or-immunities clause, were thus farsighted in attempting to equip posterity with weapons to wield against government oppression whenever officials tried to overreach in the ways that Webster and Sedgwick thought unimaginable.

True, governments have generally not regulated on which side a man may lie in his own bed or when he must rise from that bed. But governments have at times tried to dictate with whom he may lie in that bed and have also tried to outlaw certain physical positions in that bed. Contrary to Webster's sanguine expectations, governments have also sought to regulate what persons may place in their mouths—perhaps not with intrusive rules about "eating and drinking," but rather with detailed dictates about which body parts of fully consenting adults may not lawfully be brought into oral contact. Modern substantive-due-process law emerged in response to laws such as these.

Notably, the particular brand of substantive due process that was revived by Justice Harlan in *Griswold* and that has been prominently on display in unenumerated-rights case law ever since has departed in one key respect from the brand of substantive due process that characterized the so-called "*Lochner* era." *Lochner*'s watchword was "property," whereas modern substantive due process instead highlights "privacy."

Property by its very nature lends itself to many possible distribution patterns. Some of these patterns may be so highly unequal and so easily translatable into unequal political power as to threaten the Constitution's vision of proper republican equality between voters and among candidates. In the *Lochner* era (which ran, roughly, from the mid-1880s to the mid-1930s), a wide property gap had begun to open up in America separating the plutocratic haves from the proletarian have-nots. *Lochner*-style substantive due process aimed to thwart various governmental programs seeking to reduce these emerging inequalities of wealth and property.

Privacy, by contrast, is inherently more egalitarian. Whether fabulously wealthy or penniless, a person can be in only one bed at a time. Intimacy is distributed more equally across social classes than is property, and in a way far less likely to distort the nature of democratic politics.

To a blinkered literalist, property might seem to have a stronger constitutional claim than privacy. The word "property," after all, appears twice in the Bill of Rights and again in the Fourteenth Amendment, whereas the word "privacy" is altogether absent from the written Constitution. But when we read between the lines and heed the document as a whole, with particular attention to its arc across the centuries, a different picture emerges. The 1913 ratification of the Federal Income Tax Amendment, one of the notable populist events of the twentieth century, blessed redistributive economic policy by endorsing a tax that everyone understood would likely feature a progressive structure taxing the wealthy at steeper rates than the poor.[41] Many other post-Founding amendments have also reinforced the idea of equality, even though the word itself is often merely implicit. In centering modern unenumerated-rights law on "privacy," the modern Court has intuitively latched onto a concept that nicely blends the best of property and equality—a concept that has been an important element of America's lived Constitution from the Founding on, and one whose strength has only increased in American law and culture over time.

While Founding-era laws at the state and local level were often quite intrusive in claiming regulatory authority over family structures and human sexuality, not all of these laws were vigorously enforced. For instance, although edicts in the early republic formally prohibited various consensual sexual relations between adults, evidence rules at the time often prevented the "accomplices" from testifying against each other. (Both sexual partners were in a sense "interested parties" under Founding-era evidence theory.) As a result, these laws were usually enforced only when the offense had occurred in public in front of scandalized third parties who could testify to the breach of public-decency norms or in cases of coercive sex where the defendant's sexual partner was not an "accomplice" but rather a victim.[42]

In their discussions of unenumerated rights, both Webster and Sedgwick had highlighted privacy, though neither man used the word. Both had invoked the bedroom as an obvious place where government ordinarily did not belong. A similar vision animated a Pennsylvania Anti-Federalist essayist, who raised the specter that a federal constable looking for "stolen goods" might pretextually "pull[] down the clothes of a bed in which there was a woman and search[] under her shift."[43]

In an effort to assuage privacy concerns such as this, the First Congress adopted a Fourth Amendment limiting the power of government to search private places and seize private things. Though the word "privacy" does not appear on the surface of the text, the concept is strongly implicit. Indeed, shortly after the Warren Court began reorienting unenumerated-rights jurisprudence away from "property" and toward "privacy" in the 1965 *Griswold* case, the justices did the same thing to Fourth Amendment jurisprudence in the 1967 *Katz v. United States* case. Prior to *Katz*, Fourth Amendment rules had pivoted on property-law concepts, such as trespass. But in *Katz*, the Court held that the Fourth Amendment could apply even if no technical property-rights violation had occurred. An unreasonable wiretap, for example, would violate the Fourth Amendment even if government had never set foot on the private property of the search target. As the second Justice Harlan explained in his influential concurrence in *Katz*, the key Fourth Amendment issue was whether the government had violated a person's "reasonable expectations of privacy."

AT LEAST TWO WORDS OF THE FOURTH AMENDMENT itself offered strong support for this vision: "persons" and "houses." The amendment affirmed a general right of Americans to be secure against unreasonable searches and seizures of "their persons, houses, papers, and effects." The word "property" went unmentioned and was swept into the catchall category of "effects." But intrusions upon individual bodies—"persons"—raised special concerns. As with privacy more generally, bodies are distributed in egalitarian fashion. Every individual, rich or poor, has one body—is one "person" entitled to special Fourth Amendment solicitude. Similarly, "houses" were singled out above and beyond all buildings, in part because a person's house has always been a special seat of privacy, * and in part because houses in fact and folklore have been a particularly broadly distributed type of property.[44]

At the Founding, one of the most famous, and famously egalitarian, affirmations of the sanctity of houses had appeared in a 1763 speech by William Pitt, a hero to many colonists: "The poorest man may in his cottage bid defiance to all the forces of the Crown. It may be frail; its roof may shake; the wind may blow through it; the storm may enter; the rain may enter; but the King of England cannot enter—all his forces dare not

---

* In addition to "persons" and "houses," the Fourth Amendment singled out "papers" for special protections above and beyond all other stuff—"effects." The word "papers" also implicated a proto-privacy principle, as England's Lord Camden had made clear in a famous colonial-era search and seizure case, *Entick v. Carrington*. Camden notably declared that the "papers are the owner's...dearest property [and] will hardly bear an inspection;...where *private* papers are removed and carried away, the *secret* nature of those goods will be an aggravation of the trespass" (emphasis added). The special concern for "*private* papers" (emphasis added) recurred in a companion case, *Wilkes v. Halifax*; and in yet another related case, *Beardmore v. Carrington*, Camden upheld a hefty punitive-damage award against an official "who has granted an illegal warrant to a messenger who enters into a man's house, and pries into all his secret and *private* affairs" (emphasis added). For more on this famous set of cases and their obvious prefiguration of the Fourth Amendment, see Chapter 4.

cross the threshold of the ruined tenement!"[45] A similarly egalitarian vision surfaced during Reconstruction when Republicans enacted a Homestead Act subsidizing western homeownership and flirted with the idea of giving each southern freedman forty acres and a mule.[46]

In the late twentieth and early twenty-first centuries, politicians of both parties have found common ground in a national policy promoting home ownership for Americans of all races and classes. Enormous and expensive pillars of this national policy—federal facilitation of the home-mortgage market and federal tax deductions of home-mortgage interest payments and of local property taxes—are virtually untouchable politically, and in this respect resemble relatively clear constitutional texts that place particular issues politically off-limits. These pillars are politically untouchable precisely because home ownership is a broadly egalitarian American ideal open to a wide slice of the voting citizenry. (Social Security benefits are politically entrenched in modern America for similar reasons.) Home ownership is part of the American Dream and the national narrative. For many citizens, the home is the single largest family asset.[47]

True, nothing in the written Constitution explicitly demands special protection of "houses" or "privacy," but surely the document invites judges (and other interpreters) to attend to this explicit word and this implicit concept in pondering which unenumerated rights are properly claimed by the people. The explicit word "house" and the underlying privacy concept are also visible in the Third Amendment, which prohibits the peacetime quartering of troops in homes.[48]

Whether intentionally or intuitively, the justices have developed a case law of both enumerated and unenumerated rights that recognizes the special significance of houses and what happens inside them. In *Griswold*, Justice Douglas's opinion for the Court began to move in just the right direction when he mentioned the Third and Fourth Amendments in tandem and even quoted the "house" language of both amendments. Alas, Douglas did not quite close the deal. He failed to highlight the word "house" as he should have. Nor did he clearly and carefully explain how this key word could be read to signal the special sanctity of bedrooms.[49]

In an earlier case involving the same Connecticut statute, Justice Harlan, writing only for himself, offered a more careful analysis. Homing in (so to speak) on the word "house," Harlan began by noting that "the concept of the privacy *of the home* receives explicit Constitutional protection at two places" (emphasis added). Harlan then quoted the Third and Fourth Amendments. While conceding that "this Connecticut statute does not invade the privacy of the home in the usual sense, since the invasion involved here may, and doubtless usually would, be accomplished without any physical intrusion whatever into the home," Harlan nevertheless insisted that Connecticut had created "a crime which is grossly offensive to this privacy" of the home. As Harlan explained, "here we have not an intrusion into the home so much as on the life which characteristically has its place in the home....[I]f the physical curtilage of the home is protected, it is surely as a result of solicitude to protect the privacies of the life within. Certainly the safeguarding of the home does not follow merely from the sanctity of property rights. The home derives its pre-eminence as the seat of family life." (Note the post-*Lochner* distinction that Harlan explicitly draws here between "mere[]...property rights" and "the privacy of the home.")[50]

Building on a similar foundation, Justice Kennedy's majority opinion in *Lawrence v. Texas* began with the special role of the home: "Liberty protects the person from unwarranted government intrusions into a dwelling or other private places. In our tradition the State is not omnipresent in the home." Echoing both Douglas and Harlan, Justice Kennedy criticized sodomy laws for their "far-reaching consequences, touching upon the most private human contact, sexual behavior, and in the most private of places, the home."[51]

Beyond the contraception and sodomy cases, with their repeated emphasis on homes and bedrooms, the Court has crafted a series of specific house-protective doctrines in Fourth Amendment case law regarding home arrests, home surveillance, and the "curtilage" area surrounding homes; has affirmed the right of persons at home to possess sexually explicit materials otherwise unprotected by the First Amendment; has accorded constitutional protection to parents' basic choices about their children's education, including home-schooling; has championed extended family members' unenumerated rights to live together as a single household; and has upheld, in connection with the Second Amendment, the deeply rooted historical right of a homeowner to keep a gun in his home for self-protection.[52]

ONE PARTICULARLY VISCERAL AREA OF modern Court case law straddles the border between property-protection in general and house-protection in particular. Textually, the Constitution's takings clause protects all forms of property: "[N]or shall private property be taken for public use without just compensation." But judges should be particularly vigilant in enforcing the vision of this clause when private dwellings—houses—are involved.

For example, when the government forces a property owner to sell his parcel so that the government may use it for some legitimate government purpose, how much compensation is truly "just"? Where mere investment property is concerned, judges have reason to avoid giving any special bonus or premium to the owner. To a pure investor, all property is fungible: The money received from the forced sale of one parcel can be used to purchase another parcel of equal economic value. If judges generally gave investors a bonus above fair market value in setting the rate of just compensation, clever investors would have incentives to buy up land one step ahead of the government. Rewarding such strategic behavior would serve neither efficiency nor fairness.

But the matter seems different when a homeowner is displaced from his homestead. Many Americans understandably have sentimental attachments to their houses. These are not merely fungible investments. Rather, your house is your home—the place, perhaps, where you grew up, where your children were born or your parents died, where you have loved and been loved, and where many of the other most important events in your life have occurred. Putting a fair price on such a place when the government asserts a compelling need for the property involves a very different kind of calculus. If the government ends up paying a special bonus whenever a house is taken from its owner, this result is less likely to be grossly unfair or inefficient.[53]

In a high-profile 2005 case, *Kelo v. City of New London*, homeowner Susette Kelo argued that government had no right to take her home and lot—even though the city stood ready to pay "just compensation"—because, she claimed, the taking was not for a proper "public use." The government planned to use her lot by transferring it to a private real-estate developer as part of a general neighborhood redevelopment project that would, the city hoped, shore up the local tax base. The Supreme Court sided with the city and held that this proposed use was every bit as legitimate as if New London had planned to use Susette Kelo's lot as part of a public park. The Court's decision outraged grassroots activists and property-rights advocates across America, and many states and localities responded with new legislation narrowing or prohibiting the use of eminent domain in situations involving private redevelopment projects.

It is doubtful that *Kelo* would have provoked the same populist backlash had the case involved the taking of a piece of commercial property from an absentee investor. Thus, perhaps the deepest issue on the facts of *Kelo* was not how best to parse the phrase "public use" in the takings clause, but instead how homeowners deserve to be treated under the written and unwritten Constitution. In particular, a homeowner's emotional attachment to her home merits special respect, either in the compensation formula or in some other appropriate way.[54]

It matters less what specific formula judges use to vindicate the notion that forced sales of homes are matters of special sensitivity—whether the judiciary crafts a particular doctrine for homes under the law of Fifth Amendment just compensation; or instead insists upon heightened Fourth Amendment protocols when government tries to "seize" a "house"; or alternatively affirms an unenumerated right to special consideration whenever one's home is invaded or expropriated. What matters more is that faithful interpreters of the Constitution heed America's lived Constitution, both in construing the meaning of enumerated rights and in pondering possible unenumerated rights.

"unusual"

HONORING AMERICA'S LIVED CONSTITUTION requires careful counting: We must accurately assess the daily reality of rights. But how should faithful interpreters count? How many people must "live" a right for it to cross the constitutional threshold? And if the policies of, say, Wyoming and California differ dramatically on a rights-related issue, should the norms and practices of Wyoming's half-million inhabitants be given the same weight, Senate-style, as those of California's nearly 38 million residents? Or should a proper tally reflect the population differential, House-style?

Although these questions are implicated whenever courts seek to tally up actual laws and customs, the justices have not always devoted careful attention to technical issues of counting methodology. One corner of constitutional law where counting questions have pointedly arisen, and have generated explicit judicial commentary, involves the Eighth Amendment, which prohibits, among other things, "cruel and unusual punishments." Along with virtually all other provisions of the Bill of Rights, this punishment rule now fully applies against state governments thanks to the Fourteenth Amendment.

Although modern justices have splintered on various Eighth Amendment counting questions, the best approach here—as elsewhere—is one in which the written Constitution's words are taken seriously even as these words are properly supplemented by unwritten practices. Thus, "unusual" should mean what it says. If 240 million modern Americans live in states that flatly prohibit punishment X, while only 60 million live in states that vigorously practice punishment X, then X is "unusual" in the ordinary everyday meaning of that word. This is true regardless of state lines—true whether the 60 million live in the two most populous states or the 26 least populous states. Citizens, not states, should count equally in interpreting both the Eighth Amendment word "unusual" and modern America's lived Constitution more generally.[55]

The historical evolution of the Eighth Amendment confirms this plainmeaning approach to the word *unusual*, a word whose significance has varied across time and space. The Founders borrowed the phrase "cruel and unusual" from the celebrated English Bill of Rights of 1689. In England, the phrase aimed chiefly to prevent bloodthirsty judges from inflicting savage penalties that were legislatively unauthorized—that is, "unusual." If Parliament had previously approved a given punishment for a given crime, that punishment, even if unspeakably inhumane, was not "unusual" within the meaning of the 1689 declaration.[56]

Of course, in England, Parliament was sovereign. It thus made perfect sense that bills enacted by Parliament restricted not Parliament itself but the king's men—including judges, who in the 1680s still answered to the crown. The American Bill of Rights, by contrast, emerged a century later in an effort by the sovereign people to limit all federal servants, including Congress. In this new context, the Eighth Amendment punishment clause had some bite against Congress—but not much. So long as Congress routinely authorized a particular punishment that was also widely used by various states, it would be hard to say that the punishment, even if concededly cruel, was "cruel *and unusual*."

Here, as elsewhere, the meaning of the Bill of Rights shifted when its words and principles were refracted through the prism of the later Fourteenth Amendment. Section 1 of that amendment—featuring our old friend, the privileges-or-immunities clause—took special aim at the abusive practices of state governments of the Deep South, a region that had lagged behind national norms of liberty and equality. Even if a state legislature consistently authorized a given punishment, that consistency hardly made the practice "usual" when judged by the *national* baseline envisioned by the Fourteenth Amendment. Thus, a clause that originated in 1689 England as a limit on (crown) judges vis-à-vis (parliamentary) legislators morphed in 1868 America into a clause empowering (federal) judges vis-à-vis (state) legislators—and also vis-à-vis federal legislators if Congress ever tried to enact harsh punishments contrary to the broad consensus of state practice.

But how, exactly, should a proper national baseline be constructed against which the policies of any given state must be measured? In a notable 2002 death-penalty case, *Atkins v. Virginia*, Justice Scalia insisted in dissent that judges trying to construct a baseline had to count each state equally regardless of state population. According to Scalia, any survey of actual state practice that gave California more weight than Wyoming, simply because California has far more people and far more punishment cases, would be "quite absurd." What should matter is "a consensus of the sovereign States that form the Union, not a nose count of Americans for and against."[57]

Justice Scalia somehow missed the fact that the case that was before him when he wrote these words was a *Fourteenth Amendment* case—a case about whether Virginia's specific death-penalty rules violated the Reconstruction Amendment's vision of basic rights. (Indeed, almost all "cruel and unusual punishment" cases that arise today are, strictly speaking, Fourteenth Amendment cases.) The enactors of the Fourteenth Amendment surely believed that congressional legislation would provide important evidence of proper national norms and baselines. But on Scalia's logic, such legislation cannot count because it emerges from a process in which California does weigh more than Wyoming in both the House and the presidency—two of the three bodies involved in ordinary lawmaking.

Contrary to Scalia's principles, the modern Court has paid special heed to congressional legislation in measuring state penal practices. In addition, it has counted punishment practices in the national capital, which Scalia's approach, with its strict emphasis on "sovereign States," would presumably brush aside as constitutionally irrelevant. Although modern case law has not always openly paid more attention to more populous states, the justices in future cases should do precisely this in order to maximize expositional clarity and optimize the soundness of the Court's rulings. In this quadrant of case law, judges should seek to discover and channel the collective wisdom of the American people; and on certain questions, the wisest way to tap that wisdom is to survey all Americans and weight each equally.[58]

The basic idea here is that there is no reason to think that citizens of small states are any wiser than citizens of larger states about the proper meaning and scope of fundamental rights. Unless there is particular reason to believe that distinct and vital interests of small states are at special risk, the views of each small-state voter should not count for more than the views of each large-state voter. Even if it makes sense in certain contexts—say, the constitutional amendment process—to overweight small states in order to help these states preserve their proper status and separate existence against potential large-state self-aggrandizement, the domain of fundamental rights does not place small states at any distinctive risk of subjugation. As any properly recognized right would bind large states in the same way that it would bind small ones, there is little risk of large-state oppression or self-dealing in this constitutional quadrant.

Treating Americans equally need not entail simple majority rule. All members of a given jury vote equally, but a criminal jury must often be *unanimous* to convict; some civil juries, by contrast, operate by *supermajority* rules; and grand juries typically use *simple majority* rule. Similarly, different counting thresholds may be appropriate for different sorts of rights cases. If the issue is whether a given punishment is genuinely *unusual*, presumably the punishment may sometimes be upheld even if it is a minority practice. If, say, states accounting for 45 percent of the nation's population routinely use punishment X, it would be hard to say that X is truly *unusual* even though it is a minority practice. In deciding other unenumerated-rights cases not involving the Eighth Amendment word *unusual*, however, judges might sensibly strike down a practice simply because 55 percent of ordinary Americans strongly believe that this practice violates their fundamental rights. A strongly held belief by 55 percent of Americans that they have a constitutional right against abusive practice Y may suffice as a textual matter to recognize this right as a truly unenumerated right of "the people," a genuine privilege "of citizens" recognized as such by citizens.

Some scholars have suggested that a new unenumerated right should not be recognized unless it is endorsed by three-fourths of the states—the high bar set by Article V for constitutional amendments. But in recognizing new rights, judges are not *amending* the document. Rather, they are *applying* it, construing directives in the Ninth and Fourteenth Amendments that call for protection of fundamental but nonspecified rights—directives that *already* cleared Article V hurdles when these amendments were duly enacted. Part of the reason that Article V sets a high bar for ordinary constitutional amendments is that if the bar were set too low, then government-initiated amendments might end up weakening explicitly protected rights. But this concern about possible rights diminution is irrelevant when the issue is whether new rights rooted in evolving popular sentiments and practices should join the existing stock of enumerated and unenumerated entitlements.

Section 5 of the Fourteenth Amendment was clearly designed to empower Congress to enact legislation recognizing new rights, and this section envisioned only ordinary national majorities, not special Article V supermajorities. Since the Fourteenth Amendment also envisioned judicial recognition of new rights to supplement Congress whenever Congress was asleep at the switch, overwhelmed with other business, or controlled by critics of Reconstruction, section 5 provides a better benchmark for judicial rights-finding than does Article V. Thus, judges should look for the same broad national support for a new right that would warrant a properly functioning Congress to recognize the right under its own authority.[59]

IF JUDGES MAY PROPERLY strike down highly unusual state (or even federal) laws that intrude on a lived experience of liberty, there is a risk that governmental innovation and experimentation might be unduly stifled. Trigger-happy judges might kill the first glimmerings of legal reform whenever new issues arise and new approaches begin to win popular support. But this risk can be minimized if the judges proceed with caution and humility, with close attention to the danger of what might be called "judicial lock-in."

The danger is that once a particular government practice has been invalidated by judges, the practice will wither away and remain forever off-limits, even if a broad swath of Americans would like to see the practice revived at some later point. Such a judicially induced lock-in would turn proper unenumerated-rights jurisprudence on its head. Doubtful laws should be judicially invalidated because they are unusual, not unusual simply because they have been judicially invalidated.[60]

The most democratically sensitive and sophisticated version of lived constitutionalism would avoid judicial lock-in of unenumerated rights by inviting judges (or other constitutional decisionmakers) to reconsider their initial invalidations when presented with updated evidence of recent legislative patterns. For example, if many large states were to enact new laws similar to a law previously struck down—new laws with delayed start dates so as to allow for anticipatory judicial review—such enactments themselves would be new data to ponder.

The Court's death-penalty jurisprudence offers a suggestive case study. In the late 1960s, actual executions dropped to zero in America. In response to this apparent national consensus, the Court in 1972 seemed to hold the death penalty categorically unconstitutional. Over the next four years, both Congress and some thirty-five states representing an overwhelming majority of the American population pushed back against this ruling with a new round of death-penalty statutes. In response, the Court reconsidered its position and gave its blessing to the penalty when the underlying crime was particularly heinous and strict procedural safeguards were in place. Since then, the Court has imposed additional substantive and procedural limits on capital punishment with a close eye on evolving American practice.[61]

ALTHOUGH A WAVE OF NEW LEGISLATION would not ordinarily suffice to trump a precise and inflexible textual right, we must keep in mind that in this chapter we have been dealing with various rights that have not been specified in this way in the written Constitution. If the original judicial reason for deeming these rights to be full-fledged constitutional entitlements derived from the fact that American lawmakers generally respected these rights in practice, then such rights should lose their constitutional status if the legislative pattern dramatically changes. In this particular pocket of unwritten constitutionalism, what should ideally emerge is a genuine dialogue among judges, legislators, and ordinary citizens.

CHAPTER 4

CONFRONTING MODERN CASE LAW

America's "Warrented" Constitution

EARL WARREN

By acclamation, Earl Warren ranks as one of America's two greatest chief justices, standing alongside John Marshall in the American Pantheon.

IN THE COURSE OF READING between the lines of the written Constitution, probing the enacting procedures that produced the document, and taking account of the lived experiences of ordinary Americans, we have only sporadically considered modern Supreme Court case law. It is now time to directly engage the Court—for surely its rulings loom large in America's unwritten Constitution.

Although it might seem odd to speak of written judicial opinions as part of an "unwritten" Constitution, we must recall that these opinions lie outside the boundaries of the terse text itself. Case law forms no part of the written Constitution as such.

But case law does provide a powerful lens through which judges, lawyers, lawmakers, pundits, and ordinary citizens have come to read the written Constitution. The $64,000 question is, does this lens generally clarify, or does it grossly distort?

For much of the late nineteenth and early twentieth centuries, Supreme Court case law routinely misrepresented the Constitution's true contours. Today, the picture is quite different. In most (but not all) areas of constitutional law, the "unwritten" cases cohere with the written Constitution. The story of how this general coherence came about is the tale told in this chapter—the saga of the Warren Court.

WHEN EARL WARREN joined the Court as its fourteenth chief justice in 1953, Jim Crow ruled the South. Many states disfranchised blacks with impunity. The Bill of Rights did not generally apply against the states. The Court had never used the First Amendment to invalidate congressional action. Some states had succeeded in chilling core political expression. State-organized prayers were commonplace in public-school classrooms. State criminal defendants had precious few federal constitutional rights. No general right to vote existed. Almost all state legislatures were malapportioned, some grossly so.

Over the next sixteen years, Warren helped change all that, dismantling the old judicial order and laying the foundations of the basic doctrinal regime that has remained in place ever since. Warren did not act alone, of course. But it is conventional to periodize the Supreme Court by reference to its chief justices, and "the Warren Court" is an especially handy label. The term denotes a remarkable period of judicial history, beginning with the Court's deliberations and decision in *Brown v. Board of Education* and culminating in a series of landmark rulings in the 1960s that dramatically extended the reach of the Bill of Rights and revolutionized the right to vote.

A powerful triumvirate led the Court in this pivotal era: Earl Warren, a former Republican governor and vice-presidential candidate from the West; Hugo Black, a former Democratic senator from the South who had been on the Court since the late 1930s; and William Brennan, a former Democratic state court judge from the Northeast who joined the Court in 1956. In addition to their striking geographic, professional, and political complementarities, Warren, Black, and Brennan brought impressive methodological diversity to the bench. Warren inclined toward arguments from constitutional ethos and American ideals of fair play; Black liked to highlight the literal words of the Constitution and their original intent; and Brennan generally saw things through the lenses of case law and practicality.[1]

Decades after Warren's departure, his Court continues to inspire spirited debate, but most commentators have missed the real virtues, vices, and implications of the Warren Court revolution. Many conservative critics have accused Warren and his brethren of turning the Constitution upside down—dishonoring the document's text and original intent, disrespecting the considered views of coordinate branches of government, and disregarding American public opinion. In response, many of the Court's liberal admirers have glibly conceded the truth of these objections but countered that constitutional text, original understandings, congressional legislation, and popular sentiments are vastly overrated as decisional guideposts. According to these friends of the Court, the Warren-era justices were wiser and more evenhanded than the outdated constitutional text, the self-serving politicos in Congress, and the unwashed majority of ordinary Americans. Thus, the high court brethren were right to follow their own lights.

With defenders like this, who needs detractors? Even if the Warren Court justices were indeed smarter and fairer than everyone else—a doubtful proposition—these men in robes swore oaths to uphold the Constitution, and their opinions purported to apply, not amend, that document. Let us, then, review the work of the Warren Court and measure it against the words of the written Constitution.

"citizens"

PERHAPS THE MOST ICONIC MOMENT in twentieth-century American judicial history occurred on May 17, 1954, when the Court held that racial segregation in public schools was per se unconstitutional. *Brown v. Board of Education* famously ruled against state and local regimes of race separation, and a companion case, *Bolling v. Sharpe*, proclaimed that the same antisegregation principles applied to the federal government. In a widening circle of later rulings that made clear that the justices were completely repudiating the "separate but equal" doctrine underlying the 1896 case of *Plessy v. Ferguson*, the Warren Court held that apartheid had to end not just in public schools but in virtually every domain where Jim Crow laws had prevented whites and blacks from intermingling—at state beaches, on public golf courses, inside buses, and even within the bonds of matrimony.[2]

These companion rulings had deep constitutional roots. Jim Crow aimed to create two hereditary classes of Americans, with whites on top and blacks on the bottom. This racial class system was a throwback to aristocracy, assigning Americans unequal and intergenerationally entrenched legal slots on the basis of birth status. Such a regime was hard to square with the democratic social structure expressed and implied by the Philadelphia Constitution. Beyond the Preamble and the Article IV republican-government clause, the bans on federal and state titles of nobility in Article I explicitly condemned the trappings of aristocracy: "No Title of Nobility shall be granted by the United States" and "[n]o state shall...grant any Title of Nobility." Under the letter and spirit of these clauses, which promised a democratic republic and renounced a feudalism based on birth and blood, no American government could properly name some Americans "lords" and others "commoners." But in effect that was precisely what Jim Crow circa 1954 aimed to do, perpetuating a hereditary overclass of fair-skinned lords atop a hereditary underclass of dark-skinned commoners.

Alongside the antinobility clauses, another pair of Article I provisions prohibited both the state and federal governments from enacting "Bill[s] of Attainder"—statutes that singled out persons by name and pronounced them guilty of capital offenses. Beneath this specific rule ran a deeper and wider principle that forbade government from stigmatizing persons because of who they were (their status) as opposed to what they did (their conduct). When read generously, with idealistic attention to both letter and spirit, the original Constitution thus seemed to condemn a legalized racial hierarchy.[3]

However, this idealistic reading did not prevail in the early republic. Arrayed against this grand vision were antebellum arguments that on racial-equality issues, the Constitution had to be understood as a compromising and compromised document. Strong constitutional protections of chattel slavery were tightly woven into both the fabric of the document—most enduringly in the three-fifths clause, giving slaveholders extra political clout in both Congress and the electoral college—and the fabric of everyday life in antebellum America. In the old South there was in fact a legal structure of lordship and serfdom despite the antinobility clauses. Nor were these clauses unique in not meaning what they seemed to say. Slavery contradicted a huge part of the original Constitution, if the words of that document were read idealistically. For example, despite the Bill of Rights, slaves had no entitlements to worship, assemble, speak, bear weapons, or marry—indeed, no right even to eat and sleep as they pleased. In effect, each slave was sentenced to life imprisonment at birth without any ordinary due process in the form of an individualized adjudication of wrongdoing.[4]

Candid antebellum interpreters resolved the original Constitution's seeming contradictions by conceding that slaves were simply not part of "We the People" at the Founding. Rather, slaves were akin to enemy aliens, and America's Constitution aimed to protect Americans first and foremost. If protections for the American people meant privations for other peoples—whether the British, the Spanish, the French, the Mohawks, or the slaves—then so be it.

Free blacks, however, were a different story. Many had borne arms for America in the Revolution and had even voted on the Constitution itself. Thus, free blacks in antebellum America could plausibly claim all the Constitution's guarantees—or, more modestly, could claim these guarantees in any state that recognized their formal citizenship. Alas, the antebellum Supreme Court saw things differently. Chief Justice Taney's 1857 opinion in *Dred Scott* went so far as to proclaim that a free black descended from slaves could never be a citizen even if his home state said otherwise. Taney's was a twisted and ultimately temporary reading of the document. In the wake of the Civil War, America adopted a trio of amendments reaffirming the most idealistic elements of the Philadelphia Constitution and renouncing the original text's original sin.

The Thirteenth Amendment abolished slavery and empowered Congress to pass sweeping anti-caste legislation, a mission Congress immediately began to fulfill. The Fourteenth and Fifteenth Amendments made clear that the republic was being refounded on principles of free and equal citizenship. Pointedly repudiating Taney, the first sentence of the Fourteenth Amendment declared the birthright citizenship of all persons born in America, black and white alike: "All persons born or naturalized in the United States and subject to the jurisdiction thereof, are citizens of the United States and of the State wherein they reside." Notably, this clause governed the federal government as well as the states. In the next sentence, the word "equal" explicitly appeared, promising that all persons would receive "equal protection of the laws." Finally, the Fifteenth Amendment threw voting booths open, inviting blacks to participate equally with whites in the grand project of American democracy. With this trio of amendments proclaiming a new birth of freedom, the key contradictions and compromises of the Founders' Constitution melted away. No longer was it necessary or proper to read the Preamble and the other anti-aristocracy and anti-attainder clauses in a stingy way.

In light of all these constitutional clauses, all these structural considerations, and all this historical evidence, *Brown* and *Bolling* were not just correct but *clearly* correct. These iconic cases vindicated the central meaning of the Reconstruction Amendments. Jim Crow laws were not truly equal. American apartheid created a subordinated caste in violation of the vision of the Thirteenth Amendment and its early implementing legislation; perpetuated two unequal classes of citizens in defiance of the logic of the Fourteenth Amendment's first sentence; deprived blacks of the genuinely equal laws commanded by the Fourteenth Amendment's next sentence (and by the companion Fifth Amendment); and kept blacks and whites apart in a manner that renounced the premise and promise of the Fifteenth Amendment that Americans of different races would come to-gether—at polling places, in legislatures, on juries—as democratic equals.[5]

LEADING CRITICS (AND SOME FRIENDS) of the Warren Court have raised two counterarguments based on the alleged original intent of the Reconstruction Amendments. First, while the Fourteenth Amendment was pending, many congressional supporters emphatically stated that it would not prohibit segregation. Second, although the Reconstruc-tion Congress never explicitly enacted legal segregation, it did continue to fund the preexisting segregated schools in the nation's capital, and it even allowed its own public galleries in the Capitol building to be racially segregated.

Practices put in place as the ink on a newly ratified constitutional clause is still drying may properly help resolve textual ambiguities. But post-enactment practices cannot trump the central meaning of a constitutional provision as that provision was plainly understood by the public at the mo-ment of its enactment. When the Fourteenth Amendment was adopted, Americans undeniably understood that one of its central purposes was to end all "Black Codes"—laws that withheld from blacks the ordinary civil rights enjoyed by whites. Virtually all the amendment's supporters agreed that it would prohibit any law that enforced white supremacy in the do-main of civil rights.

For example, had any legislature in 1869 enacted a candid statute en-titled "An Act to Put Blacks in Their Proper Place at the Bottom of So-ciety," or "An Act to Demean and Degrade Negroes," or "An Act to Deny the Equal Citizenship and Civil Equality of Non-Whites," such a statute would have plainly violated the core meaning of the Fourteenth Amend-ment as understood by those who framed and ratified it in 1866–1868. The only question in 1954 was whether Jim Crow was legally equivalent to these hypothesized laws—equivalent in purpose, equivalent in effect, and equiv-alent in social meaning. True, Jim Crow laws, with a sly wink, purported to be "equal" and did not declare their true social meaning with the candor of our hypothetical statutes. But by 1954, honest observers understood that the "equal" part of "separate but equal" was a sham. The whole point of Jim Crow was inequality, and everyone knew it.[6]

How, then, are we to account for the fact that the Reconstruction Congress itself failed to end segregation and instead ended up perpetuating segregation in certain respects?

Actually, many Fourteenth Amendment supporters opposed racial segregation. One of the amendment's chief architects, House leader Thaddeus Stevens, established an interracial orphanage upon his death and chose to be buried alongside African Americans in an integrated graveyard. He composed his own tombstone inscription:

> I repose in this quiet and secluded spot
> Not from any natural preference for solitude.
> But, finding other cemeteries limited as to race
> by charter rules,
> I have chosen this that I might illustrate
> in my death
> The principles which I advocated
> Through a long life
> EQUALITY OF MAN BEFORE HIS CREATOR.

Stevens went to his final resting place in August 1868, less than a month after the Fourteenth Amendment became the supreme law of the land.[7]

While Stevens ranked among the most radical of Republicans on racial issues, many other Republicans were also high-minded opponents of legally imposed segregation. But some Republicans were considerably less zealous, and most Democrats refused to support an all-out crusade against segregation. In the end, faithful constitutional interpreters must investigate not merely how many segregationists existed in 1866–1868 but also what they said and did and whether their words and deeds plausibly glossed the Fourteenth Amendment. In short, we must probe how the unwritten Constitution of the mid-1860s interacted with the written Constitution itself. The question is not just whether Representative X or Senator Y supported segregation in 1867 or 1869, but how he read the Constitution's words—how he reconciled segregationism with the Constitution's express commands.

Ultimately, nothing in what segregationists actually said or did provides good grounds for revising our initial understanding of the Fourteenth Amendment's central meaning. The text calls for equal protection and equal citizenship, period. There is no textual exception for segregation, no clause that says "segregation is permissible even if unequal." Nor did most 1860s segregationists who supported the amendment argue that there was such a categorical exception. Instead, they offered up a medley of legal and factual assertions, some plausible and others less so.[8]

Many merely argued that separation was not intrinsically unequal. As a matter of logic, they were right. It is logically possible to imagine forms of separation that are not unequal. For example, separate bathrooms for men and women today are not widely understood, by either men or women, as stigmatizing or subordinating. But in some places and at some times, separate bathrooms might indeed be a way of keeping women down. In Jim Crow America, racially separate train cars, bus seats, schools, bathrooms, drinking fountains, and the like were engines of inequality in purpose, effect, and social meaning. They were ways of keeping blacks down, creating a pervasive legal system of untouchability and uncleanness that violated the basic equality ideal constitutionalized by the Fourteenth Amendment.

Put differently, this first segregationist argument accepted the correct legal meaning of the Fourteenth Amendment and simply posited that as a matter of fact—not law—separate could and would be equal in the Capitol galleries and elsewhere. Whether or not this fact was true in 1868, it hardly answered the question in 1896 or 1954. Surely the Court was entitled to draw its own factual conclusions about whether separate was actually equal. Although the *Brown* Court overstated when it proclaimed that in the field of education separate was *inherently* unequal, the Court surely could properly say, with the benefit of history, that Jim Crow in America was *inevitably* unequal. *Brown* came at the end of a decades-long string of cases in which black plaintiffs challenging regimes that claimed to be "separate but equal" had been obliged to bear the expense of proving actual inequality case by case—a string of cases in which inequality was indeed invariably found by the judiciary when it looked closely. In light of this experience, the *Brown* Court sensibly shifted the burden of proof to seg-regationist governments in all future Jim Crow cases. Henceforth, governments would need to offer compelling evidence that racial separation was indeed equal in purpose, effect, and social meaning.[9]

Segregationists in the 1860s also argued that racial separation would actually serve the interests of both races and was favored by most blacks as well as most whites. If so, then separation might indeed have been "equal" enough sociologically to be acceptable constitutionally—just as separate bathrooms and separate sports teams for males and females today pass constitutional muster precisely because a majority of each sex presumably accepts and perhaps even prefers this separation. But whether or not blacks in the 1860s truly preferred to sit separately in Capitol galleries or else-where was largely irrelevant in the 1950s, when it was clear that Jim Crow was an insulting and subordinating imposition by whites upon blacks, an imposition vigorously opposed by a wide range of black leaders and the great mass of black citizens.[10]

Another segregationist argument in the 1860s was that racial segrega-tion was formally different from the infamous Black Codes. Black Codes were formally and facially asymmetric: They heaped disabilities on blacks but not whites. By contrast, Jim Crow was formally symmetric: While blacks could not go to School X, whites were symmetrically barred from attending School Y.

Although some 1860s segregationists thought that formal symmetry rendered the Fourteenth Amendment textually inapplicable, they were clearly wrong about this. To repeat, the text does not say and cannot easily be read to say that deep and abiding inequality is permissible so long as a law is formally symmetric. Formal symmetry does not and cannot mean the law is automatically valid. Rather, formal symmetry merely means the law is not automatically (what lawyers call "facially") *in*valid, as were the Black Codes. The simple question remains: Were formally symmetric Jim Crow laws truly equal? It is possible to imagine some parallel universe where blacks as well as whites sought separation, where no stigma attached to separation, and where separation was not an instrument of subordina-tion. But that was not the world of Jim Crow in 1954 (or in 1896, when the Court wrongly upheld segregation in *Plessy v. Ferguson*).

Reconstruction-era conservatives sometimes articulated their intuition that formal symmetry decisively distinguished segregation and antimiscegenation laws from Black Codes by claiming that race-separation laws involved not "civil rights," but rather "social rights" that lay beyond the reach of the Fourteenth Amendment. But segregation laws did not merely *allow* whites to separate themselves from blacks if whites preferred this "social" arrangement. These laws *required* separation even if both whites and blacks preferred to socialize together or intermarry, and the clear purpose and meaning of such enforced separation was to boost whites and degrade blacks. Nothing in the text of the Fourteenth Amendment signaled that this species of state action was somehow categorically exempt from the amendment's general requirement of equal citizenship.[11]

A final segregationist argument was that the Fourteenth Amendment's equality norms applied only against state governments. Although this argument, if correct, could not justify state apartheid policies, it might explain segregation in various federal spaces, such as the Capitol galleries. But the Constitution's text plainly contradicts this argument. The amendment's first sentence creates rights of equal citizenship that apply against all governments, state and federal. Its text provides that "[a]ll persons born...in the United States" are by that fact alone "citizens of the United States"—and thus, equal citizens at birth. This sentence in effect constitutionalized the Declaration of Independence's "self-evident" truth—a truth that Lincoln had famously stressed (and glossed) at Gettysburg—that all men (that is, persons) are created (that is, born) equal. Any law, state or federal, heaping disabilities or dishonor upon any citizen by dint of his or her birth status—because he was born black, or because she was born female or out of wedlock—violates a core principle of the Fourteenth Amendment's opening sentence.[12]

The Civil Rights Act of 1866—a companion statute passed by the same Congress that proposed the Fourteenth Amendment, in the same season and by nearly the same vote—featured language virtually identical to this sentence and explicitly linked this language to a racial-equality rule binding both state and federal officialdom: "All persons born in the United States...are hereby declared to be citizens of the United States; and such citizens, *of every race and color*...shall have the same right, in every State *and Territory* in the United States, to...full and equal benefit of all laws and proceedings for the security of person and property, as is enjoyed by white citizens, and shall be subject to like punishment, pains, and penalties, and to none other" (emphasis added).[13]

Beyond the Fourteenth Amendment, the antinobility clauses of the Founders' Constitution explicitly applied against both state and federal officials, as did the Fifteenth Amendment, which demanded racial equality not just in Election Day voting but also in other voting venues, such as jury rooms and legislative assemblies.[14]

AND SPEAKING OF LEGISLATIVE ASSEMBLIES, we should pay close attention, as did Massachusetts Senator Charles Sumner in pointed and poignant remarks delivered shortly after the Fifteenth Amendment's ratification, to the fact that the Reconstruction Congress itself allowed its black and white members to sit side by side on a plane of perfect equality—indeed, as "brother[s]"—on the House and Senate floor. "[W]e have had in this Chamber a colored Senator from Mississippi; but according to [segregationist ideology] we should have set him apart by himself; he should not have sat with his brother Senators....[A colored man] is equal here in this Chamber. I say he should be equal in rights everywhere."[15]

In embracing Sumner's brotherly vision many decades later, the *Brown* Court not only obeyed the plain meaning of the Constitution's text but also carried forward the Reconstruction practice that best embodied the promise of the text: the integration of the floor of Congress itself.

"No State shall...abridge..."

AS ICONIC AS *BROWN* AND its progeny have been, other lines of Warren Court case law have arguably been even more significant.

Beginning in the early 1960s, the Warren Court handed down a series of decisions declaring that the Fourteenth Amendment took various provisions of the Bill of Rights that had originally operated only against the federal government and applied—"incorporated," in doctrinal jargon—these provisions against the states. In 1986, Justice Brennan ranked these incorporation opinions as the "most important" accomplishment of the

Warren era. In a 1970 essay generally critical of the Warren Court, Solicitor General (and former Harvard Law School Dean) Erwin Griswold noted that the stakes in the incorporation cases had been enormous: "I can think of nothing in the history of our constitutional law which has gone so far since John Marshall and the Supreme Court decided *Marbury v. Madison* in 1803."[16]*

The incorporation revolution was foreshadowed by a series of cases in the second quarter of the twentieth century. In this era, the justices came to agree that certain aspects of the Bill of Rights—most importantly, freedom of expression and religion—should apply against states, but not necessarily with the same strictness that would obtain in a Bill of Rights case proper involving comparable federal conduct. The explicit textual basis for applying the Bill to the states, even in watered-down form, was the Fourteenth Amendment, which the Court read as obliging states to observe fundamental rights essential to "a scheme of ordered liberty." Famous proto-incorporation cases in this pre-Warren period include *Near v. Minnesota* (prohibiting press censorship), *Powell v. Alabama* (overturning a scandalously unfair capital trial of poor black youths—the "Scottsboro boys"), *Cantwell v. Connecticut* (striking down solicitation regulations that amounted to religious censorship), *West Virginia State Board of Education v. Barnette* (invalidating compulsory flag-salutes in public schools), *Everson v. Board of Education* (upholding a religiously neutral policy subsidizing buses for private schools), and *Wolf v. Colorado* (prohibiting unreasonable state searches and seizures but declining to saddle states with the federal exclusionary rule).[17]

---

* Any reader who doubts Brennan and Griswold should play a simple parlor game: At the end of this paragraph, close your eyes and compose a mental list of what you consider to be the ten most important Bill of Rights cases in American history. Once you have your list in mind, open your eyes and continue reading this footnote.

Odds are that most of the cases on your mental list are, strictly speaking, not Bill of Rights cases at all. Rather, most are probably Fourteenth Amendment cases, where the alleged threats to liberty or equality came not from the federal government (to which the original Bill of Rights was solely directed) but rather from state or local governments. Even if your list contains a few true Bill of Rights cases involving the federal government, these cases were probably powerfully influenced by earlier incorporation cases involving state and local governments. In other words, almost all the cases on your list are probably either proto-incorporation cases, incorporation cases proper, or postincorporation cases shaped by the incorporation revolution.

Then came the incorporation revolution of the 1960s, as the Warren Court applied virtually all the provisions of the Bill of Rights against states and further held that these rights meant the same thing against the states as they did against the federal government. Most famously, *Mapp v. Ohio* applied the federal exclusionary rule, with all its rigor, to state police conduct; *Gideon v. Wainwright* insisted that the federal right of counsel—which included a right of appointed counsel for indigent criminal defendants—had to be respected by all states; *Malloy v. Hogan* applied the Fifth Amendment self-incrimination clause to states; *Miranda v. Arizona* went much further, applying the clause to police-station interrogations (even if the suspect was never obliged to answer under oath); and *Duncan v. Louisiana* required every state criminal court to honor the Sixth Amendment jury-trial right. A medley of less famous cases held that the Fourteenth Amendment incorporated, among other things, the Fifth Amendment double-jeopardy clause; the Sixth Amendment's clauses guaranteeing speedy trials, compulsory process, and the right to confront adverse witnesses; and the Eighth Amendment's bans on excessive bail and cruel and unusual punishments.[18]

These cases vastly expanded the practical scope of the Bill of Rights. For every federal felony prosecution in America today, there are more than a dozen state felony prosecutions. (That is why almost every high-schooler has heard of *Gideon* and *Miranda*; by contrast, even quiz-show winners would find it hard to name the analogous pre–Warren Court cases involving the federal government—*Johnson v. Zerbst* and *Bram v. United States*.)

Alongside its incorporation cases proper, the Warren Court handed down closely related decisions applying previously applicable rights against states, but now with special rigor rather than in watered-down form. *New York Times v. Sullivan* (an iconic free-speech case), *Engel v. Vitale* and *Abington School District v. Schempp* (a pair of decisions banning official prayer in public schools), and *Tinker v. Des Moines* (which championed the political-speech rights of students) exemplified this category.

So did *Griswold v. Connecticut*. Recall that Justice Douglas's 1965 opinion for the *Griswold* Court argued that the right of privacy could be found between the lines of the Bill of Rights—a document that the Court was increasingly deploying directly against states, thanks to the incorporation revolution in full swing when *Griswold* was decided. To the extent that Douglas's opinion in *Griswold* offered an implausible account of the letter and spirit of the first eight amendments, *Griswold*'s result could also be seen as in effect incorporating the Ninth Amendment's notion of unenumerated rights against states. As with the first eight amendments, the Ninth had originally been designed only as a limit on the federal government, but after *Griswold* the notion of unenumerated rights against states gained steam. Douglas's majority opinion made passing reference to the Ninth, and in a concurrence joined by Warren and Brennan, Justice Arthur Goldberg devoted several pages to this amendment, arguing that it served as a pointed reminder that not all citizen rights were enumerated.

By the end of the Warren era, the justices had used the Bill to strike down a vast number of state and local practices in contexts far removed from property and contract. Never before had the Court been so active in protecting liberty, privacy, and equality, and these Warren Court actions set the stage for post-Warren justices to do even more. Thus, *Griswold* provided the backdrop for *Roe v. Wade* and *Lawrence v. Texas*; *Engel* and *Abington* gave rise to a veritable cottage industry of modern litigation pricking out the proper line between church and state; and the incorporation of virtually all other parts of the Bill of Rights eventually encouraged the justices in *District of Columbia v. Heller* and *McDonald v. Chicago* to read the Second Amendment as protecting an individual right to keep a gun at home and to incorporate that right against states.

Even cases that at first seem wholly unrelated to incorporation often owe a deep debt to this doctrine. Consider, for example, the emphatic command of the First Amendment: "Congress shall make no law...abridging the freedom of speech." When Congress did make such a law early in American history—the Sedition Act of 1798—Supreme Court justices riding circuit vigorously enforced the act and swept aside First Amendment objections. When Congress made other laws abridging free speech during World War I, history repeated itself, and the justices once again sent citizens to prison for criticizing the government. (This time, the justices sat en banc, rather than on circuit.) The first time the Court ever struck down a congressional statute as a violation of free-expression principles was 1965—shortly after the incorporation revolution had begun.[19]

This timing was hardly coincidental. Thanks to the proto-incorporation free-expression cases of the preceding generation and to its own budding incorporation doctrine, the Court in the 1960s experienced a steady flow of cases inviting the justices to ponder how best to protect citizen expression against overreaching state and local governments. The recurring fact patterns in these state cases enabled the Court to begin articulating judicial rules, regulations, tests, and formulas—judicial doctrines—safeguarding free expression in a wide range of situations. Once the Court became comfortable with these doctrines, the justices were well positioned to wield these rules even against Congress, a coordinate branch of government. Thus, a 1943 proto-incorporation flag-salute case from one state (*West Virginia State Board of Education v. Barnette*) set the stage for a 1989 postincorporation flag-burning case from another state (*Texas v. Johnson*), which in turn established the basic doctrinal rules that were then easily deployed by the Court to strike down a federal flag-burning law directly under the First Amendment in a 1990 case, *United States v. Eichman*.

The same pattern can be seen in other corners of case law. In the 1951 case of *Dennis v. United States*, the Court largely blessed Congress's crusade against Communists and other allegedly subversive speakers. Only after the incorporation revolution began did the Court adamantly and unwaveringly back free expression, in a long line of cases including *Brown v. United States* (a 1965 Communist Party case), *Brandenburg v. Ohio* (a Ku Klux Klan free-expression case decided in June 1969, Warren's last month on the Court), and *New York Times Co. v. United States* (a 1971 case in which the federal government sought to block the publication of the Pentagon Papers).

In the 1971 *New York Times* case, federal censorship efforts were (unsuccessfully) defended in Court by none other than Solicitor General Griswold, who saw up close how the incorporation revolution that he had criticized was making his job of justifying federal censorship more difficult than the task that had confronted his 1950s predecessors. Notably, it was an incorporation-era case involving a state government's assault on political dissenters—the celebrated 1964 lawsuit, *New York Times v. Sullivan*—that had prompted the Court to admit for the first time in its history that the federal Sedition Act of 1798 really *had* violated the central meaning of the First Amendment. In *Sullivan*, the Court confronted repressive Alabama officials who were seeking to shut down antigovernment speech. In response, the Court declared that Alabama libel law had many of the same vices as the infamous federal seditious libel law of 1798, a law that, in the *Sullivan* Court's words, stood condemned by "the court of history." Once the justices were officially on record that President John Adams had been too thin-skinned in the midst of a naval quasi-war against France, it became easier for the justices a few years later to see that the same might be true of President Richard Nixon in the midst of a land war in Asia. Thus, *The New York Times*'s landmark Fourteenth Amendment victory against state suppression in 1964 not only foreshadowed but also facilitated *The New York Times*'s landmark First Amendment victory against federal censorship in 1971. Of the six remaining justices who had voted for the *Times* the first time around, five voted for the *Times* once again.[20]

With few exceptions, the biggest cases in the American "Bill of Rights" canon are thus either cases in which the pre-Warren Court laid the groundwork for incorporation, cases in which the Warren Court itself incorporated previously unincorporated rights against states, cases in which the Warren Court applied previously incorporated clauses with new vigor, or post-Warren cases building on this Warren Court legacy.*

FORTUNATELY FOR THE GENERAL CONDITION of the American constitutional project, the Warren Court basically got it right on incorporation.

The Court's initial critics claimed otherwise, attacking incorporation on several fronts. One camp of critics—the textualists—argued that incorporation lacked a sturdy foundation in the Fourteenth Amendment's language. But the amendment's words plainly call for incorporation of some sort: "No State shall make or enforce any law which shall abridge the privileges or immunities of citizens of the United States." Ask a roomful of Americans to name their basic rights, freedoms, privileges, and immunities as citizens and they are apt to quote or paraphrase virtually every entitlement in the Bill of Rights along with other claims of right rooted in American tradition and practice.[21]

What is true of ordinary language and American culture today was also

---

* At this point, any reader who played the parlor game set out at p. 152*n* is invited to recall the ten cases that came to mind then and determine how many of them were the seeds or the fruits of incorporation.

true in 1866, when the Fourteenth Amendment was composed. Key congressional sponsors of the Fourteenth Amendment made clear that the "privileges [and] immunities of citizens" at the amendment's core included all the individual rights found in the Bill of Rights. Ohio Representative John Bingham, the lead draftsman of this language, invoked "the Bill of Rights" more than a dozen times in one major speech, which he quickly published (in time for the congressional election of 1866) as a popular pamphlet subtitled "In support of the proposed amendment to enforce the Bill of Rights." In the Senate, fellow draftsman Jacob Howard of Michigan reported to his colleagues and his countrymen—who could follow the proceedings through detailed and high-profile press accounts—that "the privileges and immunities of citizens of the United States as such" encompassed "the personal rights guaranteed and secured by the first eight amendments of the Constitution," amendments that Howard then quoted and paraphrased in detail.[22]

Despite this compelling evidence from plain meaning and legislative history, some textualist critics of the Warren Court have remained skeptical. If the Reconstruction Congress really meant to incorporate the Bill of Rights against states, why didn't Congress say so more clearly in the amendment's text?

Actually, in 1866, the words that Congress chose to express the basic incorporation idea were clearer and more technically accurate than various alternative formulations would have been. For example, had the Fourteenth Amendment spoken explicitly of "the Bill of Rights," what would this phrase have meant? Amendments I–VIII? I–IX? I–X? Unlike many state constitutions, the federal Constitution does not contain a separate section formally captioned as a "Bill of Rights." Prior to 1866, the Supreme Court had never referred to the early amendments as a "Bill of Rights." In prominent case law, the Court had, however, described various provisions of the Bill, such as the freedoms of speech and assembly and the right to keep and carry arms, as paradigmatic "privileges and immunities of citizens." Other notable antebellum legal documents—treaties of territorial accession and statutes regulating federal territories—had likewise referred to various provisions of the Bill of Rights as "privileges" and "immunities" of "citizens."[23]

The popularity of the phrase "the Bill of Rights" in modern discourse and the synonymy of this phrase with the early amendments are themselves products of Reconstruction. In the mid-1860s, Democratic opponents of the proposed Fourteenth Amendment did not typically describe the early amendments as "a Bill of Rights" or "the Bill of Rights." Reconstruction Republicans, led by Bingham, did repeatedly refer to these amendments as the federal "Bill of Rights," thereby helping to bring the phrase into vogue. Republicans' repeated references—nearly twenty by Bingham alone in a pair of high-profile speeches—occurred as the drafters of the Fourteenth Amendment clearly explained to Congress and the American people that this amendment aimed to make all the entitlements of this "Bill of Rights" applicable against states.[24]

But not just these entitlements. Thus, any textual mention of "the Bill of Rights" and only the Bill of Rights would have fallen far short of the Reconstruction Republicans' goal of ensuring state obedience to *all* fundamental rights, freedoms, privileges, and immunities of Americans. Some fundamental rights, such as the privilege of the writ of habeas corpus, were mentioned elsewhere in the Constitution. Additional rights derived from America's lived Constitution of actual practice and from landmarks of liberty such as state constitutions and the Declaration of Independence. Still other entitlements had yet to be recognized in 1866 but were intended to be protected by future courts and especially by future Congresses tasked by section 5 to enact legislation declaring newfound fundamental civil rights.

Perhaps some problems of textual underinclusiveness might have been avoided if the framers of the Fourteenth Amendment had made clear that they meant to incorporate not simply the enumerated rights of the first eight amendments but also the unenumerated rights referred to by the Ninth Amendment. But any textual reference to, or explicit incorporation of, the Ninth Amendment as such would likely have prompted states' rights' advocates in the 1860s to cry foul: One of the animating ideas of the Ninth Amendment was to limit *federal* power in the interest of *states'* rights. After all, the Ninth Amendment textually locked arms with the Tenth: These back-to-back clauses both spoke of rights and powers retained and reserved to "the people." Undeniably, the Tenth was largely, if not wholly, a *federalism-based* provision safeguarding the structure of enumerated powers in Article I. The driving idea of the Tenth Amendment—limiting Congress so as to preserve a policy domain for state governments—made the very thought of incorporating the Tenth against the states seem perverse, if not preposterous. How could a states'-rights amendment be incorporated *against* states? And to the extent that the Ninth textually and conceptually intertwined with the Tenth—for the Ninth, too, was originally designed to ensure, among other things, that Congress did not go beyond its proper enumerated powers—how could the Ninth Amendment apply against states?

All of which leads to the second major objection to incorporation, an objection leveled by a camp of structuralist critics of the Warren Court. According to this structuralist objection, the Bill of Rights contains various states'-rights elements that cannot sensibly be applied or "incorporated" against states. The Ninth and the Tenth Amendments did not stand alone; other amendments in the Bill of Rights were also states'-rights provisions, at least in part. For example, the First Amendment establishment clause affirmed the complete absence of any express or implied federal power to regulate religion. The First Amendment words "*Congress shall make no law*" echoed (and marked the outer edge of) Article I, section 8, which said that "*Congress shall* have Power…To *make all Laws*"—but only in some domains. Religion was a domain left outside of Congress's enumerated power, and this Article I understanding was affirmatively reiterated by Amendment I. In this respect, the First Amendment resembled the Tenth Amendment, reserving an area for state regulation. How could this states'-rights clause be applied *against* states? Ditto with the Second Amendment: If a key point of this amendment was to preserve states' rights to field state-organized militias as checks against federal officialdom, then how could this states'-rights amendment be swiveled around to check states (and to empower federal officials in Congress and the Court)?

The answer to all these structural riddles can be found in the Fourteenth Amendment's text. The amendment does not say that any specific *amendment* or *clause* originally designed as a limit on the federal government must henceforth apply against states. Rather, it says that various "privileges" and "immunities" of individual "citizens" apply against states. Thus, it invites interpreters to separate and refine out the individual-rights components (that is, the "privileges" and "immunities" of "citizens") contained within the First and Second Amendments—and indeed contained within all the other parts of the Constitution, for that matter—from their comingled states'-rights components.[25]

This separation, refining the essence of individual rights from the mixed ore in which they are textually embedded, is precisely what antebellum interpreters had been obliged to do in applying the federal Constitution to the federal territories and the District of Columbia. If a particular constitutional clause was merely a federalism rule—based on the idea that federal power should be limited so that state policy could govern a given domain—then that clause did not have bite in the territories. (For example, the limits on the jurisdiction of federal courts in the federal Judicial Article were designed to let state courts hear all the remaining cases. This idea of limiting federal courts so as to protect state courts across the street made little sense in the territories, where the only sitting courts were federal courts, with no other backstop.) Conversely, if a constitutional clause was a pure individual right, then surely it should limit the federal government in D.C. or any other federal enclave just as it would in Virginia or Maryland.

Alternatively, if a clause was partly a federalism rule and partly an individual right, then interpreters would need to refine the clause in deciding exactly how to apply it in a territory. Consider, for example, the Second Amendment. To the extent this amendment merely protected official state-organized militias, it had no bite in a federal territory that lacked a state government to organize such a militia. But to the extent the amendment also protected an individual right to keep a gun at home for self-protection, the amendment did sensibly operate in this—refined—way in the territories in the same way that it operated in states.*

Reconstruction Republicans, many of whom hailed from states that had begun as territories, believed that the same refined individual-rights limits that applied when Congress legislated for the territories—and that also obviously applied against any territorial governments that Congress had established—should continue to apply when these territorial governments

---

* The Republican Party platform of 1856 evidently read the Second Amendment to go beyond purely states' rights; the platform openly criticized federal violations of "the right to keep and bear arms" in the Kansas Territory.

ripened into state governments. Hence, Republicans drafted an amendment inviting interpreters to refine the essence of individual rights from the Constitution's text and then apply these refined rights against states.[26]

The two major camps of incorporation's critics—the textualists and the structuralists—thus inadvertently canceled each other out. The very reason the Fourteenth Amendment used wording that the textualist critics found oddly indirect was that such wording elegantly avoided the perversity that troubled the structuralist critics—namely, the perversity of incorporating states' rights against states themselves. Thus, Reconstruction Republicans deftly threaded a legal needle, directing interpreters: (1) to apply the basic individual rights in the first eight amendments against states; (2) to apply all other fundamental civil rights—rights found both elsewhere in the federal Constitution and in other sources—against states; (3) not to apply states' rights against states; and (4) to refine individual-rights elements from states'-rights elements where the two were intermixed in various constitutional passages or other appropriate source material. And Republicans did all this with phrasing that also—in ways and for reasons that will soon become clear—highlighted that their proposed amendment would address only civil rights and not political rights such as voting, jury service, or office-holding. It was quite a feat of constitutional draftsmanship to codify all this in a mere twenty-one words!

YET EVEN WHILE HONORING THE central meaning of these words— "No State shall make or enforce any law which shall abridge the privileges or immunities of citizens of the United States"—the Warren Court never openly relied on this clause. Instead, the Court accomplished incorporation via the Fourteenth Amendment's immediately adjoining passage: "nor shall any State deprive any person of life, liberty, or property, without due process of law."

Textually, this was off-target. As we saw in Chapter 3, the relied-upon clause focused on fair legal procedures in lawmaking, law enforcement, and law adjudication. It focused on process, not substance. But many of the rights that the Warren Court (and its predecessor Courts) wielded against states were substantive and not merely procedural rights—a right to religious liberty, an immunity from unreasonable governmental snooping and grabbing, an entitlement to be paid a fair price for private property taken for public use, and so on. Why did the Warren Court ignore the perfectly apt clause while overworking the less apt clause?

The short answer is precedent. In the first major Fourteenth Amendment litigation to reach the justices, the *Slaughter-House Cases* of 1873, the Court in effect read the privileges-or-immunities clause—section 1's key clause—out of the amendment, suggesting that the clause merely restated principles of federal supremacy evident in the Philadelphia Constitution's Article VI and in John Marshall's basic teachings in *McCulloch v. Maryland*.[27]

Reconstruction Republicans had aimed to do much, much more than reaffirm *McCulloch*. Bingham and his allies had expressly declared on the floor of Congress that their proposed amendment would overturn another Marshall Court opinion, *Barron v. Baltimore*, which had held that the Bill of Rights limited only the federal government. In *Barron*'s place, Bingham envisioned a reconstructed America in which the basic rights of expression, religion, property, privacy, and fairness that had been promised against the federal government would apply with equal force against errant states.[28]

In the decades after *Slaughter-House*, the Court gradually came to appreciate the wisdom of Bingham's vision, first in an 1897 case obliging states to honor the right of just compensation—the very right that had been at issue in *Barron*—and then in a series of cases in the second quarter of the twentieth century involving free expression, religious liberty, and search-and-seizure issues. In this era, the Court faced a dilemma. Though unwilling to allow flagrant state violations of basic American freedoms, the justices did not want to shout from the rooftops that their predecessors had bungled *Slaughter-House* and a long line of Gilded Age cases that had followed suit. So the justices in this period simply took the path of least precedential resistance, applying a form of substantive due process to strike down the offensive state laws.[29]

By the time the Warren Court came along, *Lochner*-style substantive due process was in bad odor. The justices now understood that their *Lochner*-era predecessors had overprotected corporate and property interests in the name of due process. But the Warren Court hesitated to condemn all prior substantive uses of the due-process clause. After all, many well-respected pre-Warren opinions, such as *Near v. Minnesota* and *West Virginia State Board of Education v. Barnette* (the censorship and flag-salute cases), had used the very same due-process clause to protect important liberty interests. With only a modest amount of tweaking, the Warren Court was able to reconceptualize these proto-incorporation opinions and extend their logic to encompass virtually all the previously unincorporated provisions. The due-process clause provided a ready-made precedential tool to do the work. This tool seemed especially handy, because many of the rights that the Warren Court incorporated did relate to courtroom procedures and litigation fairness—for example, the rights of criminal defendants to confront and subpoena witnesses, to have competent counsel, and to be tried by properly constituted juries in speedy and public proceedings.[30]

Even as the Warren Court was reviving and extending substantive due process of a certain sort, the justices were also developing new doctrinal labels and jargon to highlight how their new rulings were qualitatively different from, and infinitely better than, the old *Lochner* line. Just as the *Griswold* and *Katz* Courts stressed "privacy" as distinct from "property," so the Warren Court's cases applying the Bill of Rights to states paraded under a new label—"incorporation"—so as to distinguish this project from the property fetishism and antiredistributionism of *Lochner*-era cases.

Yet there was a hefty price to be paid for this doctrinal legerdemain. By not grounding their incorporation case law upon the most apt text, and by declining to broadcast that their predecessors had taken a wrong turn at the very beginning, the Warren Court justices lost a golden opportunity to weld their doctrine to the document and to explain why the leading textualist, historical, and structuralist objections to incorporation were exactly wrong.

WHY DID THE WARREN COURT deal with incorporation clause by clause, rather than incorporating the Bill of Rights as a whole? In doctrinal jargon, why did the Court follow a "selective incorporation" rather than a "total incorporation" approach? Although the Court failed to offer a compelling answer to this question, its instincts were sound. Some clauses of the Bill of Rights were originally more entwined with states' rights than others, so it made good analytic sense to address each right separately.

A step-by-step approach also enabled the Court to fashion a workable legal framework—a Court doctrine—that could win the support of a stable and enduring Court majority. To be sure, the alternative approach of total incorporation was historically plausible and textually permissible, but it was not the only defensible way to interpret and implement the Fourteenth Amendment.

Consider the following five possible pathways to incorporation that were open to the Court in the early 1960s:

Pathway One. Rights in the Bill of Rights were included by definition within the Fourteenth Amendment's language. The phrase "the privileges or immunities of citizens" was an 1860s term of art referencing the Bill— much as the phrase "the presidents of the United States" in 1866 referenced George Washington through Andrew Johnson.

Pathway Two. Rights in the Bill of Rights were not included by definition or referenced as such. Nevertheless, these rights in 1868 were widely thought to be included precisely because they were in the Bill. The Fourteenth Amendment encompassed all fundamental rights, and any right listed in the Bill was for that very reason generally viewed as fundamental in the 1860s and should be so viewed in the 1960s.

Pathway Three. Rights in the Bill of Rights were generally included because the fact that a right was in the Bill was powerful—but rebuttable— evidence of its fundamentality. On this view, the fact that an entitlement was listed in the Bill of Rights made it presumptively, but not automatically, a fundamental right worthy of protection against states.

Pathway Four. Rights in the Bill of Rights were generally included because virtually every one of them—speech, press, religion, and so on—was understood in 1866 to be fundamental in its own right and would have been so understood even if it had not been textualized as part of the Bill of Rights.

Pathway Five. Rights in the Bill of Rights were generally included because mid-twentieth-century Americans continued to deem virtually every one of these rights fundamental, as evidenced by the fact that virtually every Bill of Rights provision had counterpart language in modern state constitutions governing most Americans.

Which of these five pathways to incorporation was the one true way?

Perhaps the best practical approach for a justice seeking to craft a majority opinion was to detour around this thorny theoretical question, since all five pathways led to incorporation of all, or virtually all, the rights in the Bill. True, the first two pathways suggested that the Court could have decided incorporation in a single case determining that all the rights in the Bill applied against states. This was the view held by Justice Hugo Black, among others. But this view never commanded five votes on the Court at any given moment. Eventually, Black was content to allow incorporation to proceed one right at a time, in a process that enabled him to collaborate with colleagues who preferred one of the last three pathways, each of which invited more careful—selective—attention to the specific right involved in the case at hand.

The best objection to the Warren Court's selective incorporation approach was that it was, well, selective—selective, that is, in a seemingly political way. Although the Warren Court incorporated every right it considered, it simply declined to consider three important rights—the right to keep a gun at home, the right to be free from prosecution unless indicted by a grand jury, and the right to have a jury trial in certain civil cases—and thus left them outside the fold, with no good explanation of the differential treatment.

Culturally, the most important of the slighted trio was the Second Amendment's right to keep and bear arms. Perhaps the Warren Court saw the Second Amendment as a pure states'-rights provision that protected organized state militias and nothing else. If so, the Court may have believed that this amendment, much like the Tenth, did not sensibly incorporate. But the Warren Court justices never agreed to take a case to carefully consider the issue. Had they done so, they would have been obliged to confront evidence that the First Amendment's establishment clause had likewise originated as a states'-rights provision that, among other things, prevented Congress from disestablishing state churches. If the Second Amendment did not properly incorporate, should the establishment clause also have been disincorporated? If, conversely, incorporating some variant of the establishment clause against states made sense despite its states'-rights roots—and as we shall see shortly, there is indeed a good case to be made for this result—then mightn't the same be true of Second

Amendment incorporation? By declining to address the Second Amendment, the Warren Court never had to answer these tough questions about its general approach to incorporation and thereby explain why its selective approach was principled across all clauses. Conservative critics may be forgiven for wondering whether the liberal members of the Warren Court were simply more personally sympathetic to antiestablishmentarianism than to gun rights.

At its best, doctrine works itself pure over time, as different judicial generations confront each other in a process that enhances the coherence of case law. So it was with incorporation, as post–Warren Court justices eventually turned to the Second Amendment and decided that it, too, had an individual-rights component applicable against both the federal and state governments. Thus, one of the most telling criticisms against the Court's incorporation doctrine as it emerged in the 1960s has now become moot.[31]

Alas, the justices have yet to explain why the remaining two unincorporated rights—the Fifth Amendment right to indictment by grand jury and the Seventh Amendment entitlement to jury trial in civil common-law suits—merit different treatment from all other rights listed in the first eight amendments. As it turns out, there may well be principled, if rather technical, reasons for treating grand juries and civil juries differently from everything else in the Bill of Rights.* The justices, however, have simply declined to hear any cases on the matter. Until the Court either extends the incorporation doctrine to protect the rights to grand juries and civil juries or clearly explains why these two rights are different from all others, the critics of incorporation will continue to have at least one valid point.[32]

---

* Unlike virtually all other clauses in the Bill of Rights, the Fifth Amendment rule that no felony case may generally proceed absent a grand-jury indictment has not been mirrored by most state constitutions. Currently, only eighteen states, making up less than 45 percent of the national population, require grand-jury indictments for all felonies. (For details, see p. 547, n. 32.) If Pathway Five is the best way to think about incorporation, the right to grand-jury indictment would seem the least attractive candidate for incorporation, precisely because it has the weakest foundations in actual modern practice at the state level, where the overwhelming majority of criminal filings occur. As for the Seventh Amendment right to civil juries in common-law cases, this right is arguably a pure states'-rights provision merely requiring a federal court to give litigants juries whenever a state court across the street would do so. On this reading, incorporation against states would merely require each state to follow its own rules about jury trials—something it would do anyway.

Yet even this point is a rather small doctrinal blemish in the grand scheme of things, given the fundamental correctness of the basic concept of incorporation. In this vastly significant quadrant of constitutional law, the doctrine and the document currently cohere remarkably well.

"press" and "religion"

TO APPLY THE BILL OF RIGHTS against states is one thing; to *correctly* interpret and enforce the meaning of the Bill—whether in incorporation cases involving states or in Bill-of-Rights-proper cases involving the federal government—is something else. Here, too, the Warren Court revolution prompted considerable criticism; and here, too, much of the criticism reflected a flawed understanding of constitutional basics. Consider, for example, two areas covered by the First Amendment: expression and religion.

In 1964, the landmark case of *New York Times v. Sullivan* struck down an Alabama libel law that had socked the *Times* with massive punitive damages for an ad that the newspaper had run criticizing Alabama officialdom. The Court likened Alabama's law to the Sedition Act of 1798, which had likewise punished printers who had opined against government policy and government policymakers.

Even some scholars who relished *Sullivan*'s result clucked that the justices had ventured far beyond the constitutional text and its original public meaning in order to do justice. According to these scholars, Blackstone's *Commentaries* had defined "liberty of the press" merely as a promise that government would not deploy licensing systems requiring would-be printers to win official approval before opening up shop. Alabama had not attempted any scheme of press licensing or "prior restraint." Instead, the state had allowed the *Times* to circulate freely, and had merely responded to what state law saw as the *Times*'s wanton abuse of the liberty that the newspaper had enjoyed.

This criticism of the landmark *Sullivan* decision misses the point—indeed, misses many points. True, Blackstone defined press freedom narrowly: "The liberty of the press is indeed essential to the nature of a free state: but this consists in laying no *previous* restraints upon publications, and not in freedom from censure for criminal matter when published.

Every freeman has an undoubted right to lay what sentiments he pleases before the public: to forbid this, is to destroy the freedom of the press: but if he publishes what is improper, mischievous, or illegal, he must take the consequence of his own temerity." It is also true that leading Americans in the early republic often invoked this stingy definition. Most notably, Federalist Party supporters of the 1798 Sedition Act leaned heavily on Blackstonian ideas in claiming that the act was perfectly constitutional, as it imposed no licensing scheme or prepublication censorship.[33]

But America's free-expression regime meant much, much more than the partisan supporters of the Sedition Act admitted. For starters, let's recall that virtually absolute freedom of political expression formed part of the process by which the Constitution sprang to life—part of the document's very enactment—even before the phrase "the freedom of the press" was added as a postscript.

Textually, the First Amendment protected not merely "freedom of the press" but also "freedom of speech." Speech freedom had never been understood in early America as confined to a no-licensing and no-prior-restraint principle, and it is hard to see how anyone at the Founding who took even a moment to muse on the differences between the words "speech" and "press" could have thought otherwise. It was at least imaginable that an eighteenth-century government might require that anyone seeking to operate a printing press—not exactly a household item back then—first obtain an official permit. (Indeed, earlier English governments had done just that.) But what would it even mean for government to insist that a person needed a permit to open his mouth and speak?

Ordinary American citizens' freedom of speech derived from sources different from and deeper than press freedom. The phrase "freedom of speech" built upon English freedom of speech and debate in Parliament. In eighteenth-century England, however, only members of Parliament could opine without fear. In post-Independence America, all citizens could do so—because in America, "We the People" were sovereign. Under the Constitution's legal hierarchy, "We" did not answer to Parliament. Rather, parliaments (Congresses and state legislatures) answered to Us. Thus, the First Amendment textualized the American Constitution's structural postulate of popular sovereignty. Here, the people would rule and were therefore free to think and opine as they wished.

The chief draftsman of the First Amendment, James Madison, said all this—first in a brief aside at the very moment he introduced his draft amendment in Congress; more clearly in 1794, when he declared that, "[i]f we advert to the nature of Republican Government, we shall find that the censorial power is in the people over the Government, and not in the Government over the people"; and most emphatically of all when he explained in 1799 why the Sedition Act of 1798 was a constitutional abomination. Note how Madison's repeated 1794 references to "the people" and its cognate word "Republican" gestured toward the Preamble and the Ninth Amendment, both of which endorsed the supreme authority of "the people," and toward the republican-government clause, whose spirit governed federal action even though its letter applied only against states. (Surely the federal government, if unrepublican, could not be trusted to guarantee the republican-government principle against states. Thus, the deep logic of the republican-government clause presupposed that the federal government would itself remain republican.)[34]

In their first opportunity to weigh in on the matter, American voters sided with Madison, vaulting his mentor and fellow free-speech champion Thomas Jefferson into the executive mansion and sweeping the Jefferson-Madison party into congressional power. These self-described Republicans immediately repudiated the 1798 precedent—Congress by refusing to revive the law when it lapsed thanks to a sunset clause, and Jefferson by pardoning every person who had been convicted under the law. On July 4, 1840, Congress made further amends by reimbursing fines that had been imposed. According to the accompanying committee report, the 1798 act was "unconstitutional, null, and void....No question connected with the liberty of the press...was ever more generally understood, or so conclusively settled by the concurring opinions of all parties, after the heated political contests of the day had passed away."[35]

And speaking of making amends—and amendments—let's not forget that the framers of the Fourteenth Amendment guaranteed a broad freedom of expression against any government that tried to suppress opinionated citizens, whether *ex ante* or *ex post*. Speech was perhaps the "privilege" most often mentioned in the Thirty-ninth Congress, which declared that states must henceforth honor all fundamental "privileges [and] immunities of citizens." In the previous decade, the Republican Party had made its core commitments unmistakably clear, as summarized in the 1856 campaign slogan, "Free Speech, Free Press, Free Men, Free Labor, Free Territory, and Fremont."[36]

To anyone with any real sense of the document and its history, the propriety of protecting a Yankee newspaper from an all-white southern government hostile to outside agitators (and to in-state blacks seeking interstate alliances) was obvious. *Sullivan* was an uncanny case of déjà vu, as democratically deficient southern governments in the 1950s and early 1960s tried to return to their playbook of the 1850s and 1860s. *Sullivan's* specific doctrinal rules protecting those opining against the government and the status quo vindicated core constitutional values that had been present at the creation and pointedly reaffirmed after the Civil War. Also apt was the Court's general insistence that America remain a land of "uninhibited, robust, and wide-open" political discourse, permitting "vehement, caustic, and sometimes unpleasantly sharp attacks on government and public officials." Here, too, the document and the doctrine cohered.

IN AFFIRMING A RIGHT OF CITIZENS to launch "vehement, caustic, and...unpleasantly sharp attacks on...public officials," the *Sullivan* justices knew whereof they spoke, for they themselves had long been the targets of just such attacks. Indeed, in the years immediately preceding *Sullivan*, criticism of the Court had reached a crescendo, thanks to two intensely controversial decisions, *Engel v. Vitale* and *Abington v. Schempp*, that had decreed an end to governmentally organized prayers in the public schools. Despite all the outrage, these cases had in fact sensibly interpreted and applied the Constitution.

Critics charged that these cases turned the establishment clause—"Congress shall make no law respecting an establishment of religion"—on its head. Codifying the general absence of Article I power to regulate religion in the several states, these words made clear that Congress could not establish a national church and made equally clear that Congress could not disestablish any state-established church. After all, any attempted disestablishment would be a federal law "respecting" (that is, regarding) "an establishment of religion." Thus, the establishment clause told the federal government to keep its nose out of religious policy and to allow such matters to be handled by the states. Yet now the Warren Court, a branch of the federal government, was interfering with state religious policy—and in the name of the First Amendment, no less!

But, strictly speaking, *Engel* and *Abington* were not First Amendment establishment-clause cases. Rather, they were Fourteenth Amendment cases. To the extent that the establishment clause was, like the Tenth Amendment, a states'-rights provision, the clause did not sensibly incorporate against the states. Yet deep principles of American religious liberty and religious equality did apply against the states as proper "privileges or immunities" of American citizenship. At the Founding, roughly half the states had government-established churches. By the time of Reconstruction, none did. The principle of genuine religious equality—and not merely toleration of dissenting sects—had thus made significant strides in the lived Constitution of actual practice circa 1866. This precept of religious equality, which continued to gain steam over the ensuing century, was the deep principle that *Engel* and *Abington* aimed to vindicate.[37]

Surely, government could not oblige a public-school child to recite a state-written or state-sponsored prayer as part of a state-run religious ritual. To force, say, a young Catholic to engage in a non-Catholic religious ceremony would violate first principles of religious liberty, principles with deep roots stretching back to the Founding. (Generally speaking, state establishments in this era were marked by religious tolerance and noncoercion of religious dissenters, even though these regimes fell short of full religious equality for all.) But once a right of dissenting students to freely opt out of state-organized prayer was recognized (as indeed it had to be under the pre-Warren landmark of *West Virginia State Board of Education v. Barnette*), hard questions arose about whether a genuinely fair opt-out system could work. For in the very act of opting out, religious dissenters would need to stand up and thus stand out. They would need to be visibly and publicly separated from the others during the state-run prayer. In effect, they would need to be segregated from the others in the public schools, at least for that instant.

As we have seen, separate is not always unequal. That is the lesson of separate bathrooms, sports teams, and gym classes for males and females in most public schools today. But separate can well be unequal; and in the wake of *Brown* and *Bolling* the justices were understandably sensitive to the constitutional problems inherent in governmental policies that physically and symbolically separated and divided America's citizens—America's equal citizens!—along formal lines of race or religion. Though perhaps not as incontrovertibly correct as the *Sullivan* decision, the *Engel* and *Abington* rulings thus reflected genuine fidelity to the Fourteenth Amendment's first principles.

"unreasonable searches…witness against himself"

THE WARREN COURT'S BIGGEST BLUNDERS came in the field of criminal procedure. These blunders proved especially costly because of the incorporation doctrine, which operated as a force-multiplier, magnifying the benefits of the Court's good decisions on individual rights and aggravating the damage of its mistaken rulings. The Court's worst decisions of all involved the so-called exclusionary rule. In case after case after case, the justices barred the government from introducing concededly reliable evidence of criminal guilt if this evidence was the product of an unconstitutional search or seizure.

It was bad enough to throw out proverbial "smoking-gun" evidence in various white-collar federal criminal cases—something that the Court had been doing ever since the 1914 case of *Weeks v. United States*. It was far worse to extend the *Weeks* doctrine to all state crimes, as the Warren Court did in the 1961 *Mapp v. Ohio* decision and a long line of post-*Mapp* cases. Unlike the tamer federal docket, state filings bristled with violent crimes—murders, rapes, robberies, arsons, aggravated assaults. When the Warren Court extended the exclusionary rule to such cases—at times suppressing literal smoking guns and not just metaphorical ones, and doing so in cases where helpless crime victims watched in anguish as their tormentors walked free, grinning—the social costs of exclusion rose not only sharply but also graphically.

Of course, if the written Constitution's letter or spirit really did support the exclusionary rule, then any justice voting to exclude was simply doing his job and honoring his oath. But the letter of the document said no such thing and its spirit discountenanced exclusion. Various criminal-procedure provisions of the document aimed to ensure that innocent souls would generally be spared, but none of these provisions supported the suppression of highly reliable physical evidence, especially of violent crime. On the contrary, the Founders mandated public criminal trials precisely so that the truth would out. This open system was designed not only to help innocent defendants win acquittals, but also to facilitate the conviction of the guilty whenever members of the general public might have incriminating testimony or physical evidence to share. Thus, the public has always had an unenumerated right to monitor criminal trials even when defendants have preferred otherwise. Truth promotion, not evidence suppression, animated the document.[38]

No leading framer ever supported exclusion, and when a defense lawyer floated the idea of exclusion in 1822, Justice Joseph Story—antebellum America's most distinguished constitutional scholar—dismissed the concept as preposterous: "In the ordinary administration of municipal law the right of using evidence does not depend, nor…has ever been supposed to depend upon the lawfulness or unlawfulness of the mode, by which it is obtained.…[T]he evidence is admissible on charges for the highest crimes, even though it may have been obtained by a trespass upon the person, or by any other forcible and illegal means."[39]

Reconstruction Republicans evidently had a similar view of the matter. With Lincoln's blessing, the Civil War Congress adopted legislation aggressively seeking evidence from criminal suspects. When Americans celebrated the centennial in 1876, no July 4 oration praised the exclusionary rule, for the simple reason that such a rule did not exist, anywhere. No state or federal judge had yet excluded evidence in the name of the Fourth Amendment or its state constitutional counterparts.[40]

Mapp claimed that without the exclusionary rule, the Fourth Amendment would be virtually meaningless—a mere "form of words," according to the Court. This hyperbole would likely have rankled the men who actually devised the amendment, men who believed its words to be muscular but who never imagined exclusion as the proper enforcement mechanism. Unlike the *Mapp* Court, whose rule benefited the guilty precisely because they were guilty—precisely because reliable evidence of their guilt had surfaced—the Founders envisioned robust remedies that would paradigmatically comfort innocent Americans. Many of these envisioned remedies—tort suits against abusive officers, punitive damages to deter future misconduct, proto-class-action devices enabling small-fry search victims to band together—had been showcased in landmark English cases known to every colonial schoolboy. The heroes of these cases, John Wilkes and Lord Camden, became synonymous with liberty. Across America, cities, counties, and later even a major-league baseball park were named in honor of these champions.[41]

The thrust of the Founders' remedial vision is visible in the text of the Fourth Amendment. It is, after all, a cluster of property law and tort law, à la Wilkes and Camden—and not any rule freeing criminals—that ordinarily operates to make persons "secure in their persons, houses, papers, and effects."

The fact that an alleged constitutional principle finds no support in the Fourth Amendment's text, spirit, or original intent does not end the matter. If exclusion were rooted in America's widespread norms or practices, in the nation's deep traditions or symbols, or in first principles of the rule of law, then *Weeks*, *Mapp*, and their progeny might make sense. But most ordinary Americans have never thrilled to the idea of springing criminals—especially violent ones. None of the other slogans used by supporters of the exclusionary rule holds up under rigorous analysis.

The strongest argument for the rule derives from the need to deter Fourth Amendment violations. But a regime of evidentiary exclusion is upside-down, providing windfalls for the guilty and nothing for the innocent—nothing to deter the abuse of various citizens whom government officials know in advance to be blameless, and indeed nothing to deter government henchmen from committing unreasonable, even brutal, deeds unrelated to the finding of evidence. [42]

The Founders' deterrence model of tort law and punitive damages, by contrast, focused precisely on the right thing—the scope of the actual property and/or privacy invasion whether or not criminal evidence happened to turn up in a given search or seizure. To the extent that post-Founding developments—for example, the rise of organized police departments across America—have warranted revisions of old remedial rules, doctrinal updating should have occurred within the framers' model of civil and proto-administrative remedies comforting the innocent, not a criminal-exclusion framework rewarding the guilty.[43]

If the aim is truly deterrence, the limits the Court has placed on the exclusionary rule from *Mapp* to the present make no sense. Exclusion has never applied to civil cases; only criminal ones. Thus, if the government finds a cache of smuggled goods in an unconstitutional search, it cannot introduce the evidence in a criminal case but can introduce everything in a civil forfeiture action brought to gain title to the goods. This bright-line rule cannot be defended on deterrence grounds. Nor does it find support in the Fourth Amendment's text, which makes no distinction between civil and criminal cases.[44]

Beyond deterrence, exclusion's supporters have invoked the principle that government must never profit from its own wrong. This sounds very nice—until one gives the matter a moment's thought. Where does this principle come from? Not Blackstone or English tradition. (England has never had an exclusionary rule.) Not early American practice. (No exclusion, anywhere.) Not modern practice, either. (As just noted, governments have always been free to bring forfeiture actions and thereby literally profit from searches, even illegal ones.)

Despite its nice sound, the idea that government may never profit from an improper search fails to survive analytic scrutiny. When government finds stolen goods in a constitutionally defective search, must it return these items to the thief? Surely not! But then, government is in fact "profiting" in a sense, if one goal of the searchers was to undo the theft and restore the stolen goods to their rightful owner. Must government return all the illegal drugs to the drug lord? Must it return a kidnapping victim to her abusers if she happens to be found in an improper dragnet?

These questions are classic *doctrinal* questions—the sort of questions lawyers and judges ask about the proper scope and application of rules and principles promulgated in judicial opinions. Yet nothing in the Court's myriad opinions excluding reliable evidence satisfactorily answered these questions or explained the actual scope of the doctrine in any plausible and principled way. For example, why does exclusion apply only in criminal cases but not civil cases? Post-*Mapp* cases have also made clear that in an illegal search of A's home that uncovers evidence against A and his nonresident partner in crime, B, government may lawfully use (and thereby profit from) this evidence in a prosecution against B but not A. How is this rule to be explained on grounds of deterrence or nonprofit?

THERE WAS, AT LEAST ARGUABLY, a principled answer to some of these questions when *Mapp* was decided. Alas, this answer, though sincere, was highly implausible in 1961 and became even more wildly so in later years.

The decisive fifth vote for exclusion in *Mapp* came from Justice Black, who in the 1949 *Wolf v. Colorado* case had voted against applying the exclusionary rule to the states despite his ardent belief in "total incorporation." In *Wolf,* Black wrote that the exclusionary rule was not implicit in the Fourth Amendment, and that states should be held to the Bill of Rights, the whole Bill of Rights, and nothing but the Bill of Rights. Since exclusion was not in the Fourth, states could do as they pleased. By 1961, Black had changed his mind. As he explained in a separate opinion in *Mapp,* he had come to believe that the exclusionary rule flowed from the Fourth Amendment in tandem with the Fifth Amendment self-incrimination clause.

The Fifth Amendment was indeed a rule of criminal exclusion—it *excluded* a defendant's compelled testimony in a *criminal* case. It thus had the right logical shape to explain: (1) where the very idea of exclusion came from; (2) why exclusion was proper in criminal but not civil cases (because the Fifth entitled a person not to be compelled to witness against himself "in any criminal case"); and (3) why the government could use stuff it found in A's house against B but not A (just as it could force A to incriminate B but not himself). A close look at the Court's pre-*Mapp* case law confirms that almost all of the key exclusionary-rule cases had in fact made at least passing reference, and often more than passing reference, to the anti-self-incrimination principle.[45]

From a twenty-first-century perspective, however, this sustained effort to fuse the Fourth and Fifth Amendments seems outlandish. How was introducing stolen goods found in a burglar's hideaway remotely like obliging the burglar to take the stand under oath in his own criminal case? The story of how some judges came to conflate the two situations is a fascinating tale of doctrinal drift—an object lesson in what can happen when supposedly "constitutional" case law loses sight of the Constitution's letter and spirit.

The story began before the Bill of Rights was even drafted. In a 1760s English cause célèbre, Crown henchmen lacking proper legal authorization invaded the home of John Wilkes, rummaged through his papers, and grabbed his person. Wilkes was a leading opposition politician, and the Crown was trying to find evidence to charge him with the crime of having anonymously authored an antigovernment essay. Thus, the Wilkes affair was not just an unreasonable search case; it was also a free-expression case in a land that had no First Amendment or any robust guarantee of free expression outside of Parliament itself. No incriminating items were found in the search, and Wilkes successfully sued the henchmen in tort, winning large civil damages designed to deter future government misconduct.[46]

The Founders obviously drafted and ratified the Fourth Amendment with the Wilkes litigation in mind. (Closely related to the suits brought by Wilkes himself was *Entick v. Carrington*, decided around the same time by the same heroic judge, Lord Camden, and raising similar search-and-seizure issues.) On the rights side, the Fourth Amendment gave special attention to searches and seizures of "persons" (Wilkes had been bodily seized and imprisoned in the Tower of London), "houses" (his private residence had been invaded), and "papers" (his private manuscripts had been rummaged). All other things that government might search or seize were referred to by the Fourth Amendment simply as general "effects." The amendment went on to condemn all warrants that failed to name a specific person or place that the government had specific reason ("probable cause") to suspect. These oppressive "general warrants" were the very instruments that the henchmen had unsuccessfully tried to hide behind in the Wilkes litigation. On the remedy side, the amendment's framers also undoubtedly legislated with the Wilkes model in mind—a model of civil damages, not criminal exclusion.

A century after the Founding, American judges seeking to understand the Bill of Rights tried to do so in light of Camden's rulings, but these jurists ultimately misread both Camden and the Bill. The fact pattern that sparked the Gilded Age judicial imagination involved a diary: Suppose the government unlawfully seized a man's diary, prosecuted him, and tried to use passages from the diary against him in that criminal prosecution. According to late nineteenth-century jurists, such a scenario was virtually identical to the *Wilkes* and *Entick* cases, and on these facts, the Fourth Amendment's rules about papers almost imperceptibly blended into the Fifth Amendment's ban on compelled self-incrimination. After all, reading a man's diary against him was tantamount to making him an involuntary witness against himself—and so judges should respond by simply excluding the diary from evidence, thereby preventing the defendant from ever becoming a witness against himself via his diary.[47]

Or so the Gilded Age judges reasoned. Actually, even in this simple diary case, the judges overlooked obvious counterarguments. Perhaps self-incrimination principles did not really apply when no oath was ever administered to the defendant—and indeed, when no direct coercion had necessarily been brought to bear upon his person. (Imagine that he had not even been present when the diary was seized.) And would the issue have been any different had the government acquired the diary lawfully? If not—if even a lawfully acquired diary should not be introduced into evidence, because reading a man's diary in open court was itself a privacy intrusion and an arguable violation of self-incrimination principles—then perhaps the antecedent paper-search was a red herring. In the end, it was highly doubtful that the Fourth Amendment really fused with the Fifth such that the two ideas were two sides of the same coin, as Gilded Age jurists argued, and as Justice Black eventually came to believe.

Also, if the issue were simply one of privacy violation, it surely mattered what the defendant was charged with. The Fourth Amendment does not bar all intrusions upon privacy—only unreasonable ones. The severe privacy violation involved in reading a man's most intimate thoughts to the world in open court might well be obviously unreasonable (and thus unconstitutional) if the government was merely trying to prove that he had scribbled a seditious libel à la Wilkes—a puny offense that in America should not even be a crime! But perhaps the same privacy invasion might be justifiable to prove the defendant guilty of murder. In such a case, the reasonableness balance might tip in the government's favor, given that incapacitating a murderer might be a good reason to do some things that would otherwise be off limits. And even if the diary itself were inadmissible, why shouldn't the government be free to use the diary to develop leads to the location of reliable physical evidence—say, the murder weapon itself?[48]

Rushing past all these complexities, judges in the late nineteenth and early twentieth centuries began their analogical and doctrinal reasoning with the premise that a court should simply exclude a criminal defendant's improperly seized diary. Thus was born the ur-exclusionary rule, which in the judicial mind came to be associated with the Fourth Amendment alongside the Fifth. From this starting point, it was an easy step for judges to exclude all "papers" improperly seized from a criminal defendant, even his business records. Never mind that such records raised far fewer reliability issues than did diaries, in which men might fantasize about things that never happened. Also, never mind that business records were far less intimate than diaries, and thus posed none of the special privacy concerns attending the reading of a personal journal in open court.

The next stop on the analogical development of treating like cases alike was to treat all the defendant's personal property—his "effects"—as equivalent to his "papers." In the *Lochner* era, judges idolized property. A man was what he owned, and thus anything that he properly owned and that had been improperly grabbed by the government could not be introduced against him. Since a criminal defendant could not be forced to speak against himself, neither could, say, his gloves be used against him.

Unless the gloves had been used in the crime, in which case they were criminal instrumentalities, and as such subject to government forfeiture! If the defendant didn't truly own them, then they could indeed be used! Or so clever prosecutors argued—but judges ultimately ruled against them. As the years wore on and jaded judges became increasingly comfortable with exclusion, courts eventually came to exclude items that defendants had never lawfully owned—contraband liquor, illegal drugs, stolen goods, murder weapons, everything.[49]

By the end of this long line of cases leading up to Justice Black's mistaken epiphany in *Mapp*, both the Fourth and the Fifth Amendments had been distorted beyond recognition. The Fourth Amendment, to be sure, is all about physical stuff—"effects." But this amendment was never designed as a rule of criminal exclusion. Indeed, the amendment says nothing at all to limit its scope to "criminal" investigations. It governs all searches and seizures for all purposes. The Fifth Amendment is indeed a rule of criminal exclusion—but it excludes only a defendant's compelled *words* and does so largely because these words might well be unreliable (and also because these words might implicate divine punishment for perjury). Physical evidence—gloves, murder weapons, stolen goods, and the like—raise none of these concerns. These two quite distinct amendments, the Fourth and the Fifth, simply do not add up to form a proper exclusionary rule. Four plus five does not equal 1961 (or 1914, for that matter).

THE WARREN COURT CASE that exposed the clear error of Fourth-Fifth fusion came exactly five years and one day after *Mapp*. This time, in the case of *Schmerber v. California*, the Court sided against an exclusionary-rule claim. California had forcibly taken a blood sample from a criminal defendant and then used that blood to convict him. *Schmerber* involved drunk driving, and the specific scientific procedure at issue was a blood-alcohol test. Later cases would apply *Schmerber* to ABO blood-typing tests and DNA tests of blood and other biological samples extracted from the defendant's person.[50]

Schmerber drove a dagger through the heart of Fourth-Fifth fusion. The defendant argued that forcing a man to give the government his very blood was an unreasonable Fourth Amendment seizure, and that using his own precious blood to convict him was tantamount to making him testify against himself in violation of the Fifth Amendment. If ever a case could be made for the Fourth and the Fifth Amendments fusing together, this was it. But the Court held that the mere taking of blood was not unreasonable, even if the purpose was to procure a criminal conviction of the blood's owner; and that no Fifth Amendment violation occurred, because blood was not really a "witness" within the meaning of the self-incrimination clause. Blood was reliable physical evidence in a way that compelled words were not. Blood did not misremember, fantasize, sweat, stutter, get confused on the stand, or easily enable a trier of fact to think it had confessed to a crime when it had not. Nor did blood tempt a defendant into damning his soul by committing perjury.

But if all this was true of blood, it was also true of bloody knives, gloves, stolen goods, and lots of other items that had been excluded thanks to an overly broad reading of the Fourth and Fifth Amendments, pre-*Schmerber*. After *Schmerber*, the entire edifice of exclusion should have collapsed, because the only principled pillar on which it had rested—Fourth-Fifth fusion—had toppled.

Nevertheless, the Warren Court and its successors mindlessly kept on excluding, in the name of precedent, without ever confronting the fact that no proper principle could support the doctrine once Fourth-Fifth fusion was decisively repudiated. Later cases continued to emphasize the demise of Fourth-Fifth fusion and cut back on the scope of the exclusionary rule, creating myriad exceptions and loopholes but never openly confessing that the whole project of exclusion had become intellectually bankrupt.[51]

The most telling fact about *Schmerber* was that four members of the Warren Court dissented; in their view, the Constitution prevented the government from using a person's compelled blood sample against him in any criminal case. Today, *Schmerber*'s basic holding—that compulsory blood testing to establish criminal guilt is not categorically impermissible—seems incontrovertibly correct. There was no government brutality involved in *Schmerber*. Nor was the policy at issue a blunderbuss; the government had specific reasons to suspect the accused of driving while intoxicated, and the blood test at issue did not generate embarrassing personal information unrelated to the legitimate governmental interest in the case. (For example, nothing in the test revealed the identity or number of Schmerber's sexual partners or whether he suffered from incontinence.) Nor did the test improperly coerce Schmerber into professing a love of the government, disclosing his theology, or taking an oath. The test did not invade his mental privacy in any way, and in fact did not even engage his faculties of mind and will. A blood test, after all, can be performed on a corpse.

Today, every state in America routinely performs tests such as this. (Nothing in *Schmerber* required this result. The five-justice majority in *Schmerber* merely enabled each state to choose how to proceed.) The federal government conducts countless *Schmerber*-style tests every day. So does every major liberal democracy in the world. Without *Schmerber* and its progeny—allowing government to compel fingerprints, handwriting samples, and voice exemplars and to extract bodily fluids and tissues for forensic analysis—a vast amount of modern crime-solving would be off limits. And yet four justices in *Schmerber* were prepared to rule against all of this crime-solving, and to do so via a constitutional holding that could not be undone even by an act of Congress. Without *Schmerber* and its progeny, countless more criminals would escape detection and thus countless more crime victims would suffer (assuming that detection leads to incapacitation and deterrence—and possibly even rehabilitation).

But this is only half of the *Schmerber* story. *Schmerber* also helps innocent persons escape conviction. Today, blood tests not only convict; they exonerate. A DNA test can prove conclusively that someone else committed the murder. Return, briefly, to the preceding chapter's Hollywood-style hypothetical. Even after our hero succeeds in introducing the bloody knife, he must still link this knife to the real perpetrator. To do this, he may need to enlist the government's assistance to compel a fingerprint or a blood sample and thereby establish the DNA match. But had the four dissenters in *Schmerber* prevailed, the government could not compel the actual murderer to submit to these tests at the insistence of our innocent hero.

The terse text, standing alone, cannot always determine how broadly or narrowly a given word should be read. Should the word "witness" be read to include blood? Yes and no. Yes in our Hollywood hypothetical. Our innocent hero's Sixth Amendment right to compel the production of "witnesses in his favor" should be read to explicitly authorize and/or to presuppose that our hero may also compel the perpetrator to undergo a blood test. And no in our Hollywood hypothetical. The perpetrator should not be allowed to thwart this blood test by claiming that he has a Fifth Amendment right not to be compelled to be a "witness" against himself in a criminal case.

Why the seeming double standard? Because both interpretations serve the largest purposes of the document and vindicate the American people's vision of justice from the Founding to the present. Both interpretations are, in the end, truth-seeking and innocence-protecting. The written words of the various amendments must be understood in light of their larger unwritten context.

Yet four dissenting justices, including both Warren and Black, utterly missed the point in *Schmerber*, reading words in a way that was textually permissible but ultimately absurd—absurd as measured both by the actual purposes of the Bill of Rights and by the unanimous verdict of democratic societies in America and around the world in the past half-century. The *Schmerber* dissents are like the thirteenth chime of a broken clock, throwing into doubt all the previous chimes. If these four justices were wildly wrong in *Schmerber*, doesn't this egregious error call into question the soundness of all closely related Fourth-Fifth fusion cases in which their votes were decisive?

Mapp of course was just such a case. And without the Fourth-Fifth fusion idea underpinning *Mapp*, the exclusionary rule cannot stand as a principled interpretation or implementation of the terse text. In this odd corner of modern case law, America's unwritten Constitution cannot be squared with the Constitution as written.[52]

"the right to vote"

THE WARREN COURT CONSTITUTIONALIZED A remarkably participatory and egalitarian system of voting rights featuring a sweeping "right to vote" and a mandate that elections for the federal House and both branches of state legislatures meet the strictly equalitarian standard of one-person, one-vote. Though the voting-rights revolution of the 1960s went far beyond what the Founders had bargained for in the 1780s, and also overread a key constitutional clause from the 1860s, the Warren Court's voting-rights rulings stand today as rock-solid pillars of modern constitutional law—and rightly so.

FIRST, SOME HISTORY. The phrase "the right to vote" nowhere appeared in the original Constitution. State law, not federal law, generally determined voting rights at the Founding. If state law (presumably state constitutional law) entitled a person to vote for his state legislature, then and only then could he vote for the federal House of Representatives. State legislatures would themselves elect U.S. senators and decide how presidential electors would be selected. Any attempted uniform constitutional voting rule would have bumped up against the fact that land values varied widely across the continent. Thus, any fixed national property qualification for voting would likely have been too high in some places and too low in others. Had the federal Constitution simply announced a blanket rule prohibiting all property qualifications for federal elections, this rule would have placed the document out of the mainstream of the 1780s, when most states employed property qualifications of one sort or another. And then there was, of course, the race issue. Some states at the Founding allowed free blacks to vote on equal terms. Others did not, and several—South Carolina springs first to mind—were fiercely unwilling to give the federal government wide authority over states on this sensitive issue.

Slavery added further complications. How should slaves be counted for apportionment purposes? The Founders devised a formula apportioning House (and electoral college) seats across state lines—the infamous three-fifths clause—but that formula said nothing about how seats should be apportioned within each state. It was thus left up to each state legislature in the first instance to determine how to balance power between slaveholding and nonslaveholding regions within that state's congressional delegation. Let us also recall that the Article IV republican-government clause was not widely understood at the Founding as giving the federal government sweeping power to restructure state legislatures in the name of reform. Had the clause been so understood, it might well have been a deal-breaker for many southerners anxious to maintain control over this most tender of topics.

In the absence of strict federal oversight of their voting and apportionment practices, antebellum states drifted apart. By the middle of the nineteenth century, most northern states had abolished property qualifications and approximated universal adult male suffrage. (Many had racial qualifications, but these exclusions did not warp the basic power structure, given that free blacks formed a tiny minority in most northern states.) Many southern states, by contrast, had developed apportionment systems that gave extra clout to their plantation belts, enabling aggressive advocates of slavery to wield added power in various state legislatures and congressional delegations.[53]

As time passed, malapportionment undermined the very foundations of these increasingly intolerant and inegalitarian southern regimes. In-state residents and out-of-state speakers who tried to speak, print, preach, petition, or assemble in opposition to slavery and the slavocracy faced a dramatic narrowing of freedom of expression. By 1860, much of the South had become a closed society controlled by slaveholding elites contemptuous of democracy, equality, and free speech. In 1861, the political leadership of the Deep South ordered the shelling of Fort Sumter because these men could not abide the results of a legitimate national election that they had lost, despite getting boatloads of extra electoral-college votes thanks to their slaves. And the war came.[54]

In its wake, the phrase "the right to vote" found its way into two of the three Reconstruction Amendments. But there was a catch. The first clause to use this phrase—section 2 of the Fourteenth Amendment—did not absolutely guarantee any right to vote, but merely penalized states that abridged this right by reducing their representation in the House and electoral college. And the second clause to use the phrase—section 1 of the Fifteenth Amendment—prohibited only disfranchisements based on "race, color, or previous condition of servitude," leaving untouched other suffrage restrictions based on property, poll-tax payment, education, literacy, and so on.

A half century later (1920, to be precise), the Nineteenth Amendment repeated the phrase "the right to vote," this time to prohibit sex-based disfranchisement. In 1964, at the high tide of the Warren Court, still another amendment—the Twenty-fourth—featured the phrase as part of its ban on poll-tax-related disfranchisements in federal elections.

ENTER THE JUSTICES, who ruled in the mid-1960s that the equal-protection clause of the Fourteenth Amendment required the enfranchisement of virtually all adult resident nonfelon citizens. Whenever a state denied the franchise to any person in this group while extending the franchise to others, the state had to justify this differential treatment with compelling policy arguments, and the Court swatted away most of the arguments that states tried to offer. Thus, in 1966, *Harper v. Virginia* held that a person could not be disfranchised, even in a state election, for failing to pay a poll tax. (The recently adopted Twenty-fourth Amendment explicitly prohibited poll-tax-based disfranchisement, but only in federal

elections.) Three years later, Warren himself delivered his final set of opinions, one of which, *Kramer v. Union Free School District*, invalidated a New
York rule that limited voting in school-board elections to those who had
children or real estate in the school district. Such a rule, said Warren, violated the equal-protection rights of the plaintiff Kramer, a bachelor who
lived in his parents' house.

By reading the equal-protection clause to encompass voting rights, the
Warren Court severed this text from its enacting context and ignored the
decisive understandings of the American people when they ratified these
words. At its core, the clause safeguarded the rights of "persons" as contradistinguished from "citizens." In other words, both this clause and its companion due-process clause affirmed a category of rights that even aliens
deserved. Voting rights were miles away from this core concept. Indeed,
voting rights were the precise obverse of this core, epitomizing the exact
kind of rights that aliens cannot constitutionally claim.[55]

Nor were voting rights encompassed by the privileges-or-immunities
clause as it was originally understood. The core rights here were seen as
"civil" rights—in pointed contrast to "political" rights such as voting. The
Constitution's Article IV had used the same cluster of words—"privileges,"
"immunities," "citizens"—to define the rights of every American when
venturing outside his home state to visit a host state. Article IV rights were
obviously civil rights, not political rights. A citizen of state A, when visit-
ing state B, could claim equality with state B's citizens in matters of free
speech, free exercise, property ownership, and so on, but could not expect
to vote in B's elections or exercise any closely related political right, such as
jury service or office-holding, in B.

These seemingly technical distinctions had bubbled up to the surface
of daily political discourse in the Civil War era thanks to the high-profile
Dred Scott case. Chief Justice Taney's notorious opinion had proclaimed
that even free blacks could not be citizens. Dissenting justices countered
that (1) at the Founding, blacks in many states had been openly recognized
as citizens, and indeed had been among those who voted on the Constitution itself, and (2) even though free blacks in many states were not allowed
to vote in the 1850s, citizenship must be distinguished from voting rights.
Women, after all, were citizens—and as such could bring diversity suits in
federal court—but women as a rule did not vote. Neither did children, yet

they, too, were citizens. Likewise, blacks were citizens even if they could not vote.[56]

The dissenters' view was embraced by the Lincoln administration during the Civil War and enacted into law at war's end in the Civil Rights Act of 1866. As its title made clear, this landmark law guaranteed civil rights as emphatically distinct from political rights. The act recognized the birth-right citizenship of all persons born in America, black and white, male and female. But citizenship rights did not entail voting rights. The *Dred Scott* dissenters had been right all along on these points, explained the act's sponsors.[57]

This was precisely the Republican Party line in presenting the Fourteenth Amendment to the American people. The amendment's first section was designed to undergird the 1866 statute; indeed, the amendment's opening sentence echoed the statute virtually verbatim. The amendment's support-ers insisted that section 1 (the section featuring the birthright-citizenship clause, the privileges-or-immunities clause, and the equal-protection clause) encompassed only civil rights, not political rights—a limit layered onto the very words of the section, given their echoes of Article IV and the "Civil Rights" statute. No prominent Republican said otherwise. The of-ficial congressional report designed to explain the amendment to ordinary Americans explicitly contradistinguished "civil" and "political" rights and reassured the nation that section 1 addressed only the former.[58]

Had the American people understood section 1 to encompass voting, they would likely have defeated the entire amendment. In 1866, the nation was not ready for a rule that every state, in the North as well as the South, must allow blacks to vote equally. When such a rule was proposed three years later in the Fifteenth Amendment, almost no one said this proposal was merely declaratory of a principle already implicit in the Fourteenth.[59]

Dissenting Warren Court justices made all these points and added one more: Section 2 of the Fourteenth Amendment spoke of "the right to vote," and surely section 1 could have done the same had it been designed to cover voting rights. Notably, section 2 did not require that any given per-son be allowed to vote; it did not create an individual right to vote as such. It merely said that any state that denied the vote to certain persons had to pay an apportionment penalty in Congress and in the electoral college.

With this last point, the dissenters inadvertently pulled the rug out from under their own feet—for section 2, it turns out, actually provides the missing foundation for the general "right to vote" championed by the Warren majority.

Section 2, in relevant part, reads as follows: "[W]hen the right to vote... is denied to any of the male inhabitants of [a] State, being twenty-one years of age, and [nonfelon] citizens of the United States,...the basis of [that State's] representation [in the House and the electoral college] shall be reduced in...proportion." This provision is triggered whenever an adult resident nonfelon citizen is denied the right to vote, regardless of the specific reason for disfranchisement. It matters not whether a person within this group of presumptive voters flunked a literacy test, failed to possess the requisite property, refused to pay a poll tax, or simply lived with his parents and had no school-age kids. Whenever disfranchisement of any sort occurs among this group of presumptive voters, a state must lose representation in proportion. For example, if 10 percent of a state's presumptive electorate is denied the vote for any reason whatsoever, the state must lose 10 percent of its seats in the U.S. House, and must also lose a corresponding number of seats in the electoral college. So saith section 2.

But in reality, section 2 has never in its history been enforced through an apportionment penalty. And here is the punch line: Since Congress has never penalized any state for disfranchisements, judges are justified in treating these disfranchisements as invalid, whether or not made on grounds of race or sex or age. In other words, if no proper section 2 loss of representation occurs, then the state simply may not disfranchise. The disfranchisement is invalid precisely because the state has not paid the proper price for this disfranchisement, as mandated by section 2.

The issue is a simple matter of remedy law. Section 2 says that no disfranchisement can occur without apportionment penalty. Thus, the apportionment penalty must be imposed—*or else the disfranchisement must end.* (If the disfranchisement ends, there is no need for the apportionment penalty, and the actual absence of such a penalty thereupon becomes wholly lawful.) Judges on their own cannot easily enforce the apportionment penalty, because judges do not control the census workers who are needed to elicit the requisite information about various state-by-state abridgments of voting rights; nor can judges redo the entire apportionment of Congress without a great deal of help from Congress itself. (For example, if state A's House delegation is to be reduced by 10 percent, should the House size simply decrease or should other states get added seats? If so, which states?) With the remedial option of judicially enforcing the apportionment penalty effectively foreclosed in court, judges must (or at least may, in their remedial discretion) instead directly set aside the disfranchisement and thereby bring the actual apportionment practice into alignment with section 2's mandate. To repeat: Section 2 says that there shall be no disfranchisement without apportionment penalty. If no apportionment penalty is actually assessed, then there can be no disfranchisement imposed upon the group of presumptive voters textually specified by section 2: "male inhabitants of such State, being twenty-one years of age, and citizens of the United States [and not criminals]."

As we shall see in more detail in later chapters, the word "male" must now be read as "male or female," thanks to the more recent Nineteenth Amendment, which banned all sex-discriminatory voting laws and thereby repealed the earlier word "male" in section 2. Likewise, after the Twenty-sixth Amendment (adopted shortly after the *Kramer* case), "twenty-one" must now mean "eighteen"—the new constitutional age line for the right to vote. Behold: a presumptive right to vote based on the Fourteenth Amendment itself, albeit not the clause the Warren Court pulled out of its hat.[60]

This interpretation kills two birds with one stone, responding to two separate objections made by those who scoff at the written Constitution. First, some mockers say that section 2 of the Fourteenth Amendment is a dead letter because its apportionment penalty has never been enforced via a reduction of a state's House and electoral-college delegation. But in fact, section 2 lives—not through direct enforcement of the apportionment penalty, but through Warren Court right-to-vote case law. Second, other mockers (and sometimes even the same mockers) say that the Court's right-to-vote case law lacks a sound textual basis. Not so. The words "right to vote" appear in section 2 and are not tethered there to any particular basis of disfranchisement, such as race. Section 2 affirms a general right to vote—as does the Warren Court's case law. The answer to each mocking objection is to be found in the other mocking objection.

A DIFFERENT FOURTEENTH AMENDMENT ARGUMENT was also available to the Warren Court justices, although they declined to use it. Recall that the best argument for robust national enforcement of democratic norms against states derives not merely from what the Fourteenth Amendment said, but also from what the amendment *did*. Its very enactment was rich with constitutional meaning and generated a new constitutional principle—or at least a new gloss on an older text. Specifically, the very process of adopting the amendment created a plausible enactment-based precedent for reading the republican-government clause extremely broadly to allow the national government to hold each state to the highest standard of democracy operating anywhere in America.

Granted, the 1860s enactment precedent could be read far more narrowly. The precedent could be understood to apply only in cases of catastrophic democratic breakdown of the sort experienced by the South in the 1850s and 1860s. But history seemed to be replaying itself in the early twentieth century: The South backslid disastrously after Reconstruction, disfranchising large masses of its citizenry and pursuing gross malapportionments that gave rural whites far more than their fair share of power, harkening back to the voting bonuses enjoyed by antebellum plantation belts. Surely it would have been poetic had twentieth-century justices explicitly revived the very "sleeping giant"—the republican-government clause—that had empowered the federal government to remedy deficient democracy in the nineteenth century.[61]

In the 1860s, Congress had been the branch of government awakening the slumbering colossus. A narrow reading of this precedent might suggest that *only* Congress could properly enforce robust democracy norms against states. However, the text of the republican-government clause does not say this. Rather, it says simply that "the United States shall guarantee to every state in this Union a Republican Form of Government," without specifying which branch of the federal government should enforce this guarantee. In any event, Congress in the 1960s was vigorously championing voting rights and explicitly encouraging the Court to do the same. The 1965 Voting Rights Act contained a provision expressly urging the Justice Department to bring lawsuits seeking the judicial invalidation of state poll-tax disfranchisements, especially whenever these disfranchisements excluded blacks disproportionately, as they almost always did. (By the time of the 1966 *Harper* case, only five states retained poll-tax-based voting rules, and all five were states in the former Confederacy with abysmal track records of race discrimination in the voting domain.) Thus, in championing a broad right to vote, the Warren Court was acting in partnership with Congress.[62]

In 1970, Congress enacted a statute entitling young adults to vote in state and federal elections. Under the leadership of Warren's replacement, Chief Justice Warren Burger, the Court struck down the state-election part of this law as beyond the scope of congressional power. Most of the Warren Court holdovers voted to uphold the act in its entirety, but newer appointees took a stricter view of Congress's power to extend the franchise. The American people responded by immediately enacting a constitutional amendment endorsing the original congressional position on young-adult voting. This amendment—the Twenty-sixth overall and the fifth to explicitly affirm "the right to vote"—vividly illustrates that, in the domain of voting rights, Warren Court jurists were generally in tune with the American people, not tuning them out as critics charged.[63]

These last points can be recast in a more textual and less sociological way, as follows. Given the emphatic repetition of the phrase "right to vote" in landmark congressional legislation and in the text of the amended and re-amended Constitution, there arose a strong argument to treat each right-to-vote amendment not as an isolated island, but as part of an archipelago. At a certain point, it became textually, historically, and structurally apt to read each affirmation of a "right to vote" not by negative implication but by positive implication. On this view, certain textually specified bases for disfranchisement were *per se* unconstitutional—race, sex, age (above eighteen)—whereas all other disfranchisements were presumptively suspect as violating a more general right-to-vote principle.[64]

BUT WHY DIDN'T THE COURT build more directly on the clauses that best supported its right-to-vote jurisprudence—namely, section 2 of the Fourteenth Amendment and the republican-government clause?

Part of the answer is precedent. Section 2 had generated no substantial case law that Warren and his brethren could profitably use, and neither had the republican-government clause. In the 1849 case of *Luther v.*

Borden, the Court had declined to decide a dispute between two political camps in Rhode Island, each claiming to be the state's proper republican government. The Court declared that Congress should decide contests such as this by judging the validity of both camps' electoral claims in the course of seating federal representatives and senators. When Congress did just that in Reconstruction, gleefully quoting *Luther* for the proposition that Congress enjoyed broad authority under the republican-government clause, Andrew Johnson forcefully objected—and managed to get himself impeached. Judicial onlookers in that era understood that they, too, should proceed with special care, lest they also provoke congressional retaliation, and the clause thus became an unwelcome guest in Court.[65]

By contrast, pre-Warren judges had used the equal-protection clause on countless occasions involving race questions and other claims of discrimination in the business world and beyond. The equal-protection clause was a familiar tool that felt comfortable in the judicial hand. So the Warren Court justices reached for it, even though it emphatically had not been designed for voting-rights issues.

ALONGSIDE RIGHT-TO-VOTE CASES SUCH AS *Harper* and *Kramer*, the Warren Court in *Baker v. Carr* and *Reynolds v. Sims* famously deployed the equal-protection clause to regulate how citizen votes should be weighted in apportioning legislative seats. In *Baker*, decided in 1962, plaintiffs challenged a Tennessee legislature that had not been reapportioned in over half a century. Vast population disparities existed in the state; some districts had ten times the population of other districts, yet each district had equal weight in the legislature. The apportionment skew generally favored rural districts that were largely white at the expense of urban districts with higher black populations. Plaintiffs asked the justices to strike down this gross malapportionment; defendants countered by claiming that earlier cases had treated apportionment issues as "political questions" beyond the ken of courts.

Writing for the Court, Justice Brennan finessed the precedent problem by noting that earlier cases had been brought under the republican-government clause, whereas the *Baker* plaintiffs were relying on an equal-protection theory that sidestepped all the earlier republican-government precedents counseling judicial restraint. In response to the defendant's arguments that no workable standards could guide judicial oversight of messy issues of apportionment, Brennan again deftly played the precedent game: "Judicial standards under the Equal Protection Clause are well developed and familiar."

Never mind that those standards had been developed in cases having nothing whatsoever to do with voting rights! Thus we see how the particular path charted by the justices in *Baker* was shaped more by the peculiar contingencies of prior precedents than by the first principles of constitutional text and history—principles that argued for reviving the republican-government clause and recognizing that the equal-protection clause was categorically inapplicable to voting rights.

And yet, as with incorporation, the Court got the big picture right. The Constitution really can be read to repudiate gross malapportionments, especially ones that meant that black votes would generally count for far less than white ones. But just as with incorporation, the Court reached this correct result by pursuing the path of least precedential resistance, which meant using the wrong clause to do the work. In both areas, the pivotal opinions—championing selective incorporation under the due-process clause and an equal-protection framework for voting rights—were authored by William Brennan. And in both areas the price to be paid was that what the Court said seemed contemptuous of the written Constitution and its original public understandings, even though what the Court did vindicated the document's deepest commitments.

Two years after *Baker*, the Court executed a midcourse correction in *Reynolds v. Sims. Baker* had signaled that the Court would use traditional equal-protection standards that had developed outside of voting-rights laws to judge apportionment maps. The Court had even pointed to the specific doctrinal standard it intended to use: Apportionment would be upheld so long as it was not "arbitrary and capricious."[66] But soon thereafter, the justices came to understand that a cleaner bright-line rule was needed. Arbitrariness seemed to lie in the eye of the beholder. A district map that one judge might think was pure hodgepodge might to another judge reflect a permissible balance of historical boundaries and multifactored modern realities. Thus, *Reynolds* minted a new rule that every district had to be equally populous. Having chosen for utterly contingent reasons to press the equal-protection clause into service, the Court unsurprisingly ended up concluding that districts had to be...equal.[67]

When the Court dropped this bombshell, more than forty state legislatures rested upon apportionment maps that flunked this strict equality test. On a single day in 1964, the Court in effect declared that almost all state governments were constitutionally defective! Yet today, no one proposes reversing *Reynolds*, because the case required only a one-time adjustment to the system. After the 1970 census, states had relatively clear guidance, thanks to *Reynolds* itself, about how to draw acceptable district lines. And once those new lines were in place, they generated elections whose winners had no particular interest in challenging the basic ground rules that had gotten them elected in the first place. The old politicians whose power bases were destroyed by *Reynolds* might rage and gnash their teeth, but they had to either adapt to the new rules or sink into political oblivion. Thus, a bloodless revolution occurred without a shot fired, and with no realistic ability of the losers to restore the old order that was gone forever.[68]

"Cases...arising under this Constitution"

AND GOOD RIDDANCE TO THAT OLD ORDER! Such has been the general attitude of post-Warren America to the Warren Court revolution. Nearly half a century after Warren's departure, the justices continue to operate on a field of constitutional argumentation mapped by the Warren Court. So do other branches of government, state and federal; so does the legal professoriate; and so does the public at large. Thus, lawyers, judges, politicians, and pundits of all stripes—liberals and conservatives, originalists and living constitutionalists—now take for granted the basic teachings of the Warren Court and argue within the Warren framework.

For example, no one today challenges the rightness of *Brown*. Rather, Americans now wrangle over *Brown*'s meaning, with both liberals and conservatives wrapping themselves in its mantle. Liberals invoke *Brown* for its affirmation of substantive equality, its vision of integration and inclusion, and its recognition of the supreme importance of public education as a gateway to equal citizenship. Conservatives deploy *Brown* and

its companion, *Bolling*, to underscore the general evil of racial classifications, even when such classifications are claimed to benefit blacks and/or
promote integration, and even when Congress itself has endorsed these
race-conscious regimes.[69]

Though some justices may (erroneously) harbor private doubts about
the rightness of incorporation, no member of the Court in the past three
decades has called this basic doctrine into question, even in passing. Every
term, the Court's docket teems with postincorporation cases, and the justices routinely use the Bill of Rights to keep states in line—sometimes to
achieve liberal results (for example, by striking down unusually troubling
death-penalty sentences and laws improperly favoring religion), other
times for more conservative ends (for instance, by invalidating ultra-strict
gun-control ordinances and confiscatory environmental regulations).[70]

Freedom of speech has never had so many friends on the Court as at
present, but conservatives and liberals have different ideas about the deep
meaning of Warren Court landmarks such as *New York Times v. Sullivan*.
Liberals have deployed *Sullivan* to explain why Congress should not be
able to insulate itself from criticism spearheaded by the Legal Service
Corporation, whereas conservatives have invoked the case to explain why
Congress should likewise be barred from regulating campaign finance in
incumbent-protective and speech-limiting ways.* So, too, current church-
state law operates within the boundaries laid down by landmarks such as
Engel and *Abington*. It is hard to imagine that the Court in the foreseeable
future would countenance a return to state-sponsored recitational prayer
in the classroom.

Voting-rights case law follows the same pattern. All justices accept the
basic teachings of *Harper*, *Kramer*, *Baker*, and *Reynolds*, even as conservatives and liberals joust over the meaning and proper application of these
Warren Court classics. Exhibit A is the Court's 2000 decision in *Bush v.
Gore*. In that case, a bare Court majority explicitly invoked *Harper* and

---

* The leading opinion on each topic—*Legal Services Corp. v. Velazquez* in 2001 and *Citizens
United v. Federal Election Commission* in 2010—was authored by the Court's current swing
justice, Anthony Kennedy. When Kennedy was a youth in Sacramento, California, Earl
Warren, who was then the governor of California, was a frequent guest at the Kennedy
home.

Reynolds to end an uneven recount then underway. Dissenters claimed Warren's legacy for themselves, arguing that the recount was actually working to mitigate Election Day inequalities that had disproportionately disfranchised poor and minority voters.[71]

The justices are not the only ones who have enthusiastically embraced Warren-style voting rights. Every state legislature today abides by the one-person, one-vote principle. So does the House of Representatives. The franchise extends to nearly all adult citizens—and Congress's Voting Rights Act of 1965, which closely harmonizes with the Warren Court's voting-rights melody, enjoys iconic status. Virtually no one—no important government official, no major political party, no mass popular movement, no notable school of academic thought, no respected group of public intellectuals or opinion leaders, no venerable think tank—forthrightly proposes a return to the old days of disfranchisement and malapportionment. (Crafty politicos today do attempt to cheat, but they loudly deny that their true purpose is to disfranchise eligible voters and/or to count votes unequally.) Ordinary Americans today broadly claim the rights to vote and to vote equally, believe that these rights are theirs, and embody these beliefs in routine practices that are nearly universally celebrated. These rights have thus become Ninth Amendment rights retained by the people and elements of proper republican government—even if they were not so when the republican-government clause and the Ninth Amendment were written.[72]

The only major post-Warren retrenchment involves the exclusionary rule, which continues to limp along, but with substantial restrictions and amid considerable anti-exclusion rhetoric on the Court. The restrictions and the rhetoric parallel broader skepticism in the American populace about the rule's basic premises.[73]

Today's world of judicial doctrine and general constitutional discourse is thus the world of Earl Warren, Hugo Black, and William Brennan. Their legacy endures.[74]

WHAT LESSONS SHOULD WE DRAW from the Warren Court cases, and from the post-Warren Court's response to this body of case law, about the proper relationship between the document and the doctrine?

Recall the basic lines of critique aimed at Warren and his brethren. First, critics have claimed that Warren Court doctrine mangled the document. But, as we have seen, the landmark cases generally got it right.

Alas, the Warren Court often reached the right result while saying odd things that confounded serious textualists and honest historians. Did "process" really mean substance? Was the key clause of the Fourteenth Amendment's opening section, affirming the privileges and immunities of citizens, irrelevant? What about the "sleeping giant" republican-government clause that had made Reconstruction possible? Did the rights of "persons," as sharply distinguished from those of "citizens," really encompass voting? (Was the Fifteenth Amendment thus unnecessary? The Nineteenth as well?) If equal-protection principles applied against the federal government (à la *Bolling*), and if these principles required equally populous districts even for state senates (as required by *Reynolds*), then why wasn't the United States Senate itself unconstitutional? (If the Court could on one day say that most states had unconstitutional governments that required major restructuring after the next census, what was to stop the Court from saying the same thing the next day about the Senate?) In the face of these questions, the Warren Court failed to explain itself satisfactorily.

The Court's case law was also a moving target, making it difficult for contemporaries to understand the Court's real principles. Thus, *Brown* said not that the pro-Jim-Crow precedent of *Plessy v. Ferguson* was overruled, but only that *Plessy* did not apply in the domain of education. But then the Court promptly issued a series of one-paragraph decisions with absolutely no explanation applying *Brown* beyond education to public beaches and to golf courses, and even to state-segregated buses—that is, to transportation, the very domain that had given rise to *Plessy* (a railroad-segregation case). Similarly, in *Baker* the Court floated one standard for voting, but then in *Reynolds* the Court followed a very different standard—one that had been expressly disavowed by a couple of the concurring opinions in *Baker*.[75]

Consider next another major charge against the Court—that it bristled with activists disrespectful of Congress. Here are the numbers: In Warren's sixteen years as chief, the Court invalidated acts of Congress in twenty-three cases—about the same clip that had prevailed in several earlier periods and a somewhat lower rate than in the ensuing Burger-Rehnquist Court, which slapped down Congress sixty-nine times in thirty-six years. Notably, the Warren Court never struck down a federal civil-rights or voting-rights act of Congress, as had early Courts and as would later Courts.[76]

In fact, the Warren Court generally partnered with Congress, especially in the area of civil rights and voting rights. True, the Court did strike down a federal policy of segregation in *Bolling*, but that policy was the ghost of Congress past. Most members of Congress in 1954 were probably opposed to federal segregation, but reformers could not overcome the intense opposition of a pro-segregation minority that enjoyed considerable congressional seniority and deployed the filibuster aggressively. Eventually, this congressional minority was overcome in the mid-1960s, and it was precisely Congress's landmark legislation under President Lyndon Johnson's leadership that burnished *Brown*'s reputation and increased compliance with *Brown*'s mandate.[77]

Critics have also erred in suggesting that the Warren Court generally defied public opinion. Had the Court done so consistently, its legacy would likely not have lasted. In the long run, old justices leave; new ones arrive; the new ones are picked by presidents (with senatorial oversight); *and the people pick presidents (and senators)*. In fact, many of the Warren cases and ideals are widely celebrated in today's popular culture—*Brown*, of course; the free-speech principles of *New York Times v. Sullivan*; the innocence-protecting vision of *Gideon v. Wainwright*; and the basic *Harper-Reynolds* notion that everyone should vote and have his or her vote counted equally. Most citizens would recoil against any proposal that states should be free to violate the Bill of Rights.

The big exceptions to this general pattern are the exclusionary rule and closely related Warren Court doctrines that freed criminals on what critics called "legal technicalities"—that is, on grounds unrelated to actual innocence or innocence-protecting procedures such as *Gideon*'s right of counsel.

THE GENERAL FIDELITY OF THE WARREN COURT to the deepest ideals of the written Constitution came at the expense of fidelity to precedent. As one tart critic put it, "the list of opinions destroyed by the Warren Court reads like a table of contents from an old constitutional law casebook."[78]

Under Warren, the Court overruled itself in some forty-five cases—more than half as many times as in the entire history of pre-Warren America. Since Warren, the Court has continued this brisk pace of overruling. For example, in the 1970s and 1980s the Court overturned its own precedents in over sixty cases. Here, too, the Warren Court established the basic judicial model that still applies.[79]

If the Warren Court was essentially right in its constitutional vision, and if earlier Courts that had rejected that vision were wrong—if, for example, *Plessy* stank and *Brown* soared; if incorporation was constitutionally correct, whereas earlier cases erred in refusing to protect Americans from state abuses; if Warren and company were right to embrace federal civil-rights and voting-rights laws that earlier justices had improperly condemned or ignored; if *Gideon* deserves to be glorified for overturning an earlier decision that was impoverished even at the moment it was handed down—then what does this say about the Court itself over time?[80]

Just this: For much of its history after John Marshall and before Earl Warren, the Court dishonored both the terse text and the American people, who enacted and who continued to embrace that text. The Warren Court's friends who urged the justices to quit worrying about the written Constitution got it backward. Reflecting the deep wisdom of the American people in their most decisive moments, the written Constitution deserves judicial fidelity, both because it is the law and because, for all its flaws, it has usually been more just than the justices. In the century and a half since the Civil War, the Court whose grand themes most closely tracked the letter and spirit of that text—the Warren Court—is the Court that has quite rightly enjoyed the most enduring influence over both its judicial successors and American society more generally.

ALL OF THIS RAISES SEVERAL HARD QUESTIONS about how precedent should generally operate in a system where ultimate authority resides in the Constitution and not the Court. The next chapter aims to sharpen and answer these questions.

CHAPTER 5

PUTTING PRECEDENT
IN ITS PLACE

America's Doctrinal Constitution

HARRY BLACKMUN (*left*) AND WILLIAM REHNQUIST (*right*) (1976).

In 1973, Justice Blackmun authored the majority opinion in *Roe v. Wade* and Justice Rehnquist dissented. In 1992, the two again squared off, as the Court in *Planned Parenthood v. Casey* pondered not merely the specific scope of abortion rights but also the proper weight to be given to precedent. Although Rehnquist by this time had become chief justice, he once again found himself in dissent.

W HEN NOT SPINNING INTO PARADOX,*self-referential statements often bring matters into sharp focus. So it is with the Constitution, whose various references to itself reveal its essence and situate us to see how and by whom it should be interpreted and executed.

The Preamble proudly proclaims that "this Constitution" was ordained and established in the late 1780s via uniquely democratic popular action. This opening proclamation signals the fundamentality of popular sovereignty and the aptness of interpreting "this Constitution" not merely as a formal written text but also as an embodied popular deed. (Hence Chapter 2's interpretive approach.) Article I explicitly reminds us of Congress's special role in effectuating powers "vested by this Constitution" in other branches. (We shall return to this reminder in Chapter 9.) Article II obliges the president to take a uniquely personal oath to "preserve, protect, and defend the Constitution" to "the best of my Ability"—a poignant reminder that our system depends upon the willingness of specific individuals to pledge fidelity to the grand constitutional project. (We shall study the uniquely personal role of America's first president in Chapter 8 and shall ponder constitutional oaths more generally in Chapter 11.) Article V tells us that each amendment forms "Part of this Constitution." Precisely because each clause, section, article, or amendment is merely a "Part," we must often step back and consider the document as a whole. (This was the animating idea of Chapter 1.) Article V's textually interrelated language that each amendment is "valid to all Intents and Purposes" bids us to heed the intergenerational nature of "this Constitution" and to ponder how later amendments harmonize with the original text and with earlier amendments. (These themes surfaced briefly in Chapter 4 and will resurface in Chapters 6, 7, 10, and 12.) The Ninth Amendment's reference to "the Constitution" confirms yet another critical fact about the document: By its own admission, the text contains a possibly incomplete enumeration of rights. (This fact lay at the heart of Chapter 3.)

As indicated by the parentheticals in the previous paragraph, every

---

* For example, this footnote is a lie.

chapter of this book on America's "unwritten Constitution" can be seen as a response to one or more key clauses in which the written Constitution revealingly refers to itself.

This chapter is no exception. As we shall see, the Constitution features no less than three major references to itself in specific connection with the judiciary. This triad of self-referential clauses will help us answer some basic questions about the proper general relationship between the written document and the judicially crafted—unwritten—doctrine. In particular: Should doctrine ever go beyond the document? Should doctrine ever go against the document? How can we tell the difference between these two situations? When it becomes clear to a court that previous judicial doctrine has mangled the true meaning of the terse text, what should the court do?

Although the three clauses in which the text speaks of itself—of "this Constitution"—in specific relation to judges furnish broad guidance concerning these big questions, the clauses leave various smaller issues underspecified. (For example, what should a lower court judge do if Supreme Court cases from different eras point in different directions? Should a lower court judge pay more heed to what the Supreme Court has said in the past, or to what it would likely say in the case at hand?) In addition to examining what the text has to say about itself in regard to judicial case law, we shall thus once again venture beyond the written Constitution to consider how something outside it—here, judicial precedent—intertwines with the document in a way that draws strength from it and in turn strengthens it.

"this Constitution"

"THIS CONSTITUTION...shall be the supreme Law of the Land." "The Senators and Representatives..., and the Members of the several State Legislatures, and all executive and judicial Officers, both of the United States and of the several States, shall be bound by Oath or Affirmation, to support this Constitution."

With this pair of self-referential sentences in the closing paragraphs of Article VI, the Constitution crowns itself king. Judges and other officials must pledge allegiance to the document. These crowning words recapitulate the Constitution's basic architecture and enactment history. In his 1803 opinion in *Marbury v. Madison*, John Marshall declared that the Constitution's supremacy would have arisen even without specific language because of the very nature of the document as approved by the American people: "Certainly all those who have framed written constitutions contemplate them as forming the fundamental and paramount law of the nation."

Of course, any document can claim to be supreme law. Something more is needed to make it so. That something is social convention. Underpinning the Constitution's self-proclaimed supremacy is the basic social fact that Americans generally accept the document's pretensions. Ordinary citizens view the Constitution as authoritative, and power-wielding officials everywhere take solemn oaths to support the Constitution, as commanded by the document itself. In particular, Supreme Court justices take these oaths, and in the pages of the *United States Reports* the justices regularly pledge allegiance to the document.

It's worth pausing to let all this soak in. Any text that self-referentially asserts its own authority can seem entirely circular to a skeptic standing outside the orb of the text's say-so. If the written Constitution asserted its own legal supremacy, while *U.S. Reports* asserted the supremacy of *U.S. Reports*, we would have two tight circles of seemingly conflicting authority. If, in addition, millions of Americans accepted the Constitution's legal pretensions, while millions of others pledged ultimate allegiance to *U.S. Reports*, then America's situation would be parlous. At the extreme, this is the stuff of civil war. But in fact this is not America's situation. *U.S. Reports* does not assert its supremacy over the written Constitution. On the contrary, case law asserts its own subordination to the Constitution, which in turn envisions the Supreme Court playing an important role in interpreting and implementing the text. In principle, at least, America's supreme law and America's Supreme Court reinforce each other.

BY PROCLAIMING ITSELF AMERICA'S SUPREME LAW, the written Constitution marked itself, and was immediately recognized in actual practice, as decisively different from its predecessor document, the Articles of Confederation. Although the Articles contained several self-referential passages, the document did not even clearly describe itself as a single holistic text as distinct from an assortment of discrete "Articles." More important, the Articles never described themselves as "law," much less as supreme law. Nowhere did the Articles describe the Confederation Congress as a "law maker" or a "legislature"—even as the Confederation document referred a dozen times to state "legislatures" or state "legislative" power. In truth, Congress under the Articles was less a legislature than an international diplomatic and military council, loosely akin to the modern-day United Nations Security Council and the NATO North Atlantic Council.

Perhaps most important of all, the Articles of Confederation contained no language whatsoever obliging any judge in America to take an oath to support the Articles or to treat the Articles as ordinary law in a courtroom, much less as supreme law applicable in courtrooms even against a state government seeking to act in contravention. Moving beyond the text to actual practice, we find that state judges did not pledge allegiance to the Articles; nor did these judges routinely enforce the Articles if their home state legislators—whose enactments were generally recognized as binding law—directed a different outcome.

THE CONSTITUTION'S REFERENCE TO ITSELF as "supreme law" in Article VI textually interlocked with an earlier self-reference in the document's Article III, its Judicial Article. Both articles specified the hierarchy of law in America and did so in virtually identical language. Consider first the text of Article III, which extends the federal judicial power to lawsuits arising under "this Constitution, the Laws of the United States, and Treaties made, or which shall be made, under their Authority." Now, compare Article VI, which specifies America's supreme law as comprising "[t]his Constitution, and the Laws of the United States which shall be made in Pursuance thereof; and all Treaties made, or which shall be made, under the Authority of the United States."

This textual interlock between Articles III and Article VI was no mere coincidence. The Philadelphia framers purposefully chose matching language to make clear that the supreme law of the Constitution would come before federal judges in garden-variety lawsuits, either at trial or on appeal from state court rulings. Thus, the clauses referring to "this Constitution" in Article III and the closing paragraphs of Article VI did not simply float freely in constitutional space; rather, they formed a tight textual triangle, with two vertices positioned in close Article VI proximity and the third located in Article III.[1]

Here is how the triangle worked: Immediately after specifying the hierarchy of America's supreme law, Article VI added that all state judges would "be bound" by this supreme law, notwithstanding any contrary command in a state law or even a state constitution. In the next sentence, Article VI went on to oblige every judge, along with other state and federal officials, to swear a personal oath to support "this Constitution." Lest state judges fail to enforce the Constitution properly—either by willfully defying the Constitution, and thus dishonoring their oaths, or by simply misconstruing the document in good faith—Article III's language stood as a backstop to Article VI, ensuring that federal courts could review and, if necessary, reverse any state court decision involving a dispute about the meaning of "this Constitution." This tight triangle of self-referential provisions thus made clear that the Constitution would operate not merely as law, not merely as supreme law, but also as everyday law—as courtroom law that could be invoked by ordinary parties in ordinary lawsuits.

The Founders understood that grand constitutional questions could arise in the humblest of places. Imagine an agreement between two small farmers, in which Jones promises to sell five acres to Smith. Before money changes hands and the deed is transferred, Jones gets a better offer and wants out of the deal. And he has an argument: Smith has recently arrived from England, and state law forbids foreigners from owning real estate. But Smith has a counterargument: Congress has enacted an immigration law giving all lawful aliens the right to hold real property despite any state rule. But is this federal law constitutional? Does it properly fall within the powers of the federal government? In a suit brought by Smith against Jones, these are the constitutional issues a court would need to address to decide whether Smith or Jones should win the case. These momentous questions, pitting state against federal power, could arise in either state or federal court, at trial or on appeal, and would need to be decided by the court even if neither the state nor the federal government formally intervened as a party to the lawsuit, and indeed even if neither government bothered to file an amicus brief.

But exactly what would and what should happen when the Constitution goes to court in this hypothetical constitutional case, or in any other case "arising under this Constitution"? How do and how should judges turn the document into workable court-law—that is, doctrine?

"The judicial Power"

VIA ITS TIGHT TRIANGLE OF self-referential clauses dealing with "law" and "judges," the Constitution envisioned that in deciding cases arising under the supreme law of the land, judges would offer interpretations of the document's meaning, give reasons for those interpretations, develop mediating principles, and craft implementing frameworks enabling the document to work as in-court law. These interpretations, reasons, principles, and frameworks are what lawyers call *doctrine*.

The basic need for doctrine arises because the terse text is and must remain terse. Concision is constitutionally constitutive. Had America's written Constitution tried to specify every detail, it would have lost its strength as a document that could be voted on in the 1780s—and that could thereafter be read and reread—by ordinary Americans. (This was John Marshall's profound insight in *McCulloch v. Maryland*, where he declared that the Constitution could not properly "partake of the prolixity of a legal code," because if it did, it would "never be understood by the public.") Because terseness is necessary, the document is importantly and intentionally underspecified. Judicial doctrine helps fill in the gaps, translating the Constitution's broad dictates into law that works in court, in keeping with the vision of Article III.

ARTICLE III "JUDICIAL POWER" comprises at least five distinct components.

First, "judicial Power" encompasses the power of constitutional interpretation and exposition—the power of judges to decide for themselves and to declare what the Constitution as law means. As Marshall famously put the point in *Marbury*, "It is emphatically the province and duty of the judicial department to say what the law is."

Marshall here built his church on the solid rock of the word "jurisdiction," a word that explicitly appeared in the Judicial Article as a facet of "judicial Power." Specifically, the Judicial Article vested "judicial Power" in federal courts; declared that this very same "judicial Power" had to extend to all legal and equitable cases arising under "this Constitution"; and then specified that the Supreme Court would generally have "appellate Jurisdiction" in these cases. Thus, "judicial Power" encompassed "Jurisdiction." "Jurisdiction" in turn encompassed the power to speak the law. As Alexander Hamilton, writing as Publius, reminded readers in *The Federalist* No. 81, the very word "jurisdiction" is "a compound of JUS and DICTO, juris, dictio, or a speaking or pronouncing of the law." Accordingly, Article III authorized any federal court hearing *Smith v. Jones* to declare its own answer to the relevant constitutional questions raised by the case.

A second and hugely significant component of "judicial Power" is the power not merely to interpret and declare the Constitution's meaning, but to implement the Constitution. This component involves taking the abstract meanings of the Constitution and making them work as actual rules of decision in the courtroom itself and in the real world beyond the courtroom. For example, in *Smith v. Jones*, what specific test should a court use to decide how broadly to construe the scope of congressional power under the Constitution? Who should bear the burden of proving what in the courtroom? What kind of evidence should count in favor of or against various factual assertions made in court? In order to decide the case at hand, a court will typically need to develop a set of tools for its own use and for the use of lawyers, litigants, and lower courts. These tools translate the core meanings of the Constitution into sub-rules, formulas, and tests that can be applied in the courtroom. Among other things, these various sub-rules and tests are necessary so that a court may go beyond abstract opining on the meaning of the Constitution and actually decide the case at hand.[2]

This need to decide also brings into view a third component of "judicial Power"—the power to adjudicate a proper constitutional case and to award a binding judgment to the prevailing party. In our hypothetical, a federal court would have the power to rule in favor of either Smith or Jones and to order that the disputed property be disposed of accordingly. So long as a lawsuit is properly before a federal court—that is, so long as the court has "jurisdiction" in the broadest sense of the word, jurisdiction as provided for in the Judicial Article and appropriate implementing legislation—the court's rulings must be respected by private citizens and enforced by public officials, even if those citizens and officials believe (quite plausibly or even correctly from a God's-eye point of view) that the court has erred and the wrong party has won. In this sense, jurisdiction and "judicial Power" encompass the judiciary's right to be wrong, its right to err and nevertheless have that error be honored as the law of the case. This is what lawyers call *res judicata*, an "adjudicated thing," the law governing the parties to the case. Thus, a federal court hearing *Smith v. Jones* could definitively determine the status of the disputed acreage between these two men.[3]

Beyond a court's legal authority to bind the parties in the case at hand, there exists a fourth component of "judicial Power," encompassing the authority to lay down a decisional precedent that will be entitled to a certain amount of legal weight in later cases. This is what lawyers call *stare decisis*. But how much weight should precedent carry? What kind of weight? Alongside the power to set precedents for the future, the judiciary also has the power to overturn past precedents. When and how should it exercise this power? We shall return to these momentous questions at the conclusion of this chapter.

Fifth and finally, the "judicial Power" encompasses authority to fashion traditional judicial remedies for the violations of legal rights. In our hypothetical, if a court rules for Smith, it will need to decide whether Smith should receive the land itself or merely money damages. If the latter, the court must also decide whether the damages should aim simply to compensate Smith for his loss or also to penalize Jones for his breach.

Although the written Constitution says little about remedies, a powerful regulatory ideal and background legal principle (rather like the precept that no man should be a judge in his own case) prevailed at the Founding: For every legal right there should be a judicial remedy. Just as Blackstone's *Commentaries* had highlighted the *nemo judex in causa sua* principle, so, too, the *Commentaries* emphasized the remedial imperative: "[I]t is a general and indisputable [!] rule, that where there is a legal right, there is also a legal remedy, by suit or action at law, whenever that right is invaded." Several Revolutionary-era state constitutions featured similar language in their bills of rights, and Madison/Publius invoked the principle—"But a right implies a remedy"—in a passage whose very casualness indicated the uncontroversial nature of the proposition.[4]

In *Marbury v. Madison*, Marshall waxed eloquent on the point. He began as follows: "The very essence of civil liberty certainly consists in the right of every individual to claim the protection of the laws, whenever he receives an injury. One of the first duties of government is to afford him that protection." After quoting Blackstone's "indisputable" rule and invoking additional language from the *Commentaries*, Marshall concluded with a flourish: "The government of the United States has been emphatically termed a government of laws, and not of men. It will certainly cease to deserve this high appellation, if the laws furnish no remedy for the violation of a vested legal right."

In short, the general authority of federal judges to fashion proper judicial remedies is a core feature of America's Constitution, whether we locate this remedial authority of judges (and the corresponding right of litigants to judicial redress) in the explicit phrase "judicial Power" or treat it as an implicit element of our unwritten Constitution in the spirit of Blackstone and the Ninth Amendment.

"Law and Equity"

WITH THIS FIVE-PART FRAMEWORK in place, let us now revisit the major Warren Court decisions canvassed in the previous chapter. Because these famous decisions have laid the groundwork for so much of modern constitutional jurisprudence, they furnish a particularly good assortment of case studies to illustrate the general usefulness of our five-part framework and the kind of constitutional insights it makes possible. Within each of the big areas addressed by the Warren Court—segregation, incorporation, free speech, religious freedom, criminal procedure, and voting rights—we shall see that some of the justices' key moves reflected considerations beyond pure constitutional interpretation. Questions of practical implementation and precedent management also figured prominently in these domains, as did subtle issues of remedial effectiveness.

BROWN AND *BOLLING* CORRECTLY UNDERSTOOD and honored the document's core meaning. Equal meant equal, and citizenship meant citizenship. Thus, on May 17, 1954, the Court read the Constitution aright and said what the law was. As cases about constitutional interpretation—about the meaning of the written Constitution and about the judiciary's province and duty of law declaration—*Brown* and *Bolling* were thus easy as pie.

The *Brown* opinion also famously said that, at least in the field of education, separate was "inherently unequal." Inherently? If understood as a claim about the meaning of the Constitution, this sentence might seem confused. Separate does not mean "unequal" in any obvious dictionary sense. Nor did the Reconstruction Republicans believe that separate was always and everywhere unequal as a matter of logic.

But if *Brown*'s famous sentence is understood as an effort to *implement* rather than simply to *interpret* the Constitution, the sentence makes perfect sense. In order to make the equality rule—the Constitution's true meaning—effective in courtrooms and in the world beyond courtrooms, the Supreme Court had to fashion implementing sub-rules to guide lawyers, lower courts (both state and federal), school administrators, state legislators, and so on. One possible implementing sub-rule could have simply required black plaintiffs in each and every case to prove that separate was unequal on the facts at hand. But given that separate was almost always unequal in the real world of 1954, would this litigation burden have been fair? Would this sub-rule have vindicated the Blackstone/*Marbury* remedial imperative? After all, this sub-rule would have imposed serious and not-fully-compensable litigation costs and time delays on those who, at the end of the day, were highly likely to prevail in court based on the actual history and practice of Jim Crow. This sub-rule would also have perversely encouraged state officials to continue to sham and wink and frustrate the real meaning of the Constitution. And would such a sub-rule have given strong guidance and cover to lower courts—especially state courts operating under pressure from segregationist state lawmakers?

The terse text did not—and could not realistically be expected to—answer all these second-order issues about how to implement the equality norm in the particular milieu of mid-twentieth-century Jim Crow. The written Constitution simply laid down the civil-equality principle and entrusted courts (among others) with the task of making that principle real in court and on the ground as the genuine law of *the land*. The rule announced on May 17, 1954—that de jure segregation would be presumed unequal in light of the actual history of Jim Crow—was a thoroughly proper way for the Court to discharge its duty of constitutional implementation.

Why, we might wonder, did *Brown* limit its ruling to the field of education? As a matter of constitutional meaning, the Court was right to note that the Fourteenth Amendment equality mandate applied only over a limited domain. (Recall, for example, that the words and the original public meaning of section 1 of the amendment did not apply to political rights, such as voting or jury service.) But nothing in the Fourteenth Amendment's idea of equal citizenship distinguished between a racial caste system in public schools, on the one hand, and a racial caste system regarding public beaches or public transportation, on the other.

The *Brown* Court nevertheless dealt only with education: "*Plessy v. Ferguson* involv[ed] not education but transportation....[In 1950] the Court expressly reserved decision on the question whether *Plessy* v. *Ferguson* should be held inapplicable to public education. In the instant cases, that question is directly presented....We conclude that *in the field of public education* the doctrine of 'separate but equal' has no place."[5]

One case at a time is an appropriate way for "judicial Power" to operate. It would also have been permissible for the *Brown* Court to have fashioned a more sweeping opinion that made clear that the Court's core idea—that Jim Crow was simply not equal—of course applied outside education as well. Alongside the cautious sensibility that judges may and often should simply decide one case at a time, there exists a background first principle—one that went without saying for the Founders and was implicit in the words "judicial Power"—that judges must decide like cases alike. If a caste system in transportation was really no different from a caste system in education, then the same constitutional rule that applied in one domain applied as well in the other.

Having opened the door in *Brown* to the possibility that education might be unlike transportation, the Warren Court correctly closed that door in a 1956 case involving Alabama buses, *Gayle v. Browder*. But the *Gayle* Court acted in a two-sentence ruling that offered no real explanation. The first sentence simply announced the result ending bus segregation, and the second sentence merely cited *Brown* and two post-*Brown* cases (neither of which involved transportation). This was problematic. Judicial doctrine and judicial power require judges to offer carefully reasoned explanations for their rulings. Having opted to write a 1954 *Brown* opinion that did not simply say "equality, equality, equality," but that seemed to

qualify the scope of the Court's holding by also saying "education, education, education," the Warren Court over the next several years failed in its
declaratory and implementational tasks of making crystal clear to lawyers,
lower courts, school administrators, state legislators, and the rest of the
citizenry what the legally operative principles truly were and why.[6]

Two factors, one backward-looking and one forward-looking, explain
this lapse. First, had the Court in 1954 simply said "equality, equality, equality" in all realms of public citizenship (political rights excepted), the justices would have had to make clear that the Court had been wrong from
day one in *Plessy*. In addition to striking down in a single day hundreds if
not thousands of federal, state, and local segregation statutes, ordinances,
and policies, the Court would have had to openly overturn its own high-
profile precedent. As shall become clearer later in this chapter, the Court
has at times been loath to admit its own past errors. Although most people
today remember *Brown* as having formally overturned *Plessy*, in fact the
Court did no such thing in May 1954. The overruling of *Plessy* became
evident only in retrospect (in the cryptic *Gayle* case).

Second, the *Brown* justices knew that massive remedial and implementational challenges lay ahead in making the Court's ruling and the underlying constitutional equality principle truly the law of the land on the
ground. Had the Court in 1954 simply said "equality, equality, equality,"
it would have been clear that state laws prohibiting interracial marriage
were also unconstitutional. This is indeed what the Constitution, properly
read, means. Equal means equal, and legally imposed racial separation in
this domain was not truly equal. In the 1967 case of *Loving v. Virginia*, the
Court said just that, in an opinion authored by Warren himself.

But when Warren said this in June 1967—at the dawn of the now-famous
"summer of love"—bans on interracial marriages were relatively rare and
were even more rarely enforced with vigor and efficacy. By 1967, Congress
and President Lyndon Johnson had jumped into the fray in full support
of *Brown*'s vision, via landmark civil rights and voting rights laws. By 1967,
blacks, who had long been disfranchised in massive numbers in some parts
of the South, were finally being allowed to vote, and could count on fair
apportionment rules after the next census. And by 1967, Martin Luther
King Jr. had delivered his iconic speech celebrating an interracial dream

of whites and blacks joining hands. America had indeed witnessed and celebrated the interracial joining of hands that was visible at the Lincoln Memorial at the very moment King spoke these words.

In 1954, however, resistance to interracial dating was intense, widespread, and politically powerful. Indeed, this resistance underlay much of Jim Crow in education: Many white parents did not want their fair-skinned girls to go to integrated schools where they might socialize (and perhaps become romantically involved) with dark-skinned boys. Had Earl Warren written *Brown* in a manner that clearly entailed the invalidity of miscegenation laws, he would have thereby made the task of ensuring actual compliance with *Brown* all the harder in the difficult days ahead. If the judicial province and duty is not merely to say what the law is, but also to make the law real, then *Brown's* narrowness becomes easier to justify.

A SIMILAR STORY CAN BE TOLD about the Warren Court's crusade to apply the Bill of Rights against the states. Here, too, the Court aced the big issue of constitutional meaning. Here, too, implementation issues complicated matters.

The idea of applying all or virtually all of the Bill of Rights against the states was at the very heart of the Fourteenth Amendment's text as understood by the men who drafted and ratified it in the 1860s. The challenge facing the justices was how best to fashion plausible second-order sub-rules to implement the amendment's central meaning. The text and history did not dictate one and only one way of "incorporating" fundamental rights. As we saw earlier, at least five different pathways to incorporation plausibly presented themselves. Had the Warren Court rejected all five approaches—as indeed the Court did for much of the pre-Warren era—then the justices would deserve our scorn for their implementational faithlessness and their interpretational stupidity. But when a court chooses one workable approach among the handful of approaches that careful and honest interpretation leave open to it, that court is properly discharging its implementational power and duty.

As with its Jim Crow case law, the most telling criticism of the Warren Court's incorporation case law is that the justices failed to explain and expound with sufficient care the relevant constitutional principles. Just as the Court did not make *Brown*'s reach crystal clear until the 1967 miscegenation case, so, too, the Warren Court failed to acknowledge the full sweep of incorporation. Not until decades after Warren's departure did the justices rule, in the 2010 case of *McDonald v. Chicago*, that the same ground rules that applied to First Amendment rights, Fourth Amendment rights, most Fifth Amendment rights, Sixth Amendment rights, and Eighth Amendment rights also applied to Second Amendment rights. (Fully a half-century after the incorporation project took flight, America is still waiting to hear what the Court has to say about Fifth Amendment grand-jury rights and Seventh Amendment rights.)

THE BASIC DISTINCTION between judicial interpretation and judicial implementation also brings the issues raised by *New York Times v. Sullivan* into sharp focus. The state of Alabama was trying to use its civil libel law to squelch political discourse in general and criticism of Alabama officialdom's race policies in particular. The state had imposed crushing liability—half a million dollars of punitive damages—upon *The New York Times* for having published a scathing political ad about state officials. Alabama law, however, purported to punish the *Times* not for the opinions expressed in the ad but for the ad's factual inaccuracies. This was a sham. The ad's slight misstatements of fact were trivial. (For example, the ad had criticized state authorities for having suppressed peaceful civil rights protesters, but had mistakenly asserted that the protestors had sung "My Country 'Tis of Thee." In fact, they had sung the national anthem.)

In striking down Alabama's gambit, the *Times* Court got the big issue of constitutional meaning absolutely right: The Constitution clearly entitles Americans to freely express their political opinions and to harshly criticize government servants in the process. The Sedition Act of 1798 had mocked this basic right, and Alabama's libel law eerily echoed this old act, which had been long discredited in the court of American history and public opinion. Like Alabama libel law, the 1798 act had purported to target only "false" statements, but both laws had operated to stifle core expressions of political opinion. (Under both legal regimes, disparaging remarks were typically presumed false, malicious, and injurious—a series of galloping presumptions that threatened free political discourse.)

Equipped with a sound understanding of the Constitution's meaning, the *Times* Court proceeded to fashion a series of implementing rules to ensure robust political discourse. Although the Constitution does not value false assertions as such, some falsity needs to be protected as a practical matter. In *Sullivan*'s words, truly free speech needs "breathing space." Without this space, citizens might hesitate to speak, chilled by the prospect of punishment or liability for innocent mistakes of fact that invariably pepper public discourse in a well-functioning democracy—a prospect exemplified by the facts of *Sullivan* itself and by America's earlier experience under the Sedition Act.

Thus, *Sullivan* held that no libel judgment could issue unless a publisher had acted with "actual malice" by having knowingly propagated a falsehood—having flat-out lied—or by having displayed a reckless disregard for the actual truth of the matter. Plaintiffs would need to show this "actual malice" by evidence possessing a "convincing clarity," and the *Sullivan* Court suggested that judges would keep juries on an especially tight leash to ensure that the evidence at trial met this heightened standard. Also, no plaintiff could prevail without evidence that he was the specific target of the libel. (In *Sullivan*, the ad had not named any Alabama official in particular, but had sweepingly condemned the oppressive state power structure in general.) These rules would apply to all libel suits brought by "a public official against critics of his official conduct." Later cases expanded *Sullivan* to encompass all "public figures," a category that at its core included all notable public servants and presumably all public office seekers, and that swept in other persons insofar as their activities were matters of legitimate public concern and commentary.[7]

Almost none of these specific sub-rules could be found in or logically deduced from the written Constitution. These were not rules of constitutional meaning; they were sub-rules of constitutional implementation. As an ensemble, they formed one sensible way, albeit not the only imaginable way, of ensuring that freedom of expression would actually prevail in court and on the ground. As such, this cluster of doctrinal rules fell squarely within the proper "judicial Power" of the Supreme Court.

Precisely because several of *Sullivan*'s doctrinal sub-rules were merely implementational, other branches of government may today properly propose alternative structures that might be equally effective or even more effective in protecting free expression overall, though less protective in certain implementational details. Imagine, for example, a congressional statute that tightly caps punitive damages for libel (thereby providing more financial protection for printers), but allows persons falsely defamed to recover token money damages and declaratory judgments that disparaging publications are false without having to prove actual printer malice (thereby providing more reputational vindication for libel victims). Had the Court itself tried to announce such rules for federal libel suits, perhaps the justices' efforts to restrain jury damages might have set off Seventh Amendment alarm bells about judges improperly limiting juries. More generally, the Court might have worried that it was democratically unseemly for unelected judges to limit the domain of juries. Congress, however, has long been understood to have broad legal authority to limit juries in the process of creating new "equitable" statutory systems replacing traditional common-law causes of action; elected members of Congress also enjoy a stronger democratic mandate to limit jury power. Thus, even though our hypothetical congressional statute in some ways would offer publishers less than *Sullivan* does, if Congress actually were to enact such a law the Court should not reject it out of hand, if indeed it would protect the core of the First Amendment as well as—or perhaps even better than—the Court was able to do acting purely on its own steam in *Sullivan*.

IN THE REALM OF RELIGIOUS RIGHTS, the Warren Court once again aced the question of constitutional meaning—affirming full religious liberty and equality against both state and federal officials—and then sensibly fashioned implementing rules to make that meaning a reality. Alas, post-Warren cases went further, laying down troubling doctrinal sub-rules organized around a poorly defined metaphor of "separation of church and state." Some of these sub-rules led to outlandish results. More recent cases have properly trimmed back some of these sub-rules, thereby returning America to the more sensible approach of the Warren Court itself.[8]

Recall that in two early 1960s cases, *Engel v. Vitale* and *Abington v. Schempp*, the Warren Court struck down organized worship services in the public schools in situations where public employees had either composed or blessed an official government prayer. In the 1985 case of *Wallace v. Jaffree*, by contrast, the post-Warren Court repeatedly invoked *Engel* and *Abington* to strike down a state law mandating a moment of classroom silence that enabled students to pray individually or simply to engage in quiet contemplation. Unlike the governments in *Engel* and *Abington*, however, the state in *Wallace* had neither written nor endorsed any kind of prayer whatsoever. Nor had the state separated children along religious lines or forced any student to opt out or stand apart. Agnostic children were free to sit at their desks in this silent moment and think about baseball. More subversive kids were even free to silently indulge atheist, heretical, or antigovernment thoughts.

In principle, a moment of silence was one way to communicate that the public schools aimed to be religiously neutral, not antireligious—to reach out to include those who had experienced *Engel* and *Abington* as assaults on and insults to their religious identities. The silent moment was meant to accommodate observance in a manner that was nevertheless wholly neutral and nonsegregative.

Some of the *Wallace* Court's hostility to moments of silence may be explained by understandable—though not admirable—institutional defensiveness. *Engel* and *Abington* provoked massive popular backlash, and in many places outright defiance of the Court's rulings. The Court responded by defending its turf, and in the process, overreacting.

More generally, post–Warren Court religion law subtly shifted away from religious equality toward separation as an organizing concept. The separation concept had been visible even before the Warren Court. The 1947 school-bus case, *Everson v. Board of Education*, had famously invoked Jefferson's 1802 metaphor of "a wall of separation" between church and state. This metaphor became an increasingly common trope in later opinions, appearing in roughly twenty Court cases in the second half of the twentieth century. But "separation" was an ambiguous concept, susceptible to profound misinterpretation and perversion of the proper principles at stake.[9]

Consider the "separation of powers." One version of this separation simply means that election to one branch of government does not automatically entitle the winner to hold a position in a different branch of government. Thus, in America—unlike England—the person elected to lead the legislature does not thereby become the chief executive. But a stronger version of separation of powers is also easily imaginable: Membership in one branch of government *disqualifies* the member from holding a position in a different branch of government. This, too, is part of the American Constitution: The incompatibility clause of Article I, section 6, prohibits any sitting member of Congress from holding a federal executive or judicial office.

Now consider analogous issues raised by the so-called "wall of separation between church and state." Under a sensibly modest version of this metaphor, no church official would automatically be entitled to sit in government. Thus, in America—unlike England—an Anglican archbishop is not automatically a member of any official legislative body, such as the "Lords Spiritual." But under a stricter version of separation, the fact that a person is a clergyman might actually disqualify him for a position in government.

Jefferson himself at times leaned in this anticlerical direction, and most states in the Founding era did indeed embrace formal disqualifications of clergymen. However, the modern Court has made clear (in a unanimous 1978 decision, *McDaniel v. Paty*) that such discrimination against religious officials is unconstitutional—a profound violation of proper principles of religious liberty and equality.

But so long as some justices use the metaphor of separation as their polestar, it becomes easier to think that rules like the one excluding the clergy are permissible, and perhaps even required, rather than being obvious affronts to America's post-Reconstruction Constitution of liberty and equality for all.

To return to the school system for a handy hypothetical, suppose that the government decides to give every child a computer so that, truly, no child will be left behind. In this hypothetical government program, every child attending a public school receives this computer, as does every child who attends a private school that is either aggressively secular or merely religiously indifferent. But what about children who attend private religious schools—schools whose curricula are otherwise comparable to the private nonreligious schools but that also add religion to the educational experience? *May* children at such schools receive the computers? *Must* they?

Anyone whose organizing metaphor is separation might be inclined to answer no to both questions. Thus, several post–Warren Court cases from the mid-1970s, when talk of Jefferson's wall reached its peak on the Court, actually held that this sort of discrimination against religious schools was not merely constitutionally permissible but constitutionally required. Fortunately, over the past decade the Court has returned to its senses, overruled several of these cases, and begun to see and say clearly that of course private religious schools should not be treated worse than otherwise comparable private nonreligious schools. The schools should be treated equally, as should the children. So long as a private school meets proper educational standards for teaching the basic 3 Rs and so on, it is simply none of the government's business whether religion is taught pervasively or in a special part of the curriculum or whether the kids are praying in school-sponsored ways.[10]

The proper touchstones are religious liberty and equality, not separation as such. If everyone else is receiving a government benefit, then so must religious folk—not because they are religious but regardless of whether they are religious. A private secular academy should never lose its government benefits merely because it later decides to add a daily prayer to its classroom regimen. Such a tax on prayer—for that is what a funding cutoff would be—would constitute an obvious violation of the ideals of liberty and equality at the heart of the Fourteenth Amendment.

To see the same point in the context of public-school education—the context that generated *Brown, Bolling, Engel,* and *Abington*—note that while governments may not properly organize prayer, *private citizens may.* If a student-organized and student-run stamp club is allowed to meet in a classroom after school, as is a student chess club, a student baseball-card club, and any other student club, then a student-organized and student-run Bible study must be allowed equal access. The key concept is not that religion must in every way be walled out of and separated from school space, but rather that religious students must be treated equally with all others. In short, the watchword is not "separate"—but "equal."

THE PROBLEM WITH THE POST-WARREN COURT'S doctrine governing church and state was not that various sub-rules were prophylactic and overprotective. As we have seen, the same could be said of *Brown*'s sub-rule that de jure segregation would be presumed unequal and improper; of *Sullivan*'s ensemble of sub-rules designed to give breathing space to free speech; and perhaps even of the virtually irrebuttable presumption in the incorporation cases that any right in the Bill of Rights was *ipso facto* fundamental.[11]

But in these other areas, arguable overprotection of core rights did not threaten any counterbalancing citizen rights. Even had *Sullivan* doomed all libel law, the Constitution does not require that libel law exist; a state would be free to eliminate all libel law. Also, in the areas of segregation, expression, and incorporation, the Court's opinions signaled that the justices understood the Constitution's central meaning and were thus building implementational rules on a sound interpretational foundation.

The post-Warren Court's deployment of separationist doctrine regarding church and state was different. At times, the Court seemed to misread the Constitution's main meaning and to elaborate a vision of separation for its own sake rather than a vision of religious freedom and equality. Because of the justices' misunderstanding of constitutional meaning and/or confusion about the proper relationship between interpretation and implementation, the post-Warren Court actually threatened Americans' right to freely exercise their religion—a right expressly guaranteed by the Constitution. When Court rulings began to suggest that the Constitution would permit or even require that private religious schools be treated worse than otherwise identical private nonreligious schools, it became clear that the justices had veered off course. Implementation must subserve—not subvert—the core meaning of the written Constitution.

MODERN CRIMINAL-PROCEDURE CASES—in particular, exclusionary-rule cases—have also veered off course, and here, the decisive wrong turns occurred on Earl Warren's watch.

The problem with the exclusionary rule is not that it overprotects the core right to some degree. To repeat, some prophylactic overprotection in implementation of a constitutional right is necessary and proper. But the exclusionary rule is wildly out of sync with the relevant constitutional principles. On reflection, we should not be surprised by this fact, because the rule was not born as a traditional and proportionate judicial remedy—

it was always and remains today an outlandish judicial remedy bearing no proper relationship to the scope of the violation. The Fourth Amendment is about the violation of actual privacy and property that occurs during a search or seizure. Whether evidence of criminality is found in such a violation is wholly irrelevant. A proper remedy would address the rights of innocents. It would punish flagrant unconstitutionality more severely than mere error. It would protect against police brutality and governmental oppression even if such misconduct had no causal connection to a search for criminal evidence. The Warren Court exclusionary rule did none of these things.[12]

Exclusion in America began not as a remedy rule, but rather as a rule about constitutional meaning—a rule deriving from a judicial interpretation that saw the Fourth Amendment and the Fifth Amendment self-incrimination clause as intimately interrelated. On this view, when a court excluded a defendant's diary in a criminal case, the judge was not primarily remedying an antecedent Fourth Amendment violation that had occurred when the government had grabbed the diary. Rather, the judge was also—and more importantly—preventing the Fourth-Fifth Amendment violation about to occur in his own courtrooms were the diary to be read to the jury. Though it was a principled interpretation of the Constitution's meaning, in the end this Fourth-Fifth-fusion view was demonstrably incorrect—indeed, preposterous—once the idea metastasized beyond diaries and personal papers to include stolen goods, murder weapons, and the like. Ever since the Court itself made that point about constitutional meaning clear in the 1966 blood-test case of *Schmerber v. California*, the exclusionary rule has been left without a principled legal leg—interpretational, implementational, or remedial—to stand on. Yet it still stands, in the name of *stare decisis*.

But why should a shaky rule that has lost its constitutional footing be perpetuated? We shall return to this key question in the concluding pages of this chapter.

CONSIDER, FINALLY, THE WARREN COURT'S revolutionary one-person-one-vote rule. Here, too, we see arguable overprotection at work, at least initially. If the true constitutional rule governing voting rights derived from the equal-protection clause, then the idea that each vote had to have exactly equal weight with every other would follow naturally. But this way of justifying *Reynolds* sits atop a faulty interpretive foundation. The equal-protection clause as originally written and understood was categorically inapplicable to voting. *Baker* and *Reynolds* were really republican-government-clause cases masquerading in equal-protection clothing.

Nevertheless, one-person, one-vote can be justified as a legitimate implementational device. True, the *Reynolds* rule arguably overprotected the constitutional principle at stake, but only after decades of judicial neglect and underprotection. Without some limit on malapportionment, a person's right to cast a vote could be rendered utterly meaningless. For example, in a state composed of one hundred districts, could the government create fifty-one "rotten boroughs"—each with a single voter (say, the fifty-one most senior leaders of the incumbent party)—and relegate all other voters in the state to the remaining forty-nine districts? If this goes too far (and it surely does), and if Tennessee had surely gone too far in *Baker*, then where and how should judges draw the line in a principled way? *Whatever its other flaws, the one-person-one-vote rule was a clean and workable implementational device.[13]

Had the justices opted to openly rely upon the republican-government clause, several alternative sub-rules might have plausibly presented themselves. First, the Court could have chosen an approach akin to today's Eighth Amendment jurisprudence, using the actual practice of the fifty states as a benchmark and proclaiming state practices that fell outside the mainstream to be unrepublican by contemporary standards. Today, applying this alternative would collapse into *Reynolds*, since all states now meet the one-person-one-vote standard. Even if states were now told that they are henceforth free to reject *Reynolds*, most would probably decline to do

---

* The federal Constitution's structure did not raise identical concerns. Even though the Senate sharply deviated from the one-person-one-vote ideal, its apportionment rules were nevertheless entrenched in a way that limited the imaginable damage. State apportionment rules, by contrast, were far more fluid and thus more in need of some additional constitutional constraint. As for federal House elections, Article I, section 2, prevented gross interstate malapportionment. After *Baker* but before *Reynolds*, the Warren Court held, in the 1964 case of *Wesberry v. Sanders*, that congressional districts within a state must be equipopulous. For more on *Wesberry*, see p. 554, n. 13.

so, because the voters themselves in most jurisdictions—along with lead-ing politicians and opinion leaders—have come to embrace the idea of equally populous districts as a basic feature of political fairness.

Another imaginable alternative in 1964 would have been to allow voters in any given state, by a statewide initiative or referendum that itself would treat all voters equally, to authorize district maps that deviated from one-person, one-vote. If, at least once every census cycle, a state's electorate had to bless any deviation from districting equality, there would likely be no systematic frustration of majority rule violative of the deep principle underlying the republican-government clause.

But what about minority rights? Suppose a 55 percent statewide ma-jority of whites approved a malapportioned statewide map giving whites majorities in 90 percent of the unevenly sized districts. Such maps might violate the spirit of the Fifteenth Amendment, but prior to *Reynolds* that amendment had proved hard for judges to enforce on their own when confronting massive state disobedience. Also, unless the Court in 1964 had decreed that every district map had to be blessed by a statewide popu-lar vote—an approach that would have obliged every state to institute a referendum or initiative process—there needed to be a doctrinal sub-rule specifying when such a popular vote would be required. Presumably the answer to this question would have been that a statewide popular vote would be needed only when a state was malapportioned. But when was that? When it departed from one-person, one-vote, of course! Our envi-sioned referendum rule was thus not a sharply distinct alternative to one-person, one-vote, but merely a softer variant that would have treated vio-lations of one-person, one-vote as presumptively unconstitutional rather than unconstitutional per se.

If some sub-rules about the permissible size of voting districts were nec-essary in order to safeguard the basic right to vote, why weren't sub-rules about the permissible shape of voting districts also necessary? In other words, once the justices decided to protect the basic right to vote in cases such as *Harper v. Virginia* and *Kramer v. Union Free School District*, and to buttress those right-to-vote rulings in the antimalapportionment cas-es of *Baker v. Carr* and *Reynolds v. Sims*, why did the Court stop there? Why didn't the justices take the additional step of regulating political "gerrymandering"—that is, the art of drawing district lines so as to favor the political group drawing the lines?

In *Reynolds*, Chief Justice Warren declared that "in a society ostensibly grounded on representative government, it would seem reasonable that a majority of the people of a State could elect a majority of that State's legislators....Since legislatures are responsible for enacting laws by which all citizens are to be governed, they should be bodies which are collectively responsive to the popular will." Alas, *Reynolds*'s simple requirement that districts be of equal size fell short of guaranteeing that a majority of statewide voters would in fact control a majority within the legislature itself. Theoretically, a statewide minority faction supported by less than 26 percent of the voters could control the state legislature by winning a bare majority of ingeniously drawn districts and winning each district by a bare majority.

If *Reynolds* alone did not guarantee republican-government-style majority rule, neither did it ensure minority rights. Even in a state that was *Reynolds*-compliant, a minority group comprising 45 percent of the statewide vote could lose every single district, 55 percent to 45 percent, if each district were cleverly drawn so as to be a microcosm of the state as a whole.

Despite these problems, the Court was wise to stop where it did. Each of the four most salient subspecies of gerrymandering—racial gerrymandering, bipartisan gerrymandering, one-party gerrymandering, and incumbent-protective gerrymandering—implicated a unique cluster of constitutional considerations, and none of these clusters supported unilateral judicial intervention.

First, when governments have tried to fashion insidious district lines to disadvantage *racial* minorities, the modern Court has not faced a pressing need to develop its own implementational sub-rules based directly on the Fifteenth Amendment. Congress has already done much of the heavy lifting, via the 1965 Voting Rights Act and a series of subsequent statutory amendments. Enacted pursuant to Congress's explicit enforcement authority under the Reconstruction Amendments, this landmark law has created an assortment of effective statutory tools—some to be wielded by courts, others by the Justice Department—to combat laws and practices that improperly dilute the voting power of racial minorities. This subspecies of gerrymandering highlights an important lesson: Federal courts are not the only branch of government tasked with faithful implementation of the Constitution; nor are courts always the branch best suited to address every constitutional issue.

Consider next the category of *bipartisan* gerrymanders. In jurisdictions where the two major parties, Republicans and Democrats, have worked together to draw district lines that favor these two parties and freeze out all third parties, these bipartisan "collusions" have generally not violated the Constitution. Rightly read, the Constitution in fact sanctions a self-perpetuating and self-stabilizing two-party system. No elaborate Court doctrine is called for here, because the practice is constitutionally proper.[14]

For different reasons, *partisan* gerrymandering designed to advantage one of the two major parties at the other party's expense also calls for judicial restraint. To begin with, any judicial intervention would be messy in the extreme. Few, if any, easy, workable, and principled sub-rules present themselves as plausible scripts for a large judicial role to neutralize partisanship in the drawing of district lines.

By contrast, in pure right-to-vote cases, such as *Harper* and *Kramer*, the basic framework was easy enough to construct: All adult-citizen, non-felon residents are presumptively eligible voters. This is the group textually identified by section 2 of the Fourteenth Amendment, as updated by the later Woman and Youth Suffrage Amendments.*It is also the lived-constitutional baseline suggested by actual modern practice in the fifty states. Some small questions have arisen at the margins—for example, how long a residency period may a state require?—but even here, actual practice and common sense have narrowed the range of plausible answers. Similarly, we have seen that the *Reynolds* rule offered a workable way to deal with malapportionment (although here, too, smallish questions at the margin needed to be addressed).[15]

But no comparably clean sub-rule exists to regulate district shape. In a sense, all districting is gerrymandering. No district map is neutral. How can principled judges treat like cases alike when each district map seems utterly unique and not easily comparable to any other map in any other

---

* For more discussion of how this updating properly operates, see Chapter 10, n. 14 and accompanying text.

state or census cycle? Perhaps the only clean approach would be to require each state to adopt some form of statewide proportional representation, but this audacious mandate would oblige every state to move beyond a single-member district system with deep historical roots almost everywhere in America.

The lesson here is that on some issues a court's implementational sub-rules may slightly underprotect certain constitutional values, just as on other issues the rules slightly overprotect. In both situations, there exists a conceptual space between the abstract meaning of the written Constitution (in the domain of interpretation) and the doctrinal sub-rules promulgated and enforced by courts (in the domain of implementation). This space arises because of institutional considerations connected to the basic features of federal courts. When the Constitution goes to court, it needs to be translated into rules that courts qua courts can properly enforce. In this process of translation—when the supreme law of the terse text becomes the detailed court-law of judicial doctrine—areas of overinclusion and underinclusion arise.

These areas form an important part of America's unwritten Constitution. As with other elements of this unwritten Constitution, these areas are not clearly mapped in the document's express words—and yet (as with other elements) they exist in close proximity to the document. In one sense, judicial sub-rules by definition range beyond and fall short of the best interpretation of the written Constitution, if the document is read in an institutional vacuum. In another sense, however, the document envisions and contemplates such areas, for they arise as a result of features built into the text itself—the affirmative scope and limitations on "judicial Power," the essential structural attributes of federal courts, the need for "one supreme Court" to supervise and suitably guide all "inferior" federal courts, and the intricate institutional relationships between the federal judiciary and other institutions created or contemplated by the Constitution.

In the case of one-party gerrymandering, whatever judicial underprotection now exists is largely harmless, because other features of modern American government have limited the potential damage. Any party seeking to maximize the number of seats it can win must minimize the number of "wasted votes" it receives—that is, votes above the necessary victory threshold of 50 percent plus one in any district and votes going to losing candidates. In other words, optimal vote maximization means that almost every vote a party gets must go to a winning candidate (because all votes going to losers are ineffectual), and that no party candidate should win by a landslide. (If any candidate does win big, then all the extra votes above the 50 percent mark are "wasted" votes that could have gone to help some other party candidate win in some other ingeniously drawn district.) But this mathematical reality means that any successful partisan gerrymander will need to tack very close to the political wind, a highly dangerous maneuver. If some modest external event arises after district lines are drawn—a party scandal, an economic downturn, a shift in district demographics—then a party could end up losing a slew of close races rather than winning them all. Parties are understandably reluctant to play the game too fine, and this reluctance makes it difficult for one party to consistently impose "wasted" votes on the other party without suffering lots of "wasted" votes itself.

Moreover, each major party typically includes powerful legislative incumbents, and every incumbent prefers to win by a landslide rather than a squeaker. Landslides facilitate fundraising and help launch future campaigns for still higher office. But landslides also waste votes, from the party's point of view. Hence, both one-party gerrymanders and incumbent-protective gerrymanders may be troubling in theory, but in practice they tend to tug hard in opposite directions, resulting in district maps that do not seriously dishonor the deep principles of republican government. Judicial intervention is thus largely unnecessary, because the political system regulates itself tolerably well with regard to gerrymandering.[16]

This was not true of the 1960s right-to-vote and malapportionment cases. Where certain persons are literally disfranchised, how are they supposed to solve the problem themselves through politics? By definition, disfranchised persons do not, as a rule, vote on whether they should get the vote in future elections, and incumbent politicos have attenuated incentives to protect the interests of nonvoters. In situations of gross malapportionment, the political power structure is itself part of the problem and thus cannot be relied upon to be part of the solution. In *Baker v. Carr*, Justice Tom C. Clark's concurring opinion stressed that the citizenry of Tennessee had no effective way to combat the state's gross malapportionment.

In particular, the state lacked an initiative process whereby a statewide majority of disgruntled voters could have changed the corrupt status quo. Electoral reform in Tennessee perversely required assistance from the very state legislature whose leaders were the chief architects and beneficiaries of the state's rotten system of vote-counting. Thus, in right-to-vote cases such as *Harper* and malapportionment cases such as *Baker* and *Reynolds*, relief needed to come from outside the voting system itself—from the federal government as the proper guarantor of state republican government. In gerrymandering situations, by contrast, the political system adequately polices itself, and thus there is less pressing need for bold judicial initiatives.

None of the considerations cataloged in the preceding paragraphs are explicitly laid out in any clear constitutional clause. Nevertheless, they flow from a careful understanding of the written and unwritten Constitution as a whole—from the implicit premises of the document; from the revitalized ideals of republicanism enacted in the amendment process during Reconstruction; from the matrix of institutions set up by the Constitution; from America's actual lived practices of voting and conducting elections; and from actual judicial doctrine rooted, by and large, in a proper vision of Article III "judicial Power."

"the supreme Court"

IT REMAINS TO ASK the biggest set of questions about Article III "judicial Power": In general, how much weight, and what kind of weight, should today's Article III judges in the proper exercise of their "judicial Power" give to past Article III exercises of "judicial Power"? In particular, when and how should the Court overrule itself? These questions are particularly momentous because many of the most famous decisions of the modern era—for instance, *Brown v. Board of Education, Mapp v. Ohio, Gideon v. Wainwright, Miranda v. Arizona, Roe v. Wade,* and *Lawrence v. Texas*—are rulings that themselves broke with prior precedent and/or cases that prominent critics have urged overruling.

In seeking to answer the biggest questions about when the Supreme Court should overrule itself, some self-described adherents of the written Constitution as originally understood have offered accounts of precedent's proper place that largely begin and end outside the text. Justice Scalia is the most famous example. Both on and off the Court—most famously in a 1989 published lecture on his philosophy of "originalism"—Scalia has argued that judges should generally follow the Constitution's original public meaning. Invoking the vision of John Marshall, Scalia has reminded us that the Constitution is America's "paramount law" and that this law has "a fixed meaning." But apparently Scalia also believes that judges need not follow this paramount law, whose meaning was fixed by its original understanding, when this paramount law sharply contradicts settled precedent. Any other approach would be impractical, he has argued.[17]

Huh? If the touchstone here is pure practicality, it is hard to see why pure practicality cannot also be the touchstone for all issues of constitutional interpretation across the board—text and original understanding be damned! Conversely, if Scalia believes that as a judge he is generally obliged to follow the supreme law, and that this law is the written Constitution as originally understood, then by artificially limiting the domain of his obligation to areas that are not settled by past precedent, Scalia would seem to be violating his own legal obligations as he understands them. Scalia errs here because he has started his thinking in the wrong place—with himself and his own philosophy—and because he has approached the written Constitution with an unsubtle understanding of how its words were actually designed to work over time.

Of course, the proper place for a faithful constitutionalist to begin analysis of precedent's weight—or any other constitutional question, for that matter—is the Constitution itself. When we start here, we shall see a pattern that by now should be familiar. The document answers some of the largest questions about precedent's weight, but leaves other questions indeterminate over a certain range. Within that range, the actual practice of American government—in particular, the practice of Article III judges themselves—has plausibly and usefully glossed the text in a manner that is invited by the text, albeit not compelled by the text. In other words, although the text does not explicitly say that this useful and plausible gloss should control, neither does the text say that it shouldn't. If we choose to attend to how the gloss actually operates, the overall Article III system works, and works well. Simply put, if we approach the text from the proper angle and with the proper interpretive methods, we can answer key questions in a way that does justice to the text itself—that is faithful to the letter and spirit of the text and that enables the text to work in court and on the ground.

CONSIDER FIRST THE "VERTICAL" ELEMENT OF PRECEDENT—the authority of some judges at the top of the judicial pyramid to impose their legal vision on judges below. The Judicial Article authorizes legal and equitable cases arising under "this Constitution" to be resolved by "one supreme Court" which presides over various "inferior" federal courts and state courts. The big idea here is that "inferior" courts should generally be bound by the interpretations, implementing frameworks, specific holdings, precedential implications, and remedial precepts—the doctrine—of the Supremes. This is so even if lower courts think that the high court is wrong about the general meaning of the written Constitution, or about the best sub-rules for implementing the document, or about how the specific case at hand or a more general category of cases must be decided, or about the proper set of legally applicable remedies. Lower courts are free to say that the high court has erred, and to offer their reasons for so believing, but disagreement does not justify a general right of disobedience. An inferior may tell his boss that she is wrong, but must nevertheless follow her instructions.

But what should a faithful inferior do when his superior seems to be in the process of changing her mind? Specifically, if the Supreme Court in case A clearly says X, but later cases B, C, and D, involving issues related to but not identical with the issue in case A, seem to point away from X, then what should an inferior court do when a case legally identical to case A—"on all fours," as lawyers would say—arises? Should it matter if none of the justices who joined the Court majority in case A is still on the Court, whereas several of the newest justices, prior to their appointment to the Court, openly criticized case A and called for its overruling?

On the one hand, the three most recent cases may well signal that principle X no longer commands the support of a current Court majority. Indeed, close analysis may suggest that cases B, C, and D were designed to lay the foundation for overruling case A, and thus the time is now ripe to declare that A no longer fits the legal landscape. Plus, the off-the-bench comments of several new justices are surely straws in the wind for any lower-court judge seeking to avoid the embarrassment of being publicly reversed by the Supreme Court. Beyond embarrassment, wouldn't legal efficiency be served if the lower-court judge made his best guess about what the Supreme Court today would actually do in the case at hand on appeal?

On the other hand, the "judicial Power" is vested in courts, not in individual justices speaking in other capacities. And though there may be hints in cases B, C, and D, let's assume that the Court did not squarely say in any of these cases that case A was being overruled, or clearly announce that principle X was no longer good law. Unless and until the Court itself speaks clearly, principle X is arguably still the Court doctrine that should be followed.

Both of these views are textually plausible. Both reflect reasonable understandings of the supremacy of the Supreme Court over inferior federal courts. One view stresses the current supremacy of the sitting justices; the other view focuses on the supremacy of past Supreme Court rulings. If a lower-court judge had only the written Constitution to guide him, the matter might well be indeterminate.

But precedent has in fact glossed the text on this very question. The Court itself has clearly held that every past Court ruling must be followed in legally identical cases until the Supreme Court itself overrules the old case in explicit language. Thus, a dutiful inferior court should: (1) note the apparent tension between case A and cases B, C, and D—ideally in a clear opinion signaling the need for eventual Supreme Court reconsideration of this area of law; (2) follow case A and principle X if the case at hand is indeed on all fours with A; and (3) leave the rest to the Supreme Court. And to highlight the fact that not all reversals are shameful, the Court in one careful 2005 case, *Eberhart v. United States*, openly praised the lower court for following this tripartite script even as the Court overruled its own prior case law—and thus reversed its faithful lieutenant![18]

SO MUCH FOR VERTICAL PRECEDENT. "Horizontal" precedent—the amount of weight and the kind of weight that past Supreme Court exercises of "judicial Power" should carry in the current Supreme Court itself—raises its own distinctive set of issues. Once again, a careful look at the document itself provides the broad outlines of a proper approach, even though the text does not provide all the answers.

The Judicial Article envisions the Court as a continuous body. The Court never automatically turns over, as the House does every two years and the presidency does every four. A continuing body would seem intentionally structured so as to give some weight to its past and some thought to its future. It does not invent itself anew each day. Given the Court's clear constitutional design, today's justices may properly give past Court decisions a rebuttable presumption of correctness. A past case may control until proved wrong, with those challenging it saddled with the burden of proof. A justice may also give a precedent persuasive weight in deciding whether the burden is met. Even if her first reaction is that the precedent wrongly interpreted the Constitution, the very fact of the prior decision may persuade her that her first reaction is mistaken: If John Marshall and his brethren thought X, perhaps X is right after all, despite initial appearances to the contrary. (For similar reasons, a deferential justice might choose to give Congress, a coequal branch, the benefit of the doubt in certain cases.)

The precise persuasive weight of a past case will vary. Not all opinions of the Court came from the likes of John Marshall or Joseph Story. It may be relevant that a particularly sound justice dissented in the allegedly erroneous case. Sometimes, a later Court will find wisdom in certain language of a past case even if its result seems wrong on the facts. Other times, its fact-specific result may distill great wisdom even if its language, on reflection, does not persuade.

Also, if the current Court believes that the past Court did not err in interpreting the Constitution, but merely chose a suboptimal set of implementing sub-rules that nonetheless fell within the range of plausible implementations, the current justices may properly choose to let the matter stand. In this conceptual quadrant, the old case law rests on a view of the meaning of the Constitution that the current Court believes is the correct one. No infidelity to a justice's oath occurs when she continues to build upon cases that are themselves firmly grounded in the written Constitution itself, rightly read.

But what if a current justice believes that a past case or line of cases misread—indeed, seriously misread—the written Constitution? Doesn't her oath of office oblige her to follow the Constitution and not the case? If the Court is generally obliged to strike down constitutionally erroneous statutes passed by Congress, why isn't it equally obliged to overturn constitutionally erroneous precedents?

In 1992, these questions came before the Court in dramatic fashion as the justices openly considered whether to overrule *Roe v. Wade*, perhaps the most controversial case of the past half century. By the narrowest of margins, 5–4, the Court in *Planned Parenthood v. Casey* decided to reaffirm *Roe*'s central holding that women have a constitutional right to obtain early-term abortions. In passing, the *Casey* Court declared that "a decision to overrule should rest on some special reason over and above the belief that a prior case was wrongly decided." Asserting that such a view had been "repeated in our cases," the Court thereupon cited two dissents, neither of which was squarely on point, leaving the careful reader with a sneaking suspicion that perhaps this view was not well established in pre-*Casey* case law.[19]

Indeed, a survey of earlier doctrine reveals at least seven twentieth-century overrulings based simply on the belief that the prior case was wrongly decided. Several of these overrulings are household names, at least in legal households: *Erie v. Tompkins* (1938), *West Virginia State Board of Education v. Barnette* (1943), and *Jones v. Alfred Mayer* (1968). In other words, if read broadly, *Casey*'s dictum about precedent was virtually unprecedented, and indeed contrary to precedent.[20]

These seven pre-*Casey* precedents stand for the proposition that, absent certain special countervailing considerations (which we shall analyze momentarily), today's Court may properly overrule yesterday's case simply because today's Court believes the old case incorrectly interpreted the Constitution. None of these seven overruling precedents has itself ever been overruled. These seven precedents span decades and cover a wide range of constitutional questions. *Casey*, by contrast, involved the hottest of hot-button issues—abortion rights, an area where the Court was under fire from critics and appears to have overreacted with ill-considered language. Thus, we should hesitate to read glib words in one case as repudiating first principles of previous case law and of the Constitution itself. Unless and until the Court emphatically and repeatedly reiterates that this *Casey* passage must be construed expansively—and thus far the post-*Casey* Court has said nothing of the sort—it makes sense to read the *Casey* dictum in a limited manner that would mesh with the case law (on case law) that *Casey* overlooked.[21]

The *Casey* dictum may well be a sensible way of thinking about precedent in areas where questions of constitutional meaning are not at issue—that is, areas where the precedents on the books concern merely common-law issues or constitutional issues revolving around implementational sub-rules. In these areas, although today's Court might choose to follow precedents that it now believes to be erroneous, the Court is not thereby privileging its own past pronouncements over the best interpretation of the Constitution itself.

Casey can also be read as highlighting the fact that the vast majority of recent overrulings have been based not solely on the fact that the earlier case was wrongly decided as a matter of pure constitutional meaning, but also on other factors. These other factors have included the general unworkability of the old precedent (as made clear by subsequent experience), the old precedent's inconsistency with other cases decided before it or after it, and the old precedent's incompatibility with later factual developments. Perhaps *Casey* simply meant to say that when these factors exist, they should be stressed by the overruling Court.

But if these factors were the only ones justifying overrulings in cases involving constitutional meaning, we would be left with a vision of constitutional law more Court-centered than Constitution-centered: A case could be overruled if it did not fit well with other cases, but would be retained if it simply did not fit well with the document.

It is understandable that, for reasons of institutional prestige, the Court might prefer, when overruling itself, to do so on grounds that downplay admission of past error. Such an approach allows the current Court to say that the past case was perhaps sensible when decided, but has been eclipsed by later legal and factual developments that could not have been perfectly foreseen when the Court first acted.

Yet even as we strive to understand the Court's institutional desire to avoid shouting from the rooftops that the Court itself has blundered badly in the past, we must also note the dangers of unchecked institutional self-aggrandizement. (The Court of late has been fond of making sweeping assertions of judicial supremacy, regularly proclaiming itself the Constitution's "ultimate" interpreter—a self-description that nowhere appeared in *Marbury*, and indeed never appeared in the *United States Reports* until the second half of the twentieth century.)[22]

If the justices generally felt free (or obliged!) to follow clearly erroneous case law concerning the core meaning of the Constitution, then the foundational document might ultimately be wholly eclipsed. Rather than simply filling the document's gaps, judicial doctrine would erase its outlines. If the written Constitution indeed contemplated this odd result, one would expect to see a rather clear statement to that effect: "This Constitution may be wholly superseded by conceded judicial misinterpretations; all branches are oath-bound to follow these misinterpretations." But the Constitution says nothing of the sort. On the contrary, it explicitly and self-referentially obliges all officials to swear oaths to itself, not to conceded misinterpretations of it.

The Constitution establishes a system of coordinate powers. If neither the legislature nor the executive may unilaterally change the document's meaning, why may the judiciary? The Constitution details elaborate checks and balances. If conceded misinterpretations become the supreme law of the land, what checks adequately limit judicial self-aggrandizement? Prior to the Constitution's ratification, none of its leading friends put forth anything like the *Casey* dictum, broadly read. Rather, the basic structure of the document suggested to ratifiers that whatever "We the People" deliberately laid down could not be changed, except by a later amendment reflecting wide and deep popular approval.

In the case that the modern Court views as the very fountainhead of judicial review, *Marbury v. Madison*, Chief Justice Marshall declared that the American people's "original right to establish, for their future government, such principles as, in their opinion, shall most conduce to their own happiness" was "the basis on which the whole American fabric has been erected." Marshall went on to observe that "[t]he exercise of this original right is a very great exertion; nor can it nor ought it to be frequently repeated. The principles, therefore, so established are deemed fundamental. And as the authority, from which they proceed, is supreme, and can seldom act, they are designed to be permanent." Given that acts of constitution and amendment require great popular exertion that cannot be expected to occur routinely, it seems perverse to insist that We the People must repeat what We said whenever judges garble what We said the first time.

Simply put, the basic structural argument against a broad reading of the *Casey* dictum is that *Marbury*-style judicial review presupposes that judges are enforcing the people's document, not their own deviations. Departures from the document—amendments—should come from the people, not from the high court. Otherwise we are left with constitutionalism without the Constitution, popular sovereignty without the people.

DOES A PROPER VIEW OF THE CONSTITUTIONAL SYSTEM, then, require that whenever the current Court believes that a past case misinterpreted the central meaning of some part of the Constitution, the justices must overrule the erroneous case? Not quite. Two moderating structural ideas come into play, both of which can be understood as "equitable" considerations that the Judicial Article allows to be taken into account. (That article features language explicitly empowering federal courts to hear cases "in Law and Equity" arising under "this Constitution.")[23]

One structural and equitable notion may be stated as follows: Once We the People have struggled to put a rule or principle in the document, that rule or principle should not be altered, except by the people themselves. An erroneous precedent that improperly deviates from the written Constitution may in some situations stand if the precedent is later championed not merely by the Court, but also by the people. When the citizenry has widely and enthusiastically embraced an erroneous precedent—when even most initial skeptics have deemed the precedent to be fundamental and admirable—a court of equity may sometimes, consistent with the document's emphasis on popular sovereignty, view this precedent as sufficiently ratified by the American people so as to insulate it from judicial overruling. This is especially true if the erroneous precedent recognized an unenumerated right before its time. If this right then catches fire and captures the imagination of a wide swathe of citizens, it thereby becomes a proper Ninth Amendment entitlement even though the Court (by hypothesis) jumped the gun.

As we have seen, unenumerated constitutional rights retained by the people under the Ninth Amendment (and the Fourteenth Amendment's privileges-or-immunities clause) encompass, among other things, those basic rights that the people at large in fact believe that they have and should have under the Constitution. If enough people believe in a given right and view it as fundamental, then that right is for these very reasons a right of the people, a basic privilege of citizenship as understood by citizens themselves. It usually does not matter how the people's belief arose—even if it arose as a result of a Supreme Court case that was wrong as a matter of text and original intent when decided.

Thus, if the Court at time T1 gets the Constitution's text and original understanding wrong and proclaims a right that does not in fact properly exist at time T1, and if the vast majority of Americans come to rejoice in this right, the Court at time T2 should affirm the originally erroneous precedent. The case, though wrong when decided, has become right thanks to an intervening change of fact—broad and deep popular endorsement—that the Constitution's own text, via the Ninth and Fourteenth Amendments, endows with special significance. Note one key asymmetry: A case that construes a textual constitutional right too narrowly is different from one that construes the right too broadly. Even if both cases come to be widely embraced by the citizenry, only the rights-expanding case interacts with the text of the Ninth and Fourteenth Amendments so as to specially immunize it from subsequent reversal.[24]

A second equitable principle, prominent in judicial decisions stretching back hundreds of years, directs judges to give due weight to the ways in which litigants who come before the Court may have reasonably relied upon prior case law. Judicial power, by its nature, is retrospective. The judiciary applies law to transactions that have already occurred. Erroneous precedents create facts on the ground that properly influence the application of retrospective judicial power. In some cases, these facts limit the Court's ability to abruptly change course, even if persuaded of past error. For example, even if the Court were tomorrow to deem erroneous its long-standing precedents upholding the constitutionality of paper money, surely the justices could not ignore the vast economic system that has built up in reliance on paper.[25]

Erroneous precedents are not unique in this respect. Prior unconstitutional conduct of other branches may likewise create *faits accomplis* that courts cannot easily undo after the fact. Unlike a broad reading of the *Casey* dictum, which treats erroneous Court precedents with more deference than erroneous statutes, a sound structural and equitable approach would respect the general coordinacy of the three branches and would recognize that judges must have due regard for facts on the ground created by prior actions of all branches and levels of government. This feature of judicial underenforcement is built into the very structure of the Judicial Article, under which judicial review can sometimes occur long after certain practices have become settled and virtually impossible for courts to reverse.

Impossible for courts to reverse—but not necessarily for legislatures. A prior erroneous Court ruling does not properly amend the Constitution, and other branches of government may be able to return to a constitutionally proper regime by acting purely prospectively in a way that judges perhaps should not. Imagine, for example, a statute proposing a gradual ten-year phase-in of a new, more constitutionally appropriate regime to replace the old case law that the Court now admits was erroneous. Were the Court itself to announce such a purely prospective phase-in, this announcement might strain the traditional boundaries of proper "judicial Power," precisely because the announcement would look purely "legislative" in nature. But legislatures, of course, typically act in precisely this purely prospective fashion, and phase-in statutes are commonplace.

It is thus important for the Court to tell the public if the justices have indeed erred in the past precisely so that the other branches may ponder their constitutionally permissible options. Justices may not relish confessing error, but they have no warrant for refusing to do so when called to account. The Court's duty, then, is not, as a broad reading of the *Casey* dictum would have it, to affirm and extend precedent without deciding whether precedent is right or wrong. Rather, the judicial duty is first to admit error whenever the Court finds that error has occurred, and then to consider whether special reliance interests apply and how those interests might limit the use of retrospective judicial power.

In other words, the Court's province and duty is to say what the law is—the law of the Constitution, of course. If, in the process, the Court decides that this supreme law has been violated, whether by a state law, a federal law, or a presidential proclamation—*or a past ruling of the Court itself*—the justices should declare that fact and then do their best to analyze how, if at all, this wrong might be righted, and by whom. When the Court itself is the source of a constitutional wrong, it has a particular obligation to help right that wrong, or at least to identify how the wrong could be righted by sister branches.

Let us now return to the *Casey* dictum one last time: "[A] decision to overrule should rest on some special reason over and above the belief that a prior case was wrongly decided." The best way to read this dictum is as follows: Even if today's Court determines that a prior case garbled the Constitution's true meaning, the judicial inquiry is not at an end. There are still two "special" questions that the Court must consider. First, have the American people themselves ratified the error in a way that cures it? Second, have litigants equitably relied upon the error in a way that immunizes it from immediate judicial reversal?

WHEN CASEY IS READ IN this way, it meshes with the actual practice of overrulings by the Court over its entire history. It also meshes with the terse text's own understanding of the proper relationship between "this Constitution" and the "judicial Power." Seen from this angle, the document and the doctrine cohere: What the Court says about "this Constitution" squares with what "this Constitution" says about the Court. Thus, this reading of *Casey*—and of the Court's case law more generally—puts precedent in its proper place.

CHAPTER 6

HONORING THE ICONS

America's Symbolic Constitution

ABRAHAM LINCOLN (NOVEMBER 8, 1863).

Less than a fortnight after posing for this photograph, Lincoln delivered a short speech commemorating the battlefield at Gettysburg.

I N A POLYGLOT NATION OF MANY FAITHS, ethnicities, and ideologies, the Constitution stands as a uniquely unifying American symbol—a New World republican version of England's Queen Elizabeth, of India's Taj Mahal. But several other iconic texts epitomizing The American Way have also helped to bind Americans together and make us a distinct people with a particular national narrative. These canonical texts have won a special place in American constitutional discourse, even though many modern Americans have never actually read these works (just as many have not read the Constitution).[1]

The most important thing to understand about America's symbolic Constitution is simply that it exists. Americans of all stripes can easily name certain texts that stand outside the confines of the written Constitution yet operate in American constitutional discourse as privileged sources of meaning, inspiration, and guidance. True, once we move beyond this core set of texts, the outer boundaries of the canon are fuzzy. But then, so are the meaning-boundaries of many of the written Constitution's clauses, whose relatively solid core applications nestle inside blurred peripheries and penumbras.*

AMERICA'S SYMBOLIC CONSTITUTION revolves tightly around *texts*. Of course, texts are not the only things that operate as symbols. England's queen is not a text, but she nevertheless symbolizes a nation. Ditto with America's president. At the Founding, George Washington functioned as a particularly important symbolic figure, shaping America's understanding of the presidency itself. But texts have certain notable features. Most

---

* Readers are welcome to test this existence claim against their own intuitions. The next five paragraphs will outline the general contours of America's symbolic Constitution. At the end of this outline, you are invited to close this book and spend a few minutes composing a list of works that you believe best fit the stated criteria. When you have finished, reopen the book and compare your list to mine, which consists of six specific texts that I believe are easy cases for inclusion in our symbolic Constitution. At the end of this chapter, you are invited to reflect once again upon which other texts might be suitable candidates to join the representative texts that I showcase.

important, the texts at the heart of America's symbolic constitutional canon closely resemble the written Constitution itself: They are public, democratic, and uniform. In other words, all these symbolic texts can easily be reprinted so that every American can have access to the same thing, with minute variations. (Different printers may follow slightly different style sheets.) By contrast, a human being operates as a more complex, privatized, and uneven symbol, as members of the public will have access to highly variable information about the person in question. In this sense, Americans will not even be reading from the same page, so to speak. Some interpreters of George Washington, for example, may know all about his childhood and marriage, while other interpreters may not. And the relationship between private life and public character raises rich but potentially distracting issues that published texts sidestep to some extent.

True, texts are not the only things that are public, democratic, and uniform. Think of uniforms themselves—the infantryman's combat outfit, the sailor's suit, the judge's robes. Or think of the American flag—a classic American symbol, rich with constitutional overtones, but not a text in the ordinary sense. Compared to the elaborate text of the written Constitution, however, symbols such as flags, uniforms, and bald eagles typically lack highly specific propositional content. Often, their beauty lies in the eye of the beholder, and they easily mean different things to different people. By contrast, each text at the center of the symbolic canon mirrors the basic frame of the written Constitution itself. Each is a specific and articulate source of linguistic meaning.[2]

Just as America's written Constitution was formally ratified and has been repeatedly amended by the American people, each element of America's symbolic Constitution at some point in American history won the hearts and minds of a wide swath of the American people, thereby helping to bind citizens together as a legal and political entity. Certain kinds of texts are unlikely to perform this function. For example, great American novels are surely articulate texts, and many of them bristle with specific ideas that might conceivably bear on constitutional issues. But novel-reading is often an intensely private or a profoundly universalizing experience rather than a public and political event tying together Americans qua Americans. Besides, which novels should qualify? On race relations, should we pick *The*

Adventures of Huckleberry Finn, To Kill a Mockingbird, Beloved—or *Gone with the Wind?* On privacy, should *Lolita* be our guide? Should property rights in America borrow a page from *Atlas Shrugged* and *The Fountainhead*, or from *The Grapes of Wrath* and *The Jungle?* By contrast, the texts at the center of America's symbolic Constitution are closer cousins to the written Constitution itself, each having been officially recognized at some point and in some way as possessing special American constitutional authority.

Thus, the hub of America's symbolic Constitution consists of works that closely relate to the written Constitution. Whereas some of these canonical works have come from official governmental sources and others have emerged from the pens or lips of private persons, each is widely read as a precursor to, an implementation of, and/or a meditation upon the written Constitution itself.

In sum, the core of America's symbolic Constitution consists of articulate texts that bear on constitutional questions, adjoin the written Constitution in some sense, and occupy a special niche in American constitutional discourse. With these parameters in mind, the next section identifies six exemplary items—six canonical texts that have in fact achieved a special constitutional authority and that, on reflection, deserve this authority.

"America"

AMERICA'S SYMBOLIC CONSTITUTION SURELY INCLUDES (but is not limited to) the Declaration of Independence, Publius's *The Federalist*, the Northwest Ordinance, Lincoln's Gettysburg Address, the Warren Court's opinion in *Brown v. Board*, and Dr. King's "I Have a Dream" speech.

These works set forth background principles that powerfully inform American constitutional interpretation. Wherever the written Constitution is fairly susceptible to different interpretations, interpreters should hesitate, and do in fact hesitate, to embrace any reading that would violate the clear letter and spirit of these other canonical texts. In short, these texts are *constitutional* in the sense that they are *constitutive*—adherence to these texts helps *constitute* Americans as a distinct people among all the peoples of the Earth. True, these special texts are not on the same legal level as the written Constitution itself. Where the terse text is clear, it trumps. But often the written Constitution is not crystal clear. Often, different interpretations are plausible, and faithful interpreters must go beyond the text to reach specific conclusions. In doing so, they must remember that they are construing *America's* Constitution, and that America stands for certain things—things set forth in other texts that we, the people, as a people, hold dear.[3]

Although each of these texts has in some sense been "ratified" by the American people in general and by faithful constitutional interpreters in particular, most of these "ratifications" have been indirect and informal. By making Martin Luther King's birthday an official holiday—a remarkable tribute to a purely private citizen who never held public office—America's lawmakers can be understood to have "ratified" King's speech, officially making King's dream America's dream. But this ratification of course differed in important ways from the ratification of express textual amendments. King's brilliant ad libs did not pass through the same elaborate screens and filters that every word in the written Constitution itself did. As we read canonical texts from the likes of Publius, Lincoln, and King, we must recall that none of these texts purported to be law. Even those who insist on strict attention to every word of the written Constitution, and who pay great heed to rules and principles of proper legal interpretation when construing that text, must understand that different and looser techniques of interpretation and literary analysis may befit several of the works in America's symbolic canon.

BEFORE EXAMINING OUR SIX TEXTS individually—explaining how each came to form part of the core of the canon and what each has come to mean—we should pause to reflect upon a few general features of America's symbolic Constitution.

For starters, these texts form a symbolic network, a system. They connect not merely to the written Constitution but to each other. Thus, Lincoln's 1863 Gettysburg Address explicitly invoked and interpreted the Declaration of Independence right out of the gate: "Four score and seven years ago"—that is, in 1776, the year of the Declaration—"our fathers brought forth upon this continent a new nation conceived in liberty and dedicated to the proposition *that all men are created equal.*" In turn, the 1963 Dream Speech, delivered in front of America's memorial to Lincoln, echoed the

Gettysburg Address right out of the gate: "Five score years ago, a great American in whose symbolic shadow we stand today...." Then, as had the Gettysburg Address itself, the Dream Speech explicitly brought the Declaration into view and quoted some of its grandest language: "When the architects of our republic wrote the magnificent words of the Constitution and the Declaration of Independence, they were signing a promissory note to which every American was to fall heir. This note was a promise that all men, yes, black men as well as white men, would be guaranteed the unalienable rights of life, liberty, and the pursuit of happiness."

Moments later, as King warmed to his task and began to describe his celebrated dream, he again conjured up the 1776 Declaration and the 1863 Address: "I say to you today, my friends, so even though we face the difficulties of today and tomorrow, I still have a dream. It is a dream deeply rooted in the American dream. I have a dream that one day this nation will rise up and live out the true meaning of its creed: 'We hold these truths to be self-evident: that all men are created equal.'" *Brown*, too, found its way into the Dream Speech, alongside an elegant invocation of the Fourteenth Amendment's guarantee of birthright citizenship: "[T]he Negro is still sadly crippled by the manacles of segregation and the chains of discrimination....There will be neither rest nor tranquility in America until the Negro is granted his citizenship rights....We can never be satisfied as long as our children are stripped of their selfhood and robbed of their dignity by signs stating 'For Whites Only.'"

Less obviously, the Dream Speech also gestured toward one of the epic themes of the Northwest Ordinance and the *Federalist* essays—namely, that America would stretch westward in an expansion process that would promote freedom. (The Ordinance itself had promised that all western lands covered by its terms would be free soil.) Whether or not King had either of these texts consciously in mind, these canonical works inflected his overall vision precisely because they are part of the general American constitutional narrative—the American dream—that King was claiming as his birthright. In precisely the spirit of *The Federalist* and the Ordinance, King took his audience on an imagined tour across the land from sea to shining sea. "So let freedom ring from the prodigious hilltops of New Hampshire. Let freedom ring from the mighty mountains of New York. Let freedom ring from the heightening Alleghenies of Pennsylvania! Let freedom ring from the snowcapped Rockies of Colorado! Let freedom ring from the curvaceous slopes of California! But not only that; let freedom ring from Stone Mountain of Georgia! Let freedom ring from Lookout Mountain of Tennessee! Let freedom ring from every hill and molehill of Mississippi. From every mountainside, let freedom ring."

To see from a different angle how America's symbolic canon forms a remarkably tight meshwork of logical and referential interconnection, note that all six of our texts directly link to Jefferson and/or Lincoln. Jefferson served as the lead author of the Declaration and also composed the first draft of what ultimately became the Northwest Ordinance. Jefferson's best friend, political lieutenant, and handpicked successor, James Madison, authored large chunks of *The Federalist*. Lincoln grew up in federal territory first governed by the Northwest Ordinance, wrote and delivered the Gettysburg Address, and inspired King, who chose to speak in Lincoln's "symbolic shadow." In *Brown*, a chief justice whose party had been co-founded by Lincoln delivered a unanimous opinion on behalf of fellow justices whose party had been cofounded by Jefferson.

The ubiquity of Jefferson and Lincoln should hardly surprise us, for America's modern Constitution is a two-party Constitution, and Jefferson and Lincoln are the patron saints of America's two parties. The historical processes by which our six texts came to enter the symbolic constitutional canon were themselves shaped by partisan politics.

Thus, Jefferson's allies in the early republic glorified the text of the Declaration as a way of advancing the popular appeal and political authority of the man from Monticello. *The Federalist* received plaudits in the 1790s and thereafter in part because both Hamiltonian Federalists and Madisonian Republicans could claim credit for the project. (By contrast, James Wilson's public defense of the Constitution, although hugely influential in 1787–1788, faded from memory in later years, in part because Wilson was too tightly linked to a party—the Federalists—that disappeared from the scene after Jefferson's and Madison's triumphs in presidential politics.) When Lincoln sought election in 1860, he and his party had strong incentives to find venerable antecedents for the biggest plank in their platform—a ban on slavery in federal territory. The Northwest Ordinance fit this political need perfectly. In 1863–1864, as Lincoln sought reelection,

Republicans' political prospects depended on persuading voters that for all its death and destruction, the Civil War had been worth fighting, because the very survival of republican self-government on the world stage was at stake. The Gettysburg Address elegantly made this case. A century after Lincoln, *Brown* and the Dream Speech won praise from persons of good-will from both political parties in the 1950s and 1960s at the very moment that leaders of both parties were wooing black voters.[4]

Later in this book we shall explore in detail how America's two domi-nant political parties infuse our daily system of governance. For now let's simply note that these two parties have influenced which texts sit atop the symbolic Constitution, much as these very same parties have influenced which presidents sit atop Mount Rushmore.

PROMINENT REFERENCES TO GOD or religion appear in five of our six representative texts. Only *Brown*, which came from a Court that would later become famous for its strict antiestablishmentarianism, was scrupu-lously secular from start to finish. Thus, the Declaration famously opened with references to "Nature's God" and the "Creator" and closed with an ap-peal to "the Supreme Judge of the World" and "divine Providence." Picking up where the Declaration left off, Publius thrice referred to "Providence" early on—in John Jay's *Federalist* No. 2, to be precise—and later echoed the Declaration's reference to "Nature's God" in Madison's *Federalist* No. 43. The Northwest Ordinance declared that "[r]eligion, morality, and knowl-edge [are] necessary to good government and the happiness of mankind." Lincoln's closing sentence referred to "this nation, under God"—words that would find their way, with minor tweaking, into the twentieth-century Pledge of Allegiance. And religious references pervaded the Reverend King's remarks, from his profuse biblical allusions and paraphrases to his thunderous conclusion: "[W]hen we allow freedom [to] ring, when we let it ring from every village and every hamlet, from every state and every city, we will be able to speed up that day when all of God's children—black men and white men, Jews and Gentiles, Protestants and Catholics—will be able to join hands and sing in the words of the old Negro spiritual, 'Free at last! Free at last! Thank God Almighty, we are free at last!'"

How, it might be asked, can any openly religious text form any part of America's constitutional order? The answer to this question begins by stressing that although America's Constitution is not itself a religious document, neither is it an antireligious document. Even as the First Amendment says that the federal government should stay out of the religion business—and as the Fourteenth incorporates the principles of religious liberty and equality against state governments—the Constitution also explicitly affirms the right of Americans to freely exercise religion. Two of our six works came from nongovernmental sources. There was nothing un-American or unconstitutional when Jay and King as private persons professed their faith even as they entered the public square.

Indeed, individuals are entitled to be religious, even if they also hold office. Beginning with Washington, many presidents have chosen to introduce religious elements, such as the Bible, at their inaugural ceremonies. In a similar vein, two of our six classic texts came from public servants speaking in unusually personal contexts. Lincoln was at Gettysburg to dedicate a cemetery. A religious reference in this setting was not out of place. The signers of the Declaration penned their names not just as representatives of America but also as individual human beings dangerously pledging their lives, their fortunes, and their sacred honor to the patriot cause. Had America lost its bid for independence, these men would have been hanged for treason. Surely, they had reason to beseech God's blessing at this terrible hour of moral choice and mortal peril. Proverbially, there are no atheists in foxholes.[5]

As for the positive references to religion and the governmental support for religion in the Northwest Ordinance, we must remember that this Ordinance originated in the Confederation Congress, which was of course not bound by the First Amendment. When the First Congress adopted the Ordinance, with a few minor tweaks, as its own, it did so before the First Amendment had even been proposed, much less ratified. Also, the First Amendment nonestablishment principle can be read in its strictest sense as applying when Congress seeks to adopt religious policy applicable in the several states. To the extent that the First Amendment resembles the Tenth Amendment, marking a domain where state policy should prevail and the federal government should refrain from legislating, the First (like the Tenth) has no proper bite in the territories: Federal power is plenary precisely because no competing state regulations exist. When legislating for the territories, Congress might thus be thought to have the same broad powers to promote morality and religion as state legislatures generally possessed in 1789. But unlike some contemporaneous state legislatures, Congress wisely avoided sectarian favoritism, promoting religion in general and not any specific denomination in particular.[6]

"in the Year...of the Independence of the United States of America the Twelfth"

EVEN BEFORE GEORGE WASHINGTON took his first oath of office, the Declaration of Independence had begun to tightly intertwine with the Constitution in both the popular and the legal mind. The two documents had both emerged from the same iconic building in Philadelphia—today known as Independence Hall—and six of the thirty-nine men who signed their names on the parchment Constitution on September 17, 1787, were especially notable at that precise moment because they had previously signed the parchment Declaration: Pennsylvania's Benjamin Franklin, James Wilson, Robert Morris, and George Clymer; Connecticut's Roger Sherman; and Delaware's George Read. The largest celebration of the Constitution's ratification—a festive affair involving some twenty thousand enthusiasts—fittingly occurred in Philadelphia itself on the Declaration's twelfth anniversary, July 4, 1788. *

The Constitution's enactment was widely understood as an implementation and extension of the Declaration's ringing language that the American people would enjoy an "unalienable" right to "alter or abolish" their governments in certain situations and to establish new governmental forms to secure society's "Safety and Happiness." Publius thrice invoked the Declaration on this precise point—once in Madison's *Federalist* No. 40, with

---

*Today, the kinship between the parchment Declaration and the parchment Constitution is dramatized by their proximity in the National Archives Rotunda. Recall that the parchment Constitution's language gesturing toward the Declaration—"done in Convention... in the Year of our Lord one thousand seven hundred and Eighty seven and of the Independence of the United States of America the Twelfth"—was not part of the official printed Constitution as ratified. This particular linkage between the two parchments was thus symbolic, not legal.

an explicit footnote reference (rare for Publius) to the Declaration; shortly thereafter in Madison's *Federalist* No. 43, referring to the people's right under "the law of nature and of nature's God" to secure their own "safety and happiness"; and yet again in Hamilton's *Federalist* No. 78, which echoed and extended the Declaration by affirming "the right of the people to alter or abolish the established Constitution, whenever they find it inconsistent with their happiness."

When Americans began altering their Constitution shortly after ratifying it, several of the provisions of the Bill of Rights reaffirmed rights, freedoms, and privileges that Americans had previously claimed for themselves in the Declaration, such as the right to petition, the freedom from peacetime troop-quartering, and the historical privilege of trial by a local jury.

In the mid-1860s, history repeated itself with a twist, as textual amendments again echoed the Declaration. If children of God really did have unalienable rights given by their Creator; and if these rights logically preceded all government, which was legitimate only if it truly protected these rights; and if all men truly were created equal—then surely slavery must end and even states must be made to honor all fundamental rights, many of which were cataloged in the Declaration itself. Or so thought the party of Lincoln. Whether or not the slaveholder Jefferson himself would have agreed with each of these points as an accurate interpretation of his own intentions, Lincoln's Republicans reglossed the Declaration and incorporated their gloss into the very text of the Fourteenth Amendment: Precisely because "all men are created equal," all persons born in America would be legally equal—and thus equally citizens—at birth, and no government could heap legal disabilities upon a person simply because of his or her birth status.

This quick summary of some of the most obvious interconnections between the Declaration and the Constitution only skims the surface. Entire books have been written on the linkages between these two iconic texts. Lest anyone doubt the special constitutional status of America's Declaration in lawyerly discourse over the centuries, a computer check of *United States Reports* should dispel all skepticism. Beginning in the 1790s and continuing into the twenty-first century, justices and advocates have expressly invoked the Declaration on hundreds of occasions across an astonishingly wide range of issues.

What is true in courtrooms is also true in classrooms and in family rooms. Every year, millions of students, parents, and teachers visit Philadelphia's Independence Hall and National Constitution Center or the National Archives in Washington, D.C. In all three of these grand civic spaces, citizens hear and speak about both the Declaration and the Constitution. When returning home from these venues, ordinary Americans often do so carrying souvenir pocket Constitutions. Many of the current popular editions reprint the Declaration alongside the Constitution, following the general format prominently adopted by the 1987 Commission on the Bicentennial of the United States Constitution.

"Ratification"

PUBLIUS'S *Federalist* ESSAYS HAVE ALSO EARNED a seat of special honor as a privileged guide to constitutional interpretation. Here, too, a document outside the written Constitution joined the canon in the earliest years of the fledgling republic and has since then continued to enjoy a special position in American constitutional discourse.

The justices and members of the Supreme Court bar began citing *The Federalist* even before John Marshall's ascension to the Court in 1801, and Marshall's extravagant praise for and deployment of Publius settled the matter for good. In his 1819 ruling in *McCulloch v. Maryland*, perhaps the most magisterial of his opinions over the course of his thirty-four-year tenure on the bench, the chief justice began his extensive discussion of Publius as follows: "In the course of the argument, *The Federalist* has been quoted; and the opinions expressed by the authors of that work have been justly supposed to be entitled to great respect in expounding the Constitution. No tribute can be paid to them which exceeds their merit."

Marshall then proceeded to accord Publius's "excellent essays" and "instructive pages" the kind of presumptive persuasive authority nowadays reserved only for previous decisions of the Court itself. Nowhere in *McCulloch* did Marshall expressly cite to or quote from any of the Court's prior precedents; but the chief did feel obliged to analyze in detail a passage from *The Federalist* that at first seemed to lean against the Court's approach. After quoting Publius at length, Marshall went on to show that, on closer inspection, *The Federalist* was actually on his side.

Two years later, in *Cohens v. Virginia*, Marshall executed another courtly bow in Publius's direction:

The opinion of *The Federalist* has always been considered as of great authority. It is a complete commentary on our Constitution; and is appealed to by all parties in the questions to which that instrument has given birth. Its intrinsic merit entitles it to this high rank; and the part two of its authors performed in framing the Constitution, put it very much in their power to explain the views with which it was framed. These essays [were] published while the Constitution was before the nation for adoption or rejection, and…written in answer to objections.

As he had in *McCulloch*, Marshall proceeded to quote Publius at length in order to illustrate that the views of the Court were in perfect harmony with the views of *The Federalist*.

All told, the justices have cited Publius in more than 300 cases. The citation rate has skyrocketed in recent decades; between 1990 and 2010, more than 100 cases explicitly cited at least one *Federalist* essay. In *Printz v. United States*, a particularly interesting 1997 case that generated several concurrences and dissents, the members of the Court cited *The Federalist* a whopping 61 times. (Despite this profusion, *Printz* counts as only a single case in the previous tallies, which do not distinguish between singular and multiple references within a case.)[7]

The Court is not alone in its respect for Publius. Over the past decade, more than 6,000 law review articles have cited *The Federalist*, and various *Federalist* essays nowadays form part of the standard curriculum of many if not most high-school and college civics courses.

Publius deserves his exalted legal status, but not quite for one of the reasons that Marshall smuggled into his courtly tribute in *Cohens*. Proper constitutional interpretation should focus not on "the views with which it [the written Constitution] was framed" behind closed doors at Philadelphia, but rather on the public understandings that prevailed when the document was later openly ratified by the American people. The Constitution, we must always remember, derived its legal authority from its ratification by the people. (Indeed, Marshall himself repeatedly stressed this theme in several of his most enduring decisions—especially in *Marbury* and *Mc-*

Culloch.) *The Federalist* deserves great weight precisely because (as Marshall also stressed in *Cohens*) Publius brought his essays before the public and expounded the Constitution at the very moment that the American people were deciding whether to consent.

Although we now know that two of the authors of *The Federalist* were indeed present at Philadelphia, *The Federalist* hid this fact from its readers and limited its analysis and defense of the proposed Constitution to materials accessible to the general public—namely, the text of the Constitution; its structural logic; its legal precursors (such as the British Constitution, colonial American practices, revolutionary state constitutions, and the Articles of Confederation); and the general challenges confronting America that the document aimed to surmount. The official author of the text was not a duo who had performed parts in the drafting of the Constitution behind closed doors, but the pseudonymous *Publius*—a self-described "public man" (for that is what *publius* means in Latin) acting *publicly* by *publishing* his analysis for the consideration of a *republican people* themselves also acting in *public*.[8]

Of course, lots of other Americans, with or without literary masks, took part in the great national conversation of 1787–1788. What makes Publius so special? Marshall's words ring true: Publius offered a remarkably "complete commentary on our Constitution"—far more systematic, disciplined, and detailed than most other contemporaneous sources—and a supremely intelligent commentary at that, with "intrinsic merit," as Marshall pithily put it.

Justice Joseph Story said much the same thing about Publius in 1833, when Story published his own multivolume *Commentaries on the Constitution*, easily the most important work of constitutional scholarship of the nineteenth century. Story laced his treatise with copious quotations from and paraphrases of *The Federalist*, and he took pains in his Preface to acknowledge that he was standing on Publius's shoulders. In Story's words, *The Federalist* towered above all other Founding-era materials as a "great work"—an "incomparable commentary" that "discussed the structure and organization of the national government, in all its departments, with admirable fullness and force."[9]

When the Constitution was pending before the American people in 1787–1788, Publius beautifully summarized and synthesized many of the

/

best arguments that other leading Federalists were making elsewhere. In turn, *The Federalist* functioned as a debaters' handbook that leading Federalists deployed in some of the later ratification debates, especially in all-important Virginia and New York. More than two centuries after the Founding, *The Federalist* thus remains a particularly handy place to begin serious constitutional analysis.[10]

"Neither slavery nor involuntary servitude"

OF THE SIX CANONICAL WORKS highlighted in this chapter, the Northwest Ordinance is doubtless the one least familiar to the average twenty-first-century American. But this document loomed large in antebellum America and continues to inspire both constitutional scholars and Supreme Court justices. Over the years, the *U.S. Reports* have recorded explicit invocations of the Ordinance in over 125 Supreme Court cases. Roughly 20 of these citations have occurred in the past half-century, mostly in high-profile cases spanning a remarkable range of topics—including the nonestablishment and free-exercise principles, the one-person-one-vote rule, the right of habeas corpus, the principle of educational equality, and the right to civil and criminal juries.[11]

Enacted by the Confederation Congress in 1787 and reaffirmed by the new Congress under the Constitution as one of the first items of business in 1789, the Ordinance formed a large link in the great chain of American constitutional history. It simultaneously connected the fledgling constitutional system back to the greatest achievement of its predecessor regime (the Articles of Confederation); provided a guiding template for how the biggest national project of the antebellum era—territorial expansion and the ultimate admission of new states into the Union—should proceed; and foreshadowed America's next great constitutional achievement (the Reconstruction). In the process, the Ordinance helped shape Americans' deepest ideas about the nature of higher law and the essence of American federalism.[12]

Much of the Ordinance's substance concerned and confirmed constitutional first principles for America's territories as distinct from states. Territories today occupy a much smaller quadrant of American land and

American law than they did in the antebellum period. Back then, a huge chunk of the national land mass had yet to be or had only recently been admitted to statehood, and questions about how that land mass should be governed—most obviously, whether, when, and how slavery should be allowed there—ranked among the most important policy and constitutional issues of the era.

Even today the Ordinance continues to serve as a source of supplementary principles in constitutional discourse concerning certain topics on which the Constitution's terse text offers less specific guidance. For example, nothing in the written Constitution itself explicitly says that when a new state joins the Union it must generally come in on equal terms and equal footing with all previous states and all future states. Yet this principle, first articulated in the Northwest Ordinance, has long been explicitly recognized by both Congress and the courts as a basic maxim of American constitutionalism—that is, as a pillar of America's unwritten Constitution, subject to case-specific provisos that Congress may properly craft in order to ensure that each new state will loyally abide by the Union's basic spirit and structure. Supreme Court case law over the centuries suggests that the "equal-footing doctrine," as it is called, has exerted a more powerful and persistent pull on the judicial mind than many an explicit constitutional clause. The justices have mentioned or applied the equal-footing doctrine in dozens upon dozens of federalism cases stretching back to the 1830s, with at least one favorable invocation of the doctrine in every subsequent decade.[13]

The modern-day status of Puerto Rico highlights the continuing relevance of the Ordinance. Were the residents of this archipelago at some future date to clearly express their desire, by a clean majority vote, to become America's fifty-first state rather than continue their current unique territorial status, nothing in America's written Constitution would compel Congress and the president to bow to this wish (or alternatively, to offer Puerto Rico complete independence if its request for statehood was rejected). Nothing, in other words, would explicitly prevent the United States from acting as a permanent colonizer of a people who do not want to be permanent colonists. But America's unwritten Constitution would surely frown upon this sort of imperialist policy, and the deep source of this disapproval may be found in the words of the Northwest Ordinance, a charter member of America's symbolic Constitution.

THE ORDINANCE WAS INITIALLY ADOPTED by the Confederation Congress meeting in New York in the summer of 1787, at the very moment that another group of continental notables was convening in Philadelphia's Independence Hall to ponder and repair the fundamental defects of the Confederation. As soon as the Constitution commenced operation in early 1789, it became necessary for the new government to assure territorial settlers that all the major promises that had been made to them in the Ordinance would be honored, even though the "United States" was now under new management. This reassurance was in keeping with the opening lines of Article VI: "All debts contracted and Engagements entered into, before the Adoption of this Constitution, shall be as valid against the United States under this Constitution, as under the Confederation."[14]

On each of the key commitments made by the 1787 Ordinance, the First Congress registered its official agreement. First, the federal government promised to secure the basic rights of territorial inhabitants. Thus, even before other Americans could claim the benefit of a federal Bill of Rights (which was proposed later in 1789 and ratified in 1791), the First Congress signed off on a proto-Bill guaranteeing northwestern settlers, among other things, the rights to worship, to claim the writ of habeas corpus, to be tried by juries, to be represented fairly in local legislatures, and to receive just compensation in eminent-domain cases. Second, the Ordinance assured settlers that their initial status of dependency on the federal government would not endure indefinitely. America would not rule its western lands as permanent colonies the way Britain had tried to rule its American coastal dependencies. Instead, the Ordinance mapped a pathway by which individual western territories would eventually win statehood "on an equal footing with the original States in all respects whatever." Third, all the federal lands governed by the Ordinance—lands north and west of the Ohio River—would be free soil. Settlers would not be allowed to bring slaves into a region that was (with small exceptions) providentially free from this blight. Fourth, the Ordinance promised that its proto–Bill of Rights was ironclad and irrepealable "as articles of compact between the original States and the people and States in the said territory and forever... unalterable, unless by common consent."[15]

As time passed, Americans poured prodigiously into the Northwest thanks in no small part to the Ordinance's inducements, and in the process settlers began to endow the Ordinance with a special symbolic sanctity. For the region's numerous residents, the Ordinance was in effect their primary constitution—their basic frame of government and their highest source of law, their Magna Carta. Indeed, to many northwesterners the promises made in this sanctified text seemed to be prior to and even higher than the federal Constitution itself. Congress had pledged not to unilaterally abandon these guarantees, and even if some future federal constitutional amendment purporting to modify the Ordinance without settler consent might be technically legal, such an act would be an unthinkable breach of fundamental first principles of fairness. The Ordinance thus reinforced the idea—an idea also clearly visible in the Declaration—that certain higher-law rights preceded all legitimate government.

Of course, the most basic of these basic rights was a universal right to be free—a right that the Declaration did not recognize in practice, and that likewise found little support in the federal Constitution as actually implemented in antebellum America. Thanks to the three-fifths clause, proslavery policies had lots of friends in high places in the national government. But the Northwest Ordinance offered antislavery Americans a much purer symbol of what America could and should be—a symbol of the West, a symbol of the future, a symbol of hope, a symbol of free soil, free men, and freedom.*

The key clause of the Northwest Ordinance—the golden apple in its

---

* Western lands were also envisioned by the Ordinance as lands free from local malapportionment. Article 2 of the Ordinance promised that northwesterners "shall always be entitled to...a proportionate representation of the people in the legislature." Article 5 went on to provide that any state constitution eventually adopted by a territory seeking statehood "shall be republican, and in conformity to the principles contained in these articles." Here, then, is intriguing evidence from the Founding era linking "republican" government to a proto-one-person-one-vote idea—an idea that could work more easily in the Northwest precisely because this region would be free from complex questions about how to count slaves in a proper/proportionate apportionment system. In the 1964 case of *Reynolds v. Sims*, Chief Justice Warren explicitly invoked Article 2 of the Ordinance in support of the Court's vision.

silver frame, to borrow a phrase—read as follows: "There shall be neither slavery nor involuntary servitude in the said territory, otherwise than in the punishment of crimes whereof the party shall have been duly convicted." If these words look vaguely familiar, they should. When the American people finally put a constitutional end to slavery in 1865, they did so via a Thirteenth Amendment whose words consciously and closely tracked—and thus paid tribute to—the great Northwest Ordinance.

The ties between the antislavery ordinance and the antislavery amendment ran even deeper than this textual similarity alone might suggest. Many of the men who pushed the amendment through were from the Northwest—men like Lincoln and Senator Lyman Trumbull from Illinois, and Congressman John Bingham and former governor Salmon Chase of Ohio. The Old Northwest—Ohio, Michigan, Indiana, Illinois, Wisconsin, Minnesota—formed much of the backbone of the Republican Party. Men from these places filled out the Union Army at every level, from Grant and Sherman on down. Without these northwesterners, there would have been no President Lincoln, no Civil War victory, and no Abolition Amendment.

The nationalism visible in section 2 of the Abolition Amendment— "Congress shall have power to enforce..."—also had deep roots in the Northwest Territory and in the Northwest Ordinance. The taming and republicanization of the Northwest was a grand nationalist and nationalizing project. Residents of this region had arrived there from many different places (especially from free states, of course) and inclined toward a distinctly nationalist worldview. Whereas nineteenth-century Virginians like Robert E. Lee gave pride of place to their home state (which had preexisted the Union by more than a century and had helped found the Union in the 1770s and 1780s), northwesterners tended to see themselves as Americans first and state residents second. America had chronologically preceded the states they now called home. Indeed, via the Ordinance, America had founded these states qua states.

"born...citizens"

SEVERAL OF THE EPIC CONSTITUTIONAL THEMES of the Northwest Ordinance—higher law, freedom, nationhood—can also be discerned in a brief 1863 address delivered by the nineteenth century's most famous northwesterner. Like the Ordinance, the Gettysburg Address gestured back to America's preconstitutional experience ("Four score and seven years ago..."). Indeed, the Address gestured back to words ("all men are created equal") composed by Thomas Jefferson, the very same man who had composed the first draft of the Northwest Ordinance. And just as the Ordinance presaged the specific language of the Thirteenth Amendment, so the Address foreshadowed the Fourteenth. Whereas Lincoln's first sentence evoked the past, his last sentence envisioned the future, calling for "a new birth of freedom."

The new birth that Lincoln foretold was nothing less than a national conversion experience in which America, under God, would seek to free itself from the original sin of slavery and inequality. Today, that conversion experience is generally referred to as the Reconstruction, a new birth of freedom that had as its constitutional centerpiece a trio of amendments that marked the first formal additions to the Constitution since Jefferson's presidency. The opening sentence of the Reconstruction's central amendment prominently featured the word "born"—a word that built on Lincoln's poetic imagery of birth and rebirth. Fittingly, this amendment's new birth of American freedom began with Americans' freedom at birth—the freedom of every American to claim citizenship on the day he or she is born. And not just citizenship, but equal citizenship, because America was, Lincoln had reminded his audience, dedicated to the proposition that all men are created—born—equal. (The imagery of birth was visible even earlier in Lincoln's opening sentence, when he noted how the nation had been "conceived" and "brought forth"—born—in 1776.)

To put the point in a more legal and less literary way: Lincoln's Gettysburg Address is a central work in America's symbolic constitutional canon because the written Constitution itself links to Lincoln and ratifies his vision. After hearing Lincoln's 1863 dream, America reelected Lincoln and his allies in 1864, and this reelection precipitated the Thirteenth Amendment.

(Lincoln in fact signed this amendment even though his signature was legally unnecessary.) When Lincoln died, America proceeded to ratify his vision even further by taking what he had claimed was America's central proposition—that all men are created equal—and textualizing this idea in the Fourteenth Amendment. Eventually, Americans adopted yet another amendment extending the franchise to black men—an idea that Lincoln himself had publicly proposed only hours before he himself became a casualty of war and went to his final resting place, spiritually joining the soldiers he had eulogized at Gettysburg. This amendment, too, was an "altogether fitting and proper" tribute to Lincoln's memory and vision, much as he had offered precisely such a tribute to the men who had died so that the nation might live.[16]

The American people's profound, albeit informal, ratification of Lincoln's Gettysburg Address did not end in the 1860s. Lincoln's dream is continuously reenacted in twenty-first-century America as millions of citizens choose every year to make the Address their own in some special way—by reading it aloud in a classroom, by committing its ultra-terse text to memory, or simply by pondering its deep meaning and highly resolving that democracy and equality must not perish from the earth—or at least, must not do so on our watch.

"equal"

SOME OF THE MOST SIGNIFICANT reenactments and ratifications of Lincoln's Address occurred in and around *Brown* and the Dream Speech, and these two texts themselves entered the American constitutional canon when they, in turn, won the hearts and minds of the American people in the 1960s. One important moment of affirmation occurred in 1957, when President Dwight D. Eisenhower—a celebrated war hero in the tradition of Ulysses S. Grant, and the most famous resident of Gettysburg, Pennsylvania—responded to violent efforts to defy *Brown*'s implementation by sending federal troops back into the South to make clear that the Union had won the Civil War and that the war had ended with the constitutional promise of a new birth of freedom.

Though Eisenhower himself did not quite say it this clearly—Ike did not have Abe's way with words—his successor did use his bully pulpit to reaffirm both Lincoln and *Brown*. Addressing the nation from the Oval Office on June 11, 1963, just weeks shy of the centennial of the battle of Gettysburg, President John F. Kennedy told his fellow Americans why he, too, had been obliged to use military troops to enforce the constitutional rights of several students "who happen to have been born Negro." His remarks are worth quoting at length, for they perfectly illustrate how America's symbolic Constitution works in tandem with the written Constitution.

Kennedy began by echoing Jefferson and Lincoln: "This Nation was founded by men of many nations and backgrounds. It was founded on the principle that all men are created equal." As had Jefferson and Lincoln before him, Kennedy then proceeded to place the issues facing America in a global and geostrategic context and to reflect on the Jeffersonian/Lincolnian/Reconstruction idea of birth equality:

> Today we are committed to a worldwide struggle to promote and protect the rights of all who wish to be free. When Americans are sent to Vietnam or West Berlin, we do not ask for whites only. It ought to be possible, therefore, for American students of any color to attend any public institution they select without having to be backed up by troops.
>
> It ought to be possible for American consumers of any color to receive equal service in places of public accommodation, such as hotels and restaurants and theaters and retail stores, without being forced to resort to demonstrations in the street, and it ought to be possible for American citizens of any color to register to vote in a free election without interference or fear of reprisal.
>
> It ought to be possible, in short, for every American to enjoy the privileges of being American without regard to his race or his color.... But this is not the case.
>
> The Negro baby born in America today, regardless of the section of the Nation in which he is born, has about one-half as much chance of completing a high school as a white baby born in the same place on the same day, one-third as much chance of completing college, one-third as much chance of becoming a professional man, twice as much

chance of becoming unemployed, about one-seventh as much chance of earning $10,000 a year, a life expectancy which is 7 years shorter, and the prospects of earning only half as much.

Building upon his earlier invocations of a southeastern proto-Democrat (Jefferson) and a northwestern Republican (Lincoln), Kennedy declared that "[t]his is not a sectional issue....Nor is this a partisan issue. In a time of domestic crisis men of good will and generosity should be able to unite regardless of party or politics....We are confronted primarily with a moral issue. It is as old as the scriptures and is as clear as the American Constitution."

JFK then reminded America of the special—symbolic—significance of the hour at hand: "One hundred years of delay have passed since President Lincoln freed the slaves, yet their heirs, their grandsons, are not fully free....Now the time has come for this Nation to fulfill its promise." The president concluded his Oval Office address with a specific call to action to reaffirm and extend the Court's teachings in *Brown*:

> I am, therefore, asking the Congress to enact legislation giving all Americans the right to be served in facilities which are open to the public—hotels, restaurants, theaters, retail stores, and similar establishments....
>
>   ...
>
> I am also asking the Congress to authorize the Federal Government to participate more fully in lawsuits designed to end segregation in public education....
>
>   ...
>
> The orderly implementation of the Supreme Court decision ... cannot be left solely to those who may not have the economic resources to carry the legal action or who may be subject to harassment.
>
> Other features will also be requested, including greater protection for the right to vote.

Speaking even more eloquently and urgently later that summer to hundreds of thousands who had thronged the national capital to demand racial progress, Dr. King made many of the same general points and called for many of the same legal actions.

When Kennedy fell to an assassin's bullet in late 1963, just as Lincoln had fallen in 1865, he, too, was succeeded by a southern vice president named Johnson. But Lyndon was no Andrew, who had fought congressional Reconstructors tooth and nail. By contrast, the second President Johnson used the memory of his slain predecessor and every other argument and implement at his disposal—including the "fierce urgency of now" that King and his crusaders had so powerfully manifested—to push through two of the most important pieces of legislation in American history, the Civil Rights Act of 1964 and the Voting Rights Act of 1965. These laws emphatically affirmed the rightness of *Brown*'s constitutional vision—and King's and Lincoln's, too.[17] *

Indeed, these laws, which remain on the books today, are qualitatively different from virtually all other legislation ever enacted by Congress. These two iconic laws are washed in the blood of American martyrs and heroes—Abraham Lincoln, John F. Kennedy, Martin Luther King Jr., John Lewis, Rosa Parks. In their actual enactment process, these statutes more closely resembled previous constitutional amendments than standard inside-the-Beltway, lobbyist-driven lawmaking. Led by Dr. King, hundreds of thousands of ordinary citizens had risen up to demand legal redress for large historical wrongs; and in the mid-1960s, all branches of the federal government heeded the voices and the vision of this extraordinary mass movement.[18]

These two statutes thus not only helped canonize *Brown* and the Dream Speech but also entered the canon in their own right as part of America's symbolic Constitution. Without these laws, it is impossible to imagine, for example, that Barack Obama could ever have been elected president. His election—as a tall, slim constitutional lawyer from Illinois, preaching and epitomizing the idea that all men are truly created equal—represents yet another symbolic affirmation of Lincoln, and yet another illustration of the uncanny ways in which various strands in America's symbolic Constitution knit together to form a fascinating network of cross-reference and allusion.

---

* In 1967, the political branches cast a further official, if indirect, vote of confidence for *Brown* when President Johnson nominated and the Senate confirmed Thurgood Marshall, the crusading lawyer who had won the *Brown* case, as America's first black Supreme Court justice. In 2010, America's first black president named a former Marshall law clerk, Elena Kagan, to the Court.

FULL RACIAL EQUALITY REMAINS A GREAT, UNFINISHED ITEM on the American agenda—and a complex one. Is actual social integration, as opposed to the ending of legal segregation, a constitutionally preferred goal? Even if it is, may governments engage in race-conscious actions to bring about this goal? What, if any, limits should apply to such actions?

The written Constitution offers us only limited guidance on these questions. To the extent that the Founders preached anything on this particular topic worthy of our allegiance today, they did not fully practice what they preached, as the slaves of Monticello and Montpelier (and even Mount Vernon) surely understood. Even the great texts and deeds of the Reconstruction generation can offer us only incomplete illumination and inspiration. In the 1860s, most American blacks had either been born slaves or born to ex-slave parents, and most American whites had little experience interacting with large numbers of free blacks. The issues of racial healing and the practical political limits confronting statesmen of goodwill in that era were surely vastly different from the racial questions that confront America in the age of Obama. (Indeed, the very word "statesmen" in the previous sentence should remind us that the political world was a different place before the advent of woman suffrage and many other twentieth-century reforms.)

In light of the limited guidance furnished by the written Constitution's text and original intent, what specific race-rules should properly govern twenty-first-century America? Some prominent scholars and judges have argued that the Constitution comfortably permits race-based "affirmative action" policies designed to help blacks—even if the government adopts or approximates a racial quota system in the distribution of benefits. Other leading constitutionalists have contended that government may never take race into account, even in supposedly benign ways aimed to help racial minorities, except when using narrowly tailored race-conscious remedies on behalf of identifiable victims of proven or provable legal violations.

Today's Court has steered a middle course between these extremes. The Court's case law has recognized that using race to integrate is different from using race to segregate, and that race-based policies aiming to promote racial equality differ from old-fashioned Jim Crow laws that aimed to secure white supremacy. More specifically, the Court has recognized that in certain realms—especially education—integration is a proper government goal that government may sometimes pursue via race-conscious means, even on behalf of racial minority members who cannot prove that they were victims of illegal racial discrimination. Nevertheless, race-conscious actions must be very carefully restricted, lest these policies treat whites unfairly, stigmatize blacks, generate white backlash, or create a racially divisive politics.[19]

While hardly compelled by the teachings of *Brown* and the Dream Speech, this middle position is broadly consistent with and consciously informed by these two iconic works. Both texts surely suggest that it is dangerous to allow government to treat any two persons differently simply because the two have different skin colors. *Brown*, after all, invalidated government policies that treated persons differently "according to race"; and its companion, *Bolling*, proclaimed that the Constitution forbade "discrimination...against *any* citizen because of his race" (emphasis added). King famously dreamed of a day when persons would "not be judged by the color of their skin but by the content of their character."

Yet, in context, both *Brown* and the Dream Speech can also easily be read as pro-integration, even if integration entails government action that is not strictly color-blind. Lower courts implementing *Brown* issued various orders requiring previously segregated public schools to take race into account in order to end a regime in which some schools were strongly identified as "black schools" and others as "white schools." Some of these race-conscious school assignments governed newly entering kindergarteners who had not been victims of any past school segregation.[20]

King dreamed of a day when "my four little children" would be judged by the content of their character, children who had been born at a disadvantage because they were black, whether or not they could ever prove that they had already become victims of some discrete and identifiable legal wrong at the hands of government. (His daughter Bernice was less than a year old at the time, and his son Dexter was two and a half.) The Dream was hardly color-blind—it was exquisitely attentive to color because America was so strongly color-coded in 1963. When King said, "[T]here is something that I must say to my people," whom did he mean by "my people"? All people? All Americans? All children of God? No. At that precise instant he was speaking as a black person about black people.

Yet King dreamed of a day when all persons of all races would unite—

would integrate. Indeed, much of the power of his dream resided in the fact that blacks and whites were uniting on that glorious day, as King himself emphasized: "The marvelous new militancy which has engulfed the Negro community must not lead us to a distrust of all white people, for many of our white brothers, *as evidenced by their presence here today*, have come to realize that their destiny is tied up with our destiny. They have come to realize that their freedom is inextricably bound to our freedom. *We cannot walk alone*" (emphasis added).

Moments later came King's final crowning vision, a vision of persons across the racial divide holding hands and singing together, a vision not merely of American liberty and American equality but also of genuine American fraternity—a vision far more strongly integrationist than anything in the terse text, yet surely a key part of America's Constitution, rightly understood.

"any Thing...to the Contrary notwithstanding"

SEVERAL SYMBOLS CONSTITUTIVE of America's constitutional identity are *negative* symbols, crystallizing what America today rejects—indeed, abhors. In particular, three specific Supreme Court opinions occupy the lowest circle of constitutional Hell and are today denounced by lawyers and judges across the spectrum: *Dred Scott v. Sanford*, *Plessy v. Ferguson*, and *Lochner v. New York*. Each case presents an example of unwritten constitutionalism run amok, and thus powerfully reminds us of the need to place principled limits on judges who venture beyond the text and original understanding of the written Constitution.[21]

Before turning to these three cases, it is worth pondering what general factors seem to be at work in shaping how the judicial actions of one era are evaluated by later generations of judges and citizens. Clearly, not all cases that are overruled by a later Court ruling or constitutional amendment come to be demonized after the overruling. For example, the 1833 case of *Barron v. Baltimore* held (correctly) that the Bill of Rights as originally written did not properly apply against state governments. No one on the modern Court or in today's academy attacks *Barron*, even though *Barron*'s vision of a world in which states and localities are free to violate the Bill of Rights with impunity is anathema to modern sensibilities.

Some might think that modern generosity toward *Barron* exists simply because its ruling is moot: The Fourteenth Amendment overruled the case, and that's that. But is it? The Fourteenth Amendment, after all, was designed to overrule not one but two major Supreme Court cases—*Barron* (on the inapplicability of the Bill of Rights to states) and *Dred Scott* (on the impossibility of black citizenship). Yet these two overruled cases receive sharply different treatment in modern constitutional discourse. *Dred Scott* is openly trashed, not merely by many of America's best scholars but by justices of all stripes on the Warren and post-Warren Courts. Not so with *Barron*.[22]

Is the answer simply that the *Dred Scott* Court's bottom line was racist and proslavery, and thus morally repugnant when judged by today's standards? This is surely part of the answer, but many other antebellum-era cases with racist and proslavery bottom lines are not demonized, or even remembered, today. Also, why is there so little modern outrage directed at *Minor v. Happersett*, which in 1875 ruled that women had no constitutional right to vote? Just as *Dred Scott*'s racist result was overruled by the Fourteenth Amendment, so *Minor*'s sexist result was overruled by the Nineteenth Amendment. Why, then, the different reputations of these two cases?

The answer is twofold. First, *Barron* and *Minor* were not merely plausible but plainly correct interpretations of the written Constitution as it existed when these cases were decided. *Dred Scott*, by contrast, was a preposterous garbling of the Constitution as that document was publicly understood when ratified, and the case was harshly criticized on precisely these grounds by notable contemporaries. In a July 1858 speech in Chicago, Lincoln called the case "an astonisher in legal history." Here, then, we see the significance of America's written Constitution. Whatever government officials might think they can get away with at the time, in the long run it does matter whether a case (think here of *Dred Scott*), a law (think here of the Sedition Act of 1798), or a president's actions (think here of Watergate) treated the document's text and structure with respect or contempt.

Second, *Dred Scott* ran counter to the Northwest Ordinance, whose free-soil spirit was declared unconstitutional by Taney, and also counter to Lincoln—who rose to fame as a result of his early criticism of *Dred*, became president on an anti-*Dred* platform, and in his opening sentence at

Gettysburg explicitly challenged *Dred*'s dismissive treatment of the equality language of the Declaration. Similarly, *Plessy* ran counter to *Brown*. Precisely because the Northwest Ordinance, the Gettysburg Address (and its gloss on the Declaration), and the *Brown* opinion are iconic elements of America's symbolic Constitution, their opposites naturally enough provoke special revulsion. Here we see additional evidence of the reality and significance of America's symbolic Constitution—and another illustration of how various constitutional symbols interconnect in an intricate semiotic network.

If this analysis is correct, *Lochner* should be viewed as a less demonic precedent than *Dred* and *Plessy* because it is not as visibly paired against a symbolic hero. And in fact, one can find scholars who praise *Lochner* and even some who call for its revival.[23]

But one does not hear such calls on the Court itself. In modern Court opinions, *Dred*, *Plessy*, and *Lochner* all function as antiprecedents—as demonized and demonic cases that are typically cited either to assert how different they were from the view being put forth by the citing justice, or as epithets and insults to hurl against the justices on the other side of a case who, according to the citer, are making a horrible mistake reminiscent of one of these three disgraced decisions. Almost none of the countless Court citations to these three cases over the past half-century have been remotely favorable, and most have been highly derogatory.

With these general observations in mind, let us now quickly survey each of these three demonized decisions.

Dred Scott. Chief Justice Taney's 1857 opinion for the Court in *Dred Scott* in effect claimed that all citizens had to be "white," a word that nowhere appeared in the Founders' text and that the Founders had pointedly omitted, in part because free blacks were in fact citizens and voters in several states at the Founding. Even more preposterous was Taney's claim that no federal territory could prohibit slavery, a rule that nowhere appeared in the Founders' document and that plainly contradicted the original understanding. *Dred Scott* also treated landmark congressional legislation—most obviously, the Northwest Ordinance and the Missouri Compromise—with contempt.

To be sure, the *Dred Scott* opinion claimed to be following the underlying premises of the Founders themselves, but this claim was untrue—the Court simply flouted the written Constitution's letter and spirit. The Court also claimed that moral considerations were wholly irrelevant to the constitutional issues under consideration. But there is room for persons of conscience to properly consult those consciences if the Constitution's written provisions are in fact fairly open to different interpretations and if one of these interpretations would lead to a grossly immoral result. The spread of slavery to virgin soil was precisely such a result, as slavery was surely an immoral institution, regardless of slavery's status as a legally protected system where it already existed.[24]

Plessy. In this 1896 case, the Court disregarded the rather plain facts that: (1) the written Constitution promised that blacks would be treated as equal citizens, and (2) the whole point of Jim Crow was to deny black equality—to treat blacks as inferior. This judicial disregard cannot be justified by appealing to some vague notion of an "unwritten Constitution" that must be given its due. America's unwritten Constitution supplements but does not supplant. It should never be a carte blanche authorizing judges (or other government officials) to ignore core commands of the written Constitution.

It is not anachronistic to condemn the *Plessy* majority in these harsh terms. After all, these are the very terms used by the first Justice John Marshall Harlan in his famous dissent, issued the same day as the infamous majority opinion. Harlan wrote that "the judgment this day rendered will, in time, prove to be quite as pernicious as the decision made by this tribunal in the *Dred Scott* case"—a remarkably prescient prediction, and an uncanny one, again illustrating linkages between different elements within the canon of America's symbolic Constitution.[25]

Lochner. Although *Lochner v. New York* is less well known outside legal circles, the very word "*Lochner*" is for legal insiders synonymous with judicial overreach. *Lochner* is thus not just a case, but an era and an attitude. In legal discourse it has even become a verb. To "Lochner" or to "Lochnerize" is to commit the same kind of judicial sin that characterized many of the

Court's rulings in what is now known as "the *Lochner* era"—roughly the mid-1880s through the mid-1930s—in which the Court, without clear textual warrant, struck down a multitude of reasonable reform statutes regulating free-market excesses.

The 1905 *Lochner* case itself, in which the Court invalidated a state maximum-hour law, was but one particularly salient example of the Court's overeagerness to invalidate progressive legislation. Nothing in the written Constitution expressly prohibited maximum-hour laws, and it is hard to make a winning argument that the Constitution implicitly did so. The Court's root objection to such laws was that they were designed to redistribute wealth from employers to laborers. But then, so was the Thirteenth Amendment itself—which redistributed slave property from masters to slaves with no compensation. Nor can it be thought that worker-health and worker-rights laws violated a pattern of lived freedom, given that a great many states (and large ones at that) repeatedly tried to enact such laws in the Progressive era. Although *Lochner* could perhaps be defended as a plausible (albeit contestable) constitutional interpretation in 1905, the Court implausibly continued to follow a strongly antiredistributionist line even after the American people in 1913 openly embraced the propriety of redistributive policies via an Income Tax Amendment that envisioned a strongly progressive—that is, redistributive—tax structure.[26]

EACH OF OUR THREE NEGATIVE ICONS not only stands as a despised symbol in its own right (perhaps "wrong" would be the better word here) but also visibly stands alongside the other two as part of a larger symbolic constitutional system. For example, all three logical pairings inherent in our trio of despised cases are visible in prominent modern opinions. Critics of the Court's early record on race have repeatedly found it useful to mention *Dred Scott* and *Plessy* in the same breath (as did Harlan in *Plessy* itself); opponents of substantive due process have invoked *Dred Scott* and *Lochner* as paired Exhibits A and B; and *Plessy* and *Lochner* have operated in tandem in modern case law as the best illustrations of the need for the Court to overrule its erroneous precedents.[27]

In short, just as the deities in the constitutional Pantheon link arms with each other in manifest and manifold ways, so do the demons in constitutional Hell.

THIS CHAPTER HAS TRIED TO SHOW that there is such a thing as America's symbolic Constitution—a set of especially significant, and indeed constitutive, texts—and that its core components are easy to spot in both case law and culture. This symbolic Constitution exists as a system of meaning and guidance, both positive and negative.

In this domain, as elsewhere, we not only must probe individual parts of the system but must also see the constitutional project as a whole and ponder larger patterns of meaning. Here is one way to connect the dots: In sharp contrast to America's most disgraced cases, which protected haves at the expense of have-nots, and insiders at the expense of outsiders, most of our icons of positive national identity have championed equality and reflected abiding concern for those at the bottom of the status hierarchy— tyrannized colonists, politically vulnerable territorial settlers, ordinary unnamed soldiers who died on a bloody battlefield, black children relegated to second-class status, the "Negro [who] is still not free." In this pattern resides a powerful lesson for how America's unwritten Constitution is best interpreted and enforced—namely, to reinforce rather than to undercut the great themes of equality and inclusion in America's written Constitution.

CHAPTER 7

"REMEMBERING
THE LADIES"

America's Feminist Constitution

"Women are too sentimental for jury duty."
—Anti-Suffrage argument.

"WOMEN ARE TOO SENTIMENTAL FOR JURY DUTY" (1915).

In the heyday of American Progressivism, some reformers met the anti-suffrage argument that "women are too sentimental for jury duty" with a reminder that men, too, could act emotionally on juries. Note the premise underlying this prong of the suffrage debate: Woman suffrage would also entail woman jury service, even though neither the federal Woman Suffrage Amendment nor its typical state constitutional counterpart explicitly enumerated the jury-service right. At least some persons on both sides in the suffrage conversation thus understood the unenumerated links between voting and jury service. But did everyone in the 1910s understand these links? What other unenumerated entailments followed from the deep logic of woman suffrage?

AMERICA'S WRITTEN CONSTITUTION DESCRIBES ITSELF as ordained by "the People" and proclaims itself "the supreme Law," superior to ordinary congressional statutes. At the Founding, these two patches of text were linked by an overarching theory of legitimacy based on popular sovereignty: The Constitution should trump an ordinary statute enacted later, because a mere statute passed by Congress is not democratically equivalent to a Constitution ratified more directly by the people themselves in a process that allowed an unusually wide slice of Americans to vote. Similarly, because a constitutional amendment needs to win the support of overwhelming supermajorities in Congress and in the states before becoming part of the Constitution, no mere congressional majority should be allowed to undo an amendment. Like the original Constitution, an amendment democratically outranks any statute, even a statute enacted more recently.[1]

But then something happened in America that the Founders did not anticipate—something with profound consequences that were neither comprehensively codified in the terse text nor immediately understood. Women got the vote via a series of reforms culminating in the Nineteenth Amendment. In 1908, almost no American woman could vote anywhere; by 1920, women voted everywhere. The Suffrage Revolution marked the largest numerical extension of the franchise in American history, complicating the standard democratic stories previously told about why the Constitution should trump a later statute.

To some extent, and perhaps unwittingly, the adoption of the Nineteenth Amendment logically undercut the democratic legitimacy of the constitutional regime that preceded the amendment. But to what extent, exactly? And what are the unwritten constitutional implications and entailments of this logical undercutting? In the aftermath of this unintentionally unsettling amendment, how should faithful constitutional interpreters make amends for the retrospectively problematic exclusions that defined the American constitutional order prior to 1920? In what other respects did the Suffrage Revolution properly precipitate later unwritten constitutional changes not wholly foreseen or textualized in 1920?*

In this chapter we shall wrestle with these weighty questions and attempt to align contemporary constitutional gender law with the written Constitution.

"We the People"

SUPPOSE THAT CONGRESS TOMORROW were to enact a sweeping new law designed to protect women's rights. Our hypothetical civil-rights statute would protect women not only against discriminatory government action, state and federal, but also against various threats to women's liberty and equality posed by private misconduct—for example, workplace harassment and violence directed against women on account of their sex. Suppose further that this new civil-rights law was thought by some to go beyond the powers given to Congress by the Founding text, and even to go beyond the powers given to Congress by the Reconstruction Amendments.

It might be thought that no one but a crank could question the constitutionality of our hypothetical law on enumerated-powers grounds. After all, there is strong reason to believe that the Reconstruction Amendments gave Congress virtually plenary authority to identify and safeguard citizens' basic rights of liberty and equality. Recall that the Fourteenth Amendment's first sentence proclaimed that all persons born in America would be equal citizens at birth, and that its last sentence empowered Congress to enforce the ideals of the amendment. The first sentence guaranteed equal citizenship not just against governments but more generally, and guaranteed this birth equality not just for blacks vis-à-vis whites, but more universally. Under a straightforward interpretation, Congress has broad power to affirm equal birthright citizenship by protecting any class of citizens at serious

---

* Other constitutional amendments expanding rights of democratic participation—for example, the Thirteenth, Fourteenth, Fifteenth, Twenty-third, Twenty-fourth, and Twenty-sixth Amendments—raise broadly similar questions that lie beyond the scope of this chapter. Here, as in other chapters, I aim to offer exemplary, not exhaustive, illustrations of how faithful interpreters may properly go beyond the text while staying true to it.

risk of being systematically harmed or demeaned on the basis of their birth status—injured or excluded because, say, they happen to have been born black or female.[2]

But let's assume that some stingy interpreters of the written Constitution are not convinced by these textual and historical arguments. These interpreters admit that the Reconstruction text could plausibly be read to broadly empower Congress; however, they believe that the legislative history of the Fourteenth Amendment, with its central focus on the rights of blacks, in particular, and on the need to prevent state misconduct, limits the power of Congress to enact civil rights for nonracial groups, such as women, and to protect any group against nonstate actors, such as private employers or prejudiced thugs. In fact, after Congress passed a real-life law resembling our hypothetical statute—the Violence Against Women Act (VAWA) of 1994—the Supreme Court, in the 2000 case of *United States v. Morrison*, held that parts of the law exceeded Congress's constitutionally enumerated power.

When these sorts of stingy interpretations prevail—when the old Constitution is read to trump a modern women's-rights statute—it is hard to see how this trumping can be said to be democratically consistent with popular sovereignty. "We the People" who voted for the Founding text and who voted for the Reconstruction Amendments did not generally include women voters. The very legislative history of Reconstruction relied upon by stingy interpreters is a history dominated by male voters and male lawmakers.

By contrast, the members of Congress who passed our hypothetical modern civil-rights law (and who passed the real-life VAWA) *were* voted for by women. Indeed, women themselves—lots of them—serve in modern Congresses even though women were generally barred from serving in the constitutional ratifying conventions of the 1780s and the legislatures that approved the Reconstruction Amendments in the 1860s.

If we are to vindicate the written Constitution's legitimating principle—popular sovereignty—we should embrace the following as a basic precept of America's unwritten Constitution: When the written Constitution can fairly be read in different ways, congressional laws that are enacted after the Nineteenth Amendment and are designed to protect women's rights merit a special measure of respect because of their special democratic pedigree. Thus, Congress should enjoy broad power to protect women's rights for the simple reason that the unwritten Constitution is a Constitution of American popular sovereignty, and popular sovereignty is perverted when more democratic, post-woman-suffrage enactments championing women's rights are trumped by less democratic, pre-woman-suffrage legal texts.

True, various pre-1920 constitutional enactments and amendments were enormously democratic for their time. Yet when these earlier enactments and amendments are viewed retrospectively through the lens of the Nineteenth Amendment, they suffer from a notable democracy deficit because they excluded women voters. The problem cannot be wished away by blithe assertions that earlier generations of men "virtually represented" women, because *the Nineteenth Amendment's underlying logic repudiated this particular version of virtual representation of women by men.* The very adoption of the Nineteenth Amendment undermined the glib assumption that before 1920, male voters and lawmakers always properly protected the legitimate interests of nonvoting females.

TO SEE THIS PROFOUND POINT about the retrospective democracy deficit more clearly, we should begin by noticing that the Nineteenth Amendment was designed to correct a past wrong. It was an amendment to make amends.

Not all amendments are of this sort. For example, nothing in the Eighteenth Amendment establishing National Prohibition in 1919 suggested that any rights violation or deep injustice had occurred when America was wet. Instead, the idea was simply that a dry America would be better. Unlike, say, murder and rape, drinking and selling alcohol were not intrinsically evil. In legalese, selling alcohol was widely understood as *malum prohibitum* (an action that was wrong only if and because the law prohibited it) and not *malum in se* (an action legally prohibited because it was wrong in itself, even before the law came along). Precisely because selling alcohol was merely *malum prohibitum*, the Eighteenth Amendment provided a special time-delay of one year after the amendment's ratification before any new federal criminal law implementing Prohibition would take effect. This year-long delay would give Americans time to adjust to a new—dry—code of conduct.

By contrast, the Allies at Nuremberg in the late 1940s applied their code of conduct to punish actions previously committed by the Nazis, and did so over the defendants' emphatic objection that this application was improperly ex post facto. Not so, said the Allies, correctly. Certain things were evil from time immemorial. Genocide and other war crimes had always been wrongful—*malum in se.* The Allies were not changing the basic human code of right and wrong; they were merely creating a new legal court to enforce the preexisting moral order, an order inscribed in the hearts of all right-thinking humans.[3]

On which side of the line did the Nineteenth Amendment fall? Did it merely create new rules that would apply purely prospectively, as with the Eighteenth Amendment? Or did it call for fully retrospective application, as with the Nuremberg prosecutions? Or was some intermediate approach called for? If so, what were its contours?

The text of the Nineteenth Amendment does not answer these questions. But here, as elsewhere, the text narrows the range of possible outcomes, and various elements of America's unwritten Constitution—structural inferences, logical entailments, principles of interpretive coherence, and common sense—narrow the range even further.

On the one hand, we should immediately reject the outlandish idea that the Nineteenth Amendment somehow pulled the rug out from under its own feet and retroactively rendered illegitimate the entire constitutional project that preceded it. The amendment's text, after all, purports to modify, not exterminate, the preexisting Constitution. It was explicitly ratified as an "amendment" to an earlier document. In the language of Article V, it forms "Part of this Constitution." In this respect, the Nineteenth Amendment differs radically from the original Constitution itself, which was designed to kill and bury its predecessor document, the Articles of Confederation.[4]

Similarly, it would be nonsensical to think the Nineteenth Amendment requires interpreters to determine how the pre-1920 Constitution would have been worded differently had women been involved in its initial enactment or its pre-woman-suffrage amendments, and to follow the presumed constitutional text that would have emerged in this alternative universe. This would be a mind-bending thought experiment of such indeterminacy that all legal constraint would be lost—and the amendment was surely about modifying a document designed to work as *law*. Likewise, no one can say whether past presidential elections would have turned out the same if women had voted, because the candidates would surely have played the game quite differently—but how, precisely? The whole world would have been different, almost unimaginably so. As the saying goes, if my aunt had wheels, she'd be a wagon.

On the other hand, it would lean too far in the other direction to limit the Nineteenth Amendment to purely prospective application, à la the Eighteenth. Such an approach would make sense if the ratification of the Nineteenth were exactly like the coming of age of an individual. When a person reaches age eighteen, she is allowed to vote, but we do not think that the fact that our new adult-voter was denied the vote last year is anything wrongful or deplorable. She couldn't vote then because she was not, in legal contemplation, old enough then. She is now older and presumably wiser. But woman suffrage was not like this. The idea was not that in 1920 women had matured and were thus fundamentally different from the women of 1919 or 1918 or 1901—or 1866 or 1787, for that matter. Rather, the very adoption of the Nineteenth Amendment was an official recognition that the previous exclusion of women from the franchise had indeed been wrong and deplorable by the more enlightened standards of the post-woman-suffrage Constitution itself. The question is how to factor this profound implication of woman suffrage into proper constitutional interpretation.

To repeat, the terse text does not prescribe a specific answer to this question. To some extent, the issue turns on basic principles of remedy law, and the text says very little about how to vindicate the venerable idea that for every legal wrong there should be some remedy.[5]

Very little, but not nothing. One clause in the Judicial Article reminds us that when judges hear cases arising under the Constitution, they are properly influenced by traditional principles of "Equity." A second clause, in the Nineteenth Amendment itself, suggests that Congress should have broad authority to enforce the amendment's letter and spirit. Indeed, the very words used—"Congress shall have power to enforce this article by *appropriate* legislation"—harked back to the letter-and-spirit test laid down by Marshall in *McCulloch*: "Let the end be legitimate, let it be within the scope of the constitution, and all means which are *appropriate*, which are plainly adapted to that end, which are not prohibited, but consist with the letter and spirit of the constitution, are constitutional" (emphasis added). Marshall himself applied this test so as to accord Congress wide discretion to promote national security. Nothing in the written Constitution said anything specific about a national bank, and a national bank was not absolutely and indispensably necessary for national security. But if Congress plausibly thought that a national bank would promote national security, that was good enough for Marshall. Similarly, if Congress tomorrow plausibly thinks that a women's-rights law might promote women's full political equality, that, too, should be good enough under an amendment that gestures toward the generous *McCulloch* test via its use of the word "appropriate."

Though the text of the Nineteenth Amendment can easily be read in this fashion, it must be admitted that the text standing alone can also be read in a more stingy way. Recall that in 2000, the *Morrison* Court in fact adopted a stingy stance and rejected the claim that Congress has plenary power to pass any and all laws genuinely aimed at promoting women's full civil and political equality.

The decisive point, then, is a deeper one implicating unwritten constitutional first principles that, alas, were not presented to the *Morrison* Court, and that the Court therefore failed even to see, much less ponder. Whenever the Constitution is read to sharply limit the power of today's Congress to protect women's rights, an ambiguous and less democratic constitutional text (from whose original enactment and early amendment women were excluded—wrongly, in retrospect) ends up trumping a clear and more democratic statutory text (in whose making women rightly enjoy political equality). Such a result undermines the popular-sovereignty foundation of the Constitution—its basic claim to legitimacy. The written text depends on the unwritten principle of popular sovereignty and must be construed in light of that principle even though the text does not quite say so in any one explicit clause.

"the right to vote"

THE NINETEENTH AMENDMENT is not the only part of the written Constitution that means more than meets the eye. Before examining several other implications of this transformative amendment, let's recall some basic truths about earlier transformative constitutional clauses that also meant more than they initially seemed to say.

Although nothing in the original Constitution explicitly declared that American citizens would be more free than British subjects to criticize officialdom, this truth was a logical implication and entailment of American popular sovereignty—a principle that underlay the entire document, beginning with its opening three words (to say nothing of its actual enactment). Not everyone at the Founding initially understood the logical implications of the new American system. This widespread failure of understanding helps to explain why so many early Congressmen voted for the Sedition Act of 1798. People who live through a revolution do not always immediately appreciate just what they have wrought.

A similar dynamic of unintended entailments unfolded during America's second great revolution, more commonly known as Reconstruction. Some Reconstructionists at first believed that the Thirteenth Amendment would suffice to repair the constitutional damage caused by slavery and secession. But once blacks became free, republicanism obliged further reforms. How could any ex-gray state be a true republic if a great mass of the state's *free men* were excluded from the franchise? On further reflection, Americans came to see that freedom without the franchise was unstable—at least if the nation was to stand by the constitutional principle that each state be an honest-to-goodness republic. Excluding slaves from voting in antebellum America had been one thing; for purposes of republican self-government, slaves were no more part of the polity than were aliens. But excluding free men was something very different—and excluding large numbers of free men was, on second thought, the very definition of unrepublicanism. Thus, Reconstruction Republicans ended up going further than many had initially intended.

What was true of America's first two great democratic revolutions was equally true of its third, the doubling of suffrage accomplished in the early twentieth century. Here, too, not all the implications and entailments were at first fully understood even by the revolutionaries themselves.[6]

FOR EXAMPLE, most suffragists probably gave little or no thought to how the Nineteenth Amendment's words should be squared with the apportionment rules laid down by section 2 of the Fourteenth Amendment, rules that had never been enforced by Congress or the courts prior to 1920. Yet simple logic dictated that the word "male" in section 2—the Constitution's first and only use of this word—would need to be modified after the Suffrage Revolution. Otherwise, section 2 itself would violate the central command of the Woman Suffrage Amendment, namely, that no law could henceforth treat males and females differently in the domain of voting rights.[7]

Exactly how far did this domain extend? For example, did voting rights entail the right to serve on juries? On this issue, too, the Suffrage Revolution implied reforms that not all suffragists may have fully understood during the revolution itself.

The Supreme Court did not recognize a right of women to serve on juries equally with men until 1975—and when the Court finally did recognize this right, in *Taylor v. Louisiana*, the Woman Suffrage Amendment went wholly unmentioned. Instead, the Court derived a right of women to serve equally on juries from the Fourteenth Amendment's equal-protection clause. As a matter of constitutional text and original understandings, this judicial reasoning left much to be desired. The equal-protection clause was written to be, and in the 1860s was universally understood to be, categorically inapplicable to voting rights. Nothing in this clause, which applied to all persons, including aliens, operated to enfranchise aliens—or blacks, or women for that matter. (In the 1875 case of *Minor v. Happersett*, a unanimous Supreme Court made mincemeat of the plaintiff's claim that the Fourteenth Amendment enfranchised women.) But if the Fourteenth Amendment gave women no right to vote outside the jury box, then how exactly did this amendment give women a right to vote inside the jury box? Conversely, if the Fourteenth Amendment equal-protection clause somehow had in fact enfranchised women, what exactly was all the fuss about in the 1910s over that Nineteenth Amendment thingy?[8]

Despite all this, *Taylor* clearly reached the right result. It simply used the wrong clause, as did so many other Warren Court and post–Warren Court cases involving voting rights and/or the Fourteenth Amendment. Once the Warren Court in the early 1960s decided to press the equal-protection clause into service as a voting-rights provision in cases such as *Harper v. Virginia* and *Kramer v. Union Free School District*, the next logical step was to treat jury service as akin to voting. Those who voted for ordinary lawmakers should as a rule also be allowed to serve—or to vote, if you will—on ordinary juries. This logic made perfect sense; but the root right of women to vote (for lawmakers or on juries) came not from the Fourteenth Amendment but from the Nineteenth.

Put another way, women's equal right to vote on juries was a simple implication of their equal right to vote generally. Even if not all suffragists and not all their opponents understood this entailment in the 1910s, many surely did;* and any other way of thinking about the question risked making a hash of the Constitution as a whole. The Nineteenth Amendment's text tracked the Fifteenth Amendment's text virtually verbatim, simply substituting "sex" for "race, color, or previous condition of servitude." Ever since the 1870s, landmark congressional legislation had made clear that the antidiscrimination rules applicable to ordinary voting for legislators (and executives and state judges) also applied to jury service. If this was true of the Fifteenth Amendment, surely it also applied to the Nineteenth, whether or not every amendment supporter or opponent understood this implication.[9]

The right to vote was generally conceptualized not merely as a right to vote for legislators but also as a right to vote within a legislature. If blacks or women could not as such be disfranchised, neither could they be excluded from the legislature on account of their race or sex. Put differently, given that the Fifteenth Amendment and the Nineteenth Amendment clearly applied to initiatives, referendums, bond measures, and other occasions when ordinary voters engaged in direct lawmaking, surely these amendments likewise applied when lawmaking and voting occurred in representative assemblies.

---

* See, e.g., the picture and caption with which this chapter begins. The linkage between woman suffrage and woman jury service was also a subtext of Susan Glaspell's brilliant 1917 short story "A Jury of Her Peers" and its accompanying one-act play, "Trifles."

But note what this means. The Nineteenth Amendment vested women with a right to run for president—for presidents are surely part of the legislative process—even though the original Constitution repeatedly used the words "he" and "his" to refer to the federal chief executive. Though the Suffrage Amendment did not expressly modify the basic rules of the Executive Article and the Twelfth Amendment, it implicitly did so. Before 1920, states could constitutionally keep women from: (1) voting for presidential electors, (2) serving as presidential electors, and (3) appearing on the ballot as presidential candidates. After 1920, states lost all three of these constitutional powers—and did so even though the Nineteenth Amendment's text might at first be thought to address only issue (1). Here, too, the amendment required a deeper restructuring of previous practices than might appear from a quick glance at the amendment's text.

THOUGH THE NINETEENTH AMENDMENT focused centrally on women's political rights and duties, it also had surprising ramifications for women's personal lives.

For example, if a married woman had an equal right to vote—if she was no longer merely represented politically by her husband—then a wife could choose to vote differently than her husband. Not only could she vote for a different candidate, but presumably she could also vote in a different jurisdiction. Politically, she was now her own man, so to speak. Thus, the Nineteenth Amendment effected an important change in traditional marriage law, which had insisted that husband and wife share a common domicile as part of the legal unity of marriage.[10]

Subtle changes within private domains such as marriage, wrought by an amendment facially concerned with public matters such as voting, have even played out within America's first families. Just as the Twelfth, Twenty-second, and Twenty-fifth Amendments reshaped the basic role of American vice presidents, so the Nineteenth Amendment worked changes in the role of the other traditional presidential running "mate"—the first lady.[11]

The notion that a president's spouse might have political ideas of her own and might function as a powerful political partner to her husband would not have shocked leading men in the Founding generation, familiar as they were with the likes of Abigail Adams (the savvy wife and mother of Presidents John and John Quincy Adams, respectively) and Mercy Otis Warren (a respected political historian married to a prominent Massachusetts politician). But in a world where women could neither vote nor hold office, political spouses often felt obliged to hide their lights under bushels and to act as traditional wives in public. Just as George Washington defined the archetypical presidential role, and Thomas Jefferson redefined this role in a world of national parties, so Martha Washington and Dolley Madison (who acted as a hostess first for Jefferson, who was a widower, and then for her husband, James) solidified the role of the first lady.

Most first ladies followed in Martha and Dolley's footsteps, supporting their men at social events and perhaps exerting political influence in private, but not asserting their intellectual independence by holding forth on the great issues of the day in newspapers or other political forums. This mold was shattered by Eleanor Roosevelt—a high-profile and highly opinionated political force in her own right, resembling Alexander Hamilton more than Martha Washington. Hillary Clinton continued in this spirit and took the new model even further, becoming a U.S. senator, presidential candidate, and cabinet officer after her tenure as first lady.

Doubtless many causes have produced this evolution in the role of first lady, but one that should not be overlooked is the Nineteenth Amendment. Just as ordinary women were freed by the amendment to vote contrary to their husbands, so women within America's first families faced a new menu of options. Had Abigail Adams spoken out in public venues, she would have offended some male traditionalists and probably damaged her husband's political prospects. Seven score years later, Eleanor Roosevelt surely did offend some traditional men, but she also electrified many women, *and women could now vote*. According to a Gallup poll, roughly 57 percent of women supported Eleanor's husband for reelection in 1936—a lower percentage than the male support for FDR that year, but still a huge vote of confidence, especially compared to 1928, when women had overwhelmingly voted Republican.[12]

In effect, Franklin and Eleanor offered themselves up as a canny post–Nineteenth Amendment two-for-the-price-of-one political pair—a kind of balanced ticket in which Franklin wooed moderates while Eleanor courted crusaders. In the very first presidential election ever held in which women could vote nationwide—in 1920—Franklin had been the Democrat's vice-presidential candidate. FDR was also the first president to have a female cabinet officer (Labor Secretary Frances Perkins) and the first to name a woman to the federal appellate bench (Florence Ellinwood Allen, who in 1922 had become the first woman ever elected to a state supreme court). In these Roosevelt appointments we see additional ripple effects of woman suffrage.

The Clintons took the Roosevelts' strategy to new heights, with implications for presidential baton-passing that are still emerging. Alexander Hamilton, Thomas Jefferson, and John Adams paid close attention to each other as potential rivals—but none of them worried about Martha Washington as a potential successor to her husband once he decided to exit the political stage. By contrast, Vice President Al Gore could not afford to overlook Hillary Clinton as President Clinton's other political "mate" and possible political successor. Thanks to the rise of women voters and women politicians—that is, thanks to the Nineteenth Amendment—dramatic new, albeit unwritten, political possibilities dwell in the old position of first lady.

"on account of sex"

THE TWO MOST FAMOUS REPRODUCTIVE RIGHTS CASES of the twentieth century—*Griswold v. Connecticut* and *Roe v. Wade*, championing unwritten rights of contraception and abortion, respectively—can also be seen in a new way if examined through the prism of the Nineteenth Amendment and the Suffrage Revolution more generally.

Both the particular Connecticut anticontraceptive law under review in *Griswold* and the specific Texas antiabortion law challenged in *Roe* were initially adopted in the nineteenth century by all-male legislatures chosen by all-male electorates. (The Texas law was adopted in the 1850s, the Connecticut law in the 1870s.) Of course, the Nineteenth Amendment did not in 1920 wipe clean the entire legal slate by sweeping off the books all previous constitutional and statutory texts. But there was a unique problem, post-1920, whenever a government continued to enforce an old statute that: (1) was initially enacted without a single woman's vote, and (2) imposed special burdens on women qua women—burdens that (3) might make it more difficult for women, even after woman suffrage was won, to be fully equal political participants, and therefore (4) might be particularly difficult for women to undo even after they won the vote.

The laws in *Griswold* and *Roe* were precisely of this sort. Both laws were adopted when no woman voted. Both laws imposed special burdens of childbearing on women, and only women, as women. Both laws probably made it harder for women to achieve full equality as legislators, governors, jurors, judges, and so on, because these women were busy being at-home mothers when some of them would have preferred to avoid conception or childbearing, and would have done so if contraception or abortion had been legally available.

Thus, under an entirely plausible vision of America's unwritten feminist Constitution, judges soon after 1920 could have held that laws such as these were valid only if reenacted by a legislature elected by women voting equally alongside men. As for *these laws*, perhaps judges should have wiped the legal slate clean in 1920, by striking down the old laws and thereby obliging states to put the matter put to a fresh vote.

An antifeminist critic of this plausible approach might say that because women were able to vote in Connecticut and Texas after 1920, the burden was properly on them to repeal these old laws if they believed that such laws discriminated against them. But the Nineteenth Amendment should be read more broadly, even though its literal words do not compel this broader reading. To repeat, this amendment sought to make amends. It sought to end a past practice of exclusion that was viewed as unfair, wrongful, erroneous. To the extent that the Connecticut and Texas laws were sex-specific remnants of that wrongful era—badges of female inequality and disempowerment—and to the extent that these laws arguably created self-entrenching effects making it harder for women to repeal these laws, even after women had formally won the vote, these laws should not have been allowed to continue after 1920. Under a robust vision of the Nineteenth Amendment, judges could have set aside the old contraception law in Connecticut and the old abortion law in Texas, obliging both states to engage in a new conversation involving men and women on a truly equal legal footing.

An opposing, ultra-feminist critic might say that courts immediately after 1920 should have decided the full meaning of women's equality for themselves, rather than merely remanding the question to the political process in Connecticut and Texas. Such a critic might be aghast at the idea of putting constitutional rights up to a vote. But surely one apt way of respecting women's equality after the adoption of the Nineteenth Amendment would simply have been for judges to precipitate and then heed broad political conversations about women's roles in which women would participate as equals. Such conversations had not been possible before woman suffrage. They might not have been possible within the judiciary itself circa 1920. As a venue for a proper conversation with and about women, the political process post-1920 was arguably preferable to a purely judicial process dominated by lawyers, and therefore by men. The world of the 1920s, after all, was a world in which women still did not attend law schools in large numbers, and a proper post-suffrage conversation about women's rights needed to involve women themselves.

AT THIS POINT IN THE ANALYSIS, it is worth pondering the similarities and differences between race-equality law and sex-equality law. There are profound but oft-overlooked parallels between the twentieth century's two most famous reproductive-rights cases and its two most famous race cases, *Brown* and *Bolling*. Recall that the Connecticut contraception law and the Texas abortion law (1) were initially enacted without a single woman's vote, and (2) imposed special gender-based burdens on women—burdens that (3) likely made it more difficult for women, even after woman suffrage was won, to be fully equal political participants, and therefore (4) were particularly difficult for women to undo even after they won the vote. Similarly, in *Brown* and *Bolling* the Court confronted Jim Crow laws that: (1) were initially enacted without the support of black voters (because blacks were widely disfranchised, often in unremedied violation of the Constitution), and (2) imposed serious race-based burdens on blacks (who were denied the chance to associate on equal terms with more privileged whites)— burdens that (3) likely made it more difficult for blacks to be fully equal political participants both in society at large and inside legislatures, and therefore (4) were particularly difficult for blacks to undo even if they later regained some measure of voting rights.

None of this is to say that racial-equality issues are identical to sex-equality issues. When it comes to race, a racial minority may not be able to protect itself fully in the legislature, even after courts have stepped in to strike down old laws from the pre-black-suffrage era. By contrast, in certain sex-discrimination situations, perhaps women, comprising half of the electorate, could have protected themselves well enough, thank you, had judges in the 1920s simply wiped the slate clean of pre-1920 laws entrenching men in power.

"equal"

OF COURSE, JUDGES DID NOT INVALIDATE such laws in the 1920s. Instead, the Supreme Court waited roughly half a century to take on sex discrimination in earnest. Only in the 1970s did the justices reinterpret the Fourteenth Amendment's equal-protection clause to approximate the then-pending Equal Rights Amendment (ERA), a proposed amendment that was never formally ratified by the requisite number of states. Having just seen how some thoughtful judges might have plausibly invoked the Nineteenth Amendment's spirit to strike down these old laws as early as the 1920s or 1930s, let's now see why the judiciary in fact waited until much later to act.

Recall that the key constitutional command of the Fourteenth Amendment is a command of birth equality: Americans should not be condemned to second-class citizenship because they were born black—or female, for that matter. Recall further that the Nineteenth Amendment envisioned women's equality across the entire range of political rights—voting, officeholding, jury service, and so on. Prior to the 1960s, some modest judges might understandably have hesitated to strike down various sex-discrimination laws (including laws regulating contraception and reproduction) because these laws were arguably not designed to treat women as inferiors or to keep them out of legislatures or off the judicial bench. Rather, many of these gender-based laws could have been viewed—and in fact were widely viewed for much of the twentieth century—as simply recognizing abiding differences between the sexes: Separate, but equal.

Though it might be tempting to scoff at this slogan, we must resist the temptation, for even today the concept remains a prominent feature of our constitutional landscape. Most public buildings continue to have separate bathrooms for males and females; and most public schools continue to operate sex-segregated locker rooms and sports programs for boys and girls. These separations go virtually unchallenged in society and in law because they are not generally viewed as invidious. They are not widely perceived as privileging males over females—or females over males, for that matter—in their design and effect. They are simply recognitions of differences between the sexes. Separate, but equal. To put the point sociologically and politically, many women as well as many men today do not find separate bathrooms and gym classes to be badges of female inferiority. Indeed, most people today—most men and most women—may well prefer separate bathrooms and gym classes.[13]

Now consider pre-1960s America. The law treated men and women differently in myriad ways, but until the 1960s perhaps judges thought that most women did not themselves find these legal differences to be markers of subordination. Men generally went off to work in the economic marketplace (with all sorts of legal encouragements), and women generally stayed home and raised kids (again, with various legal nudges), but these law-induced differences were not clearly claimed by vast numbers of women themselves to be denials of equality.

Only in the 1960s and 1970s did very large numbers of women begin to take to the streets to challenge this separate-spheres regime, labeling it invidious and unequal. Only in this era did a veritable army of feminists demand a formal federal Equal Rights Amendment. Only in this era did a substantial number of states adopt state ERAs. (Before 1970, two low-population states, Utah and Wyoming, had constitutions with explicit ERA-style provisions. By 1977, sixteen state constitutions, accounting for roughly one-third of the national population, explicitly guaranteed sex equality.) Only in this era did Congress pass major civil-rights laws prohibiting sex discrimination. Only in this era did Congress propose an ERA, which was emphatically backed by both major-party presidential platforms in 1972. Only in this era did states comprising nearly two-thirds of the national population ratify this proposal. Once these things happened, it became impossible for judges to ignore the threat to women's equality posed by a wide range of previously acceptable laws.[14]

True, the ERA was not formally ratified in the 1970s. But precisely because the Constitution already featured an amendment (the Fourteenth) explicitly promising equality and committed to equal birth-status, the ERA itself was a largely declaratory proposal—a restatement and elaboration. Many of the ERA's supporters and detractors were fully aware that the Fourteenth Amendment's language already promised equality and was pointedly not limited to racial equality, as was the language of the Fifteenth Amendment. The failure of the ERA did not repeal or erase any part of the Fourteenth Amendment. The ERA debate did, however, highlight that a strong majority of Americans now supported a robust idea of sex equality. This broad popular support was entitled to interpretive weight as a popular gloss on the Fourteenth Amendment and the Ninth Amendment, in keeping with the principles of America's lived Constitution.

TO SAY THAT JUDGES properly took the insights of feminists into account in the 1960s and 1970s is not to say that popular social movements may, as a general matter, amend the Constitution by informal actions outside Article V. For example, no informal popular movement comparable to 1970s feminism could have made thirty-three-year-olds eligible to serve as president in the absence of a formal textual amendment. Where the written Constitution is clear and fixed—as with the presidential age requirement of thirty-five years—only written amendments can ordinarily suffice to change the written rules.

The idea here is not to draw a sharp line between, say, age rules on one side and equality rules on the other side. After all, the Constitution's age rules themselves were rooted in a vision of social equality. (In their eighteenth-century context, they were anti-dynasty provisions of sorts.) Rather, the idea here is that that some constitutional applications plainly pivot on broad understandings of social meaning, whereas other constitutional applications do not.[15]

Thus, on certain equality issues, the relevant constitutional rules and principles may be so clear that social meanings and social movements are largely beside the point. The Fifteenth Amendment was violated by massive race-based disfranchisement long before Dr. King, Thurgood Marshall, and other leaders mobilized large numbers of Americans to protest this legal wrong. As with the Black Codes that facially violated the central meaning of the Fourteenth Amendment, race-based disfranchisements of blacks violated the core meaning of the Fifteenth Amendment regardless of how the disfranchised persons, or anyone else, may have understood the matter. These laws were unequal and thus unconstitutional regardless of their social meaning.

But other government practices have been properly viewed as unequal and thus unconstitutional *because* of their social meaning. In these situations, the social meaning was the basis for the legal verdict of unconstitutionality. Twentieth-century contraception and abortion laws were particularly difficult for judges to analyze under purely formal principles of equality precisely because such laws targeted features unique to women—namely, their sex-specific capacity to bear children. As to these laws, social meaning was thus particularly important—especially the social meaning of contraception and abortion laws in the eyes of women themselves.

TO GET A SENSE OF how the abortion issue looked prior to the rise of late-twentieth-century feminism, let's imagine a stylized dialogue circa 1950 between two earnest and knowledgeable constitutional scholars, Adam and Eve. Let's suppose that both Adam and Eve accept the idea that the Fourteenth Amendment was, at its core, an amendment designed to secure the birthright equality of all citizens—equality not just between blacks and whites, but also between women and men. But in 1950, Adam, who is cast as the traditionalist in this dialogue, does not have the benefit of the massive feminist consciousness-raising of the 1960s and 1970s. Let's imagine that Eve, by contrast, is familiar with avant-garde feminist theories that would soon gain wider currency. (Film buffs might profitably envision Spencer Tracy in the role of Adam, and Katharine Hepburn as Eve; recall the 1949 romantic comedy *Adam's Rib*.)[16]

ADAM: Eve, how exactly does a constitutional norm of sex-equality prohibit laws designed to protect the innocent human life of male and female babies alike? Many of these laws operate directly only upon physicians and operate equally on physicians of both sexes. This, indeed, is true of the Texas law that you find so troubling.

EVE: Adam, please get real. The primary weight of the Texas law falls not upon the physician, whoever he or she may be. Rather, the law imposes its main burden upon pregnant women who are denied access to competent medical procedures. And what a burden it is to be obliged to carry an unwanted pregnancy to term! As a practical matter, it can require a woman to end her education or career, at least temporarily. It can impose serious financial costs and medical risks. It can put her in danger of physical attack from the biological father or a man who suspects that he is not the biological father. It can dramatically interfere with her freedom of movement, her daily routine, her diet, her relations with others around her, her mental state, and her body more generally. Especially in cases of rape and incest, the pregnancy itself can impose severe mental trauma on her. After she has given birth, psychological and social pressures may make it difficult for her to give the baby up for adoption. In that event, the serious burden of an unwanted pregnancy would be only the beginning of the obligations that she will bear and the possible sacrifices she may be obliged to make.

ADAM: Nothing in Texas's abortion law requires that women keep children after birth rather than giving them up for adoption. So if women decide to keep their babies, that is their free choice—and probably a good one for all concerned. As for the burdens of pregnancy itself, there exists an obvious and indeed compelling justification for imposing these burdens, even (though I admit this might seem callous to you) in cases of rape and incest. That compelling justification is to protect the life of the unborn and innocent human life inside the pregnant woman's womb. Her liberty is abridged so as to protect the unborn baby's life. Texas and other states may properly choose life over liberty. The Constitution itself—twice!—places life ahead of liberty in its phraseology. Surely states can do the same in their policies.

EVE: The problem is that states such as Texas have chosen to impose these life-sustaining burdens only on women.

ADAM: I think your quarrel there is with God and not the state. He's the one who made the rules you are complaining about.

EVE: What makes you so sure God is a "He"? In any event, my complaint is not with the Almighty but with Texas. There are, after all, other ways of promoting unborn human life that would be more evenhanded between men and women. For example, in the case of unmarried women, the law could require the biological father to remunerate the woman for half of the total financial and physical costs that she must bear during the course of her pregnancy. This more gender-neutral approach would require him to compensate her for her childbearing expenses, work, and labor, and thus to bear his fair share of the burden. Yet Texas law does nothing of the sort.

ADAM: Your alternative scheme sounds more heavy-handed than even-handed. In fact, it sounds downright socialistic. To repeat: Nature itself imposes the burden of childbearing on the biological mother rather than the father.

EVE: Nature also makes abortion possible. If the law intervenes to limit her "natural" freedoms, why not his? Indeed, in the act of procreation itself, men would seem to bear equal if not more responsibility.

ADAM: Not always. We can imagine sexual intercourse in the absence of full male consent, as in the case of statutory rape involving an adult female and an underage male.

EVE: A cute point—but again, please get real. Sex in the absence of full consent by the woman—because of male coercion that rises to the level of legal rape, or some lower level of force or fraud—is far more common than sex in the absence of full consent by the man. Conscription of a father's income stream is actually *easier* to justify than conscription of a mother's womb. In almost every case, his commission of the sex act was voluntary; but in many cases, hers may not have been. And yet, to repeat, the Texas law saddles her with special burdens while exempting him. Texas obliges her to give up nine months of her life to sustain the unborn life, but does not oblige him to give up even nine dollars.

ADAM: Well, your plan might require the state to do lots of complicated tests to establish prenatal paternity. Surely, you will admit that a woman's pregnancy and a man's financial obligations are logically different things, even though you are trying to conflate them. The Constitution requires only that men and women be treated equally, and when it comes to pregnancy, men and women are just different. Each has a different role. Such it has always been and will always be.

EVE: Look, a uterus is a body part, but why is it so different from other body parts—body parts that even males have?

ADAM: Huh?

EVE: Once a child is in fact born, suppose that child needs a kidney or a blood transfusion, and that the only tissue that will work is the father's. Texas does not oblige him to give up even a drop of his replenishable blood or one of his kidneys, even though he has another one that suffices to meet his own biological needs. When it comes to body parts that men have, such as blood and kidneys, Texas law sides with the parent's bodily liberty even at the expense of the child's life. Only when it comes to uteri does Texas law privilege life over liberty, and Texas does so precisely because only women have uteri. In other words, Texas treats uniquely female body parts differently than all other body parts, and the state does so to women's detriment.

ADAM: All this sounds like science fiction. Formally, the law treats blood and kidneys the same for mothers as for fathers—perfect formal equality. And it treats these things the same whether the child in question who needs the blood or kidney is a boy or a girl. It's still hard for me to see the sex inequality here. True, pregnancy is treated differently than blood transfusions or kidney transplants—or nose jobs, for that matter—but that is simply because pregnancy is unique. Not all women are or ever become pregnant. The law simply treats pregnant persons differently than nonpregnant persons, and it does so for sensible reasons.

EVE: Adam, you can't really mean that last point. Surely government should not be free to subordinate women so long as it does so via laws that use women's unique biology to disadvantage them as a class! Imagine, for example, a law that said pregnant people may not vote, or serve on juries, or be elected to office. Wouldn't such a law plainly violate the Nineteenth Amendment? If so, isn't this a square admission that laws heaping disabilities on pregnant persons as such are indeed laws discriminating "on account of sex"?

ADAM: Hmm, I hadn't quite thought of the Nineteenth Amendment as relevant. But the point remains that even if abortion and other pregnancy laws are in some sense laws that treat people differently on account of sex, the different treatment is justified. *Vive la différence!* Just as boys and girls generally play on separate sports teams, so, too, men and women generally play different roles in society. These roles are not designed to subordinate women. True, abortion laws limit women's options, but other laws limit men's options. There is no grand male conspiracy here. Consider, for example, the military draft laws that have conscripted men and not women—impinging on men's liberties in order to protect the lives of all of us, in a manner that broadly counterbalances the burdens imposed on pregnant women's liberties to protect innocent unborn life.

EVE: Actually, the male-only draft tends to prove my point. When male soldiers have been drafted, our government has often furnished them with educational and other benefits after their term of service has ended. But when pregnant women are asked to disrupt their careers and education in order to protect unborn life, government has not showered comparable benefits upon them. There is no Mothers' Bill of Rights akin to the GI Bill of Rights. Indeed, in Texas and many other places, public schools and public employers have generally been allowed to expel or fire unmarried pregnant women, but have not expelled or fired the men involved. If Texas meant to minimize its imposition on the lives and liberty of women, I suspect the state could also do much more than it has done to facilitate and encourage adoption (perhaps even through publicly supported institutions that would help any woman who so desired to keep the pregnancy itself confidential as well as the later adoption). I further suspect that Texas could do far more to support public institutions providing medical assistance and other services to indigent women bearing unwanted pregnancies.

ADAM: There you go again with your heavy-handed socialistic schemes! And while we're at it, I also cannot fathom how equality principles are violated by the Connecticut contraception law that so distresses you. That law, too, is wholly evenhanded. It outlaws certain forms of contraception by both males and females.

EVE: Only a man could think that! If contraception is barred, the risk of unwanted pregnancy will be borne by women and only women. Formally, what you say is true. Both men and women are prohibited from using certain devices. But the Connecticut law specifically exempts contraceptive devices designed to prevent venereal disease. Thus, a condom is okay (as it might protect the man from unwanted infection), but a diaphragm is not (as it would only protect the woman from unwanted pregnancy). In short, Connecticut allows men to shield themselves from future disease, but women are not allowed equally to shield themselves from future "dis-ease." Pregnancy and childbirth are, after all, not exactly easy.

ADAM: Huh? Pregnancy and disease are very different things. Clever puns aside, there is a world of difference between having a baby and contracting syphilis.

EVE: Yes, there are differences, but please note how the Connecticut law entrenches traditional gender roles, implicitly treating women as baby machines and using their unique biology as a basis for legal disadvantage.

ADAM: Once you concede that pregnancy is unique, it becomes impossible for you to insist that Connecticut is improperly discriminating. Connecticut is simply recognizing the different—separate but equal—roles that men and women have always played in America.

THE LESSON OF THIS PLAYFUL VIGNETTE is that social meaning becomes especially important with regard to certain issues of gender equality because: (1) There are biological differences between the sexes that may make it hard for any purely formal and logical analysis to close the argumentative circle, and (2) the Constitution allows government to treat the two sexes differently, whereas the Constitution does not generally allow government to treat various races differently. Where pure logic runs out, social meaning often fills the gap to complete the circle of proper constitutional analysis.

Logically, it was difficult for Eve in 1950 to prove to Adam, in the way that a mathematician might undeniably prove a theorem, that the Texas and Connecticut statutes violated equality principles. And what was logically true in 1950 was of course logically true in 1975. Logic had not somehow changed in the intervening quarter century. But social norms and understandings did change in this era. *Sociologically*, Eve's task became much easier when she could point to lots of other Eves in America who now shared her once-avant-garde but increasingly mainstream views. When large numbers of women in the 1960s and 1970s began to sound increasingly like Eve, this swelling chorus of Eves prompted the Adams of the world to rethink their assumptions.

Social meaning outside the terse text thus interacts with the words of the written document in ways structured by the text itself. Even when the Constitution does not supply an unambiguous and concrete solution to a particular issue (as it does with presidential age), the document may still provide a relatively clear framework of constitutional conversation and contestation. In other words, the text at times gives later generations not the right answers but the right questions for us to ask and the right vocabulary for us as we begin thinking over and arguing about those questions.[17]

For example, we saw earlier how the word "unusual" invites interpreters to attend to national majoritarian trends in punishment. The word "unreasonable" in the Fourth Amendment also authorizes interpreters to take evolving social norms into account. What is widely viewed as reasonable in one era may not be so viewed in another period. The Ninth Amendment "rights of the people" are likewise influenced by what the people believe their rights to be at any given moment.

The word "equal" operates in a similar but not identical fashion. Like these other words, the word "equal" at times invites interpreters to go with the ebbs and flows of citizen understandings. But in looking outside the written Constitution to determine whether a borderline law should be viewed as a sex "discrimination," and, if so, whether this discrimination should be viewed as impermissibly "unequal," what matters is not merely what a majority of the entire population might think—an approach that might make more sense in parsing a word such as "unusual" or a phrase such as "the right of the people." Rather, in parsing the word "equal," faithful interpreters must pay particularly close attention to how *each side* of a given legal distinction views the law in question. If both sides think the law is sufficiently equal, that very fact might make it so. But if *either* side deems the law unacceptably unequal, then that fact may also be decisive. The mere facts that at certain moments many whites apparently convinced themselves that Jim Crow was equal, and that these whites perhaps constituted a majority, did not properly conclude the equality inquiry; the question of what blacks thought of this brand of apartheid remained. Similarly, it matters today not just whether men see various antiabortion laws as proper, but, crucially, whether women—the Eves of the twenty-first century—agree.

REGARDLESS OF IMPLEMENTATIONAL VARIATIONS and details in enforcing the written Constitution's rules regarding equal citizenship, unusual punishments, unreasonable searches and seizures, and so on, we should not lose sight of the larger methodological point: The document itself invites careful consideration of contemporary social meanings and popular understandings with regard to many issues of liberty and equality. Written words such as "equal," "unreasonable," and "unusual" direct sensitive interpreters to unwritten sources, including state practices, mass social movements, social meaning, lived experiences, and so on. Words like this, in short, are brilliantly designed to keep the American Constitution in touch with the American people even in the absence of formal Article V amendments. These words help America's written and unwritten Constitutions cohere.

THE CURRENT CHAPTER HAS TAKEN its title and its inspiration from a letter that Abigail Adams wrote to her husband in the spring of 1776: "I long to hear that you have declared an independency. And, by the way, in the new code of laws which I suppose it will be necessary for you to make, I desire you would remember the ladies and be more generous and favorable to them than your ancestors. Do not put such unlimited power into the hands of the husbands. Remember, all men would be tyrants if they could. If particular care and attention is not paid to the ladies, we are determined to foment a rebellion, and will not hold ourselves bound by any laws in which we have no voice or representation."[18]

John Adams and his fellow Founding fathers paid insufficient heed to Abigail's words, and eventually "the ladies" did "foment a rebellion"—three rebellions, in fact.

First, women played a large role in the abolition and equal-rights movements that led to the Reconstruction Revolution of the late 1860s. Happily for women, section 1 of the Fourteenth Amendment promised birth equality to all citizens in the domain of civil rights and did not limit itself to a mere promise of racial equality. Alas, section 2 constitutionalized sex-discrimination in the domain of voting rights and indeed inserted the word "male" into the Constitution for the first time.[19]

Revolted, women revolted—again. The crowning achievement of this second feminist revolution was the Nineteenth Amendment's explicit textual guarantee of equal political as well as civil rights for women.

These two revolutions left their marks in the written Constitution, but America's Constitution today also reflects, quite properly, America's third—unwritten—feminist revolution, when women in the late twentieth century added a powerful feminist gloss to the previously adopted words "citizens," "equal," and "sex." These words have come to mean even more, perhaps, than they meant to those who initially added them to the document—and rightly so, given that the political institutions that added these words to the text did not at these moments of textual addition equally represent women.

Abigail Adams was on the right track: Why, indeed, should women "hold [themselves] bound by any laws in which [they] have no [or unequal] voice or representation"? The best answer is that women today do have equal voice and representation; and that all laws, and especially those laws enacted before women achieved full political equality, must now be construed with attention to women's equality and with particularly sensitive awareness of the political exclusion of women in earlier centuries. Whether or not the written Constitution compels this feminist rule of construction, this approach redeems the document's deepest principles. Faithful interpreters today must remember Adams—and Eves.

CHAPTER 8

FOLLOWING
WASHINGTON'S LEAD

America's "Georgian" Constitution

THE INAUGURATION OF WASHINGTON (APRIL 30, 1789,
AS DEPICTED IN 1876).

As America's first "first man," Washington set precedents from his earliest moments on the job. At his 1789 inauguration he wore civilian garb and swore his oath of office on the Bible. Nothing in the written Constitution specified this protocol, yet later presidents have emulated various elements of Washington's inaugural etiquette and have closely followed many other Washingtonian precedents. Several presidents have even made a point of swearing their oaths on the same Bible that Washington used on April 30, 1789. Note also the foreground presence of two of the four men whom Washington would later bring into his first cabinet—future treasury secretary Alexander Hamilton at the far left and future war secretary Henry Knox at the far right.

LAUNCHING AMERICA'S CONSTITUTION MEANT MORE than simply discussing and approving the text of the Philadelphia plan in the several state conventions. True, Article VII of the plan proclaimed that ratification by these conventions would be "sufficient for the Establishment of this Constitution." Formally, once the state conventions said yes, the deal was done, and it remained merely for all to obey the legally binding words that the American people had approved. But in reality, the Founding process extended past the ratification period. Some patches of constitutional text raised nearly as many questions as they answered. Before these parts of the document could be obeyed, they would need to be clarified and concretized.[1]

We should therefore view the Founding as a two-part drama. First, in 1787–1788, the American people assembled in special conventions to enact—to *activate*—the Philadelphia plan. Next, newly authorized government agents appeared on the scene to reenact—to *act out*—the approved legal text, much as a theatrical troupe might act out a playwright's written script. In this post-1788 process, America's leading man, George Washington, who had waited quietly in the wings during the ratification period, now strode to center stage. During the Constitution's debut, Washington and other actors manifested the meaning of the terse text, deepening the two-dimensional print into a three-dimensional performance that set the standard for later government actors. In short, after the Founders in ratifying conventions took a mere proposal and made it law, the Founders in government took law and made it fact.[2]

Over the ensuing centuries, the constitutional understandings that crystallized during the Washington administration have enjoyed special authority on a wide range of issues, especially those concerning presidential power and presidential etiquette. Much as modern Christians ask themselves, "What would Jesus do?," presidents over the centuries have quite properly asked themselves, "What would President Washington do?" and, even more pointedly, "What did President Washington do?" In the American constitutional tradition, what Washington did—the particular way in which he handled treaties, conducted foreign affairs, dealt with the Senate, controlled his cabinet, and so on—has often mattered much more than what the written Constitution says, at least in situations where the text is arguably ambiguous and Washington's actions fall within the range of plausible textual meaning.

"Go. Washington—Presidt"

OF ALL THE TEXTUAL UNCERTAINTIES confronting America's first president, none loomed larger than the indeterminacy shrouding his own role in the new constitutional order. The Constitution's text made some things clear. America's chief executive would serve a four-year renewable term; would wield a federal veto pen (subject to override) and a federal pardon pen (except in impeachment cases); would personally oversee high executive officers whom he would handpick (with senatorial support); would make treaties (again, with senatorial involvement); could win reelection independently of Congress; and could be ousted from office only if a House majority and a Senate supermajority found him guilty of gross misconduct. In all these respects, America's president would tower far above a typical state governor circa 1787, yet remain far below England's King George III.

But the text failed to specify exactly how far above and below these distant models Washington should position himself on a variety of executive-power issues as to which the constitutional text was silent or opaque. Most important of all, uncertainty existed early on about whether a president properly had any general executive powers or privileges beyond those specifically listed in the constitutional text.

The Executive Article (Article II) opened with the following words: "The executive Power shall be vested in a President of the United States of America." This sentence appeared to confer upon the president a general residuum of "executive Power" above and beyond various specific presidential powers and duties itemized a few paragraphs later. Yet ordinary Americans during the ratification period could be forgiven for missing this point. The Legislative Article (Article I) confined Congress to an enumerated list of specified powers, and the Judicial Article (Article III) likewise limited the jurisdiction of federal courts to a textually enumerated list. Although the Executive Article used subtly different language that seemed to say that its list of specific presidential powers was exemplary rather than exhaustive, it took an eagle eye to spot the textual difference,* and few Americans during the ratification period paid attention to the powerful possibilities coiled within the Executive Article's opening clause. Eager to persuade anxious Anti-Federalists that the Constitution did not squint toward monarchy, leading Federalists, from Hamilton/Publius on down, directed the public's gaze to the limited nature of the specifically enumerated presidential responsibilities.[3]

Faithful constitutionalists seeking to honor the text as originally understood are thus yanked hard in opposite directions. On the one hand, most ratifiers may not have realized that the president would enjoy a residual "executive Power." On the other hand, the people had said yes to a text that seemed to say just that—and surely the public did understand that the Constitution would conjure up a far more muscular executive than anything they had experienced since 1776.

The seeming tension between the text and the public understanding in 1787–1788 invites a closer look at both in the hope of finding some means of reconciliation. Why didn't the text delimit the scope of presidential power more clearly and precisely? And why didn't ratifying conventions pay closer heed to every detail of Article II?

At least three things blunted the edges of the Executive Article and blurred the ratification conversation. First, no ancient or modern model closely prefigured the federal chief executive that the Founders fashioned. British monarchs had ruled by dint of noble birth and claims of divine right; most colonial governors had answered to kings; most post-Independence state governors seemed far too weak; and the presiding officer of the Confederation Congress was likewise a mere shadow of the

---

* For readers who pride themselves on their eagle eyes: Article I opened with words vesting Congress only with legislative powers specified or implied elsewhere in the document—"herein granted." Article III opened with words vesting federal courts with "the judicial Power of the United States"; and later language in Article III proceeded to itemize all the types of "cases" and "controversies" over which that very same "judicial Power" could properly "extend." Article II, by contrast, opened with words vesting a general "executive Power," and no later Article II clause textually purported to enumerate all the components of this general executive power.

new presider Americans were inventing. Though Americans could agree that their new president needed a very different blend of powers and limits from any previous executive, there remained considerable uncertainty about exactly what mix would be best.[4]

Second, the very nature of presidential power made it hard in 1787—and continues to make it hard today—to fully specify its precise boundaries in all contingencies. In a nutshell, Congress passes laws, authorizes expenditures, organizes itself, polices its own membership, and oversees the other branches via investigations and impeachments, while federal judges decide cases under law and monitor subordinates within the judicial branch. By contrast, presidents perform a far wider range of multifarious tasks. They promulgate interstitial rules, much like legislators. They find facts, construe laws, and apply laws to facts in the first instance, much like judges. But they also do much, much more. For example, they officially propose new legislation and define national reform agendas; they participate in the passage of federal statutes; they pick federal judges; they directly communicate and coordinate action with state governments; they stand atop a vast bureaucratic pyramid, filling and sometimes thinning the ranks of federal executive officialdom; they collect revenues and disburse funds; they manage federal properties; they file and defend lawsuits on behalf of the nation; they prevent, investigate, and prosecute civil and criminal misconduct; they ponder mercy for miscreants; they command armed forces in both war and peace; they respond to large-scale disasters and crises; they direct diplomacy and international espionage; and they personify America on the international stage. Even today, sophisticated commentators often define "executive Power" not affirmatively but residually. On this view, executive power encompasses all proper governmental authority that is neither legislative nor judicial in nature. Whereas legislatures and judiciaries almost always act via standard operating procedures, presidents recurrently need to improvise to handle fast-breaking situations that threaten to upend the entire system (such as the Civil War) or that present unique opportunities to promote the national welfare (such as the Louisiana Purchase). The essence of the presidential office defies easy textual specification, even after two centuries of presidential experience.

Third, even if precise textualization of every aspect of presidential power had been theoretically possible in 1787–1788, Americans were not designing the office in the abstract. Rather, they were tailoring it for its intended first occupant—George Washington. Without Washington at the helm as America's first president, it was widely believed that even a perfectly designed constitutional ship of state might founder at the launch. Conversely, with Washington in charge at the outset, even an imperfect text might work—so long as the text fit the first "first man" suitably well. An overtextualized Executive Article might not match Washington's precise proportions. Thus Americans undertextualized the presidency, trusting Washington to make sensible adjustments after wearing his custom-made constitutional uniform and testing it against the elements. The textual openness of Article II—the "give" in the garment of executive power—was not a design flaw, but a desired feature.

It is true that nothing in the official constitutional text required that George Washington be America's first president. But without the near-universal understanding that Washington would guide the new ship at the start, the Executive Article would have been drafted in a dramatically different fashion, and perhaps nothing closely resembling the Philadelphia plan would have ever won the express approval of the American people. Washington's indispensability was recognized by both the supporters and the critics of the Philadelphia plan in every state. Fittingly, the attestation section of the ceremonial parchment began with the suggestive signature of the Philadelphia Convention's presiding officer, as follows: "Go. Washington—Presidt." In many a printed version of the proposed Constitution circulating in 1787–1788, this accompanying signature was reformatted to read, "GEORGE WASHINGTON, *President.*"[5]

It is also true that nothing in the official constitutional text explicitly delegated authority to George Washington to fill in the blanks of Article II and thereby sharpen the role of all future presidents. But neither did the terse text explicitly prohibit the inference that the framers and ratifiers were deputizing Washington to clarify the Executive Article, subject to the broad advice and consent of the other branches and the American people. Though the Constitution's text does not compel this delegation-to-Washington interpretation, the text permits and even invites this reading for the simple reason that this reading makes sense. It explains the otherwise puzzling and even dangerous looseness of the Executive Article, and it turns what might otherwise seem an abject failure of draftsmanship and deliberation into something safe and clever.[6]

SEVERAL BASIC FEATURES of America's enduring presidential system have been established less by the Constitution's text than by the gloss on the text provided by President Washington's actions—actions that he initially undertook with scrupulous constitutional consciousness and that ultimately won acceptance from the other branches and the American people.

First, America's presidents today enjoy unilateral power to officially recognize and derecognize foreign governments. In 1979, for example, without any specific preauthorization from Congress as a whole or from the Senate, President Jimmy Carter established normal diplomatic relations with the (Communist) People's Republic of China, formally recognizing that regime as the official sovereign power in China. In the process, Carter cut formal diplomatic ties with the (anti-Communist) Taiwanese government, which had previously been recognized by the U.S. government as the lawful Chinese regime and, indeed, an official American treaty partner.

The text of the Executive Article's list of specific presidential responsibilities can plausibly be stretched to cover the president's powers of recognition and derecognition. In particular, the list declares that the president "shall receive Ambassadors and other public Ministers."

But this patch of text can also be plausibly read far more modestly, as simply providing that foreign diplomats from regimes already recognized by the president and Congress (or alternatively, by the president and the Senate) should as a matter of official protocol and ceremony present their credentials to the president when they arrive on American soil. In *The Federalist* No. 69, Hamilton/Publius described the reception clause as a mere matter of etiquette and convenience, more about "dignity" than "authority"—a rule of minuscule consequence whose main effect would be to avoid the need to summon the legislature or some subpart thereof into special session whenever one diplomat replaced another from a previously recognized foreign regime.

Other language in the Executive Article can be read to suggest a rather modest vision of presidential power in foreign affairs. Before dispatching an official ambassador to some foreign land, the president must ordinarily win the approval of the Senate: "He [the president] shall nominate, and by and with the Advice and Consent of the Senate, shall appoint Ambassadors." If the president must typically induce the Senate when sending official American diplomats abroad, why may the president ignore the Senate when receiving official foreign diplomats at home? Additionally, the Executive Article provides that no treaty may take effect without a two-thirds Senate vote. If the Senate plays such a prominent role in the making of treaties, why can the Senate be shoved offstage in the breaking of treaties? Also, the written Constitution broadly empowers Congress as a whole to regulate "Commerce"—that is, affairs, transactions, and general intercourse—with "foreign Nations." Why may the president act without congressional preapproval in conducting foreign affairs via diplomatic recognition or derecognition?

A structural argument on behalf of presidential power would emphasize that world events can move at lightning speed and that only the president might be in session when a critical decision must be made. (Unlike members of Congress, the president is always "in session.") Thus, a president who needs to send an ambassador on an emergency mission need not wait for the Senate to convene, thanks to another provision of the Executive Article that explicitly authorizes unilateral "Recess" appointments for temporary periods. Textually, the power to recognize new foreign regimes and to break relations with defunct treaty partners can also be defended as part of the residual "executive Power" vested solely in the president.

Beyond these plausible structural and textual arguments, however, is the strongest legal argument of all: a powerful precedent set by a powerful president. When French revolutionaries seized power and guillotined King Louis XVI on President Washington's watch, a momentous decision had to be made. America could opt to stand by the French monarchy, which had bankrolled the American Revolution and had signed treaties of amity and alliance with the United States in 1778. Alternatively, America could choose to recognize the French revolutionaries as the rightful government of France entitled to all the treaty rights of the prior regime. Or perhaps America could decide to stand aloof from all French factions in the bloody maelstrom and declare that the old treaties were now entirely void. Under this view, the French revolutionary upstarts had no automatic entitlement to treaty concessions that America had granted only to its original treaty partner, Louis, and his designated successors (starting with his young son, the dauphin Louis XVII). The competing considerations—loyalty to a friendly monarchy, solidarity with fellow revolutionary democrats, and anxiety about being sucked into an increasingly violent vortex—tugged in different directions. A wrong choice could have dreadful consequences. Were the United States to back the losing contestants in the unfolding and unpredictable tumult, the ultimate winners might well seek vengeance against the perfidious Americans.

The crucial point is that after consulting his cabinet, George Washington made the fateful decision himself—in effect, transferring official American recognition from the fallen French monarchy to the reigning French revolutionaries. Far more than any word or phrase in the written text ratified in 1787–1788, this post-1789 precedent established the basic ground rules for all subsequent presidents—for example, Jimmy Carter in 1979—trying to decide whether and how America should cut diplomatic links with displaced sovereigns and/or create diplomatic ties to new regimes.

President Carter's formal recognition of the People's Republic of China came after President Nixon's famous visit to mainland China in 1972, which in turn built on diplomatic foundations laid in 1971, when Nixon secretly sent his envoy Henry Kissinger to Beijing to parley with the Chinese Communists. In this diplomatic episode, we see a second basic feature of modern presidential power traceable back to the Washington administration, namely, the president's unilateral power to communicate, even secretly, with foreign regimes and to negotiate treaties without the Senate's foreknowledge.

Here, too, we can invoke various plausible textual and structural arguments to support presidential power, and here, too, there are plausible textual counterarguments. The matter has been settled beyond all doubt, less by the naked constitutional text than by the actual practice of presidents of all parties, with the repeated backing of Senates and Congresses when presidents have sought formal legal support for previously secret diplomatic initiatives.

Perhaps the most momentous episode occurred when President Jefferson quickly negotiated for the purchase of the Louisiana Territory as soon as this vast tract of land was unexpectedly plopped onto the bargaining table at Paris in the spring of 1803. Had Jefferson delayed negotiations in order to get detailed advice or preapproval from the Senate or House—neither of which was then in session—he would have run the risk that the mercurial Napoleon might change his mind and whisk the land off the table. Instead, Jefferson (via his handpicked diplomats, James Monroe and Robert Livingston) seized the day and closed the deal. When Congress convened in the fall, Jefferson won the support of both two-thirds of the Senate (which formally approved the treaty he had negotiated on his own initiative) and a majority of the House (which later voted, along with the Senate, to provide the legal structure for the new lands and to foot the bill).[7]

This near-doubling of the new nation's landmass, one of the most spectacular diplomatic triumphs in modern world history, followed an established constitutional script. But the script was established less by the debatable text of the written Constitution than by the definitive gloss on that text that Washington had added in the early 1790s, via diplomatic initiatives culminating in the famous Jay Treaty. The process that led to this treaty began when Washington secretly sent an unofficial emissary (Gouverneur Morris) to Britain. Later, the president decided to follow up with a formal diplomatic overture. Although the Senate confirmed Washington's choice of Envoy John Jay, senators did not preapprove the specifics of Jay's official diplomatic mission. Instead, Jay followed Washington's negotiating instructions. Only months after Jay and his English counterparts reached a tentative deal (in November 1794) was the treaty brought before American lawmakers. Eventually, both the Senate and the Congress as a whole endorsed Washington's diplomatic entrepreneurialism—the Senate by approving the Jay Treaty by the requisite two-thirds in June 1795, and the Congress by enacting the necessary implementing legislation and appropriations the following year.[8]

A third and related piece of executive power also settled squarely into place as a result of Washington's conduct in the Jay Treaty. After winning Senate approval for the treaty, Washington reserved the final legal move for himself. In the end, he alone decided whether to officially ratify the treaty in the name of the nation. Only after he decided to proceed in the wake of the Senate's yes vote did the treaty become legally binding. (Washington also needed to secure British agreement to a modification that the Senate had insisted upon as a condition of giving its advice and consent.) Although the Constitution's text could be parsed different ways on the nice questions of treaty-making raised by the power-sharing between president and Senate, what is constitutionally decisive today is not the pure text, but the institutional gloss that Washington applied to it—a gloss that was accepted then and has been accepted ever since by his countrymen.[9]

A similar story can be told about Washington's famous Neutrality Proclamation of 1793. When word reached America that France and England were officially at war, the Second Congress had just adjourned, and the Third Congress was not due to meet for several months. Washington quickly reviewed the treaties already on the books, consulted his cabinet, and then publicly announced his policy: America would steer a middle course between the belligerents and would not ally with either side. As Washington saw it, neither justice nor the strict language of existing treaties obliged America to join France's international crusade, and America's strategic interests counseled noninterference.

Washington's proclamation carried legal weight. It was not purely an exercise of free expression akin to an Inaugural Address, a State of the Union Message, or a newspaper op-ed. Rather, Washington spoke in the name of the nation, officially proclaiming that no American citizen aiding any belligerent could properly claim to be acting with the approval of the United States. On the contrary, Washington sternly warned that Americans who ran contraband war supplies or otherwise gave military help to any of the warring parties risked being criminally prosecuted or sued civilly for violating international law and breaching the peace. Although Washington did not speak particularly about Congress's constitutional role, nothing that he said denied congressional power to adopt a different policy by later statute if Congress so chose.

Here, then, was another major precedent. Much as the executive power encompassed authority to formally recognize or derecognize foreign regimes, to unilaterally and even secretly negotiate with these regimes, and to formally ratify treaties with them, so, too, the executive power encompassed authority to construe existing treaties (and international law more generally) in the first instance and to declare formal American neutrality between warring nations. In all these respects, America's presidents would officially propound America's foreign policy and act as the constitutionally authorized organ of communication between America and the world.

ONE ASPECT OF THE NEUTRALITY PROCLAMATION, however, has failed the test of time. Washington suggested that American citizens violating his neutrality policy would be immediately subject to federal prosecution. But the Supreme Court later made clear in a celebrated 1812 case, *United States v. Hudson & Goodwin*, that American presidents (and American judges, for that matter) lack authority to create federal criminal law unilaterally. This ruling accurately reflected the Constitution's grand architecture, which guarantees that ordinarily no person can be convicted of a federal crime unless Congress first defines the crime (and determines the accompanying punishment) with suitable specificity and prospectivity.[10]

Textually, the Legislative Article explicitly authorizes Congress—not the president and not the judiciary—to "define and punish...Offenses against the Law of Nations." In fact, Congress did just that in its Neutrality Act of 1794, which provided the proper legal authorization for the prosecution policy that Washington had prematurely announced in his 1793 proclamation. Thus, the justices got it just right in 1812 when they insisted that "[t]he legislative authority of the Union must first make an act a crime, affix a punishment to it, and declare the Court that shall have jurisdiction of the offence."[11]

In this landmark Marshall Court ruling, we see the proper limits of America's unwritten Constitution. Where the text and structure of the written document are clear, the written Constitution trumps the unwritten Constitution—even where George Washington is concerned.

"the Heads of Departments"

IN ALL THE WASHINGTON ADMINISTRATION EPISODES just canvassed, the president relied heavily on the advice of an inner circle of top executive-branch officials. This heavy reliance bids us take a hard look at the president's "cabinet"—a word that nowhere appears in the text of the written Constitution as ratified in 1787–1788, but an entity that has played an important role in America's actual institutional system from 1789 to the present.

Cabinet members are the president's subordinates, and have been so ever since the days of Washington. America's first president leaned on his cabinet precisely because he had reason to trust these confidants. He himself had handpicked this team, per the Constitution's explicit appointments rules. These powerful lieutenants answered directly to him under the Article II opinions clause, which encouraged presidents to require reports from the "principal Officer"—elsewhere described as the "Head[]"—of each executive department. Crucially, these men served at Washington's pleasure; he had the unilateral power to dismiss them at any time for any reason, and he was willing to wield this power. In 1795, within days of receiving intelligence raising grave doubts about the ethical and political fitness of his second secretary of state, Edmund Randolph (whom he had appointed to replace Jefferson), Washington unceremoniously muscled Randolph out of office, who resigned to avoid being fired.[12]

But where did the Constitution give presidents this unilateral, plenary, and instantaneous authority to fire the heads of executive departments? Article II explicitly made the Senate a partner in the hiring of department heads. Arguably, the document implicitly gave the Senate a symmetrical role in the firing of these department heads—a reading that would generally require the president to win senatorial consent before firing any cabinet member. (This was the interpretation offered by Hamilton/Publius in *The Federalist* No. 77.)

However, as soon as Washington took the helm, his supporters in and out of the First Congress (including Hamilton, who on second thought abandoned his earlier interpretation) insisted that the Constitution gave the president a right to fire any executive head in whom the chief executive had lost confidence. After extensive deliberation, the First Congress adopted a series of laws acknowledging this presidential authority in the course of establishing the State Department (originally named the Department of Foreign Affairs), the Department of War, and the Treasury Department.

These landmark statutes specified what should happen whenever the principal officer "shall be removed from office by the President"—phraseology artfully designed not to confer removal power upon the president by legislative grace, but rather to concede and confirm the chief executive's *constitutionally derived* authority to dismiss executive department heads at will. More than anything in the terse text or the popular understandings that had emerged in the ratification process, it was this set of landmark statutes—today often referred to as the "Decision of 1789"—that established the basic rules of executive-branch firing that govern twenty-first-century practice.[13]

Granted, a hardcore textualist can insist—as did many of Washington's supporters in the First Congress, from Madison on down—that the president's plenary authority to dismiss executive-branch underlings was simply one aspect of the president's "executive Power" vested by Article II's opening sentence. But if this sentence alone gave a president power to fire cabinet heads at will, logic would suggest that the opening sentence likewise gave a president power to fire at will all other high-level executive-branch appointees—that is, all top appointed federal officers except judges and other judicial-branch officials. This broader power, however, has not been recognized in American practice over the centuries. In a wide range of high-profile and well-settled areas, statutes have long limited and continue to limit the president's ability to remove nonjudicial officers.

For example, when Barack Obama succeeded George W. Bush in 2009, everyone understood that Bush's treasury secretary, Henry Paulson, would need to leave immediately if the new president wanted to hand the top Treasury spot to someone else. (Obama in fact let Paulson go.) Yet virtually no one thought that Obama could likewise immediately dismiss all of the governors of the Federal Reserve Board, simply because he may have preferred new persons of his own choosing. On the contrary, the statute authorizing the Federal Reserve Board—a statute whose basic framework has been in place for three-quarters of a century—pointedly limits the ability of a new president to sweep the board clean on day one. Thus the Federal Reserve Board and the Treasury are governed by different firing rules. The simple text of the Article II "executive Power" clause cannot easily explain this interesting difference in actual institutional practice.[14]

The best explanation is that in 1789, Congress squarely acknowledged presidential authority to remove certain kinds of executive appointees at will, but made no similar ruling regarding other appointees. This Decision of 1789 has, in effect, glossed the language of Article II as a whole, establishing that *individual department heads*, such as Treasury Secretaries Alexander Hamilton and Henry Paulson, must be subject to unilateral removal whenever the president loses confidence in them for any honest personal or political reason. But this Decision did not cement in place identical removal rules for all other executive appointees. Later Congresses were thus free to enact somewhat different mechanisms of accountability for these other appointees—even important executive-branch appointees such as governors of the Federal Reserve.

There are at least two ways to conceptualize the status of the Federal Reserve in light of the Decision of 1789. In one view, the governors of the Federal Reserve Board are simply not department "Heads," strictly speaking. Unlike the statutory structure establishing regular cabinet departments topped by a one-man decisional "Head" or "principal Officer," the statute creating the Federal Reserve vests legal authority in a multimember body. Thus, the Federal Reserve and certain other nonjudicial agencies whose top governing boards are not removable at will by the president may be seen as "headless" in a certain sense. The point is not that these "headless" agencies live in some mysterious fourth branch of government beyond all presidential supervision and control. Even vis-à-vis these agencies, the president remains the ultimate apex of the executive branch, retaining broad powers of appointment and additional powers of oversight and for-cause removal (as distinct from at-will removal). Rather, these agencies may be viewed as "headless" in a much narrower and more technical sense: Legal power in these agencies generally resides not in a one-man head, but instead in a multimember board or commission.

Tellingly, the written Constitution allows Congress to empower department "Heads"—but no other executive official, except the president himself—to unilaterally appoint lower-level ("inferior") executive officers. Any executive officer who could be entrusted with the honorific authority to name other executive officers had to be removable at will by the president at any time for any honest reason. Or so the First Congress could be understood as having decided after careful deliberation, and so the text of Article II as a whole could today plausibly be read, thanks to the intertwining of America's written and unwritten Constitution.[15]

An alternative interpretation of Article II as glossed by the Decision of 1789 explains the basic constitutional difference between the Federal Reserve and the Treasury in a slightly different way. Perhaps we should think of the Federal Reserve not as a "headless" department but rather as a "hydra-headed" department—that is, a department headed not by one brain but several coordinate brains. On this view, multibrain hydras qualify as "department heads," and the hydra/commission can therefore be vested with power to pick inferior officers, but the removal rules for hydra-headed departments need not be absolutely identical to the removal rules applicable to one-headed departments.[16]

From this perspective, the Decision of 1789 established that in all one-headed departments, the department head must be removable at will by the president, but this Decision simply did not reach and therefore did not resolve the different set of issues posed by hydra-headed departments. As to these departments, post-1789 presidents and Congresses have in effect decided that the president needs only the power to remove hydra heads *for cause*, rather than *at will*. In sharp contrast to a typical one-man department head who enjoys broad operational freedom within the department, each member of a hydra-headed commission is routinely subject to close monitoring by each other member for possible misconduct. Any commissioner who has concerns about a peer is well positioned to confer with other commissioners and to report these concerns to the president. As a result, the president does not need peremptory power to remove at will in order to assure commission members' due subordination and energetic performance. Removability for cause, supplemented by the additional horizontal monitoring provided by a multimember commission structure, may well suffice, if Congress and the president prefer this alternative accountability structure and embed this alternative structure into a department's enabling statute.[17]

But even if the Decision of 1789 does not require at-will removability for hydra-headed department heads, that Decision did firmly establish that neither Congress as a whole, nor the Senate, nor any subset of these bodies can participate in any specific removal decision (outside the context of impeachment or legislation subject to presidential presentment). Whatever removal power of executive officers exists—whether the removability is at will or for cause—is ultimately executive power, not legislative or senatorial power, and thus resides solely within the executive branch. That much was settled for good in 1789, even if other elements of the 1789 settlement may plausibly be read in different ways—much as constitutional texts themselves clearly settle some core issues while leaving peripheral issues unsettled and subject to differing plausible interpretations.

Thus, the opening "executive Power" language of Article II was not only clarified and qualified by the textual list of specified presidential powers that appeared later in Article II, but was additionally glossed by the basic settlement achieved between the First Congress and President Washington. Congressman Madison predicted as much to his colleagues in the First Congress even as they were deliberating: "The decision that is at this time made, will become the permanent exposition of the constitution."*[18]

CLOSELY READ, THE ARTICLE II CLAUSE sketching the role of cabinet officers gestured toward a more compartmentalized executive inner circle than what ultimately emerged in practice. Textually, the Constitution provided that "[t]he President...may require the Opinion, in writing, of the principal Officer in each of the executive Departments, upon any Subject relating to the Duties of their respective Offices." The word "respective" called to mind an image of a hub-and-spoke organizational chart, with each principal officer/department head reporting directly to the president on all matters concerning his particular executive department, but keeping mum on issues confronting other department heads.

Washington, however, routinely consulted multiple executive heads on a given issue—often in a single conference. Most of Washington's early successors followed this conference practice. Thus a new entity—the "cabi-

---

* Mid-nineteenth-century congressmen occasionally strayed from the Decision of 1789, especially when confronting ornery presidents from Tennessee named Andrew J____son. But these lapses did little to impair the legal force of the Decision of 1789, which for most of American history has enjoyed and today continues to enjoy a status akin to that of a clear constitutional text. For details, see n. 18.

net," comprising various department heads meeting together—became a notable part of actual institutional practice for much of American history (although today, meetings of the entire cabinet are less common and more ceremonial than in decades past).

Several factors explain the three-dimensional materialization of an institution that is virtually invisible in the Founders' two-dimensional blueprint. First, the real-world policy issues facing Washington often spilled across the formal boundaries separating the various executive departments. For example, the question of whether to have a federal bank surely implicated the Treasury Department, but the question also had foreign-policy aspects (should aliens be allowed to buy shares in the bank?) and raised nice issues of constitutional interpretation (did the federal government have authority to create such an institution?). When obliged to decide whether to sign or veto a bank bill that Congress passed in 1791, Washington ultimately received written opinions from Treasury Secretary Hamilton, Secretary of State Jefferson, and Attorney General Randolph. Many later issues concerning France and England likewise related to multiple departments and thus invited collective conferencing.

Second, the attorney general in some ways operated as an official liaison tying together the formal department heads and also reporting directly to the president. Strictly speaking, the attorney general himself was not a department head because he had no bureaucratic organization beneath him. (Only after the Civil War did Congress create an official executive-branch Department of Justice and thereby elevate the AG to the status of a formal department head.) Nevertheless, the 1789 statute creating the position of attorney general explicitly provided that this officer was duty-bound to provide legal opinions when so requested by the president or by the official department heads. Whether intentionally or not, this statute induced collective executive-branch deliberation, with the attorney general functioning as an interconnecting legal bridge who linked together all top executive officials by answering directly to each department head and also to the president.[19]

Third, the idea of a collective executive council drew strength from traditional practice. English monarchs had long been accustomed to receiving advice from a collective Privy Council, whose precise shape and functions had varied over time and were continuing to evolve in the Founding era. Executive councils had also featured prominently in the colonies before 1776 and in the independent states thereafter.[20]

Finally, Washington, by temperament and philosophy, was a consensus-seeker. War councils had served him well when he was a battlefield general, and in his vision of public service, patriotic officials of all stripes should ideally converge on nonpartisan solutions when presented with the same facts. Thus, he sought advice from his department heads even on topics beyond the strict boundaries of their respective departmental assignments, and later presidents followed suit.[21]

Although this collective model moved beyond the simple hub-and-spoke image suggested by the spare text of the opinion clause, Washington's practice and that of his successors did not transgress the strict letter of the written Constitution. Necessarily, the opinions clause gave the president some discretion to decide for himself which "Subject[s]" were so closely "relat[ed] to" a given department head's official portfolio as to warrant a formal opinion from that officer. And nothing in this clause or in any other clause barred presidents from seeking advice from various persons outside the official circle of department heads, if presidents deemed these other advisers wise and trustworthy. If a president could request informal advice from non-department-heads—and which president has not done this routinely?—it is hard to see why the president couldn't likewise ask a department head for informal advice on topics beyond that adviser's official bailiwick.[22]

Textual fine points aside, Washington's practice honored the animating spirit of the opinions clause, whose thrust was to concentrate accountability for presidential action on the president himself. No matter how Congress might choose to contour various executive departments and offices beneath the president, the president needed to serve as the legal hub of the executive inner circle and the apex of the executive pyramid. Even if a president chose to consult his department heads en masse, their collective judgment would not thereby trump his own. In sharp contrast to many state governors who constitutionally had to win the votes of council majorities for various proposed gubernatorial initiatives, the president would be his own man. Although the clause invited him to solicit the opinions of his department heads, it pointedly did not oblige him to do so. (Hence the phrase "the President...may require" rather than "the President...shall require.") Ultimately, the president would oversee lieutenants who answered to him—not vice versa.[23]

This was the big idea behind the opinions clause, which underscored that a president could never claim that his hands were tied because he had been outvoted or overridden by his advisers in a secret conference. In *The Federalist* No. 70, Hamilton/Publius explained that "one of the weightiest objections to a plurality in the executive...is that it tends to conceal faults, and destroy responsibility....It often becomes impossible, amidst mutual accusations, to determine on whom the blame or the punishment of a pernicious measure, or a series of pernicious measures[,] ought really to fall." According to Publius, a chief executive in a badly designed council system could always claim, truthfully or not—for the public could never be sure who had done what behind closed doors—that "I was overruled by my council" or that "The council were so divided in their opinions that it was impossible to obtain any better resolution on the point."

Though Publius in this passage did not explicitly quote the opinions clause, his telling use of the word "opinions" drove home the central purpose of this clause: to prevent presidents from evading blame by hiding behind the opinions of advisers meeting in private. As future justice James Iredell stressed with italics in his own ratification-era publication, the opinions clause would fix public attention where it belonged. "The President must be *personally responsible* for everything." In more modern parlance, the buck stops with him.[24]

Nothing in Washington's generous consultative practice violated this core principle, even as it did drift toward a collective model of advice-seeking. Everyone from Washington on down understood that even if he chose to poll various department heads or to confer with them en masse on important issues, and even if he often chose to follow their collective wisdom, he nevertheless remained personally responsible for the final decision. Legally and politically, the buck did indeed stop with him.[25]

"Advice"

TO SOME EXTENT, the cabinet's rise came at the Senate's expense.

Before the American Revolution, the upper legislative chamber in most colonies had officially doubled as the governor's executive council. After 1776, many states had either continued this double-duty system or had created new executive councils composed of select members of the upper house.[26]

As Americans pondered the proposed Constitution in 1787–1788, it seemed natural enough to many ratifiers that U.S. senators would likely play a broadly similar role vis-à-vis the president. After all, the Constitution twice spoke of the Senate as a body that would give the chief executive its "Advice and Consent"—first in the context of making treaties, and second in the context of appointing federal officers. Beyond the consultative ring of this phrase, the brute fact that presidents would ultimately need to secure senatorial approval for various executive initiatives made it plausible to predict that presidents would confer with senators early and often. Also, senators would sit as judges and jurors in any presidential impeachment trial that might occur. A cautious president would thus have yet another reason to invite senators into his confidence at the earliest opportunity: If senators were to informally approve various presidential initiatives as they were occurring, it would be harder for these counselors to later convict the chief executive of misconduct.

George Washington had little to fear from an impeachment court. Nevertheless, his natural inclination toward consultation and consensus-building prompted him to seek the Senate's advice in consiliary fashion early in his administration. In a tragicomic episode whose clumsy choreography ultimately exposed the structural inaptness of the Senate as an ideal executive council, both president and Senate tried to lead the dance, and despite honorable intentions all around, each stepped on the other's toes.

The dance began on a Saturday in August 1789 when Washington went in person to the Senate chamber. He sought the Senate's quick approval of instructions that had been drafted for a team of American negotiators preparing to parley with southern Indian tribes. Many senators, reasonably enough, wanted a little time to ponder the policy issues being presented to them. Some members felt intimidated by Washington's very presence and were bent on setting a proper precedent of senatorial autonomy. Recording his anxieties in his private journal, Pennsylvania Senator William Maclay worried that if senators said yes to the president too quickly, "we should have these advices and consents ravished, in a degree, from us....I saw no chance of a fair investigation of subjects while the President of the United States sat there...to support his opinions and overawe the timid and neutral part of the Senate."[27]

As it became clear from the meandering drift of the proceedings that the upper house would postpone the matter until Monday, a visibly impatient Washington voiced his frustration: "*This defeats every purpose of my coming here!*" Regaining his composure, Washington withdrew from the room and politely returned the next Monday, at which time he secured the approval he sought, but only after being obliged to endure hours of tedious talk. According to one account—perhaps too juicy to be true—as Washington left the chamber he was heard to say that "he would be damned if he ever went there again."[28]

In fact, Washington never again darkened the Senate's door to seek advice or consent in person. Nor did he always solicit the Senate's written advice before making momentous decisions, even decisions (for example, in treaty negotiations) that he knew would later require him to win formal senatorial approval.

The mismatch that first became apparent in August 1789 went far beyond the delicate issues of host-guest etiquette raised by the physical separation of powers between the president's regular place of business and the Senate's. Nor was the mismatch simply a function of the special admiration and fear that Washington inspired by his mere presence in a room. Had these been the only impediments to a close consultative partnership between president and Senate, a frequent practice of written advice-seeking and advice-giving between Washington and the upper chamber should have emerged. It did not. Instead, Washington increasingly turned to his department heads as his sounding board, and Washington's successors have all followed suit. For more than two centuries, America's actual institutional constitution has featured the cabinet and not the Senate as the president's de facto council. (Note that in August 1789, the advice-hungry Washington did not have the option of seeking counsel from his handpicked department heads, for the simple reason that these heads had yet to be nominated, confirmed, commissioned, and sworn in—a process that would begin a few weeks later.)

With the benefit of hindsight and structural analysis—and with special attention to the ramifications of the Decision of 1789—we can see several reasons for this shift from Senate to cabinet as the president's preferred advisory body. For starters, the Senate was too crowded to facilitate a genuinely intimate conversation. Most colonies had featured councils of twelve members, and virtually all revolutionary state councils were in the same range or smaller. By contrast, when Washington took office he faced a twenty-two-seat Senate, and by the time he left office the upper chamber had swelled to thirty-two seats, with many more future members imaginable on the western horizon in the years to come. After experimenting with different ways of handling the Senate, Washington eventually settled into a practice in which informal exchanges with a handful of trusted senators occasionally substituted for formal consultations with the entire upper chamber.[29]

Whereas senators answered to state legislatures, department heads answered to presidents. This difference had huge implications. Consider, for example, the need for strict confidentiality. An effective presidential advisory body dealing with sensitive issues of diplomacy, appointment policy, and the like will often have to keep a secret. Every member of the advisory body must cooperate: A single leak can sometimes sink a project. Not only was the Senate awkwardly large even in 1789, but each senator ultimately answered to a constituency wholly independent of the president. A leak from a political skeptic of the president might actually enhance the leaker's standing with state legislators back home, even as it compromised the national interest as understood by the president. If a department head spilled a secret, the president could deal with him severely. Thanks to the Decision of 1789, the leaker could be sacked and shamed immediately, and President Washington only had to consult his own conscience. He had no comparable control over a loose-lipped senator.

In early 1792, Secretary of State Jefferson recorded in his diary that "[t]he President had no confidence in the secresy [sic] of the Senate." The following February, when Washington asked his cabinet whether he should give senators details of his negotiating strategy vis-à-vis northern Indians, his confidants—composed entirely of Senate confirmees—unanimously advised against an early Senate briefing. According to Jefferson, "We all thought if the Senate should be consulted & consequently apprized of our line, it would become known to Hammond [a British diplomat with ties to the Indians], & we should lose all chance of saving anything more at the treaty than our Ultimatum." After Virginia's senator, Stevens Thomson Mason, violated Senate rules by handing the official text of the Jay Treaty to the press in 1795—and was not even censured by the upper chamber—Washington's early doubts hardened.[30]

Consider also the need for speed. A council works best when its members are physically proximate enough to confer in person or quickly exchange written messages. But senators hoping to be reelected—or merely hoping to explain and defend their political conduct to those who had elected them—needed to spend time in their home states. It would be a genuine political hardship for senators to be required to sit permanently in the national capital as an on-call executive council. By contrast, department heads would naturally need to remain in place to discharge their ordinary executive functions.

Here, too, the Decision of 1789 influenced the incentives. Had Congress in 1789 decided, with Washington's assent, that department heads could be fired only if both the president and the Senate agreed that removal was warranted, each head would have had reason to curry favor with leading senators—perhaps senators from the head's home state, or senators with a special policy interest in his particular department. Department heads in such an alternative universe might even have been tempted to routinely leave the national seat in order to lobby the home legislatures of their senatorial patrons. But in the actual universe created by the Decision of 1789, department heads seeking to keep their jobs have as a rule needed to please the president and only the president—not some prominent senator or some influential state legislature.[31]

Precisely because presidents over the centuries have understood all this, these chief executives have been more willing to confide in department heads than they might otherwise have been. The Decision of 1789 encouraged the emergence of a substitute body of counselors—secretaries rather than senators—who would be well positioned to evaluate presidential behavior on an ongoing basis and to sound a public alarm, via mass resignations or some other appropriate act, if a president ever revealed himself to be unfit. Thus, even as the Decision of 1789 strongly reaffirmed the unilateral powers of a unitary executive, Congress also subtly cabined those powers with...a cabinet.[32]

Thanks to the Decision of 1789, fledgling federal institutions sensibly specialized. Senators were free to periodically return home to reconnect with their constituents, secure in the knowledge that distinguished—senatorially approved!—figures would remain in the capital city to monitor and advise the president during the senatorial recess. Department heads concentrated on administering the government without the temptation to routinely abandon their posts in order to bolster their job security. And each president, beginning with Washington, has been free to confide in a council of genuinely trustworthy advisers while properly remaining personally responsible for various decisions vested by the Constitution and statutes in him and him alone.[33]

THE CONSTITUTION'S GENERALLY TERSE TEXT turns especially terse in Article II. The laconic language governing the presidency can plausibly be read in various ways. But in actual presidential practice over the centuries on a wide range of issues, the written words of Article II have been read in one quite particular way—a way that is consistent with, but by no means compelled by, the plain meaning of the words alone, a way powerfully influenced by the first president's first precedents. To understand the full meaning of Article II over the course of American history, we must read its words through a special set of lenses—the spectacles of George Washington.

CHAPTER 9

INTERPRETING
GOVERNMENT PRACTICES

America's Institutional Constitution

POTTER STEWART (1976).

Named to the Supreme Court by President Eisenhower during a Senate recess in 1958, Potter Stewart was one of a long line of recess appointees to the federal bench. The practice of judicial recess appointments began under President Washington and has continued into the twenty-first century. Since Stewart, the recess appointment process—in which an appointee provisionally takes office prior to Senate confirmation—has not been used to fill a vacancy on the Supreme Court, but has repeatedly been used for inferior-federal-court appointments.

A T BOTTOM, "CONSTITUTIONAL LAW" IS about how government is constituted. Specifically, how many and what sorts of government institutions exist? How are these institutions configured, and how do they interact with each other? How are various members of these government institutions selected and removed? What is the scope of a given institution's authority? What internal deliberation protocols and voting procedures operate within a particular institution?

Having just considered how America's presidency has functioned over the centuries, thanks in part to George Washington's clarifying precedents, we shall now survey the size, shape, and structure of the other major permanent institutions of federal governance: Congress, the Supreme Court, and administrative agencies. In this wide-ranging survey, we shall discover two abiding truths. First, institutional practice routinely goes beyond the written Constitution. Second, institutional practice rarely goes against the canonical document. Typically, the foundational text significantly constrains even if it does not exclusively control.

In general, the underspecified text and the more specific institutional practices cohere to form a single system of daily governance in which the practices gloss and clarify the text, inducing interpreters to read the otherwise indeterminate text in a highly determinate way. On a broad set of topics concerning the interactions and internal operations of government entities, post-1789 institutional practice thus furnishes a powerful lens through which to read the 1789 blueprint.[1]

"Each House may...punish its Members"

IN A SYSTEM FAMOUS FOR its detailed enumeration of congressional powers, Congress in fact enjoys some remarkable powers that are not clearly enumerated. These powers can easily be read into the Constitution—but only if its text is viewed through the prism of practice.

Today, each house of Congress can investigate virtually any subject of legitimate public interest. At times, each house can also act as policeman, prosecutor, judge, jury, and jailor all in one. For example, each house on its own motion can incarcerate an uncooperative witness, whether a public official or a private citizen, to prompt his compliance or punish disobedience that occurred earlier in the session. Each house can also adjudicate and punish other contempts against itself, such as the attempted bribery of its members. Each house has its own enforcement official, known as a sergeant at arms, and is free to use its own building as a jail so long as it is in session.

Even if the federal judiciary disagrees with a particular House or Senate contempt judgment, federal judges have only limited power to free a house detainee or otherwise reverse the house. The question for ordinary courts is not whether they concur with the substance of a particular house ruling, but whether the house in a given case acted within proper (albeit unwritten) jurisdictional bounds—by punishing only matters that may appropriately be viewed as contempts against core house functions, by following adequate adjudicatory procedures, by imposing no punishment except detention, by releasing all detainees when the house session ends, and by honoring applicable rights, such as Americans' general freedom to criticize Congress.[2]

Arguments from the Constitution's original meaning can be made both for and against these sweeping powers of inquest and punishment. On a broad reading, the Article I, section 5, clause empowering each house to "determine the Rules of its Proceedings" implicitly authorized each house to protect its core functions against outside interference or defiance. On a narrow reading, the text invited precisely the opposite conclusion. Immediately after the word "Proceedings," section 5 authorized each house to "punish its Members for disorderly Behaviour." By negative implication, each house lacked inquisitorial and punishment power over nonmembers (except in the impeachment process, outlined elsewhere in the Constitution). Of course, arguments from negative implication do not always hold true. Perhaps the power to punish nonmembers directly obstructing the basic function of a house (say, by refusing to provide the house with vital information or by trying to bribe house members) simply went without saying as an implicit element of "legislative Power."

Both the British Parliament and American state legislatures circa 1787 enjoyed broad inquisitorial and contempt powers. At least one prominent state chamber, the Virginia House of Delegates, had claimed power to punish nonmembers for contempt even though it could point to nothing in its state constitution more specific than a generic authority to "settle its own rules of proceeding." But Parliament and state legislatures were not governed by the enumerated-powers principle underlying the federal Constitution. Also, separation-of-powers limits on lawmakers were looser in England (where Parliament, sitting as an impeachment court, could try public officers and private persons alike and impose ordinary criminal sanctions) and in most states (where legislatures tended to dominate the other branches). The claim that each house of Congress had certain inherent judicial powers to punish ordinary citizens stood in tension with the federal Constitution's stricter version of separation of powers.[3]

During the Constitution's ratification process, debaters and pamphleteers paid little attention to the existence or nonexistence of these unwritten congressional powers. On the one hand, Federalists did not make clear that federal lawmakers would enjoy the same powers as those traditionally wielded by state legislators to subpoena nonmembers and to try ordinary citizens for contempt. On the other hand, Federalists did not routinely boast that the document withheld these traditional and potentially oppressive powers from Congress.[4]

On these issues, the most compelling conclusions about the meaning of America's Constitution come not from the unvarnished text as understood during the ratification process or from purely logical deductions from the document's general schema. Rather, the text was glossed almost immediately after it went into effect, and this gloss now defines how modern Americans properly read the text.

The glossing process started in the first Congress when Senator Robert Morris in 1790 requested an official congressional inquest into his own conduct as a financier during the Revolutionary War. Various accusations of financial impropriety had begun to surface against Morris, and he hoped that a formal inquest might clear his name. The House took up the matter, even though arguably the Senate would have been a fitter forum to probe the conduct and character of a sitting senator, and even though Morris lay outside the impeachment process (which covered only executive and judicial "Officers" as distinct from representatives and senators).[5]

Voicing support for a House inquest, Representative Madison articulated an expansive view of House investigatory authority: "[T]he House should possess itself of the fullest information in order to do[] justice to the country and to public officers." Although Madison did not elaborate, he could have rebutted anyone who doubted that the investigation's subject lay within the scope of Congress's Article I zones of authority by noting that Congress also had sweeping Article V power to propose constitutional amendments on virtually any subject, and that this power sensibly subsumed authority to conduct preliminary investigations of any topic of true public interest.[6]

Two years after the Morris investigation, the House launched another important inquest, backed by subpoena power, to review a failed 1791 military expedition led by General Arthur St. Clair. Supported by a unanimous cabinet, President Washington instructed his subordinates to cooperate with this inquest by supplying the investigators with relevant nonconfidential papers. In 1798, Congress passed and the president signed a federal statute regularizing oath-taking for congressional witnesses. From this era to the present day, both houses have exercised broad powers of investigation and oversight.[7]

The judiciary has endorsed this vision and in doing so has emphasized the importance of early and continuous practice. In 1927, a case came before the Supreme Court involving the Senate's arrest of a witness who had refused to appear before a Senate investigation of the Teapot Dome scandal. The Court sided with the Senate and its arresting officers in a unanimous decision, *McGrain v. Daugherty*, proclaiming that "the power of inquiry—with process to enforce it—is an essential and appropriate auxiliary to the legislative function." Although the Court waved briefly in the direction of pre-1789 state legislative practice to support this unenumerated congressional power, the justices' main argument derived from postratification federal practice: "[E]arly in their history," both houses took a broad view of the unenumerated power of legislative inquiry, "and both houses have employed the power accordingly up to the present time. The act[] of 1798... [was] intended to recognize the existence of this power in both houses and to enable them to employ it 'more effectually' than before."

All this post-1789 institutional practice, said the Court, "should be taken as fixing the meaning of [the written Constitution's] provisions, if otherwise doubtful."

POST-1789 INSTITUTIONAL PRACTICE has also refracted the 1789 text on the right of each house to punish certain private persons in situations far removed from Congress's general powers of inquest and investigation.

In 1795, several members of the House reported that a nonmember, Robert Randall, had tried to bribe them. The House promptly ordered its sergeant at arms to arrest Randall; gave the accused a three-day trial in the House; convicted him of attempted corruption, by a vote of 78–17; and incarcerated him for the next week. The Senate claimed comparable power as early as 1800. In the 1821 case of *Anderson v. Dunn*, the Marshall Court unanimously upheld the power of each house to punish nonmembers for contempts such as bribery of its members. The houses of Congress have never renounced their authority to exercise this self-help remedy even though most contempts of Congress are nowadays processed by regular Article III court proceedings. *Anderson v. Dunn* remains good law for modern judges and justices; the relevant twentieth-century opinions unanimously reaffirming *Anderson* have explicitly emphasized early practice such as the 1795 Randall matter; and the president's Office of Legal Counsel also supports this inherent contempt power of each house.[8]

The Morris, St. Clair, and Randall precedents stand in the same relation to house power as the Decision of 1789 and early presidential practices stand in relation to executive power. In both contexts, the textually uncertain scope of institutional power was clarified by early usage—in one context in favor of congressional power and in the other context in favor of presidential power. The symmetry of these examples confirms that early institutional practice is not a Trojan horse to smuggle in additional power for one or another favorite branch, but a neutral guidepost to proper constitutional interpretation. Further symmetry may be found in a long line of cases asserting the implied power of federal judges, acting on their own initiative and without direct involvement of the executive branch, to punish misconduct and contempts occurring within the litigation process— a line of cases nearly parallel to those upholding the inherent contempt powers of each congressional house.[9]

Here is yet another element of symmetry: Just as George Washington's attempt to create federal crimes by executive decree was later judicially denounced, because this aspect of his Neutrality Proclamation had plainly misread the written Constitution's letter and spirit, so, too, early congressional practices have been subsequently repudiated insofar as these practices clearly strayed from the terse text. Recall the words of the 1927 *McGrain* Court: Early practice can "fix" (that is, conclusively determine) the meaning of the written Constitution where the issue is "otherwise doubtful"—not where the practice violates the document's plain meaning or deep structure.

For example, the now-infamous Sedition Act of 1798, which criminalized the expression of antiadministration political opinion, has failed the test of time. In the twentieth century, this act was emphatically rejected by judges, lawmakers, and scholars across the political spectrum. This modern consensus is easy to defend precisely because the 1798 act did indeed flout the written Constitution's plain meaning and core principles—whether we attend to the document's explicit text (in the First Amendment's guarantee of freedom of speech), or ponder its implicit structure (founded upon popular sovereignty and the closely related principle that citizens must be free to exchange political views among themselves and to chastise their public servants), or heed the enactment process by which the document sprang to life (via an extraordinary outburst of free speech). In an adjudication infected by the same appalling judgment that had brought forth the Sedition Act, the Senate in 1800 punished publisher William Duane for contempt, merely because he had criticized the upper house in print. Like the Sedition Act itself, the Duane precedent has now been repudiated by both modern Supreme Court precedent and modern Senate practice.[10]

IF THE HOUSE, THE SENATE, AND THE FEDERAL JUDICIARY can claim certain inherent powers, so can the president, of course, as we saw in our earlier survey of presidential powers crystallized by the practices of George Washington. One more Washingtonian assertion of implied executive power deserves mention at this point, as it exists in tension with the congressional inquest power that we have just examined.

Although the written Constitution does not give the president any explicit "executive privilege" to protect confidential conversations with aides or to shield sensitive diplomatic communications, most modern lawyers and judges agree that some such privilege exists. Support for this view may be found in no less canonical a case than *Marbury v. Madison*—in an oral exchange that, curiously, is almost never assigned or even read by modern constitutional scholars. When Attorney General Levi Lincoln was summoned to give evidence before the *Marbury* Court, he told the justices that "he felt himself bound to maintain the rights of the executive....He was of the opinion, and his opinion was supported by that of others whom he highly respected, that he was not bound, and ought not to answer, as to any facts which came officially to his knowledge while acting as secretary of state." In response to Lincoln's concerns, the *Marbury* Court opined that "[t]here was nothing confidential required to be disclosed. If there had been he was not obliged to answer it; and if he thought that any thing was communicated to him in confidence he was not bound to disclose it."[11]

Executive privilege can be seen as one aspect of the Constitution's overall architecture of separation of powers, which entitles each branch to a confidential deliberative space within its own domain. Candid, freewheeling, off-the-record conversations between a president and his advisers in the Oval Office thus structurally resemble similar private deliberations that occur in the Senate cloakroom and in the confidential weekly conferences of the nine justices. These private preliminary communications are necessary for the ultimate discharge of each institution's public functions.

Legal metaphors of institutional separation have literally been built into the very physical design of the national capital, with different buildings ("houses") for different institutions ("houses"). Each institution at times claims a quasi-territorial authority to act as the lord within its own castle and to resist the efforts of other institutions to penetrate its unique physical space and zone of autonomy within its walls. We saw hints of this spatial separation-of-houses sensibility in the nice etiquette questions about where President Washington and the Senate should meet: His place or theirs? Whose man would guard the doors? Who would play host and who would play guest? Who would sit where—and who would decide this? Other elements of this spatial sensibility are visible in contempt-power doctrine, under which the House, the Senate, and the judiciary each claims special powers to punish misbehavior occurring within its own walls.

Textually, some version of "executive privilege" can also be seen as an implicit element of the catchall "executive Power...vested in [the] President" by the opening words of the Executive Article. The precise boundaries of this implicit privilege are debatable, but so are the boundaries of many an explicit constitutional provision, and indeed, the boundary might sensibly vary depending on context. For example, executive privilege vis-à-vis the House of Representatives would seem to be weakest when the House is investigating possible executive-branch misconduct in an impeachment inquiry, and much stronger when the president seeks to maintain certain diplomatic secrets in the absence of a specific showing of the House's need to know.

This was precisely the position that none other than President George Washington himself took in 1796 against none other than Representative James Madison in the wake of the Jay Treaty. After the Senate had agreed to the treaty, and Washington had officially proclaimed the treaty's validity, the matter came before the House, whose assent was needed to pass implementing and funding legislation. Initially, the House, led by Madison, balked, asking Washington to provide details of his earlier treaty negotiations with Britain. Invoking an early version of executive privilege, Washington refused to provide sensitive information that he deemed irrelevant to the issue pending before the House. In this intense inter-branch staredown, the House blinked first, passing the legislation without ever seeing the negotiating papers.[12]

This episode established that presidential claims to secrecy might sometimes prevail; however, it did not stand for the more sweeping conclusion that secrecy claims would always win out. Unlike the statutory language that emerged from the Decision of 1789, nothing in Congress's implementing legislation conceded any profound point of constitutional principle to the executive.

Later Congresses have thus remained free to challenge broad claims of executive privilege and have often exercised this freedom. When the seemingly irresistible force of congressional inquest has met the apparently immovable object of presidential privilege, the results have been all over the map. Sometimes, presidents have had to abandon their initial claims of privilege (as in the Watergate scandal of the early 1970s); other times (as in the Jay Treaty showdown between Washington and Madison), would-be congressional investigators have retreated when presidents have stood their ground. The varied results have all been within the boundaries of America's Constitution. The written document's express language and general structure do not clearly specify that one branch should invariably prevail over the other in these matters, and custom has not precipitated any clear rule or principle resolving the textual and structural indeterminacy.[13]

"Vacancies…happen"

NO ACCOUNT OF AMERICA'S CONSTITUTION would be complete without some attention to the written and unwritten rules governing the internal structure and composition—the constitution—of the House, the Senate, and the Court. One basic set of issues concerns how each entity is replenished over time as senior members leave and junior ones arrive. Given the obvious importance of institutional replenishment to the smooth operation of government, one might initially assume that the written Constitution definitively answers all the important questions. But in fact the text does not work in isolation. It works only when read through the lens of institutional practice.

FOR THE COURT, many of the rules are straightforward: A sitting justice officially leaves upon death, resignation, or removal, and a new justice officially arrives the instant her commission is signed by the president and sealed by his ministry.* But a wrinkle in this generally smooth process arises when a president makes a recess appointment to the Court. Textually, Article II entitles a president to "fill up all Vacancies that may happen during the Recess of the Senate, by granting Commissions which shall expire at the End of their next Session." Does this clause apply even to judicial vacancies—in particular, to Supreme Court vacancies?[14]

On the one hand, "all Vacancies" would seem to mean *all* vacancies, including judicial vacancies. On the other hand, the fact that the commissions of recess appointees expire in a matter of months jars with the textual

---

* The sealing of the commission, not the taking of the oath of office, is the decisive moment of investiture. Taking the oath does not make a person a judge—or a president, for that matter. Oath-taking is merely the first duty of someone who is already legally in office. On this issue, some readers may recall the flubbed oath-taking at President Obama's 2009 inauguration and the president's decision to retake the oath a few hours later out of an abundance of caution. For analysis of this episode, see n. 14.

requirement that "the Judges, both of the supreme and inferior Courts, shall hold their Offices during good Behaviour." Any judicial-recess appointee would not really hold his office for good behavior, but provisionally. In effect, he would lose his judicial office unless he received a vote of confidence from the Senate at its next session; and the Senate would be free to withhold such a vote simply because senators might dislike his initial rulings. If "all Vacancies" means *all* vacancies, shouldn't "shall hold" office during good behavior likewise mean *shall* hold? How can these two seemingly contradictory clauses be harmonized?

Had we only the text and its animating structure to guide us, the best resolution would probably be to give maximum effect to both clauses: Presidents may appoint temporary justices (and lower court judges) who either pledge at the outset to step down at the end of their temporary term or are treated by the Senate as if they had so pledged, and are thus categorically ineligible for confirmation. That way, all vacancies could be presidentially filled in prompt fashion, and all judges could freely ignore senatorial preferences and pressure.

But that is not the only plausible interpretation of the written Constitution, and that is not how practice has in fact unfolded. Rather, in 1795, George Washington himself made a recess appointment to the Court, and his appointee, John Rutledge, made no promise to sit for a merely temporary period. When the Senate chose not to confirm Rutledge because various senators apparently disliked some of the things that Rutledge had recently said, the special vulnerability of judicial-recess appointees became clear to all. Yet every one of the next seven presidents made recess appointments to the federal bench, and most presidents since then have done the same, generating more than three hundred judicial-recess appointments in all. Many judicial-recess appointees have taken the bench immediately upon being commissioned, and none have been obliged by their fellow judges to recuse themselves until confirmation. In deciding whether to confirm or reject these provisional appointees, the Senate has generally felt free to consider their initial judicial rulings. Thus, the Senate has gained a special power, not otherwise allowed, of de facto removal over these sitting but unconfirmed federal judges.

True, no recess appointment has been made to the Supreme Court since

President Eisenhower put Earl Warren, William Brennan, and Potter Stewart on the Court during Senate recesses in the 1950s. And in 1960, the Senate itself adopted a recommendatory resolution generally advising against recess appointments to the highest court in the land. But presidents of both parties have continued to name recess appointees to the lower federal judiciary, and senators have continued to confirm many of these appointees to permanent posts.[15]

The strongest argument in support of the constitutionality of these curious appointments thus comes not from text or structure, but from longstanding usage. Here, as elsewhere, an ambiguous text has been definitively glossed by what has in fact been done early and often by leaders from across the political spectrum. All three branches have blessed probationary appointments to the bench—the president by continuing to make recess appointments without extracting a public pledge of temporary tenure; the Senate by continuing to confirm some recess appointees and to reject others, based, in part, on the judicial rulings of these probationary appointees; and the judiciary by allowing these merely provisional judges to wear robes and sit on the bench.[16]

LIKE THE SYSTEM OF JUDICIAL REPLENISHMENT, the process of legislative replenishment has involved elements of both written and unwritten constitutionalism.

The senatorial renewal process usually works quite smoothly. Members leave the Senate early upon death, resignation, or expulsion. Otherwise, a senator departs the Senate whenever his term is up, unless, of course, he is reelected and reseated. New members arrive by dint of their popular election or their temporary gubernatorial appointment, pursuant to the rules of the Seventeenth Amendment. Officially, the Senate itself decides— "Judge[s]," in the phraseology of Article I, section 5—whether a newly elected (or appointed) senator was *duly* elected (or appointed) and whether he meets the Constitution's eligibility rules.[17]

The Senate is structured to ensure that it never turns over all at once in the wake of a regular biennial election. Ordinarily, two-thirds of the Senate's members remain in their seats after an election, and at any single moment the vast majority of senators are typically duly seated holdovers from previous election cycles. Thus, there is virtually always a quorum of continuing senators able to rule on any questions that might arise concerning the contested credentials of a new senator or group of new senators—even a sizable group, as when the holdover senators in late 1865 confronted a significant number of controversial southern claimants simultaneously seeking admission.

House replenishment is far more edgy, because the House is not a continuing body. Every two years, the old House legally dies and an entirely new House legally springs to life. Although many members—most members, nowadays—seek and win reelection time and again, none of these old hands, legally speaking, are holdovers from a previous election cycle. No member, not even a thirty-year House veteran who has been the speaker for the past decade, is already a member of the new House before any other member, even an incoming freshman.

The formal noncontinuity of the House raises profound theoretical questions. On Day One of the new House, who organizes it? Who sits in the chair, and who guards the doors? Who decides (at least provisionally) who has been duly elected? Who decides (at least for the moment) who meets the eligibility rules? Who decides who decides? Who decides who decides who decides? And so on. In other words, how does the new House give birth to itself? How does it bootstrap itself into operation at its first meeting?

Ordinarily, these deep questions are rather academic. Typically, only a few seats in any election cycle are plausibly subject to contestation on Day One.

But in December 1865, the issue was not merely theoretical. It was real and it was huge, as the credentials of virtually all the self-proclaimed representatives of the old South were reasonably subject to challenge on Day One. Recall that northern Republican critics of these southern claimants argued that all the underlying southern "elections" were constitutionally invalid, having been held in states that failed to meet the basic elements of proper Article IV republican government. But by what right did *some* (northern) representatives claim to be the true House on Day One, the House that would properly judge the contested credentials of the *other* (southern) self-proclaimed representatives—others who were made to

new state's senatorial electoral calendar with the senatorial calendars of the older states. Despite the textual uncertainty, the Senate has in every instance of a new state's admission followed a practice virtually identical to one first used in 1789. Under this venerable practice, most senators from new states have served initial terms of less than six years, despite the general textual rule that senators are elected for "six Years." This long-standing practice has made profound structural sense, giving proper priority to the system-stabilizing Article I, section 3, principle that "one third [of the Senate] be chosen every second Year." (Recall that this key principle happily ensures that the Senate never turns over all at once, House-style.) Here, again, we see the unwritten Constitution in action, sensibly glossing an ambiguous and underspecified text.[21]

A slightly different interaction of text and practice has occurred on the House side of the Capitol. Textually, each state must have "at Least one Representative," and "the number of Representatives shall not exceed one for every thirty Thousand" persons. In a twenty-first-century nation of some three hundred million persons distributed across fifty states, these written rules mean that the size of the House today could be as low as fifty and as high as ten thousand.

America's unwritten Constitution narrows this range. A House that was smaller than the Senate would be virtually unthinkable and arguably unconstitutional. Article I, section 2, says that to be eligible to vote for representatives to the House, voters must be eligible to vote for members of "the *most numerous* Branch of the State Legislature" (emphasis added)—a rule that implies, even if it does not expressly guarantee, that the House will be the most numerous branch of the federal legislature.

In the ratification debates of 1787–1788, a broad continental consensus emerged that the House would need to swell to somewhere around a hundred members as soon as the first census was conducted. Anything smaller would fail to provide adequate safeguards against corruption or oppression. The tinier the House, the easier it would be to bribe its members, and the less likely these members would be to embody the diversity of the citizenry and to sympathize with the concerns of ordinary Americans. Or so it was thought by a great mass of Americans during the great national ratification conversation, in which Federalists across the continent in effect promised that the written maximum House size—one representative for every thirty thousand constituents—would operate as the effective minimum House size until the House grew well past one hundred seats.

This promise formed no part of the Constitution's written text; nor was it memorialized in any other binding legal document. But without this promise, the Constitution might well have gone down to defeat in various state ratifying conventions, where the issues of House size and the need for a Bill of Rights formed the two biggest—and potentially deal-breaking— objections to the Philadelphia plan. The new Constitution derived its legitimacy from the great continental conversation of 1787–1788—not just from the formal vote at the end of each ratifying convention, but from the deliberations surrounding these votes. Had Federalists in the early 1790s walked away from the promises they had made in the ratification process, Anti-Federalists would have felt betrayed, and the entire constitutional experiment might have collapsed at the start. Instead, the document's friends in the early 1790s wisely honored the unwritten as well as the written elements of the plan that had won the approval of the American people in the great national debate of the late 1780s.[22]

As soon as the House reached the promised one hundred members in the mid-1790s, two additional dynamics came into play, preventing subsequent shrinkage. First, as new states joined the union, with each state entitled to at least one seat, it was far easier to increase the House size than to deprive an established state of an existing seat. Second, any significant diminution of House size would have required existing House members to agree to a musical-chairs game ensuring that many of them would lose their seats when the music stopped. As the nation's population increased, it was far more natural for incumbents to vote to maintain House size or to expand the House than to shrink it.[23]

In keeping with these dynamics, the size of the House has never decreased appreciably from the first census in 1790 to the present day. Ever since 1911, a landmark congressional statute has fixed the permanent size at 435, subject to temporary fluctuation to accommodate singular events, such as the admission of new states.

True, under a strict reading of the written Constitution, nothing prevents Congress from slashing the size of the House in the next decade to fifty members. But in the real world, everything prevents the Congress from doing so—tradition and trajectory; the structural role and self-image of the House as the larger, proportionate half of Congress; and the obvious incentives of existing House members to preserve their own seats and status. This predictable incentive structure forms part of America's unwritten Constitution and has operated to prevent a fifty-member House—or a five-thousand-member body, for that matter—from occurring as effectively as if these numerical boundaries had in fact been formally inscribed into the document.[24]

ALTHOUGH THE WRITTEN RULES would allow a Supreme Court of nearly any size, the unwritten rules suggest some additional constraints—but only modest ones.

An enormous difference exists between the House of Representatives and the Court: The House has an absolute policy veto on any law that changes its own size, but the Court lacks symmetric control over its own dimensions. In order to stymie any proposed legal change in House size, House members need only say they prefer the status quo. But the Court cannot thwart a change to its own size simply on the ground that the current Court deems the change undesirable. The Court may properly thwart a change only if the change is unconstitutional, and the Constitution, both written and unwritten, is best read as giving Congress considerable authority over the size of the Court.

Article I empowers Congress to make "proper" laws effectuating the powers of "the government of the United States," including the executive and judicial branches. Thus, in 1789, it was Congress—acting, of course, with bicameral assent and presidential presentment—that legally established that the first Supreme Court would have six members. Over the ensuing decades, it was Congress that episodically modified the Court's size from a low of five members to a high of ten. And ever since the 1870s, it has been Congress that has kept the Court at its present size of nine.

Today, this magic number might seem to many Americans to be an absolutely fixed feature of America's unwritten Constitution, unchangeable by ordinary legislative action for ordinary legislative reasons. But in fact, Congress need not treat the number nine as sacrosanct.

True, inertia and congressional inaction for nearly a century and a half strongly support the status quo. But inertia and inaction alone do not add up to constitutional immunity from future legislation. Between 1876 and 1950, Congress enacted no major civil-rights laws, but Congress did not thereby lose its broad powers to act in this domain. The Reconstruction Amendments conferred these broad powers in clear terms, and Congress in fact has repeatedly deployed these powers since 1950 in ways that have profoundly reshaped America. If Congress never lost its power to pass civil-rights laws, how and when did Congress lose its power to pass Court-resizing laws?

True, President Franklin Roosevelt famously tried and failed to monkey with the Court's size in 1937 when he unsuccessfully attempted to persuade Congress to enact legislation that would have "packed" the Court with several new seats. But civil-rights advocates likewise tried and failed to enact sweeping racial reforms in the FDR era. Surely these advocates retained every right to try again later on, despite their earlier failures, and the same principle applies to post-1937 advocates of judicial reform. Unsuccessful efforts to exercise an explicit power do not always—indeed, do not generally—cause the power to disappear from the document in form or in substance.

The collapse of FDR's 1937 Court-packing plan did not generate anything closely analogous to the Decision of 1789. In the 1780s, the first Congress passed a series of statutes whose language explicitly glossed an ambiguous constitutional text. In the 1930s, Congress simply declined to adopt FDR's proposed Court-packing statute. In 1789, all three key legislative actors—the House, the Senate, and the president—reached an express settlement. A century and a half later, politicians agreed to disagree. FDR never conceded any point of constitutional principle, and even many of his opponents admitted that Congress could modify the Court's size for sincere reasons of judicial administration unrelated to displeasure with the Court's rulings.[25]

Many thoughtful lawyers today believe that certain types of legislative assaults on the Court would violate the spirit of separation of powers and judicial independence. But if Congress has a sincere good-government reason for altering the Court's size, it is hard to see why Congress's views should not prevail, even if the Court sincerely disagrees about what size would be best for achieving good government. Article I's necessary-and-proper clause makes Congress the policymaker on this question and thus to some extent puts the Court at the mercy of Congress.

Even if, in a given instance of resizing the Court, Congress was retaliating against what it perceived as Court abuses—say, a string of dubious rulings and judicial overreaches—the legislature should still prevail. A strong case can be made that the written Constitution was designed precisely to allow Congress to rein in or resize a Court that Congress believes has acted improperly. Over the years, several legal changes in Court size have in fact been made by Congresses who were exquisitely aware of how the changes would likely affect the substantive rulings of the Court. For example, a lame-duck Federalist Congress in 1801 decreased the Court size from six to five in an attempt to deny the incoming president, Thomas Jefferson, an early Court appointment. The next Congress, dominated by Jeffersonians, promptly restored the size to six, so as to re-empower their man. In Jefferson's second term, he and Congress agreed to expand the Court size to seven, with the full understanding that this increase would give him an additional opportunity to mold the Court. In the late 1860s, history repeated itself. Congressional Republicans hostile to President Johnson, and seeking to limit his appointments power, reduced the size of the Court from ten to seven. Only when Johnson was out of the picture did Congress increase the Court size back to nine, thereby giving President Grant an additional opportunity to move the Court his way.[26]

Entirely different issues would arise if Congress tried not to resize the Court but to restructure it. Suppose that some future law were to provide that the Court members must generally sit in randomly generated three-justice panels, with the full nine-justice Court authorized to sit en banc and reverse individual panel decisions only in cases of "egregious panel error."

As an abstract textual matter, this hypothetical statute might pass muster. Although the Constitution does require that "one supreme Court" must exist, Court members need not always sit en banc with each other in order to truly form one Court. Today, each federal appellate court ordinarily sits in three-judge panels, with only rare en banc sittings, yet virtually no one says that this fact means that each of these courts is not really a court. Many a court at the Founding likewise did not invariably sit en banc.

Nevertheless, it is easy enough to read the Article III words "one supreme Court" to mean that the justices must tightly cohere into one highly unified and centralized entity. Ever since 1789, Congress has in fact structured the Court in just this way, as a judicial body that virtually always acts en banc. Here, custom plausibly glosses a text, and the combination of text and custom may well have created a constitutional norm that would prevent Congress from radically decentralizing the Court.

Analogously, nothing in the text of Article III requires that the justices issue written majority opinions of the Court, and prior to John Marshall the Court did not routinely produce institutional writings of this sort. But in the two centuries since Marshall, actual Court practice may well have created a soft obligation on the part of the justices to try, wherever possible, to achieve these sorts of formal institutional statements, precisely because that is what Americans have come to expect of "*one* supreme Court" (emphasis added).[27]

In sum, where customary practice attaches to and helps define a specific constitutional word or phrase, a strong synergy arises between America's written and unwritten Constitution. Whereas the venerable practices of official Court opinions and routine en banc sittings easily attach to the phrase "one supreme Court," the familiar number nine has no comparable clause to which it can comfortably adhere. Nor does the Constitution give the decision about Court size to the Court itself and thereby create a strong incentive structure that might limit the imaginable options. The long-standing tradition of a Supreme Court with exactly nine seats thus forms a rather weak aspect of America's current unwritten Constitution— a tradition doubtless cherished by the justices and many of the Court's admirers, but a tradition ultimately entrusted to other branches to maintain or modify as they see fit.

"Each House may determine the Rules of its Proceedings"

MULTI-MEMBER INSTITUTIONS, such as the House, the Senate, and the Court, can do nothing—nothing at all!—unless certain basic social-choice rules are in place within these institutions. Crucially, there must exist master rules that determine how many votes within each institution will suffice to achieve certain results. Yet the written Constitution does not textually specify the master voting rule that operates inside these three chambers. Happily, two centuries of actual practice make clear that the bedrock constitutional principle within each is simple majority rule.

Some senators today, however, think otherwise. They think that the Senate's current filibuster system cannot be abolished by a simple majority vote. They should think again, for they have misread America's Constitution, written and unwritten. To see why, let's first canvass the internal voting rules and deliberation protocols that apply within the Supreme Court and the House of Representatives and then use the evidence and insights generated by this canvass to analyze the modern Senate filibuster.

THE CONSTITUTION EXPLICITLY PROVIDES for a chief justice, but does not specify his role, except as the official who chairs presidential impeachment trials. Perhaps the chief's most important Court role, established by Court tradition, involves his power to assign opinions. Whenever he finds himself in the initial majority after oral argument, he decides which justice shall take the lead in trying to compose an opinion on behalf of the Court. Of course, he may opt to assign the opinion to himself, as John Marshall did in most important cases of his day, and as Earl Warren did in landmark cases such as *Brown v. Board of Education* and *Reynolds v. Sims*.

Thanks to the necessary-and-proper clause, Congress has also vested the chief justice with sundry administrative and supervisory responsibilities for the federal judiciary as a whole—but none of these congressional statutes has done much to clarify the chief's authority within the Supreme Court itself. And although Congress has defined the jurisdiction of the Court and has enacted various rules of evidence and procedure for litigants who come before the justices, federal lawmakers have opted to leave a great deal of the internal protocol among the justices to be worked out by the justices themselves.[28]

But by what voting rule? Although the written Constitution left the matter unspecified, four interrelated factors pointed to simple majority rule as the master norm among the justices, at least in the absence of some contrary protocol prescribed by Congress.

First, majority rule has unique mathematical properties that make it the obvious answer. When an uneven number of voters (or justices) are deciding between two simple alternatives, such as whether to affirm or reverse a lower-court decision or whether to rule for the plaintiff or the defendant in a trial situation, there is always an alternative that commands the support of a majority, but there might be no alternative that enjoys more than majority support.

Second, anyone who had studied John Locke's canonical *Second Treatise of Government*—as had most of the leading American revolutionaries—knew that majority rule was considered the natural default principle of all assemblies. In Locke's words: "[I]n assemblies impowered to act by positive laws, where no number is set by that positive law which impowers them, the act of the majority passes for the act of the whole and, of course, determines, as having by the law of nature and reason the power of the whole."[29]

Other Founding-era authorities said the same thing. Building on this broad tradition, Thomas Jefferson's mid-1780s booklet *Notes on the State of Virginia* declared that "*Lex majoris partis* [is] founded in common law as well as common right. It is the natural law of every assembly of men, whose numbers are not fixed by any other law." In written remarks read aloud to the Philadelphia Convention, Benjamin Franklin described majority rule as "the Common Practice of Assemblies in all Countries and Ages." None of his fellow delegates said otherwise.[30]

Third, the Constitution's text evidently incorporated this majoritarian premise, albeit by implication. Whenever a federal institution was authorized by the Constitution to make a certain decision using some principle other than simple majority rule, the exception to the (implicit) rule was specified in the document itself. For example, the text made clear that a two-thirds vote was necessary for the Senate to convict an impeachment defendant or approve a proposed treaty, or for either house to expel a member, approve a constitutional amendment, or override a presidential veto. For other actions, majority rule simply went without saying.

Several of the Constitution's provisions prescribing supermajorities make the most sense only if we assume that majority rule was the self-evident background principle that applied in the absence of a specific clause to the contrary. Thus, Article I presupposed that each house would "pass" legislative bills by majority vote—except when trying to override presidential vetoes, which would require a *special* supermajority. The supermajorities explicitly required for constitutional amendments likewise were designed to be *more demanding* than the simple majorities implicitly prescribed for ordinary statutes; and the Senate supermajority needed for treaty ratification was meant to erect a *higher* bar than the rule for ordinary Senate agreement to ordinary legislation—a higher bar meant to offset the absence of the House in the formal treaty-making process. Similarly, the provisions empowering each house to exclude improperly elected or constitutionally ineligible candidates were meant to operate by simple majority rule—as distinct from the *exceptional* supermajority rule that applied when a house sought to expel duly elected and fully eligible members.[31]

But if majority rule truly went without saying, then why did the framers feel the need to specify, in Article I, section 5, that a majority of each house would constitute a quorum? The obvious answer is that state constitutions and British practice had varied widely on the quorum question, and thus, *on this special issue*, there did not exist an obvious default rule from universal usage or mathematical logic. For example, Pennsylvania set the quorum bar at two-thirds, whereas the English rule in effect since the 1640s had provided that any forty members could constitute a quorum of the House of Commons. But neither Parliament nor any state circa 1787 generally required more than simple house majority votes for the passage of bills or the adoption of internal house procedures, even though, in many of the states, no explicit clause specified this voting rule. In America circa 1787, majority rule in these contexts truly did go without saying.

We should also note that the Constitution's electoral-college clauses explicitly speak of the need for a majority vote. In this context, involving candidate elections, majority rule did not go without saying as the obvious and only default rule. Plurality rule furnished a salient alternative (and indeed is the rule that even today remains the dominant one for candidate contests in America). But this point about candidate elections, which might involve voting on three or more persons simultaneously, did not apply to the enactment of house rules or the exclusion of members under Article I, section 5, or the enactment of laws under Article I, section 7—all of which involved *binary* decisions against the status quo. (As noted, majority rule has unique mathematical advantages in situations of binary choice.)

Fourth, as we saw in Chapter 2, majority rule was not only implicit in the Constitution's text, but also visible in its very enactment. Nothing in Article VII explicitly said that ratification conventions should act by simple majority rule, but this is what every convention did, and in a manner that suggested that the issue was self-evident.

Thus, in a wide range of constitutional contexts, majority rule went without saying. For the same reason that this background rule applied to ratifying conventions and to each house of Congress, it also applied to the Court.

From its first day to the present day, the Court has routinely followed the majority-rule principle without even appearing to give the matter much thought. As a rule, when five justices today say that the law means X, and four say it means Y, X it is. Over the years, the Court has invalidated dozens of congressional laws by the slimmest of margins: 5–4.

Politicians and commentators have occasionally urged Congress to respond with a statute forbidding the Court to strike down federal legislation unless the Court vote is at least 6–3. Yet Congress has never followed this advice—and with good reason, for hidden within this proposal there lurk at least two distinct and insuperable Article VI supremacy-clause problems. First, in situations not governed by the proposed statute, the Court would presumably continue to operate by majority rule. For example, Congress surely would not want the Court to enforce state laws violating congressional statutes so long as the state got four of the nine Court votes. But if a simple majority vote would suffice to vindicate a federal statute over a state law, the same simple majority vote should suffice to vindicate the Constitution over a federal statute. By trying to change the Court's voting rule *selectively*, the proposed statute would violate the legal hierarchy laid down in Article VI, which privileges the Constitution over federal statutes in exactly the same way that it privileges (constitutionally proper) federal statutes over mere state laws. Second and more generally, any statute that gave a jurist brandishing a mere congressional law (or any other subconstitutional law) a weightier vote than a dueling jurist wielding the Constitution would improperly invert the clear prioritization of legal norms established by the supremacy clause.[32]

Could the justices themselves decide by simple majority rule to abandon Court majority rule in some situations where these sorts of supremacy-clause problems do not arise? In fact, the Court has done just that, but in a manner that has preserved the ultimate authority of majority rule. By Court tradition, four justices—a minority—can put a case on the docket and, ordinarily, can guarantee that the petitioner seeking review will be able to press his case via full briefing and oral argument. But ultimately, the Court majority of five has the last word—not just on the merits of the case, but on whether the Court itself will in fact issue any opinion. At any time, a simple Court majority of five can dismiss any case on the docket, even if the remaining four justices adamantly object. In short, minority rules such as the "Rule of Four" nest within a framework of simple majority rule.[33]

A SIMILAR ANALYSIS APPLIES to the voting rules followed by the House of Representatives. In general, the House follows the Constitution's implicit directive of simple majority rule in performing its basic constitutional functions: enacting legislation, authorizing expenditures, organizing itself, judging its members' elections and qualifications, issuing subpoenas, adjudicating contempts, maintaining order within its own walls, and impeaching executive and judicial officers. True, a labyrinth of House rules—most obviously, a set of rules enabling committees and the House leadership to dictate the House agenda and another set of rules regulating parliamentary procedure—may prevent a given matter from ever reaching the House floor for a simple majority vote. But these internal rules are themselves authorized at the biennial beginning of each new Congress under the aegis of Article I, section 5—and they are authorized by a simple chamber majority in keeping with the Constitution's letter and spirit.[34]

NOT SO WITH what has now become perhaps the most dysfunctional aspect of modern American institutional practice: the Senate filibuster. Thanks to an internal Senate rule allowing filibusters—Senate Rule 22, to be precise—the de facto threshold for enacting a wide range of legislation has in recent years become 60 votes instead of the constitutionally proper 51 votes. Under Rule 22, a mere 41 senators can prevent a typical bill from ever reaching the Senate floor for a final vote, even if 59 senators on the other side are intensely eager to end debate and approve the bill. Can you spell "gridlock"?*

---

* The filibuster analysis that follows is taken verbatim from this book's first edition, published well before the Senate effected major filibuster reform in late 2013. This remarkable reform closely tracked the line of analysis presented herein—dramatic support of this book's interpretive method. For a quick update, see my 11/21/13 posting in Slate.com, "The Nuclear-Option Genie Is Out of the Bottle."

The filibuster rule itself is not approved biennially at the outset of each new congressional term. Rather, this old rule, initially adopted by the Senate in the 1910s and significantly revised in the 1970s, simply carries over from one Congress to the next by inertia, under the notion that the Senate, unlike the House, is a continuing body. Senate rules, once in place, need never be formally reenacted. Similarly, Senate leaders, once in place, need never be formally reelected.[35]

But the Senate does generally retain the right to oust any holdover leaders at any time and to do so by a simple majority vote—and this majoritarian principle, which clearly applies to holdover Senate leaders, should also apply to holdover Senate rules. All Senate rules, including the filibuster rule, are valid *if and only if a majority of the Senate at any time may change the old rules by simple majority vote.*[36]

But some senators today seem to believe that a simple Senate majority cannot change the old filibuster rule, even if this Senate majority emphatically wants change. Why not? Because the old filibuster rule says so. That's some catch, that catch-22.[37]

This circular logic will not do. The filibuster rule, like every other American law or regulation, is ultimately subordinate to America's Constitution. If the Constitution requires ultimate majority rule in the Senate, no purported Senate rule may properly say otherwise. And in fact, America's Constitution, correctly understood, does require ultimate majority rule in the Senate. Insofar as the old filibuster rule claims the status of an entrenched protocol that cannot be altered by an insistent current Senate majority, then the old filibuster rule is to this exact extent unconstitutional and should be treated as such by the senators themselves acting as the proper promulgators and judges of their own procedures. Concretely, if a simple majority of the Senate ever did take steps to repeal the filibuster rule, the Senate's presiding officer should rule this repeal to be in order, and this ruling from the chair should be upheld by a simple Senate majority. And that would be that: No more filibusters.

We need not insist that a current Senate majority has the right to change its rules instantaneously and peremptorily. The Senate's presiding officer may properly allow each side ample time to make its case before holding a vote on a Senate rule change. But any attempt to prevent a reform vote altogether via dilatory tactics—that is, any attempt to indefinitely filibuster attempted filibuster reform—would violate the applicable written and unwritten constitutional principles.

THIS CONCLUSION MAY ASTONISH, coming as it does in the middle of a survey of American institutional practice. Some might think that if the name of the game is actual governmental practice, the fact that the filibuster exists, and the fact that many senators claim that it cannot be altered by a simple majority, are unanswerable game-winners.

It is precisely at this point that this book's general framework proves its worth. Let us, then, carefully apply this framework to the filibuster issue.

Begin by noting that even though majority rule is not always explicitly specified in various clauses of the written Constitution, it surely forms part of America's *implicit* Constitution in certain respects. If the Senate may entrench (that is, enact and insulate from simple majoritarian repeal) a rule that 60 votes are required to pass a given bill, then the Senate could likewise entrench a rule that 70 votes are required. But such a rule would plainly violate the letter and logic of Article I, section 7, which provides that a two-thirds Senate majority always suffices, even when the president vetoes a particular bill. Surely it follows *a fortiori* that something less than a two-thirds vote suffices in the absence of a veto.

And that something is majority rule, as is powerfully evident from America's *enacted* Constitution, which teaches us that majority rule does indeed go without saying in the Constitution, in the absence of strong implicit or explicit contraindication. Majority rule supplied the self-evident master norm for state ratifying conventions organized under Article VII. This key fact provides a compelling reason to believe that majority rule likewise provides the self-evident master norm for senatorial legislation under Article I, section 7, and also for senatorial internal rulemaking under Article I, section 5. Thus, unless we find in the written or unwritten Constitution some strong contraindication, majority rule is the Constitution's proper voting protocol when the Senate decides whether to keep or scrap the filibuster rule.[38]

Nothing in America's *lived* Constitution provides strong contraindication. Although it would be surprising if the daily rhythms and routines of average Americans decisively answered technical questions concerning the Senate's internal procedures, it is perhaps noteworthy that when average Americans participate in various clubs and the like, they quite often and without much ado practice majority rule.

Likewise, nothing in America's *doctrinal* Constitution, either pre-Warren or post-Warren, supports the entrenched filibuster. Not only have the justices themselves always followed majority rule, but in the 1892 case *United States v. Ballin*, the Court explicitly embraced majority rule as the background master norm for each house of Congress: "[T]he general rule of all parliamentary bodies is that, when a quorum is present, the act of a majority of the quorum is the act of the body. This has been the rule for all time, except so far as in any given case the terms of the organic act under which the body is assembled have prescribed specific limitations.... No such limitation is found in the Federal Constitution, and therefore the general law of such bodies obtains."

Nor does anything in America's *symbolic* Constitution argue for an entrenched Senate filibuster rule. Many ordinary citizens today disdain Senate Rule 22, and this disdain has a long history. The most memorable filibusters in the American experience occurred in the 1950s and early 1960s, when various southern senators tried to thwart much-needed civil-rights legislation—legislation that eventually passed in the mid-1960s and became the pride of the nation, reaffirming the equality of all races (and also of both sexes). In short, key elements of America's *symbolic* Constitution (and also America's *feminist* Constitution) came about despite the filibuster, not because of it.

Nor, finally, does the history of actual *institutional* practice—from the *Georgian* period to the present—provide solid support for an entrenched filibuster rule. Properly construed and contextualized, the history of Senate practice in fact supports modern-day filibuster reformers.[39]

Nothing like Rule 22's catch-22 was in place in the age of George Washington or in the Jeffersonian era that followed. Throughout the 1790s and early 1800s, the Senate practiced and preached simple majority rule. Under the procedures that governed the Senate during its earliest years, a senator could move "the previous question" and thereby end debate if a majority of senators agreed; and senators could also call an unruly orator to order at any time and thereby oblige him to "sit down," subject to a ruling by the chair and, if necessary, an appeal to the Senate as whole.[40]

Although some scholars have quibbled about the precise operation of these initial rules, the history of the Senate prior to the 1830s offers no notable examples of organized and obstructionist filibustering—and absolutely nothing like a pattern of systematic, self-perpetuating, entrenched frustration of Senate majority rule. Thomas Jefferson, the Senate's presiding officer from 1797 to 1801, was thus describing actual senatorial norms and usages when he penned the following passages of his 1801 *Manual of Parliamentary Practice for the Use of the Senate of the United States*: "No one is to speak impertinently or beside the question, superfluously or tediously....The voice of the majority decides. For the *lex majoris partis* is the law of all councils, elections, &c. where not otherwise expressly provided."[41]

For much of the mid-nineteenth century, even as Senate minorities began to develop and deploy dilatory tactics, these tactics typically occurred with the indulgence of the Senate majority. Long-winded speechifying occasionally delayed the Senate's business, but orations usually did not prevent majorities from ending debate at some point and taking a vote. The Senate in those days was smaller than it is today and had less business to transact. The upper chamber often opted to indulge individual senators as a matter of courtesy. In turn, the indulged senators did not routinely try to press their privileges so as to prevent Senate majorities from governing. For example, in 1850, politicians of all stripes from all regions understood that California's admission—giving free states a narrow but decisive majority over slave states in the Senate—mattered hugely, *precisely because the Senate's operative principle in the mid-nineteenth century was in fact simple majority rule*. According to one expert treatise, prior to the 1880s virtually every obstructed measure eventually prevailed against the opposition's stalling tactics.[42]

In the late twentieth and early twenty-first centuries, routine filibustering practices have skyrocketed. Yet senators in the modern era have failed to achieve a general consensus via a compelling line of clean, consistent Senate rulings on the key constitutional question. Properly framed, this question is not whether the Senate may choose by inaction and inertia to keep the filibuster, nor whether the Senate may choose to keep the filibuster by readopting it via a fresh majority vote. Rather, the question is whether the current Senate is simply stuck with the old filibuster rule, even if a current majority emphatically wants to change the rule and explicitly votes to do so. This issue has only intermittently arisen in a clean parliamentary fashion. Over the years, various senators may have quietly favored the old filibuster rule but have not wanted to publicly take the blame for this position, preferring instead to shroud the issue in layer upon layer of procedural complexity.

In 1975, a majority of the Senate in fact upheld a constitutional ruling of the vice president, sitting in the chair, that a mere majority could rightfully end debate on filibuster reform and overturn the old filibuster rule. Shortly thereafter, however, the Senate voted to reconsider its earlier action, leaving us today with a Rorschach-blot precedent whose meaning is largely in the eye of the beholder. In the early twenty-first century, Republican senators, frustrated by the success of the Democratic minority in blocking votes on various judicial nominations, loudly threatened to revise the old filibuster rule by a simple majority vote. This threatened revision, popularly nicknamed "the nuclear option," never came to a conclusive floor vote. Instead, Democrats moderated their obstructionism and Republicans sheathed their sword.

Precursors of this "nuclear option"—also known as "the constitutional option"—were forcefully advocated by prominent senators throughout the twentieth century, and at various moments over the past sixty years these precursors have in fact won the considered support of vice presidents and Senate majority leaders of both parties. Many of the most important filibuster reforms of the twentieth century came about when reformers first threatened the "constitutional option" and then compromised by effectuating their desired reforms in an endgame process that formally obeyed the Senate's catch-22 rule structure.[43]

If a Senate majority truly were powerless to set things right, then Senate practice would be wildly out of step with the practice of its sibling body, the House of Representatives. In the House, majority-rule rules today and has always ruled. Although this fact alone does not prove that majority rule is required by Article I, section 5, it surely confirms that majority rule is consistent with this section. The long-standing practice of the House should also remind us that, in sharp contrast to the 1860s, when the House got the Senate and the president to bless its use of old House clerks to birth new Houses, the modern filibuster rule has not received any encouragement from the lower house or the executive branch.[44]

THE POLITICALLY CONVENIENT ASSERTION that today's Senate majority is simply a powerless captive of ghosts of Senates past should ring particularly hollow to British ears—and this hollowness deserves special attention in any analysis of how America's Constitution might look to a proper British constitutionalist. Although Britain has never had an American-style written Constitution, the British have developed a deep understanding of the proper relationship among Parliaments over time. It is a bedrock principle of British constitutionalism that one Parliament cannot bind a later Parliament. Otherwise, the inalienable right of parliamentary self-government would be lost. Indeed, what makes a right *inalienable* is precisely the fact that it is incapable of being waived, even by an actual practice of apparent waiver.

Just as Americans at the Founding surely understood that no person could be a judge in his own case, thanks in part to Blackstone's clear formulation of the basic principle, so, too, the Founders were intimately familiar with and embraced what Blackstone had to say about the relationship between one legislature and its successor: "Acts of parliament derogatory from the power of subsequent parliaments bind not." Why not? Because, Blackstone explained, prior Parliaments are not legally superior to subsequent Parliaments. By what voting rule would each Parliament proceed? Here, Blackstone was clear: "In each house the act of the majority binds the whole."[45]

The same logic applies on this side of the Atlantic. Each house can make rules for itself. But neither house can entrench rules in a way that prevents a later house from governing itself. Only the Constitution can create entrenched rules of this sort. And on this issue, the rule that the Constitution has entrenched for each house is majority rule.[46]

Because this protocol is established by the Constitution itself, the protocol cannot be changed by either house or by statute. Just as Congress may not properly enact an ordinary statute that changes the constitutional rules governing how future ordinary statutes are to be enacted, so, too, neither house may properly enact a house rule that changes the constitutional rules governing how future house rules are to be enacted.

HERE IS ONE FINAL WAY of pulling together the basic argument. It is obvious that some specific voting rule must be used to operationalize the Article I, section 5, power and duty of each House to determine its own rules of proceeding. If majority rule is not the implicit rule, what is? Without some jumpstarting rule, the first House and the first Senate in 1789 would have faced an insoluble infinite regress problem. (By what initial voting rule would each house decide what voting rule to use in determining its rules of proceedings? By what pre-initial voting rule would that initial voting rule be decided? By what pre-pre-initial voting rule would the pre-initial voting rule be decided? And so on, without end.) But no such infinite regress in fact occurred in the first Congress because majority rule did in fact go without saying in each house in 1789, just as it had gone without saying in each ratifying convention in 1787–1788. This first set of Article I, section 5, votes thus established the first key point of actual practice.

Just as the first House and the first Senate each used majority rule to decide its procedures, every subsequent House and Senate may and must do the same, for nothing in the Constitution made the Congress of 1789 king over later Congresses. All Congresses are equal in this respect. In fact—and this is a second key point about actual practice—neither house has ever formally required a supermajority for amendment of its rules. Not even Senate Rule 22 has the audacity to openly assert that it cannot be repealed by simple majority vote. Rather, Rule 22 says only that *debate* on its own repeal cannot be ended by simple majority vote.

The question thus becomes, is this supermajoritarian aspect of Rule 22 a genuine rule of debate or a de facto rule of decision? If Rule 22 simply means that the rule itself should not be repealed without a fair opportunity to debate the repeal, then Rule 22 is fully valid. But insofar as Rule 22 in fact allows repeal opponents to stall interminably so as to prevent a majoritarian repeal vote from ever being held, then Rule 22 is to that precise extent operating as an unconstitutionally entrenching supermajority rule of decision rather than a proper rule of debate. It is the right and duty of each senator to adjudicate for herself whether Rule 22 has in fact come to operate as an improper rule of decision rather than a proper rule of debate. And in adjudicating that question, the Senate, operating as a constitutional court of sorts, acts by majority rule, just as the Supreme Court itself does when adjudicating constitutional (and other) questions.

"This Constitution...shall be the supreme Law"

AMERICA DELIGHTS IN ITS INVENTIONS. From bifocals at the Founding to light bulbs, flying machines, and iPhones in the modern era, we constantly quest for the holy grail of the next new thing. America's lawyers over the centuries have proved especially inventive in crafting new institutions and institutional devices to respond to perceived problems. As postbellum America's economy, society, and laws became increasingly complex, requiring more scientific expertise and bureaucratic rationality within government to regulate both private actors and the government itself, new "independent agencies" arose. And as legislators felt obliged to give more policymaking authority to administrators, Congress sought to reserve a checking role for itself via a newfangled contraption called the "legislative veto." In the wake of Watergate, a new breed of judicially appointed "independent counsels" emerged to keep all the president's men in line.

This much is well understood by lawyers and scholars of all stripes. What is not well understood is why certain modern institutional innovations have endured while others have imploded. A glance at four of the past century's most notable institutional innovations will suggest a startlingly simple answer: Innovations that utterly disregarded the written Constitution's blueprint ultimately proved structurally unsound and collapsed of their own weight. Innovative institutions carefully erected inside the flexible (but not infinitely flexible) lines of the blueprint remain standing.

CONSIDER FIRST THE *legislative veto*, a device that modern Congresses have insinuated, in some form or other, into hundreds of statutes. A legislative-veto clause purports to vest one or both houses of Congress, or some subset thereof (say, a House or Senate committee) with the legal authority to block—to "veto," in effect—certain attempted executive-branch implementations of the statute. Imagine a statute that says that all persons who meet conditions A, B, and C will be eligible for a certain benefit (say, a sizable rebate on their income taxes). A legislative-veto clause in this statute might say that whenever the executive branch decides that a person meets the statutory conditions and thus deserves the statutory benefit, either house (or some committee) may unilaterally nullify this decision.

This familiar device, in all its variants, is constitutionally preposterous—a flamboyant negation of the Constitution's basic structure. As advertised by its honest and oxymoronic label, the device improperly aims to vest quintessential executive (and/or judicial) powers in legislators. The written Constitution's rules and principles are clear. Congress's job is to enact general and prospective laws—to decide, in our example, whether to require A, B, and C, or D, E, and F instead. Once the law is on the books, it is for other branches, namely, the executive and the judiciary, to implement and interpret it. If Congress wishes to change the law, Congress must enact a new law, with both houses agreeing and the president assenting (or being duly overridden). Only in a few specific situations defined by text and tradition may Congress play executive or judge, or may a single house act unilaterally on outsiders—for example, in impeachments, in judging house elections, in conducting inquests, in disciplining its members, in imposing contempt punishments, and in controlling physical space in the Capitol. These are the proverbial exceptions that prove the rule that in other situations, Congress must stick to lawmaking and leave law execution and law adjudication to others.*

---

* Here are two formal proofs of the unconstitutionality of the legislative veto. Proof number 1: The federal government has only three kinds of power—legislative, executive, and judicial (per the Constitution's first three articles and Tenth Amendment). Hence the legislative veto must fit into one of these three boxes. If it is an exercise of legislative power, it requires bicameralism and presentment. If, conversely, it is an exercise of executive or judicial power, it may not be carried out by the Congress, which is not given such powers (outside a few carefully specified contexts). Either way, the legislative veto fails. QED. Proof number 2: In voting to block the executive's determination that conditions A, B, and C are met and that a given person thus deserves the statutorily prescribed benefit, Congress is doing one of two things—either applying the ABC standard specified in the earlier statute, or laying down a new standard. In the former case, this effort to apply a prior law to a later and specific fact situation is an impermissible effort to wield executive or judicial power. In the latter case, this effort to adopt a new legislative standard requires bicameralism and presentment. Either way, the legislative veto fails. QED.

Nothing in the Constitution's ratification debates or in early federal practice offers any support for a legislative veto, a statutory device that first appeared in federal statute books in 1932, nearly a century and a half after the ink had dried on the Constitution.[47]

When the legislative-veto issue finally reached the justices in a landmark 1983 case, *INS v. Chadha*, a broad coalition of jurists from across the spectrum laughed the device out of court. Only one justice, Byron White, voted to uphold the constitutionality of the device, and even he joined a later opinion that reaffirmed and extended *Chadha's* basic teaching.[48]

How, then, are we to make sense of the fascinating fact that even after *Chadha*, Congress has continued to slip legislative-veto clauses into statutes? Two points are key. First, even as presidents both before and after *Chadha* have signed omnibus bills containing these dubious devices, America's chief executives have routinely attacked these clauses and at times publicly announced that they would treat attempted legislative vetoes as legal nullities. Unlike other innovations that have endured (such as independent agencies), the legislative veto never won the considered and consistent support of all the branches of government. In *Chadha* itself, the Court noted that "11 Presidents, from Mr. Wilson through Mr. Reagan, who have been presented with this issue have gone on record at some point to challenge congressional vetoes as unconstitutional." In the years since *Chadha*, America's presidents have continued this tradition of official opposition.[49]

Second, post-*Chadha* legislative-veto clauses may operate politically even if they do not create valid law that courts will respect or that presidents will routinely follow. Imagine, for example, an omnibus bill funding the federal judiciary that contains a clause purporting to give the senior senator from Nebraska the right to pick the next federal district judge from Nebraska. Legally, such a provision is preposterous and unenforceable, because the Constitution is clear: Presidents, not senators, select judges. Nevertheless, as politics actually play out, a president might choose to give Nebraska's senior senator de facto authority to call the shots on a judicial nomination from the senator's home state, perhaps in order to win the senator's support for other elements of the president's agenda. Although the official nomination would always come from the president himself, everyone might know that it was the senior senator who unofficially made the selection. Thus, the hypothetical Nebraska clause, though *legally* invalid, might nevertheless work *politically*, memorializing an informal arrangement that this president (or a future president) may hesitate to dishonor even if the chief executive has an absolute constitutional right to do so. Post-*Chadha* legislative-veto clauses may similarly operate politically today even though they are, from a strictly legal point of view, obviously invalid.

CONSIDER NEXT THE POST-WATERGATE REGIME of *independent counsels*—an institution that ultimately led to the only impeachment of an elected president in American history.*

Ordinarily, federal criminal investigations and prosecutions occur within the Justice Department, headed by the attorney general, who serves at the pleasure of the president. But in the early 1970s, shocked Americans came to learn that several prominent members of the Nixon administration—including the president himself, several of his top White House aides, and his attorney general, John Mitchell—were themselves criminal wrongdoers. In situations such as this, could the Justice Department be trusted to properly investigate and prosecute?

Obviously not, thought many reformers. Thus, a 1978 statute and successor legislation authorized a special panel of Article III judges to appoint a lawyer independent of the Justice Department to make the key investigatory and prosecutorial decisions in certain specified situations where the department was arguably untrustworthy. Between 1978 and 2000, judicial panels appointed at least eighteen independent counsels in low- and high-profile cases alike—most famously, Ken Starr, who was tapped to investigate possible wrongdoing by officials in the Clinton administration, including the president himself. At the end of the millennium, Counsel Starr's ever-widening investigation provided the basis for Clinton's impeachment by the House. The Senate ultimately acquitted.[50]

Despite its good intentions, the 1978-style independent-counsel regime violated the Constitution's plain meaning and warped the document's ba-

---

* Recall that Andrew Johnson was never elected president in his own right and became president only by dint of an assassin's bullet.

sic structure. This poorly designed system ultimately imploded, and this implosion in turn occurred precisely because of the 1978 statute's failure to mesh with the carefully calibrated institutional gears created by the written Constitution.

True, the Constitution's text allows Congress by law to empower courts to make certain appointments—but only of "inferior" officers. Independent counsels were not truly inferior. How, indeed, can one be both truly independent and truly inferior? Like the legislative-veto device, the independent-counsel regime wore its unconstitutionality on its sleeve.

Elsewhere in the Constitution, whenever the word "inferior" appeared, it conjured up a *relational* idea. Each inferior had a superior. Thus the document described lower federal courts as "inferior to" the Supreme Court, which would in turn be supreme over the inferior courts (and not, as some might think, over the other branches or over the Constitution itself). Analogously, the plain purpose of the inferior-officer-appointment clause was to allow a court, pursuant to statute, to appoint officers inferior to the appointing court, such as law clerks or special-purpose magistrates.

This plain purpose was confirmed and clarified early on, when Congress and President Washington implemented the appointments clause's companion language allowing an executive department head/principal officer to name an "inferior" officer whenever federal law so provided. In the ensemble of statutes enacted as part of the Decision of 1789, Congress first authorized the secretary of foreign affairs (soon renamed the secretary of state) to appoint an "inferior officer" who would serve as the "chief Clerk in the Department," and thereafter authorized the three other department heads (the war secretary, the treasury secretary, and the postmaster general) to appoint similar assistants within their respective departments. The obvious principle put into practice here was that statutes could allow each appointing authority to pick its own assistants.[51]

Judicial appointments of prosecutors under the 1978 system shattered this Founding-era principle and precedent, for the simple reason that federal prosecutors are not now and never have been proper judicial assistants. On the contrary, prosecutors wield quintessentially executive power— prosecutorial power. Allowing judges to pick prosecutors was almost as outlandish as authorizing them to appoint admirals or ambassadors.[52]

Read at face value, the appointments clause preserved political account-ability. If an inferior goofed, the public could blame the superior who ap-pointed him, and who was responsible for monitoring his conduct. But the 1978 law blurred accountability. Once picked, an independent counsel effectively answered to no one. Had the judicial panel that appointed a particular independent counsel genuinely tried to supervise his actions as his investigation and prosecutorial decision-making proceeded, the judges would have thereby transformed themselves into super-prosecutors, in ob-vious violation of basic precepts of separation of powers.

Further compounding the constitutional perversity of the 1978 system, judges making these decidedly unjudicial appointments decisions oper-ated wholly outside the traditional framework governing ordinary judicial decision-making. When adjudicating "cases" and "controversies," judges are ordinarily expected to explain their rulings via written opinions (or some other public statement of reasons), to deploy the tools of legal analysis in rendering their decisions, and to sharply limit their off-the-record ex parte communications with interested government officials. But picking prosecu-tors turned this regime topsy-turvy. Deciding which of the countless lawyers in America should be chosen above all others to serve as an independent counsel was essentially a political act, not a legal one. This decision called for a suitably political selection process in which judges, acting as an appoint-ments panel, needed to, and presumably did, confer confidentially with top politicos to decide which candidates had the most political and prosecutorial credibility. (Shortly before naming Ken Starr as the special counsel to inves-tigate Bill and Hillary Clinton, the head of the three-judge panel, Judge Da-vid Sentelle, lunched privately with two prominent critics of the Clintons, Republican senators Lauch Faircloth and Jesse Helms.)[53]

Some of the constitutional defects of the 1978 law were curable, per-haps, via aggressive use of the president's pardon pen. A counsel might in some sense be inferior (albeit not to the panel that appointed him) if the president himself kept the counsel in line. A president could ordinarily do so by pardoning the target of an independent counsel's investigation if the counsel ever went too far by spending too much time and money chasing trivial misconduct that did not merit Javert-style justice. Some post-1978 presidents did in fact use their pardon power—most notably, President George H.W. Bush, who pardoned former cabinet officer Caspar Weinberger before trial and thereby obliged the independent counsel in the case, Lawrence Walsh, to fold his tent.

As this episode illustrated, no person could ever be prosecuted by the independent counsel or by anyone else so long as the president strongly objected and was willing to act on that objection. The 1978 statute promised something that it could never really deliver. So long as the pardon power meant what it said—and nothing in the 1978 regime took direct aim at the pardon power—no prosecution could be legally independent of the chief executive.

With one notable exception: A president could never properly pardon himself. Such gross self-dealing was obviously unconstitutional, akin to a man sitting in judgment of his own case. Thus, uniquely among independent counsels, Ken Starr could not be controlled via the actual or threatened use of the presidential pardon pen, because Starr's investigation focused in part on the possibly criminal conduct of the president himself. Starr correctly recognized that he could not properly initiate an ordinary criminal prosecution against a sitting president. But this self-restraint hardly meant that Starr was a truly "inferior" officer.

Although the Supreme Court in the 1988 case of *Morrison v. Olson* initially winked at the constitutional flaws of the 1978 statute, Justice Antonin Scalia penned a powerful dissent that has come to prevail in both political and legal circles. Politically, no American president either before or after *Morrison* was ever willing to agree to the 1978 regime except as a temporary statutory experiment that would require periodic reassessment and reenactment. In 1992, the experiment lapsed when the first President Bush successfully opposed reenactment; but his successor, Bill Clinton, unwisely agreed to give the statute another run in 1994. Several years and several independent counsels later, the Clinton administration came to its senses. In testimony before Congress signaling that any additional attempt to reenact the law would meet a constitutionally based presidential veto, Attorney General Janet Reno repeatedly invoked Scalia's dissent. She concluded that the Independent Counsel Act was "structurally flawed, and... these flaws cannot be corrected within our constitutional framework." No veto proved necessary; Congress allowed the law to lapse in 1999, and no president or congressional leader since then has shown much interest in reviving this failed experiment.[54]

Legally, the Supreme Court has all but overruled *Morrison*, treating it as a dubious decision strictly limited to its unique facts. According to one of the Court's most recent pronouncements on the appointments clause, *Edmond v. United States*, "the term 'inferior officer' connotes a relationship with some higher ranking officer." As a rule, "whether one is an 'inferior' officer depends on whether he has a superior." This test and much of the other language of *Edmond* came directly from Justice Scalia's *Morrison* dissent, and Scalia himself was indeed the author of the *Edmond* majority opinion. None of the justices from the *Morrison* majority remains on the Court today.

The collapse of the 1978 experiment does not mean that America in the twenty-first century must do wholly without independent counsels, and must simply trust the Justice Department and the president to do the right thing out of the goodness of their hearts. Rather, the demise of the 1978 statute has simply restored the *political* system of independent counsels that had worked beautifully in Watergate itself.

Under that system, whenever doubt arose about the propriety of a Justice Department investigation of one of its own officials or some other sensitive target, political and professional pressure would build until the attorney general or the president himself named a special prosecutor outside the department and informally promised that prosecutor some zone of autonomy. If no such person was named, or if the zone of autonomy was unduly constricted, Congress could use or threaten to use its own vast powers of inquest and impeachment to prod the executive branch into action. If the special prosecutor, once appointed, went too far too fast, she could be legally dismissed by the superior officer who had appointed her (either the AG or the president himself); but if dismissal occurred for some seemingly corrupt reason, it would generate a political backlash. Politics kept the system in balance via the interplay of vigorous press oversight, congressional powers of inquest and impeachment, and executive powers of appointment, removal, supervision, and pardon. The game's ultimate umpires were not some tiny clump of judges meeting secretly, but the American people themselves in the press and at the ballot box.

Under this system, Richard Nixon's administration was obliged to hire a renowned Harvard law professor, Archibald Cox, to conduct a credible outside investigation of alleged administration wrongdoing. When Cox pushed very hard very fast, Nixon had Cox fired, in the so-called Saturday Night Massacre. But Nixon paid an enormous political price and was politically obliged to replace Cox with another respected outsider, Leon Jaworski, who completed the job and indeed brought down the administration. Had Nixon tried to fire Jaworski or to pardon the targets of investigation in an effort to oblige Jaworski to close up shop, Nixon would have been quickly impeached and removed from office in exactly the way that the framers sketched the system on the drawing board, with Congress—not a judicial panel—making the key decisions.

Although this Watergate system of political independence offered less formal legal independence than the 1978 statute that arose to replace it, it actually worked better, and did so precisely because it did not stretch the roles and rules laid down in the terse text. Viewed from one angle, Archibald Cox and Ken Starr were almost identical twins. Cox was a well-respected Democrat who had served as a distinguished solicitor general to the man who had run against Nixon—John F. Kennedy. Starr, in turn, was a well-respected Republican who had served as a distinguished solicitor general to the man who had run against Clinton—George H.W. Bush. Starr's appointment was thus perfect poetic justice. Why, then, was Clinton much more successful in discrediting Starr than Nixon had been in his attempt to demonize Cox?*

One big reason was that Starr started off with less credibility than Cox precisely because Clinton himself had not picked Starr. In addition, Starr's appointment had arguably involved judges doing nonjudicial things in nonjudicial fashion. (Recall, for example, the controversial lunch between Judge Sentelle and leading anti-Clinton senators.) Had Clinton, like Nixon, been politically obliged to name an outside lawyer such as Starr, the outside lawyer would have had special political authority from the start, having been chosen not by a clump of mostly Republican-appointed judges, but by the Democrat president himself. After completing his service as independent counsel, Starr echoed Scalia and Reno in criticizing the basic structure of the 1978 act.

The complete collapse of the statutory independent counsel system

---

* Full disclosure: Ken Starr has been my friend for many years, and we regularly taught classes together at Pepperdine Law School from 2005 to 2010. However, I have never discussed with him anything closely connected to his service as independent counsel.

should teach us that modern reformers ignore the written Constitution at their peril. Innovations that work within or work around the document's formal rules survive. Innovations that run roughshod over these rules do not. A Watergate-style system of special prosecutors has worked before and can work again precisely because nothing in this political improvisation violates the Constitution's text—or, more precisely, because this improvisation nicely meshes with the written document's schema of institutions and incentives. By contrast, the 1978 system of legally independent counsels failed precisely because it dishonored the proper written roles of each of the three branches by placing too little reliance on congressional oversight and impeachment; putting too much confidence in judges, even as it obliged them to do nonjudicial things; and paying no heed to how presidents may usually control prosecutors via the pardon pen.

HAVING JUST SEEN A COUPLE OF FAILED twentieth-century institutional improvisations, let's conclude with a couple of modern success stories.

One clever, albeit highly technical, separation-of-powers gadget is known to beltway insiders as the *Saxbe fix*. Here's how it works: Under Article I, section 6, "[n]o Senator or Representative shall, during the Time for which he was elected, be appointed to any civil Office under the Authority of the United States…the Emoluments whereof shall have been increased during such time." The obvious aim of this anticorruption provision is to prevent members of Congress from improperly inflating the salaries of executive or judicial offices and then benefiting personally by resigning from Congress and being appointed to those overpaid offices. The strict letter of the rule could be read to disqualify any member of Congress from any executive or judicial office for which the salary was increased during the member's current term. But the spirit of the clause is satisfied by a more sensible, if less literalistic, approach—the Saxbe fix—that allows the appointment so long as the appointee receives only the old (pre-increase) salary and thus does not pocket any salary increase that may have been recently adopted.

For example, if the salary for a given cabinet office swells from $100,000 to $105,000 on a senator's watch, and the president thereafter wants to appoint that senator to this office, a literalist might say the appointment would be irremediably illegal (since the salary was indeed upped on the senator's watch). But under the less literalistic Saxbe-fix approach, the appointment would be proper so long as the salary is reduced—"Saxbe fixed"—back to $100,000 before the senator takes office.[55]

While the letter and the spirit of the emoluments clause arguably tug in opposite directions on this nice question, actual practice—approved by all three branches and both major political parties over a long stretch of time—sensibly breaks this interpretational tie. No justice ever refused to sit alongside ex-senator Hugo Black, who would have been ineligible for appointment to the Court under a hyper-literalist reading. Also, for more than a century, presidents and senators of both parties have continued to appoint and confirm resigned or resigning members of Congress to cabinet positions for which salaries had recently been increased, so long as the new appointee would not receive the increase. Indeed, outgoing presidents have repeatedly signed on to statutory "Saxbe fixes" aimed at accommodating the cabinet preferences of incoming presidents—even presidents of the other party. Cabinet members appointed under this approach include Treasury Secretary Lot Morrill in the Grant administration, Secretary of State Philander Knox in the Taft administration, Attorney General William Saxbe in the Nixon administration (whence the phrase, "Saxbe fix"), Secretary of State Edmund Muskie in the Carter administration, Treasury Secretary Lloyd Bentsen in the Clinton administration, and Secretary of State Hillary Clinton and Interior Secretary Ken Salazar in the Obama administration.

On reflection, the general acceptance of the Saxbe fix makes perfect sense precisely because this particular institutional improvisation rests on a plausible—albeit not incontestable—reading of the terse text. To see this clearly, let's imagine a hypothetical Senator Smith elected to serve a six-year term beginning at Time T_1. Early in his term (at Time T_2), Congress increases the attorney general's salary from $100,000 to $105,000. (It matters not whether Smith voted for or against this increase—the relevant constitutional rule in no way hinges on this fact.) Still later (at Time T_3), the president makes clear that he would like to name Smith as the next attorney general. Congress then (at Time T_4) passes a "Saxbe-fix" statute restoring the AG salary to $100,000. (It matters not how Smith votes on this, or, indeed, whether he is still in the Senate or has already resigned in anticipation of his executive service.) The Senate then confirms Smith at

Time T5, and Smith, after resigning from the Senate (if he has not already done so), assumes his $100,000 office at Time T6. A replacement senator, Jones, is named to fill out the remainder of Smith's Senate term, which ends exactly six years after T1. Call this end date T7. Did Smith's appointment violate the emoluments clause?

Recall the relevant words: "No Senator…shall, during the Time for which he was elected, be appointed to any civil Office under the Authority of the United States…the Emoluments whereof shall have been encreased during such time." A hyper-literalist might say that Smith's appointment was indeed unconstitutional. The AG's "emoluments" (i.e., salary) were indeed "encreased" at T2—and the fact that these emoluments were later decreased at T4 cannot change what did in fact occur at T2. And the $5,000 increase did occur on Smith's watch—"during the Time for which [Smith] was elected." The obvious counterargument is that the AG's salary really had not "encreased" *on balance* and *for Smith* between T1 and T6—a characterization that captures the two legally relevant moments in time and properly focuses on the "Senator" himself in keeping with the letter and logic of the clause. The salary was $100,000 both when Smith started his Senate term (T1) and when he entered office (T6). This is a perfectly sensible way to understand the word "encreased"—especially once we understand the need to read the Constitution not literally but faithfully.

Even if we did not have the benefit of Chapter 1's extended case study of vice-presidential impeachment, the emoluments clause itself makes clear that constitutional words must be read sensitively and in context, with reference to their obvious spirit and purpose. First, what does the opening phrase "during the Time for which he was elected" mean? Suppose at Time T1 Smith is beginning his *second* term, and that he was in fact first elected to serve a term beginning six years before T1. If the AG's salary had been increased in that *first* term—from, say, $96,000 to $100,000—why couldn't it be said that Smith was ineligible to be appointed even during the interval between T1 and T2? True, before T2, Congress had not "encreased" the AG's "emoluments" during Smith's *second* term. But these "emoluments" had increased "during the Time for which [Smith] was elected," if that phrase is read in a literalistic, flatfooted way. The clause is not sensibly read that way, however, because this reading does not make good common sense or structural sense and because the clause can be construed more sensibly.

(The reason why this flatfooted reading makes no sense is that it would disqualify Smith between T1 and T2, but in this very same time period it would not disqualify ex-senator Smythe, who served alongside Smith in Smith's first term, and who then left the Senate at T1. What sense does it make to treat Smith worse than Smythe? Indeed, Smythe may have voted for the $4,000 increase, whereas Smith may have voted against it. And before T2, nothing in Smith's second term has happened in Congress that seems relevant to the emoluments clause.)

Now consider the emolument clause's final phrase: "during such time." During what time? Under a literal reading, "such time" obviously refers to earlier language, namely, "during the Time for which [Smith] was elected." In Smith's case, this first "during" phrase clearly covers the precise six-year period between T1 and T7. But upon reflection, it cannot be right that the final "during" phrase means the same thing as the opening "during" phrase. Suppose Congress had never raised the AG's salary at Time T2 in Smith's second term. If so, there would have been no problem whatsoever with his appointment at T6—and no need for any sort of Saxbe fix at Time T4. But what if Congress *later* increases the AG's salary on Jones's watch—that is, sometime after T6 but before T7? Surely this increase does not somehow retroactively oust Smith from office. Even though the first "during" phrase covers the entire period from T1 to T7, the second phrase only covers the period until Smith's appointment—T1 to T6. The closing phrase "during such time" cannot sensibly be read to mean the same thing as the opening phrase "during the Time for which [Smith] was elected," even though this might at first seem to be the literal meaning.

Just as other phrases in the emoluments clause—the opening "during" phrase and the closing "during" phrase—must be read with reference to their purpose and spirit, so, too, must the word "encreased" be construed functionally. The Saxbe fix is thus a highly plausible gloss on a genuinely ambiguous text—a classic illustration of how America's written and unwritten Constitutions generally cohere.

CONSIDER, FINALLY, THE ROLE OF various *independent agencies* that have been created over the past century, such as the Federal Trade Commission, the National Labor Relations Board, the Federal Reserve Board, and the Consumer Products Safety Commission. All told, several dozen such agencies currently exist, making up a substantial portion of the federal government's regulatory apparatus. Many casual observers and even some scholars who should know better have suggested that the very existence of these agencies proves that real institutional practice in America broke free from the written Constitution long ago, and remains as free as ever today. A close look at both the text and the practice suggests otherwise.

The very label "independent agency" can be read in different ways, and some readings lead only to confusion. "Independent" agencies are of course not independent of the Constitution itself. Nor are they independent of the document's tripartite scheme. Constitutionally speaking, they are executive-branch agencies of a certain sort.

True, some of these agencies perform multiple functions—promulgating rules of conduct (as does a legislature), enforcing civil laws and prosecuting violations of criminal statutes (in classic executive fashion), and also performing adjudicatory tasks between government and individuals and sometimes even between private parties (much like a court). But this fact does not suffice to relegate these agencies to some counter-constitutional "fourth branch" outside the written Constitution's three-branch structure. Rather, this mixture of functions places "independent agencies" squarely within the second branch—the executive branch, a branch that has always performed a wide range of tasks. Interstitial rule-making within the bounds of a vague or ambiguous statute is a common executive function, as is applying law in the first instance to specific facts involving specific persons.

The label of independence may also mislead some into thinking that actual agencies either freely float between the Congress and the president or can be statutorily sited anywhere along the continuum between legislature and executive. In fact, these agencies conform to a strict pattern.

Note first how agency officials are *appointed*. The top members of so-called independent agencies are never directly named by Congress or by any subpart thereof. Rather, these officials are invariably appointed by the president, with Senate confirmation, in precisely the manner prescribed by Article II for all high-level executive-department officers. The point is not that Congress has never attempted to overleap these constitutional walls. It has indeed tried—and dramatically failed. For example, in 1974 Congress enacted an intricate federal campaign-finance law and created a Federal Election Commission, which was vested with the classic executive functions of enforcing the statute and filling in statutory gaps via the promulgation of legally binding rules and regulations. These are precisely the sort of tasks that may be given to executive officers under Article II, yet under the terms of the statute, none of the six voting members of the commission were to be appointed in the constitutionally correct way. Rather, the statute said that two members were to be formally named by a *Senate leader*, two others by *the speaker of the House*, and the final two by the president—with all six members to be confirmed by *both* houses of Congress. When the statute reached the Court, the justices disagreed about several knotty campaign-finance issues raised by the law, but were united in striking down these outlandish appointments rules, which were quickly corrected by new legislation.[56]

Note next how independent-agency officials may be *removed*. Nothing in the written Constitution allows both houses of Congress, acting together without the president, or either house acting alone, or any subset of either house, to remove any executive officer—except, of course, via the impeachment process. Ordinarily, Congress must act by law—via bicameralism and presentment. In perfect harmony with this basic structure, independent-agency officers have never been removable by the legislature alone or by any subpart. Nor has the Senate succeeded in reserving to itself a role alongside the president in making removal decisions. Though the written Constitution might arguably be read to require the Senate to say yes to every ordinary removal, just as the Senate must say yes to every ordinary appointment, this reading was repudiated by the Decision of 1789. Whatever power exists to remove executive officers—including officers of independent agencies—is solely executive power. Nearly all of actual American practice from Washington's era to our own has honored this vision.[57]

In sum, so-called independent agencies are in reality executive agencies. These entities wield executive power. Their high-ranking officials are all appointed by the chief executive in much the same way that various cabinet heads are appointed—a process that ordinarily involves the Senate as well. The top officials of these agencies are removable by the president acting without any legislative involvement, in much the same way that various cabinet heads are removable.[58]

One key difference, however, is that cabinet heads are removable *at will*, whereas independent-agency officials are removable only *for cause*, and are in this sense more independent of the president. This modest form of independence is easy to justify precisely because it does not contravene the written Constitution, which, as we have seen, says nothing explicit about removal (outside of impeachment). Nor does this modest form of independence contravene the Decision of 1789, which only addressed departments akin to the State Department, the War Department, and the Treasury Department—departments with single heads.[59]

True, we could read the Constitution to imply that all top executive officials must be removable at will. We could further read the document to imply that wherever a statute creates any executive-branch discretion or decisional authority, the president may always substitute his own personal discretion or decision for that of any high-level executive official—even when the statute explicitly vests the discretion or decisional authority in the official and not the president. But this is not a required reading of the text, which qualifies its grant of "executive Power" to the president in a variety of ways. A later clause in the Executive Article says that the president "shall take care that the laws be faithfully executed." This clause does not say that the president shall *personally* execute all the laws. It says that he shall oversee others and take care that the laws "*be* faithfully executed"—by others, who may indeed be vested by necessary and proper congressional statutes with certain discretion or decisional authority in domains where these independent officials possess distinctive expertise or impartiality.[60]

Or so the terse text may plausibly be read. And so government has operated for decades and perhaps centuries. And so the boundaries of presidential power have come to be accepted by a long line of presidents of both parties and all political stripes. And so the text and the practice have actually come to cohere and mutually reinforce.[61]*

Although a president may not dismiss an independent officer at will, he may dismiss any "independent" official who is not faithfully executing the law—anyone who is corrupt, careless, lazy, or lawless, for example.

---

* Even if the line between cabinet departments and independent agencies was not clearly established in constitutional text prior to 1967, the Twenty-fifth Amendment, which was adopted in that year, constitutionalized this line and thus implicitly endorsed the propriety of independent agencies. For details, see n. 61.

A president may also dismiss an independent official who is insubordinate to the proper role of the president as the superintendent-in-chief of the entire administration and the wielder of a broad set of powers that the Constitution itself vests in the president personally. For example, if a president orders an "independent" prosecutor not to pursue a certain target of investigation, and the prosecutor defies this order, the president could ordinarily nullify the prosecutor's actions by pardoning the target. Given this greater power of pardon, it would seem sensible that a president also has a lesser power of mere non-prosecution. And if, in fact, the president does rightly enjoy a power of non-prosecution—a power vested in him and him alone by the Executive Article itself in a specific clause beyond its opening "executive Power" grant—then any "independent" prosecutor who thumbed his nose at a presidential order to cease prosecution would have overstepped his subordinate authority and committed a removal-worthy act of insubordination. (If the official cannot in good conscience carry out the president's orders, the path of honor is generally not defiance but resignation.)[62]

The casual labels distinguishing cabinet officers from "independent" agency officials should thus not obscure the fact that both sets of officials fall wholly within the executive branch, albeit with varying rules of composition, authority, and removal.

Viewed through the prism of practice, the Constitution allows independent agencies to be created when three factors converge: first, when an executive entity is best headed up by a committee rather than by a single officer; second, when it makes sense to create continuity-enhancing fixed-tenure offices embodying technical expertise or nonpartisanship in a specific policy domain; and third, when an executive agency does not routinely interfere with specific constitutional grants of personal presidential authority, such as the powers to command the military, to personally monitor all cabinet heads, to pardon criminals, to parley with foreign leaders, to make appointments, to define an overall national agenda, and, more generally, to superintend the entire executive branch.[63]

Although the powers vested in independent agencies and the limited removability of these agency officials do constrain presidents, virtually all modern presidents have accepted these constraints. By contrast, many presidents have loudly objected to improvisations such as the legislative veto or the 1978-style independent counsel. Those improvisations weakened presidents vis-à-vis Congress and courts, whereas limitations on the removal of independent-agency officials have merely reshuffled power among presidents over time. Although President A may not remove at will all the officials he inherits on his first day in office, his successor, President B, will likewise be unable to remove at will all the officials that A manages to appoint during his tenure. Each president thus gets his fair share of presidential power, albeit with a time lag. Put a different way, independent agencies do not involve any legislative vetoes in removals; nor do they give judges nonjudicial power to appoint executive officials. Unlike legislative vetoes or the 1978 independent-counsel statute, laws establishing independent agencies do not vest members of other branches with any executive power whatsoever. Rather, these laws, in keeping with the necessary-and-proper clause, merely allocate authority within the executive branch between the president and his subordinates.

Many presidents over the years may not have even wanted truly plenary power to remove and/or countermand all executive officials. The responsibility to review on a clean slate each policy decision made by every underling might well have weakened modern presidents by overloading them, making it harder for them to concentrate on the issues that mattered most, especially in areas where the Constitution or statutes vested them with personal decisional authority. In this respect, modern presidents confront a qualitatively different supervisory situation from the one faced by George Washington, who stood atop a federal bureaucracy of infinitesimal size, by modern standards. In the end, the simple fact that modern presidents themselves have embraced independent agencies furnishes a strong reason for the rest of us to make room for these agencies as we ponder the laconic language of Article II.

A REMARKABLE AND COMPREHENSIVE PATTERN has emerged in the preceding pages. On issue after issue and in institution after institution, America's unwritten Constitution and America's written Constitution mutually reinforce one another. For example, modern unenumerated-rights jurisprudence does justice to the words of the Ninth and Fourteenth

Amendments, which in turn invite judges to listen carefully to what ordinary Americans in word and deed claim as their rights. In judicial decisions far afield of unenumerated rights, large sectors of Warren Court and post–Warren Court constitutional case law build upon the written Constitution's basic blueprint. (The exclusionary rule is the major exception.) In their actual organization and operation, all three branches of the federal government gloss the terse text.

America's written Constitution lives—in America's unwritten Constitution.

CHAPTER 10

JOINING THE PARTY

America's Partisan Constitution

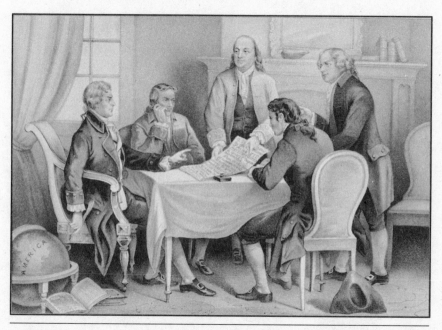

THE DECLARATION COMMITTEE (1776, AS DEPICTED IN 1876).

In 1776, even if Thomas Jefferson (far left) and John Adams (far right) were on opposite sides of a table, they were definitely on the same side of the great issue of American independence that lay before them. Twenty years later, these former friends vied for the presidency. Adams won, and Jefferson, as runner-up, became vice president. During Adams's presidency, a national two-party system intensified, making it hard for the two men to collaborate as before. After Jefferson bested Adams in a rematch in 1800–1801, the Twelfth Amendment restructured the election process for presidents and vice presidents.

A NATIONAL TWO-PARTY SYSTEM IS AS indelible a feature of modern America's landscape as the Great Plains, the Rocky Mountains, the Grand Canyon, or the Columbia River—though none of these things was part of George Washington's America. Although several prominent scholars have claimed that the written Constitution fails to address political parties, a close look at the text proves otherwise. A national two-party system in fact forms a vital part of the connective tissue tightly binding America's written and unwritten Constitution into a coherent and workable whole.[1]

The key point is that, where parties are concerned, today's Constitution dramatically differs from the document that Publius described in *The Federalist* in 1787–1788 and that Washington swore to preserve, protect, and defend in 1789. Washington strove mightily to stand above party, but in this regard today's presidents cannot and should not emulate Washington, despite the general teachings of Chapter 8. On certain issues, modern presidents must follow Jefferson and Lincoln, Andrew Jackson and Theodore Roosevelt, FDR and Reagan—partisans, all—because today's Constitution openly embraces a permanent national two-party system that was at odds with Washington's Constitution (and Washington's constitution).

The point extends far beyond modern presidents. Most of the rules and roles textually delineated in the original Constitution—for House members, senators, department heads, vice presidents, members of the electoral college, and so on—must today be reread through the prism of America's two-party system, even though the terse text does not quite say all this in so many words.

"Electors shall…vote…for two Persons"

THE INTRICATE ARTICLE II presidential-selection system cobbled together at Philadelphia was a calamity waiting to happen, because the framers failed to anticipate all the ways in which this system might malfunction once two antagonistic presidential parties appeared on the scene.

Under the Philadelphia plan, whoever came in second in the voting for president would automatically become vice president. Even if the leading presidential prospects did not run for election but merely stood quietly—with no organized attempts to mobilize supporters or to disparage rivals—some friction or frigidity would likely exist between two prominent leaders who had never chosen to stand together as a political team. Unless the electoral margin between America's leading man and his constitutional understudy was overwhelming (as indeed it was between Washington and Adams), it would not be unreasonable to imagine that at the next election the nation might well vault the current number two into the number one slot. This thought could hardly endear the vice president to the president. It would be a rare chief executive who would want to share his power or his secrets with a man whom he had not picked, whom he could not fire, who presumably coveted the top job, and who embodied perhaps the biggest obstacle to the president's own reelection. The vice president, in turn, was apt to have mixed emotions about the only man in America who outranked him. As Gouverneur Morris wryly observed at Philadelphia, any vice president who truly revered the president would be the world's "first heir apparent that ever loved his father."[2]

And then, even before Washington left the political stage, a national two-party system started to take shape. What had begun as a merely clumsy contraption for selecting the nation's two top men quickly became a dangerously dysfunctional device—a faulty constitutional gearbox apt to fail catastrophically. If a president from one party ended up with a vice president from the other party, and if each had won his seat only after fiercely opposing the other in a turbulent popular contest, relations between the nation's top two officers would likely be severely strained. Extremists seeking to reverse the election's outcome might even begin to dream about assassinations or partisan impeachments, whereby number two could become number one.

The fraught relationship between John Adams and Thomas Jefferson perfectly illustrated the structural problem. In 1796, these onetime friends had run against each other, but the Founders' rules ended up forcing these two now-rivals to cohabit, so to speak, as president and vice president, respectively. As frosty as relations between these two men were during their four years of enforced political cohabitation, the situation would have been infinitely worse had both men been reelected—in either order—in their bitter rematch of 1800–1801. Yet such split tickets were easy to imagine under the Philadelphia framers' elaborate election rules. Any national party trying to capture both the presidency and the vice presidency had to find clever but risky ways of manipulating constitutional machinery that had been designed precisely to thwart electoral manipulation and interstate coordination. Even if both political parties—Federalists and Republicans, as they came to be known—strongly preferred that the top two executive-branch spots go to teammates rather than enemies, the Philadelphia rules could not guarantee that the outcome would be either two compatible Federalists or two compatible Republicans. King Solomon in his storied wisdom had never truly sought to split the baby, but the Philadelphia rules in their stark unwisdom actually could lead, time and again, to painful split verdicts and odd inversions that almost no one wanted.[3]

WHY DID THE PHILADELPHIA FRAMERS fail to foresee what seems to us in hindsight inevitable, namely, the emergence of two highly organized national parties that would routinely vie for the presidency (and lots of other positions as well) in energetic electoral contests that might well inflame the passions of political leaders and ordinary voters alike? After all, Whigs and Tories existed in eighteenth-century England, and many states were home to political competitions between various coalitions.

In fact, political competitions in the Anglo-American world circa 1787 were often patterned, but not always organized—at least by today's standards of political organization. Elections and politicking were not tightly configured around large-scale, institutionalized parties with stable membership lists, official nominees, written platforms, issue-oriented campaigns, and well-oiled mechanisms for mass fund-raising and fund-disbursement. Instead, political life was typically connected to shifting personalities and local concerns. For much of the eighteenth century, an unelected English king picked his own ministers as he saw fit, using a grab bag of monarchial prerogatives to manage, manipulate, flatter, bribe, and punish members of Parliament into supporting his pets. Only in the next century would a new English system visibly and enduringly emerge in which Parliament would elect the prime minister and his cabinet, and organized parties would openly compete to control Parliament and the machinery of government.

In most post-Independence states, political life was also local and personal, often pitting allies of a charismatic governor (John Hancock in Massachusetts, George Clinton in New York, Patrick Henry in Virginia, and so on) against a wide and loose assortment of adversaries. No permanent interstate political networks existed, and few places had anything like today's modern two-party system, with two long-standing and highly visible political organizations routinely fielding competing slates of candidates, and each party winning some of the time.[4]

To see the framers' world from another angle, we should recall that, although the politics of the 1760s and early 1770s had become more organized—and had witnessed the first iteration of intercolonial coordination and coalition-building—the two main "parties" that had emerged were the Patriots, who would ultimately revolt, and the Loyalists, who continued to back King George. After 1776, the Loyalists dissolved as a viable political force in independent America. Political power flowed to the Patriots, who had all been on the same side—in the same "party," so to speak—during the great sorting-out that was the American Revolution.[5]

Most likely, the Constitution's framers did not envision a modern national two-party system for the simple reason that this system began to take shape only after and because of the Constitution itself. Before 1789, no strong interstate two-party competition existed because no strong interstate offices existed. Each state picked its own members of the Confederation Congress, and Congress lacked a strong continental presidency worth fighting for via the two-party system as we now know it. The Constitution itself created a powerful national government with powerful national offices—beginning with the presidency—and a national two-party system soon emerged in response.

AT THIS POINT IN OUR STORY, it might seem that the scholars who claim that the written Constitution makes no mention of parties are dead right. But wait. What these scholars miss is that America's written Constitution is not now—and for more than two centuries has not been—the text drafted at Philadelphia. Rather, America's written Constitution consists of the original text *and its written amendments*.

"distinct ballots"

FROM START TO FINISH, both on the surface and between the lines, these amendments are all about political parties.

The first ten amendments—generally known today as the Bill of Rights, although this caption does not explicitly appear in the federal text—began with a textual affirmation of the right of citizens to organize politically via "speech," "the press," "assembl[ies]," and "petition[s.]" Although the term "political parties" does not explicitly appear in this amendment, the idea is nevertheless implicit. After all, parties engage in "speech." Parties publish their opinions and appeals via "the press"—and when these words were written into the Constitution, many of America's leading printers were political operatives. Parties routinely coordinate signatures in "petition" drives and "assemble" in parks, street rallies, meeting halls, convention centers, and so on. More generally, the grand idea unifying all these First Amendment clauses is that citizens have a right to communicate with each other and to criticize government officials even if these expressions are one-sided—even if, that is, the speakers, printers, assemblers, and petitioners are *partisan*.

The man who played the largest role in getting the First Amendment enacted, James Madison, is also the man who shortly thereafter cofounded America's oldest continuous national political party—the Republican Party of the 1790s, the forerunner of today's Democrats—which succeeded in delivering the vice presidency in 1796 and the presidency in 1800–1801 to the party chieftain, Thomas Jefferson. Tellingly, the partisan politician Madison and his partisan partner Jefferson were the most vigorous champions of the First Amendment when its principles (and its principals) came under assault from the Sedition Act of 1798, at the precise moment that these two men were building their party. And as soon as Jefferson and Madison ascended to the presidency and the cabinet, respectively, in 1801, the stage was set for another written constitutional amendment, the Twelfth, that would further enact and further entrench the prominent and legitimate role of political parties in the American constitutional system.[6]

PROPOSED IN LATE 1803 and ratified in mid-1804, the Twelfth Amendment rewrote the rules for picking presidents and vice presidents. Although the term "political parties" does not appear in the amendment's explicit text, here, as elsewhere, we must read between the lines. When we do, we quickly see that this amendment was designed precisely to accommodate the recent emergence of a system of two national presidential parties in the Adams-Jefferson/Federalist-Republican elections of 1796 and 1800–1801.

The key Twelfth Amendment reform allowed each member of the electoral college to cast two "distinct ballots"—one ballot for the president and a wholly separate ballot for the vice president. This amendment freed each national political party to run a slate of two candidates openly presenting themselves to the voters as a team, one running for president and the other for vice president, with no need to manipulate balloting, as had become necessary under the Philadelphia plan. If a national party had enough clout to get its top man elected president, the party could ordinarily rest assured that its second man would win the vice presidency, so long as this team win was indeed what most American voters truly wanted. No more would Americans have to routinely risk dysfunctional political cohabitations of the sort exemplified by Adams and Jefferson in the late 1790s.

Once the president and the vice president began to see themselves as "running mates"—as men who had successfully partnered up to win a three-legged race in the last election and who might need to partner up again in the next election—it became somewhat less awkward for the president to bring his vice president into his inner circle of confidants and counselors. Still later amendments adopted in the twentieth century (amendments that we shall explore momentarily) intensified the relationship between America's top two executive-branch officers, with the result that today's vice presidents typically have much closer relationships with presidents than Adams had with Washington or than Jefferson had with Adams. In actual government practice in the twenty-first century, the vice president is ordinarily a key member of the president's inner circle, and by statute plays an important role in National Security Council deliberations.[7]

The Twelfth Amendment did not merely bring a national two-party system into the written Constitution because of what the amendment said, explicitly and implicitly. The amendment also constitutionalized parties in a deeper way, via what it did. Its very enactment was partisan, with the fledgling two-party system playing a large and visible role in the amendment's drafting and ratification. Jefferson's Republican Party backed the proposed new rules, and the main opposition came from New England members of the Federalist Party.

These Federalists were right to resist. The amendment's new rules, while designed to fix several problems that had been highlighted by the Adams-Jefferson rivalry (and by the complicating ambitions of Jefferson's supposed teammate, Aaron Burr), left intact and thereby entrenched one of the Philadelphia system's most glaring defects. Via the three-fifths clause of Article I, section 2, the Constitution gave slave states extra seats in the House of Representatives—and therefore also in the electoral college—above and beyond the proper allotment warranted by these states' free population. As the elections of 1796 and 1800 had made clear, this disgraceful rule of extra seats for extra slaves had generally benefited Jefferson's party—the Republicans.[8]

Unsurprisingly, Republicans ignored the pleas of New England Federalists to fix this Philadelphia flaw along with other Philadelphia flaws being repaired. Once the amendment's new rules were ratified, the Federalists, who had in effect won the first three presidential elections—and perhaps might have won the fourth, absent the proslavery skew of the Philadelphia plan—never again won the presidency. The next three presidential elections were won by the cofounders of the Republican Party, Jefferson and Madison. This party and its eventual successor, the Jacksonian Democrats, dominated presidential politics until 1860, thanks in no small part to the rules of the Twelfth Amendment that had been drafted by this party and for this party.

Thus, the Twelfth Amendment, both in process and in result, was partisan hardball. Pretty or not, this amendment proves that a national two-party system has been a central feature of the written Constitution, both in its amendatory texts and in its amendatory deeds, for more than two centuries.

"race...sex...age"

WHAT GOES AROUND COMES AROUND. The next three amendments were even more partisan in both the substance of their constitutional vision and the enactment process by which they sprang to life. This time, however, a different Republican Party—the party of Lincoln, not Jefferson—prevailed.

Proposed in early 1865 and ratified later that year, the Thirteenth Amendment abolished slavery and thereby marked the fulfillment of the official 1864 Republican Party platform: "[W]e are in favor...of such an amendment to the Constitution, to be made by the people in conformity with its provisions, as shall terminate and forever prohibit the existence of Slavery within the limits of the jurisdiction of the United States." The Democrats' official platform had offered voters a starkly different vision: "[T]he aim and object of the Democratic party is to preserve the Federal Union and the rights of the States unimpaired."

In the Senate, which had passed the amendment before the November election, all Republicans had said yes, while most Democrats had voted no. In the House, which passed the amendment after the election, virtually every Republican supported the amendment, and roughly three-quarters of the Democrats opposed it. The few Democrats who voted yes were generally latecomers to the parade—men who had previously voted against the amendment and who reversed course only after the voters handed the Republican Party a sweeping victory.[9]

When the next Congress convened in late 1865, it quickly became obvious that the Republican Party could not simply rest on its laurels. The abolition of slavery meant that freed slaves would now count for five-fifths in apportioning congressional and electoral-college seats, even though the freedmen were generally not allowed to vote. Unless something was done, and done soon, southern antiblack politicians—Democrats committed to undoing the Republican Party's vision of liberty and justice—could end up with more seats and more power than ever. Republicans thus cobbled together another constitutional amendment, the Fourteenth, which was proposed by a true-blue Congress in mid-1866 and ratified by three-quarters of all the states in mid-1868.

This amendment was a partisan product from start to finish. Its opening paragraph sweepingly guaranteed a broad range of basic rights against state governments, including the rights to speak, to print, to assemble, and to be treated fairly. The most obvious and immediate intended beneficiaries of this sweeping guarantee were Republicans and Republican sympathizers in the South. For years, various Democrat-controlled state governments in this region had trampled basic rights, in effect criminalizing the Republican Party. The amendment's second paragraph reduced congressional and electoral-college apportionment for any state that disfranchised adult male citizens. This provision penalized states that refused to let freedmen vote; put differently, the provision incentivized states to enfranchise freedmen. Freedmen, of course, were likely to vote for the party that had voted for them—Republicans. Thus, states that enfranchised likely Republicans would get more seats than states that did not. The third section of the amendment barred various rebel leaders from high-level public service. Almost all the banned leaders were Democrats, and the only federal branch authorized by this section to lift the ban was the one branch controlled overwhelmingly by Republicans: Congress. (Democrats at the time not only held the presidency, in the person of Andrew Johnson, but also retained a slim majority on the Court.) The amendment's fourth section repudiated debts that had been incurred by rebel (that is, Democrat-controlled) governments—debts especially apt to be held by rebel sympathizers (again, largely Democrats)—while guaranteeing repayment of federal debts that had been incurred by previous Republican Congresses. The amendment's fifth and final section gave Congress sweeping enforcement powers at the very moment that Republicans enjoyed veto-proof majorities in both houses.

The amendment's enactment process was even more partisan than its substance. Much of the amendment was hammered out in a Republican Party caucus that closed its doors against Democrats. Ultimately, not a single congressional Democrat voted for the amendment, and only one congressional Republican voted against it. In the 1866 elections, the proposed amendment functioned as the Republicans' de facto party platform, much as the hoped-for Thirteenth Amendment had furnished a large plank in the official quadrennial platform two years earlier. In several state legislatures deciding whether to ratify the proposed amendment, Republicans rammed the measure through with minimal deliberation and little direct engagement of the objections raised by Democrats, whose party chieftain, Andrew Johnson, was crusading against the proposed amendment with unprecedented venom and vigor. And let's not forget that many southern political leaders, overwhelmingly Democrats, were excluded from the Congress that drafted the Fourteenth Amendment and were barred from reentry until their states said yes to the measure and also agreed to enfranchise blacks, who would likely vote Republican. In blistering language, the Democratic Party Platform of 1868 proclaimed that Congress's recent interferences with state suffrage laws via the Reconstruction Acts of 1867 were "an usurpation, and unconstitutional, revolutionary, and void."[10]

In the first general election held after the Fourteenth Amendment became law, Republican Ulysses Grant won the presidency even though a majority of whites nationwide had apparently backed the Democratic candidate, Horatio Seymour. Aware that newly enfranchised southern blacks had voted overwhelmingly for their party, Republicans responded with yet another constitutional amendment, this one guaranteeing race-neutral voting laws in state and federal elections. Proposed in early 1869 and ratified in early 1870, the Fifteenth Amendment aimed not merely to reinforce the rights of blacks who were already voting in the South, but also, and more pressingly, to extend the vote to disfranchised blacks in the North—blacks apt to join their southern cousins in voting Republican. Almost all congressional Republicans supported this final Reconstruction Amendment, and virtually every congressional Democrat opposed it. In the ratification process, Republican whips in state legislatures generally ensured that party members followed the party line.

To stress that all three Reconstruction Amendments were intensely partisan measures is not to condemn these provisions, but rather, to give credit to the role that political parties at their best can play and have played in the American constitutional order. The Reconstruction Amendments contain some of the noblest elements of the American Constitution. These provisions should remind us that a national two-party system does not exist at odds with the written Constitution, but has long operated in sync with it, and has indeed been the main engine driving formal changes to its text over time.

THE PRECISE ROLE PLAYED BY PARTIES within the amendment process has changed in important ways over the centuries. As we have seen, America's first set of amendments—the Bill of Rights—emerged from a *pre-partisan process*. While Americans at the Founding had witnessed an epic continental debate between Federalists and Anti-Federalists, it was not immediately clear that these two temporary camps would harden into permanent parties. In fact, many backers of the Bill of Rights in the First Congress were hoping to find common ground that could reunite the camps. The next momentous set of amendments—the Twelfth through the Fifteenth—emerged from a *strictly partisan process* in which one party simply steamrolled to victory under the banner of reform. As we shall now see, America's most recent amendments have generally emerged from a *bipartisan process* in which both major parties have worked together to achieve the political supermajorities ordinarily required by Article V—two-thirds of each house of Congress plus three-quarters of the states.

The Sixteenth Amendment, explicitly authorizing a federal income tax, was endorsed by the Democratic Party platforms of 1908 and 1912 and by Republican presidents Theodore Roosevelt and William Howard Taft. (Although presidents have no formal vote or veto in the amendment process, they nevertheless command considerable authority as de facto leaders of their party.) Even politicians who were skeptical of a federal income tax found it hard to resist the prevailing political winds. In 1909, the amendment breezed through the Senate unanimously, and passed the House on a vote of 318 to 14. Over the next four years, the amendment received enough state ratifications to become the first textual addition to the Constitution since Reconstruction.

Both Democrats and Republicans had found it in their interest to appeal to a rising twentieth-century progressive movement whose members generally favored a progressive income tax. A few years later, an analogous dynamic unfolded on the issue of woman suffrage. As it became increasingly imaginable that suffragists might ultimately prevail, the prophecy became self-fulfilling, thanks in part to partisan competition. Both parties wanted to win the allegiance of the new voters, and support for a Woman Suffrage Amendment was crucial to winning that allegiance.

In 1916, the parties hedged their bets. Each party platform endorsed both the principle of woman suffrage and the right of every state to decide for itself. Four years later, competition for women's allegiance intensified and the parties raised their bids. The Republican Party platform reminded voters that "the Republican Congress...submitted to the country the constitutional amendment for woman suffrage, and furnished twenty-nine of the thirty-five legislatures which have ratified it to date." Not to be outdone, Democrats—whose outgoing party leader, President Woodrow Wilson, had crusaded for the federal Suffrage Amendment—inserted the following plank in their 1920 platform:

> We endorse the proposed 19th Amendment of the Constitution of the United States granting equal suffrage to women. We congratulate the legislatures of thirty-five states which have already ratified said amendment and we urge the Democratic Governors and Legislatures of Tennessee, North Carolina and Florida and such states as have not yet ratified the Federal Suffrage Amendment to unite in an effort to complete the process of ratification and secure the thirty-sixth state in time for all the women of the United States to participate in the fall election.

Later that summer, the parties' wish came true when Tennessee became the decisive thirty-sixth state to say yes.

Similar stories can be told about more recent amendments. In the middle years of the twentieth century, American blacks were a swing constituency wooed by both parties. Before 1932, blacks voted overwhelmingly for Republicans; by 1972, they had generally become reliable Democrats. In the years in between, neither party could confidently count them in or count them out. Unsurprisingly, this era witnessed three voting-rights amendments that disparately benefited black voters—the Twenty-third Amendment, folding the District of Columbia (with its large black population) into the electoral college; the Twenty-fourth Amendment, condemning various systems of tax-based disfranchisement (systems that had notoriously been used to dampen black suffrage); and the Twenty-sixth Amendment, which guaranteed the right to vote to young adults (who were then and who still are disproportionately nonwhite). All three amendments won broad support among both Democrats and Republicans.

THREE OTHER TWENTIETH-CENTURY AMENDMENTS intertwined even more tightly with party politics, with the written Constitution's formal rules both reflecting and reinforcing specific protocols of America's two dominant political parties.

By providing for direct popular election of senators, the Seventeenth Amendment, ratified in 1913, constitutionalized a practice that was already in place in various states where one party dominated the political landscape and routinely held primary elections to determine its choice for senator. In such states, these primaries functioned as direct senatorial elections, de facto, even before the amendment came along.

A similar story can be told about the vice-presidential selection process. For most of the nineteenth and early twentieth centuries, party conventions did not invariably rubber-stamp the running mate most preferred by the presidential nominee himself. More recently, both major parties have consistently invited the presidential nominee to handpick his vice-presidential running mate. In perfect harmony with this emerging party practice, the Twenty-second Amendment, ratified in 1951, limited presidents to two terms, thereby giving presidents more reason to work closely with their vice presidents. For a second-term president seeking to extend his policies and cement his legacy, personal reelection is no longer an option, but election of his own handpicked running mate remains permissible. Whereas the vice president under the Philadelphia plan was apt to embody the president's biggest obstacle, the vice president under the new rules is apt to embody the president's best opportunity—an opportunity to win a third (and even fourth) term by proxy.

The Twenty-fifth Amendment, ratified in 1965, further tightened the relationship between presidents and vice presidents by encouraging presidents undergoing routine surgeries and the like to temporarily hand off power to their handpicked running mates. Another section of the amendment formalized the highly personal tie between America's two top officers by providing that in the event of a vice-presidential vacancy, the president would name his own protégé, subject to congressional confirmation—a written rule mirroring unwritten party norms giving a presidential nominee the right to name his running mate, subject to the approval of the party convention.

ALAS, THE CURRENT PRESIDENTIAL-SUCCESSION STATUTE violates the spirit of the Twenty-fifth Amendment, not to mention the letter of the original Constitution. Enacted in 1947, this statute provides that if both the president and vice president are unable to function because of death, disability, removal (via impeachment), or resignation, presidential power devolves to the speaker of the House. The first big problem with this statute is textual: It runs counter to the Constitution's succession clause—Article II, section 1, paragraph 6, which empowers Congress to specify "what Officer" should take over in succession situations. A member of Congress, such as the House speaker, is simply not an eligible "Officer" within the meaning of the succession clause, which was designed to enable cabinet officers, not congressmen, to step up to fill the breach.

The second big problem with the statute implicates the spirit of the Constitution—the "post-Georgian" Constitution, the one we must nowadays read through the prism of America's party system. Above and beyond the formal textual separation of powers—the distinction between Article I legislators and Article II "officers"—we must also attend to the informal but no-less-important separation of *parties*. Crucially, the president and the speaker may often be leaders of opposing parties. Indeed, except for Jimmy Carter, every one of America's eight most recent presidents has for at least part of his time in office faced an opposition-party speaker. The 1947 statute threatens to return America to the instability of the original Philadelphia plan, with a potential political enemy of the president improperly positioned to gain presidential power in the event of mishap. Shades of Adams and Jefferson! (And let's not forget Ben Wade in the Johnson impeachment trial.) Cabinet succession, by contrast, coheres with the officer-means-officer letter of the original succession clause and with the executive-branch-teamwork and party-continuity spirit of the Decision of 1789, the Twelfth Amendment, and the Twenty-fifth Amendment. In general, if a president cannot complete his term, it should be completed by a party mate whom he has chosen, either personally or by proxy.[11]

It might be thought that the very existence of this 1947 statute represents a large exception to this book's thesis that America's actual system of government generally coheres with America's written Constitution. But, in fact, this statute has never been triggered. This law thus lacks the authority enjoyed by statutes that have passed the tests of time and implementation and thereby acquired the weight of custom and practice. The statute's serious and multiple departures from the written Constitution's letter and spirit make it doubtful that things will actually work smoothly in a future crisis. Ours remains a culture that worships at the shrine of a written Constitution. Those who are serious about the American constitutional project, and who would like to see the document's text mesh with actual practice in a way that ultimately strengthens both text and practice, should strive to repeal and replace this misshapen statute before anyone gets hurt.

"any primary...election"

ALTHOUGH THE ROLE OF POLITICAL PARTIES in nominating presidents and vice presidents was not explicitly visible in the text of the Twenty-second and Twenty-fifth Amendments, that role lay only inches below the surface of the text for those with eyes to see. In the intervening Twenty-fourth Amendment, political parties actually found their way into the text itself. Proposed in 1962 and ratified in 1964, the Twenty-fourth Amendment outlawed poll-tax-related disfranchisement in all federal elections, including "any *primary*...election" (emphasis added)—that is, any election in which a *political party* teamed up with government to let voters decide whom the party would nominate in the general election.

The explicit language of the Twenty-fourth Amendment invites us to revisit four other amendments, all of which feature the same key phrase as the Twenty-fourth—"the right of citizens of the United States to vote"—or a close variant. None of these four other amendments explicitly mentions primary elections. Were it not for the language of the Twenty-fourth, it might well be an open question whether these other citizen-right-to-vote amendments in fact properly apply in government-run party primary elections. But thanks to the explicit language of the Twenty-fourth, all five citizen-right-to-vote amendments should indeed apply to primary elections, even though in four of the five instances, this application is... unwritten. Put a different way, although the Twenty-fourth Amendment's words explicitly apply only to the narrow question of poll-tax-related disfranchisement, the amendment's unwritten spirit invites us to read all preceding and subsequent citizen-right-to-vote language as applicable to both primary and general elections alike.[12]

The Twenty-fourth Amendment does not apply to all elections. Rather, it proclaims that poll taxes may not operate to abridge the right of citizens of the United States to vote in the following elections: "any primary or other election for President or Vice President, for electors for President or Vice President, or for Senator or Representative in Congress." Left conspicuously unmentioned were, among other things, elections for state and local positions (such as state governors, state legislators, state judges, mayors, city councilmen, and county sheriffs) and noncandidate elections (such as initiatives, referendums, and bond measures).* By contrast, the Fifteenth, Nineteenth, and Twenty-sixth Amendments sweepingly proclaim that the right of citizens of the United States to vote may never be abridged on account of race, sex, or age, respectively—in *any* election of *any* sort at *any* level of government. These amendments clearly cover more elections than does the Twenty-fourth. Given that the Twenty-fourth Amendment plainly applies to primaries, surely it follows—*a fortiori*, in legalese—that these three universal amendments must also apply to primaries.[13]

The only other citizen-right-to-vote provision in the Constitution is located in section 2 of the Fourteenth Amendment. That section reduced congressional and electoral-college apportionment for states that disfranchised various adult male citizens. The more widespread the disfranchisement in a given state, the greater the apportionment penalty. But only certain elections counted for this apportionment-penalty clause, namely, "any election for the choice of electors for President and Vice President of the United States, Representatives in Congress, the Executive and Judicial officers of a State, or the members of the Legislature thereof."

Are primary elections encompassed by this clause? Imagine that a state, in tandem with a political party, disfranchises some group in a state-run presidential primary election, but allows this group to vote in the general presidential election. Should the state pay an apportionment penalty under

---

* Nothing in the amendment explicitly endorsed or authorized poll-tax-related disfranchisement in nonfederal elections. Instead, the amendment left these elections to be addressed by state and federal statutes and by earlier federal constitutional provisions, including the republican-government clause and the Reconstruction Amendments. In mid-1965, a year and a half after the ratification of the Twenty-fourth Amendment, Congress passed a sweeping Voting Rights Act that invited the judiciary to invalidate all poll-tax-related disfranchisements. In 1966, the Warren Court, in *Harper v. Virginia*, accepted that invitation, striking down state poll-tax disfranchisements as violative of the Fourteenth Amendment. The 1965 act and the 1966 case are discussed in more detail in Chapter 4, text accompanying nn. 55–62.

section 2? If we simply laid section 2 alongside the Twenty-fourth Amendment for comparison, we might at first think that section 2 was plainly designed to be inapplicable to primary elections. After all, section 2 speaks only of "any election for the choice of electors for President," and, strictly speaking, primary elections do not directly pick presidential "electors"—that is, members of the electoral college. These electors are picked only in the general (November) election. Indeed, the Twenty-fourth Amendment itself can be read as plainly contradistinguishing "a primary...election for President" from the general (November) "election...for *electors* for President."

Had section 2 and the Twenty-fourth Amendment been adopted at the same moment, we might have good reason to view this key textual distinction as decisive, and it might make sense to read section 2 as purposefully excluding primaries by pointed negative implication. But section 2 was in fact adopted a century before the Twenty-fourth Amendment. The latter amendment took pains to clarify that government-run primary elections and general elections should be governed symmetrically precisely because the twentieth-century experience had demonstrated that primary elections might well be the main event. (Were it not for the 1960 primary elections, which JFK swept in dramatic fashion, it is doubtful that he would have persuaded enough party insiders to support him, despite his youth and Catholicism. And in many notable twentieth-century electoral contests for state and congressional positions, the decisive races had occurred in party primary elections, not the November general elections.)

If primaries and general elections merited symmetric treatment under a 1960s amendment safeguarding "the right of citizens of the United States to vote," then they also merited symmetric treatment under an 1860s amendment that also aimed to safeguard "the right to vote" of "citizens of the United States." The omission of any specific mention of primaries in the 1860s amendment was not purposeful or pointed. Rather, primary elections were neither specifically mentioned nor explicitly omitted for the simple reason that these elections were not a particularly prominent feature of American politics in the 1860s, and only became so later on.

True, if we interpolate "primary elections" into the express provisions of section 2 of the Fourteenth Amendment, we are, in effect, reading between the lines. But if we do not do so, the Constitution as a whole fails to make sense. Like the Fifteenth, Nineteenth, and Twenty-sixth Amendments, section 2 of the Fourteenth has a far wider textual catchment basin than does the Twenty-fourth Amendment. Ordinary state elections for state legislators, executives, and judges fall within the plain sweep of section 2 but lie beyond the explicit scope of the Twenty-fourth Amendment. Unless we interpolate "primary elections" into section 2, we reach the perverse result that section 2 covers less ground than the Twenty-fourth Amendment.[14]*

In short, later amendments often contain a powerful, albeit unwritten, gravitational pull that invites reinterpretation of earlier amendments so that the Constitution as a whole coheres as a sensible system of rules and principles. To borrow a phrase from John Marshall, we must never forget that it is a Constitution—a single rational document, as opposed to a pile of unconnected clauses—that we are expounding. In previous chapters, we confronted the question of gravitational pull where voting rights and women's rights were concerned. For now, let us not lose sight of the remarkable fact that no fewer than five of the fifteen amendments ratified after Jefferson's tenure in office explicitly or implicitly address primary elections, and therefore directly address political parties.[15]

"The...Manner of holding Elections for Senators and Representatives"

A SIMILAR PICTURE COMES INTO VIEW when we venture beyond the words and deeds of America's constitutional amendments to examine the formal and informal structure of daily governance in America. Here, too, political parties have in fact tightly and enduringly woven themselves into the very fabric of the American system—so tightly and enduringly that we

---

* Nor is this the only aspect of section 2 that needs to be reread through the prism of later amendments. Section 2 explicitly penalizes states only when they disfranchise *males*. Surely this pointed and purposeful exclusion of females from the scope of protection cannot survive the subsequent adoption of the Woman Suffrage Amendment, ratified in 1920—an amendment explicitly prohibiting the federal government from discriminating on the basis of sex in the domain of voting rights. After 1920, any literalistic federal enforcement of section 2—protecting the right of males to vote more vigorously than the right of females to vote—would itself violate the letter and spirit of the Suffrage Amendment. Similarly, section 2's age limit of "twenty one years" was silently repealed by the Twenty-sixth Amendment, ratified in 1971, which in effect (albeit not expressly) substituted the new age limit of eighteen years into the penalty clause of section 2. For more analysis, see n. 14.

should regard the current two-party system as a basic element of America's Constitution.

For over a century, framework statutes regulating the American administrative state have explicitly taken political parties into account in an effort to maintain a carefully balanced two-party system. The Federal Election Commission, which was redesigned after the Court's 1976 ruling in *Buckley v. Valeo*, contains an even number of voting members—six, to be precise. By law, no more than three commissioners "may be affiliated with the same political party." Various other statutes governing commissions comprising an uneven number of members—typically five or seven—have tried to prohibit any political party from controlling more than a bare majority of commissioners. Of the seven seats on the United States Sentencing Commission, for example, no more than four may be held by "members of the same political party." Likewise, the notable 1914 law creating the Federal Trade Commission provides that no more than three of its five commissioners "shall be members of the same political party." Identical language appears in the statutes creating the Federal Energy Regulatory Commission (a reorganized version of the earlier Federal Power Commission), the Equal Employment Opportunity Commission, the Commodity Futures Trading Commission, the Nuclear Regulatory Commission, and several other independent agencies—including the Securities and Exchange Commission, whose enabling statute also provides that "in making appointments members of different political parties shall be appointed alternately as nearly as may be practicable." The Federal Communications Commission statute has slightly different wording, but it, too, prohibits any party from having more than three out of five members. The statute structuring the Consumer Product Safety Commission features language regulating party "affiliat[ion]" rather than "member[ship]"; thus, no more than three of the five commissioners may be "affiliated with the same political party." Deploying yet another verbal formula echoing the landmark 1887 act that established the once famous, but now defunct, Interstate Commerce Commission, the enabling statute of the Federal Maritime Commission proclaims that no more than three of its five members may be "appointed from the same political party." This language also appears verbatim in the statute creating the National Transportation Safety Board.[16]

Most of these statutes might at first seem easy to evade. Formally, a clever president is free to propose an appointee who is only nominally connected to (or independent of) a given party. In practice, however, opposition-party senators are often able to deter any sly evasions that presidents might envision.[17]

The law of bipartisan replenishment of independent agencies is thus enforced through congressional party politics, which in turn are shaped by bipartisan rules and laws regulating the structure of Congress and the election of congresspersons. For a century and a half, Congress has been dominated by the same two major parties, Republicans and Democrats, who have alternated in power. In an intricate meshwork of statutes, house rules, and customary practices, this two-party system has threaded itself into durable formulas and folkways determining how many seats and staffers each party will have on each house committee, how party leaders will interact on committees and on the floor, and so on. These formulas and folkways both presuppose and help ensure that at any given moment, each house of Congress will consist of two main groups—one "majority" party and one "minority" party.[18]

This basic dichotomy is visible in the very architecture of each house chamber, with members of one party traditionally sitting together on one side of the chamber and members of the other party likewise clustered on the other side, with an aisle literally and metaphorically separating the two groups. This remarkably steady, stable, stolid two-party system stands in sharp contrast to the kaleidoscopic arrangements one sees in many leading democracies around the globe, where three or more parties routinely win a significant number of seats in the national legislature, new parties arise with some frequency, and major parties occasionally collapse.

AMERICAN ELECTION LAW has created conducive conditions for this entrenched Republican-Democrat duopoly. The cornerstone of this legal foundation is a simple rule in the United States Code that disaggregates each state into single-member congressional districts. For example, if a state is entitled to twelve seats in the House of Representatives, it must have twelve congressional districts, each of which picks one House member. The state may not divide itself into, say, three districts, each of which elects four House members. Nor may the state create a system in which all twelve seats are filled in a single statewide election, with each voter allowed to cast one vote. Each district must have one and only one representative, and in this system it is hard for more than two parties in any district to thrive in long-term equilibrium.

Students of political science will recognize this empirical regularity as "Duverger's Law." The basic mechanisms driving the regularity identified by Professor Duverger are not hard to understand. When one and only one seat is up for grabs in a given congressional district, the victor must win a majority, or at least a plurality, within this district. Most sophisticated voters understand that a vote for a third-party candidate is usually a wasted vote, for several reasons.[19]

First, a start-up party, by definition, has no track record of past victory—only the two established parties can claim such a track record—and the need to achieve a district-wide majority or plurality sets the bar of success quite high for the start-up entrant. Second, even a voter who sincerely prefers a third-party candidate should understand that a vote for this candidate, instead of a vote for the lesser-evil of the two major-party candidates, may increase the odds that the voter's least favorite (greater-evil) major-party candidate will prevail.* Third, even if these two factors do not initially sway a given voter, that voter should understand that these factors will likely sway other sophisticated voters, and that fact, in turn, provides an additional reason to think that a third-party vote would be a wasted or perverse vote. Thanks to the dynamic and reinforcing interplay of these three factors, the prophecy that the two established parties will continue to be the only realistic options becomes largely self-fulfilling—a stable equilibrium that can be disrupted only by a massive external jolt, the political equivalent of an asteroid strike.

Separation of powers and federalism further reinforce this equilibrium. Because America has one and only one president, and because this one-

---

* Consider a simple example from the presidential contest of 2000: Any ultraliberal voter who cast his ballot for his first-choice candidate, Ralph Nader, instead of his second choice, Al Gore, thereby increased the odds that his least favorite candidate, George W. Bush, would prevail. Symmetrically, any ultraconservative voter who cast his vote for his first choice, Pat Buchanan, instead of his second choice, Bush, thereby increased the odds that his least favorite candidate, Gore, would win. Similar dynamics operate in any single-member-district House election.

man executive is elected independently of Congress, Duverger's Law predicts that two and only two major presidential parties will survive in the long run. A similar dynamic ensures that within any given state two parties will routinely vie for gubernatorial control. The great majority of state legislatures also use single-member districting systems. The fact that virtually every congressional district has the *same* two parties today—Republicans and Democrats—is a product of certain electoral economies of scale and the ticket-system facilitated by the tight coordination of state and national elections.

In a multi-member districting system, by contrast, more parties may be able to thrive if friendly voting rules are in place. Imagine a district with four seats to be filled, and suppose further that each voter is given only one vote. In this system, any party with slightly over 20 percent of the vote is guaranteed to win a seat. (If Party X has more than 20 percent, it must necessarily be among the top four parties; if there were four other parties, each of which got more votes than Party X, the total votes would exceed 100 percent—a mathematical impossibility.) The victory threshold is thus much lower than a district-wide majority or plurality. In such a multi-member district, as many as five different parties could survive in long-term equilibrium, in a musical-chairs game with, say, three parties at 21 percent apiece and two slightly smaller parties credibly vying for the last remaining chair. More generally, any multi-member district with n seats and friendly voting rules can sustain, in the long run, as many as n + 1 parties. Multi-member district systems and variants thereof are used throughout the world, and many national elections abroad feature robust multiparty competitions year after year.

American congressional elections, by contrast, narrow the playing field to two major parties. In any given district, there is one seat to be won in the musical-chairs game, and thus in the general election there are typically only two contestants—one Democrat and one Republican—plausibly vying for the seat. (We should recall here the critical winnowing role of primary elections and/or party caucuses, which enable the typical general election to become a focused contest between one Republican and one Democrat.)

The federal law that laid the foundation for this two-party congressional system was first enacted in 1842, pursuant to Article I, section 4, which authorizes Congress to legislate rules governing the "manner" of congressional elections. According to this statute, House members were to be elected "by districts composed of contiguous territory equal in number to the number of Representatives to which said State may be entitled, *no one district electing more than one Representative.*" Over the ensuing century, Congress repeatedly revisited its election laws in connection with the decennial House reapportionment mandated by Article I, section 2. Most of the time, Congress reenacted the 1842 statute or some close cousin, but occasionally Congress allowed the single-member-district law to lapse, only to revive the law in a later reapportionment cycle. Since 1967, the single-member-district statute has been a fixed feature of the U.S. election code, a politically entrenched and politically entrenching provision cementing in place the current two-party system about as effectively and enduringly as any explicit constitutional text could ever hope to do.[20]

To be clear: There is no constitutional text that explicitly or implicitly requires a two-party system. Nor is there any constitutional text that explicitly or implicitly requires single-member districts, with or without the gloss of the past 170 years of actual government practice. Congress has the power to create single-member House districts, but not the duty to do so. Nothing in the 1842 law, or the 1967 law, or any of the districting laws in between invites us to read any specific constitutional clause in a manner that suggests that House members must be elected this way or that way. Rather, this long string of laws merely confirms that Congress can choose to require single-member House districts if it wants to.

But that is enough, for once single-member districts took root and solidified a two-party system in Congress, Congress lost almost all incentive to change the basic structure. Thus, this structure became deeply entrenched—a self-perpetuating element of America's unwritten Constitution far harder to change than, say, the current size of the Supreme Court. To change the Court size, Congress need only pass an ordinary law, and it is actually imaginable that some future Congress might wish to do this—imaginable precisely because such a change in law would not necessarily harm congressional incumbents in any obvious way. To change the current two-party system, Congress likewise need only pass an ordinary law, but it is almost unimaginable that a future Congress might wish to do this—almost unimaginable because such a change would indeed harm incumbents by opening the door to new parties that might threaten the existing duopoly enjoyed by the two major parties tied to these incumbents.* If ever it makes sense to call something a "constitutional" rule even though this rule does not in fact appear in the written Constitution, America's basic two-party system is such a thing.

DESPITE ALL THAT WE HAVE seen, it cannot be said that the Constitution directly addresses political parties in a comprehensive fashion. Is this because, as some scholars have claimed, the document's rules concerning elections and the political process—especially its provisions governing presidential politics and presidential authority—are the petrified fossils of an eighteenth-century world, wholly ill-fitting the political realities of modern America?

The evidence suggests otherwise. At the very moment that national parties arose, they began to integrate themselves into the Constitution in both text and deed. America's modern presidency is not the product of eighteenth-century mistakes that later Americans have simply been unable to comprehend or correct. Although the presidency was originally designed for a nonpartisan figure—George Washington—the office was repeatedly redesigned, via many different amendments adopted over the course of many decades, to fit the rise of more partisan chief executives, including Thomas Jefferson, Abraham Lincoln, Franklin Roosevelt, and Lyndon Johnson. Most of the rules of presidential power are robust. These rules first worked without an entrenched two-party system and now work within such a system.

To put the point another way, virtually all states have created governorships that look amazingly like the presidency, and most states created these presidential look-alikes after the rise of America's two-party system. Almost no state constitution comprehensively regulates political parties, even though many written state constitutions are quite detailed and relatively easy to amend.

All this evidence suggests that there is a different reason why politi-

---

* In this book's final chapter, I shall try to imagine the virtually unimaginable by sketching one theoretical scenario in which incumbent members of Congress might see fit to change the existing two-party duopoly.

cal parties receive rather spotty treatment in America's fifty-one written constitutions, state and federal. The explanation, quite simply, is that it is far from clear what a more comprehensive constitutional regulatory framework should look like.

True, several advanced democracies across the oceans feature more detailed constitutional regulations of political parties, but few of these foreign constitutions provide models for easy American emulation. Most foreign regimes lack America's special combination of an entrenched two-party system and an executive elected independently of the legislature. The fifty state constitutions are more obvious models for possible federal constitutional rules, precisely because all fifty-one constitutions, state and federal, share a great deal in common (including electorally separated branches and two major parties). But, to repeat, virtually no state constitution regulates political parties in dramatically different fashion than does the federal Constitution. Unless and until several state constitutions come along and demonstrate a better mousetrap for addressing American-style political parties, most Americans are unlikely to view the federal Constitution as defective in this regard.

There may well be deep wisdom in America's piecemeal approach to political parties, which are, after all, multifarious, protean, and complex creatures. Consider just a few of the complications that could confound a proposal to regulate parties in a more truly systematic fashion: America's two alternating governing parties are qualitatively different from its wide assortment of fringe parties. The boundaries between official political parties and broader social movements are porous. At any instant, official party membership lists will only imperfectly reflect real partisan allegiance and inclination. Sometimes a particular party may be tightly knit and ideologically pure; at other times, less so. A party that opens its primaries to independent voters will likely act differently than one that operates only closed primaries. Other matters of internal party governance—whether the party favors primaries or caucuses, whether it strongly privileges party chieftains or is more open to insurgents, whether it embraces plurality rule or proportional representation in picking delegates to its conventions, whether conventions in turn follow majority rule or supermajority rule in selecting party nominees—introduce additional wrinkles. Parties often operate differently within Congress than within the executive branch.

In periods of "unitary" government when one party controls both Congress and the presidency, distinctive political possibilities and pathologies arise that are usually dormant in eras of "divided" government, which present their own classic routines and rhythms. Within any chamber of government, the ruling party often confronts opportunities and temptations not faced by the loyal opposition, and vice versa. Partisanship may play out differently in moments of extreme ideological polarization and high-stakes reform—as during the Jeffersonian revolution of the early 1800s or the Reconstruction of the 1860s—than in eras of relative quiescence, when party ideologies are blurred and patronage looms larger than principle.

Sometimes parties need to stand wholly outside government with clear rights against the formal legal order. (Think of the First Amendment.) Other times, a government works so closely with a party that it may be hard to determine where one ends and the other begins. (Think of certain kinds of primary elections covered by the five citizen-right-to-vote amendments.) In still other ways, parties operate as unique intermediary institutions, formally operating outside government even as the law specially facilitates or specially restrains partisanship within government. (Think of the Twelfth and Twenty-fifth Amendments, or the string of independent agencies with party-membership rules.)

Given all these complications and complexities, the absence of a more comprehensive constitutional grid regulating American political parties is not some horrible and incurable eighteenth-century goof, but the considered choice of many generations of Americans ever since Jefferson's ascension—and a sensible choice at that.

CHAPTER 11

DOING THE RIGHT THING

America's Conscientious Constitution

WILLIAM BRENNAN (*left*) AND
THURGOOD MARSHALL (*right*) (1976).

Beginning in the 1970s, Justices Brennan and Marshall refused to
support any death sentence, state or federal, that came before them.

Enacted and amended at epic moments by a collective people noisily politicking on a grand public stage, the Constitution in the interim has often unfolded through the actions of individuals and institutions in smaller and quieter settings. While the presidency is the Constitution's most personal office—with one individual sitting atop an entire branch—Congress members, judges, and jurors are persons, too. How does the Constitution enlist the consciences of all these individuals? Once enlisted, how is conscience to be constrained? How should a conscientious person act when his conscience and the statute books tug in opposite directions?

Over the centuries, these questions have had special urgency for jurors when they have been confronted with a criminal defendant who is clearly guilty, but who faces a punishment that seems unconscionably savage. The written Constitution does not explicitly specify the proper role of juror conscience in such situations. Nevertheless, the document is best read as presupposing an unwritten right of jurors in certain situations to show mercy by acquitting the defendant and thereby "nullifying" an unduly harsh criminal statute. Alas, this deeply rooted right of juror conscience has not been properly nourished and pruned in modern courtrooms. Current doctrines of jury composition and jury control must thus be tweaked to both facilitate and discipline the exercise of conscience in the jury box.

As for judges and other public servants who find certain penal policies unconscionably harsh, here, too, there is a proper place for *conscience*—a concept that forms part of the necessary, albeit unwritten, substratum of American constitutionalism.

"Oath"

THE SUCCESS OF our national constitutional project requires that certain things must always exist, and exist in abundance, in America. *Virtue, honor,* and *conscience* rank high among these essential elements.

In every generation, vast numbers of ordinary citizens must willingly keep the constitutional machinery running—by voting on Election Day, by serving on juries when summoned, by doing their best to obey the law (and to pay their taxes) in ordinary circumstances, and by defending the Constitution, by force of arms, if need be. Also, a significant slice of America's most able and admirable citizens must willingly serve in government if called to do so by their peers. This willingness to serve the public good was a key component of what the Founding generation referred to as "virtue."

Writing as "Publius"—the "public man"—in *The Federalist* No. 55, James Madison observed that although "there is a degree of depravity in mankind which requires a certain degree of circumspection and distrust, so there are other qualities in human nature which justify a certain portion of esteem and confidence." According to Madison/Publius, "[r]epublican government presupposes the existence of these qualities in a higher degree than any other form" of government and necessarily presumes that "there is…sufficient virtue among men for self-government."[1]

What sorts of men and women are needed as public servants to run the Constitution on a daily basis? Obviously, persons of discernment and ability, but also—crucially—persons of honor, rectitude, and conscience. Anyone who doubts the salience of honor in the Founding era need only recall the stirring words at the close of America's other iconic parchment, adopted on July 4, 1776: "And for the support of this Declaration, with a firm reliance on the protection of divine Providence, we mutually pledge to each other our Lives, our Fortunes and our sacred Honor."

Though the word "conscience" did not appear on the surface of the text that emerged from Independence Hall eleven years later, three different passages of the original constitutional text obliged public servants to take special oaths; later, the Fourteenth Amendment contained an entire section addressing the issue of oaths. Thus, Article I mandated that whenever the Senate sat as an impeachment court, its individual members had to take an "oath or affirmation" to do proper justice as judges and jurors of the impeachment defendant.* Even as Article II left many of the details

---

* This was the oath that Ohio Senator Ben Wade was accused of dishonoring during the 1868 impeachment trial of Andrew Johnson. Recall from Chapter 1 that Wade would have automatically gained the presidency itself upon Johnson's conviction and thus, claimed critics, faced a disqualifying conflict of interest that precluded him from sitting in judgment of Johnson.

of executive power unspecified, it took pains to insist that a president's first task—before performing any other official function—was to take an oath of office, an oath whose exact content Article II proceeded to prescribe verbatim. Article VI obliged every important state or federal official to take an oath to support the federal Constitution; and section 3 of the Fourteenth Amendment imposed special political disqualifications on officials who had not merely sided with the Confederacy, but in the process betrayed previously sworn oaths.

Oaths also figured prominently in the Fourth Amendment, which allowed search warrants to issue only when supported by an informant's "oath or affirmation." On June 1, 1789, the very first statute ever enacted by the very first Congress specified the text of the oath to be taken by various officials. In his two most celebrated opinions, *Marbury v. Madison* and *McCulloch v. Maryland*, Chief Justice John Marshall fittingly used the existence of these constitutional and statutory oaths to illustrate constitutional first principles. In *Marbury*, Marshall stressed the judicial oath; in *McCulloch*, he highlighted the power of Congress to add new oaths, even though such power was not expressly enumerated in the written Constitution.[2]

ACCORDING TO THE SELF-REFERENTIAL LANGUAGE of Article VI, key government officials would be "*bound* by Oath or Affirmation to support this Constitution" (emphasis added)—but what did the word "bound" mean here? Oaths do not bind in the same way that chains do. When Article IV referred to persons "held to Service or Labor," this language did in fact refer to human beings—slaves—who were physically bound and literally held in bondage. But Article VI oaths bound persons via a very different mechanism.

Much of the force of an oath arises as a matter of internalization. An oath creates a felt duty of obedience and obligation that resides within the breast of the oath-taker. Thus, the Constitution envisioned that oaths would work largely because most Americans were virtuous and would struggle to keep their oaths as a matter of honor and conscience. For some oath-takers, religious beliefs would reinforce the sanctity and sacredness of a sworn oath; for others, religion would have nothing to do with it. The document aimed to accommodate conscientious persons of all stripes by allowing any public servant unwilling or unable to swear an oath to instead commit himself to support the Constitution via an honor-based "affirmation."

In some situations, may a man of honor and conscience break his solemn oath? In certain contexts, must he do so? These were not purely abstract questions in Independence Hall in the summer of 1776, as men who had previously pledged allegiance to the British Crown now publicly renounced their old vows in the very process of making new promises to stand together in opposing the tyrant King George. Concerns about oaths and their moral boundaries also animated discussions in that legendary hall during the summer of 1787. Knowing that an out-of-touch government that asked too much and gave too little might lose its just claims to the people's allegiance, the Philadelphia framers aimed to build a new system that would tap into the deepest convictions of its citizens, a system in which honorable oath-takers would almost never have occasion to regret or renounce their vows. This new system strengthened itself not only by broadly enlisting public support via an extraordinary series of ratification elections in the late 1780s and routine elections thereafter, but also by requiring officials to bind themselves to the precise text that the people had endorsed. As we shall now see, the new system also built some bend into these bonds, enabling public officials and ordinary citizens in certain situations to follow their own consciences without thereby violating their legal oaths, rightly understood.

"Jury"

THE SYSTEM'S SUPPLE STRUCTURE was especially notable where jurors were concerned. The very word, "juror," suggested the high stakes involved and hinted at the subtle tension between oaths and law. In one sense, a proper "juror"—from the French *jurer* and the Latin *jurare*, to swear—was a person who honored his sworn oath to return a true verdict. (The word "verdict" meant a speaking of the truth.) Thus, anyone who swore falsely, betrayed his oath, or returned a false verdict was a "perjurer," with *per* referring to the Latin word for destruction. The word-stem *jur* also connoted law more generally, as reflected in, for example, the word "jurisprudence"— the study of law.

But if a criminal law enacted by men was profoundly unjust across the board, or if strict application of this law in a particular case would be profoundly unjust, would a juror who acted to indict or convict a defendant under that law be a false swearer to God or to some ultimate moral truth? In the converse situation, could a juror properly vote to indict or convict a man who had not violated the letter of any actual law on the books, but had indeed violated the true moral code as the juror understood that code?

America's Constitution has always treated these two cases differently, in keeping with other pro-defendant asymmetries in the criminal-justice system, such as the *Winship* rule that whenever reasonable doubt exists, a criminal defendant must be acquitted. Jurors in criminal cases have always enjoyed an absolute right to say no, and when the jury has said no, the no is decisive, and the defendant goes free. But jurors have never had symmetric authority to compel criminal punishment if other governmental actors favor mercy. In such cases, despite a jury's willingness to say yes to punishment, other actors, including judges, may properly say no, absolutely and irreversibly.[3]

The Constitution does not say all this in so many words. But this is the best way to understand the document in light of the post-Tudor history of the Anglo-American jury, a history familiar to the document's drafters and ratifiers. Even when seventeenth- and eighteenth-century English juries refused to convict defendants who seemed guilty to the presiding judges, English law treated the resulting acquittals as sacrosanct. When some judges tried to force jurors to return guilty verdicts, and/or to punish jurors for acquitting obviously guilty defendants, these judicial efforts were rebuffed—most famously in a 1670 lawsuit known as *Bushell's Case*, which made clear that the bench could neither coerce nor punish a jury bent on acquittal, even if the defendant's technical guilt under the law as written was obvious. Thus, if a resolute English jury believed that the defendant should prevail, it could vote its conscience with impunity, and the defendant would go free regardless of the views of the Crown or the bench.[4]

These jury privileges and immunities were acted out on a grand stage in 1688, when the soon-to-be-deposed King James II prosecuted certain Anglican clerics who had expressed opposition to his religious policies. While the trial judges disagreed among themselves about the relevant legal issues, the twelve jurors in the *Seven Bishops Case* unanimously acquitted, delivering one of the most celebrated rebukes to the Crown in English history and setting the scene for the Glorious Revolution that soon followed.

In more prosaic cases, English juries often showed mercy to guilty defendants by convicting prisoners only of noncapital offenses even when capital crimes had occurred. For example, certain acts of theft were punishable by hanging, but petty thefts received more lenient treatment. Officially, the difference between life and death hinged on the value of the stolen item, which was ostensibly a simple matter of fact to be decided by the trial jury. Exercising his conscience under the guidance of the presiding judge, many an English juror pretended that valuable goods were not so valuable in order to spare the life of a pitiable soul, a practice that Blackstone famously described as "a kind of pious perjury" that reflected the humanity and decency of English juries. Blackstone's memorable phrase is telling. In one sense, the jurors were acting falsely—committing perjury. But at an even higher level they were acting nobly and virtuously, conscientiously—piously.[5]

These basic English rules also applied in eighteenth-century America. In the 1730s, two successive New York grand juries refused to indict the publisher John Peter Zenger, who had printed tracts harshly critical of the colonial governor, William Cosby. When Cosby's attorney general used another legal device (an "information") to detour around grand jurors and trigger a criminal trial, the twelve-man trial jury famously acquitted, despite Zenger's technical guilt under extant libel law as expounded by the trial judge. The acquittal stuck and Zenger went free, thereby dramatizing the authority of pro-defendant jurors to uphold truth and justice (as they understood these things) against law (as understood by the judge). History repeated itself in the 1760s and early 1770s, as colonial grand jurors refused to indict and colonial trial jurors refused to convict leaders of the Stamp Act protests and other patriot speakers and printers.[6]

Though this jury power to just say no to a criminal indictment or prosecution was not explicitly written into the original Constitution or the Bill of Rights that immediately followed, it surely formed part of the implicit understanding of the words "jury" and "grand jury" that did appear in these documents. These words did not describe wholly new institutions being conjured into existence. (Compare, for example, the novel American presidency.) By using words with deep roots in American practice, the framers implied that these traditional American institutions would continue to operate under the new system much as they had before—unless, of course, some other implicit or explicit element of the Constitution indicated otherwise on some particular issue of jury law.

ALTHOUGH JURORS under traditional Anglo-American law had the last word whenever that word was "acquittal," the matter was entirely different if the jury wanted to convict. Through a variety of procedural techniques, English presiding judges could effectively spare defendants in the interests of justice, as the judges conscientiously understood those interests, even if jurors seemed bent on a more punitive course.

For starters, a trial judge who believed that a defendant did not merit punishment—as a matter of either strict legal interpretation or more equitable considerations of justice and fairness—could simply quash an indictment or use other procedural tools to dismiss a case before it ever reached the jury. Some of these judicial rulings functioned as acquittals, effectively ending the litigation in the defendant's favor; other kinds of rulings allowed the prosecutor to try again in a fresh proceeding. Alternatively, a trial judge could send a case to the jury with strongly pro-defendant commentary upon the evidence and pro-defendant legal instructions, reserving to himself authority to do justice even if the jury convicted. In any capital felony case in which the jury brought in a guilty verdict, the presiding judge could postpone ("respite") the execution and submit a report to the king, who thereupon issued a pardon as a matter of course.[7]

Different procedures applied in misdemeanor cases, but here, too, judges could effectively overrule jurors so long as these overrulings were pro-defendant. Thus the King's Bench regularly set aside jury verdicts of guilty, sometimes setting the defendant free and other times setting the case for retrial. This basic pro-defendant asymmetry was highlighted by Blackstone's *Commentaries*: "[I]n many instances, where contrary to evidence the jury have found the prisoner guilty, their verdict hath been mercifully set aside, and a new trial granted by the court of king's bench....But there hath yet been no instance of granting a new trial, where the prisoner was *acquitted* upon the first. If the jury therefore find the prisoner not guilty, he is then for ever quit and discharged of the accusation."[8]

"No person shall be held to answer for a...crime, unless..."

THE BASIC PRO-DEFENDANT ASYMMETRY within the judicial branch fits snugly within the Constitution's general structure, which situates the irreversible pro-defendant powers of judges and juries alongside irreversible pro-defendant powers of other government organs. In a nutshell, federal criminal-law punishments must clear a unique set of six hurdles—two in the legislature, two in the executive branch, and two in the judicial system. Unless the federal government clears each and every one of these hurdles, the criminal defendant walks free. Every hurdle is thus positioned in favor of the criminal defendant's life and liberty and in a manner that privileges the merciful consciences of the persons involved in ordaining and executing punishment. Animated by broad themes of populism, bodily liberty, and conscience, the system is designed so that no criminal will be subject to severe pain, extended imprisonment, or death unless the American people as a whole approve of the general punishment policy and various especially attentive and conscientious American individuals approve of the particular punishment imposed upon a given person.

NO PERSON MAY BE criminally punished in federal court for misconduct unless both houses of Congress have affirmatively voted to criminalize this particular misconduct. This basic structural postulate marks federal criminal law as distinct from both federal noncriminal law and state criminal law.[9]

On the noncriminal side of the docket, federal courts have long been free to fashion certain legal rules regulating misconduct even in the absence of specific congressional authorization. For example, the Supreme Court has itself promulgated a rule allowing victims of improper governmental searches and seizures to recover civil damages from the federal officers involved even though nothing in the Constitution or in federal statutory law explicitly creates this species of federal civil liability. This civil-liability rule is simply one component of what is generally referred to as "federal common law"—a set of judge-made regulations that Congress may modify or repeal but need not affirmatively enact in the first instance.[10]

Such "federal common law" has never had any proper place on the *criminal* side of the federal docket. No federal court may hold a federal officer criminally liable for an improper search or seizure, even one that flagrantly violates the Fourth Amendment, unless Congress affirmatively provides for such criminal liability. Structurally, this rule has guaranteed that no person may be sent to the gallows or to prison unless both houses of Congress—and especially members of the lower house, the one most directly accountable to the people—have specifically authorized this grave intrusion upon bodily liberty.

The mere ability of the Congress to overturn a judge-promulgated criminal law code would not have adequately guaranteed broad populist approval of federal penal policy. Imagine a counterfactual world in which federal courts were permitted to promulgate a (possibly harsh) federal criminal code on their own authority—a world in which Congress is allowed to repeal the judges' criminal code but need not affirmatively enact the code itself. In such a counterfactual world, harsh penal policies might prevail even if the American people as a whole broadly disapproved of these policies: Even if every single member of the House and nearly two-thirds of the Senate voted to repeal the judge-fashioned criminal code, the code could nevertheless remain in force so long as the president used his veto pen to side with the judges. But thanks to our Constitution's actual structure, bodily liberty has received far more protection. Noncriminalization is the universal starting point, a default rule that can be displaced only if all three elected branches—the House, the Senate, and the president—affirmatively agree that certain specified criminal misconduct justifies death or imprisonment.[11]

Many scholars have suggested that the Constitution's general requirement of bicameralism and presentment for ordinary lawmaking was designed to produce fewer federal laws—and especially fewer intrusive federal laws—than would have been generated by a single unicameral process with no possibility of veto. Stated this sweepingly, such suggestions overlook the fact that America's segmented lawmaking process can at times lead to more law, not less. If the House favors intrusive rule A while the Senate prefers intrusive rule B, and the president fancies intrusive rule C, perhaps nothing will pass all three chambers. But perhaps A, B, and C will all pass as part of an omnibus package. A priori, it is hard to say whether a three-pronged lawmaking process will lead to more or fewer intrusive rules.

Whether it leads to more or fewer laws in general, or more or fewer intrusive laws in particular, however, is not the point. This three-pronged system was designed to result in fewer *unconstitutional* or *unconscionable* laws than other systems. If any one of the three lawmaking chambers deems a particular proposal not merely intrusive but actually unconstitutional or truly unconscionable, then an omnibus bill including that proposal is not likely to pass—so long as each chamber comprises individuals of strong conscience and constitutional fidelity.

The structural principles that we have been analyzing distinguish federal *criminal* law (where judges may never take the initiative in defining and proscribing misconduct) from federal *civil* law (where judges may sometimes do so). These principles also differentiate *federal* criminal law from *state* criminal law, which has typically recognized the propriety of judge-fashioned common-law crimes. In almost no state has the judiciary been as insulated from popular sentiments as in the federal system, where judges reach the bench with no direct input from the lower house of Congress and then serve for life. If one key structural idea is that criminal law works best when it has broad popular support, it stands to reason that unelected and insulated federal judges cannot and should not play the same broad role that more democratically accountable state judges play in defining criminal liability.

THE ESPECIALLY STRICT REQUIREMENT of *legislative* bicameralism in federal criminal law is mirrored by unique rules of *executive* bicameralism that apply whenever potential bodily punishment is at issue.

Let's first recall the general rules that apply outside the criminal context. Ordinarily, even if a president strongly opposes a given statutory proposal to burden American citizens in some way, that burden might nonetheless win out. True, once the burden-creating statute passes both houses of Congress, a president can veto the bill. But Congress can override this veto, and after that the president's hands might well be tied. If the law specifically requires the president to take certain enforcement measures, the president must typically enforce the law, howsoever distasteful to him enforcement might be. If the president, after careful legal analysis, deems the burdensome statute not merely distasteful but affirmatively unconstitutional, perhaps he might initially decline to enforce the statute, in keeping with his oath to obey the Constitution above all else as the supreme law of the land. But if the Supreme Court later rules against the president's constitutional objections and orders him to carry out the law as written, any continued presidential refusal to enforce the statute would be virtually unprecedented, and might well merit presidential impeachment and removal. Moreover, the burdensome law might be structured so that presidential enforcement is unnecessary. Many federal noncriminal laws enable ordinary citizens outside the federal executive to sue directly to enforce the laws' commands. (Antitrust laws and antidiscrimination laws are obvious examples.) In all these ways, private citizens might be intruded upon even though the president emphatically opposes the intrusion.[12]

But within the special realm of federal criminal law, wholly different rules apply. Here, so long as a private citizen can count on the emphatic support of the president, the citizen's bodily liberty is absolutely safe from intrusion, even if Congress members and Supreme Court justices overwhelmingly favor the intrusion and oppose the president. If the intrusive bill in question is a criminal prohibition, the president has not one but two constitutional pens in his quiver—a veto pen and a pardon pen—and the latter pen cannot be overridden or overwritten by Congress or the Court. Thus, even after Congress has overridden the president's veto, and even after the Supreme Court has declared that the bill in question is constitutionally flawless, a president can still "just say no" to criminal punishment, and make that "no" stick, simply by providing a pardon to any private citizen whose conduct may have run afoul of the law. Assuming that the pardon issues in good faith—that it springs from the president's conscience and not, for example, from a bribe—no court could ever properly undo the pardon. Nor should any member of Congress think it appropriate to impeach and convict the president for the good-faith exercise of a power that was precisely designed to focus one honorable man's conscience and to invite him in the name of that conscience to just say no to bodily punishment.

The greater power to issue a criminal pardon generally subsumes the lesser power simply to decline to criminally prosecute. Although the latter is typically referred to as "prosecutorial discretion," it is best understood as a power of *non*prosecutorial discretion—an asymmetric and unilateral power to favor potential criminal defendants. Here, too, we see a sharp contrast between the rules that ordinarily apply to federal law and the especially protective rules operative in the sphere of federal *criminal* law. No one doubts that the Supreme Court may generally oblige the president to carry out a noncriminal statute as written, but the Court has never claimed for itself authority to oblige a president to prosecute a criminal case. Nor may Congress simply detour around an immovable president by deputizing private citizens to act as criminal prosecutors. America's Constitution does not permit private prosecutions, even as it does allow widespread private enforcement of noncriminal laws.[13]

Ordinary citizens do, however, have a role to play in criminal prosecutions, and this role further highlights the pro-defendant asymmetry of the criminal-justice system. In seeking to enforce federal *civil* statutes, a president typically need only manage persons within his own branch—persons generally appointed by him personally or by his underlings or his predecessors. As we saw in Chapter 9, so-called independent agencies are really executive-branch agencies of a certain sort. But if a president decides to enforce a *criminal* statute, he must persuade members of a truly independent agency—namely, a grand jury composed of ordinary citizens whom he did not pick and cannot remove. These citizens have every right and power to just say no to any proposed prosecution on the simple ground that they believe that prosecution would be unwise or unjust, even if technically lawful. Thanks to the explicit wording of the Fifth Amendment, if these citizen-jurors stand on conscience and just say no, no prosecution for serious federal (nonmilitary) crime can ever be brought, even if the House, the Senate, the president, and the judiciary are all pro-punishment.

Grand jurors thus share half of the power of nonprosecutorial discretion. Just as a president who says no can be reversed only by a later president (and even then only if the statute of limitations has not run), so, too, a grand jury that just says no can be reversed only by a later grand jury.

In short, the pro-defendant asymmetry visible in the special requirement of legislative bicameralism plays out in similar fashion within the executive branch. The upper and lower houses of Congress must both agree before any federal criminal law may exist; likewise, both the upper house of the executive branch (the president) and the lower house of the criminal executive-enforcement branch (the grand jury) must also both say yes. If any of these four houses says no—perhaps as a mere matter of policy or perhaps as a matter of conscience—that single no trumps all else. In this way, the Constitution aims to ensure that no serious American bodily punishment occurs without the blessing of the American body politic.

WITHIN THE THIRD BRANCH, a similar bicameral rule favoring criminal defendants applies: If either the upper judicial house (the bench) or the lower judicial house (the jury) sides with the criminal defendant, the defendant wins. As we have seen, eighteenth-century trial jurors could say no to punishment with irreversible finality; and so, too, could eighteenth-century judges, as a rule. If anything, this English approach, as described by Blackstone, is even more fitting in America, because this pro-defendant judicial bicameralism in criminal cases mirrors especially strict American rules for legislative bicameralism in criminal cases (rules that prohibit English-style common-law crimes) as well as especially strict American rules for executive bicameralism in criminal cases (rules that prohibit English-style private prosecutions and English-style evasions of grand juries via "information").

EARLY FEDERAL PRACTICES generally reinforced the Constitution's basic structure, and many of these practices have continued unbroken to the present day. American trial juries have always enjoyed the right and power to acquit against the evidence, with no reprisals against the nullifying jurors and no possibility for retrial of the defendant so long as the jurors have acted in good faith. (In a case where a defendant or his lawyer bribed the jury, perhaps the bought acquittal might properly be set aside on equitable grounds.) Likewise, American grand juries have always had complete discretion to nullify a proposed prosecution with impunity, and there is no easy end-run around this institution for ordinary federal prosecutions.* Good-faith presidential pardons are similarly sacrosanct. (Here,

---

* State prosecutions are a different matter. Many states do not require grand-jury indictments for all serious crimes, and the Fifth Amendment's rule for federal grand juries is one of the few provisions of the Bill of Rights that has not (at least, not yet) been incorporated against states. For details, see Chapter 4, n. 32 and accompanying text.

too, bribery would raise special issues.) Federal judges have always had unilateral power to stop a prosecution from even reaching the jury and to overrule any jury conviction deemed by the bench to be contrary to law or justice. The modern law of federal jurisdiction gives convicted defendants broader avenues to challenge their punishments on appeal and via habeas corpus than did the Founding-era rules of jurisdiction and appeal. And for the past two centuries, the American constitutional system has recognized that no person may be punished for a federal offense without the specific approval of the people's House. Thus, no treaty has ever created self-executing criminal sanctions; nor has any subsequent president emulated Washington's mistaken effort in the Neutrality Proclamation of 1793 to create federal criminal law by executive decree.[14]

In sum, the Constitution gave wide room to the consciences of the individuals personally responsible for inflicting pain or death on fellow creatures. The system privileged consciences inclined toward mercy. However, the precise situations warranting mercy were not, and probably could not have been, exhaustively codified in a compact document designed for the ages. Hence, the terse text structured several spaces for uncodifiable clemency and conscience.

"Amendment"

ALAS, THE FOUNDERS' ELABORATE CONSCIENCE-PROTECTING, mercy-tending, pro-defendant, pro-populist system currently lies in a state of modest doctrinal disrepair. Although criminal grand jurors remain free to just say no to an indictment if they find the statutorily authorized punishment overly harsh, these jurors are not always explicitly told of this conscience-based prerogative and its distinguished pedigree. Even worse, criminal trial jurors are sometimes today told (incorrectly) by the presiding judge that if the evidence points overwhelmingly toward guilt, they "must" convict. And they are almost never told that they have an absolute legal right to acquit even in cases of overwhelming guilt if they feel as a matter of conscience that the legal punishment is obscenely harsh. Nor are jurors told that they may properly engage in "pious perjury" by convicting on a lesser charge, even if the defendant is actually guilty of a greater charge, if they find the punishment for the greater charge unconscionably severe. Nor, in many cases, are jurors today told by the judge—or allowed to be told by defense attorneys—of the brutal penal consequences that may or must follow upon a jury verdict of guilty. These failures to tell jurors the whole truth are especially troubling in cases of rigid mandatory minimum-sentencing laws requiring strong punishment upon conviction, and draconian three-strikes laws that automatically send men to prison for life upon their third felony conviction, even if the felony in question is shoplifting a baseball glove. In these respects, Founding practice was different—more generous to defendants and more respectful of jurors.

True, the power of mercy and the particular authority of a jury to acquit against the evidence—to "nullify" a criminal law in the case at hand—may be abused. The specter of bigoted white jurors refusing to convict Klansmen and other murderous thugs who have preyed on black folk looms large in the minds of modern jury critics—and with good reason, given much of American history prior to the Second Reconstruction of the 1960s. Countless specific illustrations might be offered. Perhaps the most infamous involved the murder in the mid-1950s of Emmett Till, a black youth savagely beaten and then shot dead for having reportedly flirted with a white woman in a small town in the Mississippi Delta. The all-white jury took just sixty-seven minutes to deliberate before reporting its verdict of acquittal. One juror later said, "If we hadn't stopped to drink pop, it wouldn't have taken that long."[15]

The haunting image of racist verdicts such as this should remind us that faithful modern constitutionalists must do more than ponder the letter and spirit of Founding-era texts. Holistic interpreters must also take account of the vision underlying the three Reconstruction amendments that revolutionized race law in America and various twentieth-century amendments that expanded upon the Reconstruction vision. Although the terse amendatory clauses of the past century and a half do not detail precisely how the Founders' jury rules are to be modified, this textual underspecificity should not daunt us. Having already trained our senses to detect America's unwritten Constitution alongside its written counterpart in other contexts, we need simply to put these skills to work here.

As we have already glimpsed in previous chapters, the fact that post-

1789 Americans have added textual amendments as discrete and sequential postscripts to the original document poses a significant interpretive challenge. Almost no amendment fully enumerates which preceding words in the document must now be deemed wholly inoperative or must in certain respects bend to the amendment's letter and spirit. The precise manner in which words adopted in different decades and centuries are to be synthesized to form one single coherent Constitution is to some extent left... unwritten.

Thus arises a classic challenge of American constitutionalism: gauging the constitutionally proper gravitational pull of later amendments on earlier constitutional clauses.*

BEGIN AT THE BEGINNING: Many Founders were partial to local juries and somewhat skeptical of judges chosen and paid by the central government. The American Revolution had been won by a coalition of independent state governments arrayed against imperial officialdom. In the 1760s and 1770s, local juries and local militias staffed by American patriots had protected American liberties against judges picked by the king's men and against imperial redcoats who also danced to the king's tune.

Proposed in 1789 and ratified in 1791, the Bill of Rights reflected the localist spirit of 1776. It championed rights against the central government while saying nothing about rights against states and localities. It began with the words: "Congress shall make no law..." and ended with a Ninth Amendment that reinforced the limited scope of enumerated federal power and a Tenth Amendment that reserved various powers "to the States respectively, or to the people." The Second Amendment celebrated local militias as "necessary to the security of a free state," impliedly treating the central government's professional army as a constitutionally disfavored in-

---

* In this spirit, Chapter 4 traced how the first eight amendments needed to be refracted through the Fourteenth Amendment language of "privileges" and "immunities"—a refraction process in which Founding meanings sometimes bent as they passed through Reconstruction's prism; Chapter 7 pondered various ways in which the Nineteenth Amendment also implicitly bent earlier constitutional clauses and principles even though the amendment's words did not precisely enumerate the full scope of these implicit changes; and Chapter 10 aimed to show that section 2 of the Fourteenth Amendment had to be creatively reinterpreted in light of the later right-to-vote amendments.

strument. The Third Amendment likewise reflected special anxiety about a federal standing army in peacetime.

Four of the five remaining amendments explicitly or implicitly exalted the local militia's close cousin, the local jury.* The Fourth Amendment envisioned civil juries of the people protecting "the right of the people"—in particular, the people's right to be secure against unreasonable intrusions, a right that jurors would safeguard by hitting abusive government searchers and seizers with punitive damages in tort suits brought by victimized citizens. The Fifth likewise contemplated civil juries determining what compensation would be just whenever government took private property for public use. The Fifth also explicitly provided that no nonmilitary criminal defendant could be forced to face serious federal criminal charges "unless on a presentment or indictment of a Grand Jury." The amendment went on to strengthen the power of the criminal trial jury by making clear that any jury acquittal in a serious case would be final, because any second prosecution for the same offense would improperly place the defendant "twice in jeopardy of life or limb." The Sixth Amendment specified that criminal defendants had a right not only to a trial jury, but to a local jury, at that—a jury drawn from the "district" (though not necessarily the traditional "vicinage") where the crime had transpired. The Seventh Amendment promised to "preserve[]" the right of "trial by jury" in virtually all civil suits "at common law" and to limit the power of federal judges to overturn any fact properly tried by a civil jury.

FOUR SCORE AND SOME YEARS after the American Revolution, Reconstruction Republicans layered the Fourteenth Amendment atop the

---

* In many ways, the jury is to the judiciary what the militia is to the military. Both jurors and militiamen are amateurs counterbalancing professionals (judges and army soldiers, respectively); both juries and militias are organized locally; jury service and militia service are linked duties of citizenship (alongside voting, and both duties are mainly addressed to the subset of the population eligible to vote); both juries and militias typically elect their own officers (foremen and captains, respectively); both entities are classic embodiments of republican virtue. Both entities exist as points on a wider spectrum of kindred premodern law-enforcement bodies encompassing the neighborhood hue and cry, the local posse comitatus, the militia, the grand jury, and the trial jury. In some ways, militiamen can be seen as jurors with guns in their hands.

Founders' Bill of Rights. Like the Founders, the Reconstrutors valued juries, but theirs was a far more nationalistic vision.

Recall that in the very process of adopting the Fourteenth Amendment, Americans celebrated and redefined the role of the nation's army and subordinated the Founders' vaunted local militia. Beyond the military realm—indeed, across the board—the Reconstruction vision reposed more confidence in organs of the central government than did the Bill of Rights. Whereas the First Amendment had begun by stressing that "Congress shall make no law" of a certain sort, each of the Reconstruction Amendments ended by proclaiming that "Congress shall have power to enforce" the Reconstruction vision, which of course included at its very core the notion that "[n]o State shall make or enforce any law" violating fundamental rights as defined by national institutions.

The right to be tried by a jury was precisely one of these fundamental rights—a civil right that was thus properly incorporated against states thanks to the Fourteenth Amendment. But a mere civil right of criminal *defendants* offered insufficient protections to certain *victims* of crime—in particular, blacks—who were placed at risk if bigoted juries chose to wink at crimes committed against these vulnerable victims.

Enter the Fifteenth Amendment, which in 1870 promised to restructure both state and federal juries—civil, grand, and petit—in a manner designed to reduce the risk of racist jury nullification. The Founders had allowed states to choose juries howsoever they pleased, much as states had broad authority to define their electorates, subject only to the Article IV republican-government clause, which was never seriously enforced prior to 1860. And the war came—and came precisely because of antebellum America's failure to hold states to high republican standards. With the Fifteenth Amendment (which built on and extended earlier Reconstruction statutes requiring race-neutral voting laws in the old South), Republicans took direct aim at race discrimination in the domain of political rights: "The right of citizens of the United States to vote shall not be denied or abridged by the United States or by any State on account of race, color, or previous condition of servitude." Through this right-to-vote amendment, Republicans reconstructed not merely the ballot box but also the jury box. In neither venue would states be allowed to discriminate as they had before the Civil War. In theory, blacks would have an equal right to vote in every election and an equal right to serve on and vote in every jury—a principle expressly reaffirmed by a landmark 1875 congressional statute whose jury-trial provisions have remained in effect to the present day.[16]

In actual practice, much of the promise of the Fifteenth Amendment lay dormant until this amendment was effectively reawakened by the vigorous tag team of the Voting Rights Act of 1965 and the Warren Court. Prior to 1965, blacks in many parts of America—especially the Deep South—were kept off the voting rolls and out of the jury box, in unremedied defiance of the Constitution. Since 1965, the picture has dramatically improved. And wherever and whenever the full letter and spirit of the 1870 amendment, the 1875 act, and the 1965 act have been followed, racist jury nullification has not been a grave problem; blacks have been able to serve alongside whites in the jury box and thereby thwart racist nullification.

The root problem of racist jury nullification in cases such as the murder of Emmett Till was never the jury as such, nor nullification as such. It was racism pure and simple—and, in particular, racist rules that allowed all-white juries as a matter of course. Now that the jury box has truly opened itself to all races on equal terms, racist jury nullification has largely faded away as a decisive argument for depriving jurors of their traditional right to acquit against the evidence as a matter of conscience.

AND "RIGHT" IS THE RIGHT WORD. For more than two centuries, the deep logic of American constitutional law has recognized not merely the brute *power* of criminal trial juries to just say no and get away with it by escaping perjury charges, but also the legal *right* of these juries to acquit against the evidence—to "nullify" a particular criminal prosecution. This logic emerges from a simple side-by-side comparison of certain technical rules of civil and criminal procedure and a quick review of the asymmetric rules within criminal cases.

In a civil jury trial, if the evidence and testimony overwhelmingly establish the defendant's civil liability, the judge, on his own motion, may enter judgment against the defendant, without even submitting the matter to the jury. If the judge instead allows the case to go to the jury, he may in the process "direct"—order—the jury to find for the plaintiff, or he may cabin the jury by insisting that it answer a series of specific factual inquiries and thereby render a "special verdict" rather than a simple general verdict of "liable" or "not liable." In other situations, even after a jury has found for the defendant, the trial judge may simply set aside this verdict and enter his own verdict for the plaintiff, if indeed the defendant had no good legal justification. In still other cases, the judge may instead opt for a new trial, giving the plaintiff a second chance against the defendant.

Precisely and only because criminal juries have a legal right to acquit against evidence, judges in criminal cases have never had authority to do any of the things that they may automatically do on the civil side of the docket—in criminal law, there are no summary judgments, no directed verdicts, no special verdicts, no judgments notwithstanding the verdict, and no second prosecutions for the same offense. Or, to be more precise, judges have never had authority to do any of these things *to the detriment of the criminal defendant*. Bench rulings favoring criminal defendants—for example, summary judgments against the prosecution and decisions setting aside jury verdicts of guilty—have never been constitutionally prohibited.

Together, these and a cluster of other closely related legal doctrines add up to a clear, if implicit, constitutional right, and not merely a lawless power, of criminal juries to acquit against the evidence—to nullify a specific prosecution. These constitutional rules are about as well settled as any in America's Constitution, written or unwritten. Not only were these rules in place prior to the Founding, and thus embedded in the word "jury" as its role and rights were understood by the framing generation, but these rules have remained in place ever since as definitive glosses on the document.

THE QUESTION THUS BECOMES, if these are in fact the rules of America's Constitution, written and unwritten, why shouldn't jurors be told the truth about them? Some jurors (for example, all those who have read this book) will enter the jury box knowing these truths. Other jurors will arrive as blank slates. Still other jurors will come into courtrooms with garbled misunderstandings of first principles. This state of affairs betrays one the deepest purposes of jury trial, namely, the proper legal education of citizens as they are drawn into temporary public service. Juries should be devices to reconnect the people's law, the Constitution, with the people themselves. Instead, the status quo calls to mind an unhappy image of a Constitution that is in effect written in a foreign language known only to a few legal insiders. If modern America can Mirandize every criminal suspect taken into custody, surely we can Zengerize and Tillize every juror by properly informing her of her true legal rights and responsibilities.

Jury nullification thus needs to be brought into the open, with honest bench instructions and morally serious judicial commentary about this right and power. Ideally such judicial guidance would include explicit references to occasions when the past exercises of this right have become celebrated parts of the American story (as in the *Zenger* case) as well as to instances when jury nullification has been the shame of the nation (as in the *Till* case). The precise wording could emerge from the Supreme Court itself, much as the now-famous *Miranda* warnings built upon the Court's own opinion in *Miranda v. Arizona*. Alternatively, the Department of Justice, in cooperation with the American Bar Association, could compose a short video to be shown to all prospective grand jurors and petit jurors. Such a video would vindicate the essence of the American jury, reconnecting ordinary citizens to the Constitution and enlisting them in the grand American project of morally serious self-government.

Current practice, by contrast, does not invariably draw jurors into this project. Rather, modern officialdom all too often instrumentalizes and infantilizes jurors by disrespecting or derailing their moral judgment. When a juror finds a man guilty of having shoplifted a baseball glove and only later finds out from the local newspaper or a lawyerly acquaintance that what she really voted for in the jury room was to send this poor soul to prison for life (and at taxpayer expense), she is apt to feel ill-used—as is the defendant, of course. In such situations, the basic constitutional framework has been warped. To repeat, the very point of jury trial is to ensure that American penal policy, both in gross and in micro, commands broad support among the citizenry.

To see the problem from another angle, let us return to the key idea of *conscience*. Jurors are supposed to be persons of independent conscience, persons neither beholden to government officialdom nor tied to the defendant. Before dooming the defendant to death or severe bodily punishment, jurors need to assure themselves of the defendant's clear culpability, his guilt beyond a reasonable doubt—his guilt to a moral certainty. This high bar of required certitude serves to protect not only the lives, limbs, and liberty of innocent defendants, but also the consciences of the jurors themselves. For a juror to condemn a man to death in the face of real and substantial moral doubt about his guilt would be for the juror to possibly damn his own soul, to participate in a kind of judicialized murder. The high proof bar thus serves to salve the conscience of the juror, to enable him to sleep at night, and to respect himself and his government, even after having voted to inflict severe harm or death upon another human being.

But when the juror is not told what punishments she is actually voting to inflict and not told that she has a legal right to just say no and a legal duty to consult her conscience, then the moral foundations of the entire system begin to crumble.

THE FOUNDATIONS OF THE SYSTEM—or at least the foundations of the system as it needs to be reconceived in light of various right-to-vote amendments—also begin to crumble when lawyers are allowed to peremptorily challenge prospective jurors and thereby keep them out of the jury box. A peremptory challenge need not be justified; it can be exercised on a whim or a hunch or even because of a deep-seated prejudice entertained by a litigant or lawyer. That, indeed, is what makes such a challenge "peremptory" and what distinguishes it from a challenge for "cause"—that is, for juror bias asserted and established in the courtroom.

Although peremptory challenges were part of Founding-era practice, there is reason to suspect that in that era peremptories often functioned merely as polite challenges for cause. In a world characterized by small-town trials, many a prospective juror might have been a personal acquaintance—perhaps a friend, perhaps a rival—of the defendant, the prosecutor, and/or one of the witnesses. Proving actual disqualifying bias in such situations might have been legally difficult and socially awkward. Peremptories enabled lawyers to eliminate actual bias in a more graceful fashion. As America's population grew and juries were drawn from increasingly populous districts, the need for peremptory challenges declined. A lower percentage of prospective jurors was likely to have any personal connections to litigants or witnesses, and judges could easily dismiss all such persons for cause without seriously depleting or skewing the pool of prospective jurors.[17]

More importantly, the post-Founding constitutional amendments transformed jury service into a federal constitutional right. It was one thing for a prosecutor (or a defense attorney, for that matter) to peremptorily exclude dark-skinned jurors in, say, 1859. It was quite another thing to do so twenty years later, because by that time the Fifteenth Amendment was on the books, an amendment that promised an end to all racial exclusions in the political world, not just at the ballot box but in the jury box as well. The later Nineteenth, Twenty-fourth, and Twenty-sixth Amendments, written in nearly identical language, likewise promised jury equality alongside other forms of voting equality.

In 1965—the same year that saw the enactment of the transformative Voting Rights Act—the Warren Court announced that peremptory challenges could not be used systematically to keep blacks out of jury boxes. (Alas, the Court invoked the Fourteenth Amendment, rather than the more apt Fifteenth Amendment, as the basis for this limitation.) The post-Warren Court has begun to put teeth into this doctrine, extending it to prohibit sex-based peremptories (once again by relying on the Fourteenth Amendment, even though the Nineteenth would have been the more solid foundation for the extension).[18]

So-called "peremptory" challenges in the early twenty-first century are thus no longer peremptory. Prosecutors and defense attorneys must be prepared to show that they are not in fact bouncing citizens off juries because of the prospective jurors' race or sex or indeed for any other unconstitutional reason. In fact, clever lawyers seeking to win cases do use race and sex all the time in exercising their allotted peremptory challenges, while pretending that nothing of the sort is happening in the hallowed halls of justice. Full vindication of the post-Founding right to vote will be achieved when peremptories are abolished altogether—a move that Justice Thurgood Marshall called for long ago and that has received more recent reinforcement from Justices Stephen Breyer and David Souter. Voting registrars and poll workers are not allowed to peremptorily deny adult resident citizens their basic right to vote on Election Day; neither should trial lawyers be allowed to deny these same individuals their basic right to serve and to vote on juries when duly summoned.[19]

FULLY RECONSTRUCTED JURIES OF THE FUTURE will feature more demographic diversity than ever before, and this unprecedented diversity may well require modification of the Founding ideal of jury unanimity.

Jurors from disparate backgrounds and with differing consciences may need to agree to disagree about some things. A sensible response to this unprecedented degree of jury diversity would allow nonunanimous criminal jury verdicts, but only after a minimum period of full deliberation—say, three days for a routine case, longer for a case of unusual complexity. Such a system would give an initial dissenting juror—movie buffs should recall Henry Fonda's character in *Twelve Angry Men*—a fair opportunity to make his case to his fellow jurors, while allowing a strong supermajority to ultimately overrule a truly eccentric minority and reach closure. In this reconstructed regime, unanimity would be required for any verdict brought in within the initial deliberation period. After the expiration of that period, and once the jury has reported that no more deliberations would be fruitful, a final vote of, say, nine to three should suffice to convict, but anything short of this should count as a case-ending acquittal.

This openly asymmetrical voting rule would give some criminal defendants more protection than they receive under the current regime. Federal juries today must be unanimous to convict *or acquit*.* Any vote short of unanimity counts as a hung jury permitting retrial. Thus, even if a jury today hangs in the defendant's favor—say, with eleven votes favoring acquittal and only one vote to convict—the defendant may be put through the wringer again and face death or imprisonment if unanimously convicted in a second trial.

Would nonunanimous juries pass constitutional muster? The Constitution does not explicitly require unanimity, but of course proper analysis cannot simply leave it at that. After all, the document does not explicitly authorize jury acquittals against the evidence. Nor does the Constitution explicitly require a jury of twelve persons. But surely most Americans at

---

* State criminal juries are a different story, and some states do not require unanimity. In this corner of doctrine, a fractured Court in a 1972 case, *Apodaca v. Oregon*, in effect held that the criminal-jury rules of the Sixth Amendment apply more flexibly against states than against the federal government. As we shall see, a better approach would openly acknowledge that the Sixth Amendment, as reconstructed by later right-to-vote amendments, does not invariably require unanimity, even in federal proceedings.

the Founding understood that these elements were built into the very word "jury." The petit jury, as the Founding generation knew and used this institution, comprised twelve men empowered to find guilt or to just say no as a matter of fact or conscience. By the same token, some might argue that the word "jury" as understood at the Founding implicitly connoted a body that needed to act unanimously in any criminal trial.

Modern Supreme Court case law has garbled these matters and has slighted various original understandings. The most egregious garbling has occurred in case law concerning the proper size of a petit jury. May a jury properly consist of five persons? Certainly not: Five or fewer persons do not a jury make, said the Court in the 1970s. But a six-person jury—that's okay, said the Court in that very same decade.[20]

Huh? The distinction between five and six is of course completely arbitrary, with almost nothing behind it. Where in heaven's name did this line come from?

Of course, the line between eleven and twelve might also look arbitrary as a matter of pure logic—but this line has a vast amount of pre- and post-Founding history behind it. Virtually all eighteenth-century criminal juries in England, the American colonies, and the newly independent states had twelve members. Thus, the number twelve was implicit in the word "jury" itself, as that word was generally understood and embodied in 1787: A criminal trial jury was, in a phrase dating back to the seventeenth century, "*twelve* good men, and true." The post-1787 gloss placed on the word "jury" by early and unbroken federal practice, and the kindred practices of almost every state, operating under similarly worded state constitutions, further confirm that twelve is the magic number. Although some erosion occurred in various states long after the Founding, even in 1970, when the Court read the Sixth Amendment to permit six-person juries in serious felony cases, the overwhelming majority of states—forty-five, to be precise, accounting for roughly 85 percent of the nation's population—used twelve-person juries for all serious crimes, as did the federal government.[21]

The issue of jury unanimity, however, is rather different from the issue of jury size. First, any move away from unanimity does not logically unravel in the same way that any move away from twelve jurors does. Once a jury is allowed to comprise fewer then twelve members, there is no logical and principled stopping point. (Yes, modern Court case law stops the unraveling at the number six, but there is absolutely no principled or logical basis for this made-up number.) But there are indeed logical and principled stopping points short of unanimity. Surely a criminal conviction requires at least a majority vote—at least seven of the twelve jurors—if the pro-defendant asymmetries of *Winship* and of the criminal-justice system as a whole mean anything. Indeed, at least eight out of twelve votes would seem to be structurally required to convict: It should take at least as high a percentage vote to take a man's life or to put him in prison as it does to oust him from office in an impeachment trial (where the Constitution requires a two-thirds vote to convict, and asymmetrically treats any lesser vote as an acquittal).

Second, for centuries actual practice has permitted nonunanimous verdicts of a certain sort. As previously noted, whenever the first jury hangs, the government has generally been allowed to reprosecute the defendant and to convict him if all twelve jurors in the second trial so vote. But to say that the jurors were truly unanimous in these situations is to indulge in a counting trick. The claimed unanimity simply ignores the juror or jurors (perhaps eleven of them!) in the first trial who voted against conviction.

Most important of all, moving away from jury unanimity may simply be the necessary consequence of full enforcement of the post-Founding right-to-vote amendments. Once modern America, in a dramatic break with the Founders, fully guarantees all adult resident (nonfelon) citizens a federal constitutional right to vote, on juries and elsewhere, the increased demographic diversity on juries resulting from this full implementation of post-Founding amendments may well entail further necessary adjustments of the Founders' jury vision. The Founders' juries could typically reach unanimity in part because so much of American society was excluded from these decision-making bodies. Once all are properly included, in keeping with post-Founding amendments, it may be as unrealistic to expect jury unanimity as it is to expect House unanimity or Senate unanimity—or Supreme Court unanimity, for that matter.

"Judges"

SPEAKING OF THE COURT, let us now conclude our general discussion of conscience by turning away from jurors and toward judges and justices. What role does and should conscience play in judicial decision-making?

Most lawyers and scholars would probably agree that a judge interpreting the Constitution may properly consult her conscience as a tiebreaker if the purely legal sources at hand are perfectly balanced. If all the legal considerations are in exact equipoise, something is needed to tip the scales, and the judge's heartfelt sense of right and wrong seems a far better tiebreaker than, say, a coin flip. Also, the judge's social conscience provides a lens through which she views all legal materials. In deciding, for example, whether a particular patch of statutory or constitutional text truly means what it seems to say, background understandings of social conscience and common sense come into play. It is precisely factors such as these that underlie the Blackstonian rules of interpretation demanding that the law must speak with distinctive clarity before it will be read to make a man a judge in his own case, to punish conduct that was innocent when committed, or to prevent a defendant from introducing reliable evidence of his innocence at trial—or, indeed, to do any number of things that would seem to the faithful interpreter to be absurd as a matter of common sense or common decency.[22]

Structurally, the judicial conscience should play an especially large role in the criminal-justice system. Judges may not be better than the rest of us in deciding the excruciatingly hard moral questions raised by, say, abortion or assisted suicide, but they do have special expertise concerning a criminal-justice system that operates in their own courtrooms and that pivots on their own personal signatures on death warrants and harsh prison sentences. Having wrongly prevented jurors from giving full vent to conscience and mercy, judges should in various situations use their own consciences to fill the conscience gap that they themselves have helped to create.

For example, trial judges should be recognized as having broad discretion to be merciful to criminal defendants. *Cruel* and unusual punishments are expressly prohibited by the Constitution; *merciful* and unusual punishments are not. Although current doctrine often gives effect to trial-court mercy, it does so in indirect and legalistic ways that are simultaneously overbroad and underinclusive. Currently, when a trial judge at the close of evidence dismisses the jury and declares that a criminal defendant is "acquitted," that acquittal is immune from appellate review and reversal—even if the acquittal was based on a clear statutory misreading or other legal gaffe on the part of the trial judge. (Imagine, for example, that the trial judge erroneously thinks that the criminal statute applies only in cases of premeditated misconduct, when the statute actually contains no such premeditation requirement.) There is nothing in the double-jeopardy clause, rightly read, or in first principles of justice, giving a defendant a vested legal right to walk free whenever the trial court misreads the statute books. The Constitution could instead be sensibly read to allow appellate courts to treat all pro-defendant dismissals by trial judges as provisional—as "pre-acquittals" that ripen into true case-ending acquittals only when the underlying legal rulings are confirmed as legally correct by the appellate bench. Going too far in the other direction, current doctrine today withholds from a trial judge a general power to openly set the defendant free on the simple ground that this judge—the only judge who has heard all the evidence and seen the defendant herself—sincerely believes that harsh punishment would be utterly unconscionable.

Similarly, Supreme Court justices today who are morally troubled by certain death-penalty cases that come before them often feel obliged to announce that a death sentence in the case at hand would be "unusual" given the underlying crime and the circumstances of the defendant, when what they really sense is that, in their personal view, a death sentence would be unconscionable—something that they cannot in good conscience personally sign on to. In recent decades, four justices—William Brennan, Thurgood Marshall, Harry Blackmun, and John Paul Stevens—at various times and with various degrees of absolutism, have condemned the death penalty across the board. Perhaps these condemnations are better understood as personal statements of conscience than as earnest interpretations of society-wide morality and practice. Consider the strikingly personal words of Harry Blackmun, who, after years of struggling with the death penalty, announced near the end of his tenure on the bench that he would henceforth vote against any capital sentence that came before him: "From this day forward, I no longer shall tinker with the machinery of death."[23]

A heartfelt statement like this is closer to judicial civil disobedience than to standard judicial review. Like other forms of civil disobedience, judicial statements of this sort are dangerous medicine. In a well-functioning democratic society, such civil disobedience must ultimately aim to prick the consciences of the disobedient's fellow citizens. As an act of one conscientious objector appealing to the consciences of other presumptively virtuous members of society, this disobedience should be openly expressed, and the disobedient should be prepared to suffer personal consequences if his fellow citizens strongly disagree. Indeed, this courageous willingness to suffer personally is part of the principled logic and nobility of civil disobedience.

Whereas a simple good-faith legal interpretation of the word "unusual" is obviously not a proper basis for impeachment, the case of a judge who openly and routinely votes against death sentences as a pure matter of personal conscience seems different. Here, America's unwritten constitutional traditions offer no ironclad immunity from the possibility of impeachment—personal punishment for a personal stand. What the good-faith judge hears as the voice of conscience may strike some congresspersons as judicial willfulness. House and Senate members might plausibly think that a judge who cannot in good conscience apply the criminal law as written should simply recuse himself, rather than sit in judgment and nullify the law for purely personal reasons. In an ideally functioning system, however, the threat of actual impeachment should be extremely remote, so long as all political actors understand the special role that conscience and mercy may properly play in the criminal-justice system.

It must be stressed that encouraging judges to openly disregard certain harsh criminal laws or sentences in cases of conscience is very different from inviting judges to invalidate laws generally because of the judges' policy views or even their moral compasses. What is under consideration here is a special category of cases where judges (1) with their own hands are being asked to do things they consider (2) absolutely unconscionable (as opposed to merely unwise) to (3) vulnerable human beings (4) who are personally standing before them in the courtroom, and (5) are all the more vulnerable because the judiciary itself has erroneously eliminated various rights of jurors to give full effect to conscience and mercy.

PERHAPS UNWITTINGLY, THE BEST CASE for judicial (and juror) conscience in the criminal-justice system was made by a jurist who is well known for his hard-nosed view of the law and the ordinary judicial role:

> What if some state should enact a new law providing public lashing, or branding the right hand, as punishment for certain criminal offenses? Even if it could be demonstrated unequivocally that these measures were not cruel and unusual measures in 1791, and even though no prior Supreme Court decision has specifically disapproved them, I doubt whether any federal judges—even among the many who consider themselves originalists—would sustain them against eighth amendment challenge....I confess that in a crunch I may prove a faint-hearted originalist. I cannot imagine myself, any more than any other federal judge, upholding a statute that imposes the punishment of flogging.

With this public confession in a 1988 address to law students, Antonin Scalia outed himself as not merely "a faint-hearted originalist" but also a good-hearted human being. The long-term success of America's system of government depends in no small part on the willingness of good-hearted humans to serve as judges and justices. Although no explicit clause in the terse text itself says so in so many words, America's Constitution should thus be read to allow, and even to invite, judges (and others) to just say no to savage punishments, and to do so in the name of conscience and humanity.

CHAPTER 12

ENVISIONING THE FUTURE

America's Unfinished Constitution

THE LAST ASPECT OF AMERICA'S UNWRITTTEN CONSTITUTION that we shall explore is the Constitution still to be written, the hoped-for Constitution of 2020—and of 2121 and 2222.

What should our future Constitution contain? What in fact will it contain? Must all momentous changes be accomplished by express textual amendments, or could some transformative revisions occur through other—unwritten—reform processes? If political and legal power in America today is in certain respects unfairly distributed, could the individuals and institutions currently benefiting from this unfair status quo ever be induced to support justice-seeking reforms? Is it truly realistic to think that the future will overcome the iniquities of the present?

AT FIRST, IT MIGHT BE WONDERED whether anything truly *constitutional* can be said about which future amendments should be adopted. After all, We the People are free to adopt just about any amendments we like. On one view, the existing Constitution says very little of a binding nature about what the future Constitution ought to look like.

What this view misses is that America's Constitution is designed not merely to bind but also to enlighten. Even if the written Constitution merely mandates, its unwritten twin teaches. Yes, we today are free to change the Constitution in almost any direction, but we are also free not to do so. In exercising this vast freedom and responsibility, we would be wise to note that some proposed changes would radically reverse the trajectory of our constitutional story thus far, whereas others would fulfill the existing Constitution's spirit, even as they changed its letter. Careful study of the past can guide and persuade us, giving our generation powerful reasons for preferring certain sorts of proposed amendments over other sorts.

Thus, future amendments to criminalize flag-burning or to restrict the equality rights of same-sex couples should be viewed with special skepticism because these amendments would do violence to the trajectory of the American constitutional project over the past two hundred years. By contrast, an amendment to allow certain immigrant Americans to be eligible for the presidency should be viewed more favorably, precisely because it would be a far better fitting next chapter to our unfolding constitutional saga.

Of course, not all important elements of American governance have left explicit marks in the terse text. For example, it is virtually unthinkable that a modern state legislature would itself pick presidential electors, with no regard for the views of the voters. But the formal constitutional text would allow this result; over the centuries, the actual power of the people on presidential Election Day has come about informally, via norms and customs. Dramatic future reforms of our presidential election system could likewise arise informally, without the need for a formal constitutional amendment. Under our current written Constitution, it is easy to imagine a way—two ways, in fact—by which Americans in the year 2020 could pick presidents by direct national popular election.

Studying how our existing Constitution was in fact enacted, how it has actually been glossed by past interpreters and implementers, and how it truly operates today can also help us to make sound scientific predictions about which amendment proposals have the best odds of prevailing in the days and decades ahead. Precisely because state constitutions closely mirror their federal counterpart, the fifty states are the most likely laboratories in which future federal constitutional reforms will initially be tested. Precisely because America has a party-based system of government, successful amendment proposals will typically need to align with the interests of America's two major political parties.

And whenever certain justice-seeking amendment proposals would run counter to current entrenched interests, we must keep in mind one extraordinary but largely unnoticed tool that earlier reformers used to overcome some of the injustices of their era—and that today's reformers can use to right the wrongs of our own times.

"Amendments...shall be valid...as Part of this Constitution"

FROM THE FOUNDING TO THE PRESENT, America's written Constitution has traced a clear and remarkable trajectory, visible at every moment of enactment and amendment along the way. With the ill-fated exception of Prohibition, none of its amendments has aimed to diminish liberty or reduce equality. On the contrary, most amendments have expanded freedom and egalitarianism.

So, yes, Americans today are free to amend the Constitution to criminalize flag-burning, and thus repudiate the basic constitutional principle that sovereign, self-governing citizens have a robust right to mock basic symbols of government authority. Americans are also free to amend the Constitution to ban gay marriages, and thereby constrict the scope of the grand idea that government should not demean a person because of his or her birth status—because she was born out of wedlock or he was born black or she was born female or he was born gay. But these illiberal amendments would be radical departures from our national narrative thus far.

Here, then, is a classic *conservative* argument for substantively *liberal* amendments: Most of the amendments from the Founding to the present were adopted by the liberals of their era—liberty-loving supporters of the Bill of Rights, Reconstruction Republicans, early twentieth-century Progressives, and late twentieth-century crusaders for civil rights.

THE UNITED STATES SENATE held a hearing on October 5, 2004, to consider a proposed constitutional amendment—then known as Senate Joint Resolution 15—that would allow long-standing naturalized citizens to run for president.

I was one of the expert witnesses invited by the Senate to testify at that hearing. As a child, grandchild, and spouse of immigrant Americans, I had (and continue to have) my own personal views about American immigration policy. However, I was being asked to testify not as a second-generation American but as a constitutional scholar. So I tried to analyze how Senate Resolution 15 would fit into the larger story of American constitutionalism thus far.

I testified that although the proposed amendment would surely change the existing rules, it would do so in a pro-immigrant direction—*just as the Founders themselves changed older English rules in pro-immigrant ways*. Indeed, I went a step further: Given that the reasons the eighteenth-century Founders themselves barred certain naturalized citizens from running for president no longer apply in the twenty-first century, modern Americans would best *vindicate* the spirit of the Constitution by formally *amending* it.

I pointed out that the Founders' Constitution was, by the standards of its time, hugely pro-immigrant. Under the famous English Act of Settlement of 1701, no naturalized subject in England could ever serve in the House of Commons, or Lords, or the Privy Council, or in a wide range of other offices. The Constitution repudiated this tradition across the board, opening the House, Senate, cabinet, and federal judiciary to naturalized and native citizens alike. Seven of the thirty-nine signers of the Constitution at Philadelphia were foreign-born, as were countless thousands of the voters who helped ratify the Constitution in the enactment process that gave birth to the document. Immigrants accounted for eight of America's first eighty-one congressmen, three of our first ten Supreme Court justices, four of our first six secretaries of the treasury, and one of our first three secretaries of war. Only the presidency and vice presidency were reserved for birth-citizens, and even this reservation was softened to recognize the eligibility of all immigrants who were already American citizens in 1787— men who had proved their loyalty by remaining in or coming to America during the Revolution.[1]

Of course, these generally pro-immigrant Founders did exclude later immigrants from the presidency. But they did so because some at the time feared that a scheming foreign earl or duke might cross the Atlantic with a huge retinue of loyalists and a boatload of European gold, and then try to bully or bribe his way into the presidency. In a young America that lacked campaign-finance rules, when a fledgling New World democracy was struggling to establish itself alongside an Old World dominated by monarchy and aristocracy, this ban on future foreign-born presidents made far more sense than it does in the twenty-first century.[2]

In 2004, I argued that a rule widening presidential eligibility would not only vindicate the Founders' general principles of immigrant equality but also nicely fit the trajectory of post-Founding amendments. By treating naturalized citizens as the full equals of natural-born citizens, and by allowing a person of obvious merit to overcome a legal impediment created merely because he or she was born in the wrong place at the wrong time or to the wrong parents, the proposed amendment would widen and deepen the grand principle of birth equality at the heart of the Fourteenth Amendment. By making a new class of Americans eligible to be president, the proposed amendment would also echo and extend the spirit of the Fifteenth and Nineteenth Amendments, which entitled blacks and women not merely to vote on equal terms on Election Day but also to be voted for on equal terms and to vote and veto equally in matters of governance.

In short, I argued in 2004, and I continue to believe today, that what the suffragist movement did for women, America should now do for naturalized citizens. This country should be more than a land where everyone can grow up to be…governor.

THE VERY STRUCTURE of these 2004 hearings highlighted a basic teaching of America's Constitution—namely, that successful amendments must typically win bipartisan support. The sponsor of Senate Joint Resolution 15 was a leading conservative Republican, Utah Senator Orrin Hatch, who had enlisted the formal support of leading liberal Democrats such as the House Judiciary Committee's ranking minority member, John Conyers. Another leading liberal Democrat, Vermont Senator Patrick Leahy, who has jousted with Senator Hatch on many issues over many years, had this to say about the proposed Hatch Amendment in the hearings: "I believe this amendment is far worthier of consideration than the amendments the Chairman has made a priority during this Congress—the Federal Marriage Amendment [banning gay marriage] and the Flag Desecration Amendment [allowing the criminalization of flag-burning]."

In turn, Hatch himself reached across the aisle in his own testimony, noting that the current rules of presidential eligibility had excluded highly credentialed patriots of both parties—for example, the Republican Henry Kissinger and the Democrat Madeleine Albright. Although Hatch did not explicitly refer to the proverbial elephant in the room—foreign-born Republican Arnold Schwarzenegger, who had recently been elected governor of California, the home base of three of the seven most recent Republican presidents—the senator did mention and quote a rising foreign-born Democratic star: "Michigan Governor Jennifer Granholm, who was born in Canada, also supports this amendment. She explained: 'You can't choose where you are born, but you can choose where you live and where you swear your allegiance.'"

Precisely because America's Constitution is a partisan Constitution—indeed, a bipartisan Constitution, with two entrenched parties, neither of which typically has enough votes in Congress and the states to push an amendment through on its own—successful constitutional amendments in the foreseeable future must follow the bipartisan strategy exemplified by Senator Hatch in 2004.

Nothing has yet become of Hatch's proposed amendment, perhaps because the politics of immigration have become more radioactive over the past eight years, especially within Hatch's own Republican Party, and because the election of Barack Obama in 2008 intensified anxiety in certain segments of Hatch's party about possibly nefarious foreign influences over American presidential elections. (Obama's Kenyan father was not an American citizen when the future president was born in the state of Hawaii in 1961.) But the long-term prospects for an eventual amendment along the lines of Hatch's proposal remain good, because it is easy to imagine a future moment when both parties will find it politically advantageous to compete for the allegiance of immigrants and their allies, just as there were many past moments when both parties found it in their interest to demonstrate their liberality toward women and blacks.

"The person having the greatest Number of votes for President, shall be President"

CAREFUL STUDY OF OUR EXISTING CONSTITUTION and its history can also help us to identify areas where dramatic changes can occur even without formal textual amendments.

For example, the manner of selecting presidents over the years has shifted substantially in various ways not explicitly codified in the written Constitution. As late as 1820, it was a relatively common practice for state legislatures to pick presidential electors themselves, without soliciting the presidential preferences of the state's electorate. Today, it is almost impossible to imagine a state doing this, but this sea change in actual practice has come about as a result of ordinary laws and established customs rather than a formal textual amendment. Similarly, long before the Seventeenth Amendment formally decreed that state voters would directly elect United States senators, political parties and states had begun to devise a series of subconstitutional mechanisms approximating this result.[3]

With these two examples of past informal change in mind, on December 28, 2001, I posted an essay on a website in order to illustrate just how much additional change in America's current system of presidential election is similarly imaginable in the absence of a formal textual amendment. The essay was not much more than a theoretical daydream—a "thought experiment"—but several years later, a variant of this daydream, the National Popular Vote (NPV) Initiative, actually began to take shape as part of a serious national political movement to reform the electoral college. As I now write these words in mid-2012, eight states and the District of Columbia, collectively comprising 132 electoral votes—49 percent of the magic 270 needed to activate the plan—have formally ratified the NPV Initiative.*

What follows is a revised version of my 2001 daydream, updated to take account of the intervening census of 2010.

IMAGINE THIS: Americans could pick the president by direct national election, in 2016, 2020, and beyond, without formally amending our Constitution.

A small number of key states—eleven, to be precise—would suffice to put a direct-election system into effect. Alternatively, an even smaller number of key persons—four, to be exact—could approximate the same result, with a little help from their friends.

Begin with the key-state scenario. Article II of the Constitution says that "[e]ach state shall appoint, in such Manner as the Legislature thereof may direct," its allotted share of presidential electors. Each state's legislature thus has discretion to direct how state electors are appointed. The legislature is theoretically free simply to name these electors itself. It is likewise free to direct by law that electors be chosen by direct popular state vote, winner-take-all. This is what almost all states do today.

So, too, each state legislature is free to direct that its state electors be chosen by direct popular national vote. Each state could thus pass the

---

* At the same time that I was daydreaming, so was Professor Robert Bennett. See Robert W. Bennett, "Popular Election of the President Without a Constitutional Amendment," *Green Bag 2d* 4 (2001): 241; Robert W. Bennett, "State Coordination in Popular Election of the President Without a Constitutional Amendment," *Green Bag 2d* 5 (2002): 141.

following statute: "This state shall choose a slate of electors loyal to the presidential candidate who wins the national popular vote." The eleven most populous states together now have 270 electoral votes, exactly the majority needed to win (out of a total of 538). Thus, if all eleven passed this statute, the presidency would go to the candidate who won the national popular vote.

For those who are counting, the eleven states are California (with 55 electoral votes), Texas (38), New York (29), Florida (29), Pennsylvania (20), Illinois (20), Ohio (18), Michigan (16), Georgia (16), North Carolina (15), and New Jersey (14). There is nothing magical about these eleven states; advocates of direct national election need not draw the poker equivalent of a royal flush. If some of the big eleven were to opt out, their places could be filled by any combination of smaller states with as many (or more) total electoral votes. The number eleven is highlighted merely to illustrate how few states might be needed, in theory, to effectuate direct national election.

It's worth pausing to let this soak in. Under the Constitution's Article V, a constitutional amendment providing for direct national election would as a practical matter require two-thirds support in the House of Representatives, a two-thirds vote in the Senate, and the further support of thirty-eight state legislatures. Thus, under the Constitution, any thirteen states—even the thirteen tiniest—could block an Article V amendment. In contrast, our hypothetical plan could succeed even if as many as thirty-nine states and Congress (which directs how the District of Columbia's three electors are to be chosen) opted out.

If the eleven biggest states were to pass our law, an odd theoretical possibility would arise: A candidate could win the presidency, by winning the national popular vote, even if he or she lost in every one of these big states! (Imagine a scenario where the candidate narrowly loses in each of these states, but wins decisively most other places.) Should this theoretical possibility deter big states from passing this law?

After all, the current electoral-college landscape reflects an effort by virtually every state to maximize its own clout by awarding all of its electoral votes to the candidate who wins the state, rather than dividing its electoral votes proportionately among candidates based on their percentage shares of the statewide popular vote. Take Pennsylvania, with its twenty electoral votes. The Keystone State has traditionally been a "battleground" jurisdiction in the presidential sweepstakes, a state in which one party rarely bests the other by a wide margin. A proportional-voting Pennsylvania would likely have a maximum of four electoral votes truly at stake—the difference between a 12–8 blowout victory and an 8–12 blowout defeat. This would make Pennsylvania no more important than a tiny winner-take-all state like Rhode Island (offering either a 4–0 win or a 0–4 defeat). A winner-take-all Pennsylvania means that not four but twenty electoral votes are at stake, so candidates must pay more attention to the state. For Pennsylvania to abandon winner-take-all when Rhode Island and almost all other states are retaining it would be the electoral equivalent of unilateral disarmament.

A similar concern might discourage Pennsylvania from unilaterally embracing our envisioned national-popular-vote law. This law, too, is a form of unilateral disarmament, telling a candidate not to worry about winning votes in Pennsylvania. Indeed, a candidate could lose Pennsylvania's popular vote badly and still get all of its electoral votes by winning nationwide. Even worse, Pennsylvania would be unilaterally disarming with no assurance that the presidency would in fact go to the national-popular-vote winner. Acting alone, Pennsylvania cannot guarantee that its twenty electoral votes would be enough to put the national-popular-vote winner at or over the 270 electoral-vote mark.

But Pennsylvania need not act unilaterally. Its law could provide that its electors will go to the national-popular-vote winner if and only if enough other states follow suit. Until that happens, Pennsylvania and every other likeminded state could continue to follow current (self-aggrandizing) methods of choosing electors. Thus, our revised model state law would look something like this: "This state shall choose a slate of electors loyal to the presidential candidate who wins the national popular vote, if and only if other states, whose electors taken together with this state's electors total at least 270, also enact laws guaranteeing that they will choose electors loyal to the presidential candidate who wins the national popular vote."

Acting in this coordinated way, a consortium of states with electoral votes adding up to 270 would not really be disarming themselves. Although it would be theoretically possible for a candidate to win a national vote while losing in all (or almost all) of the consortium states, this is an unrealistic scenario. In general, candidates would pay attention to consortium states collectively comprising roughly half or more of the American electorate. As a practical matter, one couldn't win nationally without winning, or at least coming very close to winning, lots of states.

Of course, any coordinated state-law effort would require specifying key issues: Majority rule or plurality rule? How should recounts and challenges be handled? It would be hard to rely completely on the laws and courts of each state, many of which might not be part of the cooperating group of states. For example, the national vote might be close even though the state vote in some noncooperating state was not, and that state might refuse to allow a state recount. Indeed, a noncooperating state might theoretically try to sabotage the system by refusing to allow its citizens to vote for president! What if some state let seventeen-year-olds vote in an effort to count for more than its fair share of the national total? Also, even if all states generally behaved themselves, wouldn't the considerable variation in actual state election administration—for example, with some states allowing easy registration and absentee voting and other states adopting much stricter rules—mock the reformist idea of genuine equality for all American votes and voters? And what about Americans who live abroad or in the federal territories?

These questions suggest an even more mind-boggling prospect: Our national-vote system need not piggyback on the laws and machinery of noncooperating states at all! Let these noncooperating states hold their own elections, but so long as the number of their electors adds up to less than 270, these elections would be sideshows. The cooperating states could define their own rules for a uniform "National Presidential Vote" system. In that case, our law would read something like this: "Section 1. This state shall choose a slate of electors loyal to the presidential candidate who wins the 'National Presidential Vote,' if and only if other states, whose electors taken together with this state's electors total at least 270, also enact laws guaranteeing that they will choose electors loyal to the presidential candidate who wins the 'National Presidential Vote.' Section 2. The 'National Presidential Vote' shall be administered as follows...."

Section 2 of this model law would proceed to specify the precise rules of this National Presidential Vote. For example, section 2 could provide that

Americans everywhere who want to be counted must register in a system to be administered by a nongovernmental election commission—made up, say, of a panel of respected political scientists and journalists. Section 2 could also specify its own uniform rules of voting eligibility, its own regulations regarding uniform presidential ballots, and even its own simple or elaborate election-dispute procedures. Alternatively, section 2 might contemplate that the National Presidential Vote should be administered by a new interstate election council or directly by the federal government, and Congress could then pass a statute blessing this more elaborate interstate agreement.

Some might dismiss all this as mere academic daydreaming, but this daydream dramatizes a remarkable truth about America's current Constitution: Significant change is sometimes possible within the lines of the existing constitutional blueprint, short of formal amendment. A system of direct national election would surely mark an important departure from the current presidential-selection regime, yet this shift could be accomplished without changing a single word of the written Constitution.

Here is a final daydream: Imagine that the two leading presidential contenders in 2016 or 2020 both believe that the current system of presidential election fails to do justice to the bedrock democratic principle of one person, one vote. Imagine, that is, that both candidates believe that every American voter—whether in a big state or a small state or a midsize state; whether in a red state or a blue state or a purple state; whether in a state at all, or instead in a territory, or in D.C.—should count exactly the same as every other American voter. If so, both candidates could in fact put their ideals into action. *For the two major presidential candidates and their two running mates have it within their power to move us to direct national election.*

A candidate could publicly pledge that, if he loses the national popular vote, he will ask his electors to vote for the national-popular-vote winner. Having taken this public pledge, the candidate could then challenge his rival to take a similar pledge. Each candidate could likewise insist that his vice-presidential running mate take the pledge. Ideally, the candidates' handpicked electors would honor their respective candidates' solemn pledges when the electoral college met; but if not, no matter. The candidates and running mates should simply include in their initial pledge an additional ironclad promise to resign immediately after inauguration in favor of the national-popular-vote winner.

The candidates themselves can make their pledges stick via the Twenty-fifth Amendment, which allows a president and Congress to fill a vacant vice presidency. Suppose, for example, that Smith somehow is inaugurated even though Jones won the national popular vote. On Inauguration Day, Smith's vice-presidential running mate would resign immediately. Smith would then name Jones the new vice president under the Twenty-fifth Amendment, and Congress could then confirm Jones in a matter of minutes. Jones is, after all, the man with the mandate in our hypothetical, having won under the ground rules the candidates themselves publicly embraced before the election and that the public fully understood at the time of the vote. Minutes after Jones's pro-forma confirmation as vice president, Smith would step down in favor of Jones.

If this scenario seems odd, it is useful to recall that it is not that different from the one that made Gerald Ford president in 1974: Vice President Spiro T. Agnew resigned, and then was replaced by Ford, who in turn became president upon Richard Nixon's resignation.

Another analogy: Beginning with George Washington, who resigned after eight years even though he would have easily won a third term, for which he was fully eligible, early presidents gave America a strong tradition of a two-term limit on the presidency. Likewise, presidential candidates today could, via preelection pledges and (if necessary) postinauguration resignations, establish a strong tradition that the presidency should go to the person who actually won the national popular vote. Just as the informal two-term limit ultimately became specified in constitutional text—in the Twenty-second Amendment, to be specific—so, too, a series of candidate pledges could eventually pave the way for a formal direct-election amendment.*

---

* In 1916, President Woodrow Wilson toyed with a similar way to hand presidential power to the candidate with the true mandate. Running against Charles Evans Hughes, Wilson, the incumbent, imagined that if Hughes won the election, he (Wilson) could appoint Hughes secretary of state—the officer next in line after the vice president under the presidential-succession law then in effect. If Wilson and his vice president, Thomas Marshall, were then to resign, Hughes could then take over as president. In the actual event, Wilson beat Hughes and nothing ever came of Wilson's musings.

And all it would take to get the ball rolling is for four persons to take the pledge in 2016. Imagine that.

"any Thing in the Constitution…of any State"

WHETHER IT WOULD BE ACCOMPLISHED by formal constitutional amendment or by informal adaptation, direct election of the president is an especially imaginable modification of the status quo because the current version of the electoral college can be seen as downright un-American—indeed, doubly so. First, America's present method of electing presidents obviously violates the grand principle of one person, one vote—a principle that was not at the center of American constitutional practice prior to the Warren Court's ruling in *Reynolds v. Sims*, but that has become central ever since that landmark decision. Second, the current version of the electoral college seems intuitively odd because all fifty states have governors who look remarkably like presidents, yet no state picks its governor via an electoral-college system. Rather, each state chooses its chief executive by a statewide popular vote, winner-take-all—thus raising the question of why the presidency should not likewise be selected by a national popular vote, winner-take-all.[4]

This second point ramifies far beyond the issue of how twenty-first-century Americans should elect the chief executive. Precisely because America's fifty state constitutions so strongly resemble America's fifty-first—federal—Constitution, the interesting respects in which the states diverge from the federal model provide plausible versions and visions of potential federal reform.

To fully appreciate the role that state constitutions have played and will probably continue to play in shaping the American constitutional imagination, we need to take a quick peek at the fifty terse—and sometimes not so terse—texts that collectively embody America's other major experiment in written constitutionalism.

WHEN WE DO, a striking pattern emerges: Across a large number of large issues, virtually all state constitutions have converged on a single distinct model of government. When it comes to at least ten fundamental constitutional features, virtually every state for the past half-century has resembled every other state, and the federal model, too. As to these features, there is a distinctly American Way, with elements that differ dramatically from those at work in various prominent foreign constitutions. Here, then, are ten basic features of American constitutionalism:

First, a written constitution adopted and amendable by some expression of popular sovereignty above and beyond enactment by an ordinary legislative majority. (Beyond America's shores, Britain and Israel, among others, are notable contrasts.)

Second, a bill of rights, which is typically textually separate from the rest of the document. The fifty-one American bills of rights also overlap a great deal in their language and substantive coverage, generally including freedom of expression and religion; the right to keep and bear arms; protections against unreasonable searches and seizures; procedural rights of criminal defendants; and safeguards of jury trial. (Great Britain and Australia, by contrast, have traditionally lacked strongly entrenched bills of rights.)

Third, a bicameral legislature (except in Nebraska), with fixed rather than variable legislative terms. (Compare the modern British Westminster model with a functionally unicameral legislature and with traditions obliging early elections when the party in power loses a parliamentary vote of no confidence. In some foreign jurisdictions, the party in power may also call an early "snap" election on its own motion, merely to solidify its current political advantage.)

Fourth, a legislative lower house typically composed entirely of representatives from equally populous single-member districts, each of which picks its representative via majority rule or plurality rule. (A minority of states do have multimember districts in the lower state house.) All geographic districts are redrawn at least once a decade to maintain equal population. Unlike the proportional-representation systems in place in countries such as Germany and New Zealand, no jurisdiction-wide vote-tallying system exists to ensure that the number of legislative seats held by a political party closely tracks the overall percentage of party votes across the entire jurisdiction. Unlike multiparty regimes that operate in many other leading democracies, each American legislature is dominated by two main political parties—indeed, the same two parties across the continent, with minor variations.

Fifth, a strong presidential/gubernatorial system with a one-person chief executive elected independently of the legislature, at fixed terms, wielding powers of pardon, appointment, and non-absolute veto. (By contrast, in classic parliamentary systems in places such as Britain, the legislature chooses the chief executive, who has no formal veto power and serves only so long as she continues to command a legislative majority. Even in some strong presidential systems abroad—for example, the French system—the president lacks a muscular veto.)

Sixth, an executive understudy (vice president/lieutenant governor) explicitly provided for in the constitution (with a few notable state exceptions) who automatically takes over when the chief executive is disabled, dies, or resigns. Although this understudy usually has few other powers of his own, he does enjoy a fixed term of office coextensive with the chief executive; he is not simply appointable and removable at will by the chief executive or by the legislature. Rather, the understudy is typically elected by the people at the same time they elect the chief executive. (Here, too, parliamentary models abroad structure things very differently, with no constitutionally designated second-in-command, and no fixed terms or independence from parliament for executive understudies.)

Seventh, a universal understanding that the constitution is judicially enforceable law capable of being invoked in ordinary courtrooms, even between two private litigants in lawsuits in which the government is not formally a party. (By contrast, many modern European systems feature an official "Constitutional Court" in which constitutional issues are often treated differently from ordinary legal questions arising in ordinary private litigation.)

Eighth, a system blending judicial independence and accountability in a distinctive way. Although judges, once chosen, may not simply be fired at will by the executive or the legislature, the process of selecting and promoting judges is highly political. Judges do not generally appoint other judges; nor is promotion to a higher court based strictly on seniority or on one's reputation among fellow judges (unlike the German and French systems, in which the judiciary is much more self-regulating, and closer to a bureaucratic civil service).

Ninth, a common-law style of adjudication featuring judicial precedent as an important source of law. (Here, the civil-law system of France presents an obvious contrast.)

Tenth, juries, which are a prominent feature of both civil and criminal litigation. (Again, not so in a place such as France.)

WHAT FOLLOWS FROM THIS STRIKING PATTERN? Not any strong claim that every state must slavishly adhere to this Basic American Model in every respect as a matter of federal constitutional law. It would be silly, for example, to think that Nebraska is under any constitutional obligation to repudiate its unicameral tradition. But in a less rigidly legal and more sociological sense, this Basic American Model defines the boundaries of realistic constitutional reform in America. Proposed federal amendments based on state variations *within* the Basic American Model described above are much more likely to be taken seriously than amendment proposals originating outside of this Basic American Model—proposals that are apt to be viewed as "foreign," "alien," or "un-American."[5]

Examples of "alien" concepts include early "snap" elections or no-confidence elections for legislatures as a whole (as opposed to individual recall elections); multiparty regimes; cumulative voting or other proportional-representation systems for anything other than local elections; parliamentary systems involving legislative selection of chief executive officers; and civil-service models of self-appointing and self-perpetuating judiciaries. Although in the abstract there may be much to commend some or all of these concepts, none of them will likely take America by storm anytime soon.

By contrast, certain proposals to amend the federal Constitution will be taken seriously if comparable proposals have already been adopted and road-tested at the state level. In fact, most of the federal amendments that have thus far succeeded were copycats or adaptations of preexisting state constitutional texts or practices. Thus, the federal Bill of Rights tracked various state antecedent documents; the Reconstruction Amendments borrowed from the best constitutional practices of various enlightened free states; Woman Suffrage won at the continental level only after prevailing in many state constitutions; and so on.

Even before any formal amendments to the Philadelphia Constitution took shape, the Philadelphia document itself obviously built upon state constitutional templates. The basic structure of the Philadelphia plan—a written "Constitution" with a bicameral legislature and three branches of government—distilled the essence of extant state constitutions. On detail after detail, the Philadelphia framers in effect began by canvassing state constitutional practices and then eventually opted for what the delegates considered the best state practice. Thus, in the decision to put the federal Constitution to a special ratification vote of the people—a vote that would ideally encompass an especially broad electorate—the framers copied the models of the Massachusetts Constitution of 1780 and the New Hampshire Constitution of 1784. The idea of a federal census borrowed from the Pennsylvania Constitution of 1776 and the New York Constitution of 1777. The elimination of property qualifications for federal public servants likewise borrowed from Pennsylvania, as did provisions for all federal lawmakers to be compensated from the public fisc. The broad outlines of federal executive power combined the best of the Massachusetts and New York Constitutions. Various elements of federal judicial independence drew upon several state constitutional antecedents, as did Article III's basic commitment to jury trial. In short, America's federal constitutional project has tightly intertwined with her state constitutions from day one.

Notably, the framers' biggest blunder—their fateful mistake to give slave states a large bonus in all future House and presidential elections, via the three-fifths clause—occurred precisely because this was an issue where no guidance could be drawn from the state experience. None of the states with large slave populations had yet devised a general formula for apportioning slaves in legislative (or executive) elections. Lacking any helpful state templates or good data from actual state practice, the Philadelphia delegates in effect plucked the number three-fifths from the nearest hat they could find. Alas, this hat had been tailored to fit a very different problem—how much each state under the Confederation should pay into continental coffers, an issue utterly irrelevant to the question of how many seats each state under the new Constitution should properly claim in a proportionate House or in a newfangled electoral college.

WITHIN THE BASIC AMERICAN MODEL DESCRIBED ABOVE—indeed, amazingly enough, within *each* of the ten observed similarities across American constitutions—there are also important variances between the federal Constitution, on the one hand, and certain widespread state practices, on the other.

Let us, then, revisit our ten basic elements, note the interesting variances between state and federal constitutionalism, and use these differences to generate a checklist of basic questions for further academic research and political discourse—the kinds of questions that serious scholars and statesmen should ask themselves as they ponder possible state or federal constitutional amendment. In general, whenever a variance exists between state and federal constitutional practice, Americans should ask whether states should change to fit the federal model more closely; whether the federal Constitution should instead be amended to fit the contrary state practice; or whether, if we are already living in the best of all possible constitutional worlds, there might well be reasons why the two levels of American constitutions should differ.

First, written state constitutions are typically much longer and more clearly amendable by direct majoritarian popular action (via initiative or referendum) than their federal counterpart. Most state constitutions interweave amendatory textual additions and deletions directly into the prior constitutional text, rather than appending amendments as sequential postscripts in federal fashion. Also, many states have periodically promulgated entirely new constitutions wholly superseding their predecessor documents.[6]

These differences raise interesting questions for possible legal reform: Are state constitutions too easy to amend by direct popular action? Or is the federal Constitution too hard to amend? Or perhaps the system of majoritarian state amendment and supermajoritarian federal amendment is just right as is: Precisely because the federal Constitution sets the basic ground rules that states cannot violate, state amendments are already constrained by a stable framework of fundamental freedom, and frequent state amendment is thus not as great a threat to liberty—especially given that it is easier for state dissenters to move to a sister state than for national dissenters to move to a foreign country. The lower thresholds for state constitutional amendments also enable states to function as effective laboratories of constitutional experimentation, with successful experiments offering useful guidance to sister states and, eventually, would-be reformers of the federal Constitution.

Even if the general difficulty level of federal constitutional amendment is about right, Article V of the federal Constitution gives unequally sized states equal weight both in the Senate (which effectively operates as a veto-gate alongside the House in proposing amendments) and in the ratification process. States, by contrast, generally do not feature gross malapportionment in their amendment process. Should Article V itself be changed by revising the structure of the Senate and by weighting states by population in the ratification process? Or perhaps by providing for a national popular ratification referendum with a supermajority requirement for adoption, thereby bringing Article V into closer alignment with state amendment procedures? (But even if such an amendment of the federal amendment rules were widely conceded to be fairer than the current Article V system, wouldn't small states always be able to block an amendment amendment out of pure self-interest?)

Second, compared to the federal Constitution, state constitutions are conventionally viewed as having more explicit "positive" and "social" rights, such as the right to education. Given this fact, should the federal Constitution be construed to protect more "positive" rights? Or has the state experience shown that courts (and other governmental enforcers) do a rather bad job of protecting such rights?[7]

Third, many states have term limits for legislators and also allow voters to "recall" individual lawmakers (making state legislators' terms slightly less fixed, formally). Some states also have direct-democracy processes of initiative and referendum that enable voters to supplant or supplement the legislature in the enactment of certain kinds of statutes.[8]

Has the state experience with recalls and with statutory initiatives and referenda been a happy one worthy of federal emulation, or a mistake that states should repudiate? (Note that emulation might well require considerable federal oversight of direct-lawmaking elections to ensure uniformity of suffrage rules and voting procedures across the various states.) Should states abandon term limits for state legislators? Or should the federal Constitution be amended to provide for term limits? (If so, how could members of Congress ever be induced to support such a Congress-limiting amendment under Article V?)

The current asymmetry between long-serving federal lawmakers and rotating state legislators might give Congress "repeat-player" advantages in the federal-state tug of war, and also a stronger position vis-à-vis a powerful president. On one view, because the president is so much stronger than state governors, we need a more experienced group of federal legislators to counterbalance him than is needed at the state level. Thus, one argument for the status quo might be that it leads to a strong federal government that is not overly tilted toward the president.

Fourth, under the Supreme Court's landmark ruling in *Reynolds v. Sims*, no state is allowed to malapportion either branch of its legislature on the model of the U.S. Senate. Thus, no state can have an upper house in which each county has an equal number of seats, regardless of population. If the deep principle of *Reynolds v. Sims* is right—if states should not be allowed to malapportion their senates by giving unequally populated counties equal seats—then is the basic apportionment principle of the U.S. Senate a vicious one? Or is federalism the answer to the seeming discrepancy? Some would say yes: Federalism is the answer, and counties are not the same as states in an inherently federal system. Others would counter that giving Wyoming and California equal representation may benefit some political interest groups (at the expense of other groups), but does little to protect states qua states. On this view, the federal Constitution should be changed to reduce Senate malapportionment—say, by giving each state at least one senator and capping even the largest state at eight senators. Such a scheme would keep the Senate at roughly its present size and would respect the existence of states qua states while dramatically reducing the current degree of malapportionment. (But could small states ever be induced to agree to such a federal amendment?)[9]

Fifth, each state chief executive is elected by direct popular vote rather than by something akin to the federal electoral college. Some state governors are subject to popular recall. State governors have no strong foreign affairs powers. Most important, virtually no state has a strongly "unitary" executive. Almost every state, for example, has an attorney general elected separately from the governor rather than appointed by him. Many states feature a wide variety of cabinet-like positions elected by the people rather than handpicked (and removable) by the governor. In these respects, state governors seem much weaker than presidents, but in one other respect, governors are stronger: Almost all of them now enjoy a line-item veto when presented with spending bills.[10]

These differences should prompt reformers to ask a range of questions: If the federal electoral college is so good, why does no state (or foreign country, for that matter) closely follow it? Here, examination of state constitutions helps us see with distinctive clarity a good candidate for federal constitutional reform. Might a popular recall system be a useful additional check on presidential power? Also, can state experience with line-item vetoes inform the federal debate over the proper allocation of power between Congress and the president? Finally, even if (for reasons explained in Chapter 9) the 1978 federal independent-counsel statute was plainly unconstitutional, should we formally amend the federal Constitution to permit such a device, which has worked well at the state level? If we do so, should we adopt special rules about investigations that affect foreign policy? Or, instead, should we try to develop informal traditions of independence within the Justice Department?[11]

In connection with the proposed Hatch Amendment, it is also worth mentioning that naturalized citizens are virtually everywhere eligible to serve as governors—as dramatized by Arnold Schwarzenegger and Jennifer Granholm. Although skeptics of the Hatch Amendment correctly note that governors are not directly involved in foreign affairs, surely senators and cabinet secretaries are involved in these matters, and, as noted earlier, naturalized Americans have served in these posts ever since the days of George Washington.

Sixth, many states allow voters to vote separately for governor and lieutenant governor, but at the federal level, voters have generally been denied the option to split their ticket by voting for Party A for president and Party B for vice president. Also, in many states, when the governor leaves the jurisdiction, her powers automatically devolve upon the lieutenant until she returns.

A few obvious law-reform questions: Is the current federal practice of selecting a vice president as a mere adjunct to the president—without allowing ticket-splitting—a sensible way of conferring legitimacy on the person who, if tragedy strikes, may need to be the national leader? Conversely, should state rules automatically conferring power on the lieutenant governor whenever the governor leaves the state be abandoned? The lack of a federal counterpart (combined with the fact that many state constitutions omit this categorical rule) might suggest that this rule is of doubtful utility.[12]

Seventh, unlike the U.S. Supreme Court, several state supreme courts can issue "advisory" opinions directly to the legislature before a law is passed or a private lawsuit crystallizes. Doesn't the state experience show that these opinions are sometimes useful and rarely harmful? In light of this experience, should federal courts be allowed to render anticipatory opinions before a proposed law has been adopted by Congress (or, indeed, by a state legislature)? Would the federal Constitution need to be amended here, or just reinterpreted?[13]

Eighth, state judges typically lack life tenure, and many must come directly before the general electorate at the time of initial appointment or in a later retention context—sometimes in contested elections featuring full-blown media campaigns and explicit party endorsements.[14]

These large differences between state and federal practice should prompt us to wonder whether federal judges enjoy too much independence, or whether state judges enjoy too little. Perhaps both are true, and the best model would give judges more independence than they get in various states but less than they get under the federal Constitution. Imagine, for example, a system in which judges are appointed for fixed eighteen-year nonrenewable terms.

Ninth, state court precedents misconstruing state constitutions are easier to overturn by state constitutional amendments. With this fact in view, we see all the more clearly why the U.S. Supreme Court must remain open to reconsider its own previous constitutional rulings that are alleged to be in error, given the special difficulty of using the federal amendment process to correct the Court's misrulings.

Tenth, many states have done away with grand juries, and a few have moved away from a unanimity requirement in criminal cases. But why shouldn't states be required to use grand juries, just as they are required to honor virtually all the other guarantees of the Bill of Rights via the Fourteenth Amendment? If the argument is that the grand jury has truly outlived its usefulness, then should the federal Constitution be amended to relieve the federal government of this "nuisance"? Also, a good case can be made that state experiments with nonunanimous criminal juries should be emulated by the federal government, and that this reform may properly occur (as was argued in the preceding chapter) by federal statute, with no need for a formal constitutional amendment.[15]

SEVERAL OF THE IMAGINABLE FEDERAL constitutional amendments suggested by the pattern of America's current state constitutions would reduce the power of individuals and institutions who today have the ability to block constitutional amendments, should they so choose. As a matter of realpolitik, why would these veto-wielders ever allow these amendments to pass, even if these individuals and institutions were convinced of the genuine justice and wisdom of such amendments in principle?

For example, why would voters or legislators in Wyoming ever vote to reduce the Senate's malapportionment, given that the existing rules favor Wyoming? Why would a U.S. senator from Wyoming ever sign his own electoral death warrant? Or why would Congress ever support an amendment to limit congressional terms? In short, how could certain justice-seeking amendments ever escape the powerful gravitational force of an arguably unjust status quo?

To answer these far-reaching questions about America's future, let us turn, one last time, to America's past for guidance.

"to...secure the Blessings of Liberty to...our Posterity"

JUSTICE-SEEKING REFORMERS CAN ULTIMATELY PREVAIL in time, using time—in particular, using the key device of a long time-delay between the vote on a visionary amendment and the effective start date of such an amendment. Americans are accustomed to laws (the Bush tax cuts, for example) that automatically lapse—that "sunset"—after a certain time period. Henceforth, we need to envision a different species of rules that should properly go into effect—that should "sunrise"—only after a substantial time delay.

For ordinary elections, long time-delays would make no sense: It would be an Alice-in-Wonderland world if we voted today, by democratic procedures, for lawmakers whose terms of office would start in, say, twenty or forty years. The idea of long time-delays for most ordinary statutes is likewise odd. But constitutional law often operates on a different timeline from ordinary statutory law, and for certain kinds of constitutional amendments—especially amendments that aim to establish the most just and fair decision procedures possible—long time-delays make a great deal of sense.

It is hard for a single generation to decide all issues of fair procedure for itself. Who decides which procedures are the best? Who decides who decides? By what vote? Who decides *that* question? And by what vote? And so on. There is, in principle, an infinite regress problem if a democracy is truly to bootstrap itself off the ground.* If ever there were a proper role for the "dead hand of the past"—the fixing of certain ground rules by Generation 1 for the benefit of Generation 2—it is in the setting of fair decisional procedures, precisely because Generation 2 cannot easily do this for itself.

---

* As we saw in Chapters 2 and 9, at several points at the Founding majority rule presented itself as a preexisting focal point and default rule, a rule in effect inherited from previous theory and practice.

And the setting forth of fair decisional procedures is, of course, one of the basic aims of the American Constitution.[16]

Once Americans understand that in adopting certain constitutional amendments, they are setting up fair procedures not so much for themselves as for their unborn grandchildren and great-grandchildren, they should be more likely to focus on what is truly right rather than what is in their own current interest. If Jefferson Smith is a senator from Wyoming, it may well run hard against his current self-interest to vote for an amendment that will mean one senator from Wyoming rather than two—unless the amendment has a decades-long time-delay clause. But if the amendment does have such a distant-sunrise clause, it cannot hurt Smith personally, because he will be gone before the sunrise. So perhaps Smith will then be somewhat more likely to concentrate on whether the amendment is truly fair. He may focus on the fact that his own grandchildren and great-grandchildren might not be Wyoming residents. Indeed, they may be more likely to be Californians. Why should Smith favor his Wyoming posterity over his California posterity? Ideally, Smith should favor neither and should instead consider what is truly fair and just, standing behind what the famous twentieth-century philosopher John Rawls called a "veil of ignorance" shielding Smith from biased considerations of personal self-interest.[17]

Such generational veils of ignorance were powerfully and self-consciously at work at the Founding itself. For example, George Mason argued at Philadelphia that the rich should care about the poor because the posterity of the rich would one day come to fill even the lowest social ranks:

> We ought to attend to the rights of every class of the people. [I have] often wondered at the indifference of the superior classes of society to this dictate of humanity & policy, considering that however affluent their circumstances, or elevated their situations, might be, the course of a few years, not only might but certainly would, distribute their posterity throughout the lowest classes of Society. Every selfish motive therefore, every family attachment, ought to recommend such a system of policy as would provide no less carefully for the rights and happiness of the lowest than of the highest orders of Citizens.[18]

In a similar philosophical spirit, Gouverneur Morris urged his fellow Philadelphia delegates to rise above parochialism, because they or their posterity would one day likely inhabit other states. Other leading lights—including James Wilson, James Madison, and Alexander Hamilton—voiced related thoughts in the summer of 1787, explicitly imagining themselves to be representatives of a wide posterity across time and space.[19]

What was true at America's Founding moment has likewise been true of amending moments in American history. Indeed, from one point of view, the "Founders" themselves were amenders; they were, after all, modifying their own preexisting legal system in proposing the Constitution itself.

A close look at the original Constitution and its amendments reveals clever, albeit too-rare, use of the sunrise device to overcome immediate entrenched interests and injustices and thereby achieve a more disinterested and just future state of affairs. Although the Deep South refused to give up the power to import transatlantic slaves for the first twenty years of the new Constitution's operations, this region was willing to allow precisely such importations to be banned by Congress beginning in 1808—and forevermore. Had the framers been equally clever in the use of sunrise rules on other slavery-related issues—for example, had the original Constitution prohibited slavery in all western territory after 1808, or prohibited three-fifths apportionment credit for all slaves after 1808—perhaps Americans might have ultimately ended slavery without the unspeakable carnage of the Civil War. In the mid-twentieth century, Americans adopted a new amendment limiting presidents to two terms, but did so in a way that did not deprive any current or past president of perpetual reeligibility.

Various states in the Founding era likewise used sunrise rules to achieve the gradual abolition of slavery itself. Under these rules, existing slaves would not be liberated—but eventually their future children would walk free. In this way, the arc of history, though long, bent toward justice.

In the same spirit, amendment-minded Americans should imagine ourselves today to be virtual representatives of our twenty-second-century posterity, tasked with the awesome challenge of framing just rules for that society even though we will never live to see the brighter day that we aim to bequeath. If it makes sense for modern American constitutionalists to attend to words written and deeds done centuries ago to form a more perfect union, then it also makes sense for us to struggle to envision and help birth a still more perfect union centuries hence. Much of American history remains to be written, and much of American constitutional law remains to be framed.

FAITHFUL CONSTITUTIONALISTS labor under a twofold constitutional responsibility. We must look backward in time and claim our constitutional inheritance, and we must also look forward in time and make our constitutional donation. Though this second responsibility does not reside on the clear surface of any explicit constitutional text, surely it forms an integral part of America's unwritten Constitution.[20]

AFTERWORD

A T SOME POINT IN THE PRECEDING PAGES, it will doubtless have struck the reader that this book, whose title promised to explain and explore "America's Unwritten Constitution," is also chock-full of detailed claims about the written Constitution itself.

If there is any contradiction here, it is only skin-deep. In order to establish that some specific rule or principle is properly understood as part of America's *unwritten* Constitution, surely it must be shown that the rule or principle in question is not in America's *written* Constitution, read at face value. But how could I prove this to the reader without parsing the document itself? And how could I further prove that a particular unwritten rule or principle forms part of America's *Constitution*—and is thus roughly on a par with or somehow akin to the canonical text—without still more examination and elaboration of the document itself?

Precisely because America's unwritten Constitution and America's written Constitution fit together to form a single system, no proper account of the former should ever lose sight of the latter: The terse text is inextricably intertwined with the implicit principles, the ordaining deeds, the lived customs, the landmark cases, the unifying symbols, the legitimating democratic theories, the institutional settlements, the framework statutes, the two-party ground rules, the appeals to conscience, the state-constitutional counterparts, and the unfinished agenda items that form much of America's unwritten Constitution.

Even if twenty-first-century Americans unanimously agreed that the written Constitution had no binding legal authority whatsoever over us, we would nevertheless do well to dwell on it. The American Revolution, the Civil War, the Progressive Era, and the Second Reconstruction of the 1960s have all left their explicit marks on this unfolding document. The convenient manner in which amendments are layered one atop another in chronological sequence adds special transparency to this intergenerational project and invites readers to view the terse text in light of the grand narrative of American history. Even a casual reader can see when each textual change was made and can thus easily trace the temporal trend-line of American constitutionalism. Like a miniature Grand Canyon, the written Constitution exposes America's colorful history to the eye of the ordinary observer.

The document's brevity and its intimate relation to America's storyline make it a brilliant focal point drawing together ordinary twenty-first-century citizens coming from all directions. The genetic forebears of today's citizenry arrived in the New World at different times from different lands, professing different faiths, speaking different tongues, and displaying different skin colors. Yet in the written Constitution itself, we can all find a common vocabulary for our common deliberations and a shared national narrative—an epic saga of ordinary and ever more inclusive Americans binding themselves into one people, one posterity.

For all these reasons and many more, no sensitive account of America's unwritten Constitution could ever stray far from its written counterpart. At every turn, I have thus tried to keep the document in view even as I have invited readers to go beneath, behind, and beyond it. The organizational schema of this book—with subheadings in each chapter consisting of phrases drawn from the written Constitution—has aimed to highlight this general approach. Rarely does the featured phrase, if read in isolation and at face value, definitely answer the various legal questions that I have tried to analyze. But the featured phrase typically meshes with various elements of America's unwritten Constitution to direct faithful interpreters to sound constitutional solutions.

THE CAREFUL READER may also have noticed that the very word "constitution" is a chameleon that takes on different hues in different contexts. The canonical text, of course, repeatedly describes itself as "this Constitution," but once we come to understand that this text is crucially incomplete in various ways, exactly what sorts of things outside the text are sensibly viewed as genuinely "constitutional" things? The preceding pages have suggested that, beyond the written Constitution itself, at least three other understandings of America's "constitution" are useful.

First, America's "constitution" encompasses cherished principles of higher law that are widely understood to limit American governmental officials, even if these specific principles do not appear explicitly in the terse text. Some of these higher-law rights and rules are fully enforceable by courts. Others may not be, but are still commonly recognized as binding in legal conscience upon nonjudicial actors.

Second, America's "constitution" comprises the practices, protocols, procedures, and principles that constitute the government. Especially noteworthy are those aspects of governmental organization and operation that are somehow entrenched—that is, rendered immune from easy and ordinary legislative modification. Some kinds of entrenchment are highly legal and formal. For example, a court might bar certain attempted governmental restructurings violative of unwritten constitutional principles of federalism or separation of powers. Other sorts of organizational entrenchment operate informally and politically, via incentive structures and power allocations that make the current system functionally self-perpetuating in certain respects. (America's two-party duopoly is an example.)

Both of these understandings of America's real, albeit unwritten, "constitution" have deep roots in Founding-era American discourse. Both understandings are also widespread among modern American lawyers, legal scholars, and judges. To these two conventional understandings of America's actual unwritten "constitution," this book has added a third thought: America's unwritten "constitution" should also be understood to encompass the basic tools and techniques by which faithful interpreters tease out the substantive meaning of the written Constitution and unwritten rights and structures.

The main aim of this book has been to illustrate how these four elements of America's Constitution—the terse text, unwritten higher-law principles, unwritten constitutive structures, and unwritten tools and techniques of constitutional interpretation—fit together.

DESPITE MY OPENING PROMISE to present a panoramic picture of American constitutional law,* I have not devoted sustained attention to foreign and international law; nor have I invited readers to give serious thought to how a new form of *world* constitutionalism, American style, might be imaginable in, say, 2121 or 2222. My excuse for this large lapse is that I have come to believe that the issues involved are too broad to be handled in one or two chapters. Serious analysis would probably require yet another book, and I am doubtful that I am the best person to write such a book.

That said, the reader deserves to know how I might begin to think about some of these issues. For starters, what role, if any, should foreign law and norms play in construing the American Constitution? A real but limited one, I think. Foreign law is of course relevant if we are deciding whether to amend our Constitution in order to be more like some other regime. Foreign law is also relevant if we want to understand certain empirical truths about the world—laws of X sort generally have effects Y and Z—that might bear on proper constitutional interpretation. But given that many foreign constitutions are so different from our own, international comparisons may be of limited empirical value. The same kind of law might empirically operate very differently in two regimes with profoundly divergent institutional structures, cultural traditions, party systems, and so on. Judges (and other constitutional interpreters) may often be better off looking at state constitutional experiences, which have played out within a basic model much closer to the federal one.

Beyond the domain of empirical prediction, international norms and ideals are key features of America's unwritten Constitution to the extent they have in fact been widely embraced by the American people and have thereby woven themselves into the fabric of America's lived experience or America's symbols, or to the extent that these foreign ideals and norms have touched the conscience of Americans. For example, Martin Luther King Jr. borrowed openly from Mahatma Gandhi. Through King and his

---

* The various hypotheticals and case studies in this book have, by design, been drawn from a broad cross-section of American constitutional law—at times involving advanced topics that have been hived off from introductory constitutional-law courses into more specialized classes on criminal procedure, civil procedure, federal jurisdiction, legislation, administrative law, election law, treaty law, remedies, property, and so on.

movement, the non-American Gandhi—who himself had studied Americans such as Henry David Thoreau—became part of the American constitutional story.

Foreign norms and laws may also become *negative* symbols in the American constitutional conversation. Thus, one way to understand the 1942 case of *Skinner v. Oklahoma*, in which the Supreme Court struck down a state statute that called for the sterilization of certain convicted criminals, is to see the link between this statute and Hitler's eugenics program, which served as a powerful symbol of precisely what modern America had come to repudiate when it declared war on the Nazis. In the famous (now infamous) 1927 case of *Buck v. Bell*, the Court had seemed to smile on eugenics, upholding the sterilization of a young woman who had committed no crime. But by 1942, the Court strained conventional doctrinal categories to invalidate a sterilization program targeted at certain felons. This newly voiced hostility to government sterilization came about not just because judges as a matter of individual conscience decided that Hitler's ideas were evil and unconscionable, but also because the American people as a whole had sharply turned against Hitler and had come to react to his twisted vision with horror. Hitler in effect became another powerful negative symbol, another *Dred Scott*.[1]

Finally, to the extent that America's Constitution aspires to set an enlightened example for the rest of the world, the Supreme Court may in various situations properly ask itself whether the practices of certain individual state governments are likely to bring the nation as a whole into international disrepute. However, if Congress or the president has already addressed this issue, the Court should hesitate to upset these determinations made by the branches of the federal government tasked with primary responsibility for conducting foreign affairs and protecting the good name of the United States abroad.

Those branches, in turn, would do well to heed Madison/Publius's *Federalist* No. 63, which identified two reasons for paying attention to "the judgment of other nations." First, national hubris ill serves America's image. Regardless of "the merits of any particular plan or measure," American actions "should appear to other nations as the offspring of a wise and honorable policy." Second, no matter how wise or how strong America might become, it should always be open to the teachings of enlightened humankind beyond our shores: "[I]n doubtful cases, particularly where the national councils may be warped by some strong passion, or momentary interest, the presumed or known opinion of the impartial world, may be the best guide that can be followed."

PERHAPS THE MOST DIFFICULT AND INTERESTING questions of all concern not the role of global law in reshaping America's Constitution, but rather the reverse: How might America's Constitution, written and unwritten, serve as a model for the world? America's Constitution was originally designed as a kind of World Constitution—a Constitution, that is, for the New World, separated by vast oceans from the Old. But at the dawn of a new millennium it is clear that planet earth is one world, and that global solutions are needed to solve genuinely global problems—climate change, famines, genocide, pandemic viruses, international terrorism, trade imbalances, nuclear proliferation, and on and on.

Many of the existing world institutions are not fully adequate to solve these problems—and they are inadequate in ways that call to mind the similar inadequacies of the Articles of Confederation to solve the problems of the New World in the 1780s. The United States of 1785 looked rather like today's United Nations, whose General Assembly bears an uncanny resemblance to the Confederation Congress: one-state, one-vote, in a body that declares a lot and does much less, where member states sometimes obey and sometimes don't. The Founders' solution was to create a strong community of New World democracies. In today's world, there is no true international counterpart of any importance. The UN—in both the General Assembly and the Security Council—seats thuggish regimes alongside admirable ones. The North Atlantic Treaty Organization (NATO) focuses overwhelmingly on military issues and excludes non-European nations. The European Union is likewise just a regional body. The Group of Twenty (G-20) features the world's economic powerhouses, whether or not they are democratic. The Organization of Petroleum Exporting Countries (OPEC) is only for the oil-rich, the Arab League for Arabs, and so on.

Perhaps what is needed is a new international group that would start out quite informally and gradually gain legitimacy and authority as a powerful moral force in the world—a genuinely international community of democracies encompassing rich and poor nations, North and South, East and West. This organization would include the United States, of course, but also India and Costa Rica, Old Europe and New Europe—but only the world's truly democratic countries. In effect, this organization would emulate the American Constitution's "sleeping giant," the republican-government clause, which requires individual states in the Union to meet minimum standards of democratic decency—free speech, fair votes, respect for minorities, and so on.

Or at least, that is my current thinking on the matter. My specific reform ideas are highly tentative, and in the spirit of *The Federalist* No. 63 I welcome enlightenment from abroad.

The best ideas may well come from the young. Madison and Hamilton were both in their mid-thirties when they composed the lion's share of *The Federalist* essays championing world government for the New World. Whereas Publius was a joint product of three men (John Jay rounded out the trio), today's technology makes it possible for many minds across the planet to collaborate. If the blessings of liberty are to be secured for posterity—not just for Americans but for all God's children—young visionaries must speak up.

Publius II, where are you? The world awaits your proposals.

AMERICA'S WRITTEN CONSTITUTION[*]

We the People of the United States, in Order to form a more perfect Union, establish Justice, insure domestic Tranquility, provide for the common defence, promote the general Welfare, and secure the Blessings of Liberty to ourselves and our Posterity, do ordain and establish this Constitution for the United States of America.

ARTICLE. I.

Section. 1. All legislative Powers herein granted shall be vested in a Congress of the United States, which shall consist of a Senate and House of Representatives.

Section. 2. The House of Representatives shall be composed of Members chosen every second Year by the People of the several States, and the Electors in each State shall have the Qualifications requisite for Electors of the most numerous Branch of the State Legislature.

No Person shall be a Representative who shall not have attained to the Age of twenty five Years, and been seven Years a Citizen of the United States, and who shall not,

---

[*] In deference to the general convention among modern lawyers, judges, and scholars, the version of the 1787 text reprinted here tracks the hand-signed National Archives parchment of September 17, 1787, as distinct from the September 28, 1787, typeset version of the Constitution sent out to the state ratifying conventions. For more discussion of these two versions, see Chapter 2. The amendment texts reprinted here derive from S. Doc. 103-6 (1992, reprint 1996).

when elected, be an Inhabitant of that State in which he shall be chosen.

Representatives and direct Taxes shall be apportioned among the several States which may be included within this Union, according to their respective Numbers, which shall be determined by adding to the whole Number of free Persons, including those bound to Service for a Term of Years, and excluding Indians not taxed, three fifths of all other Persons. The actual Enumeration shall be made within three Years after the first Meeting of the Congress of the United States, and within every subsequent Term of ten Years, in such Manner as they shall by Law direct. The Number of Representatives shall not exceed one for every thirty Thousand, but each State shall have at Least one Representative; and until such enumeration shall be made, the State of New Hampshire shall be entitled to chuse three, Massachusetts eight, Rhode-Island and Providence Plantations one, Connecticut five, New-York six, New Jersey four, Pennsylvania eight, Delaware one, Maryland six, Virginia ten, North Carolina five, South Carolina five, and Georgia three.

When vacancies happen in the Representation from any State, the Executive Authority thereof shall issue Writs of Election to fill such Vacancies.

The House of Representatives shall chuse their Speaker and other Officers; and shall have the sole Power of Impeachment.

5–6, 11, 350–351   Section. 3. The Senate of the United States shall be composed of two Senators from each State, chosen by the Legislature thereof, for six Years; and each Senator shall have one Vote.

Immediately after they shall be assembled in Consequence of the first Election, they shall be divided as equally as may be into three Classes. The Seats of the Senators of the first Class shall be vacated at the Expiration of the second Year, of the second Class at the Expiration of the fourth Year, and of the third Class at the Expiration of the sixth Year, so that one third may be chosen every second Year; and if Vacancies happen by Resignation, or otherwise, during the Recess of the Legislature of any State, the Executive thereof may make temporary Appointments until the next Meeting of the Legislature, which shall then fill such Vacancies.

No Person shall be a Senator who shall not have attained to the Age of thirty Years, and been nine Years a Citizen of the United States, and who shall not, when elected, be an inhabitant of that State for which he shall be chosen.

The Vice President of the United States shall be President of the Senate, but shall have no Vote, unless they be equally divided.

The Senate shall chuse their other Officers, and also a President pro tempore, in the Absence of the Vice President, or when he shall exercise the Office of President of the United States.

The Senate shall have the sole Power to try all Impeachments. When sitting for that Purpose, they shall be on Oath or Affirmation. When the President of the United States is tried, the Chief Justice shall preside: And no Person shall be convicted without the Concurrence of two thirds of the Members present.

Judgment in Cases of Impeachment shall not extend further than to removal from Office, and disqualification to hold and enjoy any Office of honor, Trust or Profit under the United States: but the Party convicted shall nevertheless be liable and subject to Indictment, Trial, Judgment and Punishment, according to Law.

412–413   Section. 4. The Times, Places and Manner of holding Elections for Senators and Representatives, shall be prescribed in each State by the Legislature thereof; but the Congress may at any time by Law make or alter such Regulations, except as to the Places of chusing Senators.

The Congress shall assemble at least once in every Year, and such Meeting shall be on the first Monday in December, unless they shall by Law appoint a different Day.

6, 81, 336, 345, 359, 361, 363, 366, 368

Section. 5. Each House shall be the Judge of the Elections, Returns and Qualifications of its own Members, and a Majority of each shall constitute a Quorum to do Business; but a smaller Number may adjourn from day to day, and may be authorized to compel the Attendance of absent Members, in such Manner, and under such Penalties as each House may provide.

Each House may determine the Rules of its Proceedings, punish its Members for disorderly Behaviour, and, with the Concurrence of two thirds, expel a Member.

Each House shall keep a Journal of its Proceedings, and from time to time publish the same, excepting such Parts as may in their Judgment require Secrecy; and the Yeas and Nays of the Members of either House on any question shall, at the Desire of one fifth of those Present, be entered on the Journal.

Neither House, during the Session of Congress, shall, without the Consent of the other, adjourn for more than three days, nor to any other Place than that in which the two Houses shall be sitting.

35–36, 38–39, 45, 220, 378, 380

Section. 6. The Senators and Representatives shall receive a Compensation for their Services, to be ascertained by Law, and paid out of the Treasury of the United States. They shall in all Cases, except Treason, Felony and Breach of the Peace, be privileged from Arrest during their Attendance at the Session of their respective Houses, and in going to and returning from the same; and for any Speech or Debate in either House, they shall not be questioned in any other Place.

No Senator or Representative shall, during the Time

for which he was elected, be appointed to any civil Office under the Authority of the United States, which shall have been created, or the Emoluments whereof shall have been encreased during such time; and no Person holding any Office under the United States, shall be a Member of either House during his Continuance in Office.

359, 363 Section. 7. All Bills for raising Revenue shall originate in the House of Representatives; but the Senate may propose or concur with Amendments as on other Bills.

Every Bill which shall have passed the House of Representatives and the Senate, shall, before it become a Law, be presented to the President of the United States; If he approve he shall sign it, but if not he shall return it, with his Objections to that House in which it shall have originated, who shall enter the Objections at large on their Journal, and proceed to reconsider it. If after such Reconsideration two thirds of that House shall agree to pass the Bill, it shall be sent, together with the Objections, to the other House, by which it shall likewise be reconsidered, and if approved by two thirds of that House, it shall become a Law. But in all such Cases the Votes of both Houses shall be determined by yeas and Nays, and the Names of the Persons voting for and against the Bill shall be entered on the Journal of each House respectively. If any Bill shall not be returned by the President within ten Days (Sundays excepted) after it shall have been presented to him, the Same shall be a Law, in like Manner as if he had signed it, unless the Congress by their Adjournment prevent its Return, in which Case it shall not be a Law.

Every Order, Resolution, or Vote to which the Concurrence of the Senate and House of Representatives may be necessary (except on a question of Adjournment) shall be presented to the President of the United States; and before the Same shall take Effect, shall be approved by him, or being disapproved by him, shall be repassed by two thirds of the Senate and House of Representatives, according to the Rules and Limitations prescribed in the Case of a Bill.

Section. 8. The Congress shall have Power To lay and collect Taxes, Duties, Imposts and Excises, to pay the Debts and Provide for the common Defence and general Welfare of the United States; but all Duties, Imposts and Excises shall be uniform throughout the United States;

To borrow Money on the credit of the United States;

To regulate Commerce with foreign Nations, and among the several States, and with the Indian Tribes;

To establish an uniform Rule of Naturalization, and uniform Laws on the subject of Bankruptcies throughout the United States;

To coin Money, regulate the Value thereof, and of foreign Coin, and fix the Standard of Weights and Measures;

To provide for the Punishment of counterfeiting the Securities and current Coin of the United States;

To establish Post Offices and post Roads;

To promote the Progress of Science and useful Arts, by securing for limited Time to Authors and Inventors the exclusive Right to their respective Writings and Discoveries;

To constitute Tribunals inferior to the supreme Court;

To define and punish Piracies and Felonies committed on the high Seas, and Offences against the Law of Nations;

To declare War, grant Letters of Marque and Reprisal, and make Rules concerning Captures on Land and Water;

To raise and support Armies, but no Appropriation of Money to that Use shall be for a longer Term than two Years;

To provide and maintain a Navy;

To make Rules for the Government and Regulation of the land and naval Forces;

To provide for calling forth the Militia to execute the

Laws of the Union, suppress Insurrections and repel Invasions;

To provide for organizing, arming, and disciplining, the Militia, and for governing such Part of them as may be employed in the Service of the United States, reserving to the States respectively, the Appointment of the Officers, and the Authority of training the Militia according to the discipline prescribed by Congress;

To exercise exclusive Legislation in all Cases whatsoever, over such District (not exceeding ten Miles square) as may, by Cession of Particular States, and the Acceptance of Congress, become the Seat of the Government of the United States, and to exercise like Authority over all Places purchased by the Consent of the Legislature of the State in which the Same shall be, for the Erection of Forts, Magazines, Arsenals, dock-Yards, and other needful Buildings; — And

To make all Laws which shall be necessary and proper for carrying into Execution the foregoing Powers, and all other Powers vested by this Constitution in the Government of the United States, or in any Department or Officer thereof.

102, 125   Section. 9. The Migration or Importation of such Persons as any of the States now existing shall think proper to admit, shall not be prohibited by the Congress prior to the Year one thousand eight hundred and eight, but a Tax or duty may be imposed on such Importation, not exceeding ten dollars for each Person.

The Privilege of the Writ of Habeas Corpus shall not be suspended, unless when in Cases of Rebellion or Invasion the public Safety may require it.

No Bill of Attainder or ex post facto Law shall be passed.

No Capitation, or other direct, Tax shall be laid, unless in Proportion to the Census or Enumeration herein before directed to be taken.

No Tax or Duty shall be laid on Articles exported from any State.

No Preference shall be given by any Regulation of Commerce or Revenue to the Ports of one State over those of another: nor shall Vessels bound to, or from, one State, be obliged to enter, clear, or pay Duties in another.

No Money shall be drawn from the Treasury, but in Consequence of Appropriations made by Law; and a regular Statement and Account of the Receipts and Expenditures of all public Money shall be published from time to time.

No Title of Nobility shall be granted by the United States: And no Person holding any Office of Profit or Trust under them, shall, without the Consent of the Congress, accept of any present, Emolument, Office, or Title, of any kind whatever, from any King, Prince, or foreign State.

30 Section. 10. No State shall enter into any Treaty, Alliance, or Confederation; grant Letters of Marque and Reprisal; coin Money; emit Bills of Credit; make any Thing but gold and silver Coin a Tender in Payment of Debts; pass any Bill of Attainder, ex post facto Law, or Law impairing the Obligation of Contracts, or grant any Title of Nobility.

No State shall, without the Consent of the Congress, lay any Imposts or Duties on Imports or Exports, except what may be absolutely necessary for executing it's inspection Laws: and the net Produce of all Duties and Imposts, laid by any State on Imports or Exports, shall be for the Use of the Treasury of the United States; and all such Laws shall be subject to the Revision and Controul of the Congress.

No State shall, without the Consent of Congress, lay any Duty of Tonnage, keep Troops, or Ships of War in time of Peace, enter into any Agreement or Compact with another State, or with a foreign Power, or engage in War, unless actually invaded, or in such imminent Danger as will not admit of delay.

ARTICLE. II.

Section. 1. The executive Power shall be vested in a President of the United States of America. He shall hold his Office during the Term of four Years, and, together with the Vice President, chosen for the same Term, be elected, as follows.

Each State shall appoint, in such Manner as the Legislature thereof may direct, a Number of Electors, equal to the whole Number of Senators and Representatives to which the State may be entitled in the Congress: but no Senator or Representative, or Person holding an Office of Trust or Profit under the United States, shall be appointed an Elector.

The Electors shall meet in their respective States, and vote by Ballot for two Persons, of whom one at least shall not be an Inhabitant of the same State with themselves. And they shall make a List of all the Persons voted for, and of the Number of Votes for each; which List they shall sign and certify, and transmit sealed to the Seat of the Government of the United States, directed to the President of the Senate. The President of the Senate shall, in the Presence of the Senate and House of Representatives, open all the Certificates, and the Votes shall then be counted. The Person having the greatest Number of Votes shall be the President, if such Number be a Majority of the whole Number of Electors appointed; and if there be more than one who have such Majority, and have an equal Number of Votes, then the House of Representatives shall immediately chuse by Ballot one of them for President; and if no Person have a Majority, then from the five highest on the List the said House shall in like Manner chuse the President. But in chusing the President, the Votes shall be taken by States, the Representation from each State having one Vote; A quorum for this Purpose shall consist of a Member or Members from two thirds of the States, and a Majority of all the States shall be necessary to a Choice. In every Case, after the Choice of the President, the Person having the greatest Number of Votes of the Electors shall be the Vice President. But if there should remain two or more who have equal Votes, the Senate shall chuse from them by Ballot the Vice President.

The Congress may determine the Time of chusing the Electors, and the Day on which they shall give their Votes; which Day shall be the same throughout the United States.

No Person except a natural born Citizen, or a Citizen of the United States, at the time of the Adoption of this Constitution, shall be eligible to the Office of President; neither shall any Person be eligible to that Office who shall not have attained to the Age of thirty five Years, and been fourteen Years a Resident within the United States.

In Case of the Removal of the President from Office, or of his Death, Resignation, or Inability to discharge the Powers and Duties of the said Office, the Same shall devolve on the Vice President, and the Congress may by Law provide for the Case of Removal, Death, Resignation or Inability, both of the President and Vice President, declaring what Officer shall then act as President, and such Officer shall act accordingly, until the Disability be removed, or a President shall be elected.

The President shall, at stated Times, receive for his Services, a Compensation, which shall neither be encreased nor diminished during the Period for which he shall have been elected, and he shall not receive within that Period any other Emolument from the United States, or any of them.

Before he enter on the Execution of his Office, he shall take the following Oath or Affirmation:— "I do solemnly swear (or affirm) that I will faithfully execute the Office of President of the United States, and will to the best of my Ability, preserve, protect and defend the Constitution of the United States."

Section. 2. The President shall be Commander in Chief of the Army and Navy of the United States, and of the Militia of the several States, when called into the actual Service of the United States; he may require the Opinion, in writing, of the principal Officer in each of the executive Departments, upon any Subject relating to the Duties of their respective Offices, and he shall have Power to grant Reprieves and Pardons for Offences against the United States, except in Cases of Impeachment.

He shall have Power, by and with the Advice and Consent of the Senate, to make Treaties, provided two thirds of the Senators present concur; and he shall nominate, and by and with the Advice and Consent of the Senate, shall appoint Ambassadors, other public Ministers and Consuls, Judges of the supreme Court, and all other Officers of the United States, whose Appointments are not herein otherwise provided for, and which shall be established by Law: but the Congress may by Law vest the Appointment of such inferior Officers, as they think proper, in the President alone, in the Courts of Law, or in the Heads of Departments.

The President shall have Power to fill up all Vacancies that may happen during the Recess of the Senate, by granting Commissions which shall expire at the End of their next Session.

Section. 3. He shall from time to time give to the Congress Information of the State of the Union, and recommend to their Consideration such Measures as he shall judge necessary and expedient; he may, on extraordinary

Occasions, convene both Houses, or either of them, and in Case of Disagreement between them, with Respect to the Time of Adjournment, he may adjourn them to such Time as he shall think proper; he shall receive Ambassadors and other public Ministers; he shall take Care that the Laws be faithfully executed, and shall Commission all the Officers of the United States.

Section. 4. The President, Vice President and all civil Officers of the United States, shall be removed from Office on Impeachment for, and conviction of, Treason, Bribery, or other high Crimes and Misdemeanors.

ARTICLE. III.

Section. 1. The judicial Power of the United States, shall be vested in one supreme Court, and in such inferior Courts as the Congress may from time to time ordain and establish. The Judges, both of the supreme and inferior Courts, shall hold their Offices during good Behaviour, and shall, at stated Times, receive for their Services, a Compensation, which shall not be diminished during their Continuance in Office.

Section. 2. The judicial Power shall extend to all Cases, in Law and Equity, arising under this Constitution, the Laws of the United States, and Treaties made, or which shall be made, under their Authority; — to all Cases affecting Ambassadors, other public Ministers and Consuls; — to all Cases of admiralty and maritime Jurisdiction; — to Controversies to which the United States shall be a Party; — to Controversies between two or more States; — between a State and Citizens of another State; — between Citizens of different States, — between Citizens of the same State claiming Lands under Grants of different States, and between a State, or the Citizens thereof, and foreign States, Citizens or Subjects.

In all Cases affecting Ambassadors, other public Ministers and Consuls, and those in which a State shall be Party, the supreme Court shall have original Jurisdiction. In all the other Cases before mentioned, the supreme Court shall have appellate Jurisdiction, both as to Law and Fact, with such Exceptions, and under such Regulations as the Congress shall make.

The Trial of all Crimes, except in Cases of Impeachment, shall be by Jury; and such Trial shall be held in the State where the said Crimes shall have been committed; but when not committed within any State, the Trial shall be at such Place or Places as the Congress may by Law have directed.

Section. 3. Treason against the United States, shall consist only in levying War against them, or in adhering to their Enemies, giving them Aid and Comfort. No Person shall be convicted of Treason unless on the Testimony of two Witnesses to the same overt Act, or on Confession in open Court.

The Congress shall have Power to declare the Punishment of Treason, but no Attainder of Treason shall work Corruption of Blood, or Forfeiture except during the Life of the Person attainted.

ARTICLE. IV.

Section. 1. Full Faith and Credit shall be given in each State to the public Acts, Records, and judicial Proceedings of every other State. And the Congress may by general Laws prescribe the Manner in which such Acts, Records and Proceedings shall be proved, and the Effect thereof.

Section. 2. The Citizens of each State shall be entitled to all Privileges and Immunities of Citizens in the several States.

A Person charged in any State with Treason, Felony, or

other Crime, who shall flee from Justice, and be found in another State, shall on Demand of the executive Authority of the State from which he fled, be delivered up, to be removed to the State having Jurisdiction of the Crime.

No Person held to Service or Labour in one State, under the Laws thereof, escaping into another, shall, in Consequence of any Law or Regulation therein, be discharged from such Service or Labour, but shall be delivered up on Claim of the Party to whom such Service or Labour may be due.

Section. 3. New States may be admitted by the Congress into this Union; but no new State shall be formed or erected within the Jurisdiction of any other State; nor any State be formed by the Junction of two or more States, or Parts of States, without the Consent of the Legislatures of the States concerned as well as of the Congress.

The Congress shall have Power to dispose of and make all needful Rules and Regulations respecting the Territory or other Property belonging to the United States; and nothing in this Constitution shall be so construed as to Prejudice any Claims of the United States, or of any particular State.

81–82

Section. 4. The United States shall guarantee to every State in this Union a Republican Form of Government, and shall protect each of them against Invasion; and on Application of the Legislature, or of the Executive (when the Legislature cannot be convened) against domestic Violence.

ARTICLE. V.

136, 203, 283, 296, 304, 338, 401, 458, 469–470

The Congress, whenever two thirds of both Houses shall deem it necessary, shall propose Amendments to this Constitution, or, on the Application of the Legislatures of two thirds of the several States, shall call a Convention for

proposing Amendments, which, in either Case, shall be
valid to all Intents and Purposes, as Part of this Constitution, when ratified by the Legislatures of three fourths
of the several States, or by Conventions in three fourths
thereof, as the one or the other Mode of Ratification may
be proposed by the Congress; Provided that no Amendment which may be made prior to the Year One thousand
eight hundred and eight shall in any Manner affect the
first and fourth Clauses in the Ninth Section of the first
Article; and that no State, without its Consent, shall be
deprived of it's equal Suffrage in the Senate.

ARTICLE. VI.

73, 74–75, 77–78,
162, 204–206,
260, 421

All Debts contracted and Engagements entered into, before the Adoption of this Constitution, shall be as valid
against the United States under this Constitution, as under the Confederation.

This Constitution, and the Laws of the United States
which shall be made in Pursuance thereof; and all Treaties made, or which shall be made, under the Authority of
the United States, shall be the supreme Law of the Land;
and the Judges in every State shall be bound thereby, any
Thing in the Constitution or Laws of any State to the
Contrary notwithstanding.

The Senators and Representatives before mentioned,
and the Members of the several State Legislatures, and all
executive and judicial Officers, both of the United States
and of the several States, shall be bound by Oath or Affirmation, to support this Constitution; but no religious
Test shall ever be required as a Qualification to any Office
or public Trust under the United States.

ARTICLE. VII.

The Ratification of the Conventions of nine States, shall be sufficient for the Establishment of this Constitution between the States so ratifying the Same.

Done in Convention by the Unanimous Consent of the States present the Seventeenth Day of September in the Year of our Lord one thousand seven hundred and Eighty seven and of the Independence of the United States of America the Twelfth In witness whereof We have hereunto subscribed our Names,

    Attest William Jackson Secretary

    Go. Washington—Presidt. and Deputy from Virginia.

New Hampshire	John Langdon
	Nicholas Gilman
Massachusetts	Nathaniel Gorham
	Rufus King
Connecticut	Wm: Saml. Johnson
	Roger Sherman
New York	Alexander Hamilton
New Jersey	Wil: Livingston
	David Brearley.
	Wm. Paterson.
	Jona: Dayton
Pennsylvania	B Franklin
	Thomas Mifflin
	Robt Morris
	Geo. Clymer
	Thos. Fitzsimons
	Jared Ingersoll

	James Wilson
	Gouv Morris
Delaware	Geo: Read
	Gunning Bedford jun
	John Dickinson
	Richard Bassett
	Jaco: Broom
Maryland	James McHenry
	Dan of St Thos. Jenifer
	Danl. Carroll.
Virginia	John Blair—
	James Madison Jr.
North Carolina	Wm. Blount
	Richd. Dobbs Spaight.
	Hu Williamson
South Carolina	J. Rutledge
	Charles Cotesworth Pinckney
	Charles Pinckney
	Pierce Butler.
Georgia	William Few
	Abr Baldwin

AMENDMENT I [1791]

Congress shall make no law respecting an establishment of religion, or prohibiting the free exercise thereof; or abridging the freedom of speech, or of the press; or the right of the people peaceably to assemble, and to petition the Government for a redress of grievances.

AMENDMENT II [1791]

A well regulated Militia, being necessary to the security of a free State, the right of the people to keep and bear Arms, shall not be infringed.

AMENDMENT III [1791]

No Soldier shall, in time of peace be quartered in any house, without the consent of the Owner, nor in time of war, but in a manner to be prescribed by law.

AMENDMENT IV [1791]

The right of the people to be secure in their persons, houses, papers, and effects, against unreasonable searches and seizures, shall not be violated, and no Warrants shall issue, but upon probable cause, supported by Oath or affirmation, and particularly describing the place to be searched, and the persons or things to be seized.

AMENDMENT V [1791]

No person shall be held to answer for a capital, or otherwise infamous crime, unless on a presentment or indictment of a Grand Jury, except in cases arising in the land or naval forces, or in the Militia, when in actual service in time of War or public danger; nor shall any person be subject for the same offence to be twice put in jeopardy of life or limb; nor shall be compelled in any criminal case to be a witness against himself, nor be deprived of life, liberty, or property, without due process of law; nor shall private property be taken for public use, without just compensation.

AMENDMENT VI [1791]

In all criminal prosecutions, the accused shall enjoy the right to a speedy and public trial, by an impartial jury of the State and district wherein the crime shall have been committed, which district shall have been previously ascertained by law, and to be informed of the nature and cause of the accusation; to be confronted with the witnesses against him; to have compulsory process for obtaining witnesses in his favor, and to have the Assistance of Counsel for his defense.

AMENDMENT VII [1791]

In Suits at common law, where the value in controversy shall exceed twenty dollars, the right of trial by jury shall be preserved, and no fact tried by a jury, shall be otherwise re-examined in any Court of the United States, than according to the rules of the common law.

AMENDMENT VIII [1791]

Excessive bail shall not be required, nor excessive fines imposed, nor cruel and unusual punishments inflicted.

AMENDMENT IX [1791]

The enumeration in the Constitution, of certain rights, shall not be construed to deny or disparage others retained by the people.

AMENDMENT X [1791]

The powers not delegated to the United States by the Constitution, nor prohibited by it to the States, are reserved to the States respectively, or to the people.

AMENDMENT XI [1795]

The Judicial power of the United States shall not be construed to extend to any suit in law or equity, commenced or prosecuted against one of the United States by Citizens of another State, or by Citizens or Subjects of any Foreign State.

AMENDMENT XII [1804]

The Electors shall meet in their respective states and vote by ballot for President and Vice-President, one of whom, at least, shall not be an inhabitant of the same state with themselves; they shall name in their ballots the person voted for as President, and in distinct ballots the person voted for as Vice-President, and they shall make distinct lists of all persons voted for as President, and of all persons voted for as Vice-President, and of the number of votes for each, which lists they shall sign and certify, and transmit sealed to the seat of the government of the United States, directed to the President of the Senate;—The President of the Senate shall, in the presence of the Senate and House of Representatives, open all the certificates and the votes shall then be counted;— The person having the greatest Number of votes for President, shall be the President, if such number be a majority of the whole number of Electors appointed; and if no person have such majority, then from the persons having the highest numbers not exceeding three on the list of those voted for as

President, the House of Representatives shall choose immediately, by ballot, the President. But in choosing the President, the votes shall be taken by states, the representation from each state having one vote; a quorum for this purpose shall consist of a member or members from two-thirds of the states, and a majority of all the States shall be necessary to a choice. And if the House of Representatives shall not choose a President whenever the right of choice shall devolve upon them, before the fourth day of March next following, then the Vice-President shall act as President, as in the case of the death or other constitutional disability of the President.—The person having the greatest number of votes as Vice-President, shall be the Vice-President, if such number be a majority of the whole number of Electors appointed, and if no person have a majority, then from the two highest numbers on the list, the Senate shall choose the Vice-President; a quorum for the purpose shall consist of two-thirds of the whole number of Senators, and a majority of the whole number shall be necessary to a choice. But no person constitutionally ineligible to the office of President shall be eligible to that of Vice-President of the United States.

AMENDMENT XIII [1865]

Section 1. Neither slavery nor involuntary servitude, except as a punishment for crime whereof the party shall have been duly convicted, shall exist within the United States, or any place subject to their jurisdiction.

Section 2. Congress shall have power to enforce this article by appropriate legislation.

AMENDMENT XIV [1868]

Section 1. All persons born or naturalized in the United States and subject to the jurisdiction thereof, are citizens of the United States and of the State wherein they reside. No State shall make or enforce any law which shall abridge the privileges or immunities of citizens of the United States; nor shall any State deprive any person of life, liberty, or property, without due process of law; nor deny to any person within its jurisdiction the equal protection of the laws.

Section 2. Representatives shall be apportioned among the several States according to their respective numbers, counting the whole number of persons in each State, excluding Indians not taxed. But when the right to vote at any election for the choice of electors for President and Vice President of the United States, Representatives in Congress, the Executive and Judicial officers of a State, or the members of the Legislature thereof, is denied to any of the male inhabitants of such State, being twenty-one years of age, and citizens of the United States, or in any way abridged, except for participation in rebellion, or other crime, the basis of representation therein shall be reduced in the proportion which the number of such male citizens shall bear to the whole number of male citizens twenty-one years of age in such State.

Section 3. No person shall be a Senator or Representative in Congress, or elector of President and Vice President, or hold any office, civil or military, under the United States, or under any State, who, having previously taken an oath, as a member of Congress, or as an officer of the United States, or as a member of any State legislature, or as an executive or judicial officer of any State, to support the Constitution of the United States, shall have engaged in insurrection or rebellion against the same, or given aid or comfort to the enemies thereof. But Congress may by a vote of two-thirds of each House, remove such disability.

Section 4. The validity of the public debt of the United States, authorized by law, including debts incurred for payment of pensions and bounties for services in suppressing insurrection or rebellion, shall not be questioned. But neither the United States nor any State shall assume or pay any debt or obligation incurred in aid of insurrection or rebellion against the United States, or any claim for the loss or emancipation of any slave; but all such debts, obligations and claims shall be held illegal and void.

Section 5. The Congress shall have power to enforce, by appropriate legislation, the provisions of this article.

AMENDMENT XV [1870]

Section 1. The right of citizens of the United States to vote shall not be denied or abridged by the United States or by any State on account of race, color, or previous condition of servitude.

Section 2. The Congress shall have power to enforce this article by appropriate legislation.

AMENDMENT XVI [1913]

The Congress shall have power to lay and collect taxes on incomes, from whatever source derived, without apportionment among the several States, and without regard to any census or enumeration.

AMENDMENT XVII [1913]

The Senate of the United States shall be composed of two Senators from each State, elected by the people thereof, for six years; and each Senator shall have one vote. The electors in each State shall have the qualifications requisite for electors of the most numerous branch of the State legislatures.

When vacancies happen in the representation of any State in the Senate, the executive authority of such State shall issue writs of election to fill such vacancies: Provided, That the legislature of any State may empower the executive thereof to make temporary appointments until the people fill the vacancies by election as the legislature may direct.

This amendment shall not be so construed as to affect the election or term of any Senator chosen before it becomes valid as part of the Constitution.

AMENDMENT XVIII [1919]

282–284

Section 1. After one year from the ratification of this article the manufacture, sale, or transportation of intoxicating liquors within, the importation thereof into, or the exportation thereof from the United States and all territory subject to the jurisdiction thereof for beverage purposes is hereby prohibited.

Section 2. The Congress and the several States shall have concurrent power to enforce this article by appropriate legislation.

Section 3. This article shall be inoperative unless it shall have been ratified as an amendment to the Constitution by the legislatures of the several States, as provided in the Constitution, within seven years from the date of the submission hereof to the States by the Congress.

185, 189, 197, 271, 279, 281–294, 300, 305, 401–402, 406, 408, 434n, 441, 455

AMENDMENT XIX [1920]

The right of citizens of the United States to vote shall not be denied or abridged by the United States or by any State on account of sex.

Congress shall have power to enforce this article by appropriate legislation.

AMENDMENT XX [1933]

Section 1. The terms of the President and Vice President shall end at noon on the 20th day of January, and the terms of Senators and Representatives at noon on the 3d day of January, of the years in which such terms would have ended if this article had not been ratified; and the terms of their successors shall then begin.

Section 2. The Congress shall assemble at least once in every year, and such meeting shall begin at noon on the 3d day of January, unless they shall by law appoint a different day.

Section 3. If, at the time fixed for the beginning of the term of the President, the President elect shall have died, the Vice President elect shall become President. If a President shall not have been chosen before the time fixed for the beginning of his term, or if the President elect shall have failed to qualify, then the Vice President elect shall act as President until a President shall have qualified; and the Congress may by law provide for the case wherein neither a President elect nor a Vice President elect shall have qualified, declaring who shall then act as President, or the manner in which one who is to act shall be selected, and such person shall act accordingly until a President or Vice President shall have qualified.

Section 4. The Congress may by law provide for the case of the death of any of the persons from whom the House of Representatives may choose a President whenever the right of choice shall have devolved upon them, and for the case of the death of any of the persons from whom the Senate may choose a Vice President whenever the right of choice shall have devolved upon them.

Section 5. Sections 1 and 2 shall take effect on the 15th

day of October following the ratification of this article.

Section 6. This article shall be inoperative unless it shall have been ratified as an amendment to the Constitution by the legislatures of three-fourths of the several States within seven years from the date of its submission.

AMENDMENT XXI [1933]

Section 1. The eighteenth article of amendment to the Constitution of the United States is hereby repealed.

Section 2. The transportation or importation into any State, Territory, or possession of the United States for delivery or use therein of intoxicating liquors, in violation of the laws thereof, is hereby prohibited.

Section 3. This article shall be inoperative unless it shall have been ratified as an amendment to the Constitution by conventions in the several States, as provided in the Constitution, within seven years from the date of the submission hereof to the States by the Congress.

AMENDMENT XXII [1951]

41*n*, 289, 403, 405, 462

Section 1. No person shall be elected to the office of the President more than twice, and no person who has held the office of President, or acted as President, for more than two years of a term to which some other person was elected President shall be elected to the office of the President more than once. But this Article shall not apply to any person holding the office of President, when this Article was proposed by the Congress, and shall not prevent any person who may be holding the office of President, or acting as President, during the term within which this Article becomes operative from holding the office of President or acting as President during the remainder of such term.

Section 2. This Article shall be inoperative unless it shall have been ratified as an amendment to the Constitution by the legislatures of three-fourths of the several States within seven years from the date of its submission to the States by the Congress.

AMENDMENT XXIII [1961]

402

Section 1. The District constituting the seat of Government of the United States shall appoint in such manner as the Congress may direct:

A number of electors of President and Vice President equal to the whole number of Senators and Representatives in Congress to which the District would be entitled if it were a State, but in no event more than the least populous State; they shall be in addition to those appointed by the States, but they shall be considered, for the purposes of the election of President and Vice President, to be electors appointed by a State; and they shall meet in the District and perform such duties as provided by the twelfth article of amendment.

Section 2. The Congress shall have power to enforce this article by appropriate legislation.

AMENDMENT XXIV [1964]

185, 402,
405–408, 441

Section 1. The right of citizens of the United States to vote in any primary or other election for President or Vice President, for electors for President or Vice President, or for Senator or Representative in Congress, shall not be denied or abridged by the United States or any State by reason of failure to pay any poll tax or other tax.

Section 2. The Congress shall have power to enforce this article by appropriate legislation.

AMENDMENT XXV [1967]

Section 1. In case of the removal of the President from office or of his death or resignation, the Vice President shall become President.

Section 2. Whenever there is a vacancy in the office of the Vice President, the President shall nominate a Vice President who shall take office upon confirmation by a majority vote of both Houses of Congress.

Section 3. Whenever the President transmits to the President pro tempore of the Senate and the Speaker of the House of Representatives his written declaration that he is unable to discharge the powers and duties of his office, and until he transmits to them a written declaration to the contrary, such powers and duties shall be discharged by the Vice President as Acting President.

Section 4. Whenever the Vice President and a majority of either the principal officers of the executive departments or of such other body as Congress may by law provide, transmit to the President pro tempore of the Senate and the Speaker of the House of Representatives their written declaration that the President is unable to discharge the powers and duties of his office, the Vice President shall immediately assume the powers and duties of the office as Acting President.

Thereafter, when the President transmits to the President pro tempore of the Senate and the Speaker of the House of Representatives his written declaration that no inability exists, he shall resume the powers and duties of his office unless the Vice President and a majority of either the principal officers of the executive department or of such other body as Congress may by law provide, transmit within four days to the President pro tempore of the Senate and the Speaker of the House of Representatives their written declaration that the President is unable to discharge the powers and duties of his office. Thereupon Congress shall decide the issue, assembling within forty-eight hours for that purpose if not in session. If the Congress, within twenty-one days after receipt of the latter written declaration, or, if Congress is not in session, within twenty-one days after Congress is required to assemble, determines by two-thirds vote of both Houses that the President is unable to discharge the powers and duties of his office, the Vice President shall continue to discharge the same as Acting President; otherwise, the President shall resume the powers and duties of his office.

AMENDMENT XXVI [1971]

189, 191, 402, 406, 408, 441

Section 1. The right of citizens of the United States, who are eighteen years of age or older, to vote shall not be denied or abridged by the United States or by any State on account of age.

Section 2. The Congress shall have the power to enforce this article by appropriate legislation.

AMENDMENT XXVII [1992]

No law varying the compensation for the services of the Senators and Representatives shall take effect, until an election of Representatives shall have intervened.

NOTES

WORKS FREQUENTLY CITED

Amar, *ACAB*	Akhil Reed Amar, *America's Constitution: A Biography* (2005).
Amar, *Bill of Rights*	Akhil Reed Amar, *The Bill of Rights: Creation and Reconstruction* (1998).
Amar, *CCP*	Akhil Reed Amar, *The Constitution and Criminal Procedure: First Principles* (1997).
Annals†	Joseph Gales, Sr., *The Debates and Proceedings in the Congress of the United States*...(1834–), 24 vols. ("Annals of the Congress of the United States").
Blackstone's Comm.	William Blackstone, *Commentaries on the Laws of England*, 4 vols. Note: This book cites to Blackstone's first edition, volume 1 of which was published in 1765.
CG†	*Congressional Globe.*
Cong. Rec.†	*Congressional Record.*
DHRC	Merrill Jensen, John P. Kaminski, and Gaspare J. Saladino, eds., *The Documentary History of the Ratification of the Constitution* (1976–), 20 vols.
Elliot's Debates†	Jonathan Elliot, ed., *The Debates in the Several State Conventions on the Adoption of the Federal Constitution.*...(1888), 5 vols.
Farrand's Records†	Max Farrand, ed., *The Records of the Federal Convention of 1787* (rev. ed. 1966), 4 vols.
Ford, *Essays*	Paul Leicester Ford, ed., *Essays on the Constitution of the United States* (1892).
Ford, *Pamphlets*	Paul Leicester Ford, ed., *Pamphlets on the Constitution of the United States* (1888).

Hamilton, *Papers*	Harold C. Syrett, ed., *The Papers of Alexander Hamilton* (1961–), 27 vols.
JCC[†]	*Journals of the Continental Congress.*
Jefferson, *Papers*	Julian P. Boyd, ed., *The Papers of Thomas Jefferson* (1950), 30 vols.
Jefferson, *Writings* (Ford)	Paul Leicester Ford, ed., *The Writings of Thomas Jefferson* (1895), 10 vols.
Maclay's Journal[†]	Edgar S. Maclay, ed., *Journal of William Maclay* (1890).
Madison, *Papers*	William T. Hutchinson, William M. E. Rachal, et al., eds., *The Papers of James Madison* (1962), 17 vols.
Madison, *Writings* (Hunt)	Gaillard Hunt, ed., *The Writings of James Madison* (1910), 9 vols.
Reg. Deb.[†]	*Register of Debates.*
Sen. Exec. J[†]	*Senate Executive Journal.*
Sen. J[†]	*Senate Journal.*
Stat.[†]	*Statutes at Large.*
Storing's Anti-Fed.	Herbert J. Storing, ed., *The Complete Anti-Federalist* (1981), 7 vols.
Story, *Commentaries*	Joseph Story, ed., *Commentaries on the Constitution of the United States* (1833; rev. ed. 1991), 3 vols.
Washington, *Writings*	John C. Fitzpatrick, ed., *The Writings of George Washington, from the Original Manuscript Sources, 1745–1799* (1939), 39 vols.

CHAPTER I: READING BETWEEN THE LINES

1 *New York Times*, March 6, 1868, 1; *Sen. J*, 40-2: 809 App. (March 5, 1868).

2 A strict constitutional textualist might view the matter differently. According to Article II, "In Case of the Removal of the President from Office, or of his Death, Resignation, or Inability to discharge the Powers and Duties of the said Office, the Same shall devolve on the Vice President." Did "the Same" in this sentence mean merely the "Powers and Duties" of the office, or the "Office" itself? A strong textual case could be made that upon the death of the president, the vice president remained vice president, but simply

---

[†] Available online on the Library of Congress website, "A Century of Lawmaking." Many of these LOC databases are word-searchable. Detailed citations are generally omitted for other easily web-searchable materials, such as the *Federalist* essays, Jefferson's *Manual of Parliamentary Practice*, the collected works of Abraham Lincoln, famous speeches in American history, national political party platforms, and prominent Supreme Court opinions.

inherited various presidential "Powers and Duties"—just as he would in the case of a debilitating presidential illness. The text makes no devolution distinction between a death and a disability, and surely in the case of a mere disability (which might prove temporary), the vice president never becomes president. On this strict textualist view, Andrew Johnson never became "president" but was always simply a vice president wielding various presidential powers—exactly as if Lincoln lay in a coma rather than in a vault. If so, perhaps Chief Justice Chase should not have presided, because the Senate was trying a vice president, not a president, and the constitutional text provides for the chief justice's presence only in cases where "the President of the United States is tried."

But this is not what happened. When President William Henry Harrison died in 1841, Vice President John Tyler eventually claimed that he was president, and this claim was accepted by the other branches of government and by the people. (Thus, Tyler was entitled to a president's salary, rather than the smaller vice-presidential stipend.) After the death of President Zachary Taylor, Vice President Millard Fillmore likewise saw himself as president and was treated as such. Andrew Johnson followed suit, and no serious question arose in 1868 about treating his impeachment as a *presidential* impeachment triggering the presence of the chief justice. The articles of impeachment prepared by the House themselves repeatedly referred to "Andrew Johnson, President of the United States." *Sen. J*, 40-2: 800–807 App. (March 2, 1868). All of which reminds us that America's constitutional experience goes beyond a narrow, literalistic constitutional textualism. The practical precedents set by Tyler and Fillmore definitively glossed the ambiguous language of Article II. After President Kennedy's assassination, this understanding was formally codified in section 1 of the Twenty-fifth Amendment: "In case of the removal of the President from office or of his death or resignation, the Vice President shall become President." For additional examples of actual governmental practices glossing and clarifying initially ambiguous constitutional clauses, see Chapters 8 and 9.

3 *Trial of Andrew Johnson, President of the United States, Before the Senate of the United States, on Impeachment by the House of Representatives for High Crimes and Misdemeanors* (1868), 3:360–361.

4 For a clever—tongue-in-cheek?—argument that a vice president may preside over his own impeachment trial, see Michael Stokes Paulsen, "Someone Should Have Told Spiro Agnew," in William N. Eskridge Jr. and Sanford Levinson, eds., *Constitutional Stupidities, Constitutional Tragedies* (1998), 75–76. For a powerful counterargument, see Joel K. Goldstein, "Can the Vice President Preside at His Own Impeachment Trial? A Critique of Bare Textualism," *St. Louis U. LJ* 44 (2000): 849.

5 Consistent with these bedrock principles, in the very first days of the very first meeting of the House of Representatives, that body adopted rules forbidding any member from voting on a matter in which he was "immediately and particularly interested." *Annals*, 1:104 (April 7, 1789). In his famous *Manual of Parliamentary Practice,* Thomas Jefferson later linked this rule to "the fundamental principles of the social compact, which denies to any man to be a judge in his own cause." Sec. XVII.

6 *Dr. Bonham's Case*, 8 Co. Rep. 107a, 77 Eng. Rep. 638 (C.P. 1610).

7 Donald S. Lutz, *A Preface to American Political Theory* (1992), 134–140. For representative references in 1787–1788, see *Farrand's Records*, 1:472 (Hamilton: "the celebrated Judge Blackstone"); *Federalist* Nos. 69 and 84 (Hamilton/Publius: "the judicious Blackstone"); *Elliot's Debates*, 2:423–424, 432, 437, 455 (Wilson), 518 (Smilie and Wilson); ibid., 3:501 (Madison: "a book which is in every man's hand"), 544 (Henry: "the learned judge Blackstone, so often quoted"), 506 (George Nicholas), 512–513 (Henry), 510 (Corbin); ibid., 4:63 (Maclaine: "admirable Commentaries"), 278 (C. C Pinckney: one of "the best writers on the laws and constitution of England"); ibid., 1:504 (R. H. Lee to Edmund Randolph, Oct. 16, 1787, reprinted in the Petersburg *Virginia Gazette* on Dec. 6, 1787, *DHRC*, 8:59–60); "The Address and Reasons of Dissent of the Minority of the Convention of Pennsylvania to Their Constituents" (Dec. 18, 1787), in *Storing's Anti-Fed.*, 3:160; A Columbian Patriot, "Observations on the New Constitution, and on the Federal and State Conventions" (1788), in ibid., 4:276; "Essays by a Farmer (III)" (June 6, 1788), in ibid., 4:213 ("Justice Blackstone, who is one of the most celebrated Authors now extant"); "Essays by Hampden" (Jan. 26, 1788), in ibid., 200 ("Judge Blackstone's excellent Commentary").

8 *Blackstone's Comm.*, 1:91, 60–61 (emphasis added) (footnote citing *Bonham's Case* omitted).

9 *Farrand's Records*, 2:375–376. See also *Calder v. Bull*, 3 U.S. (3 Dall.) 386, 389 (1798) (Chase, J.) ("The prohibition against their making *any ex post facto laws* was introduced for *greater* caution"). By contrast, the *nemo judex in causa sua* principle was not a prominent textual feature in revolutionary state constitutions. (In practice, all the states did of course accept the validity of the basic *nemo judex* principle.) Had the federal Constitution omitted a textual affirmation of the ban on ex-post-facto laws, this omission perhaps might have been more easily misunderstood by some as a purposeful rejection of the ban as it had been expressed in various foundational state texts.

10 *Blackstone's Comm.*, 1:45–46. For an invocation of this very passage at the Philadelphia Convention, see *Farrand's Records*, 2:448–449 (Dickinson).

11 Ibid., 2:495 (comma deleted).

12 See *Elliot's Debates*, 4:44 (Maclaine) ("[I]f the Vice-President should be judge, might he not look at the office of President, and endeavor to influence the Senate against him?"); William Rawle, *A View of the Constitution of the United States of America* (2d ed. 1829; reprint 2003), 216 ("[I]t would be inconsistent with the implied purity of a judge that a person under a probable bias of such a nature, should participate in the trial"). See also Story, *Commentaries*, 2:247, sec. 775 (similar).

13 Cf. Philip Bobbitt, *Constitutional Fate: Theory of the Constitution* (1982), 142 (explaining how a constitutional text may sometimes be properly read "not for its own force, but rather as evidence of a more general [ethical] principle").

14 For representative comments on the vice presidency at Philadelphia, see *Farrand's Records*, 2:537. The First Congress provided by statute that the vice president receive an annual salary of $5,000. Act of Sept. 24, 1789, 1 Stat. 72.

15 Leading Anti-Federalists evidently took the Federalists at their word here. Maryland's Samuel Chase, who had opposed Wilson, Ellsworth, Madison, and Hamilton in 1787–1788, echoed these men a decade later. Sitting as a justice of the U.S. Supreme Court, Chase declared that American governments must honor not only the "express" limitations on their power found in state and federal constitutions, but also "great first principles of the social compact." Chase proceeded to offer a handful of examples of impermissible government action, including both ex-post-facto laws and violations of *nemo judex in causa sua. Calder v. Bull*, 3 U.S. (3 Dall.) 386, 387–388 (1798) (opinion of Chase, J.).

In John Locke's influential writings, the *nemo judex* principle had formed part of the very basis for the existence of civil government. According to Locke, in a state of nature each person seeking to avoid wronging others and to remedy others' violations of his own rights might routinely be obliged to be a judge in his own case, which was a result strongly to be avoided. "Civil Government is the proper Remedy for the inconveniences of the State of Nature, which must certainly be great, where Men may be Judges in their own Case." John Locke, *Second Treatise of Government* (1690), Ch. II, sec. 13. See also supra n. 5.

16 For an illustration of precisely this sort of contestability, see *Trial of Andrew Johnson*, 3:375–378 (Sen. Sumner).

17 John G. Nicolay and John Hay, *Abraham Lincoln: A History* (1890), 9:394.

18 Though Chase was a leading Republican in the 1860s, he had begun his career as a Democrat and was willing to revert under the right conditions.

19 Of the first sixteen presidents to serve after Washington, nine were former senators: James Monroe, John Quincy Adams, Andrew Jackson, Martin Van Buren, William Henry Harrison, John Tyler, Franklin Pierce, James Buchanan, and Andrew Johnson. Washington himself, of course, could not have been a senator because the Senate did not exist before 1789.

20 For Morris's proposal, see *Farrand's Records*, 2:427. In 1789, Washington received 69 electoral votes; Adams, 34; Jay, 9; and Rutledge, 6. Maryland's Robert Harrison—another man whom Washington would name to the Supreme Court (but who declined appointment) also received 6. On Marshall's scheming, see Bruce Ackerman, *The Failure of the Founding Fathers: Jefferson, Marshall, and the Rise of Presidential Democracy* (2005), 36–54.

21 Act of March 1, 1792, ch. 8, sec. 9, 1 Stat. 239, 240.

22 Annals, 2:1902 (Rep. White, Jan. 10, 1791); ibid., 3:281 (Reps. Sturges and Giles, Dec. 22, 1791); Madison to Edmund Pendleton, Feb. 21, 1792, in Madison, *Papers*, 14:235.

23 Senator James Dixon argued that the framers' *nemo judex* rationale for excluding the vice president from a presidential impeachment applied equally to Senator Wade, and that "the character and meaning and spirit of the Constitution" prohibited Wade from sitting in judicial judgment of the president. The framers "knew that in the very nature of things, in common justice, a man could not be a judge in his own case. They knew that the provisions of the common law prohibited a man from being a judge in his own

case. They probably remembered what has been said by one great commentator, (Blackstone,) that the omnipotence of Parliament was limited in this respect, and that body could not make a man a judge in his own case." *Trial of Andrew Johnson*, 3:397. For other senatorial statements explicitly arguing that the Constitution gave the chief justice the presidential-impeachment gavel for *nemo judex* reasons, and that the spirit of this *nemo judex* clause applied to Wade as well, see ibid., 360, 365 (Sen. Hendricks), 362–363 (Sen. Reverdy Johnson—no relation to Andrew), 363–364 (Sen. Davis), 373–374 (Sen. Bayard), 385 (Sen. Buckalew). For the text of the impeachment oath, see *Sen. J*, 40-2:809 App. (March 5, 1868). For general background, see Michael Les Benedict, *The Impeachment of Andrew Johnson* (1973), 118.

24 In 1862 Congress imposed a special 3 percent salary tax on a wide range of federal officials, including judges. In response, Chief Justice Roger Taney limited himself to penning and publishing a letter of protest to Treasury Secretary Chase: "I should not have troubled you with this letter, if there were any mode by which the question could be decided in a judicial proceeding. But all of the judges of the courts of the United States have an interest in the question, and could not therefore with propriety undertake to hear and decide it." Taney to Chase, Feb. 16, 1863, in 157 U.S. 701, 702 (1895) (challenging Act of July 1, 1862, ch. 119, sec. 86, 12 Stat. 432, 472). For more recent case law, see, e.g., *United States v. Will*, 449 U.S. 200, 213–217 (1980). Cf. *Evans v. Gore*, 253 U.S. 245, 247–248 (1920); *O'Malley v. Woodrough*, 307 U.S. 277 (1939). See generally John T. Noonan Jr., "Making the Case One's Own," *Hofstra LR* 32 (2004): 1139. For defenses of Wade invoking the two-senator-per-state rule, see, e.g., *Trial of Andrew Johnson*, 3:360, 371–372 (Sen. Sherman), 361 (Sen. Howard), 379 (Sen. Howe), 382 (Sen. Thayer). Note that no necessity problem arises in any situation when the vice president must recuse himself as the Senate's presiding officer; Article I, section 3, expressly provides that the Senate may designate a substitute presiding officer in the vice president's absence.

25 Act of Jan. 19, 1886, ch. 4, sec. 1, 24 Stat. 1; Act of July 18, 1947, Public Law (Pub. L. hereafter) No. 80-199, sec. (a)(1), (b), 61 Stat. 380, 380 (codified at 3 U.S.C. sec. 19[a][1], [b]). For more on this deeply flawed 1947 statute, see Chapter 10, text accompanying n. 11.

26 Cf. Hadley Arkes, *Beyond the Constitution* (1990) and *Constitutional Illusions and Anchoring Truths* (2010).

27 Professor Sanford Levinson has provocatively identified a nineteenth-century pattern in which Justice Brockholst Livingston participated "in circuit court litigation involving the New York steamboat monopoly even though his brother Robert Livingston was the holder of the monopoly in question"; Justice Levi Woodbury "once heard on circuit an important case in which a lawyer for one of the litigants was his son, Charles Woodbury"; Chief Justice Taney declined to recuse himself when his brother-in-law Francis Scott Key argued before his Court; and "David Dudley Field…argued three of the most important cases involving national power over the defeated Confederacy before a Court that included his brother, Stephen J. Field." Sanford Levinson, Book Review, *Virginia LR* 75 (1989): 1429, 1439–1440. And of course, in *Marbury v. Madison*, 5 U.S. (1 Cranch) 137 (1803), a case brought before the justices as trial judges, John Marshall declined to

would immediately pass a loosely worded framework statute inviting the courts back in to keep doing pretty much what they have been doing. Put another way, Congress today legislates against the backdrop of rules generated by the Court's dormant-commerce-clause doctrine and appears by its actions and inactions over many decades to have embraced the federal judiciary as its partner in keeping states under control. Thus, current dormant-commerce-clause doctrine is a proper part of America's unwritten Constitution—indeed, quadruply so, with deep roots in this chapter's implicit-Constitution approach, in proper precedential principles as outlined in Chapter 5, in the iconic Declaration featured in Chapter 6, and in actual institutional practice of the sort highlighted in Chapter 9.

38 Act to Prevent Circulation of Seditious Publications, N.C. Rev. Code, ch. 34, 16 (1854) (revising 1830 N.C. Sess. Laws, ch. 5, at 10–11); 1860 N.C. Sess. Laws, ch. 23, at 39 (1860). See, generally, Michael Kent Curtis, "The 1859 Crisis over Hinton Helper's Book, *The Impending Crisis*: Free Speech, Slavery, and Some Light on the Meaning of the First Section of the Fourteenth Amendment," *Chicago-Kent LR* 68 (1993): 1113.

39 Here, as elsewhere, I am indebted to Black, *Structure and Relationship*. Black himself graciously credited the seminal work of Alexander Meiklejohn in *Free Speech and Its Relation to Self-Government* (1948).

40 The legal maxim of interpretation at issue here is known to lawyers as *expressio unius est exclusio alterius*: The expression of one thing is the exclusion of other things. Thus, when the law says "A, B, and C," this maxim suggests that the law should be read to mean *only* "A, B, and C" and nothing else. Sometimes *expressio unius* is a sound textual inference; sometimes not. Whether this inference makes good constitutional sense in any given constitutional situation will depend, among other things, on the document as a whole, on its larger structures and purposes, and on how the clause in question was understood by Americans when they framed and ratified it. In other words, any claim that a given constitutional clause contains a negatively implied "only" is *itself* an argument within the general framework of America's implicit Constitution and should be analyzed by reference to the general criteria that this chapter seeks to bring to light. For Marshall's repeated rejection of *expressio unius* arguments in *McCulloch*, see, e.g., 17 U.S. at 416–417, 425–426, 427.

41 Although the Fourteenth Amendment was designed to affirm free speech and free press rights—and many other rights—against states, and was so understood by its ratifiers, that amendment was still waiting to be born in 1858.

42 Thus, the first Congress provided its members with newspapers at public expense and openly justified this measure as properly promoting a free press. Even as a joint House-Senate Committee (unsuccessfully) proposed reducing this subsidy to economize on public expenses, the Committee acknowledged that "the publication of newspapers [was] highly beneficial in disseminating useful information throughout the United States, and deserving of public encouragement." *Annals*, 1:427 (May 28, 1789). See, generally, David P. Currie, *The Constitution in Congress: The Federalist Period* (1997), 73 n. 137.

43 But see *Hutchinson v. Proxmire*, 443 U.S. 111 (1979). This case is powerfully critiqued in

Josh Chafetz, *Democracy's Privileged Few: Legislative Privilege and Democratic Norms in the British and American Constitutions* (2007), 103–104.

44 In a similar vein, Justice Story suggested that the petition and assembly rights "would seem unnecessary to be expressly provided for in a republican government, since it results from the very nature of its structure and institutions." Story, *Commentaries*, 3:745, sec. 1887.

45 As American history actually unfolded, of course, North Carolina's government purported to join the Confederacy in late May 1861, after serious hostilities had commenced in mid-April. Presumably nothing prevented North Carolina in March or early April from claiming its full rights as a state in good standing under the U.S. Constitution. And presumably there were at least some proslavery fanatics in the Tar Heel State who might have been willing to swear out all manner of charges against Lincoln, if given the chance.

46 On the importance of institutional muscle, as opposed to textual declarations—"parchment barriers"—see, e.g., *Federalist* Nos. 48, 51 (Madison).

47 *Spalding v. Vilas*, 161 U.S. 483, 495 (1896) (quoting *Scott v. Stansfield*, 3 L.R. Exch. 220, 223 [1868]). The Court has not had occasion to consider whether the implicit constitutional immunity from state defamation law that federal judges enjoy might be subject to abrogation by Congress. Note that when the *judiciary* pronounces the existence of certain *judicial* immunities, this pronouncement might itself seem to be in tension with the *nemo judex* principle, but might nevertheless be valid in light of the rule of necessity: If the central idea of a properly impartial judge—an idea tightly intertwined with the *nemo judex* principle—entails broad judicial freedom of speech and independence from libel law within the courtroom itself, then the seeming conflict of interest visible whenever a judge pronounces the existence of this judicial freedom/independence/immunity would not be unique to the specific judge in this particular case, but would be true of all judges in all cases, and thus permissible under one sensible understanding of the rule of necessity.

48 On Burr, see *New-York Evening Post*, Feb. 6, 1805, 3 (quoting "The World Upside Down," *Trenton Federalist*, Feb. 4, 1805, 3 [quoting *New-England Palladium*, Jan. 15, 1805, 1]).

49 Civil litigation against a sitting president does not raise the same risk, given that a president does not typically face the threat of a bodily coercion in civil litigation; he remains free to simply boycott the litigation and pay damages if found liable. In the famous case of *Clinton v. Jones*, 520 U.S. 681 (1997), the Supreme Court unanimously ruled that a sitting president had no general immunity from a civil suit brought against him in federal court. Prior to this ruling, some scholars (myself included) did express concern that civil litigation might improperly distract a president from attending to the people's business. See, e.g., Akhil Reed Amar and Neal Kumar Katyal, "Executive Privileges and Immunities: The *Nixon* and *Clinton* Cases," *Harvard LR* 108 (1995): 701. The *Jones* Court brushed aside these concerns, declaring that "if properly managed by the District Court, [the Paula Jones suit] appears to us highly unlikely to occupy any substantial amount of [the president's] time." 520 U.S. at 702.

50 Any statute of limitations should be tolled by the president's invocation of immunity.

51 As a structural matter, presidential immunity from state prosecution should be waivable; in certain situations a sitting president might prefer an immediate trial to clear his name from an obviously baseless charge. A sitting president could of course also choose to temporarily cede presidential power to his vice president during the pendency of a criminal trial.

52 *Federalist* Nos. 69, 77.

53 *Farrand's Records*, 2:500; *Elliot's Debates*, 4:37. See also "Letter of Americanus (I) to the Virginia Independent Chronicle" (Dec. 5, 1787), reprinted in *DHRC*, 8:200, 203 (president "is liable to be impeached…and *afterwards* he is subject to indictment, trial, judgment, and punishment according to law") (emphasis added).

54 *Elliot's Debates*, 2:480 (emphasis deleted). James Iredell in North Carolina echoed Wilson: "If the President does a single act by which the people are prejudiced, he is punishable himself, and no other man merely to screen him. If he commits any misdemeanor in office, he is impeachable, removable from office, and incapacitated to hold any office of honor, trust, or profit. If he commits any crime, he is punishable by the laws of his country, and in capital cases may be deprived of his life." Ibid., 4:109. See also Alexander Contee Hanson, "Remarks on the Proposed Plan of a Federal Government, Addressed to the Citizens of the United States of America, and Particularly to the People of Maryland" (Jan. 1, 1788), in Ford, *Pamphlets*, 226, 233 ("Like any other individual, [the president] is liable to punishment.…Not even his person is particularly protected."); James Iredell, "Answers to Mr. Mason's Objections to the New Constitution, Recommended by the Late Convention" (Jan. 1788), in ibid., 352 ("[The president] is not exempt from a trial, if he should be guilty or supposed guilty, of [treason] or any other offence"). As with Wilson's remarks, none of these discussions focused with precision on whether impeachment and removal would ordinarily need to precede regular criminal prosecution of a sitting president. Iredell, in particular, aimed to contradistinguish presidents from kings—who of course were not subject to ordinary criminal prosecution and were also immune from impeachment or any other regular mechanism of removal from power. As Iredell himself explained, "There are no courts to try him [the king] for any high crimes; nor is there any constitutional method for depriving him of his throne." *Elliot's Debates*, 4:109. By contrast, the U.S. Constitution did provide an obvious mechanism for removing a president first, and then prosecuting him in an ordinary criminal court. Read in context, Iredell's comments should thus not be seen as squarely rejecting the proposition that impeachment and removal (or resignation or waiver) would ordinarily need to precede regular criminal prosecutions of a president.

Relatedly, Federalist Tench Coxe asserted that the president "is not so much protected as that of a member of the house of representatives; for he may be proceeded against like any other man in the ordinary course of law." "An Examination of the Constitution for the United States of America (I)," in Ford, *Pamphlets*, 139. It is not entirely clear whether Coxe was discussing civil or criminal cases or both in juxtaposing presidential

and congressional privileges. His sweeping language seems to encompass both categories, rendering his hasty analysis highly doubtful. For example, Coxe seemed to imply
that a president could be sued for common-law libel even for remarks contained within
a veto message to Congress or a State of the Union message. If so, presidential messages
that the Constitution itself authorizes and requires would receive less protection from
state libel law than do ordinary judicial utterances in court or in published opinions.
Here, too, great caution is warranted before deriving sweeping conclusions from mere
negative implication.

55 *Elliot's Debates*, 2:480, 523 (emphasis deleted). For more on *Marbury* and executive privilege, see Chapter 9, text accompanying n. 11.

56 *Maclay's Journal*, 167 (Sept. 25, 1789); Jefferson to George Hay, June 20, 1807, in Paul
Leicester Ford, ed., *The Works of Thomas Jefferson* (1905), 10:404 n. 1 (emphasis deleted).

57 Story, *Commentaries*, 3:418–419, sec. 1563 (emphasis added). The hedging language suggested that the president's "person must be deemed, in civil cases at least, to possess an
official inviolability." Ibid. The potentially limiting language about "civil cases" suggests
that Story here may have been analogizing to the scope of congressional immunity from
civil arrest under Article I, section 6. See Amar and Katyal, "Executive Privileges and
Immunities," 711–717.

58 For more on the difference in unitariness between state and federal executive branches,
see Chapter 12. Note also that although governors typically wield pardon pens, a governor may not pardon himself without violating the *nemo judex* principle. For discussion
of the similar (albeit implicit) ban on presidential self-pardons, see Chapter 9.

59 For similar reminders that satisfying textual arguments must attend to the larger structural and institutional contexts within which textual fragments are located, see Black,
Structure and Relationship, 31; Laurence H. Tribe, "Taking Text and Structure Seriously:
Reflections on Free-Form Method in Constitutional Interpretation," *Harvard LR* 108
(1995): 1221, 1233.

60 It is at precisely this point where leading critics of presidential immunity veer furthest
off course. See, e.g., Eric M. Freedman, "The Law as King and the King as Law: Is a
President Immune from Criminal Prosecution Before Impeachment?," *Hastings Constitutional Law Quarterly* 20 (1992): 7; Eric M. Freedman, "On Protecting Accountability,"
Hofstra LR 27 (1999): 677, 709–710; Jonathan Turley, "'From Pillar to Post': The Prosecution of American Presidents," *American Criminal LR* 37 (2000): 1049. The real question
is not whether a sitting president is absolutely and utterly immune from all criminal
proceedings that might be brought against him. Rather, the question is whether the
screening of the accusations against him and the judgment about his guilt should be
made in the first instance by officials and jurors from a single locality or instead by the
great national inquest of Congress. Thus, the most eminent constitutional structuralist
of the twentieth century thought that a sitting president should not be fair game in an
ordinary criminal court. Charles L. Black Jr., *Impeachment: A Handbook* (1974), 40.

CHAPTER 2: HEEDING THE DEED

1 On the importance of "symbolic expression"—paintings, flags, processions, liberty poles, costumes, effigies, and so on—and a survey of Founding-era legal protections of these forms of expression, see Eugene Volokh, "Symbolic Expression and the Original Meaning of the First Amendment," *Georgetown LJ* 97 (2009): 1057. For discussion of one episode in which Anti-Federalists burned effigies of Federalist leaders, see Pauline Maier, *Ratification: The People Debate the Constitution, 1787–1788* (2010), 121–122. Maier also argues that the Federalists were able to use their economic and organizational advantages to dominate certain press outlets. See ibid., 70–95, 99–101. Maier further notes that the ratification process was marred by occasional threats of mob violence, and she highlights one instance in which a printer actually fell victim to a significant act of illegal repression. (Interestingly, this episode occurred *after* eleven states had ratified the document. Ibid., 398.) Fisticuffs and rioting sometimes closely accompanied elections in late eighteenth-century America, and the year-long and continent-wide ratification process was not entirely free from these electoral blemishes. Ibid., 406–408. Notwithstanding these lapses, the fact that no one died or was seriously injured in America's Great Debate of 1787–1788 stands in remarkable contrast to the American Revolution of the 1770s and the French Revolution of the 1790s.

2 On Adams and Ames, see *Elliot's Debates*, 2:11, 178–181. For additional examples of persuasion at this convention, see ibid. 160 (Nathaniel Barrell), 183 (Benjamin Swain).

3 *Elliot's Debates*, 2:432 (emphasis and punctuation altered), 458 (emphasis added). Contemporary foreign observers also took note of the epic continental conversation unfolding before them. See, e.g., *DHRC*, 8:205 (Dec. 6, 1787, letter from Diego de Gardoqui to Conde de Floridabalanca); ibid., 14:229 (Nov. 26, 1787, letter from Louis-Guillaume Otto to Comte de Montmorin).

4 For English law and practice, see *Blackstone's Comm.* 4:151–152; see also infra Chapter 4. For American practice after the Revolutionary War, see Leonard W. Levy, *Emergence of a Free Press* (1985), 186–189; David A. Anderson, "The Origins of the Press Clause," *U.C.L.A. LR* 30 (1983): 455, 510–515. The war years were a different story.

5 *Elliot's Debates*, 4:570–571 (Madison's 1799 Report on the Virginia Resolutions).

6 The fact that Congress enacted an expression-suppressing Sedition Act in 1798, only a decade after the ink had dried on the Philadelphia Constitution, might be thought to undercut the basic enactment argument for robust free speech. But many of the claims made by supporters of the 1798 act flatly contradicted claims and promises made by leading Federalists in the great national debate of 1787–1788 and in the conversation surrounding the drafting and ratification of the First Amendment. Indeed, the amendment's chief draftsman was Madison, whose reminder that the very act of constitution itself had depended on and solidified robust free-expression rights occurred precisely as he was explaining why the 1798 act was a constitutional abomination. The American people sided with Madison on this issue in the election of 1800, and his views have also

been affirmed by the court of history. Today, the unconstitutionality of the Sedition Act of 1798 is a first principle of free-expression law. For more on this, see Chapter 4, text accompanying nn. 20, 33–35, and Chapter 7, text accompanying n. 6; see also Amar, *Bill of Rights*, 36; Amar, *ACAB*, 102–104.

It might be argued that robust free speech must be allowed, by analogy to the enactment principles that operated in 1787–1789, only when the American people are amending the Constitution, just as special voting rules might apply only to amendments. But since the people have a right to amend at any time, and since speech is part of the agenda-setting process, free speech at every moment is necessary to vindicate the basic principle that the Constitution is open to amendment at all times.

7 Mass. Const. (1780), pt. II, ch. VI, art. X. In the actual adoption of the 1780 Constitution, certain flaws in the tally were deftly swept under the rug with Yankee ingenuity.

8 *Storing's Anti-Fed.*, 4:172 (emphasis deleted).

9 On Warren as the likely author, see ibid., 162. For Anti-Federalist deference to majority rule in Massachusetts, see *Elliot's Debates*, 2:181–182 (Abraham White) ("[N]otwithstanding he had opposed the Constitution, yet, as a majority had seen fit to adopt it, he should use his utmost exertions to induce his constituents to live in peace under and cheerfully submit to it"); ibid., 182 (William Widgery) ("[H]e should return to his constituents, and inform them that he had opposed the adoption of this Constitution; but that he had been overruled, and that it had been carried by a majority of wise and understanding men; that he should endeavor to sow the seeds of union and peace among the people he represented;…for, said he, we must consider that this body is as full a representation of the people as can be convened"); ibid. (Daniel Cooley) ("[A]s it [the Constitution] had been agreed to by a majority, he should endeavor to convince his constituents of the propriety of its adoption"); ibid., 182–183 (Benjamin Randall) ("[H]e had been uniformly opposed to the Constitution…but as he was beaten, he should sit down contented, hoping the minority may be disappointed in their fears, and that the majority may reap the full fruition of the blessings they anticipate"); ibid., 183 (Benjamin Swain) ("[A]lthough he was in the minority, he should support the Constitution as cheerfully and as heartily as though he had voted on the other side of the question"). For similar gracious concession speeches, see ibid., 182 (Joshua Whitney, John Taylor, and Samuel Nasson). For young Adams, see entry of Feb. 7, 1788, *DHRC*, 14:220. For similar statements from Anti-Federalists Elbridge Gerry and Robert Yates, see Maier, *Ratification*, 432–433.

10 Pa. Const. (1776), sec. 47; "The Address and Reasons of Dissent of the Minority of the Convention of Pennsylvania to Their Constituents" (Dec. 18, 1787), in *Storing's Anti-Fed.*, 3:149 (emphasis added).

While aggressive, Pennsylvania Federalists' parliamentary tactics did not cross the line into blatant illegality. The Pennsylvania assembly used its sergeant at arms and other allies to track down and arrest a pair of Anti-Federalist assembly members who tried to absent themselves from the assembly chamber and thereby defeat a quorum.

Once found, these would-be quorum breakers were physically obliged to return to the chamber and take their seats. For colorful accounts, see Maier, *Ratification*, 63–64; Bruce Ackerman, *We the People: Transformations* (1998), 55–56. This use of physical force fell comfortably within the sweeping traditional powers enjoyed by all legislative assemblies to enforce discipline over assembly members and to oblige the members' attendance at legislative sessions (see Chapter 9). Also, Pennsylvania's 1776 Constitution contained a highly unusual assembly quorum rule of two-thirds—perhaps to compensate for the state's lack of a bicameral upper house. See Mark Kruman, *Between Liberty and Authority: State Constitution Making in Revolutionary America* (1997), 52, 149. This unusually high quorum rule created incentives for minority lawmakers to game the system by boycotting the assembly; in response, majority lawmakers resorted to aggressive procedures to enforce the basic republican principle of majority rule. For a discussion of analogous issues raised by modern Senate filibuster practices and the threatened use by Senate majorities of a majority-rule "nuclear option" to curtail these antimajoritarian practices, see Chapter 9. In recent years, similar quorum-breaking tactics and forcible majoritarian countertactics occurred in Texas in 2003 and in Wisconsin and Indiana in early 2011.

11 *Storing's Anti-Fed.*, 3:150.

12 Va. Const. (1776), Declaration of Rights, secs. 2–3 (emphasis added). For citations to and discussion of counterpart provisions in other Revolution-era state constitutions, see Akhil Reed Amar, "The Consent of the Governed: Constitutional Amendment Outside Article V," *Columbia LR* 94 (1994): 457, 477–481.

13 A few quotations on the Federalist side: "[T]he Constitution of a particular State may be altered by a majority of the people of the State." *Farrand's Records*, 2:92 (Morris). The "fundamental maxim of republican government…requires that the sense of the majority should prevail" and the federal Constitution's republican-government clause "could be no impediment to reforms of the State constitution by a majority of the people in a legal and peaceable mode. This right would remain undiminished." *Federalist* Nos. 22, 21 (Hamilton/Publius). "[T]he majority in each State must bind the minority" in framing a Constitution. "Were [the federal Constitution] wholly national, the supreme and ultimate authority would reside in the *majority* of the people of the Union; and this authority would be competent at all times, like that of a majority of every national society, to alter or abolish its established government." *Federalist* No. 39 (Madison/Publius). "As to the people, however, in whom sovereign power resides,…[f]rom their authority the constitution originates.…If so; can it be doubted, that they have the right likewise to change it? A majority of the society is sufficient for this purpose." Robert Green McCloskey, ed., *The Works of James Wilson* (1967), 1:304 (1790 Lectures on Law). A few quotations on the Anti-Federalist side: "It will not be denied, that the people have a right to change the government when the majority chuse it, if not restrained by some existing compact [i.e., treaty]." Letters from the Federal Farmer (XVII) in *Storing's Anti.-Fed.*, 2:336. "'A majority of the community hath an indubitable, unalienable, and indefeasible right to reform, alter, or abolish' [government].…This, sir, is the language of democracy—that a majority

of the community have a right to alter government when found to be oppressive....We now act under a happy system, which says that a majority may alter government when necessary." *Elliot's Debates*, 3:50, 595 (Patrick Henry, quoting in part the Virginia Declaration of Rights authored by George Mason).

14 *Elliot's Debates*, 2:495.

15 For a list of thirty-four conventions held prior to 1917 in eighteen states whose constitutions did not expressly authorize such conventions, see Roger Sherman Hoar, *Constitutional Conventions: Their Nature, Powers, and Limitations* (1917), 39–40. See also Ackerman, *We the People*, 80 ("On sixteen occasions before the Civil War, state legislatures refused to read [state constitutional] silence to imply exclusivity"). By the end of the twentieth century, "only one state [New Hampshire] required a supermajority of voters [two-thirds, to be specific] to approve amendments." John J. Dinan, *The American State Constitutional Tradition* (2009), 57–58, 312 n. 115. Among the other states, simple majority rule typically prevailed whenever a proposed constitutional amendment was submitted to the electorate, with most states requiring merely that the proposed amendment receive more yes votes than no votes; five states—Hawaii, Illinois, Minnesota, Tennessee, and Wyoming—generally required an absolute majority of all votes cast in that particular election (thus treating any voter who showed up on election day and who weighed in on other ballot contests, but left blank the amendment-proposal section of the ballot, as if he had explicitly voted no). Ibid. For discussion of the notably inclusive suffrage and delegate-eligibility rules that operated federally in 1787–1788—rules nowhere specified by the text of the written Constitution, but a dramatic feature of its actual enactment—see Amar, *ACAB*, 5–7, 308–311. For discussion of how later state constitutional revisions have often been enacted via especially inclusive elections that widened preexisting suffrage rules, see Hoar, *Constitutional Conventions*, 205–212. For a different account of the "birth logic" of the Constitution itself—the procedures and protocols of the Constitution's enactment—and the proper legal implications of this birth logic, see Lawrence G. Sager, *Justice in Plainclothes* (2004), 161–193.

16 *Farrand's Records*, 2:665 (Convention resolution of Sept. 17, 1789).

17 Cf. Laurence H. Tribe, *The Invisible Constitution* (2008), 6–7 ("[N]othing in the visible text can tell us that what we are reading really *is* the Constitution, rather than an incomplete or otherwise inaccurate facsimile....[I]t's the *invisible* Constitution that tells us what text to accept as the *visible* Constitution of the United States."). See also ibid., 149–154.

18 *Farrand's Records*, 2:633–634 (McHenry); ibid., 3:81 (Washington).

19 For signing-ceremony details and qualifications, see Amar, *ACAB*, 536 n. 74. The parchment's engrosser was a Philadelphia clerk named Jacob Shallus—a fact not widely known at the Founding.

20 *JCC*, 33:549. Unlike some other printed versions floating around in mid-September, both the September 18 Convention print and the September 28 congressional print used notably larger lettering for the Preamble than for the rest of the document. Unlike the engrossed parchment, both the Convention and the congressional prints capitalized the first word

of Article I, section 1 ("ALL"), consistently abbreviated and italicized each section caption as "*Sect.*" and hyphenated "New-Hampshire," "Rhode-Island," "New-York," "New-Jersey," "North-Carolina," and "South-Carolina" in the third paragraph of Article I, section 2.

21 Senate Document (S. Doc. hereafter) No. 87-49, 59 n. 32 (July 17, 1961) (historical notes by Denys P. Myers). These ratification instruments are reproduced in *Documentary History of the Constitution of the United States* (1894), 2:24–160, 174–203, 266–320.

22 See Francis Childs and John Swaine, eds., *Acts Passed at a Congress of the United States, Begun and Held at the City of New-York, on Wednesday the Fourth of March in the Year M, DCC, LXXXIX* (1789), iii (emphasis added) (quoting resolution of July 6, 1789); ibid., i.

23 S. Doc. No. 87-49, 89, 60, 49. This document was based on the research of Denys P. Myers, a former State Department official who carefully examined historical records after the department received an inquiry from a foreign government for an "official" copy of the Constitution of the United States.

24 Ibid., 53 & n. 17, 89.

25 Ibid., 61.

26 Ibid., 54. See also ibid., 49, 91–92.

27 References to the particular physical document that was under consideration—that is, the September 28 print sent by the Confederation Congress—were especially thick in the closing days of the Virginia ratifying convention, where both Federalists and Anti-Federalists repeatedly conjured up the same imagery. See, e.g., *Elliot's Debates*, 3:577 (Henry) ("that paper before you"); 583 (Madison) ("the declaration on that paper"); 584 (Mason) ("the paper before you"); 586 (Henry Lee) ("the paper on your table"), 618 (Madison) ("the paper on the table"); 628 (Harrison) ("that paper on your table"); 633, 636 (Innes) ("the paper on the table"); 639 (Tyler) ("that paper'); 651 (Henry) ("the paper on the table"). For a similar invocation by the president of the ratifying convention at the outset, see ibid., 38 (Pendleton) ("the paper on your table").

28 Of the nine states that included a transcript of the text being ratified in their formal instruments of ratification, three—Pennsylvania, New Jersey, and Maryland—caught and corrected the "inferior court" typo. *Documentary History of the Constitution*, 2:39, 57, 117. The other six—Georgia, South Carolina, Virginia, New York, North Carolina, and Rhode Island—did not. Ibid., 77, 135, 157, 185, 287, 304.

29 Act of Nov. 13, 2002, Pub. L. 107-293, 116 Stat. 2057, 2060.

30 Both Article I, section 9, and Article V make explicit reference to "the Year one thousand eight hundred and eight"—the year when Congress was first allowed to prohibit the international slave trade (although the document scrupulously avoided the word "slave" itself in these two passages, using euphemism here as elsewhere).

31 Other language in the parchment directly below Article VII and above the autographs was not reprinted in the September 28 print. This language, which appears on the parchment directly alongside the "Year of our Lord" sentence, catalogs various earlier places in the parchment where the scrivener had made handwritten corrections and interlineations. The September 28 print obviously did not need to, and thus did not, include any

of this parchment language. Rather, the printer simply made all the noted corrections in the initial typesetting, with no interlineations or erasures.

32 For a brief survey of some of the written Constitution's most notable references to itself, see the opening paragraphs of Chapter 5.

33 *Farrand's Records*, 2:665–667.

34 The five states that omitted the attestation and signature section were New Jersey, Maryland, South Carolina, Virginia, and North Carolina. See *Documentary History of the Constitution*, 2:60–61 121, 138, 160, 290. Four states included the attestation and signatures in their ratification instruments: Pennsylvania, Georgia, New York, and Rhode Island. See ibid., 43–44, 81–82, 189–190, 307–309.

35 See *Elliot's Debates*, 1:319 (Delaware), 319–320 (Pennsylvania), 321 (New Jersey), 324 (Georgia), 325 (South Carolina), 329 (New York), 337 (Rhode Island). See also ibid., 321 (Connecticut) ("A.D. 1788"), 323 (Massachusetts) ("Anno Domini 1788"). The remaining states were Maryland, New Hampshire, Virginia, and North Carolina.

36 On Blackstone, see Chapter 1, text accompanying n. 8.

37 For state constitutions, see Amar, *ACAB*, 557 n. 2 (quoting Revolution-era constitutional provisions of Pennsylvania, Delaware, Georgia, Massachusetts, and New Hampshire, and neglecting to mention S.C. Const. [1778], art. XXXVI ["So help me God"]). Although some revisionists have recently challenged the traditional view that Washington solemnly uttered the phrase "so help me God" at his first inauguration, it is undeniable that religion and religiosity pervaded various other parts of this event. Multiple eyewitness accounts, some penned shortly after the inauguration, noted that Washington kissed the Bible on which he swore his oath. After the oath came his Inaugural Address, nearly a third of which was devoted to America's relationship to the Almighty. *Annals*, 1:27–29 (April 30, 1789). Washington and other dignitaries then proceeded by prearrangement to a religious service at Saint Paul's Chapel, where prayers were delivered by Senate Chaplain Samuel Provost, an Episcopal bishop. Ibid., 25–29 (April 27–30, 1789). Revisionists have also argued that the phrase "so help me God" was not used at a presidential swearing-in until the late nineteenth century, and that only in the twentieth century did the phrase become a typical part of presidential inaugurations. There is widespread agreement that the vast majority of inaugurations have used the Bible and that many have featured Bible-kissing and/or other religious trappings.

38 On the signing ceremony, note that George Read signed by proxy for John Dickinson. See *Farrand's Records*, 3:587.

39 Even today, it remains common for witnesses in public settings to invoke God in some way, and in particular to add the words "so help me God" when these persons are formally sworn in as witnesses, or to swear on a Bible even though the law today generally does not (and cannot) require these religious trappings.

40 Amar, *ACAB*, 166.

41 First Reconstruction Act of March 2, 1867, 14 Stat. 428. Strictly speaking, the act did not require the excluded states to do anything; it merely mapped out a safe harbor. If states

did the things specified in the statute, they would thereby win readmission.

42 The act envisioned disfranchisement of certain felons and former rebels.

43 See, e.g., Pinckney G. McElwee, "The 14th Amendment to the Constitution of the United States and the Threat That It Poses to Our Democratic Government," *South Carolina Law Quarterly* 11 (1959): 484.

44 See Proclamation of Andrew Johnson, July 27, 1868, 15 Stat. 708; Certification of William H. Seward, July 28, 1868, 15 Stat. 708–711.

45 Felix Frankfurter, "John Marshall and the Judicial Function," *Harvard LR* 69 (1955): 217, 229.

46 William M. Wiecek, *The Guarantee Clause of the U.S. Constitution* (1972), 13.

47 On speech suppression in the 1850s, see Clement Eaton, *The Freedom-of-Thought Struggle in the Old South* (rev. ed. 1964); Russell B. Nye, *Fettered Freedom* (1963); W. Sherman Savage, *The Controversy over the Distribution of Abolitionist Literature, 1830–1860* (1938); Michael Kent Curtis, "The 1859 Crisis over Hinton Helper's Book, *The Impending Crisis*: Free Speech, Slavery, and Some Light on the Meaning of the First Section of the Fourteenth Amendment," *Chicago-Kent LR* 68 (1993): 1113.

48 See *CG* 39-1, 430 (Bingham) ("There was then [at the Founding] no State in this Union wherein any considerable portion of the free persons of the United States, being male persons over twenty-one years of age, were disfranchised"). For more statements, see Amar, *ACAB*, 603–604 n. 37.

49 See, generally, Amar, *Bill of Rights*, 137–294; Amar, *ACAB*, 376–378, 385–392. See also infra Chapter 4.

50 On the 1864 electoral-college tally, see Joint Resolution of Feb. 8, 1865, 13 Stat. 567. For more on true-blue mathematics—making mid-February 1867 the key pivot point—see *CG*, 40-1:64 (Bingham, March 11, 1867), 40-2:475 (Bingham, Jan. 13, 1868), 41-2:494 (Bingham, Jan. 14, 1870).

51 The ellipsis here is ironic: Two quite distinct constitutional passages are being playfully joined, the first in Article I, and the second in Amendment II. The Founding generation said in Amendment II that militias—not armies—were necessary to the security of a free state. But post–Civil War America has reasons to read the constitutional text in a quite different way—reasons that are not fully textual but entirely constitutional, thanks to the role that the Union Army played in the war and its constitutional aftermath.

52 See, generally, Amar, *Bill of Rights*, 53–58.

53 For more on Webster, see ibid., 57–58.

54 Act of March 3, 1863, 12 Stat. 731.

55 For a transcript of Taney's draft opinion—"Thoughts on the Conscription Law of the United States"—see Martin Anderson, ed., *The Military Draft* (1982), 207–218.

56 Subsequent military reconstruction legislation also merits mention. See, e.g., Supplementary Reconstruction Act of March 23, 1867, 15 Stat. 2. For general discussion of military reconstruction legislation and of the military's role in Reconstruction, see Michael Les Benedict, *A Compromise of Principle: Congressional Republicans and Reconstruction, 1863–1869* (1974), 223–243; Eric Foner, *Reconstruction: America's Unfinished Revolution,*

1863–1877 (1988), 271–277, 307–308, 438; Kenneth M. Stampp, *The Era of Reconstruction, 1865–1877* (1965),144–147; Joseph B. James, *The Ratification of the Fourteenth Amendment* (1984), 210–211.

57 Perhaps it might be said that the permissibility of the draft was truly settled on the battlefields of 1863–1865, rather than in the enactments of 1866–1870. But did the Civil War battlefield experience justify even a peacetime draft?

58 *Selective Draft Law Cases*, 245 U.S. 366, 389 (1918).

CHAPTER 3: HEARING THE PEOPLE

1 Recall the suggestion in Chapter 1 that a negative-implication argument should never be decisive absent additional, fine-grained reasons to support its application in a given situation. To fully persuade, these fine-grained reasons will typically need to reference something beyond the mere words of the clause—for example, history, structure, common sense, or the interrelation between the clause and some other textual provision(s) of the Constitution.

2 See Amar, *CCP*, 116–144 (explicating the Sixth Amendment's truth-seeking and innocence-protecting architecture); see also *Holmes v. South Carolina*, 547 U.S. 319, 324 (2006) ("Whether rooted directly in the Due Process Clause of the Fourteenth Amendment or in the Compulsory Process or Confrontation clauses of the Sixth Amendment, the Constitution guarantees criminal defendants a 'meaningful opportunity to present a complete defense'" [quoting earlier case law]).

3 *Calder v. Bull*, 3 U.S. (3 Dall.) 386, 387–388 (1798) (opinion of Chase, J.). Chase's reference to the impropriety of punishing an innocent man appeared in the specific context of his condemnation of ex-post-facto criminal laws. Because the reason such laws are violations of first principles is that they enable government to punish men for actions that were innocent when done, the same principle condemns punishment of an innocent man via a different procedural trick—namely, preventing him from presenting his defense. For thoughtful analyses of how procedural rules in court must be structured so as not to undermine broadly accepted norms of primary conduct outside the courtroom, see Meir Dan Cohen, "Decision Rules and Conduct Rules: On Acoustic Separation in Criminal Law," *Harvard LR* 97 (1984): 625; Charles Nesson, "The Evidence or the Event? On Judicial Proof and the Acceptability of Verdicts," *Harvard LR* 98 (1985): 1357.

4 See Amar, *Bill of Rights*, 108.

5 On the necessary-and-proper clause, see Chapter 1, nn. 30, 33, and accompanying text; on free speech, see ibid., text accompanying nn. 38–44, and Chapter 2, text accompanying nn. 1–6. Likewise, the Tenth Amendment textualized principles of federalism and popular sovereignty obviously implicit in the original Constitution and embodied in the enactment process.

6 On constitutional redundancy in general, see Akhil Reed Amar, "Clarifying Clauses and Constitutional Redundancies," *Valparaiso U. LR* 33 (1998): 1. On the declaratory nature of the Bill of Rights, see Department of State, Bureau of Rolls and Library, *Documentary*

History of the Constitution of the United States of America (1894), 2:321; Amar, *Bill of Rights*, 147–149. On Wilson and Ellsworth, see Chapter 1, text accompanying n. 9.

7 See, generally, Amar, *Bill of Rights*. See also infra Chapter 4.

8 The premier exponent of this general approach to constitutional interpretation is Professor Barry Friedman. See, generally, Barry Friedman, *The Will of the People: How Public Opinion Has Influenced the Supreme Court and Shaped the Meaning of the Constitution* (2009), and Barry Friedman, "Dialogue and Judicial Review," *Michigan LR* 91 (1993) 577, 590–605. Professor Jeffrey Rosen's work also merits special mention here. See, generally, Jeffrey Rosen, *The Most Democratic Branch: How the Courts Serve America* (2006). For yet another interesting discussion, see David A. Strauss, "The Modernizing Mission of Judicial Review," *U. of Chicago LR* 77 (2009): 859. For path-breaking work on the importance of American ethos more generally in constitutional interpretation, see Philip Bobbitt, *Constitutional Fate: Theory of the Constitution* (1982), 93–177.

9 See *Ferguson v. Georgia*, 365 U.S. 570, 573–575 (1961); Joel N. Bodansky, "The Abolition of the Party-Witness Disqualification: An Historical Survey," *Kentucky LJ* 70 (1981): 91.

10 See, generally, Albert W. Alschuler, "A Peculiar Privilege in Historical Perspective: The Right to Remain Silent," *Michigan LR* 94 (1996): 2625, 2641–2646.

11 See *Ferguson*, 365 U.S. at 577; Alschuler, "Peculiar Privilege," 2660–2664; Bodansky, "Abolition," 93; Amar, *CCP*, 73–74, 83–88. See also *Wilson v. United States*, 149 U.S. 60, 66 (1893).

12 In *Holmes v. South Carolina*, 547 U.S. 314, 326 (2006), a unanimous Court cited *Rock* with approval and built upon its central teaching. *Holmes*, incidentally, was the maiden opinion of Justice Samuel Alito, himself a former prosecutor.

13 In the extremely unusual case in which a fair federal trial simply cannot be held in the crime-scene state, a defendant is entitled to move the trial to some other state where a fair trial can be had. Although unenumerated, the right to a fair trial is obviously implicit in the Fifth and Sixth Amendments, and indeed in the entire Constitution read as a whole. As noted in Chapter 1, even seemingly literal and absolute legal commands may sometimes yield in unusual cases that were not contemplated by the law's enactors. A narrow rule moving federal criminal trials beyond the crime-scene state only when required by a fair-trial imperative can be brought within the scope of this background interpretive principle. A sweeping rule mandating a trans-state venue change any time a defendant so requests cannot be; this latter rule is simply a blanket negation of the "main object" of the venue clause of the Judicial Article, which aims to prescribe a fixed trial location regardless of the defendant's preferences—or the prosecutor's or the judge's preferences, for that matter. Before a federal trial is properly moved to another state, all legitimate in-state options—relocation to another district within the state, extra-strict rules of juror selection, extra-careful jury instructions—must be unavailing. If one of these alternatives is workable, there is no conflict between the crime-scene-state-venue command of the Judicial Article and the fair-trial command of the Constitution as a whole, and both commands should be followed.

14 A possible objection: Whereas the written Constitution recognizes a defendant's right

to remain silent, the unwritten Constitution recognizes his right to speak. Since silence and speech are opposites, isn't this a contradiction? No. A contradiction would arise if, for example, judges recognized an unwritten constitutional right of a violent crime victim to force the criminal defendant to take the stand at his own criminal trial and answer all relevant questions propounded by the victim. Such an interpretation of the unwritten Constitution would indeed negate the written Constitution, which plainly declares that a criminal defendant cannot be compelled to testify in his own criminal trial. But there is no contradiction in saying that the Constitution recognizes a defendant's right to stand mute or to take the stand, as he chooses. On this reading, the Constitution simply gives him the option, the freedom to decide for himself—a waivable right and a right to waive. Had the Constitution explicitly guaranteed the defendant the right to testify or be silent, no contradiction would have arisen. The matter is no different merely because the Constitution explicitly guarantees his right to silence while only implicitly guaranteeing his right to testify.

15 In the words of Dr. Benjamin Rush, a signer of the Declaration of Independence, at the Pennsylvania ratifying convention: "Our rights are not yet all known. Why should we attempt to enumerate them?" *DHRC*, 2:440 (Nov. 30, 1787) (Wilson's notes).

16 Specific historical evidence exists that the Thirty-ninth Congress envisioned a system in which both Congress and the courts would protect rights and in which citizens in general could claim the benefit of the more generous view of a given right. See Michael Kent Curtis, *No State Shall Abridge: The Fourteenth Amendment and the Bill of Rights* (1986), 128–129; Akhil Reed Amar, "Intratextualism," *Harvard LR* 112 (1999): 747, 826. And as a matter of simple common sense, it would be odd to think that Congress could generally license states to flout basic Fourteenth Amendment rights, given that most of these rights are also guaranteed against Congress itself. See also *Katzenbach v. Morgan*, 384 U.S. 641, 651 n. 10 (1966). On Congress's power to create new rights under section 5, see Amar, *Bill of Rights*, 175 n*; Amar, "Intratextualism," 821–825.

17 See *Barron v. Baltimore*, 32 U.S. (7 Pet.) 243 (1833); Amar, *Bill of Rights*, 195–196 & n. *, 281–282 & n. *.

18 For an important qualification of this generalization, see the concluding paragraph of this chapter.

19 Amar, *CCP*, 132–138; Amar, *Bill of Rights*, 117–118.

20 For capital defendants, see Federal Crimes Act of 1790, ch. 9, sec. 29, 1 Stat. 112, 118. On the judge as counsel, see John H. Langbein, "The Historical Origins of the Privilege Against Self-Incrimination at Common Law," *Michigan LR* 92 (1994): 1047, 1050–1052. See, generally, Amar, *CCP*, 140–141.

21 For the state figures, see Brief for Petitioner Clarence Earl Gideon, Nov. 21, 1962, 1962 *WL* 115120, 29–31; *McNeal v. Culver*, 365 U.S. 109, (1961) 120–121 (Appendix to the opinion of Douglas, J., concurring). The five outlying states were Alabama, Florida, Mississippi, North Carolina, and South Carolina.

22 *Blackstone's Comm.*, 4:352 (emphasis added).

23 *Regina v. Leatham*, (1861) 8 Cox Crim. Cas. 498, 501 (Q.B.) (Crompton, J.). On the absence of an exclusionary rule in state courts early on, it should be kept in mind that while the federal Bill of Rights did not directly apply against the states prior to the Civil War, most state bills of rights featured language paralleling the federal Fourth Amendment's ban on unreasonable searches and seizures.

24 The classic rebuttal is that the exclusionary rule does not truly benefit guilty defendants or create any windfall but merely restores the status quo ante: Had the cops followed the Constitution and refrained from the search, no evidence would have been found, and the exclusionary rule simply puts the defendant in the position he would have occupied had the Constitution been obeyed. This rebuttal ignores all the ways in which the evidence surely would have surfaced or might well have surfaced even had no Fourth Amendment violation ever occurred. In other words, there is a massive "causation gap" in the exclusionary rule as currently practiced. For example, if police could have obtained a needed warrant but did not, today's judiciary excludes the evidence even though it would have been easy enough to get the warrant and with the warrant the evidence would have been discovered just the same. Although the Court has allowed in some evidence on an "inevitable discovery" exception to the exclusionary rule, the exception is currently far too narrow in application, leading to boatloads of exclusionary windfalls that make guilty defendants much better off than they would have been had the police fully complied with the Fourth Amendment.

25 See *Wolf v. Colorado*, 338 U.S. 25, 33–34 (1949).

26 *Elkins v. United States*, 364 U.S. 206, 224–225 (1960); *Mapp v. Ohio*, 367 U.S. 643, 651 (1961).

27 Sometimes, the Constitution vests a defendant with a supplemental implicit right to do the opposite (testify) of what he has an explicit right to do (decline to testify). Similarly, a defendant has an explicit right to legal counsel and an implicit right to forgo all counsel and represent himself. He has an explicit right to compel and cross-examine witnesses and an implicit right to decline to do so. But not all of his explicit criminal-procedure rights are matched by supplemental implicit rights to the opposite thing. For example, a defendant has a constitutional right to a jury trial, but no constitutional right to insist upon a bench trial. Nor does he have an implicit right to an unspeedy trial or a nonpublic trial. Why the different standards for different rights when the Sixth Amendment's text does not clearly signal these differences?

By now, the answer should be clear: The text must be read against various background legal principles derived from history, structure, spirit, justice, and common sense. In the domain of criminal procedure, for example, some rights are rooted in a vision of defendant autonomy and are thus best understood as giving each defendant a constitutional option to choose X or not-X. Other rights are not pure autonomy rights of the defendant alone, and thus are not best read to entail a defendant's right to do the opposite thing. The people themselves—members of the general public apart from the defendant—have implicit constitutional rights to, or legitimate interests in, public trials, speedy trials, and jury trials. Hence these areas are not governed simply by the preferences of the defendant.

28 On assembly, see Amar, *Bill of Rights*, 26–32. On Fifth Amendment immunity, see Amar, *CCP*, 65–66. Douglas's reliance on the Fifth Amendment self-incrimination clause built upon earlier cases that tried to read the clause as intimately interrelated with the Fourth Amendment. In particular, Douglas cited the Court's then-recent decision in *Mapp v. Ohio*, which had relied on both the Fourth and Fifth Amendments, and quoted *Mapp*'s explicit affirmation of "a "right to privacy, no less important than any other right carefully and particularly reserved to the people." *Griswold v. Connecticut*, 381 U.S. 479, 484–485 (1965) (quoting *Mapp v. Ohio*). For more discussion of this judicial attempt to fuse the Fourth and Fifth Amendments, and analysis of the basic errors of this effort, see Chapter 4.

29 *Poe v. Ullman*, 367 U.S. 497, 554–555 (1961) (Harlan, J., dissenting). In *Griswold*, Justice Harlan in effect incorporated by reference his *Poe* opinion. See *Griswold*, 381 U.S. at 500 (Harlan, J., concurring in the judgment).

30 *Griswold*, 381 U.S. 479, 481–482 (1965). For more on *Dred* and *Lochner* as *negative* elements of America's symbolic Constitution—high-profile cases that help define the boundaries of modern American constitutional discourse by exemplifying what faithful interpreters should *not* say or do—see Chapter 6.

31 See Amar, *Bill of Rights*. See also infra Chapter 4, text accompanying nn. 16–32.

32 See Amar, *Bill of Rights*, 171–173.

33 See, e.g, *McDonald v. City of Chicago*, 130 S. Ct. 3020, 3091–3092 (2010) (Stevens, J., dissenting); John Paul Stevens, "The Bill of Rights: A Century of Progress," *U. of Chicago LR* 59 (1992): 13, 20; John Paul Stevens, "The Freedom of Speech," *Yale LJ* 102 (1993): 1293, 1298–1299.

34 According to the Eisenstadt Appellee Brief: "The prescription and use of contraceptive devices, at least under some circumstances, is now lawful in all fifty of the states. More significant [to] the issue here, in many states and localities the government operates positive programs to make contraceptive devices available for persons desiring to use them." 1971 WL 133617.

35 *Lawrence v. Texas*, 539 U.S. 558, 562–575 (2003) ("Freedom extends beyond spatial bounds. Liberty presumes an autonomy of self that includes freedom of thought, belief, expression, and certain intimate conduct.…Equality of treatment and the due process right to demand respect for conduct protected by the substantive guarantee of liberty are linked in important respects, and a decision on the latter point advances both interests.… When homosexual conduct is made criminal by the law of the State, that declaration in and of itself is an invitation to subject homosexual persons to discrimination both in the public and in the private spheres. The central holding of *Bowers*…demeans the lives of homosexual persons.").

36 See Laurence H. Tribe, *Abortion: The Clash of Absolutes* (1992), 13; for additional tallies, see Friedman, *Will of the People*, 297; Rosen, *The Most Democratic Branch*, 92–93.

37 *Washington v. Glucksburg*, 521 U.S. 702, 710–711 (1997) (citations and footnotes omitted).

See also Michael W. McConnell, "The Right to Die and the Jurisprudence of Tradition," *Utah LR* (1997): 665.

38 *Gonzales v. Raich*, 545 U.S. 1 (2005).

39 *DHRC*, 15:199 (Noah Webster, writing as "America," *N.Y. Daily Advertiser*, Dec. 31, 1787).

40 *Annals*, 1:759–760 (Aug. 5, 1789).

41 For documentation of the expected progressivity of taxation under this amendment, see Amar, *ACAB*, 408–409.

42 *Lawrence v. Texas*, 539 U.S. 558, 569–570 (2003).

43 See *Storing's Anti-Fed.*, 3:58, 61 ("Essay of a Democratic Federalist").

44 *Entick v. Carrington*, 19 Howell's State Trials 1029, 1066 (C.P. 1765); ibid., 1063; *Wilkes v. Halifax*, 19 Howell's State Trials 1406, 1408 (C.P. 1769); *Beardmore v. Carrington*, 19 Howell's State Trials 1405, 1406 (C.P. 1764), 95 Eng. Rep. 790, 793–794.

45 Quoted in *Miller v. United States*, 357 U.S. 301, 307 (1958).

46 On ideas of houses and homesteads in the 1860s, see Homestead Act of 1862, 12 Stat. 292; Eric Foner, *Reconstruction: America's Unfinished Revolution, 1863–1877* (1988), 70–71.

47 Joan Williams, "The Rhetoric of Property," *Iowa LR* 83 (1988): 277, 326.

48 See Amar, *Bill of Rights*, 62–63, 267; Laurence H. Tribe, *The Invisible Constitution* (2008), 190. On the way in which this amendment was, even at the Founding, understood as connected to sexual privacy issues, see, e.g., Robert A. Gross, "Public and Private in the Third Amendment," *Valparaiso U. LR* 26 (1991): 215, 219 (quoting colonist expressing hostility to Parliament's Quartering Act placing soldiers "abed" with America's "Wives and Daughters"). Note that an early version of Professor Tribe's argument linking the Third Amendment to issues of domestic privacy occurred in his oral argument in the 1986 sodomy case of *Bowers v. Hardwick*—a case that rejected Tribe's approach but that was later famously reversed in *Lawrence v. Texas*.

49 *Griswold v. Connecticut*, 381 U.S. 479, 484–485 (1965). At this precise point in his opinion, Douglas also quoted earlier Court language explicitly building on the proto-privacy reasoning of *Entick v. Carrington*, a case discussed at text accompanying n. 44. For more on *Entick*, see Chapter 4, text accompanying nn. 41, 46–47.

50 *Poe v. Ullman*, 367 U.S. 497 (1961). See also *Griswold*, 381 U.S. at 500 (Harlan, J., concurring in the judgment) (reaffirming his views as expressed in *Poe*). For a recent reminder of the importance of Harlan's analysis, see Tribe, *The Invisible Constitution*, 189–190. For a more general analysis of the kind of argument Harlan here exemplifies—in which the constitutional interpreter identifies the constitutional "ethos" standing behind a particular patch of constitutional text—see Bobbitt, *Constitutional Fate*, 142–143. Note also how Harlan's claim that Connecticut's contraception law offended constitutional values even in the absence of a "physical intrusion" foreshadowed Harlan and the Court's ultimate move in Fourth Amendment law away from physicalist ideas of trespass and toward a broader privacy approach in the 1967 *Katz* case. See text accompanying n. 43.

51 Seen from this perspective, Justice Kennedy's opinion in *Lawrence* would seem more faithful to the paradigm-case method championed by Yale professor Jed Rubenfeld—

with *Griswold* functioning as a key paradigm and a landmark case—than Rubenfeld himself recognizes. See Jed Rubenfeld, *Revolution by Judiciary: The Structure of American Constitutional Law* (2005), 16, 184–190.

52 In the Fourth Amendment case law, see, e.g., *Payton v. New York*, 445 U.S. 573 (1980) (generally requiring warrants for home arrests, but not for arrests outside the home); *United States v. Dunn*, 480 U.S. 294 (1987) (reaffirming and defining special protection for curtilage around home); *Kyllo v. United States*, 533 U.S. 27, 38 (2001) (demonstrating special sensitivity to high-tech surveillance of homes, especially of bathrooms and bedrooms, and stressing that the high-tech search technique at issue would enable the government to determine "at what hour each night the lady of the house takes her daily sauna and bath—a detail that many would consider 'intimate'"). On First Amendment rights at home, see *Stanley v. Georgia*, 394 U.S. 557 (1969). On the rights of parents to home-school children, cf. *Meyer v. Nebraska*, 262 U.S. 390, 399 (1923) (recognizing a constitutionally protected right to "establish a home and bring up children"); *Pierce v. Society of Sisters*, 268 U.S. 510, 534–535 (1925) (reaffirming that "under the doctrine of *Meyer v. Nebraska*, [there exists a] liberty of parents and guardians to direct the upbringing and education of children under their control"); *Wisconsin v. Yoder*, 406 U.S. 205, 217 (1972) (exempting Amish children from compulsory secondary-education laws in a context in which "modern compulsory secondary education in rural areas is now largely carried on in a consolidated school, often remote from the student's home and alien to his daily home life"). Note that both *Meyer* and *Pierce* were prominently invoked in Justice Douglas's opinion for the Court in *Griswold*, 381 U.S. at 481–483. On the rights of an extended family to live together as one household, see *Moore v. City of East Cleveland*, 431 U.S. 494 (1977). On the right of a homeowner to keep a gun at home, see *District of Columbia v. Heller*, 554 U.S. 570 (2008); *McDonald v. City of Chicago*, 130 S. Ct. 3020 (2010); cf. *Semayne's Case*, (1604) 77 Eng. Rep. 194 (K.B.) 198; 5 Co. Rep. 91 a, 93 a ("The house of every one is his castle, and if thieves come to a man's house to rob or murder, and the owner or his servants kill any of the thieves in defense of himself and his house, it is no felony and he shall lose nothing").

53 Margaret Jane Radin, "Property and Personhood," *Stanford LR* 34 (1982): 957, 1013.

54 See, generally, John Fee, "Eminent Domain and the Sanctity of Home," *Notre Dame LR* 81 (2006): 783. See also Daniel A. Farber, *Retained by the People* (2007), 166–170. In floating the idea of special eminent-domain rules to protect houses above and beyond other real property, Farber astutely highlighted several key facts about Susette Kelo: "The house had been in her family for more than one hundred years. She was born in the house in 1918; her husband, petitioner Charles Dery, moved into the house when they married in 1946. Their son, who also joined in the lawsuit, lived next door with his family in the house he was given as a wedding gift." Ibid., 168–169.

55 Note that whether hypothetical punishment X is "cruel" as well as unusual is a separate question. Perhaps punishment X, although unusual, is less cruel than counterpart punishments in other places.

56 Amar, *Bill of Rights*, 82, 87, 279.

57 *Atkins v. Virginia*, 536 U.S. 304, 346 (2002) (Scalia, J., dissenting).

58 For cases counting congressional and/or D.C. laws, see, e.g., *Atkins v. Virginia*, 536 U.S. 304, 313–314 & n. 10 (majority opinion); *Kennedy v. Louisiana*, 554 U.S. 407, 421–425 (2008); *Kennedy*, 554 U.S. at 455–457 & n. 4 (Alito, J., dissenting, joined inter alia by Scalia, J.); *Kennedy v. Louisiana*, 129 S. Ct. 1, 3 (2008) (denying rehearing); *Graham v. Florida*, 130 S. Ct 2011, 2024 (2010). In ordinary language, the word "unusual" focuses not merely on laws on the books but also on the law as actually applied. Laws exist allowing jaywalkers to be jailed; but being jailed for jaywalking in America is surely "unusual." (Whether it is also "cruel" is another question.) Examining law as actually applied properly brings constitutional institutions other than the legislature into the frame of Eighth Amendment analysis. Criminal laws are often written in overbroad ways precisely because it is understood—and in some respects constitutionally required (see Chapter 11)—that such laws will be softened in practice by merciful discretion exercised by prosecutors, grand juries, criminal trial juries, trial judges, governors, and parole boards. Each of these institutions represents the public, too, and helps define what modern America really does believe and practice when it comes to punishment.

59 On Congress's broad power to find new rights, see Amar, *Bill of Rights*, 175 n *; Amar, "Intratextualism," 821–825.

60 For a wide-ranging discussion, see Michael Abramowicz, "Constitutional Circularity," *U.C.L.A. LR* 49 (2002): 1.

61 See *Furman v. Georgia*, 408 U.S. 238 (1972); *Gregg v. Georgia*, 428 U.S. 153 (1976); *Penry v. Lynaugh*, 492 U.S. 302 (1989); *Stanford v. Kentucky*, 492 U.S. 361 (1989); *Atkins v. Virginia*, 536 U.S. 304 (2002) (in effect overruling *Penry*); *Roper v. Simmons*, 543 U.S. 551 (2005) (overruling *Stanford*); *Kennedy v. Louisiana*, 128 S. Ct. 2641 (2008).

CHAPTER 4: CONFRONTING MODERN CASE LAW

1 For more on these distinct styles of constitutional argument, see Philip Bobbitt, *Constitutional Fate: Theory of the Constitution* (1982).

2 *Brown v. Board of Education*, 347 U.S. 483 (1954); *Bolling v. Sharp*, 347 U.S. 497 (1954); *Mayor of Baltimore v. Dawson*, 350 U.S. 877 (1955) (per curiam) (beaches); *Holmes v. City of Atlanta*, 350 U.S. 879 (1955) (per curiam) (golf courses); *Gayle v. Browder*, 352 U.S. 903 (1956) (per curiam) (buses); *Loving v. Virginia*, 388 U.S. 1 (1967) (matrimony).

3 See Akhil Reed Amar, "Attainder and Amendment 2: *Romer's* Rightness," *Michigan LR* 95 (1996): 203.

4 On "extra" clout for slave-holders, see Amar, *ACAB*, 87–98, 148–159, 344–347.

5 Both the Fifth and the Fourteenth Amendment promised "due process of law"—the Fifth vis-à-vis the federal government and the Fourteenth vis-à-vis states. As understood by the Reconstruction generation, who in effect reglossed the Fifth Amendment by adopting a later amendment echoing it, "law" in its nature was general, equal, and

impartial; and the "due process" that generated "law" had to respect that nature by ensuring that lawmaking would be general and prospective and that the execution and adjudication of law would be impartial. Thus, implicit in due process, as understood by the Reconstruction generation, was an equality idea of sorts. Indeed, an early draft of the Fourteenth Amendment spoke of "equal protection in the rights of life, liberty, and property." *CG*, 39-1:1034 (Feb. 26, 1866). The final draft, which featured separate equal-protection and due-process clauses, aimed not to sharply contradistinguish these two related concepts but to elaborate their interrelatedness as two sides of the same coin: Proper "law" had to be equal and pursuant to fair process. To punish or stigmatize a person on the basis of his birth status violated this vision, which the Reconstruction Congress understood as a first-principles limit that derived from the nature of law and thus bound all levels of government.

6 See Charles L. Black Jr., "The Lawfulness of the Segregation Decisions," *Yale LJ* 69 (1960): 421.

7 Hans L. Trefousse, *Thaddeus Stevens: Nineteenth-Century Egalitarian* (1997), xi (quoting tombstone), 244 (discussing orphanage).

8 Although each of the main segregationist arguments persuaded some Republicans in the 1860s, none appears to have won over a majority of Republicans at that time. In embracing or accepting segregation, various Republican Congressmen in the 1860s did not need to agree upon one single plausible legal theory. Various minority theories, even if each was ultimately implausible, nevertheless gave rise to a powerful political bloc that was reinforced by diehard Democrats, who stood united in their opposition to the Fourteenth Amendment and its promise of racial equality in civil rights. But if the *Brown* Court had sought to defend segregation in a judicial opinion, the justices would have needed to articulate a particular legal reason, a principled and doctrinally acceptable reason. It would have been odd for *Brown* to have adopted one or another eccentric theory that was in fact rejected by most Republicans and that also reflected an implausible understanding of the amendment's text.

9 Pre-*Brown*, see, e.g., *Missouri* ex rel. *Gaines v. Canada*, 305 U.S. 337 (1938); *Sipuel v. Board of Regents of the University of Oklahoma*, 332 U.S. 631 (1948); *Sweatt v. Painter*, 339 U.S. 629 (1950); *McLaurin v. Oklahoma State Regents*, 339 U.S. 637 (1950). Many lower-court decisions in this era also identified fact-specific inequality.

10 See Michael J. Klarman, *From Jim Crow to Civil Rights* (2004); Randall Kennedy, "Martin Luther King's Constitution: A Legal History of the Montgomery Bus Boycott," *Yale LJ* 98 (1989): 999.

11 Beyond the issues raised by formally symmetric laws, the distinction between civil rights and social rights that was prominent in Reconstruction-era discourse was reflected in two additional Fourteenth Amendment ideas. First, certain commands of the amendment did not apply of their own self-executing force to various nongovernmental activities. (Hence the so-called "state action" doctrine, whose textual font is the opening "No State shall" language of the amendment's second sentence.) Second, although Con-

gress would have power under section 5 to enforce the equal-birth-citizens idea of the amendment's opening sentence (which does not use the phrase "No State shall") against various nongovernmental practices and institutions that might threaten a regime of equal citizenship, there would remain real boundaries to this congressional power. Congress, for example, could not under section 5 require private persons to refrain from race discrimination in private dinner parties and dating. Such "social" practices lay outside the domain of equal citizenship, which could extend beyond the strictly governmental sphere (especially if Congress so provided) but which would not encompass highly private spaces governed by individual associational and social freedom.

12 Perhaps it might be argued that in regulating its own galleries, neither house was thereby *legislating*; and that each house was therefore not bound by ordinary principles applicable to ordinary laws. But if so, segregation in the Capitol galleries loses virtually all precedential significance for other forms of segregation backed by actual legislation. More generally, America's implicit Constitution surely imposes many obligations on Congress to abide by first principles even when Congress is not, strictly speaking, legislating. If the First Amendment's free-speech principles apply to presidents and courts who seek to censor—notwithstanding the amendment's limited textual command that "*Congress* shall make no *law*"—then surely these principles also constrain Congress even when Congress is not legislating but, say, regulating its galleries via the internal rules of each house. And what is true of free-speech principles is likewise true of equal-citizenship principles.

13 Act of April 9, 1866, 14 Stat. 27. Congress enacted this statute to implement the Thirteenth Amendment's antislavery and anti-caste principles and also to overrule the *Dred Scott* case, which had claimed that free blacks were not citizens. Democrat critics claimed that the statute went beyond Congress's powers under the Thirteenth Amendment. Ending slavery, they argued, did not entail citizenship for all and race-neutral civil rights, as provided for in this act. Andrew Johnson vetoed the bill, and Congress overrode him by a two-thirds vote of each house—the first major override in American history. Once it became clear that Reconstruction Republicans could muster a two-thirds vote on a matter of supreme consequence, reformers proceeded to propose the Fourteenth Amendment, in part to provide an unquestionable constitutional foundation for the still-contested Civil Rights Act. The act has always been understood by lawyers and judges as intimately linked to the amendment. Under the framework of Chapter 2, the act can even be seen as part of the amendment's very enactment process.

14 On the Fifteenth Amendment, see Amar, *ACAB*, 400–401 & n.*, 612–613 n. 106; Amar, *Bill of Rights*, 273–274 & n.*. Consider also the equality component of the Fifth Amendment's due-process clause, as glossed by the Fourteenth Amendment's equal-protection and due-process clauses. See supra n. 5. See also Amar, *Bill of Rights*, 281–283; Akhil Reed Amar, "Intratextualism," *Harvard LR* 112 (1999): 747, 766–773.

15 *CG*, 42-2:242 (Dec. 20, 1871).

16 William J. Brennan Jr., "The Bill of Rights and the States: The Revival of State

Constitutions as Guardians of Individual Rights," *New York U. LR* 61 (1986): 535, 535–536; Erwin N. Griswold, "Due Process Problems Today in the United States," in Bernard Schwartz, ed., *The Fourteenth Amendment* (1970), 161, 164 (citation omitted).

17 For the Court's "ordered liberty" test, see *Palko v. Connecticut*, 302 U.S. 319, 322–329 (1937).

18 *Robinson v. California*, 370 U.S. 660 (1962) (cruel and unusual punishment); *Pointer v. Texas*, 80 U.S. 400 (1965) (confrontation); *Klopfer v. North Carolina*, 386 U.S. 213 (1967) (speedy trial); *Washington v . Texas*, 88 U.S. 14 (1967) (compulsory process); *Benton v. Maryland*, 395 U.S. 784 (1969) (double jeopardy). See also *Schlib v. Kuebel* (bail) (dictum), 404 U.S. 357 (1971), decided shortly after Warren left the Court.

19 In the 1798–1801 period, see Act of July 14, 1798, 1 Stat. 596; *Lyon's Case*, 15 F. Cas. 1183 (C.C.D. Vt. 1798) (No. 8,646) (Paterson, J.); *United States v. Callender*, 25 F. Cas. 239 (C.C.D. Va. 1800) (No. 14,709) (Chase, J.); *United States v. Cooper*, 25 F. Cas. 631 (C.C.D. Pa. 1800) (No. 14,865) (Chase, J.); *United States v. Haswell*, 26 F. Cas. 218 (C.C.D. Vt. 1800) (No. 15,324) (Paterson, J.). In the World War I era, see Espionage Act of 1917, 40 Stat. 217; Sedition Act of 1918, 40 Stat. 553; *Schenck v. United States*, 249 U.S. 47 (1919); *Debs v. United States*, 249 U.S. 211 (1919); *Abrams v. United States*, 250 U.S. 616 (1919). Postincorporation, see *Lamont v. Postmaster General*, 381 U.S. 301 (1965). For an astute reminder of *Lamont*'s firstness and of the fact that "actual Bill-of-Rights invalidation of congressional legislation is a fairly recent phenomenon," see Laurence H. Tribe, *American Constitutional Law* (1978), 3–4 & n. 8.

20 The five were Justices Black, Douglas, Brennan, Potter Stewart, and Byron White; the sixth was Justice Harlan. Two of the three justices who voted against the *Times* in 1971—Chief Justice Burger and Justice Blackmun—had not been on the Court in 1964. Nor had Justice Thurgood Marshall, who sided with the *Times* in 1971. The 1964 *New York Times* case was cited twice in the 1971 *New York Times* case. *New York Times Co. v. United States*, 403 U.S. 713, 720 n. 1, 724 (1971) (Douglas, J., concurring, joined by Black, J.). For more on the first *Times* case, see Harry Kalven Jr., "The New York Times Case: A Note on 'The Central Meaning of the First Amendment,'" *Supreme Court Review* 1965: 191.

21 The four words—rights, freedoms, privileges, and immunities—are virtually interchangeable today and have been so for centuries. For example, the Sixth Amendment refers to a criminal defendant's "right" to a jury trial, but Continental Congresses in 1774 and 1775 flayed the British for dishonoring the "inestimable privilege" of jury trial. *JCC*, 1:69 (Resolutions of the First Continental Congress, Oct. 14, 1774); ibid., 2:145 (Declaration of the Causes and Necessity of Taking Up Arms, July 6, 1775). Similarly, freedom of speech has long been described as a "right" and/or a "privilege"; and a criminal defendant's "rights" to remain silent at trial and to prevent retrial after acquittal are often referred to as "immunities" from compulsory process and reprosecution.

22 *CG*, 39-1:1088–1094 (Bingham, Feb. 28, 1866), 2765–2766 (Howard, May 23, 1866). For much more evidence and analysis, see Amar, *Bill of Rights*, 163–214.

23 See Amar, *Bill of Rights*, 166–171 (citing, among other things, *Dred Scott v. Sanford*, 60 U.S. [19 How.] 393, 416–417, 449–450 [1857]); Matthew J. Hegreness, "Note, An Organic Theory of the Fourteenth Amendment: The Northwest Ordinance as the Source of Rights, Privileges, and Immunities," *Yale LJ* 120 (2011): 1820.

24 For more evidence and analysis, see Amar, *Bill of Rights*, esp. 284–288. For Bingham's speeches, see *CG*, 39-1:1088–1094 (Feb. 28, 1866), 1291–1293 (March 9, 1866).

25 See Amar, *Bill of Rights*, 215–230.

26 Ibid., 157–158, 167–169, 277–278; Hegreness, "Note."

27 *The Slaughter-House Cases*, 83 U.S. 36, 73–80 (1873). For more analysis, see Amar, *Bill of Rights*, 212–213.

28 Compare *Barron v. Baltimore*, 32 U.S. (7 Pet.) 243 (1833), with *CG*, 39-1:1089–1090 (Bingham, Feb. 28, 1866), 39-2: 811 (Bingham, Jan. 28, 1867). For more, see Amar, *Bill of Rights*.

29 See *Chicago, Burlington & Quincy Railroad Co. v. City of Chicago*, 166 U.S. 266, 236–241 (1897). See also supra n. 17 and accompanying text.

30 For the key cases, see supra n. 18 and accompanying text.

31 *McDonald v. Chicago*, 130 S. Ct. 3020 (2010).

32 According to the National Center for State Courts, the eighteen states requiring grand-jury indictments for all felonies are: Alabama, Alaska, Delaware, Georgia, Kentucky, Maine, Massachusetts, Mississippi, New Hampshire, New Jersey, New York, North Carolina, Ohio, South Carolina, Tennessee, Texas, Virginia, and West Virginia. For more discussion of the possible twists and turns of Seventh Amendment incorporation, see Amar, *Bill of Rights*, 88–93, 275–276, 391 n. 171. Note also that the Third Amendment has not been held applicable against states; but then, this amendment is almost never invoked by modern litigants against any government official, state or federal.

33 *Blackstone's Comm.*, 4:151–152.

34 *Annals*, 1:453–454 (June 8, 1789); ibid., 4:934 (Nov. 27, 1794); *Elliot's Debates*, 4:569–577 (Madison's Report on the Virginia Resolutions—discussed in more detail in Chapter 2, text accompanying nn. 5–6).

35 Act of July 4, 1840, c. 45, 6 Stat. 802, accompanied by H. R. Rep. No. 86, 26th Cong., 1st Sess. (1840), *CG*, 26-1:411 (May 23, 1840).

36 Amar, *Bill of Rights*, 235, 380 n. 10.

37 See ibid., 32–42, 246–254.

38 See Amar, *CCP*, esp. 89–144.

39 *United States v. La Jeune Eugenie*, 26 F. Cas. 832, 843–844 (C.C.D. Mass. 1822) (No. 15, 551).

40 Act of Jan. 24, 1862, ch. 11, 12 Stat. 333. For details and analysis see Amar, *CCP*, 79.

41 On Wilkes and Camden, see *Wilkes v. Wood*, 19 Howell's State Trials 1153 (C.P. 1763), 98 Eng. Rep. 489; *Entick v. Carrington*, 19 Howell's State Trials 1029 (C.P. 1765), 95 Eng. Rep. 807; *Wilkes v. Halifax*, 19 Howell's State Trials 1406 (C.P. 1769). See also *Huckle v. Money*, 19 Howell's State Trials 1404 (C.P. 1763), 95 Eng. Rep. 768; *Beardmore v. Carrington*, 19 Howell's State Trials 1405 (C.P. 1764), 95 Eng. Rep. 790; *Money v. Leach*, 19 Howell's State Trials 1001 (K.B. 1765), 97 Eng. Rep. 1075. For more on Wilkes and

Camden, see Akhil Reed Amar, *The Law of the Land: A Constitutional Travelogue* (forthcoming 2013), Chapters 2 and 7. Notable American venues named for these heroes include Wilkes-Barre, Pennsylvania; Wilkes County, Georgia; Wilkes County, North Carolina; Camden, New Jersey; Camden, South Carolina; Camden, Maine; and historic Camden Yards, home of the Baltimore Orioles.

42 Exclusionary-rule advocates often claim that the rule in no way benefits a guilty defendant but simply restores the status quo that would have existed had no Fourth Amendment violation ever occurred. Wrong: See Chapter 3, n. 24.

43 On what proper updating should look like, see Amar, *CCP*, 28, 31, 40–45.

44 See *United States v. Janis*, 428 U.S. 433, 447 (1976) ("In the complex and turbulent history of the [exclusionary] rule, the Court never has applied it to exclude evidence from a civil proceeding, federal or state").

45 For a list of nearly twenty key cases, with specific page citations to their invocations of the Fifth Amendment alongside the Fourth, see Amar, *CCP*, 250 n. 28. The single major exclusionary-rule case that omitted mention of the Fifth Amendment self-incrimination rule was *Silverthorne Lumber Co. v. United States*, 251 U.S. 385 (1920). For analysis and criticism of *Silverthorne*, see paragraph 2 of the above-mentioned n. 28.

46 See supra n. 41.

47 See *Boyd v. United States*, 116 U.S. 616, 630, 634–635 (1886):

> [A]ny forcible and compulsory extortion of a man's own testimony, or of his private papers to be used as evidence to convict him of crime…is within the condemnation of [Lord Camden's] judgment. In this regard the fourth and fifth amendments run almost into each other.…[A] compulsory production of the private books and papers of the owner…is compelling him to be a witness against himself, within the meaning of the fifth amendment to the constitution, and is the equivalent of a search and seizure—and an unreasonable search and seizure—within the meaning of the fourth amendment.

48 See Amar, *CCP*, 46–88. See also Akhil Reed Amar, "Paper Chase," *The New Republic*, Dec. 15, 1997.

49 For details, see Amar, *CCP*, 22–23, 190 n. 115.

50 *Schmerber v. California*, 384 U.S. 757 (1966). See also *United States v. Wade*, 388 U.S. 218 (1967) (obliging criminal suspect to stand in a line-up); *Gilbert v. California*, 388 U.S. 263 (1967) (obliging suspect to provide handwriting exemplar); *United States v. Dionisio*, 410 U.S. 1 (1973) (obliging suspect to provide voice-print).

51 See, e.g., *Fisher v. United States*, 425 U.S. 391, 407 (1976) (proclaiming that the Fourth-Fifth fusion idea underlying the 1886 *Boyd* case [see supra n. 47]—the only truly principled basis for the exclusionary rule—had "not stood the test of time"); *Stone v. Powell*, 425 U.S. 465 (1976) (holding the exclusionary rule inapplicable in federal habeas corpus cases reviewing state court convictions); *United States v. Janis*, 428 U.S. 433, 447 (1976) (refusing to extend the exclusionary rule to civil cases); *United States v. Havens*, 446 U.S.

620 (1980) (creating an exception to the exclusionary rule in order to impeach a criminal defendant's testimony); *United States v. Leon*, 468 U.S. 897, 905–906 (1984) (echoing *Fisher* verbatim and carving out an exception to the exclusionary rule for certain violations of the Fourth Amendment involving "good faith" behavior of police officers); *Hudson v. Michigan*, 547 U.S. 586 (2006) (applying the "inevitable discovery" exception to the exclusionary rule); *United States v. Herring*, 555 U.S. 135 (2009) (broadly reading the *Leon* good-faith exception doctrine).

52 Three of the four *Schmerber* dissenters—Warren, Black, and Douglas—had been on the Court in *Mapp* and had been crucial to forming the *Mapp* majority of five votes for exclusion. (The other two votes came from Justices Tom C. Clark and Brennan.) In particular, Justice Black's decisive fifth vote in *Mapp* was explicitly based on the precise Fourth-Fifth fusion idea squarely rejected by the Court in the later *Schmerber* decision.

53 For a few specifics, see Amar, *ACAB*, 97–98.

54 See Chapter 1, n. 38, and Chapter 2, n. 47 and accompanying text. See, generally, Amar, *Bill of Rights*, 160–161, 235–239, and sources cited therein; Amar, *ACAB*, 371–372, and sources cited therein.

55 Recall that the privileges-or-immunities clause incorporated all the basic rights of the early amendments, among other things. Such rights surely encompassed the right to due process. Yet the amendment immediately proceeded to enumerate due process. As Bingham and other sponsors explained, the amendment did so to make clear that certain rights—rights to fair legal procedures—belonged to all persons whether citizens or not (contra *Dred Scott*). Thus, the amendment's text and enactment history reflect exquisite sensitivity to the citizen/person distinction. See Chapter 3, n. 32 and accompanying text. See also Amar, *Bill of Rights*, 171–174. Note that I do not say that aliens cannot vote or assert that aliens have never voted; I say only that voting is hardly a paradigmatic right of aliens qua aliens. For an interesting historical survey, see Jamin B. Raskin, "Legal Aliens, Local Citizens: The Historical, Constitutional and Theoretical Meanings of Alien Suffrage," *U. of Pennsylvania LR* 141 (1993): 1391.

56 Compare *Dred Scott v. Sanford*, 60 U.S. (19 How.) 393, 403–427 (1857) (opinion of the Court, per Taney, C.J.) with ibid., 583 (Curtis, J., dissenting).

57 *Opinions of the Attorney General*, 10:382 (1862); Act of April 9, 1866, 14 Stat. 27, quoted supra text accompanying n. 13.

58 See *Report of the Joint Committee on Reconstruction* (1866), xiii, xviii, xxi; Amar, *Bill of Rights*, 216–218 & n. *, and sources cited therein; Amar, *ACAB*, 391–392.

59 Recall that section 1 of the Fourteenth Amendment clearly took aim against the Black Codes—laws that openly discriminated against blacks. Had section 1 been understood to encompass political rights, then all race-based suffrage laws would have been legally equivalent to Black Codes and thus unconstitutional. These suffrage laws were not so understood in 1866–1868 precisely because 1860s discourse sharply distinguished between laws affecting civil rights—Black Codes—and regulations of political rights, such as voting and jury service. Note also that if the equal-protection clause encompassed

voting rights for blacks, it would also seem to do so for women. Yet when suffragists brought suit in the 1870s claiming that they had been enfranchised by the Fourteenth Amendment, the justices in *Minor v. Happersett* unanimously laughed the claim out of Court, making many of the points summarized here. Plaintiffs in *Minor* had relied on the privileges-or-immunities clause; no one even thought to invoke the equal-protection clause as the font of voting rights. For more on woman suffrage, see Chapter 7. On what changed decisively between 1866–1868 and 1869–1870, enabling the Fifteenth Amendment to accomplish what the Fourteenth had not dared to propose, see Amar, *ACAB*, 395–399.

60 See Chapter 10, n. 14 and accompanying text; see also Chapter 7.

61 At the height of Reconstruction, Senator Charles Sumner famously likened the republican-government clause to "a sleeping giant in the Constitution, never until this recent war awakened, but now it comes forward with a giant's power." *CG*, 40-1:614 (July 12, 1867).

62 Act of Aug. 6, 1965, sec. 10; 79 Stat. 437, 442; Amar, *ACAB*, 443, 623–624 n. 22.

63 *Oregon v. Mitchell*, 400 U.S. 112 (1970). Of the seven Warren Court holdovers, four—Justices Douglas, Brennan, White, and Marshall—voted to sustain the 1970 statutory amendments to the Voting Rights Act in their entirety, and a fifth, Justice Black, voted to uphold broad congressional power to enfranchise young adults in federal elections but not state elections. Two Warren Court holdovers—Justices Harlan and Stewart—voted to strike down both the state-election provision that Black found troubling and also the federal-election provision. In this willingness to broadly set aside Congress's handiwork, these two jurists were joined, for the most part, by the two recent post-Warren appointees, Chief Justice Warren Burger and Justice Harry Blackmun. With Black thus emerging as the swing justice in the case, the Court, by separate votes of 5–4, upheld Congress's power to enfranchise young adults in federal elections and struck down Congress's efforts to enfranchise these young adults in state elections.

64 Cf. John Hart Ely, *Democracy and Distrust* (1980), 6–7, 99, 123 (advocating a proper interpretive "line of growth" based on "the ways our constitutional document has developed in the two centuries since the Republican Form Clause was drafted"—a line of growth dramatized by a string of "right-to-vote" amendments); Laurence H. Tribe, *The Invisible Constitution* (2008), 69–70 ("[V]oting is itself constitutionally 'core' in what the Constitution had become by 1964 or at the very latest 1971, if not by 1920").

65 See Akhil Reed Amar, "The Central Meaning of Republican Government," *U. Colorado LR* 65 (1994): 749, 753–754, 776–777, 780.

66 *Baker v. Carr*, 369 U.S. 186, 226 (1962). See also ibid., 244–245 (Douglas, J., concurring) ("Universal equality is not the test; there is room for [unequal] weighting [of votes]"); 258 (Clark, J., concurring) ("No one—except the dissenters...—contends that mathematical equality among voters is required by the Equal Protection Clause").

67 For additional reasons supporting *Reynolds*'s strict equalitarian approach—reasons centered more on implementation than pure interpretation—see Chapter 5, n. 13 and accompanying text.

68 See Barry Friedman, *The Will of the People* (2009), 268 (quoting Senator Strom Thurmond's claim that the Warren Court rulings doomed the existing political structures of at least forty-four states).

69 Compare the contrasting visions of *Brown* on pervasive display in *Parents Involved in Community Schools v. Seattle School District No. 1*, 551 U.S. 701 (2007), in which Chief Justice John Roberts and Justice Clarence Thomas offered politically conservative readings of *Brown*, Justices Stephen Breyer and John Paul Stevens offered politically liberal readings, and Justice Anthony Kennedy's swing opinion split the difference. For more discussion of *Brown*'s special status, which made this fierce debate over its legacy both fraught and inevitable, see Chapter 6.

70 While Justice Thomas has raised questions about the incorporation of the establishment clause, in particular—see, e.g., *Newdow v. United States Congress, Elk Grove Unified School District, et al.*, 542 U.S. 1, 49–54 (2004) (Thomas, J., concurring)—he has elsewhere vigorously applied and, in the context of the Second Amendment, extended the basic principles of incorporation. *McDonald v. Chicago*, 130 S. Ct. 3020, 3058–3088 (2010) (Thomas, J., concurring).

71 Compare *Bush v. Gore*, 531 U.S. 98, 104–105 (2000) (per curiam) (citing *Harper* and *Reynolds*), with ibid., 124–125 (Stevens, J., dissenting, joined by Ginsburg and Breyer, JJ.) (citing *Reynolds*).

72 See Chapter 3. Voting rights might also be understood as part of America's actual institutional Constitution, à la Chapter 9, insofar as these rights are foundational elements of the institutionalized system of government as it in fact operates in America. But unlike most of the inside-the-Beltway governmental issues that will be canvassed in Chapter 9, the basic rights of adult American citizens to vote and to have their votes count equally form part of the actual lived experiences of ordinary persons, who go to the polls year after year expecting these basic principles to be respected by government officials.

   Note also that although popular understandings do not generally suffice to subtract from expressly enumerated or structurally implicit constitutional rules and rights, the beliefs of the American people over time are especially relevant in glossing open-ended clauses, especially those that explicitly reference "the people," as the Ninth does in so many words and as the republican-government clause does via the cognate word "republican," which both etymologically and conceptually revolves around the principle of popular/populist/public/people-based government. (For more details on these etymological and conceptual connections, see Amar, *ACAB*, 276–281.)

73 See supra n. 51.

74 Most commentators agree that the key constitutional contributions of the Warren Court occurred in the six fields covered in this chapter: race, incorporation, speech, religion, criminal procedure, and voting rights. Although two other fields in today's constitutional discourse—privacy law and sex-equality law—have more obvious origins in the 1970s Burger Court, as reflected in cases such as *Roe v. Wade* and *Frontiero v. Richardson* (both decided in 1973), some see the 1965 Warren Court decision in *Griswold v. Connecticut* as the forerunner of these later cases. For discussion of *Griswold* as signaling an egalitarian

switch away from "property" in favor of "privacy" as the proper center of judicial solicitude, see Chapter 3, text accompanying nn. 40–41, 50. For a view of *Griswold* through the prism of post-*Griswold* feminism, see Chapter 7, text after n. 16. For *Griswold* as an incorporation-era case, recall the present chapter's discussion at text following n. 18.

75 See supra n. 66; supra n. 2 and accompanying text. See also Chapter 5, nn. 5–6 and accompanying text.

76 From 1865 through 1888, the Court struck down acts of Congress in sixteen cases (one of which—one of the *Legal Tender Cases*—was later overruled within this window); from 1899 through 1912, the Court invalidated congressional action in fourteen cases; from 1920 through 1936, the Court tossed out Congress's handiwork in over thirty cases. The data here derive from compilations in Lee Epstein, Jeffrey A. Segal, Harold J. Spaeth, and Thomas G. Walker, *The Supreme Court Compendium: Data, Decisions, and Development*, 4th ed. (2007), 176–180 (Table 2-15). There is some imprecision in these numbers. Nice classification questions arise when a very small part of a large statute is judicially disregarded, and also when a statute is not held to be "facially" unconstitutional in all applications but is rather found to be unconstitutional only as applied to certain facts. Moreover, judicial review resulting in the "invalidation" of a statute exists on a continuum with judicial techniques "avoiding" invalidation by construing a statute in an exceedingly narrow—and perhaps textually implausible—way.

77 See Bruce Ackerman, *We the People: The Civil Rights Revolution* (forthcoming).

78 Philip B. Kurland, *Politics, the Constitution, and the Warren Court* (1970), 90–91. Though Professor David Strauss is far more celebratory of the Warren Court than was Kurland, Strauss has not successfully explained how that Court's reversal of precedents across the wide range of topics canvassed in this chapter squares with his own advocacy of "common law constitutionalism." See David A. Strauss, "Common Law Constitutional Interpretation," *U. of Chicago LR* 63 (1996): 877. For a valiant effort to provide such an explanation—which, alas, fails to discuss huge portions of the Warren Court revolution and nowhere confronts the breathtaking sweep of the revolution as a whole—see David A. Strauss, "The Common Law Genius of the Warren Court," *William and Mary LR* 49 (2007): 845. Strauss claims that "the Warren Court's most important decisions cannot be easily justified on the basis of the text of the Constitution or the original understandings" and that, "[i]f you look only to those sources of law, you will not find justification for what the Warren Court did." Ibid., 845, 850. The present chapter has defended the Warren Court against precisely these sorts of claims. The only Warren-era decisions that this chapter has declined to defend are exclusionary-rule rulings such as *Mapp*—a quadrant of case law unmentioned by Strauss.

79 Johnny H. Killian and George A Costello, eds., *The Constitution of the United States: Analysis and Interpretation* (1996), 2245–2255 (appendix prepared by Congressional Research Service compiling "Supreme Court Decisions Overruled by Subsequent Decisions") (listing eighty-eight cases overruling precedents pre-Warren, forty-five cases from the Warren years, and sixty-one cases in the 1970s and 1980s). As with the data pre-

sented in n. 76 and accompanying text, the figures here are the products of the compilers' interpretive judgments. For example, at what point are we to say that a given disfavored case has been, in effect, overruled *sub silentio*—rejected by the Court even though not expressly overruled? When certain language in case 1 is cast aside in later case 2, does it matter whether that discarded language is the "holding" of the case or merely "dicta"? If so, how is the line to be drawn between "holding" and "dicta"?

80 *Gideon v. Wainwright*, 372 U.S. 335 (1963), overruled *Betts v. Brady*, 316 U.S. 455 (1942). See Jerold H. Israel, "Gideon v. Wainwright: The 'Art' of Overruling," *Supreme Court Review* 1963: 211.

CHAPTER 5: PUTTING PRECEDENT IN ITS PLACE

1 *Farrand's Records*, 2:389, 417, 430–431 (rewording the Judicial Article and the supremacy clause so as to "conform[]" and interlock); Amar, *ACAB*, 576–577 n. 47.

2 Important scholarly analyses of the need for and significance of doctrine of this sort include Keith E. Whittington, *Constitutional Construction: Divided Powers and Constitutional Meaning* (1999); Richard H. Fallon Jr., *Implementing the Constitution* (2001); Richard H. Fallon Jr., *The Dynamic Constitution: An Introduction to American Constitutional Law* (2004); Jed Rubenfeld, *Revolution by Judiciary: The Structure of American Constitutional Law* (2005); Kermit Roosevelt, *The Myth of Judicial Activism: Making Sense of Supreme Court Decisions* (2006); Jack M. Balkin, *Living Originalism* (2011); David A. Strauss, "The Ubiquity of Prophylactic Rules," *U. of Chicago LR* 55 (1988): 190; Mitchell N. Berman, "Constitutional Decision Rules," *Virginia LR* 90 (2004): 1. Special mention must also be made of the extraordinary contributions of Professors Tribe, Bobbitt, and Currie. See Laurence H. Tribe, *American Constitutional Law* (1978); ibid., 2d ed. (1988); ibid., 3d ed. (2000); Philip Bobbitt, *Constitutional Fate: Theory of the Constitution* (1982); Philip Bobbitt, *Constitutional Interpretation* (1991); David P. Currie, *The Constitution in the Supreme Court: The First Hundred Years, 1789–1888* (1992); David P. Currie, *The Constitution in the Supreme Court: The Second Century, 1888–1986* (1994).

3 See William Baude, "The Judgment Power," *Georgetown LJ* 96 (2008): 1807.

4 *Blackstone's Comm.* 3:23; Del. Const. (1776), Declaration of Rights, sec. 12; Md. Const. (1776), Declaration of Rights, art. XVII; Mass. Const. (1780), pt. I, art. XI; *Federalist* No. 43. See also *Elliot's Debates*, 3:658 (twelfth item of proposed bill of rights of the Virginia ratifying convention).

5 *Brown v. Board of Education of Topeka*, 347 U.S. 483, 491–495 (1954) (citations omitted; emphasis altered).

6 See also *Mayor of Baltimore v. Dawson*, 350 U.S. 877 (1955) (beaches); *Holmes v. City of Atlanta*, 350 U.S. 879 (1955) (golf courses).

7 See, e.g., *Gertz v. Robert Welch, Inc.*, 418 U.S. 323, 336 n. 7 (1974) ("Chief Justice Warren stated the principle for which [post-*Sullivan*] cases stand—that *The New York Times* test reaches both public figures and public officials").

8 See, e.g., *Meek v. Pittenger*, 421 U.S. 349 (1975), overruled by *Mitchell v. Helms*, 530 U.S. 793 (2000); *Wolman v. Walter*, 433 U.S. 229 (1977), overruled by *Mitchell*; *Aguilar v. Felton*, 473 U.S. 402 (1985), overruled by *Agostini v. Felton*, 521 U.S. 203 (1997); *Agostini*; *Mitchell*; *Zelman v. Simmons-Harris*, 536 U.S. 639 (2002).

9 The last time a Court majority invoked the metaphor of a "wall of separation" was over a quarter-century ago—and this final invocation was far more equivocal than previous enthusiastic invocations by Court majorities in *Everson* and many other pre-1980 cases. See *Lynch v. Donnelly*, 465 U.S. 668, 673 (1984). For more on the rise and fall of Jefferson's metaphor in *U.S. Reports*, see Ian Bartrum, "The Constitutional Canon as Argumentative Metonymy," *William & Mary Bill of Rights J* 18 (2009): 327, 331–346.

10 See supra n. 8.

11 If the Fourteenth Amendment's words simply incorporated by reference the rights of the Bill, via Pathway One mapped out in Chapter 4, then Warren Court doctrine did not overprotect the amendment's core textual meaning. But if the amendment's words had a logically and semantically looser link to the Bill of Rights—such as Pathway Five—then the Warren Court doctrine could indeed be seen as slightly overprotective.

12 For most of the twentieth century prior to *Mapp*, the Court neutered a key Reconstruction-era federal statute—42 U.S.C. section 1983—aimed at remedying state constitutional wrongs via civil damages and equitable injunctions. State law had failed to fill the breach, creating a remedial gap that obviously concerned the *Mapp* Court. But only months before *Mapp* was (incorrectly) decided, the Court (correctly) revived section 1983 in *Monroe v. Pape*, 365 U.S. 167 (1961). The *Mapp* Court did not wait to see how this superior remedial structure might be made to work. To the extent that the section-1983 structure has fallen short of its promise, several of its limitations are due to niggardly Court interpretation of section 1983's provisions—provisions that establish a structurally sound (and congressionally authorized) foundation for a civil-remedy system in the tradition of the Wilkes-Camden cases that inspired the Fourth Amendment.

13 In *Wesberry v. Sanders*, 376 U.S. 1 (1964), the Court, per Justice Black, held that the congressional districts within any given state had to be equipopulous, thanks to the command of Article I, section 2, that House members be elected "by the People." Without more, this argument was implausible, because the Founders took care not to specify any fixed apportionment rule within each state. A fixed rule would have awkwardly required the document to decide how slaves should be counted within a state for congressional districting purposes. Amar, *ACAB*, 88–89, 537 n. 94. *Wesberry*'s reading of Article I became possible only after and because of the Reconstruction, which: (1) rendered the slave-apportionment issue moot, (2) obliged southern states to enfranchise blacks on a massive scale, and (3) eventually obliged all states to adopt race-neutral voting laws. Beyond Article I, it is possible to interpret malapportionment as an "abridge[ment] of the right to vote" within the meaning of the Fourteenth Amendment's section 2, and/or as a violation of general principles of republicanism, construed very broadly post-Reconstruction. Thus, *Wesberry* is best justified as a *Bolling v. Sharp*–like reverse-incorporation

case, in which the Court read rights regarding the federal government in light of Reconstruction rights against states. In turn, *Reynolds* resembled a standard incorporation case, in which the Court simply made *Wesberry*'s rules for federal legislative elections equally applicable to state legislative elections. *Reynolds* itself framed the issue in just this way. See *Reynolds v. Sims*, 377 U.S. 533, 560–561 (1964).

14 See Chapter 10.

15 At one end of the plausible range, a state surely has a legitimate interest in ensuring that registered voters are bona fide residents. A constitutionalized sub-rule requiring that every state offer instantaneous registration to anyone claiming to be a new resident on Election Day might result in considerable fraud and tactical vote-shopping by persons who never were and never would become actual residents. At the other end of the plausible range, any state voting rule requiring more than, say, six months of previous state residence would undermine Americans' basic right to change their state citizenship by moving—a right explicitly guaranteed by the opening sentence of the Fourteenth Amendment. Within this range of plausible interpretation, the modern Court has held that states can require up to fifty days of previous residence—a reasonable sub-rule that cannot be uniquely derived from the written Constitution but that sensibly operationalizes its relevant principles. See *Dunn v. Blumstein*, 405 U.S. 330 (1972); *Marston v. Lewis*, 410 U.S. 679 (1973). Here are some of the "marginal" questions raised by the general equalitarian formula of *Reynolds*: How much population deviation from strict equality should be permitted? Less than 1 percent? More than 10 percent? In exactly what respect must districts be equally populous? In actual population? Legal population? Citizen population? Eligible voting population? Registered voting population?

16 For recent data supportive of this assessment—at least for House elections—see David Mayhew, *Partisan Balance* (2011), 22–26.

17 See Antonin Scalia, "Originalism: The Lesser Evil," *U. of Cincinnati LR* 57 (1989): 849, 854, 861.

18 *Rodriguez de Quijas v. Shearson/Am. Express, Inc.*, 490 U.S. 477, 484 (1989); *Eberhart v. United States*, 546 U.S. 12, 19–20 (2005) (per curiam).

19 *Planned Parenthood of Southeastern Pennsylvania v. Casey*, 505 U.S. 833, 864 (1992) (citing *Mitchell v. W. T. Grant Co.*, 416 U.S. 600, 636 [1974] [Stewart, J., dissenting]; *Mapp v. Ohio*, 367 U.S. 643, 677 [1961] [Harlan, J., dissenting]). The Stewart dissent focused only on overrulings linked to changing Court membership; the Harlan dissent merely urged full briefing and argument before overruling, stressing the unwisdom of overruling based on a contrary "disposition" as opposed to a settled and deliberately reached sense of prior error.

20 See, e.g., *Fox Film Corp. v. Doyal*, 286 U.S. 123 (1932) (overruling *Long v. Rockwood*, 277 U.S. 142 [1928]) (federal immunity from state taxation); *Erie R.R. Co. v. Tompkins*, 304 U.S. 64 (1938) (overruling *Swift v. Tyson*, 41 U.S. [16 Pet.] 1 [1842]) (federal common law); *O'Malley v. Woodrough*, 307 U.S. 277 (1939) (overruling *Evans v. Gore*, 253 U.S. 245 [1920]; *Miles v. Graham*, 268 U.S. 501 [1925]) (taxation of Article III salary); *West Virginia State*

Board of Education v. Barnette, 319 U.S. 624 (1943) (overruling *Minersville School District v. Gobitis*, 310 U.S. 586 [1940]) (free expression); *Jones v. Alfred H. Mayer Co.*, 392 U.S. 409 (1968) (overruling *Hodges v. United States*, 203 U.S. 1 [1906]) (congressional power under the Thirteenth Amendment); *Michelin Tire Corp. v. Wages*, 423 U.S. 276 (1976) (overruling *Low v. Austin*, 80 U.S. [13 Wall.] 29 [1871]) (state taxation of imports); *Daniels v. Williams*, 474 U.S. 327 (1986) (overruling *Parratt v. Taylor*, 451 U.S. 527 [1981]) (due process).

21 Since 1992, the *Casey* dictum has appeared only once in *U.S. Reports*—in a dissent complaining that the Court in that case was overruling precedent in violation of the *Casey* dictum. See *Citizens United v. F.E.C.*, 130 S. Ct. 836, 938 (Stevens, J., dissenting) (2010). The Court's majority opinion, which took no notice of the *Casey* dictum, was authored by Justice Kennedy, who himself was one of the joint authors of *Casey*. For other notable post-*Casey* decisions that discuss the importance of *stare decisis* but do not repeat this specific passage from *Casey*, see *Adarand Constructors v. Pena*, 515 U.S. 200, 231–235 (1995); *Agostini v. Felton*, 521 U.S. 203, 235–236 (1997); *Dickerson v. United States*, 120 S. Ct. 2326, 2336 (2000); *Lawrence v. Texas*, 539 U.S. 558, 577 (2003). See also ibid., 587–591 (Scalia, J., dissenting) ("Today's opinions in support of reversal do not bother to distinguish—or indeed, even bother to mention—the paean to *stare decisis* coauthored by three Members of today's majority in *Planned Parenthood v. Casey*....[T]the Court has chosen today to revise the standards of *stare decisis* set forth in *Casey*. It has thereby exposed *Casey*'s extraordinary deference to precedent for the result-oriented expedient that it is."). Note that elsewhere in *Casey*, the Court said various things about precedent that were better rooted in prior case law and constitutional structure and that have been echoed in later cases. The sole focus of analysis here is one particularly loosely worded dictum—namely, that "a decision to overrule should rest on some special reason over and above the belief that a prior case was wrongly decided."

22 This phrase first appeared in an opinion of the Court in *Baker v. Carr*, 369 U.S. 186, 211 (1962). Cf. *Cooper v. Aaron*, 358 U.S. 1, 18 (1957) (proclaiming, in a context involving state defiance of the Court's mandate rather than congressional or presidential disagreement with the Court's judgment, that "the federal judiciary is supreme in the exposition of the law of the Constitution"); *Youngstown Sheet & Tube Co. v. Sawyer*, 343 U.S. 579, 595 (1952) (Frankfurter, J., concurring) (describing "judicial process as the ultimate authority in interpreting the Constitution"). For more recent statements, see, e.g., *Nixon v. United States*, 506 U.S. 224, 238 (1993); *Miller v. Johnson*, 515 U.S. 900, 922 (1995); *United States v. Morrison*, 529 U.S. 598, 616–617 n. 7 (2000).

23 The idea of "equity" is especially apt in pondering how best to remedy constitutional violations. The written Constitution says relatively little about remedies, and in both England and America, the historical concept of equity has featured prominently in a wide range of remedial contexts. Here, we deal with the interesting question of how best to "remedy" a judicial decision that was, by hypothesis, a mistake, a "violation" of sorts of the best reading of the Constitution.

24 An exception to this general approach might be warranted if expanding a nontextual right would somehow contract a textual right.

25 In fact, federal paper money has always been perfectly constitutional. See Amar, *ACAB*, 123. The example thus serves as a reminder that any approach that welcomes judicial overrulings when the current Court is persuaded that a past Court has erred risks false-positives—that is, situations in which today's Court erroneously ends up overruling past decisions that in fact correctly interpreted the Constitution.

Although reliance interests obviously loom large in certain transactional areas involving property and contract, legitimate reliance interests in certain other contexts may well be less significant or even nonexistent. Consider the exclusionary rule. What legitimate reliance interests should impede a Court that is convinced that past cases excluding reliable evidence were plainly erroneous and should thus be overturned? The interest of an especially calculating criminal in getting out of jail free if the cops ever err in procuring compelling evidence against him? Merely to state this interest is to see its absurdity: This is not the stuff of proper reliance worthy of equitable protection. Even if this interest were to be protected, it would offer no shield to any crime committed after the Court made clear that the exclusionary rule must go.

CHAPTER 6: HONORING THE ICONS

1 On the importance of constitutional narratives, see Jack M. Balkin, *Constitutional Redemption: Political Faith in an Unjust World* (2011), 25–32.

2 The American flag has proved to be a particularly protean and slippery symbol—a kind of Rorschach blot that has seduced some otherwise disciplined constitutionalists to drift into embarrassing solipsism rather than deep engagement with the concrete message of a specific text. For details, see Akhil Reed Amar, "The Case of the Missing Amendments," *Harvard LR* 106 (1992): 124, 132–146 (critiquing the unlawyerly—nearly lawless—dissenting opinions of Chief Justice Rehnquist and Justice Stevens in the flag-burning case, *Texas v. Johnson*, 491 U.S. 397 [1989]).

3 For a kindred effort to draw attention to and muse on various exemplary texts that constitute the constitutional canon, see Philip Bobbitt, "The Constitutional Canon," in J. M. Balkin and Sanford Levinson, eds., *Legal Canons* (2000), 331–373.

4 On Jefferson, see Pauline Maier, *American Scripture: Making the Declaration of Independence* (1998), 160–175; Philip F. Detweiler, "The Changing Reputation of the Declaration of Independence: The First Fifty Years," *William & Mary Quarterly* 19 (1962, 3d ser.): 557. On Wilson, see Pauline Maier, *Ratification* (2010), 78–81. On the mid-twentieth-century political competition for black votes, see Amar, *ACAB*, 441. See also infra Chapter 10, text accompanying nn. 10–11.

5 On Washington's and other presidents' inaugurations, see Chapter 2, n. 37 and accompanying text. For an artistic depiction of Washington's use of the Bible at his 1789 swearing-in, see the opening picture of Chapter 8.

6 See Amar, *Bill of Rights*, 247–250.

7 For citation data, see Dan T. Coenen, *The Story of the Federalist: How Hamilton and Madison Reconceived America* (2007), 208–215, and sources cited therein.

8 Beyond its generic meaning of "the public man," "Publius" also referred to a particular Roman hero, Publius Valerius Publicola, who had helped to found the Roman Republic.

9 Story, *Commentaries*, 1:v–vi.

10 True, Publius was typically not cited by name or by *Federalist* number in the ratification debates, and thus does not appear in crude computer word-searches. But a close look at the words and themes of several ratifying convention speeches—especially in Virginia and New York—suggests that several leading delegates literally had *The Federalist* in hand or at hand. See, e.g., Amar, *ACAB*, 69, 81, 536 n. 76.

11 The fact that the Northwest Ordinance is not prominent in today's pop culture does not disqualify it from inclusion in the constitutional canon. After all, many specific clauses of the written Constitution no longer capture the popular imagination, despite the fact that several of these clauses were at earlier moments in American history at the very center of popular discourse (as was the Ordinance itself). Recall that America's symbolic Constitution encompasses texts that "*at some point in American history* won the hearts and minds of a wide swath of the American people, thereby helping to bind citizens together as a legal and political entity," supra text accompanying n. 2. For modern citations to the Ordinance, see, e.g., *Engel v. Vitale*, 370 U.S. 421, 442–443 & n. 9 (1962) (Douglas, J., concurring) (establishment clause); *Reynolds v. Sims*, 377 U.S. 533, 573 & n. 54 (1964) (one-person, one-vote); *Williams v. Florida*, 399 U.S. 78, 97–98 n. 44 (1970) (criminal jury trial); *Furman v. Georgia*, 408 U.S. 238, 244 & n. 6 (1972) (Douglas, J., concurring) (death penalty); *Milliken v. Bradley*, 418 U.S. 717, 794 (1974) (Marshall, J., dissenting, joined by Douglas, Brennan, and White, JJ.) (educational equality); *Parklane Hosiery Co., Inc., v. Shore*, 439 U.S. 322, 341 n. 5 (1979) (Rehnquist, J., dissenting) (collateral estoppel in civil jury suits); *Immigration and Naturalization Service v. Chadha*, 462 U.S. 919, 982–984 n. 18 (1983) (White, J., dissenting) (legislative vetoes); *Wallace v. Jaffree*, 472 U.S. 38, 100 (1985) (Rehnquist, J., dissenting) (establishment clause); *Rosenberger v. Rector and Visitors of the University of Virginia*, 515 U.S. 819, 862–863 (1995) (Thomas, J., concurring) (establishment clause); *City of Boerne v. Flores*, 521 U.S. 507, 538–539 (1997) (Scalia, J., concurring in part, joined by Stevens, J.) (free exercise of religion); *Kelo v. City of New London*, 545 U.S. 469, 509–510 (2005) (Thomas, J., dissenting) (takings clause); *Boumediene v. Bush*, 553 U.S. 723, 756 (2008) (habeas corpus). The citation number mentioned in the text—125—does not include the many dozens of Court cases in which justices have built upon precepts of the Ordinance, such as the equal-footing doctrine, but have not explicitly cited the Ordinance as the deep source of these precepts.

12 *JCC*, 32:334–343 (July 13, 1787); Act of Aug. 7, 1789, 1 Stat. 50.

13 See Eric Biber, "The Price of Admission: Causes, Effects, and Patterns of Conditions Imposed on States Entering the Union," *American Journal of Legal History* 42 (2004): 119.

14 Note how this intriguing self-referential clause simultaneously distinguished "this Constitution" from and linked "this Constitution" to its predecessor regime of "the Confederation." Note also that the main function of the congressional statute of August 7, 1789, reaffirming the Ordinance of 1787 was to integrate the Ordinance into the new Constitution's system of separation of powers. Whereas the 1787 Ordinance had vested the Confederation Congress with power to appoint various territorial officials, the 1789 law made clear that, per Article II, these powers would henceforth be exercised by the president, subject to Senate advice and consent. The power to remove these officials, which had also been vested in the Confederation Congress, was "hereby declared" to be vested in the president alone, in keeping with the so-called "Decision of 1789"—a fact highlighted by the Court in its landmark removal-power ruling in *Myers v. United States*, 272 U.S. 52, 145 (1926) (citing 1 Stat. 50, 53).

15 On the Washington administration's interpretation of the Ordinance as not requiring the emancipation of preexisting slaves in the Northwest, see Amar, *ACAB*, 356.

16 For details, see ibid., 594–595 n. 7, 396.

17 Johnson's celebrated "We Shall Overcome" speech—delivered to a joint session of Congress on March 15, 1965—is also worth quoting at length, both in its own right and for its powerful echoes of Jefferson, Lincoln, Kennedy, and King:

> This was the first nation in the history of the world to be founded with a purpose. The great phrases of that purpose still sound in every American heart, North and South: "All men are created equal"—"government by consent of the governed"— "give me liberty or give me death." Well, those are not just clever words[;] those are not just empty theories. In their name Americans have fought and died for two centuries, and tonight around the world they stand there as guardians of our liberty, risking their lives.
>
> Those words are a promise to every citizen that he shall share in the dignity of man. This dignity...rests on his right to be treated as a man equal in opportunity to all others....To apply any other test—to deny a man his hopes because of his color or race, his religion or the place of his birth—is not only to do injustice, it is to deny America and to dishonor the dead who gave their lives for American freedom.
>
> ...
>
> [A] century has passed—more than a hundred years—since the Negro was freed. And he is not fully free tonight. It was more than a hundred years ago that Abraham Lincoln, a great president of another party, signed the Emancipation Proclamation, but emancipation is a proclamation and not a fact. A century has passed—more than a hundred years—since equality was promised. And yet the Negro is not equal. A century has passed since the day of promise. And the promise is unkept. The time of justice has now come....It is right in the eyes of man and God that it should come.

18 See James Gray Pope, "Republican Moments: The Role of Direct Popular Power in the American Constitutional Order," *U. of Pennsylvania LR* 139 (1990): 288; Bruce Ackerman, *We the People: The Civil Rights Revolution* (forthcoming). In the recent case of *Northwest Austin Municipal Utility District No. 1 v. Holder*, 557 U.S. 193 (2009), several justices at oral argument seemed not to understand the iconic status of the Voting Rights Act. Happily, the Court came to its senses in its final written decision, declining to endorse the appellant's frontal assault on this special statute.

19 See *Regents of the University of California v. Bakke*, 438 U.S. 265, 269–324 (1978) (swing opinion of Powell, J., announcing the judgment of the Court); *Grutter v. Bollinger*, 539 U.S. 306, 311–344 (2003) (opinion of the Court, per O'Connor, J.); *Parents Involved in Community Schools v. Seattle School District No. 1*, 551 U.S. 701, 782–799 (2007) (opinion of Kennedy, J., concurring in part and concurring in the judgment).

20 See *Swann v. Charlotte-Mecklenburg Board of Education*, 402 U.S. 1 (1971), and cases cited therein.

21 See Laurence H. Tribe, *The Invisible Constitution* (2008), 20.

22 See, e.g., *Boumediene v. Bush*, 553 U.S 723 (2008) (opinion of the Court per Kennedy, J., joined by Stevens, Souter, Ginsburg, and Breyer, JJ.) (describing the *Dred Scott* case as "notorious"); *Planned Parenthood of Southeastern Pennsylvania v. Casey*, 505 U.S. 833, 998 (1992) (Scalia, J., dissenting, joined by Rehnquist, C.J., and White and Thomas, JJ.) ("[T]he Court was covered with dishonor and deprived of legitimacy by *Dred Scott v. Sanford*, an erroneous (and widely opposed) opinion that it did not abandon, rather than by *West Coast Hotel Co. v. Parrish*, which produced the famous 'switch in time' from the Court's erroneous (and widely opposed) constitutional opposition to the social measures of the New Deal") (citations omitted); *Fullilove v. Klutznick*, 448 U.S. 448, 516 (1980) (Powell, J., concurring) ("[O]ur own decisions played no small part in the tragic legacy of government-sanctioned discrimination. See *Plessy v. Ferguson*; *Dred Scott v. Sanford*.") (citations omitted); *Bell v. Maryland*, 378 U.S. 226, 253 (1964) (separate opinion of Douglas, J., joined by Goldberg, J.) (describing *Dred Scott* as "ill-starred" and implying that the case "exalt[ed] property in suppression of individual rights"); *Cohen v. Hurley*, 366 U.S. 117, 142 n. 23 (1961) (Black, J., dissenting, joined by Warren, C.J., and Douglas, J.) (mocking *Dred Scott* and *Plessy* as "renowned" decisions that ignored "the words of the Constitution").

23 It might be thought that Justice Oliver Wendell Holmes Jr.'s dissent in *Lochner* could function as the paired symbolic "hero." But the status of this dissent and of Holmes more generally in modern constitutional discourse is rather complicated. Holmes has his admirers, but also has eminent critics. See, e.g., Alexander Meiklejohn, *Free Speech and Its Relation to Self-Government* (1948). Holmes memorably told us in *Lochner* that "the Fourteenth Amendment does not enact Mr. Herbert Spencer's Social Statics." *Lochner v. New York*, 198 U.S. 45, 75 (1905) (Holmes, J., dissenting). Fair enough—the Constitution indeed does not mandate laissez faire or condemn all redistribution. But Holmes was much less helpful in explaining exactly what the Fourteenth Amendment *does* do. Holmes's obtuse arguments that state governments could brazenly defy the Fifteenth

Amendment with no judicial repercussions, could properly penalize core political expression, could lawfully enforce a system of peonage-labor, and could legitimately sterilize women as officials saw fit—see, e.g., *Giles v. Harris*, 189 U.S. 475 (1903); *Patterson v. Colorado*, 205 U.S. 454 (1907); *Bailey v. Alabama*, 219 U.S. 219, 245–250 (1911) (Holmes, J., dissenting); *Buck v. Bell*, 274 U.S. 200 (1927)—have not aged well. These pronouncements from Holmes form no part of today's symbolic Constitution. On the contrary, these and related Holmesian pronouncements are widely viewed today as deplorable. Yet their underlying vision of bland deference to majority will, even if tyrannical, cannot be cleanly separated from the vision on display in Holmes's *Lochner* dissent.

24 *Dred Scott v. Sanford*, 60 U.S. 393, 405 (1857).

25 Though *Plessy* now stands as a disgraced opinion, the Court of late has unfortunately had rather kind things to say about an earlier landmark ruling in *The Civil Rights Cases* of 1883, a ruling whose logic and voting line-up foreshadowed *Plessy*'s logic and line-up. In *The Civil Rights Cases*, 109 U.S. 3 (1883), the Supreme Court—over the sharp solo dissent of Justice Harlan—invalidated major portions of Congress's Civil Rights Act of 1875, which required racial equality in railroads, steamships, and various other facilities open to the public, such as inns, theaters, and other places of public amusement. Had the Court in 1883 simply upheld the 1875 Civil Rights Act, then the Louisiana Jim Crow law in *Plessy* could have been struck down on the easy ground of federal preemption. Thus, the negative symbol of *Plessy* also reinforces the wisdom of paying special deference to congressional civil rights laws, especially the civil rights laws enacted during the first and second Reconstructions. Much as the Philadelphia framers, led by presiding officer George Washington, drafted the language of Article II in a way that effectively delegated broad power to shape the presidency to the first president, who of course would be Washington himself (see Chapter 8 for more details), so the Reconstruction Congress drafted the Thirteenth, Fourteenth, and Fifteenth Amendments in a manner that gave Congress itself broad authority to shape the full meaning of these amendments.

26 The *Lochner* Court sharply distinguished between what it saw as legitimate and illegitimate government purposes. Protecting workers' health and safety was a legitimate purpose; but it was illegitimate for government to enhance workers' bargaining power for its own sake or to intentionally shift economic surplus from employers to employees. Thus the Court condemned any law that was a "labor law, pure and simple," in which government openly favored Labor at the expense of Capital. *Lochner v. New York*, 198 U.S. 45, 57 (1905). See also *Coppage v. Kansas*, 236 U.S. 1, 17–18 (1915), in which the *Lochner*-era Court condemned legislative efforts to level "inequalities of fortune." For similar readings of the antiredistributive essence of the *Lochner* case and the *Lochner* era, see, e.g., Laurence H. Tribe, "The Supreme Court, 1972 Term—Foreword: Toward a Model of Roles in the Due Process of Life and Law," *Harvard LR* 87 (1973): 1, 6–7, 12–13 & n. 69; Jed Rubenfeld, "The Anti-Antidiscrimination Agenda," *Yale LJ* 111 (2002): 1141, 1146–1147. For a recent effort to end the demonization of *Lochner*, see David E. Bernstein, *Rehabilitating* Lochner: *Defending Individual Rights Against Progressive*

Reform (2010). Bernstein succeeds in establishing that Justice Holmes and several other extreme contemporary Progressive critics of *Lochner* should not be viewed as heroic figures; their unduly dismissive vision of individual constitutional rights should not have prevailed in the *Lochner* era and should not prevail today. Alas, much of the rest of Bernstein's book fails to engage the best criticisms of *Lochner*, preferring instead to knock down an army of straw men. Bernstein fails to highlight the fact that the most admirable cases of the *Lochner* era, on which modern case law continues to build, were all joined in relevant part by Justice Louis Brandeis. Bernstein also oddly tries to claim Justice Harlan for his own team, even though Harlan famously dissented in *Lochner*. Ibid., 123–127. Despite the title of his book, Bernstein fails to rehabilitate *Lochner* even though he does defrock Holmes. Bernstein would have done better to write a book lauding *Lochner*'s most admirable and trenchant critics, including the first Justice Harlan, Justice Brandeis, and Justice Black. Although these three men disagreed about many things, each of these judicial icons contributed a great deal to what is best about modern constitutional law.

27 For the pairing of *Dred Scott* and *Plessy*, see, e.g., *Parents Involved in Community Schools v. Seattle School District No. 1*, 551 U.S. 701, 781 (2006) (Thomas, J., concurring). Earlier opinions authored or joined by Justices Powell, Black, and Douglas and Chief Justice Warren also paired *Dred* and *Plessy*. See supra n. 22. For the pairing of *Dred Scott* and *Lochner*, see, e.g., *Planned Parenthood of Southeastern Pennsylvania v. Casey*, 505 U.S. 833, 998 (1992) (Scalia, J., dissenting, joined by Rehnquist, C.J., and White and Thomas, JJ.). For the pairing of *Plessy* and *Lochner*, see, e.g., ibid., 957. For a thoughtful discussion of related issues, see Richard Primus, "Canon, Anti-Canon, and Judicial Dissent," *Duke LJ* 48 (1998): 243.

CHAPTER 7: "REMEMBERING THE LADIES"

1 On the especially inclusive voting rules that governed the Constitution's ratification in the late 1780s, see Amar, *ACAB*, 5–7 and accompanying notes.

2 For more discussion and documentation, see ibid., 381–383.

3 See Akhil Reed Amar, "The Supreme Court, 1999 Term—Foreword: The Document and the Doctrine," *Harvard LR* 114 (2000): 26, 96–102.

4 Joint Resolution of June 5, 1919, 41 Stat. 362.

5 The attentive reader will by now have noticed that several of the most interesting areas of interplay between America's written and unwritten Constitution involve questions of remedy and related issues of severability. In a nutshell, what should happen when the Constitution's rules are not properly followed? For example, when states unlawfully try to exit the Union? (See Chapter 2, text accompanying nn. 41–50.) What about when improper searches and seizures in fact occur? (See Chapter 3, text accompanying nn. 23–26; Chapter 4, text accompanying nn. 38–52; and Chapter 5, text accompanying n. 12.) Or when the rights of blacks to enjoy equal citizenship and voting rights are massively violated by a pervasive regime of segregation, disfranchisement, and oppression? (See

Chapter 5, text accompanying nn. 5–6.) Or when the Court itself garbles the Constitution? (See Chapter 5, text accompanying nn. 19–25.) Or when certain sentences of the Constitution would violate later amendments unless some old words are in effect excised or some new words in effect interpolated? (See Chapter 10, text accompanying n. 14.)

6 Cf. Jack M. Balkin, *Living Originalism* (2011), 261–262 ("New amendments may alter the relationships between other parts of the Constitution, sometimes…in quite unexpected ways.…[S]tructural principles might emerge from the constitutional system that no single person or generation intended.").

7 For more, see Chapter 10, n. 14 and accompanying text.

8 It is, of course, logically possible to envision a declaratory amendment that merely restates more clearly a principle already implicit in the Constitution—and, indeed, we encountered a few examples in previous chapters. But almost no one in the 1910s believed that the proposed Woman Suffrage Amendment was merely declaratory of a voting right already implicit in the equal-protection clause. Note that in one of the first post-suffrage Supreme Court cases involving sex discrimination on juries, the Court did make passing reference to the Nineteenth Amendment. See *Fay v. New York*, 332 U.S. 261, 290 (1947).

9 In 1875, Congress evidently relied on the letter and spirit of the Black Suffrage Amendment to support enforcement legislation affirming the right of blacks to serve equally on juries. Compare U.S. Const. amend. XV ("The right of *citizens of the United States* to vote shall not be denied or abridged by *the United States or by any State on account of race, color, or previous condition of servitude*") (emphasis added) with the Act of March 1, 1875, ch. 114, sec. 4, 18 Stat. 335, 336 ("no *citizen*…shall be disqualified for service as grand or petit juror in any court *of the United States or of any State, on account of race, color, or previous condition of servitude*") (emphasis added). For much more elaboration and documentation, see Vikram David Amar, "Jury Service as Political Participation Akin to Voting," *Cornell LR* 80 (1995): 203. See also Amar, *Bill of Rights*, 272–274 & n *; Amar, *ACAB*, 400 & n *, 426–428 and accompanying notes; Akhil Reed Amar, "Intratextualism," *Harvard LR* 112 (1999): 747, 789.

10 See Reva B. Siegel, "She the People: The Nineteenth Amendment, Sex Equality, Federalism, and the Family," *Harvard LR* 115 (2002): 947, 1016–1018.

11 For details on the changing shape of the vice presidency, see Chapter 10, text accompanying nn. 7, 11. See also Amar, ACAB, 342–343, 437–438, 449–451.

12 Jo Freeman, "Gender Gaps in Presidential Elections," *P.S.: Political Science and Politics* 32 (1999): 191.

13 If these separations one day come to be perceived by large numbers of men or women as invidious, then that change in public perception could provide a basis for declaring these now-permissible separations to be unequal and therefore unconstitutional.

14 On state constitutions, see Dawn C. Nunziato, "Gender Equality: States as Laboratories," *Virginia LR* 80 (1994): 945, 975–977; Beth Gammie, "Note, State ERAs: Problems and Possibilities," *U of Illinois LR* (1989): 1123, 1125–1126. Not counting various states that clearly or arguably rescinded their prior ratifications, the following thirty states said

yes to the ERA before March 1979 (and thus within the initial seven-year ratification window proposed by Congress): Alaska, California, Colorado, Connecticut, Delaware, Hawaii, Indiana, Iowa, Kansas, Maine, Maryland, Massachusetts, Michigan, Minnesota, Montana, New Hampshire, New Jersey, New Mexico, New York, North Dakota, Ohio, Oregon, Pennsylvania, Rhode Island, Texas, Vermont, Washington, West Virginia, Wisconsin, and Wyoming. On the legality of state rescissions and congressional extensions of the ratification window, see Amar, *ACAB*, 455–445, and accompanying notes.

15 On the anti-dynastic logic of Founding-era age rules, see Amar, *ACAB*, 70–72, 159–164. Briefly, the idea was that in a world without age limits for public service, sons of famous fathers would have an unfair and unrepublican inside track to early election. Age limits would oblige political scions to develop political records of their own before they could win high posts and would give lower-born men of merit time to rise and shine.

16 Ever since Plato immortalized Socrates (and perhaps earlier), the dialogic form has been a familiar genre to explore questions of law and justice. Modern legal classics using hypothetical dialogue to present the analytic thrust and parry include Henry M. Hart, "The Power of Congress to Limit the Jurisdiction of Federal Courts: An Exercise in Dialectic," *Harvard LR* 66 (1953): 1362; Bruce A. Ackerman, *Social Justice in the Liberal State* (1980); and Philip Bobbitt, *Constitutional Interpretation* (1991), 111–112. Note that in the movie, Hepburn played "Amanda" (not "Eve") opposite Tracy's "Adam."

17 See Balkin, *Living Originalism*, 31.

18 Charles Francis Adams, *Familiar Letters of John Adams and his Wife Abigail Adams, During the Revolution* (1876), 149–150 (letter of March 31, 1776).

19 See Amar, *Bill of Rights*, 216–218, 239–241, 245–246, 257 n *, 260–261 & n *, 293–294, 305; Amar, *ACAB*, 393–395, 401; Akhil Reed Amar, "Women and the Constitution," *Harvard Journal of Law and Public Policy* 18 (1995): 465.

CHAPTER 8: FOLLOWING WASHINGTON'S LEAD

1 Cf. *Federalist* No. 37 (Madison) ("All new laws, though penned with the greatest technical skill, and passed on the fullest and most mature deliberation, are considered as more or less obscure and equivocal, until their meaning be liquidated and ascertained by a series of particular discussions and adjudications"). See, generally, Caleb Nelson, "Originalism and Interpretive Conventions," *U. of Chicago LR* 70 (2003): 519.

2 Washington was acutely aware of his unique role and responsibility as a precedent-setter. On May 5, 1789, he wrote as follows to Madison: "As the first of every thing, in our situation will serve to establish a Precedent, it is devoutly wished on my part that these precedents may be fixed on true principles." Washington, *Writings*, 30:310–311. In a similar vein, Washington noted in a letter of May 17, 1789, to John Adams that "[m]any things, which appear of little importance in themselves and at the beginning, may have great and durable consequences from their having been established at the commencement of a new general government." Charles Francis Adams, ed., *The Works of John Adams* (1853), 8:490.

3 See, e.g., *Federalist* No. 69.

4 Only weeks before the opening of the Philadelphia convention, Madison confessed, in a letter to Washington, to having "scarcely ventured as yet to form my own opinion" about the nature and structure of proper federal executive power in an ideal Constitution. Paul H. Smith et. al., eds., *Letters of Delegates to Congress, 1774–1789* (1976–2000), 24:231 (Letter of April 16, 1787).

5 See *Farrand's Records*, 3:302 (May 5, 1788, letter of Pierce Butler to Weedon Butler) ("[M]any of the members [of the Philadelphia convention] cast their eyes towards General Washington as President; and shaped their Ideas of the Powers to be given to a President, by their opinions of his Virtue"); *Elliot's Debates*, 1:506 (Oct. 30, 1787, letter from Gouverneur Morris to George Washington) ("[Y]our name to the new Constitution has been of infinite service.…[I]f you had not attended that Convention, and the same paper had been handed out to the world, it would have met with a colder reception, with fewer and weaker advocates, and with more, and more strenuous, opponents. As it is, should the idea prevail that you will not accept the Presidency, it would prove fatal in many parts."). "[B]e assured," James Monroe wrote Thomas Jefferson shortly after the Constitution squeaked through the Virginia ratifying convention, Washington's "influence carried this government." *DHRC*, 10:1705 (July 12, 1788, letter from Fredericksburg).

6 It is an interesting question precisely how much of the weight of early executive-branch precedents derives from Washington's personal authority. Had lightning killed America's first president moments after he took office—and had virtually all the major practices and precedents that in fact arose under Washington instead arisen under Vice-President-turned-Acting-President John Adams, would these Adams administration precedents have carried the same weight in American history as the real-life Washington administration precedents have in fact carried?

7 Treaty Between the United States of America and the French Republic, April 30, 1803, 8 Stat. 200; *Sen. Exec. J*, 1:450 (Oct. 20, 1803); Act of Oct. 31, 1803, 2 Stat. 245; Act of Nov. 10, 1803, 2 Stat. 245.

8 Treaty of Amity, Commerce and Navigation Between his Britannic Majesty and the United States of America, by their President, with the Advice and Consent of their Senate, Nov. 19, 1794, 8 Stat. 116; Additional Article, May 4, 1796, 8 Stat. 130; *Sen. Exec. J*, 1:186 (June 24, 1795); Act of May 6, 1796, 1 Stat. 459.

9 Unlike a presidential nomination, which cannot be "amended" by the Senate, a presidentially negotiated treaty can be modified by the Senate, subject to approval by the president and by America's treaty partner(s). This difference helps explain the subtle variance in phraseology in the two adjoining Article II clauses that refer to Senate advice and consent—the first clause addressing treaties and the second, appointments. Thus, the textual variance should not imply the blanket impermissibility of presidential treaty negotiation in the absence of prior consultation with the Senate—a textual reading that has been repudiated by long-standing practice dating back to Washington.

For the March 1, 1796, presidential promulgation of the Jay Treaty, see *Annals*, 5:48.

For more on this treaty, see Amar, *ACAB*, 192, 564 n. 38. In earlier episodes, the Senate had foreshadowed its acceptance of the principle that the president would decide whether and when to formally ratify a senatorially approved treaty. One episode concerned a consular agreement that had been negotiated with France under the Articles of Confederation in November 1788, and that was presented to the Senate by Washington in July 1789. *Sen. Exec. J,* 1:8–9 (July 29, 1789) (*"Resolved,…*That the Senate do consent to the said convention, and advise the President of the United States to ratify the same"). Other episodes involved treaties made with certain Indian tribes. The Senate used varying verbal formulas in giving its approval. Compare ibid., 28 (Sept. 22, 1789) (*"Resolved,* That the Senate do advise and consent that the President of the United States ratify the treaty concluded at Fort Harmar"), with ibid., 61–62 (Aug. 12, 1790) (*"Resolved…*That the Senate do consent to the aforesaid treaty, and do advise the President of the United States to ratify the same"), and ibid., 89 (Nov. 10, 1791) (*"Resolved,…*That the Senate consent to the aforesaid treaty, and advise the President of the United States to ratify the same"). See also ibid., 116 (March 26, 1792) (*"Resolved,…*That they advise and consent to the stipulation"); ibid., 170 (Jan. 8, 1795) (*"Resolved,…*That they do advise and consent to the ratification thereof"); ibid. (Jan. 9, 1795) (*"Resolved,…*That they advise and consent to the ratification of the treaty above-mentioned"). The Jay Treaty highlighted Washington's post-Senate role in a much more visible and high-stakes chapter in American diplomacy, thereby cementing the emerging understanding of American treaty practice. Ibid., 186 (June 24, 1795) (*"Resolved,…*That they do consent to, and advise the President of the United States, to ratify the treaty…, on condition that…").

10 For structural support for this vision, see Amar, *ACAB*, 63–64, 190, 304, 592–593 nn. 37–38; Amar, *Bill of Rights*, 102, 344 n. 85. See also Chapter 11. For exceptions to this general structural principle in situations involving contempt of Congress or contempt of court, see Chapter 9.

11 Act of June 5, 1794, 1 Stat. 381. Note that the earlier Judiciary Act of 1789 had not specified any elements of criminal misconduct or delimited the extent of permissible criminal punishment in its bland section 11 language empowering federal circuit courts to adjudicate various "crimes and offenses cognizable under the authority of the United States" (1 Stat. 73, 78–79). This section is thus best read at face value; it did not itself create criminal liability or delegate the power to do so to federal courts, but rather, merely conferred jurisdiction over crimes defined elsewhere in the federal criminal code.

12 It has been suggested that the Constitution was designed not to equate the "principal Officer in each of the executive Departments" with "the Heads of Departments," but rather, to contradistinguish these two categories. Lawrence Lessig and Cass R. Sunstein, "The President and the Administration," *Columbia LR* 94 (1994): 1, 35–38. There is strong reason to doubt this suggestion. The terse text links the two descriptions via the word "Departments," which in context clearly means *executive* departments in both phrases. (The two phrases appear in consecutive sentences in the Article outlining executive power. Nowhere does the Constitution itself speak of the "legislative department" or

the "judicial department.") No major ratification speaker or essayist sharply contradistinguished "heads" from "principal officers" or clearly suggested that these two clauses in Article II referred to different categories. Both Federalists and Anti-Federalists generally used the terms interchangeably in the great debate of 1787–1788. See, e.g., "The Federal Farmer (XIV)," in *Storing's Anti-Fed.*, 2:308; see also Steven G. Calabresi and Saikrishna B. Prakash, "The President's Power to Execute the Laws," *Yale LJ* 104 (1994): 541, 626–634 & n. 393, 647–654. One major ratification pamphlet—authored by Oliver Ellsworth, who would later serve as the nation's third chief justice—is particularly notable. Paraphrasing the opinions clause, Ellsworth substituted the words "heads of the departments" for the words "principal officer in each of the executive departments." "Letters of a Landholder (VI)," in Ford, *Essays*, 163. America's first chief justice, John Jay, did virtually the same thing in a landmark 1793 communication to the Washington administration on behalf of the entire Supreme Court. (For more details of this correspondence, see infra n. 22).

True, the 1789 statute establishing the Treasury Department did not explicitly describe it as an "executive department"—unlike earlier statutes denominating the "executive" Department of Foreign Affairs (later renamed the "executive" Department of State) and the "executive" Department of War. But only days after creating the Treasury, Congress enacted yet another statute, the Salary Act of 1789, whose title explicitly referred to Treasury officers as "executive" officers no different from those in the other executive departments. Act of Sept. 11, 1789, 1 Stat. 67. True, Congress described the treasury secretary as a "head" while describing the secretary of each of the other two departments as a "principal officer," but once again the two labels were in effect synonyms: The ensemble of 1789 statutes explicitly recognized that all three secretaries were removable at will by the president. See infra n. 13. Both Hamilton and Washington clearly understood that Hamilton was an executive department principal officer who answered to Washington under the opinions clause. See Hamilton's "Opinion as to the Constitutionality of the Bank of the United States," in John C. Hamilton, ed., *The Works of Alexander Hamilton* (1851), 4:104 (beginning his now-famous opinion of Feb. 23, 1791, by referring to the fact that Washington had issued an "order" to him—presumably under the opinions clause—to provide the president with his views regarding the bank bill). In *McCulloch*, John Marshall specifically described Hamilton's role as a key member of Washington's "*executive* cabinet." *McCulloch v. Maryland*, 17 U.S. 316, 402 (1819) (emphasis added).

13 See Act of July 27, 1789, 1 Stat. 28, 29 (secretary of foreign affairs—later renamed secretary of state); Act of Aug. 7, 1789, 1 Stat. 49, 50 (secretary of war); Act of Sept. 2, 1789, 1 Stat. 65, 67 (secretary of treasury). See also Act of Aug. 7, 1789, 1 Stat. 50, 53 (recognizing presidential removal power over territorial officers). See Saikrishna Prakash, "New Light on the Decision of 1789," *Cornell LR* 91 (2006): 1021. On Hamilton's change of heart, see George C. Rogers Jr., ed., "The Letters of William Loughton Smith to Edward Rutledge," *South Carolina History Magazine* 69 (1968): 1, 6–8 (reprinting letter of June 21, 1789; also reprinted in Charlene Bangs Bickford et al., eds., *Documentary History of the First Federal Congress* (2004), 16:831, 832–833).

14 The Federal Reserve Board was created in 1913; the restrictions on presidential removal at will were added to the statute in 1935. Act of Aug. 23, 1935, sec. 203(b), 49 Stat. 684, 704–705 (giving board members fourteen-year terms "unless sooner removed for cause by the President"). A later statutory change eliminated the president's ability to unilaterally designate the chairman of the Federal Reserve Board; the statutory revision requires a separate nomination and confirmation for the four-year position of chairman of the board. Act of Nov. 16, 1977, sec. 204(a), 91 Stat. 1388.

15 This suggestion is offered up as a friendly alternative to the approach advocated by Justice Scalia in *Freytag v. Commissioner*, 501 U.S. 868, 920–922 (1991) (Scalia, J., concurring in part and concurring in the judgment, joined by O'Connor, Kennedy, and Souter, JJ.), an approach recently embraced by a Court majority in *Free Enterprise Fund v. Public Company Accounting Oversight Board*, 130 S. Ct. 3138 (2010).

16 The Supreme Court has recently embraced this approach. See supra n. 15. On alternative interpretations of the Decision of 1789, cf. Jerry L. Mashaw, "Governmental Practice and Presidential Direction: Lessons from the Antebellum Republic?," *Willamette LR* 45 (2009): 659, 663 ("deriving uncontested meaning from the practice of any period is almost impossible").

17 For more on the Federal Reserve and other so-called independent agencies, see Chapter 9.

18 For Madison's remarks, see *Annals*, 1:514 (June 17, 1789). Regarding ornery presidents from Tennessee, the facts are as follows. In 1833, Andrew Jackson fired his treasury secretary, William Duane, who had defied presidential directives concerning the Bank of the United States. In response, various senators assailed Jackson and urged Congress to repudiate the Decision of 1789. See, e.g., *Reg. Deb.*, 10:834–836 (March 7, 1834, statements and proposed resolutions of Sen. Henry Clay). No repudiationist legislation ensued, but in March 1834 the Senate passed a resolution censuring Jackson for his general conduct vis-à-vis the bank without specific mention of his removal of Duane. Ibid., 1187 (March 28, 1834). On April 15, 1834, Jackson countered with a blistering protest message insisting, among other things, that the Decision of 1789 had settled the removal question. Jackson described the Decision of 1789 as "a full expression of the sense of the Legislature" supported by "the concurrent authority of President Washington, of the Senate, and the House of Representatives, numbers of whom had taken an active part in the convention which framed the Constitution and in the State conventions which adopted it." Jackson also invoked the "numerous removals made by" his predecessors in pursuance of the Decision of 1789. In early 1836, the man whom Jackson had initially picked to replace Duane at Treasury, Roger Taney, was confirmed by the Senate as the nation's fifth chief justice, and in early 1837 the Senate expunged its earlier censure resolution. See ibid., 13:504–505 (Jan. 16, 1837). In 1867, over the veto of President Andrew Jackson—oops, Johnson—Congress enacted a Tenure of Office Act that in certain instances required the president to win Senate approval before firing executive department heads. Act of March 2, 1867, 14 Stat. 430. Roughly a third of Johnson's veto message—the first third—

focused almost entirely on the Decision of 1789. *CG*, 39-1:1964–1966 (March 2, 1867). Johnson also stressed an unbroken tradition of practice honoring this Decision. Johnson later unilaterally dismissed Secretary of War Edwin Stanton. The House impeached him for this alleged statutory violation and for his more general defiance and obstruction of duly enacted Reconstruction legislation. Johnson was acquitted by the Senate in 1868, and in 1887 Congress repealed the 1867 act. See Act of March 3, 1887, ch. 353, 24 Stat. 500.

In *Myers v. United States*, a landmark 1926 decision authored by Chief Justice (and former president) William Howard Taft, the Supreme Court emphatically reaffirmed the Decision of 1789 and proclaimed the defunct 1867 act unconstitutional in the course of invalidating another law, enacted in 1876, that obliged the president to win Senate approval before removing postmasters. Although later cases have limited *Myers* by allowing statutes to insulate various non-cabinet officials wielding quasi-judicial authority from at-will removal—see, e.g., *Humphrey's Executor v. United States*, 295 U.S. 602 (1935)—the core of *Myers* has remained rock-solid, and the case continues to be cited with approval by all the members of the modern Court—left, right, and center. Thus, the Court, citing *Myers*, has forcefully insisted that, outside the impeachment context, neither the Senate, nor Congress as a whole, nor any other subpart may play any role in the removal of any executive-branch officers. This insistence is self-consciously in keeping with the Decision of 1789 and contra *The Federalist* No. 77. See, e.g., *Free Enterprise Fund v. Public Company Accounting Oversight Board*, 130 S. Ct. 3138 (2010) (citing the "landmark case" [p. 3152] of *Myers* early and often in both majority and dissenting opinions); ibid., 3153 n. 3 (opinion of the Court, per Roberts, C.J., declaring that the legislative-veto aspect of the 1867 Tenure of Office Act is today "universally regarded" as unconstitutional); ibid., 3151–3152 ("'Th[e] Decision of 1789 provides contemporaneous and weighty evidence of the Constitution's meaning since many of the Members of the First Congress had taken part in framing that instrument.' And it soon became the 'settled and well understood construction of the Constitution.'") (quoting previous cases; citations omitted); *Morrison v. Olson*, 487 U.S. 654, 685–686 (1988) (citing *Myers* with strong approval for the proposition that "Congress' attempt to involve itself in the removal of an executive official [is] sufficient grounds to render [a] statute invalid"). Outside the Court, there is likewise a broad political consensus today—in both the legislative and executive branches and in both political parties—that cabinet officers serve at the pleasure of the president.

19 Act of Sept. 24, 1789, sec. 35, 1 Stat. 73, 92–93.
20 See Jackson Turner Main, *The Upper House in Revolutionary America, 1763–1788* (1967).
21 On Washington's early use of war councils, see David McCullough, *1776* (2005). On his ideal of nonpartisanship, see Glenn A. Phelps, *George Washington and American Constitutionalism* (1993); Ralph Ketcham, *Presidents Above Party: The First American Presidency, 1789–1829* (1987). Note that Washington also sought advice early on from the Senate and the Supreme Court, but with less success. On the Senate, see text accompanying nn. 27–28 ; on the Court, see infra n. 22.

22 It's worth repeating a point from Chapter 1: Faithful constitutionalists should not draw broad negative inferences from the terse text absent particular good reasons for doing so—reasons, for example, derived from the specific historical understanding of the text as it was being ratified or from general considerations of constitutional structure. The opinions clause offers an apt case study. Although it would make little sense to infer that presidents may never seek advice (even informally) from persons other than cabinet heads, it does make sense—good structural sense—to infer that presidents may not compel formal advice from federal judges. Unlike cabinet heads, judges are not part of the executive branch and are not unilaterally removable by the chief executive. Judges are supposed to be independent, and thus they emphatically do not answer to the president as do his executive department heads. In this respect, the opinions-clause text and the Constitution's overall structure marked a decisive break with English practice, whereby judges served on the monarch's Privy Council. In the summer of 1793, justices of the Supreme Court interpreted the text of the opinions clause in precisely this negative-implication fashion when they wrote a private letter to President Washington firmly declining to furnish him ex parte advice even though he had requested their views about various treaty-law and international-law issues precipitated by the French Revolution. In rejecting Washington's request, the justices noted that "the Lines of Separation drawn by the Constitution between the three Departments of government," and the fact that the branches were "in certain Respects checks on each other," were "strong arguments" against judicial participation in what would later be referred to as the president's kitchen cabinet—"especially as the Power given by the Constitution to the President, of calling on the Heads of Departments for opinions, seems to have been *purposely* as well as expressly united to the *executive* Departments" as pointedly distinct from the judiciary (emphasis in original). Hamilton, *Papers*, 15:111 (excerpting August 8, 1793, letter of John Jay, James Wilson, James Iredell, and William Paterson to President Washington). This now-famous episode in effect glossed the text, and its lessons have been studiously followed ever since by lawyers and judges. Here we see yet another Washington-era precedent resolving an arguable ambiguity in the written Constitution and operating thereafter with a kind of peremptory argument-ending legal force akin to that of a relatively clear textual provision. As this episode illustrates, the Washington-era precedents that have endured did not simply result from unilateral executive actions but instead reflected interbranch settlements in which other branches sometimes embraced executive initiatives and sometimes resisted them.

23 *Elliot's Debates*, 4:108 (Iredell) ("He is only to consult them if he thinks proper"); *Farrand's Records*, 2:329 (Pinckney) ("[T]he President shd. Be authorized to call for advice or not as he might chuse").

24 "Observations on George Mason's Objections to the Federal Constitution," in Ford, *Pamphlets*, 348. For a similar statement behind closed doors at Philadelphia, see *Farrand's Records*, 2:542 (Gouverneur Morris) ("The question of a Council was considered in the Committee, where it was judged that the Presidt. by persuading his Council—to concur

in his wrong measures, would acquire their protection for them"). For more evidence and analysis, see Amar, *ACAB*, 197–198 and sources cited therein.

25 See Leonard D. White, *The Federalists: A Study in Administrative History* (1961), 41 ("Although Washington uniformly asked for advice, he retained the power to decide all matters except...when away from the seat of government. Cabinet opinions were not infrequently divided....Washington did not debate a case with advisors, but listened to their arguments or read their written opinions and then decided the issue."). In a June 12, 1807, letter to William Short, Jefferson claimed that as president he had never overruled his cabinet even though a president "certainly" had a right to do so, and colorfully noted, "[M]y predecessor [Adams] sometimes decided things against his counsel [*sic*—council] by dashing and trampling his wig on the floor." Paul Leicester Ford, ed., *The Works of Thomas Jefferson* (1905), 10:414. For an account of President Adams's decision to pardon the convicted traitor John Fries despite the unanimous advice of his cabinet to execute Fries, see John Quincy Adams and Charles Francis Adams, *The Life of John Adams* (1871), 2:314–318. This account makes no mention of trampled wigs. For a description of Washington's practices emphasizing the first president's personal control over department heads, see Jefferson's own Nov. 6, 1801, Circular to Department Heads, in Jefferson, *Papers*, 35:576–578.

After 1791 Washington routinely involved the attorney general in the cabinet despite the fact that the AG was not a formal department head; however, the president did not usually bring the postmaster general into collective cabinet deliberations, even though the postmaster general was legally a department head, vested by Congress (as only department heads could be vested) with the power to appoint inferior departmental officers. See Act of Feb. 20, 1792, 1 Stat. 232, 234. Washington's choices remind us that, strictly speaking, his "cabinet" was an informal entity, not an official assembly of all executive department heads. Note also that, for reasons that will become clear in Chapter 10, Vice President Adams did not play a large role either in cabinet deliberations or as a close presidential confidant. See Henry Barrett Learned, *The President's Cabinet: Studies in the Origin, Formation, and Structure of an American Institution* (1912), 118–130.

26 Examples include Massachusetts, Rhode Island, Connecticut, New York, and New Jersey. See, generally, Main, *Upper House*.

27 *Maclay's Journal*, 129–130 (Aug. 22, 1789).

28 Ibid., 131 (emphasis in original); Charles Francis Adams, ed., *Memoirs of John Quincy Adams* (1875), 6:427 (diary entry of Nov. 10, 1824). Adams was transcribing a tale told to him by William H. Crawford, whose source was probably James Monroe. Monroe had joined the Senate a year after Washington's famous visit. See Stanley Elkins and Eric McKitrick, *The Age of Federalism* (1993), 765 n. 44.

29 See Main, *Upper House*, 3; Joseph Ralston Hayden, *The Senate and Treaties, 1789–1817* (1920), 62–92.

30 "The Anas," in Jefferson, *Writings*, 191 (Apr. 9, 1792), 218–220 (Feb. 26, 1793); Hayden, *The Senate and Treaties*, 88–93.

31 True, Congress might seek to enact legislation removing an executive-branch official— for example, by eliminating his cabinet office altogether, or defunding his office, or simply excising him in an even more surgical fashion. But if the president supports the beleaguered official, the president can simply veto any attempted removal legislation, and it has generally proved quite difficult for Congress to override a president's veto. See Saikrisha Prakash, "Removal and Tenure in Office," *Virginia LR* 92 (2006): 1779.

32 Shortly after the assassination of President Kennedy in 1963, the written Constitution was formally amended to empower the cabinet in one very specific context to vote as a collectivity—and with that vote to override the president, and, indeed, to oust him from power, if a majority of the group, prompted by the vice president, deems the president unable to discharge his office. See U.S. Const., amend. XXV, sec. 4. This extraordinary power, vested in "a majority of…the principal officers of the executive departments," is carefully hedged by a series of safeguards designed to prevent palace coups. Nevertheless, the very existence of this power serves as a sharp contrast to the pointed absence of any official collective cabinet decisionmaking in the Founders' Constitution. This clause also illuminates the risks to presidential power latent in an overly strong model of collective cabinet governance.

33 Over the centuries, presidents have varied considerably in the use of their cabinets. Andrew Jackson, the first president to treat the postmaster general as a regular cabinet member, also famously relied on various informal advisers who functioned as his "kitchen cabinet." Abraham Lincoln organized his cabinet so as to bring within his administration a talented group of ambitious politicians and presidential aspirants. Franklin Roosevelt was known for playing cabinet officials off one another as a means of testing loyalty and extracting better performances. Dwight Eisenhower publicly presented himself as a strong believer in cabinet government. In the perilous hours of the Cuban Missile Crisis, John F. Kennedy relied not on his full cabinet but rather on an "Executive Committee"—an ad-hoc collection of National Security Council members and other key foreign policy and intelligence advisers. Today, the cabinet typically includes more than twenty members—Washington's original four, plus the heads of newer departments and agencies, including the Department of Homeland Security and the Environmental Protection Agency. Also notable is the larger role of the vice president in modern American cabinets, which has been reflected in various twentieth-century framework statutes and in a pair of twentieth-century constitutional amendments. These amendments are discussed in more detail in Chapter 10.

CHAPTER 9: INTERPRETING GOVERNMENT PRACTICES

1 It might be thought that the jury system is also a "permanent" institution of federal governance, even though individual juries are typically quite transient. On the proper size, structure, and scope of juries, see Chapter 11.

2 Some uncertainty surrounds the required end-date of incarceration when a house holds

multiple "sessions" within the two-year term allotted to each successive Congress. Also, there are questions about how the temporal limits applicable to House incarceration apply to the Senate. It might be thought that because the Senate operates as a continuing body that does not lapse and revive biennially in the same manner as does the House, senatorial incarceration power need not lapse every two years. But structurally, why should the Senate enjoy greater contempt-punishing power than the House? Since House contempt power necessarily lapses biennially, so should Senate contempt power. More importantly, a large threat to liberty would arise if the Senate could reach back into the distant past, to identify prior acts of contempt against its younger self, and could furthermore project punishment for any contempt, whether recent or ancient, infinitely into the future. Any future assertion of such a nearly boundless power would find little support in actual senatorial practice. For more on the Senate, see Aaron-Andrew P. Bruhl, "Burying the 'Continuing Body' Theory of the Senate," *Iowa LR* 95 (2010): 1401.

3   Va. Const. (1776), para. 27 (beginning, "The right of suffrage…)"; Josh Chafetz,. "Executive Branch Contempt of Congress," *U. of Chicago LR* 76 (2009): 1083, 1125–1126.

4   Josh Chafetz, *Democracy's Privileged Few: Legislative Privilege and Democratic Norms in the British and American Constitutions* (2007), 208 ("[T]he Houses' power to punish non-Members does not seem to have been considered in…the states' ratifying conventions, or the press"). In the secret Philadelphia Convention, George Mason did on August 7 raise the issue of a general power of investigation and inquest, opining that members of Congress "are not only Legislators but they possess inquisitorial powers. They must meet frequently to inspect the Conduct of the public offices." *Farrand's Records*, 2:206.

5   Though former officers are also arguably subject to impeachment, Morris had not served as an officer under the U.S. Constitution, but rather as a secretary under the Articles of Confederation. On the limited circle of impeachable persons, see infra n. 17.

6   *Annals*, 2:1514–1515 (March 19, 1790).

7   See David P. Currie, *The Constitution in Congress: The Federalist Period, 1789–1801* (1997), 163–164; Act of May 3, 1798, 1 Stat. 554.

8   See, generally, Chafetz, *Democracy's Privileged Few*, 212–214, 226–235. On Randall, see Chafetz, "Executive Branch Contempt," 1128. In the case law, see *Marshall v. Gordon*, 243 U.S. 521 (1917); *Jurney v. MacCracken*, 294 U.S. 195 (1935); cf. *Groppi v. Leslie*, 404 U.S. 496, 501 (1972). On the Office of Legal Counsel's position, see 8 U.S. Op. Off. Legal Counsel 101, 124 (May 30, 1984). For contrary views, see Jefferson's *Manual of Parliamentary Practice*, sec. 3; St. George Tucker, *View of the Constitution of the United States, with Selected Writings* (1803, Liberty Fund 1999), 146–150.

9   For another example of early practice glossing an ambiguous text in Congress's favor and to the disadvantage of the president, see Amar, *ACAB*, 594–595 n. 7 (discussing how early practice and case law glossed an ambiguous Article V by establishing that proposed constitutional amendments need not be presented to the president).

On the implicit constitutional power that the judiciary claims that it has to punish in-court contempts, see *Young v. United States ex rel. Vuitton et Fils S.A.*, 481 U.S. 787, 804

(1987). Recall two related points from Chapter 1. First, federal judges have long claimed implied immunity from state libel laws for any judicial utterance in an opinion or in the courtroom, much as members of Congress have always enjoyed express immunity under the Article I speech-or-debate clause. Second, executive officials such as the president and vice president deserve similarly absolute immunity for certain expressions in their official capacity.

If courts and the houses of Congress have "inherent" power to punish past acts of contempt, may a president pardon a judicial or congressional detainee who is being punished for a past act of contempt? Textual and structural considerations seem to point in both directions. If presidents may pardon in these contexts, then the House and Senate are not as independent over their own proceedings as they might think, and the president has the effective power to countermand prosecutors who, unlike ordinary federal prosecutors, do not derive their prosecutorial powers from presidential appointment. If presidents may not pardon, then there exists an unwritten exception to the Article II pardon power above and beyond the one exception explicitly mentioned in the Constitution's text for cases of impeachment, and the additional exception, implicit in the *nemo judex* principle, that a president may never pardon himself. Relying in part on a long line of actual practice, the Court in 1925, per Chief Justice (and former president) Taft, held that the president may indeed pardon for criminal contempt of court, something that previous presidents had done twenty-seven times over an eighty-five-year period. *Ex Parte Grossman*, 267 U.S. 87, 118 (1925). A different result might obtain regarding attempted pardons for contempts of houses of Congress. See ibid. (noting 1830 opinion of Attorney General Berrien).

10 See *Marshall v. Gordon*, 243 U.S. 521 (1917). One final fact about actual practice during the free-expression controversy of the late 1790s merits mention: At the precise moment that the explicit free-speech guarantee of America's written Constitution—the First Amendment—was being punctured by the Sedition Act, an implicit free-speech guarantee of America's unwritten Constitution emerged to minimize the damage. While many printers and speakers in 1798 and 1799 were deterred from criticizing the federal Sedition Act, lest they be prosecuted under that very statute, the Virginia and Kentucky legislatures felt free to criticize the act with impunity. That criticism, of course, occurred via the now-famous Virginia and Kentucky Resolves. Nothing in the written Constitution explicitly guaranteed state legislatures the same virtually absolute freedom of speech and debate expressly guaranteed members of Congress under Article I, section 6. Yet this symmetric freedom for state lawmakers apparently went without saying. In the 1760s and early 1770s, colonial legislatures across the continent had claimed their rights, as American parliaments, to absolute parliamentary freedom to criticize the king, and indeed, to criticize Parliament itself. These colonial legislatures had not merely claimed this absolute freedom of speech and debate; they had wielded this freedom in actual practice, and with great effect. A generation later, this established usage helped ground the assumption that American state legislatures could exercise sweeping freedom of

speech and debate against the new central government. Some printers in the late 1790s apparently felt themselves free to republish with impunity these state legislative resolves, even as these same printers thought twice about publishing comparable tracts that could not claim the absolute expressive immunity enjoyed by state legislative resolves. In this remarkable episode, America's unwritten Constitution outperformed its written counterpart. At a dark hour when, despite the seemingly clear words of the First Amendment, the sword seemed mightier than the pen, the practice of free speech in legislative assemblies proved mightiest of all. And it did so even though no specific clause in the written Constitution expressly buttressed the practice-based argument that state legislatures existed as special free-speech enclaves wholly immune from federal censorship laws.

11 Note also that Marbury's lawyer, Charles Lee, had conceded that "confidential communications between the head of the department and the President" were privileged.

12 Washington acted on March 1, 1796. See Chapter 8, n. 9. See also Act of March 6, 1796, 1 Stat. 459. For details of the stare-down, see Currie, *The Constitution in Congress*, 211–215. Note that Washington explicitly emphasized that the House request for information was not made as part of any impeachment inquiry. *Annals*, 5:760 (reprinting Washington letter to House of March 30, 1796).

13 For discussion of a recent controversy involving Congress's efforts to compel testimony from executive-branch officials Josh Bolton and Harriet Miers, see Chafetz, "Executive Branch Contempt."

14 Physical delivery of the commission is not required. Although this nondelivery rule does not explicitly appear in the written Constitution, it was proclaimed by no less a case than *Marbury v. Madison*, and thereafter became settled usage.

   As for the Obama oath re-do in 2009, here are the key points to keep in mind: A new president-elect receives his official designation—his commission-equivalent—from Congress as a whole, which bears responsibility for counting electoral votes, resolving any disputes (such as those which arose in 1876–1877), and, if necessary, choosing among the top electoral-vote-getters (if no candidate has enough electoral votes to prevail, as occurred in 1824–1825). The president-elect, by dint of the explicit command of the Twentieth Amendment, legally becomes president at the precise stroke of noon on January 20. The clock and not the oath does the work. In this explicit text, we see on display the perfect seamlessness and continuity of the American presidency, which, unlike courts and Congress, never goes out of session—an obvious carryover from the seamlessness of the British system ("The [old] king is dead; long live the [new] king!"). Textually, it is clear from the words of Article II that the oath is a duty imposed on the person who is already president, not a magic spell that makes him president: "Before he [the president] shall enter on the Execution of his Office, he shall take the following Oath or Affirmation...." In Britain, it was not uncommon for months or even years to elapse between the start of a monarch's official reign and the taking of the official Coronation Oath with all its pomp and ceremony. Prior to the ratification of the Twentieth

Amendment, which contains the word "noon," a nice question had arisen about whether the magic moment of presidential transition was midnight or noon (or some other instant). The original text did not specify an hour, but early unwritten practice identified midnight as the magic moment. Hence the storied efforts of John Adams and his staff to sign and seal judicial commissions late into the evening of his final hours on the job in an effort to vest his "midnight judges" with the proper authority.

15 For the Senate's expressed views in 1960, see S. Res. 334, 86th Cong., 2d sess., 106 Cong. Rec. 18145 (Aug. 29, 1960): "*Resolved,* That it is the sense of the Senate that the making of recess appointments to the Supreme Court of the United States...should not be made except under unusual circumstances and for the purpose of preventing or ending a demonstrable breakdown in the administration of the Court's business." The Resolution's sponsor, Senator Philip Hart of Michigan, expressly conceded that the gloss of history had established the constitutionality of recess appointments to the Court, in particular, and the federal judiciary, in general. Ibid., 1830. For tallies of actual judicial recess appointments, see Second Supplemental Brief of the United States, *United States v. Woodley,* No. 82-1028, Ninth Circuit, at A1–A25, cited in Louis Fisher, *Federal Recess Judges* (CRS Report of Feb. 2, 2005, RS 22039); Brief for the United States, at app., *Miller v. United States,* 2004 WL 2112791 (No. 04-38) (Supreme Court 2004). Fisher also mentions the recess appointments of Judge Roger Gregory by President Clinton in December 2000 and of Judges Charles Pickering and William Pryor by President George W. Bush in early 2004. See also Edward Hartnett, "Recess Appointments of Article III Judges: Three Constitutional Questions," *Cardozo LR* 26 (2005): 377; Thomas A. Curtis, "Note, Recess Appointments to Article III Courts: The Use of Historical Practice in Constitutional Interpretation," *Columbia LR* 84 (1984): 1758.

16 Beyond the nice questions raised by recess appointments of judges and justices, two other questions concerning recess appointments in general deserve mention. First, may a president use his special recess-appointment power to fill any vacancy that happens to *exist* during a particular Senate recess, or only those vacancies that happen to *arise or open up* during that recess? Washington's attorney general, Edmund Randolph, took the narrow view of presidential power in 1792, whereas President Madison apparently acted in accordance with the broad view. In 1823, Attorney General William Wirt clearly embraced the latter interpretation. Since then, the overwhelming mass of actual practice has supported the broad view, generating another example of how customary usage can operate to gloss an ambiguous text. On this question, the definitive gloss has emerged from a process involving all three branches. Specifically, for nearly two centuries presidents and senators have recognized the broad view in the give-and-take of the nomination-and-confirmation process. In addition, framework statutes (enacted with ordinary bicameralism and presentment) have presupposed the propriety of the broad view while establishing salary rules applicable to recess appointees. Finally, the judiciary has consistently recognized the legitimacy of officers appointed under the broad view. For an informative debate, compare Hartnett, "Recess Appointments," with Michael B.

Rappaport, "The Original Meaning of the Recess Appointments Clause," *U.C.L.A. LR* 52 (2005): 1487. Note that in upholding the broad view—that a president may use the recess-appointment power to fill any vacancy that exists during a Senate recess, even if the vacancy first arose during a Senate session—Judge (later Justice) William Burnham Woods explicitly relied upon "the practice of the executive department for nearly 60 years, the acquiescence of the senate therein, and the recognition of the power claimed by both houses of congress." *In re: Farrow*, 3 F. 112, 115 (C.C. N.D. Ga. 1880). To this we should now add another 130 years of confirmatory practice, acquiescence, and supportive legislation. See, generally, Patrick Hein, "In Defense of Broad Recess Appointment Power: The Effectiveness of Political Counterweights," *California LR* 96 (2008): 235.

Second, what counts as a Senate recess? In particular, should we distinguish between the Senate's traditional *intersession* recess (the break between its first session and its second session) and the *intrasession* recesses that have become increasingly common as technology has made it easier for senators to bounce back and forth between their house and their homes? Should we distinguish between long recesses and short ones, and, if so, where should we draw the line? Should nominees who were recently bottled up in the Senate confirmation process be treated differently from other possible recess appointees? Here, actual usage has not always precipitated fixed rules, but instead has structured a conversation between presidents and senators resulting in evolving understandings, conventions, and truces. In general, recent presidents and senators have often recognized broad presidential authority to treat even relatively short intrasession Senate breaks as formal opportunities to make recess appointments. Similar negotiations between presidents and Congress have resulted in elaborate arrangements specifying which congressional bills are properly subject to ordinary veto rules and which are instead governed by pocket-veto rules triggered by congressional adjournments of one sort or another.

17 Senators as such are not officers and are thus not impeachable as senators or removable from the Senate via the impeachment process. Under Article II, section 4, only "civil Officers" are impeachable. (Presidents and vice presidents are also mentioned separately in this clause, perhaps to blunt any argument that their role atop—or in the VP's case, potentially atop—the military chain of command removes them from the category of "civil" officers.) Although the word "only" does not expressly appear in Article II, section 4, the word is implicit, as strongly confirmed by both structure and history. Unless Article II is read as limiting impeachment to civil officers, even private persons would be subject to impeachment and potential disqualification from future officeholding without the usual safeguards of trial by local jury, proof beyond reasonable doubt, and so on. And unless "civil Officers" means *only* civil officers, the House would play an improper role in Senate membership decisions, and vice versa. Article I, section 5, envisions each house policing its *own* membership via its powers to judge elections and qualifications and to expel by a two-thirds vote. Also, Article I, section 3, is emphatic that punishment in impeachments "shall not extend further than...removal from Office, and disqualification

to hold and enjoy any [federal] Office." Since it is clear that ordinary membership in Congress is not an office—see Article I, section 6 ("[N]o Person holding any Office under the United States, shall be a Member of either House")—how could impeachment effect the ouster of a member of Congress from the House or Senate? See Akhil Reed Amar, "On Impeaching Presidents," *Hofstra LR* 28 (1999): 291. Senate practice coheres with the foregoing analysis. Early on, the Senate correctly determined that Senator William Blount was not a proper subject of impeachment. For details, see Currie, *The Constitution in Congress*, 275–281. For more on the distinction between "officers" and members of Congress, see Akhil Reed Amar and Vikram David Amar, "Is the Presidential Succession Law Constitutional?," *Stanford LR* 48 (1995): 113.

18 Act of March 3, 1863, ch. 108, 12 Stat. 804. On Day One and the days immediately preceding and following it, see "From Washington. The Roll List of the Members of the House Completed. None of the Southern Delegations Included in the List," *New York Times*, Dec. 3, 1865, 1; "The New Congress. Completion of the Roll List of the House of Representatives. Exclusion of the Members from the Lately Rebellious States," *New York Herald*, Dec. 3, 1865, 1; "The Meeting of Congress—The Republican Programme," *New York Herald*, Dec. 4, 1865, 4; "The Thirty-Ninth Congress—Movements Preliminary to the Organization To-Day," *Boston Herald*, Dec. 4, 1865, 2; "The New Congress," *New York Herald*, Dec. 5, 1865, 1; "The Opening of Congress—The Organization," ibid., 4; "Letter from Washington," *Daily Picayune*, Dec. 10, 1865, 1; "A Peep Behind the Political Coulisses," *New York Herald*, Dec. 11, 1865, 1; Benjamin J. Kendrick, *The Journal of the Joint Committee of Fifteen on Reconstruction* (1914), 37, 133–154; Eric L. McKitrick, *Andrew Johnson and Reconstruction* (1960), 258–259; Eric Foner, *Reconstruction: America's Unfinished Revolution* (1988), 239; Bruce Ackerman, *We the People: Transformations* (1998), 166–169.

19 See Act of March 3, 1863, ch. 108, 12 Stat. 804; Act of Feb. 21, 1867, 14 Stat. 397. For the current version, see 2 U.S.C. 26. See also John Harrison, "The Lawfulness of the Reconstruction Amendments," *U. Chicago LR* 68 (2001): 375, 399 n. 125.

20 A similar vision underlies the power of each house to act as a judge in adjudicating contested elections and qualifications of its members and in exercising disciplinary power over its members.

21 For details, see S. Doc. No. 89-103 (Aug. 19, 1966) (analysis of "The Classification of United States Senators," by Floyd M. Riddick, Senate Parliamentarian).

22 On the centrality of the House-size issue in the ratification debates, see Amar, *Bill of Rights*, 8–17; Amar, *ACAB*, 76–84.

23 The use of certain particular apportionment formulas and rounding rules might occasionally generate the paradoxical result that an increase of overall House size might actually reduce the absolute number of seats that a given state might get. See George G. Szpiro, *Numbers Rule* (2010), 119–133.

24 The only drop of note occurred in 1842, when Congress passed an Apportionment Act shrinking the overall size of the House by about 5 percent and also obliging states to

elect representatives in single-member districts. Act of June 25, 1842, 5 Stat. 491. See Johanna Nicol Shields, "Whigs Reform the 'Bear Garden': Representation and the Apportionment Act of 1842," *Journal Early Republic* 5 (1985): 355. For more on the single-member-district issue, see Chapter 10, text accompanying nn. 19–20. For the 1911 statute, see Act of Aug. 8, 1911, ch. 5, 37 Stat. 13, 14. When Alaska and Hawaii became states, the number of representatives temporarily increased to 437, then dropped back to the traditional 435 after the next census. Note that a House of gargantuan size would foreclose the sort of face-to-face deliberation that the House was obviously intended to effectuate and would also eliminate the ability of individual House members to retain any status as national leaders. Why would House members ever agree to this form of institutional and personal disarmament? True, it is possible to imagine House members agreeing to a drastic shrinkage in House size so long as the shrinkage were to go into effect after a very long time delay—long enough so as not to disturb the hopes of most incumbents to secure indefinite reelection. But this delayed-shrinkage hypothetical suggests that a radical reduction in House size would operate more like a typical constitutional amendment—that is, as a long-term change designed for posterity rather than as a typical statute designed for immediate effect. For more on the classic time horizons applicable to constitutional amendments as distinct from ordinary statutes, see Chapter 12.

25 In August 1937, Congress passed and FDR signed a law that did reform the federal judiciary in small ways, but nothing in the text of this law addressed the constitutional propriety of Court-packing. Act of Aug. 24, 1937, ch. 754, 50 Stat. 751.

26 Act of July 23, 1866, 14 Stat. 209; Act of April 10, 1869, 16 Stat. 44.

27 Likewise, if lower federal court judges today were generally to stop announcing in public the legal reasons supporting their rulings on the merits, this refusal would violate the Article III text as glossed by centuries of practice, even though Article III nowhere specifies that judges must ordinarily make public the reasons for their decisions. Whether or not this norm can be deduced as an implicit background principle of Article III as originally envisioned, today it forms an indispensable element of "judicial Power" as that phrase appears in Article III and has come to be operationalized by actual practice.

28 For general discussion of the various powers of the chief justice, see Judith Resnik and Lane Dilg, "Responding to a Democratic Deficit: Limiting the Powers and the Term of the Chief Justice of the United States," *U. of Pennsylvania LR* 154 (2006): 1575. Note that while the written Constitution refers to "the Chief Justice," it describes the other members of the Supreme Court as "Judges" and not "Justices." It is conventional today to describe all the members of the Supreme Court as "justices" because the Judiciary Act of 1789 used that phrasing and later congressional statutes have followed suit. See Act of Sept. 24, 1789, 1 Stat. 73, sec. 1. Early practice has thus glossed the text on this nice question of title and etiquette.

Current federal law authorizes the Supreme Court to sit, in effect, as an agency to promulgate procedural rules that will operate in all federal civil litigation. 28 U.S.C. 2072. Although this power of judges to act outside of cases and controversies and to proceed in a legislative/administrative fashion might be thought to raise serious separation-of-powers issues, if only the Constitution's text and its underlying conceptual logic were relevant, the decisive fact is that such rulemaking authority traces back to section 17 of the landmark Judiciary Act of 1789, 1 Stat. 73, 83—a section passed by the First Congress, signed into law by George Washington, and explicitly upheld by Chief Justice Marshall speaking for a unanimous Court in *Wayman v. Southard*, 23 U.S. (10 Wheat.) 1, 43–44 (1825). Here, too, early practice has definitively glossed the text and turned what might otherwise be a hard constitutional question into an easy one.

29 John Locke, *The Second Treatise of Government,* Thomas P. Peardon, ed. (1952), sec. 96. See Willmoore Kendall, *John Locke and the Doctrine of Majority-Rule* (1959); Bernard Wishy, "John Locke and the Spirit of '76," *Political Science Quarterly* 73 (1958): 413.

30 Thomas Jefferson, "Notes on the State of Virginia," in *Writings,* 3:229–230 (citing Brooke, Hakewell, and Puffendorf); *Farrand's Records,* 1:198.

31 On the enactment of ordinary laws by simple majority, see *Federalist* Nos. 22, 58, 62; Jed Rubenfeld, "Rights of Passage: Majority Rule in Congress," *Duke LJ* 46 (1996): 73. On the basic difference between statutes and constitutional amendments, see Bruce Ackerman, *We the People: Foundations* (1991). On the way in which treaty supermajority rules help offset the absence of the House, see Amar, *ACAB,* 190. On the key differences between house exclusion by majority vote and house expulsion by supermajority, see *Powell v. McCormack*, 395 U.S. 496 (1969).

32 Could Congress enact a statute requiring that no federal law be held unconstitutional unless the court hearing the case is unanimous? If so, were Congress to structure a Court of one hundred members (as the Constitution allows), the Court would have to enforce a federal law even if ninety-nine of the one hundred justices found that law clearly unconstitutional. At this point, judicial review would have effectively been undone by a mere statute. The proper stopping point on the slippery slope is to insist that Congress may pass no law giving any judge who sides against a constitutional claim more weight than a judge who sides with a constitutional claim—a principle implicit in the supremacy clause itself.

Two state constitutions have provisions preventing their respective state supreme courts from declaring state legislation unconstitutional unless the court acts by supermajority. In North Dakota, the state constitution authorizes a majority of a quorum of the state supreme court to act for the court in all situations "provided that the supreme court shall not declare a legislative enactment unconstitutional unless at least four [of the five] of the members of the court so decide." N.D. Const., art. VI, sect. 4. This clause has been understood to apply only when the issue is whether a North Dakota statute violates the state constitution. Thus read, it raises no major federal problem. North Dakota is not obliged to have a state constitution that trumps ordinary state statutes; nor is the state obliged to provide for strong judicial enforcement of its state constitution. The Nebraska Constitution features a similar clause: "A majority of the [state supreme court] members sitting shall have authority to pronounce a decision except in cases involving the constitutionality of an act of the Legislature. No legislative act shall be held unconstitutional except by the concurrence of five [of the court's seven] judges." Nebr. Const., art. V, sect. 2. The Nebraska clause apparently has been held by the state supreme court to apply to cases involving claims that a state statute violates the federal Constitution. See *DeBacker v. Brainard*, 161 N.W. 2d 508 (Neb. 1968), *appeal dismissed*, 396 U.S. 28 (1969); *DeBacker v. Sigler*, 175 N.W. 2d 912, 914 (Neb. 1970) (Spencer, J., dissenting). To the extent that this clause might direct the state's highest court to affirmatively enforce a state statute despite the fact that a court majority deems the statute contrary to the U.S. Constitution, this clause plainly violates the federal supremacy clause, which specifically addresses state judges and obliges them to prioritize the U.S. Constitution over a mere state statute. No other state follows the North Dakota or Nebraska model. Instead, majority rule generally prevails on state courts. For an excellent discussion, see Evan H. Caminker, "Thayerian Deference to Congress and Supreme Court Supermajority Rule: Lessons from the Past," *Indiana LJ* 78 (2003): 73. For more on the interplay between federal and state constitutional law, see Chapter 12.

33 For a subtle analysis of how the Court's majority has ultimately exercised its power to manage and/or dismiss cases docketed by a Court minority, see Richard L. Revesz and Pamela S. Karlan, "Nonmajority Rules and the Supreme Court," *U. of Pennsylvania LR* 136 (1988): 1067.

34 Although in recent years the House occasionally adopted internal rules requiring supermajority votes in the enactment of certain types of laws—laws raising taxes, for example—leading constitutional scholars have condemned these rules as unconstitutional under Article I, section 7. See Rubenfeld, "Rights of Passage," 83. Other thoughtful scholars have defended these rules by arguing that each house has always retained the inalienable right to suspend supermajority requirements at any time, and to do so by a simple majority vote—a theory honoring the Constitution's basic requirement of house majority rule, but relocating the effective locus of this constitutional norm from Article I, section 7, to Article I, section 5. See John O. McGinnis and Michael B. Rappaport, "The Rights of Legislators and the Wrongs of Interpretation: A Further Defense of the Constitutionality of Legislative Supermajority Rules," *Duke LJ* 47 (1997): 327. One noteworthy limit on the agenda-setting power of House leaders and committees is embodied in the device of the discharge petition. Through this theoretically important, if little-used, safety valve, a majority of the entire House—218 members—may bypass committee veto-gates and bring a bill to the floor. For the argument that all House rules are and indeed must be modifiable at all times by a later House majority, see ibid. and *United States v. Ballin*, 144 U.S. 1, 5 (1892).

35 The specific ways in which the Senate operates as a "continuing body" are complex. Senate bills passed during one congressional term all die at the end of the term and must be repassed in a new Senate, but the same is not true of Senate rules. Rules are thus treated differently from bills. This difference is not spelled out in the written Constitution but instead has formed a notable feature of actual government practice from the Founding

to the present. A structural argument explaining this feature of actual practice might run as follows: When enacting a bill, the Senate is operating in tight bicameral partnership with the House. When the old House dies at the end of its two-year term, all House bills obviously die as well, and the same should hold true bicamerally for Senate bills. But when enacting its internal rules, the Senate is acting in more unicameral fashion and need not coordinate with House practice to the same extent. This reasoning makes sense but goes beyond narrow textualism. Here, then, is yet another example of how America's written and unwritten Constitutions cohere.

A further example comes from House practice. Until each new House adopts rules for proceeding, which procedural rules apply? The terse text does not say. Customary usage fills in this textual gap with…customary usage. Thus, the House tradition has been to follow "general parliamentary law" in its opening moments—law derived from customary Anglo-American parliamentary practices. (Between 1860 and 1890, a contrary, quasi-senatorial approach emerged in which the rules of the prior—defunct—House were said to apply in the new House until superseded.) For details, see Aaron-Andrew Bruhl, "Burying the Continuing Body Theory," 1411 & n. 19.

36 Thus, although the Senate need not reenact its standing rules every two years—as the House has generally felt it must—the Senate, like the House, must be free to repeal any standing rule and must be free to do so by simple majority vote.

37 According to Senate Rule 22—I swear I am not making up this number!—a motion to end debate "shall be decided in the affirmative by three-fifths of the Senators duly chosen and sworn—except on a measure or motion to amend the Senate rules, in which case the necessary affirmative vote shall be two-thirds of the Senators present and voting."

38 On majority rule as the obvious command of Article I, section 7, see Rubenfeld, "Rights of Passage." On majority rule as the obvious command of Article I, section 5, see McGinnis and Rappaport, "The Rights of Legislators."

39 For a wise reminder that practices do not typically interpret and contextualize themselves, and that different opinions are apt to exist about how best to interpret a practice, see Jerry L. Mashaw, "Governmental Practice and Presidential Direction: Lessons from the Antebellum Republic?," *Willamette LR* 45 (2009): 659, 663.

40 *Sen. J*, 1:13 (April 16, 1789).

41 See Richard R. Beeman, "Unlimited Debate in the Senate, the First Phase," *Political Science Quarterly* 83 (1968): 419; Sarah S. Binder and Steven S. Smith, *Politics or Principle? Filibustering in the United States Senate* (1997).

42 Franklin L. Burdette, *Filibustering in the Senate* (1965), 39. See also Beeman, "Unlimited Debate"; David R. Mayhew, "Supermajority Rule in the U.S. Senate," *PS: Political Science and Politics* 36 (2003): 31 (for most of its history, the Senate never "had any anti-majoritarian barrier as concrete, as decisive, or as consequential as today's rule of 60").

43 For discussion of the 1975 rulings, see John C. Roberts, "Majority Voting in Congress: Further Notes on the Constitutionality of the Senate Cloture Rule," *Journal of Law and Politics* 20 (2004): 505, 516–517. For a contrasting account claiming the existence of a clear senatorial pattern rejecting prototypes of the nuclear option, see Michael J. Ger-

hardt, "The Constitutionality of the Filibuster," *Constitutional Commentary* 21 (2004): 445, 476–478. Gerhardt's own narrative, however, provides evidence that the Senate has in fact flip-flopped on the key issue. For an illuminating account of the strong senatorial and vice-presidential support for the nuclear/constitutional option for much of the past century, and a sophisticated discussion of how the strong threat of the nuclear/constitutional option has repeatedly operated to win filibuster reforms that formally followed the catch-22 voting rules laid down by previous Senates, see Martin B. Gold and Dimple Gupta, "The Constitutional Option to Change Senate Rules and Procedures: A Majoritarian Means to Overcome the Filibuster," *Harvard Journal of Law & Public Policy* 28 (2004): 205. For the early twenty-first-century Republicans' argument for the nuclear option, see John Cornyn, "Our Broken Judicial Confirmation Process and the Need for Filibuster Reform," *Harvard Journal of Law & Public Policy* 27 (2003): 181; Orrin G. Hatch, "Judicial Nomination Filibuster Cause and Cure," *Utah LR* (2005): 803.

44 For a qualification and clarification of my claim about House practice, see supra n. 34. Note that the majority-rule principle operates slightly differently for each half of Congress. In the House, new rules are affirmatively adopted by majority vote at the start of every new congressional term. In the Senate, the old rules need not be adopted by majority vote at the start, but must be repealable by majority rule. Under an alternative characterization, the old Senate's rules do lapse at the end of each Congress, just like the old House's rules, but the new Senate need not formally vote to readopt the old Senate rules at the outset of a new Congress. Instead, the new Senate may implicitly readopt the old Senate rules simply by acting in conformity with them. On this view, the new Senate at the beginning of its session may, in House fashion, adopt a wholly new set of rules, and may do so by following "general parliamentary law"—which enables a simple majority to end debate—until these new rules are adopted. See Gold and Gupta, "The Constitutional Option," 220–222 (explaining this theory—an early version of the constitutional option—as put forth by Senator Thomas J. Walsh in 1917). On the role of "general parliamentary law" in jumpstarting the new House, see supra n. 35.

In Chapter 10, we shall consider the role that political parties have played in shaping America's *partisan* Constitution. In this context, it is worth noting that at different points in the past, each party has attacked the entrenched filibuster, and that sometimes both parties have done so simultaneously. In 1960, when Democrats and Republicans combined to nominate four Senate figures (three sitting senators and the sitting vice president, himself an ex-senator) to top their tickets, *both* parties featured strong filibuster-reform planks in their official platforms.

45 *Blackstone's Comm.*, 1:90, 174. For analysis of British practice and theory strongly supportive of the approach advocated in this book, see Josh Chafetz's remarks in his debate with Michael Gerhardt, "Is the Filibuster Constitutional?," *U. of Pennsylvania LR PEN-Numbra* 158 (2011): 245, 250. On the equality of legislatures across time, see also *Federalist* No. 78 (Hamilton) ("[T]he last [statute] in order of time shall be preferred to the first… from the nature and reason of the thing.…[B]etween the interfering acts of an *equal* authority, that which was the last indication of its [the legislature's] will, should have

the preference."); *Newton v. Comm'rs*, 100 U.S. 548, 559 (1879) (similar). On majority rule within each house, see *United States v. Ballin*, 144 U.S. 1, 6 (1892) quoted supra text accompanying nn. 38–39.

46 Clear evidence that the Founding generation accepted this logic comes from the text of Virginia's 1786 Bill of Religious Freedom, a landmark statute enacted largely thanks to the efforts of Jefferson and Madison : "[W]e well know that this Assembly, elected by the people for the ordinary purposes of Legislation only, have no power to restrain the acts of succeeding Assemblies constituted with powers equal to our own, and that therefore to declare this act irrevocable would be of no effect in law."

47 The first federal legislative veto provision was in the Act of June 30, 1932, ch. 314, sec. 407, 47 Stat. 382, 414. See *Immigration and Naturalization Service v. Chadha*, 462 U.S. 919, 944 (1983); ibid., 969 (White, J., dissenting).

48 In this later case, the Court made clear that neither Congress as a whole nor any subset thereof could be vested with a statutory role in the performance of inherently executive acts such as the firing of executive officers—a position evidencing the enduring strength of both *Chadha* and the Decision of 1789. See *Morrison v. Olson*, 487 U.S. 654, 685–686 (1988) ("Congress' attempt to involve itself in the removal of an executive official [is] sufficient grounds to render [a] statute invalid").

49 *Chadha*, 462 U.S. at 942 n. 13. On post-*Chadha* statutes with legislative veto clauses, see, e.g., President George H.W. Bush's formal statement on November 3, 1989, in the course of signing the Treasury, Postal Service and General Government Appropriations Act of 1990: "[N]umerous provisions of H.R. 2989…constitute legislative veto devices of the kind declared unconstitutional in *INS v. Chadha*. Accordingly, I will treat them as having no legal force or effect in this or any other legislation in which they appear."

50 For a list of seventeen statutory independent counsels appointed from 1978 to 1998, see Cass R. Sunstein, "Bad Incentives and Bad Institutions," *Georgetown LJ* 86 (1998): 2267, 2283–2286. To this list we should add Robert Ray, who replaced Ken Starr.

51 See Act of July 27, 1789, 1 Stat. 28, 29 (secretary of foreign affairs—later renamed secretary of state); Act of Aug. 7, 1789, 1 Stat. 49, 50 (secretary of war); Act of Sept. 2, 1789, 1 Stat. 65 (secretary of treasury). See also Act of Feb. 20, 1792, 1 Stat. 232, 234 (postmaster general).

52 But cf. 28 U.S.C. 546(d) (providing for interim appointments of U.S. attorneys by federal district courts).

53 See Henry J. Reske, "A Judge's Lunch Debated: Five Former ABA Presidents Criticize Meeting with Senators," *ABA Journal*, Nov. 1994, 32. The other two members of the Special Division that appointed Ken Starr were Judge Joseph Sneed and Judge John Butzner. Anxiety about the propriety of extensive ex parte exchanges between judges and the executive branch lay at the heart of the 1793 decision by the early justices to decline President Washington's request that they serve as his informal legal advisers. For details, see Chapter 8, n. 22.

54 Testimony of March 17, 1999, Before the Senate Committee on Governmental Affairs.

55 Though Saxbe fixes have not generated an extensive academic literature, they have not escaped the eagle eyes of two of America's preeminent scholars of constitutional method. See Philip Bobbitt, *Constitutional Fate: Theory of the Constitution* (1982), 226; Michael Stokes Paulsen, "Is Lloyd Bentsen Unconstitutional?," *Stanford LR* 46 (1994): 907. The current discussion aims to allay the concerns about Saxbe fixes raised by these scholars.

56 *Buckley v. Valeo*, 424 U.S. 1 (1976). For an argument that congressional leaders continue to call the shots informally, see Jamin B. Raskin, "'A Complicated and Indirect Encroachment': Is the Federal Election Commission Unconstitutionally Composed?," *Administrative LR* 52 (2000): 609, 615–618. For an explanation of how the informality of this revised arrangement can make all the difference constitutionally, see supra text accompanying nn. 48–50.

57 The most notable exception—the Tenure of Office Act of 1867—is discussed in detail at Chapter 8, n. 18. In brief, this act was repealed by Congress in the late nineteenth century, was emphatically repudiated by the Supreme Court in a landmark case early in the twentieth century, and has no visible advocates on the current Court. No modern president has ever supported this act or its underlying principles.

58 Whereas statutes establishing cabinet offices have typically allowed the president virtual carte blanche in picking the person of his choice, the laws creating independent agencies have often provided for a partisan balance on the agency, restricting the number of commissioners or board members who may be picked from any single political party. For more on this aspect, see Chapter 10.

59 See, e.g., Federal Trade Commission Act of 1914, sec. 1, 38 Stat. 717, 718, 15 U.S.C. 41 (giving Federal Trade Commissioners seven-year terms subject to presidential removal for "inefficiency, neglect of duty, or malfeasance in office"); National Labor Relations Act of 1935, sec. 3(a), 49 Stat. 449, 451, 29 U.S.C. 153(a) (1935) (giving NLRB members five-year terms subject to removal for "neglect of duty or malfeasance in office, but for no other cause"); Banking Act of 1935, sec. 203(b), 49 Stat. 684, 704–705, 12 U.S.C. 242 (giving Federal Reserve board members fourteen-year terms "unless sooner removed for cause by the President"); Consumer Product Safety Act of 1972, sec. 4, 86 Stat. 1207, 1210, 15 U.S.C. 2053 (giving Consumer Product Safety Commissioners seven-year terms subject to removal for "neglect of duty or malfeasance in office but for no other cause"). Similar rules apply to many other agencies, including the Federal Energy Regulatory Commission, 42 U.S.C. 7171 ("Members shall hold office for a term of 5 years and may be removed by the President only for inefficiency, neglect of duty, or malfeasance in office"), and the Nuclear Regulatory Commission, 42 U.S.C. 5841 ("Each member shall serve for a term of five years....Any member of the Commission may be removed by the President for inefficiency, neglect of duty, or malfeasance in office."). Although some other agency-creating statutes are silent on the removal question, the overall structure of these statutes and the specific mission of these agencies have been thought to limit the president to for-cause removal. The Federal Election Commission is a case in point. See 2 U.S.C. 437c(a); *FEC v. NRA Political Victory Fund*, 6 F.3d 821, 826 (D.C. Cir. 1993).

In the mid-1970s, administrative law scholar Kenneth Culp Davis listed some sixty independent entities with some amount of protection from at-will presidential removal. Kenneth C. Davis, *Administrative Law of the Seventies* (1976), 14. This general picture remains true today, and we should note the especially important role of the independent agencies enumerated by the Paperwork Reduction Act, 44 U.S.C. 3502 (5).

60 On the "horizontal" sweep of the Article I, section 8, necessary-and-proper clause—its broad empowerment of Congress to make various decisions about how best to structure the executive and judicial departments within the broad outlines laid down by the terse text, as distinct from the clause's "vertical" confirmation of broad federal power vis-à-vis the states—see Amar, *ACAB*, 110–111. For an argument that various congressional laws have in fact vested executive-branch officials with powers to make decisions as to which the president may not simply substitute his own judgment or discretion, see Kevin M. Stack, "The President's Statutory Powers to Administer the Laws," *Columbia LR* 106 (2006): 263, 270–273, 276–283 (2006). For a different reading of some of these statutes, see Elena Kagan, "Presidential Administration," *Harvard LR* 114 (2001): 2245.

61 For a partial list of twentieth-century statutes stretching back to 1914, see supra n. 59. For a late nineteenth-century precursor of these statutes, see the Interstate Commerce Act of 1887, 24 Stat. 379, 383 (creating an Interstate Commerce Commission whose members were to serve six-year terms, and who were removable "by the President for inefficiency, neglect of duty, or malfeasance in office," but without any suggestion of a plenary presidential power to countermand commission decisions). For Attorney General William Wirt's much earlier endorsement of congressional power to create statutes giving certain executive department underlings decisional autonomy, see The President and Accounting Officers, 1 Op. Att'y Gen 624, 625 (1823); The President and the Comptroller, 1 Op. Att'y Gen. 636 (1823); The President and Accounting Officers, 1 Op. Att'y Gen. 678 (1824); The President and Accounting Officers, 1 Op. Att'y Gen. 705 (1825); The President and Accounting Officers, 1 Op. Att'y Gen. 706 (1825). For an even earlier statement of this point of view, see Letter from Thomas Jefferson to Benjamin Latrobe (June 2, 1808), in Thomas Jefferson and the National Capital, Saul Padover, ed. (1946), 429, 431 ("[W]ith the settlement of the accounts at the Treasury, I have no right to interfere in the least. The Comptroller is the law officer. He is the sole & supreme judge in all claims for money against the US and would no more receive direction from me as to his rules of evidence than one of the judges of the supreme court."). For criticism of this point of view, see Steven G. Calabresi and Christopher S. Yoo, *The Unitary Executive* (2008), 89–90.

Section 4 of the Twenty-fifth Amendment—which was ratified well after the high-profile emergence of independent agencies—singles out "the principal officers of the executive departments" for special responsibilities. Unless statutes specify otherwise, these officers initially decide whether a president is so disabled as to warrant his displacement by the vice president. Although section 4 does not speak directly to the issue of whether a president may unilaterally oust all high-level executive-branch officials, it does address a similar—indeed, a symmetric—question: whether high-level executive-branch officials may ever oust the president. And the officials who are specified by section 4 to make this ouster decision are "principal officers of the executive departments"—cabinet heads, and not board members or commissioners of independent agencies. According to the key congressional report, "[o]nly officials of Cabinet rank should participate in the decision as to whether presidential inability exists....The intent...is that the Presidential appointees who direct the 10 executive departments named in 5 U.S.C. 1[now codified as sect. 101], or any executive department established in the future, generally considered to comprise the President's Cabinet, would participate...in determining inability." H.R. Rep. No. 203, 89-1, 3 (1965).

In essence, this amendment blesses the distinction between cabinet departments and independent agencies—and does so in a way fitting Chapter 8's functional account. Because presidents are responsible for monitoring cabinet officers—monitoring that includes the power of at-will removal—these cabinet officers are symmetrically best positioned to monitor the president for signs of disability. Independent-agency officials are not in the same position to personally monitor the president, and this is precisely because they are not, as a rule, personally monitored by the president. The commissioners of independent agencies monitor and are monitored by each other, rather than monitoring and being monitored by the president in cabinet-style fashion.

62 Cf. Washington, *Writings*, 32:386 (March 13, 1793, letter to William Rawle, a U.S. district attorney, "instruct[ing]" Rawle to cease prosecution of a specified case and "enter a Nolle prose qui on the indictment aforesaid"). See Leonard D. White, *The Federalists: A Study in Administrative History* (1961), 31 n. 15, 408 & n. 10.

63 The specific provisions vesting the president personally with these respective powers are the commander-in-chief clause, the opinions clause, the pardon clause, the ambassador-receiving clause, the appointments clause, the state-of-the-union and recommendation clauses, and the take-care clause. Under this framework, it makes perfect sense that in 1789, the War Department and the State/Foreign Affairs Department were structured as cabinet-style departments directly answerable to the president, and that they have remained so structured ever since. It also makes perfect sense that the attorney general answered directly to the president in 1789 and has done so ever since.

CHAPTER 10: JOINING THE PARTY

1 For the erroneous claim that the written Constitution omits all mention of and/or is hostile to political parties, see, e.g., Samuel Issacharoff and Richard H. Pildes, "Politics as Markets: Partisan Lockups of the Democratic Process," *Stanford LR* 50 (1998): 643, 713–714 ("[T]he constitutional structure was specifically intended to preclude the rise of political parties, which were considered the quintessential form of 'faction.' Yet political parties have become the principal organizational form for mass democracy."); Samuel Issacharoff and Richard H. Pildes, "Election Law as Its Own Field of Study: Not by

'Election' Alone," *Loyola of Los Angeles LR* 32 (1999): 1173, 1175–1176 ("No constitutional framework for enabling modern democratic self-government can neglect the role of political parties, yet the Constitution is not only silent about parties but designed to preclude their emergence"); Ernest A. Young, "The Constitution Outside the Constitution," *Yale LJ* 117 (2007): 408, 419 (proclaiming that "our two dominant political parties" are "left entirely out of the canonical document"). Note that Professor Young defines the phrase "canonical document" to mean the terse text "ratified in 1789, formally amended several times since, and passed out in handy pocket-size booklets by the Federalist Society." Ibid., 415. See also ibid., 409 (referring to "the language of a certain Document of 1789, together with a severely select coterie of additional paragraphs called Amendments"). None of these articles contains any qualifying reference to the vision of national political parties undergirding the Twelfth Amendment (adopted by the Founding generation) or to the later Twenty-fourth Amendment, which explicitly covers party "primary" elections. The Twelfth Amendment is also painfully absent from a prominent article by another outstanding scholar, who declares that "the Jacksonian ascendance of popular democracy and political parties" took place "without any authorizing or triggering constitutional amendment." David A. Strauss, "Common Law Constitutional Interpretation," *U. of Chicago LR* 63 (1996): 877, 884. For yet another acclaimed scholar trying to use the emergence of political parties to challenge the written Constitution's fit with actual practice, see Barry Friedman, "The Will of the People and the Process of Constitutional Change," *George Washington LR* 78 (2010): 1232, 1236.

2   *Farrand's Records*, 2:537.

3   On how these odd outcomes could easily occur, Amar, *ACAB*, 336–341.

4   See, generally, Richard Hofstadter, *The Idea of a Party System* (1969), 41–42 ("British politics in the era of George III, with its cabinet system not yet developed, with its relatively small electorate, its pocket boroughs, its connections of leading families, its management by purchase and arrangement, its lack of highly focused issues, its multiple, shifting factions, its high proportion of unaligned members of Parliament, bore only a vague germinal relation to the highly developed modern British party system"). In fascinating unpublished work, Professor Philip Bobbitt has suggested that Hofstadter's portrait may be overdrawn and that, by the late eighteenth century, parliamentary politics were more modern than Hofstadter suggested. Bobbitt also maintains that in America, political parties of a certain sort were well underway by the time the Constitution was adopted in 1789.

5   See Amar, *ACAB*, 9: "Virtually no arch-loyalist went on to become a particularly noteworthy political leader in independent America."

6   For an outstanding recent biography that captures Madison's essence as a politico—and in later life, a party man—see Richard Brookhiser, *James Madison* (2011).

7   On the vice president's expanding role and increased proximity to the president, see Joel K. Goldstein, "The New Constitutional Vice Presidency," *Wake Forest LR* 30 (1995): 505, 531; Richard Albert, "The Evolving Vice Presidency," *Temple LR* 78 (2005): 811; Richard

Friedman, "Some Modest Proposals on the Vice-Presidency," *Michigan LR* 86 (1988): 1703. On the vice president's statutory role in the National Security Council, see NSA Amendments of Aug. 10, 1949, ch. 412, sec. 3, 63 Stat. 578, 579, 50 U.S.C. 402(a).

8 On extra seats and Jefferson, see Amar, *ACAB*, 87–98, 148–159, 344–347. On Burr, see ibid., 168, 313, 338–343.

9 I have intentionally used imprecise language in reporting these voting lineups because party affiliations were complex and fluid at this moment.

10 The one Republican no vote on the Fourteenth Amendment came from Senator Peter G. Van Winkle of West Virginia. This tally excludes three ex-Republicans who were in the process of switching parties. The three former Republicans who by mid-1866 had become de facto or de jure Democrats were Edgar Cowan of Pennsylvania, James R. Doolittle of Wisconsin, and Daniel S. Norton of Minnesota. Special thanks to Les Benedict for his help on this tally.

11 For more discussion, see Amar, *ACAB*, 170–173, 452–453; Akhil Reed Amar and Vikram David Amar, "Is the Presidential Succession Law Constitutional?," *Stanford LR* 48 (1995): 113; Akhil Reed Amar, "Applications and Implications of the Twenty-fifth Amendment," *Houston LR* 47 (2010): 1.

12 Section 2 of the Fourteenth Amendment addresses situations in which "the right to vote" is "denied" or "abridged" to various persons who are "citizens of the United States." Section 1 of the Fifteenth Amendment, section 1 of the Nineteenth Amendment, and section 1 of the Twenty-fourth Amendment all use the same phrase: "[t]he right of citizens of the United States to vote." Section 1 of the Twenty-sixth Amendment uses the phrase "[t]he right of citizens of the United States…to vote." All four of the later amendments also gesture toward section 2 of the Fourteenth in their explicit use of the phrase "denied or abridged."

13 There is no substantial historical evidence that primary elections were purposefully omitted from the scope of the Twenty-sixth Amendment in order to limit the sweep of this amendment. Rather, the Twenty-sixth was symbolically phrased to track the iconic Fifteenth Amendment's text. If this earlier amendment's sweeping text (which simply did not focus on primary elections because such elections were not particularly salient in the 1860s) is best read after the adoption of the Twenty-fourth Amendment to apply to all government elections, including primary elections, then, in the absence of strong legislative history to the contrary, the Twenty-sixth Amendment's equally sweeping text should likewise apply to all such elections. For some of the interesting methodological questions at stake here, see Amar, "Intratextualism," *Harvard LR* 112 (1999): 747, 789 n. 173.

14 Imagine an 1868 federal statute awarding each state an annual federal subsidy based on the number of "adult male citizens" who voted in the most recent general statewide election. The adoption of the Nineteenth Amendment would surely require federal officials to reinterpret this annual subsidy law—presumably by simply ignoring the word "male" in the statute. The same result should apply if the word "male" appears in an 1868

constitutional amendment instead of an 1868 statute. After all, the Woman Suffrage Amendment was designed to trump all previous legal pronouncements—state laws, federal statutes, administrative regulations, judicial rulings, and even previous constitutional clauses—that contradicted the amendment's core command that the sexes must stand equal before the law wherever the right to vote is involved.

(Parenthetically, the word "male" does appear in an 1872 statute closely tracking the language of section 2 of the Fourteenth Amendment and formally operative today: "[S]hould any State, after the passage of this act, deny or abridge the right of any of the male inhabitants of such State, being twenty-one years of age, and citizens of the United States, to vote at any election named in the amendments to the Constitution, article fourteen, section two, except for participation in the rebellion or other crime, the number of Representatives apportioned in this act to such State shall be reduced in the proportion which the number of such male citizens shall have to the whole number of male citizens twenty-one years of age in such State." Act of Feb. 2, 1872, sec. 6, 17 Stat. 28, 29. The current version of this old act, codified at 2 U.S.C. 6, reads slightly differently but still includes the word "male.")

As a matter of logic, the sex equality required by the Nineteenth Amendment could be guaranteed either by ignoring the word "male" in section 2 (and thereby functionally extending section 2's protective scope to women as well as men), or instead by ignoring section 2 altogether (and thereby, in effect, excising this section from the Constitution). Either solution would treat the sexes equally in voting law. The choice between these two options presents a nice question of what lawyers call "severability": How much of a constitutionally deficient provision should be ignored by "severing" it from adjoining legal language? In the specific case of section 2 of the Fourteenth Amendment, it seems far more appropriate to ignore the word "male" than to ignore the entire section. It would be extremely perverse to read the Constitution's third citizen-right-to-vote amendment (the Nineteenth) as inviting a functional excision rather than a functional extension of the Constitution's first citizen-right-to-vote provision (section 2 of the Fourteenth Amendment).

A virtually identical analysis applies to the Twenty-sixth Amendment, which insists that the federal government treat young adults aged eighteen through twenty no worse than it treats older adults insofar as "the right of citizens of the United States...to vote" is concerned. It would also be odd, after the 1913 enactment of the Seventeenth Amendment, to treat disfranchisements for House races any differently than disfranchisements for Senate races, even though the explicit text of section 2 applies only to the former. Direct elections for the Senate simply did not exist in the 1860s, and the obvious aim of section 2 was to cover all elections for major state and federal positions. Hence the need to read Senate elections into section 2's catchment provision, even though this specific application is undeniably...unwritten.

For an earlier spotting of the fascinating intergenerational issues teed up by section 2 in light of later voting-rights amendments, see Laurence H. Tribe, *The Invisible Constitution* (2008), 75–77.

15 Cf. Jack M. Balkin, *Living Originalism* (2011), 261–262 ("New amendments may alter the relationships between other parts of the Constitution, sometimes…in quite unexpected ways.…[S]tructural principles might emerge from the constitutional system that no single person or generation intended.").

16 For the FEC, see 2 U.S.C 437c(a)(1); for the USSC, see 28 U.S.C. 991(a); for the FTC, see 15 U.S.C. 41; for FERC, see 42 U.S.C. 7171(b)(1); for the EEOC, see 42 U.S.C. 2000e-4; for the CFTC, see 7 U.S.C. 2(a)(2)(A); for the NRC, see 42 U.S.C. 5841(b)(2); for the earlier FPC, see the Federal Power Commission Reorganization Act of 1930, 46 Stat. 797; for the SEC, see 15 U.S.C. 78d(a); for the FCC, see 47 U.S.C. 154(b)(5); for the CPSC, see 15 U.S.C. 2053(c); for the old ICC, see sec. 11 of the Interstate Commerce Act of 1887, 24 Stat. 379, 383; for the FMC, see 46 U.S.C. 301(b)(1); for the NTSB, see 49 U.S.C. 1111(b). Note also that "not more than 3 of the members of the Board of Directors [of the Federal Deposit Insurance Corporation] may be members of the same political party." 12 U.S.C. 1812(a)(2). For still more statutes with similar provisions, see Jamin B. Raskin, "'A Complicated and Indirect Encroachment': Is the Federal Election Commission Unconstitutionally Composed?," *Administrative LR* 52 (2000): 609, 621–622 & n. 51.

17 See Neal Devins and David E. Lewis, "Not-so Independent Agencies: Party Polarization and the Limits of Institutional Design," *Boston U. LR* 88 (2008): 459.

18 For example, House Rule X5(a)(3)(A) provides for equal party membership on a key ethics committee, regardless of which party happens to control the chamber as a whole. House Rule X5(a)(1) and X5(b)(1) dramatize the formal role that party membership plays in committee assignments generally: "Membership on a standing committee during the course of a Congress shall be contingent on continuing membership in the party caucus or conference that nominated the Member." The Senate's rules governing its committees also formally pivot on party membership. For example, under Senate Rule XXVI(3), "If the chairman of any such committee is not present at any…meeting of the committee, the ranking member of the majority party on the committee who is present shall preside." On the formal role of parties in structuring the allocation of committee staffers, see Senate Rule XXVII(3) and House Rules X9(a)(2) and X9(i). For complementary statutory provisions concerning congressional committee staff, with elaborate references to the respective entitlements of the majority and the minority, see 2 U.S.C. 72a.

19 See Maurice Duverger, *Political Parties*, 2d ed., Barbara North and Robert North, trans., (1962 [1951]), 216–228; V. O. Key, *Politics, Parties, and Pressure Groups* (1952), 224–231; Anthony Downs, *An Economic Theory of Democracy* (1957), 114–125; Doug Rae, *The Political Consequences of Electoral Laws* (1967), 95–96.

20 Act of June 5, 1842, sec. 2, 5 Stat. 491 (emphasis added); Act of Dec. 14, 1967, 81 Stat. 581, 2 U.S.C. 2c.

CHAPTER 11: DOING THE RIGHT THING

1   For the canonical modern account of the importance of virtue in late eighteenth-century American republican ideology, see Gordon S. Wood, *The Creation of the American Republic, 1776–1787* (1969), 34, 65–70, 413, 425. For the canonical eighteenth-century treatment of virtue as the mainspring ("ressort") of a true republic—a treatment that Madison/Publius likely had specifically in mind as he penned *The Federalist* No. 55 and that was surely familiar to many of his readers in 1788—see Montesquieu, *De L'Esprit des Lois, Livre III* (first published in 1748). Montesquieu was the single most cited postantiquity authority in late eighteenth-century American political discourse, edging out Blackstone and leaving Locke a distant third. See Chapter 1, n. 7 and accompanying text.

2   1 Stat. 23.

3   On the need for Congress to affirmatively authorize federal criminal punishment, see *United States v. Hudson & Goodwin*, 11 U.S. (7 Cranch) 32 (1812); Amar, *ACAB*, 63–64, 190, 304, 592–593 nn. 37–38; Amar, *Bill of Rights*, 102, 344 n. 85. On exceptions to *Hudson's* general rule in contempts of Congress and contempts of court, see Chapter 9, nn. 2–10 and accompanying text.

4   *Bushell's Case*, 124 Eng. Rep. 1006 (C.P. 1670). Though Blackstone mentioned the theoretical possibility of a suit of "attaint" brought by the Crown to punish jurors and set aside their verdict, *Blackstone's Comm.*, 4:354, writs of attaint had generally fallen into disuse in England and have played no important role under America's Constitution. Leading scholars have suggested that writs of attaint never applied to jurors in criminal cases. See, e.g., James C. Oldham, "The Origins of the Special Jury," *U. of Chicago LR* 50 (1983): 137, 162 n. 122; James B. Thayer, "The Jury and Its Development," *Harvard LR* 5 (1892): 244, 377.

5   *Blackstone's Comm.*, 4: 238–239. See also ibid., 19 ("[J]uries, through compassion, will sometimes forget their oaths, and either acquit the guilty or mitigate the nature of the offense").

6   See Amar, *Bill of Rights*, 84–85 and sources cited therein.

7   See *R. v. The Inhabitants of the County of Oxford*, 104 Eng. Rep. 429, 432 (K.B.1811) (reporter's note [b]); *United States v. Gibert*, 25 F. Cas. 1287, 1297 (C.C.D. Mass. 1834) (No. 15,204) (Story, Circuit J.); Joseph Chitty, *A Practical Treatise on the Criminal Law* (1819), 1: * 654; John H. Langbein, *Origins of the Adversary Criminal Trial* (2006), 325 ("So effective was this judicial remedy that it seems to have virtually eliminated the conviction against direction as a sphere of conflict between judge and jury").

8   *Blackstone's Comm.*, 4:355 (emphasis in original). Though Blackstone's passage addressed only King's Bench proceedings—typically misdemeanor prosecutions—the basic asymmetry between jury convictions (which judges could undo, in effect) and jury acquittals (which judges could not undo) also applied to ordinary felony cases in other courts. Blackstone noted an obscure exception to this general rule of acquittal finality in the case of "appeal[] of felony"—a medieval practice in which a private party and not the

Crown brought criminal suit and as to which the Crown had no pardon power. This practice was already nearly obsolete in Blackstone's day (ibid., 308) and is not permitted under America's Constitution, which as a rule does not recognize the propriety of purely private federal prosecutions immune from presidential pardon power.

9 This basic postulate was ringingly affirmed by the Supreme Court in the 1812 case of *United States v. Hudson & Goodwin* and has never thereafter been called into question by the Court. For more on that case, recall the discussion in Chapter 8, text accompanying nn. 10–11.

10 On *Hudson's* deep structure, see supra n. 3; on noncriminal federal common law, see, e.g., *Bivens v. Six Unknown Named Agents*, 403 U.S. 388 (1971).

11 See Amar, *ACAB*, 58–64. If the president vetoes a criminal law, this veto may be overridden; but in such a case the president reserves a nondefeasible pardon power.

12 See William Baude, "The Judgment Power," *Georgetown LJ* 96 (2008): 1808.

13 Contempt of federal court marks a partial exception to this general rule against private prosecution. See Chapter 9, n. 9.

14 Again, note the curious exceptions of contempt of court and contempt of Senate, Chapter 9, nn. 2–10 and accompanying text. On the early flirtation with a federal common law of crimes prior to the definitive 1812 *Hudson & Goodwin* case, see Amar, *Bill of Rights*, 344 n. 85.

15 "Trial by Jury," *Time*, Oct. 3, 1955, 19.

16 See Chapter 7, n. 9 and accompanying text.

17 On small-town and/or self-informing juries, see *Blackstone's Comm.*, 3:375 ("[I]f a juror knows any thing of the matter in issue, he may be sworn as a witness, and give his evidence publicly in court"); Langbein, *Origins*, 319–320.

18 *Swain v. Alabama*, 380 U.S. 202 (1965); *Batson v. Kentucky*, 476 U.S. 79 (1986) (putting some teeth in the rule prohibiting race-based peremptories); *Georgia v. McCollum*, 505 U.S. 42 (1992) (extending *Batson's* limits on race-based peremptories to jury challenges by criminal defense counsel); *J.E.B. v. Alabama ex rel. T. B.*, 511 U.S. 127 (1994) (extending *Batson's* approach to sex-based peremptories).

19 For arguments that peremptories should be abolished, see *Batson*, 476 U.S. 102–108 (Marshall, J., concurring); *Miller-El v. Dretke*, 545 U.S. 231, 266–273 (2005) (Breyer, J., concurring); *Rice v. Collins*, 546 U.S. 333, 342–344 (2006) (Breyer, J., concurring, joined by Souter, J.).

20 See *Williams v. Florida*, 399 U.S. 78 (1970) (six is okay, even in a case involving a sentence of life imprisonment...); *Ballew v. Georgia*, 435 U.S. 223 (1978) (...but five is too small).

21 See *Williams*, 399 U.S. at 98–99 n. 45.

22 The phrase "social conscience" is used as a reminder that the judge is indeed part of a larger *society*—a person who has been *socialized* by the norms of society in general and especially by the norms of America's written and unwritten Constitution. For more on conscience, see Philip Bobbitt, *Constitutional Fate: Theory of the Constitution* (1982); Philip Bobbitt, *Constitutional Interpretation* (1991).

23 *Callins v. Collins*, 510 U.S. 1141, 1145 (1994) (Blackmun, J., dissenting from denial of cert.). Justice Stevens was more guarded; he announced his opposition to the death penalty except in cases where settled Court precedent dictated otherwise. *Baze v. Rees*, 553 U.S. 35, 86–87 (2008) (Stevens, J., concurring in the judgment). See also *Thompson v. McNeil*, 129 S. Ct. 1299–1301 (2009) (Stevens, J., respecting the denial of cert.).

CHAPTER 12: ENVISIONING THE FUTURE

1 These data are also discussed in Amar, *ACAB*, 69–70, 164–165, 219.

2 Ibid., 164–165.

3 For details, see ibid., 342, 409–412.

4 Actually, Mississippi has a variant of the electoral college: Unless a gubernatorial candidate wins both a statewide popular majority and a majority of legislative districts, the race is decided by the state legislature. Miss. Const., secs. 140–141. But this system, designed in 1890, was conceived in sin—craftily crafted to prevent a black from ever winning the governorship. A close look at the federal electoral college shows that its roots, too, lie in political racism, with states being allowed to disfranchise blacks without penalty in presidential elections. See generally Amar, *ACAB*, 156–159, 344–347.

5 To put the point in the language of Professor Bobbitt, certain amendment proposals are likely to be seen as "un-ethical" in the sense that they run strongly counter to the "ethos" of the American people as expressed in the mass of state constitutions. See Philip Bobbitt, *Constitutional Fate: Theory of the Constitution* (1982), 93–177.

6 See Chapter 2, n. 15 and accompanying text. See John J. Dinan, *The American State Constitutional Tradition* (2009), 30–31, 55–63.

7 Ibid., 184–221.

8 Ibid., 94–96.

9 Some might wonder whether such an amendment is even permissible. Article V, which lays down general rules for constitutional amendment, explicitly provides that "no State, without its Consent, shall be deprived of its equal Suffrage in the Senate."

Formally, this proviso does not prohibit our envisioned amendment, but merely requires that every state "Consent" to such an amendment—presumably during the ratification process, in which all fifty states (rather than the usual thirty-eight) would need to say yes. In reality, however, it would be almost impossible to achieve unanimity among the states for our envisioned amendment—or almost any proposed amendment on any topic, for that matter. Under the Articles of Confederation, whose amendment clause required unanimity among the thirteen extant states, unanimity was never achieved. Indeed, the Articles failed precisely because the amendment bar was set too high, inducing reformers to abandon the Confederation altogether in favor of the Philadelphia Constitution, whose ratification required only nine states to say yes.

But wait. Read at face value, the Article V unanimity proviso turns out to be an easily outflanked Maginot Line. The proviso's words do not apply to an amendment that preserves the Senate's existing apportionment while transferring virtually all current Senate powers to a newly created, more proportionately representative entity. In response, it might be thought that unwritten constitutional principles—the spirit of the proviso—should bar any such outflanking. But several substantial "spiritual" principles argue otherwise. First, although small states are lawfully entitled to what they were able to bargain for or extort in 1787–1788, it is doubtful that they are entitled to any more. In this view, a deal is a deal, and the Article V proviso deal means exactly what it says and not one ounce more. Second, the Article V proviso is a remnant of the failed Articles of Confederation system, and that very failure provides a strong cautionary note against reading the proviso broadly. Third, a proper account of the Constitution's spirit must factor in the enhanced nationalism of post-Founding deeds and texts—especially the Reconstruction Amendments and the egalitarian ideology underlying *Reynolds v. Sims* and its progeny. Fourth, the Constitution has in fact already been amended at least once, using ordinary (thirty-eight-state) amendment rules, in a way that drained some power from the Senate in favor of a more proportionately representative entity. (For details, see Amar, *ACAB*, at 589 & n. 13.) Fifth, once we move past the clear (but easily outflanked) words of the proviso, there is no comparably clear line separating special amendments that require fifty-state approval from ordinary amendments that require thirty-eight-state approval. Finally, small states are well protected by the ordinary rules of Article V, in which Wyoming counts equally with California in both the existing Senate and the ratification process. In a world where two-thirds of the Senate, as currently composed, and three-fourths of the states actually adopted our envisioned amendment in the ordinary way, wouldn't this fact itself be decisive evidence of America's spirit?

Regardless of one's ultimate position on the theoretical questions raised by the Article V proviso, one point should be clear to all: Proper constitutional interpretation here pivots not only on the Constitution's explicit words, but on a sensitive interpretation of America's unwritten Constitution, based on implicit principles, past amendment practices and protocols, bedrock ideas from the Warren Court era, and so on.

10 Dinan, *The American State Constitutional Tradition*, 98, 122–123. Note also that in roughly one-quarter of the states, the legislature needs less than a two-thirds vote to override a gubernatorial veto. Ibid., 113. And note further the distinctive gubernatorial election rules in Mississippi. See n. 4.

11 Although the federal independent-counsel statute ill fit the architecture of the federal Constitution, it initially seemed not "foreign" but natural, because it resembled schemes that had worked in various state constitutions that seemed at first almost identical to the federal model. In fact, however, these constitutions are different in key respects, and so piecemeal borrowing here was a big mistake. See Akhil Reed Amar, "Scandalized," *The New Republic*, Oct. 11, 1999.

12 See Basile S. Uddo, "'Who's in Charge?': The Louisiana Governor's Power to Act in Absentia," *Loyola LR* 29 (1983): 1.

13 For more details on the sources of the federal ban on advisory opinions, see Chapter 8, n. 22.

14 Dinan, *The American State Constitutional Tradition*, 98.

15 For one possible argument against incorporation of the grand-jury right, see Chapter 4, n. 32 and accompanying text.

16 Cf. Jed Rubenfeld, *Freedom and Time* (2001).

17 See John Rawls, *A Theory of Justice* (1971). See also Lawrence G. Sager, *Justice in Plainclothes* (2004), 8–9, 161–193.

18 *Farrand's Records*, 1:49 (punctuation altered).

19 Ibid., 529, 531 (Gouverneur Morris, claiming that "he came here as a Representative of America; he flattered himself he came here in some degree as a Representative of the whole human race," and urging fellow delegates to rise above parochialism because they or their posterity would one day likely live elsewhere); 405, 413 (Wilson, noting likely impact of Convention on the entire planet and distant, "multiplied posterity"). See also ibid., 2:125 (Wilson: "We should consider that we are providing a Constitution for future generations, and not merely for the peculiar circumstances of the moment"). For similar musings of James Madison and Alexander Hamilton, see ibid., 1:421–224. See also ibid., 2:3 (Sherman, noting that "We are providing for our posterity, for our children & our grand Children, who would be as likely to be citizens of the new Western States, as of the old States. On this consideration alone, we ought to make no [unfair] discrimination"). For a similar statement during the ratification process, see *ACAB*, 272 (quoting Wilson in Pennsylvania: "We are representatives, sir, not merely of the present age, but of future times; not merely of the territory along the sea-coast, but of regions immensely extended westward").

20 Although Article V addresses the general topic of constitutional amendment, its text does not explicitly speak of the "responsibility" of each generation to ponder amendments with specific reference to the needs and interests of "posterity." Nor does Article V explicitly address various ways of adding to or subtracting from America's unwritten Constitution as distinct from modifying the terse text itself.

AFTERWORD

1 See Victoria F. Nourse, *In Reckless Hands:* Skinner v. Oklahoma *and the Near Triumph of American Eugenics* (2008).

ACKNOWLEDGMENTS

BEYOND GOD AND COUNTRY, my family and Yale University have made me who I am. Regarding my family, the most important things go without saying. As for Yale, many years ago *alma mater* took an unformed youth and changed his life. Homes are important (see Chapter 3), and Yale has been my home for more than three decades. I still can't believe I get paid to work here.

Two former deans of Yale Law School straddle the family/Yale divide, for they have become de facto kin. Guido Calabresi, who gave me my first law-teaching job and so much more, has long been my Fairy Godparent; and Harold Koh, who gave me my current chair—a chair that was rightfully his to claim—has been my Godbrother (if that is a word) since the day we met. Other Yale colleagues who must be mentioned here are my occasional coauthors—Ian Ayres, Jack Balkin, Jed Rubenfeld, and Reva Siegel—and my wise mentors, Owen Fiss and John Langbein.

And then there is Yale's incomparable Bruce Ackerman, whose influence on me has been so wide and deep that I feel obliged to distinguish my views from his at every anxious turn.

Outside Yale's Ivy-covered walls, my sometime coauthor and all-time friend Sandy Levinson has long been an Ackerman-like inspiration and provocation. Two other role models merit extra-special mention. Laurence Tribe's profound insights about constitutional law—particularly the teachings of his recent book *The Invisible Constitution*—were never far from my mind as I composed the preceding chapters. Ditto for Philip Bobbitt's brilliant meditations on the nature of constitutional interpretation, especially in his books *Constitutional Fate* and *Constitutional Interpretation*. Bobbitt's thinking about the constitutional *ethos* of the American people is a particularly rich vein of thought. Several of this book's chapters aim to profile distinct species of the genus that Bobbitt labels "ethical" argument.

Among the recently departed, Charles Black and John Hart Ely first opened my eyes to the importance of holistic as distinct from clause-bound constitutional interpretation; and David Currie's detailed analyses of the Constitution in Congress helped ground Chapters 8 and 9.

Many friends generously provided commentary on early drafts. Special thanks to Sean Barney, Will Baude, Jon Blue, Jonathan Bressler, Rebecca Brown, Aaron-Andrew Bruhl, Steve Calabresi, Josh Chafetz, Travis Crum, Greg Dubinsky, Gus Eyler, Barry Friedman, Josh Geltzer, Heather Gerken, Matthew Hegreness, Neal Katyal, Jaynie Lilley, Fred Liu, Pauline Maier, Nick Makarov, John Manning, Jerry Mashaw, David Mayhew, Chris Michel,

Trevor Morrison, Victoria Nourse, Nick Parrillo, Matthew Pearl, Saikrishna Prakash, Aniko Richheimer, Kermit Roosevelt, Tom Schmidt, Kevin Stack, Kathy Streckfus, Richard Tao, Aaron Tidman, Adrian Vermeule, and Lindsey Ohlsson Worth. Thanks also to the editors of the *Yale Law Journal* for their help with an early version of Chapter 3.

In the publishing world, my literary agents, Glen Hartley and Lynn Chu, went beyond the call of duty. I am lucky to have them as friends and counselors. I am also grateful to the legendary Bob Loomis, now retired, for his expert editorial advice early on. My current editor, Lara Heimert, is quite simply the best in the business. She has redeemed my faith in the future of books.

THE ENUMERATION IN THIS BOOK of certain thanks should not be construed to deny or disparage other thanks owed to various persons and institutions. Some of my biggest debts remain unwritten. I hope there will be other occasions for me to acknowledge all who have helped me. For now, I simply say (as I have said before), you know who you are and so do I. Bless you.

ILLUSTRATION CREDITS

Chapter 1, page 1: *The Impeachment Trial of Andrew Johnson* (1868). Sketch by Theodore R. Davis. Originally published in *Harper's Weekly*. Courtesy of the Library of Congress.

Chapter 2, page 49: *Don't Wait for the Draft* (1917). Courtesy of the Library of Congress.

Chapter 3, page 95: *Home Sweet Home* (1877). Lithograph by G. F. Gilman. Courtesy of the Library of Congress.

Chapter 4, page 139: *Earl Warren* (date unknown). Courtesy of the Library of Congress.

Chapter 5, page 201: *Harry Blackmun and William Rehnquist* (1976). Color negatives by Robert S. Oakes. Courtesy of the Library of Congress.

Chapter 6, page 243: *Abraham Lincoln* (November 8, 1863). Photo by Alexander Gardner. Courtesy of the Library of Congress.

Chapter 7, page 277: *"Women Are Too Sentimental for Jury Duty"* (1915). Lithograph by Chamberlain. Originally published in *Puck*. Courtesy of the Library of Congress.

Chapter 8, page 307: *The Inauguration of Washington* (April 30, 1789, as depicted in 1876). Lithograph by Currier & Ives. Courtesy of the Library of Congress.

Chapter 9, page 333: *Potter Stewart* (1976). Color negative by Robert S. Oakes. Courtesy of the Library of Congress.

Chapter 10, page 389: *The Declaration Committee* (1776, as depicted in 1876). Lithograph by Currier & Ives. Courtesy of the Library of Congress.

Chapter 11, page 417: *William Brennan and Thurgood Marshall* (1976). Color negatives by Robert S. Oakes. Courtesy of the Library of Congress.

Chapter 12, page 449: *March for Women's Liberation, Washington, D.C., August 26, 1970.* Photo by Warren K. Leffler. Courtesy of the Library of Congress and U.S. News & World Report, Inc.

INDEX